T0183503

Lecture Notes in Computer Science 13446

More information about this series at https://link.springer.com/bookseries/558

Lucio Tommaso De Paolis · Pasquale Arpaia ·
Marco Sacco (Eds.)

Extended Reality

First International Conference, XR Salento 2022
Lecce, Italy, July 6–8, 2022
Proceedings, Part II

Editors
Lucio Tommaso De Paolis
University of Salento
Lecce, Italy

Pasquale Arpaia
Università di Napoli Federico II
Naples, Italy

Marco Sacco
CNR-STIIMA
Lecco, Italy

ISSN 0302-9743 ISSN 1611-3349 (electronic)
Lecture Notes in Computer Science
ISBN 978-3-031-15552-9 ISBN 978-3-031-15553-6 (eBook)
https://doi.org/10.1007/978-3-031-15553-6

This Springer imprint is published by the registered company Springer Nature Switzerland AG
The registered company address is: Gewerbestrasse 11, 6330 Cham, Switzerland

Preface

In recent years, there has been a huge research interest in virtual reality (VR), augmented reality (AR), and mixed reality (MR) technologies that now play a very important role in various fields of application such as medicine, industry, cultural heritage, and education. The boundary between the virtual and real worlds continues to blur, and the constant and rapid spread of applications of these technologies makes it possible to create shortcuts that facilitate the interaction between humans and their environment and to encourage and facilitate the process of recognition and learning.

Virtual reality technology enables the creation of realistic looking worlds and enables users to completely isolate themselves from the reality around them, entering a new digitally created world. User inputs are used to modify the digital environment in real time and this interactivity contributes to the feeling of being part of the virtual world.

Augmented reality and mixed reality technologies, on the other hand, allow the real-time fusion of digital content into the real world to enhance perception by visualizing information that users cannot directly detect with their senses. AR and MR complement reality rather than replacing it completely and the user has the impression that virtual and real objects coexist in the same space.

Extended reality (XR) is an umbrella term encapsulating virtual reality, augmented reality, and mixed reality technologies.

Thanks to the increase in features that allow us to extend our real world and combine it with virtual elements, extended reality is progressively expanding the boundaries of how we live, work, and relate.

The potential of XR technology is amazing and can transform consumers' everyday experiences and generate benefits in many market sectors, from industrial manufacturing to healthcare, education, and retail.

This book contains the contributions to the 1st International Conference on eXtended Reality (XR SALENTO 2022) held during July 6–8, 2022, in Lecce (Italy) and organized by the Augmented and Virtual Reality Laboratory (AVR Lab) at the University of Salento (Italy). To accommodate many situations, XR SALENTO 2022 was scheduled as a hybrid conference, giving participants the opportunity to attend in person or remotely.

The goal of XR SALENTO 2022 was to create a friendly environment leading to the creation or strengthening of scientific collaborations and exchanges between participants and, therefore, to solicit the submission of high-quality original research papers on any aspect and application of virtual reality, augmented reality, or mixed reality.

We received 84 submissions, out of which 58 papers were accepted for publication, 16 of which are short papers. Each submission was reviewed by at least two reviewers. We used the OCS-Unisalento Conferences system for managing the submission and review process. The Scientific Program Committee, with the help of external reviewers, carefully evaluated the contributions considering originality, significance, technical soundness, and clarity of exposition.

We are very grateful to the members of the Scientific Program Committee for their support and time spent in reviewing and discussing the submitted papers and doing so in a timely and professional manner.

We would like to sincerely thank the keynote speakers who gladly accepted our invitation and shared their expertise through enlightening speeches, helping us to fully meet the conference objectives. We were honored to have the following invited speakers:

- Vincenzo Ferrari – University of di Pisa, Italy
- Nicola Masini – CNR, Institute of Cultural Heritage Sciences, Italy
- Christian Sandor – Paris-Saclay University, France

We cordially invite you to visit the XR SALENTO 2022 website (www.xrsalento.it) where you can find all relevant information about this event.

We hope the readers will find in these pages interesting material and fruitful ideas for their future work.

July 2022

Lucio Tommaso De Paolis
Pasquale Arpaia
Marco Sacco

Organization

Conference Chair

Lucio Tommaso De Paolis	University of Salento, Italy

Program Chairs

Pasquale Arpaia	University of Naples Federico II, Italy
Marco Sacco	STIIMA-CNR, Italy

Scientific Program Committee

Andrea Abate	University of Salerno, Italy
Sara Arlati	STIIMA-CNR, Italy
Selim Balcisoy	Sabanci University, Turkey
Sergi Bermúdez i Badia	University of Madeira, Portugal
Monica Bordegoni	Polytechnic University of Milan, Italy
Andrea Bottino	Polytechnic University of Turin, Italy
Pierre Boulanger	University of Alberta, Canada
Andres Bustillo	University of Burgos, Spain
Silvia Mabel Castro	Universidad Nacional del Sur, Argentina
David Checa Cruz	University of Burgos, Spain
Rita Cucchiara	University of Modena, Italy
Yevgeniya Daineko	International Information Technology University, Kazakhstan
Egidio De Benedetto	University of Naples Federico II, Italy
Mariolino De Cecco	University of Trento, Italy
Valerio De Luca	University of Salento, Italy
Giovanni D'Errico	Polytechnic University of Turin, Italy
Giuseppe Di Gironimo	University of Naples Federico II, Italy
Tania Di Mascio	University of L'Aquila, Italy
Aldo Franco Dragoni	Polytechnic University of Marche, Italy
Ugo Erra	University of Basilicata, Italy
Ben Falchuk	Peraton Labs, USA
Vincenzo Ferrari	University of Pisa, Italy
Emanuele Frontoni	Polytechnic University of Marche, Italy
Luigi Gallo	ICAR-CNR, Italy
Carola Gatto	University of Salento, Italy

Fabrizio Lamberti	Polytechnic University of Turin, Italy
Mariangela Lazoi	University of Salento, Italy
Leo Joskowicz	Hebrew University of Jerusalem, Israel
Tomas Krilavičius	Vytautas Magnus University, Lithuania
Vladimir Kuts	Tallinn University of Technology, Estonia
Salvatore Livatino	University of Hertfordshire, UK
Luca Mainetti	University of Salento, Italy
Eva Savina Malinverni	Polytechnic University of Marche, Italy
Matija Marolt	University of Ljubljana, Slovenia
Nicola Masini	CNR, Institute of Cultural Heritage Sciences, Italy
Fabrizio Nunnari	German Research Center for Artificial Intelligence (DFKI), Germany
Tauno Otto	Tallinn University of Technology, Estonia
Üyesi Yasin Ortakci	Karabük University, Turkey
Miguel A. Padilla Castañeda	Universidad Nacional Autónoma de México, Mexico
Volker Paelke	Bremen University of Applied Sciences, Germany
Roberto Paiano	University of Salento, Italy
Giorgos Papadourakis	Technological Educational Institute of Crete, Greece
Alessandro Pepino	University of Naples Federico II, Italy
Eduard Petlenkov	Tallinn University of Technology, Estonia
Roberto Pierdicca	Polytechnic University of Marche, Italy
Sofia Pescarin	CNR ITABC, Italy
Paolo Proietti	MIMOS, Italy
Arcadio Reyes Lecuona	Universidad de Malaga, Spain
Christian Sandor	Paris-Saclay University, France
Andrea Sanna	Polytechnic University of Turin, Italy
Jaume Segura Garcia	Universitat de València, Spain
Huseyin Seker	Birmingham City University, UK
Franco Tecchia	Scuola Superiore Sant'Anna, Italy
Antonio Emmanuele Uva	Polytechnic University of Bari, Italy
Aleksei Tepljakov	Tallinn University of Technology, Estonia
Kristina Vassiljeva	Tallinn University of Technology, Estonia
Krzysztof Walczak	Poznań University of Economics and Business, Poland

Panel Committee

Alessandro Pepino	University of Naples Federico II, Italy
Paolo Proietti	MIMOS, Italy
Ersilia Vallefuoco	University of Naples Federico II, Italy

Award Committee

Lucio Tommaso De Paolis	University of Salento, Italy
Pasquale Arpaia	University of Naples, Italy

Organizing Committee

Ilenia Paladini	University of Salento, Italy
Silke Miss	XRtechnology, Italy

Local Organizing Committee

Silvia Liaci	University of Basilicata, Italy
Laura Corchia	University of Salento, Italy
Sofia Chiarello	University of Salento, Italy
Federica Faggiano	University of Salento, Italy
B. Luigi Nuzzo	University of Salento, Italy
Giada Sumerano	University of Salento, Italy

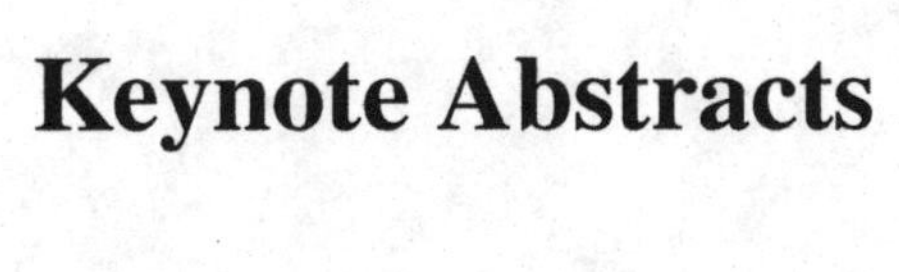

Keynote Abstracts

Extend Human Performances with Augmented Reality

Vincenzo Ferrari

Università di Pisa, Italy

AR allows the integration of spatial relation between visible and invisible information under a natural naked eye view. Furthermore, the augmented information could guide the user's hand during precision tasks improving human efficiency and accuracy. This improvement could bring human performance closer to that of the robot with a higher level of flexibility and humanization of the task. For tasks unfeasible with the sole hands, AR becomes particularly useful in robotics applications where the humans are engaged for remote controlling or cooperative working. In current AR displays, the augmentation lacks geometrical coherence along the three dimensions between real and virtual information that determine perceptual issues as wrong spatial, focus, and depth cues for both eyes. These issues will be detailed during the talk and possible solutions will be explained.

Past and Coming 20 Years with Augmented Reality

Christian Sandor

Paris-Saclay University, France

Augmented Reality embeds spatially-registered computer graphics into a user's view of the real world. During the last 20 years, AR has progressed enormously from a niche technology to a widely investigated one. This keynote consists of two parts. First, I speak about how major challenges for AR have been solved over the last 20 years. Second, I speculate about what the next 20 years are going to bring. The goal is to present a Birdseye view of the AR domain, including the balance of power between the major AR forces US and China. In my view, Europe has a very big, possibly almost impossible, challenge ahead to catch up. I hope that my talk will contribute to laying the seeds of a major European AR initiative.

Remote and Close Range Sensing, Imaging and eXtended Reality for the Interpretation and Conservation of Cultural Heritage

Nicola Masini

CNR, Institute of Cultural Heritage Sciences, Italy

Cultural heritage is not only the legacy of tangible and intangible heritage assets of a community inherited from past generations, to be maintained and transmitted to future generations, but it is also a domain of study and research where multidisciplinary skills compare, combine and contaminate each other, stimulating the development of new technologies and methods of analysis and study that can be re-applied in other domains. The reason is due to the heterogeneity of data to be analysed (from historical sources to imaging), phenomena to be observed (from chemical degradation to structural risks), objectives (from safeguarding to conservation). Effective tools to enrich knowledge of Cultural properties are remote and close range sensing, for diagnostic purposes, which provide a number of data on biophysical parameters without any contact with the object/artefact/site to be investigated. However, the heterogeneity of the data and the difficulty of transforming them into useful information for knowledge and conservation of CH, makes it necessary to use tools aimed at facilitating their interpretation. To this end, a useful tool for this purpose is the creation of combined real and virtual environments, i.e. extended reality capable to cover the entire spectrum from "completely real" to "completely virtual" in the concept of reality-virtuality continuum. This approach allows to interrelate data and results of the different diagnostic imaging techniques (from thermal infrared to high frequency georadar) with the spatial and architectural contexts of reference, in its constructive components and materials, facilitating their interpretation to improve the knowledge and to support decisions for restoration.

Contents – Part II

eXtended Reality for Learning and Training

Mixed Reality Agents for Automated Mentoring Processes 3
Benedikt Hensen, Danylo Bekhter, Dascha Blehm, Sebastian Meinberger, and Ralf Klamma

Asynchronous Manual Work in Mixed Reality Remote Collaboration 17
Anjela Mayer, Théo Combe, Jean-Rémy Chardonnet, and Jivka Ovtcharova

A Virtual Reality Serious Game for Children with Dyslexia: DixGame 34
Henar Guillen-Sanz, Bruno Rodríguez-Garcia, Kim Martinez, and María Consuelo Saiz Manzanares

Processing Physiological Sensor Data in Near Real-Time as Social Signals for Their Use on Social Virtual Reality Platforms 44
Fabio Genz, Clemens Hufeld, and Dieter Kranzlmüller

Developing a Tutorial for Improving Usability and User Skills in an Immersive Virtual Reality Experience 63
Ines Miguel-Alonso, Bruno Rodriguez-Garcia, David Checa, and Lucio Tommaso De Paolis

Challenges in Virtual Reality Training for CRBN Events 79
Georg Regal, Helmut Schrom-Feiertag, Massimo Migliorini, Massimiliano Guarneri, Daniele Di Giovanni, Andrea D'Angelo, and Markus Murtinger

A Preliminary Study on the Teaching Mode of Interactive VR Painting Ability Cultivation 89
YanXiang Zhang and Yang Chen

eXtended Reality in Education

Factors in the Cognitive-Emotional Impact of Educational Environmental Narrative Videogames 101
Sofia Pescarin and Delfina S. M. Pandiani

Instinct-Based Decision-Making in Interactive Narratives 109
Tobías Palma Stade

The Application of Immersive Virtual Reality for Children's Road Education: Validation of a Pedestrian Crossing Scenario 128
Giulia De Cet, Andrea Baldassa, Mariaelena Tagliabue, Riccardo Rossi, Chiara Vianello, and Massimiliano Gastaldi

Collaborative VR Scene Broadcasting for Geometry Education 141
YanXiang Zhang and JiaYu Wang

Collaborative Mixed Reality Annotations System for Science and History Education Based on UWB Positioning and Low-Cost AR Glasses 150
YanXiang Zhang and LiTing Tang

Artificial Intelligence and Machine Learning for eXtended Reality

Can AI Replace Conventional Markerless Tracking? A Comparative Performance Study for Mobile Augmented Reality Based on Artificial Intelligence 161
Roberto Pierdicca, Flavio Tonetto, Marco Mameli, Riccardo Rosati, and Primo Zingaretti

Find, Fuse, Fight: Genetic Algorithms to Provide Engaging Content for Multiplayer Augmented Reality Games 178
Federico Aliprandi, Renato Avellar Nobre, Laura Anna Ripamonti, Davide Gadia, and Dario Maggiorini

Synthetic Data Generation for Surface Defect Detection 198
Déborah Lebert, Jérémy Plouzeau, Jean-Philippe Farrugia, Florence Danglade, and Frédéric Merienne

eXtended Reality in Geo-information Sciences

ARtefact: A Conceptual Framework for the Integrated Information Management of Archaeological Excavations 211
Damianos Gavalas, Vlasios Kasapakis, Evangelia Kavakli, Panayiotis Koutsabasis, Despina Catapoti, and Spyros Vosinakis

Geomatics Meets XR: A Brief Overview of the Synergy Between Geospatial Data and Augmented Visualization 224
Roberto Pierdicca, Maurizio Mulliri, Matteo Lucesoli, Fabio Piccinini, and Eva Savina Malinverni

Utilization of Geographic Data for the Creation of Occlusion Models in the Context of Mixed Reality Applications 236
Christoph Praschl, Erik Thiele, and Oliver Krauss

Development of an Open-Source 3D WebGIS Framework to Promote Cultural Heritage Dissemination 254
Alessandra Capolupo, Cristina Monterisi, and Eufemia Tarantino

Industrial eXtended Reality

A Framework for Developing XR Applications Including Multiple Sensorial Media 271
M. Bordegoni, M. Carulli, and E. Spadoni

Augmented Reality Remote Maintenance in Industry: A Systematic Literature Review 287
David Breitkreuz, Maike Müller, Dirk Stegelmeyer, and Rakesh Mishra

Virtual Teleoperation Setup for a Bimanual Bartending Robot 306
Sara Buonocore, Stanislao Grazioso, and Giuseppe Di Gironimo

eXtended Reality in the Digital Transformation of Museums

Virtualization and Vice Versa: A New Procedural Model of the Reverse Virtualization for the User Behavior Tracking in the Virtual Museums 329
Iva Vasic, Aleksandra Pauls, Adriano Mancini, Ramona Quattrini, Roberto Pierdicca, Renato Angeloni, Eva S. Malinverni, Emanuele Frontoni, Paolo Clini, and Bata Vasic

"You Can Tell a Man by the Emotion He Feels": How Emotions Influence Visual Inspection of Abstract Art in Immersive Virtual Reality 341
Marta Pizzolante and Alice Chirico

Augmented Reality and 3D Printing for Archaeological Heritage: Evaluation of Visitor Experience 360
Valeria Garro and Veronica Sundstedt

Building Blocks for Multi-dimensional WebXR Inspection Tools Targeting Cultural Heritage 373
Bruno Fanini, Emanuel Demetrescu, Alberto Bucciero, Alessandra Chirivi, Francesco Giuri, Ivan Ferrari, and Nicola Delbarba

Comparing the Impact of Low-Cost 360° Cultural Heritage Videos Displayed in 2D Screens Versus Virtual Reality Headsets 391
Bruno Rodriguez-Garcia, Mario Alaguero, Henar Guillen-Sanz, and Ines Miguel-Alonso

eXtended Reality Beyond the Five Senses

Non-immersive Versus Immersive Extended Reality for Motor Imagery Neurofeedback Within a Brain-Computer Interfaces 407
Pasquale Arpaia, Damien Coyle, Francesco Donnarumma, Antonio Esposito, Angela Natalizio, and Marco Parvis

Virtual Reality Enhances EEG-Based Neurofeedback for Emotional Self-regulation 420
Pasquale Arpaia, Damien Coyle, Giovanni D'Errico, Egidio De Benedetto, Lucio Tommaso De Paolis, Naomi du Bois, Sabrina Grassini, Giovanna Mastrati, Nicola Moccaldi, and Ersilia Vallefuoco

Psychological and Educational Interventions Among Cancer Patients: A Systematic Review to Analyze the Role of Immersive Virtual Reality for Improving Patients' Well-Being 432
Maria Sansoni, Clelia Malighetti, and Giuseppe Riva

Author Index 455

Contents – Part I

Virtual Reality

Rehabilitation of Post-COVID Patients: A Virtual Reality Home-Based Intervention Including Cardio-Respiratory Fitness Training ... 3
Vera Colombo, Marta Mondellini, Giovanni Tauro, Giovanna Palumbo, Mauro Rossini, Emilia Biffi, Roberta Nossa, Alessia Fumagalli, Emilia Ambrosini, Alessandra Pedrocchi, Franco Molteni, Daniele Colombo, Gianluigi Reni, Marco Sacco, and Sara Arlati

Comparison of the Effect of Exposing Users for Height While Being Active Versus Passive in a Virtual Environment - A Pilot Study ... 18
Günter Alce, Felicia Hanserup, and Kornelia Palm

A Proposal for a Computational Framework Architecture and Design for Massive Virtual World Generation and Simulation ... 37
Zintis Erics and Arnis Cirulis

Evaluating Forms of User Interaction with a Virtual Exhibition of Household Appliances ... 48
Mikołaj Maik, Paweł Sobociński, Krzysztof Walczak, and Tomasz Jenek

TryItOn: A Virtual Dressing Room with Motion Tracking and Physically Based Garment Simulation ... 63
Gilda Manfredi, Nicola Capece, Ugo Erra, Gabriele Gilio, Vincenzo Baldi, and Simone Gerardo Di Domenico

Automatic Generation of 3D Animations from Text and Images ... 77
Alberto Cannavò, Valentina Gatteschi, Luca Macis, and Fabrizio Lamberti

Design Process of a Ceramic Modeling Application for Virtual Reality Art Therapy ... 92
Carola Gatto, Kim Martinez, and Lucio Tommaso De Paolis

Computer Simulation of a Spectrum Analyzer Based on the Unity Game Engine ... 104
Ye. A. Daineko, A. Z. Aitmagambetov, D. D. Tsoy, A. E. Kulakayeva, and M. T. Ipalakova

The Influence of Method of Control and Visual Aspects on Exploratory Decisions in 3D Video Games Environments ... 113
Aneta Wiśniewska, Jedrzej Kołecki, Adam Wojciechowski, and Rafał Szrajber

Collaborative Virtual Reality Environment for Training Load Movement with Overhead Bridge Cranes ... 121
David Checa, Ines Miguel-Alonso, Henar Guillen-Sanz, and Andres Bustillo

A VR Multiplayer Application for Fire Fighting Training Simulations ... 130
Irene Capasso, Chiara Bassano, Fabrizio Bracco, Fabio Solari, Eros Viola, and Manuela Chessa

Effects of Head Rotation and Depth Enhancement in Virtual Reality User-Scene Interaction ... 139
S. Livatino, A. Zocco, Y. Iqbal, P. Gainley, G. Morana, and G. M. Farinella

Are We Ready for Take-Off ? Learning Cockpit Actions with VR Headsets ... 147
S. Livatino, M. Mohamed, G. Morana, P. Gainley, Y. Iqbal, T. H. Nguyen, K. Williams, and A. Zocco

Virtual Reality as a Collaborative Tool for Digitalised Crime Scene Examination ... 154
Vincenzo Rinaldi, Lucina Hackman, and Niamh NicDaeid

A Virtual Reality Application for Stress Reduction: Design and First Implementation of ERMES Project ... 162
Carola Gatto, Giovanni D'Errico, Fabiana Nuccetelli, Benito Luigi Nuzzo, Maria Cristina Barba, Giovanna Ilenia Paladini, and Lucio Tommaso De Paolis

Efficient and Secure Transmission of Digital Data in the 5G Era ... 174
Bruno Carpentieri and Francesco Palmieri

Augmented Reality

Hand Interaction Toolset for Augmented Reality Environments ... 185
Ilias Logothetis, Konstantinos Karampidis, Nikolas Vidakis, and Giorgos Papadourakis

Assessing Visual Cues for Improving Awareness in Collaborative Augmented Reality ... 200
Francesco Strada, Edoardo Battegazzorre, Enrico Ameglio, Simone Turello, and Andrea Bottino

Human Augmentation: An Enactive Perspective 219
Agnese Augello, Giuseppe Caggianese, and Luigi Gallo

XRShip: Augmented Reality for Ship Familiarizations 229
Yogi Udjaja, Muhamad Fajar, Karen Etania Saputra, and Samsul Arifin

Coupling Mobile AR with a Virtual Agent for End-User Engagement 239
Tina Katika, Ioannis Karaseitanidis, and Angelos Amditis

3D Audio + Augmented Reality + AI Chatbots + IoT: An Immersive Conversational Cultural Guide 249
Michalis Tsepapadakis, Damianos Gavalas, and Panayiotis Koutsabasis

eXtended Reality

Regulating the Metaverse, a Blueprint for the Future 263
Louis B. Rosenberg

Do Presence Questionnaires Actually Measure Presence? A Content Analysis of Presence Measurement Scales 273
Olivier Nannipieri

Self Assessment Tool to Bridge the Gap Between XR Technology, SMEs, and HEIs 296
Ahmet Köse, Aleksei Tepljakov, Saleh Alsaleh, and Eduard Petlenkov

An Overview on Technologies for the Distribution and Participation in Live Events 312
Vito Del Vecchio, Mariangela Lazoi, and Marianna Lezzi

How to Improve Vehicle Lateral Control: The Effect of Visual Feedback Luminance 324
Riccardo Rossi, Giulia De Cet, and Federico Orsini

Extended Reality Technologies and Social Inclusion: The Role of Virtual Reality in Includiamoci Project 335
Carola Gatto, Silvia Liaci, Laura Corchia, Sofia Chiarello, Federica Faggiano, Giada Sumerano, and Lucio Tommaso De Paolis

Author Index 347

eXtended Reality for Learning and Training

Mixed Reality Agents for Automated Mentoring Processes

Benedikt Hensen(✉), Danylo Bekhter, Dascha Blehm, Sebastian Meinberger, and Ralf Klamma

Advanced Community Information Systems, Chair of Computer Science 5, RWTH Aachen University, Aachen, Germany
hensen@dbis.rwth-aachen.de

Abstract. Mentoring processes can enhance education by providing personalized advice and feedback to students. A challenge of mentoring is that with a rising number of students, more mentors are required. As it is oftentimes infeasible to employ such a high number of mentors, automated tools can support the activities of mentors by e.g., answering common questions. However, such tools can impact the students' engagement as they can feel impersonal. Therefore, we developed mixed reality mentoring agents. They personify these automated tools, can interact directly with the students, and demonstrate practical tasks to them as a guide. On the technical level, this is realized by a behavior tree structure with blackboards that simulate the agent's memory. With such a visual representation of the behavior, developers, teachers, and mentors alike can edit and define the mentoring capabilities of the agent. The implementation results are open-source and we added them to our Virtual Agents Framework that allows developers to quickly add agents to cross-platform mixed reality applications. Moreover, we conducted a user study with the mentoring prototype. The results are promising as students perceived the mixed reality agents in a positive way, with high usability, and as helpful advisors. Therefore, mixed reality mentoring agents have the potential to become widespread companions for students during their studies.

Keywords: Mixed reality · Virtual agents · Mentoring

1 Introduction

A mentoring system can improve the quality of education as students are assigned a mentor who can guide them in their studies [16]. The mentor can provide personalized help, both regarding content and emotional support. One challenge of such a mentoring system is that it does not scale well [12]. With the rising number of students, more mentors are required to make sure that a mentor has enough time and dedication to keep the quality of advice at a high level. However, it is oftentimes not feasible to find such a large number of mentors who are trained and skilled enough to supervise the students. A possible

L. T. De Paolis et al. (Eds.): XR Salento 2022, LNCS 13446, pp. 3–16, 2022.
https://doi.org/10.1007/978-3-031-15553-6_1

solution to this is to automate mentoring processes, for example with the help of intelligent mentoring systems. These bear their own challenges as students are not interacting with another human anymore, but instead only look at an impersonal application or chat interface. To provide more meaningful interactions that raise the user acceptance, mixed reality can be used. Mixed Reality provides an intuitive user interface in 3D. It combines virtual elements with real-world elements [15], meaning that virtual humans can be added to the real world. In the mentoring context, we can use such virtual mixed reality agents as a natural user interface where the student is directly talking to a character. A major challenge for mixed reality mentoring agents is making them appear intelligent and empathic enough. The agent needs to be able to respond to various scenarios and contextual situations. Here, inspiration can be found in non-player characters (NPCs) in games that can use behavior trees as a flexible and extendable logic representation [14]. This technique can be coupled with other known concepts from cognitive modeling like blackboards which store key-value pairs as the agent's memory. This way, complex and powerful mixed reality mentoring agents can be created which can still be edited by developers, designers, and mentors.

In this paper, we create an example mixed reality mentoring agent. It consists of a reusable framework as a technological foundation which allows authors to create their own mentoring experiences. We present a possible architecture for constructing a mixed reality mentoring agent and explore a possible example use case to support automated mentoring.

The rest of this paper is structured as follows. In Sect. 2, we present related approaches. Section 3 describes the realized framework and the implementation of a prototype for a sample use case. In Sect. 4, we evaluate this prototype and show the results. In Sect. 5, we discuss our results. Finally, Sect. 6 concludes the paper and outlines possible future work.

2 Related Work

A common use case for simulating virtual humans can be found in video games. Here, virtual agents are inserted as NPCs to populate the virtual worlds of the game. There are various techniques for authoring and managing the behaviors of such NPCs such as behavior trees [14], goal-oriented action planning, or utility-based systems [2]. The goal of these approaches is similar in creating believable, complex life-like virtual lifeforms that can easily be authored. However, Lankoski and Björk [13] already analyzed that is neither feasible nor necessary to strive for a perfect simulation of virtual humans but instead, engagement can already be achieved if specific factors are fulfilled and by following a series of patterns. However, virtual agents can also be applied in more serious use cases. For this, Gratch et al. defined the work frontiers that need to collaborate in order to realize virtual agents [7]. To realize a virtual agent, developers need to work on the aspects of full-body animations, facial expressions, perceiving the environment, modeling behavior, simulating emotions, and communicating via speech understanding and speech synthesis.

In mixed reality, virtual humans have also been applied. Here, Holz et al. were one of the first to systematically characterize and organize the field of mixed reality agents [10]. They defined a taxonomy with the three dimensions of agency, corporeal presence, and interactive capacity. In the agency category, weak agency and strong agency are differentiated. The corporeal presence describes whether the agent has a representation that is purely in the virtual world, solely in the real world, or in both worlds. Similarly, the interactive capacity classifies whether the agent is capable of interacting with objects in virtuality or the real environment, e.g., by robotics.

One main area for mixed reality agents is their use in education. Here, they can be used as virtual guides in museums that can repeatedly convey the same experience to a large number of visitors [8]. This guiding ability can also be used to demonstrate construction tasks that require interactions with real objects. Apart from conveying information, mixed reality agents are used in simulations where human interaction is required. This can concern different kinds of simulations like presentation training where the virtual audience can give automated feedback about their level of engagement during the talk [17]. Additionally, virtual agents have been used to train teachers to react to specific situations in a classroom [6]. The agent can also act as a user interface. For instance, in a mixed reality vocabulary learning application, an agent was added as an additional mean of interaction [11].

3 Realization

We implemented our mixed reality mentoring agents using the 3D engine Unity. The prototype is based on our Virtual Agents Framework, which is an open-source project on GitHub[1]. With this prototype implementation, we were also able to extend the Virtual Agents Framework's feature set.

3.1 Virtual Agents Framework

The Virtual Agents Framework provides a core architecture for creating virtual humans. The framework delivers a base agent visualization in the form of a rigged 3D character as shown in Fig. 1, but it can be switched out by different 3D models, e.g., a 3D scan of a real person. Moreover, the Virtual Agents Framework consists of building blocks which define the agent's logic and provide an application programming interface (API) for other scripts to control the agent. To achieve this, actions are scheduled on a task queue. A single task can, e.g., instruct the agent to walk to a specific place or to play a specific animation. A priority queue is used to determine which tasks must be executed first. For tasks with the same priority, the first-in-first-out principle is applied. Tasks can be grouped in a sequential manner in composite tasks. This way, complex action sequences can be coded. Each task object consists of a starting method,

[1] https://github.com/rwth-acis/Virtual-Agents-Framework.

an update method which is called every frame, and an event to inform other components once the task is finished. Because of this interface, developers can extend the system with their own tasks and actions. The agent's API also provides aliases for common actions like walking to a specific location. This way, developers do not need to create the task object every time but can instead call a method which automatically creates the correct task object, initializes it with the context values, and schedules it on the agent.

The currently executed task must be visualized to the user. This is done by animations. They are organized by a Unity animator controller which is a state machine to transition between different animations. The Virtual Agents Framework provides a base animator controller which can be adapted and extended. Its central component for movement is a blend tree which can continuously transition between an idle animation and a walking animation based on a given speed parameter. Hence, once the agent starts moving, the blend tree automatically fades into a walking animation which corresponds to the agent's movement speed. Here, we created custom animations for common actions such as walking and packaged them with the framework. All animations use Unity's humanoid rig target. This means that the animations can be transferred to any other character model which is compatible with Unity's humanoid rig target. Additional animations can be added to the animator controller's state graph.

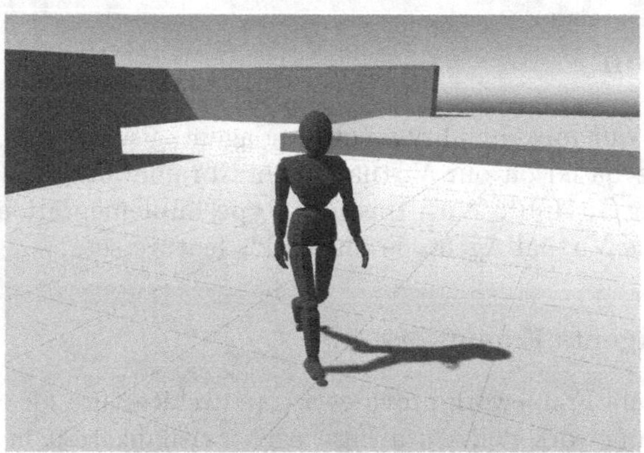

Fig. 1. The agent of the Virtual Agents Framework during a walking animation

3.2 Architecture of the Mixed Reality Mentoring Agent

The mixed reality mentoring agent is realized using the Virtual Agents Framework. The framework provides a configurable core structure of the agent as shown in Fig. 2. Here, the 3D mesh representation and its skeleton can be switched with a custom model. The changed skeleton is then mapped to a general definition so that it works with the pre-defined animations. The agent executes a task that can output an animation action or speech. In the case of an action, the agent schedules a task which accesses its animator. There, the animation state is switched accordingly. The animation is then performed by the agent in the augmented reality setting where it can be observed by the user. The second option for an output is speech. We use Microsoft's text-to-speech engine to convert a written answer into spoken text. The answer is then read out to the user. This output option of the spoken text is also realized using specific, implemented tasks that are given to the agent. To select a currently executed task, the cognitive model layer of the agent is used. Here, developers can define how the agent should plan tasks or react to the environment. In the Virtual Agent Framework, we provide different alternatives that can be chosen like a prioritized task queue where tasks are executed in a given order or a behavior tree which evaluates the current situation and determines a suitable task. Moreover, this part is extendable as developers can implement and add their own task planners. The cognitive model works with tasks which are given to the core agent. The framework provides predefined tasks like walking to a given position but developers can also add own tasks for their specific purposes. For the mentoring agent, we also added own application logic which reads the environment state. Moreover, speech input can be collected which causes tasks to be scheduled on the agent. We use the dictation manager and the speech commands by the mixed reality toolkit (MRTK) to capture speech input by the user.

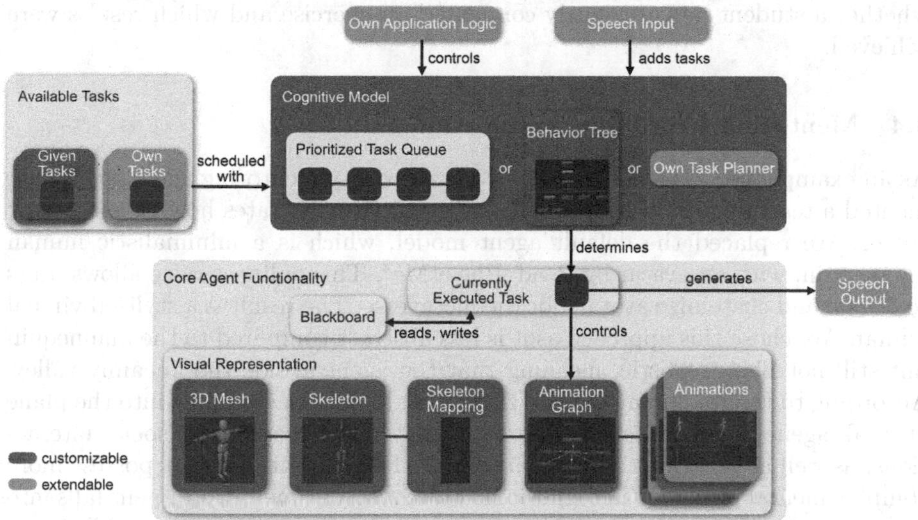

Fig. 2. The architecture of the Virtual Agents Framework

3.3 Extensions for Mentoring: Behavior Trees

The task system forms the base layer where commands are directly given to the agent. As a separate layer above this, we have added behavior trees which enable autonomous behavior. Within such a tree, developers can encode the behavior of the agent. It allows them to define different cases and the reactions by the agent. The behavior tree is evaluated every frame in order to find the currently applicable leaf node. The leaf node then adds its corresponding task object to the task queue and makes sure that it is executed directly.

With the visual representation in the Unity editor, developers gain an overview of the coded scenario and can easily adapt and adjust it using the visual tool. Hence, with this visual representation, non-developers, like designers or teachers can create their own scenarios. This is especially useful for the mentoring use case. The regular evaluation of the behavior tree allows the agent to react to the current situation. However, additional measures are required to give the agent a memory. Here, we use blackboards. They are implemented as key-value stores. Values are added or updated as task actions are executed. Moreover, the decision nodes of the behavior tree have access to the blackboard and so the agent can make decisions based on previous knowledge. To ensure that agents have persistent knowledge, the blackboard is stored in a JavaScript Object Notation (JSON) file on application exit and it is reloaded at the next startup. Therefore, the blackboard can hold information about the user or specific data about the exercise that the student has to take. It can, e.g., remember whether a student has previously completed an exercise and which results were achieved.

3.4 Mentoring Prototype Application

As an example use case and to test our mixed reality mentoring agent, we implemented a teaching application where the agent demonstrates how to use a laser cutter. We replaced the default agent model, which is a minimalistic human mannequin, with an avatar by ReadyPlayerMe[2]. This online service allows users to design and customize avatars for the metaverse. The result is a stylized virtual human. We chose this approach as it is less abstract compared to the mannequin but still not photorealistic, meaning that the agent avoids the uncanny valley. According to the taxonomy cube of Holz et al. [10], our agent falls into the plane of weak agency since it can act autonomously and is capable of social interactions, as well as reacting to the environment. However, it does not possess more complex mental processes like emotions. Moreover, our mentoring agent falls into the category of virtual corporeal presence and virtual interaction capabilities as the agent exists in a virtual space.

To encourage interaction of the participants in the subsequent user evaluation with the mentoring agent, we added a 3D model of a laser cutter. With this virtual device, users are supposed to gain knowledge about how to operate it.

[2] https://readyplayer.me.

By design, we chose a device that most of the evaluation participants do not know and the 3D model of the device is deliberately not accurate to a real-world device. This way, we guarantee that users do not know how to use it and therefore, the help of the agent is required. We defined a series of exercises which can be loaded by the agent as JSON files. In these exercises, the individual task steps of the agent are defined. For instance, there is an exercise where the agent demonstrates to the user how to start a laser cutting process. Here, we defined the different steps for inserting material into the device, starting the laser cutting process, and finally retrieving the finished cut. This JSON file is loaded by the agent if the agent's behavior tree detects a corresponding question about this topic and chooses to activate this exercise. After that, the steps of the agent are inserted into the task queue of the agent. The agent will then run through this process as shown in Fig. 3. The agent concludes the task by memorizing in the blackboard that the user has viewed the exercise. This is helpful in recognizing whether a student asks for the same demonstration multiple times which can be a signal that additional help by a human mentor is required. Apart from exercises, the agent is prepared to answer a series of pre-defined questions which can also be adjusted by mentors.

Fig. 3. The mentoring agent demonstrating the use of the laser cutter

4 Evaluation

The resulting mentoring prototype was tested with 11 users on the Microsoft HoloLens. All of them are students enrolled at the RWTH Aachen University.

4.1 Preparations and Setup

Participants were first briefed about the Microsoft HoloLens. They were then introduced to the application and were given the task to understand how the virtual 3D laser cutter is restocked with new material. Hence, they can ask any question to the mentoring bot and should at some point ask for the demonstration exercise. Finally, users filled out a questionnaire to judge this system regarding its usability and their impression of the agent. Therefore, we utilized the system usability scale (SUS) [3]. This established questionnaire consists of ten statements to which users should express their level of agreement on a five-point Likert scale. Here, smaller values show disagreement and higher values agreement. With the results, an overall usability score between 0 and 100 can be computed where higher values indicate better usability. A study showed that a result of 68 is regarded as average and signals an ok usability [1,4]. Good usability can be attested for systems with scores of 80 and above [1]. Since the statements alternate between positive and negative formulations, users have to concentrate on the content of the statement and the calculation in the end has to invert half of the statement's results. The questionnaire also contained a part which aimed at evaluating the educational performance. Here, the main question is whether students understood the demonstrations and whether they think that it was helpful to them. They were also asked so asked to comment about the agent itself, e.g., its appearance and its behavior. We observed the users while interacting with the application and noted any comments that the users made.

4.2 Results

Regarding the usability, an average SUS score of 83.6 was achieved. This indicates that the usability can be assessed as good and is just short of the SUS range with excellent usability which starts at 85. The lowest usability score that an individual response recorded is 70 which is still above average. The detailed results are visualized in Fig. 4. With a mean value of four on the five-point Likert scale, participants expressed that they would like to use the system frequently. Moreover, strong and agreeing opinions are found in the statements whether the system is unnecessary complex and whether a lot had to be learned before using the system. Here, a mean value of 1.18 and a standard deviation of 0.4 are achieved, meaning that participants think that the system is intuitive to understand. Participants commented that the system is easy to use as all participants rated this aspect with four or five points on a five-point Likert scale. The statement where opinions are most spread regards requiring the help of a technical person. Here, a mean value of 2.09 and a standard deviation of 1.51 is recorded. This means that the answers are spread on the Likert scale but overall, participants tend to think that they do not require technical help. The integration of functions into the mentoring system was well-received with an average score of 4.09. The results also indicate that the users found the system to not be inconsistent as the average score here is 1.64. Mixed results were recorded regarding the cumbersome usage of the system. Here, a mean score of 2.09 with a standard deviation of 0.94 was obtained in the results. This means that some participants found the application cumbersome but overall, participants still disagreed with the statement. A question with a positive result where participants only answered with four or five points on the Likert scale regards the question whether others can learn the system quickly. With a mean value of 4.64, participants agree that the system can be understood quickly. This is also indicated by the tenth question where the users indicated that they themselves did not have to learn much as the statement scored an average of 1.18. Users signaled that they were confident with the application as this statement also only recorded agreement or strong agreement with a mean value of 4.36.

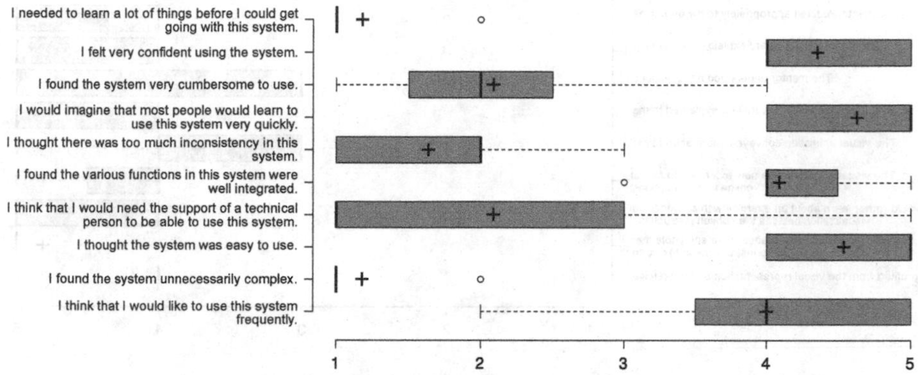

Fig. 4. Boxplot of the results regarding the system usability scale

In the questionnaire about the educational experience, students agreed that the visual demonstration of a process with the agent is better than a textual description. Here, a mean value of 4.82 and a standard deviation of 0.4 was scored on a five-point Likert scale. The overall results are also illustrated in Fig. 5. Students also agreed with an average of 4.18 and a standard deviation of 0.4 that they profited from a visual representation. Regarding the mentoring design, students expressed their desire for additional visual elements that support the vocal instructions. Here, an average result of 4.64 was obtained with a standard deviation of 0.5. Moreover, opinions were more scattered and less agreeing about the statement whether the shown animations help convey additional information. Here, a mean of 3.73 was scored with a standard deviation of 0.9, meaning that students were slightly in favor of the used animations to learn about the laser cutting process. When asked whether students see these animations as an extension of online learning, they agreed with a mean of 4.09 and a standard deviation of 0.7. The results also indicate that the users understood the agent's explanations as all participants either chose four or five on the five-point Likert scale, expressing agreement or strong agreement. This leads to a mean agreement value of 4.55 and a standard deviation of 0.52 for this statement. Regarding the abilities of the agent, options were mixed about how well the mentor understood questions. Here, a mean of 3.73 and a standard deviation of 1.01 was scored, meaning that opinions are spread out. Similarly, the support provided by the agent was scored with an average of 3.64 and a standard deviation of 0.81, indicating that students were not fully satisfied with the support capabilities of the agent. There was also a large spread of opinions on the question whether the mentor appropriately reacted to questions with a standard deviation of 1.03. However, the mean value of this question still indicates overall agreement with a value of 4.36. Similarly, the spoken language was perceived as clear. Here, students gave the agent a 4.64 mean score with a standard deviation of 0.5.

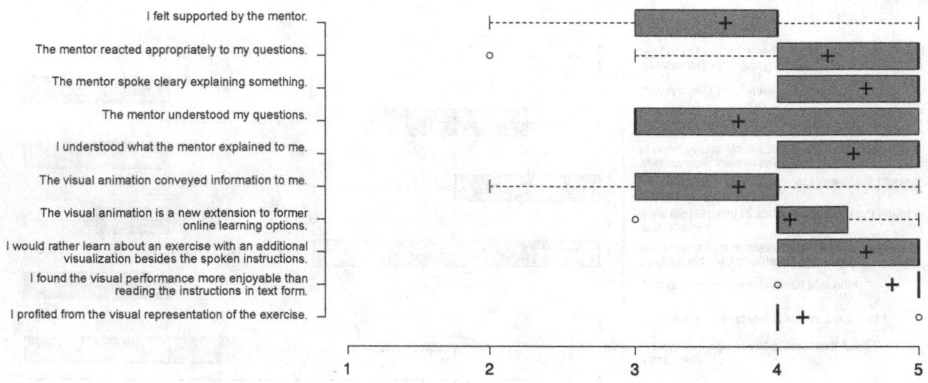

Fig. 5. Boxplot of the results regarding the educational experience

In the last part of the questionnaire, we evaluated the agent's appearance and behavior. The results are illustrated in Fig. 6. Here, mixed results were recorded regarding the human-like appearance of the agent with an average agreement value of 3.73. With a standard deviation of 1.27, options were spread out. Students could identify that the agent was controlled by the computer. When asked if the mentor could be controlled by a person, they disagreed with a mean of 1.64 and a standard deviation of 0.5. Largely varying feedback was gathered regarding the question whether participants recognized unrealistic behavior of the agent during the interaction. Here, a mean value of 3.64 indicates that on average, students found unrealistic behavior but with values recorded on every stage of the Likert scale and a standard deviation of 1.29, a large discrepancy between answers was found. We also saw a tendency of users to perceive the agent's movement as robotic with a mean value of 3.36 and a standard deviation of 0.81. The participants were also undecided about whether the agent was paying attention to them. With a standard deviation of 0.98 around a mean of 3.82, opinions about this varied. However, the results indicate that students felt immersed as they expressed on average with 4.18 and a standard deviation of 1.17 that they perceived the agent as being in the same room. Few comments regarded uncanniness as students disagreed with a mean value of 2.36 and a standard deviation of 0.92 that the agent felt uncanny. However, there was agreement that the agent seems friendly as an average answer score of 4 with a standard deviation of 0.77 was recorded. The spoken answers could also clearly be perceived as students thought that the agent's voice sounds clear with an average value of 3.46 and a standard deviation of 0.67.

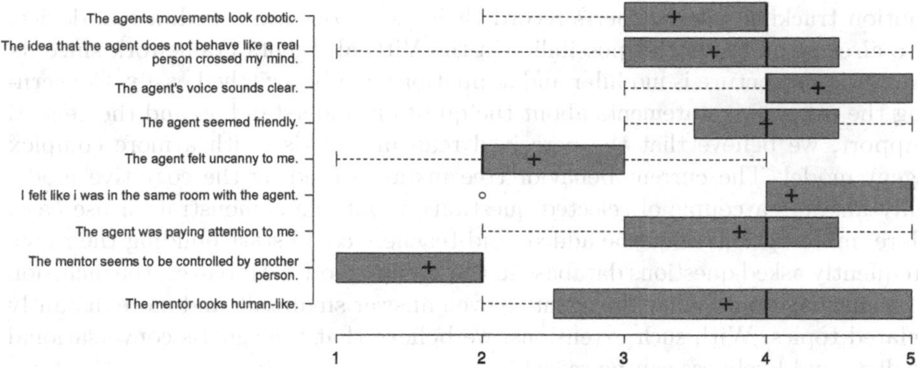

Fig. 6. Boxplot of the results regarding the agent's appearance and behavior

5 Discussion

The results indicate good to excellent usability. A main reason for the positive usability score is that users can interact naturally with the agent by talking to it. The later questionnaire parts show that the answers were well-perceived and so the text-to-speech module is working well. The only two usability questions where opinions were spread out, regard the need for technical help and the cumbersomeness of the system. The technical help can be explained by the fact that participants had to learn how to use the Microsoft HoloLens and its interaction gestures. This is also in line with previous research, which also stated that the relatively new technology can influence the participant's experience of the learning technology [5]. As the answers vary, some participants could also have misunderstood the question and answered whether they needed technical help from the agent to fulfill the laser cutting task. Some participants perceived the application as cumbersome which can be attributed to the technological setup. They must move around in the 3D space to follow the life-size agent and they have to make sure that they are standing in the right place to see the detailed aspects of the demonstration. This is more demanding than e.g., watching a demonstration video while sitting in front of a screen. In the future, we will try out different settings to reduce the physical demand. One option would be to explore miniature-sized agents that perform their demonstrations on a desk. This way, the user has to move around less, and it could also help with accessibility as students could immediately start the application on their own smartphone.

The results of the user evaluation also indicate that the students appreciated the advice of the mentoring agent and found it helpful. Out of the ten statements about the educational experience, an average agreement above four was scored on seven occasions. The three other questions regarded the amount of information conveyed by the animations, the agent's understanding of questions, and general support provided capabilities by the mentor. More detailed animations could be provided that are tailored towards the specific use case instead of generic ones from a database. A possible avenue to explore in the future would be motion tracking where experts record their own movements with a real device. We already prepared this possibility in the Virtual Agents Framework since its animation structure is modular and animations can be switched easily. Concerning the other two statements about the question understanding and the general support, we believe that the perceived realism will rise with a more complex agent model. The current behavior tree instance used by the cognitive model only answers a couple of selected questions about the demonstration use case. Here, more options could be added, and teachers could start building their own frequently asked questions database in the agent's model. Moreover, the inclusion of a chatbot would allow the agent to even answer small talk and more distantly related topics. With such extensions, we believe that the agent's conversational realism and liveliness can be raised.

Similarly, the realism of the agent is an aspect of future research. We deliberately did not strive for a photorealistic agent to avoid the uncanny valley. The results show that we succeeded in this as the agent was perceived as friendly and not as uncanny. However, one particular aspect to explore in the future is how to allow for more complex and natural behaviors. Again, custom-made, motion-tracked animations could contribute to the perceived behavioral realism. Moreover, the agent's behavior tree instance could be extended as it is currently limited to the central actions and commands for the demonstration use case. We believe that the behavior trees are already a suitable tool to author complex decisions. However, there is the possibility known from games that users learn the patterns of behavior trees and can therefore foresee how an agent will react to a given stimulus. Possible extensions to the behavior trees or more complex methods of simulating virtual humans that introduce a factor of randomness can be tried out. However, for such tools, it is an important requirement that mentors are able to precisely author and control behaviors in a visual manner and without coding. This would e.g., make approaches like goal-oriented action planning or even neural nets less viable as these approaches make it more difficult to fine-tune the minute details of the agent's behavior.

Overall, we are satisfied with the modular architecture of the Virtual Agents Framework and the way how we could adjust both the visual appearance, animations, and behavior for the mentoring use case. We believe that the study shows a large potential for mixed reality mentoring agents as students indicated that the agent was helpful to them and that it was perceived positively.

6 Conclusion and Future Work

In this paper, we presented a mixed reality mentoring agent based on our Virtual Agents Framework. The agent uses behavior trees with blackboards as a cognitive behavioral model. Students can communicate with the agent via speech input and text-to-speech output in order to ask questions and get demonstration exercises by the agent. We implemented the base architecture of the agents in our open-source Virtual Agents Framework which provides an API for giving tasks to the agents. The active task is then visualized, e.g., as animations. We then took this basis and created the mixed reality mentoring prototype on the Microsoft HoloLens where life-sized agents demonstrate how to use a laser cutting device. The user evaluation showed good to excellent usability and that the mixed reality mentoring agents are accepted by students. Our prototype avoided the uncanny valley and students gave the feedback that the agent was helpful to them. The study highlights the potential that mixed reality mentoring agents can become personal assistants for students in their learning activities.

In future work, we would like to explore more aspects of the created mixed reality mentoring agents and how they influence the learning experience. For instance, this includes exploring how the degree of realism influences learning outcomes. Moreover, we would like to expand the agent's range of answers by connecting it to existing mentoring systems that rely on chatbots. Another aspect is the extension of the cognitive model. For instance, experiments can be conducted with more autonomous agents that can, e.g., plan their actions with regard to their environment. We also plan to incorporate the agents into a collaborative environment, e.g. in our shared project management application VIAProMa to gain insights how agents can support multiple participants in parallel [9]. Based on such prototypes and findings, we would like to expand the Virtual Agents Framework to further support its ability to quickly generate mixed reality mentoring agents in new projects. Future research can also look at the potential of mixed reality mentoring bots in different use contexts. Apart from higher education institutions, they can also be useful in professional or vocational training, in research training but also in museums. With the positive indications of the given evaluation, we will continue the work on the agents and conduct further studies of the mentoring agent in university courses.

Acknowledgements. We thank the German Federal Ministry of Education and Research for their support within the project "Personalisierte Kompetenzentwicklung durch skalierbare Mentoringprozesse" (tech4comp; id: 16DHB2110).

References

1. Bangor, A., Kortum, P., Miller, J.: Determining what individual SUS scores mean: adding an adjective rating scale. J. Usabil. Stud. **4**(3), 114–123 (2009). http://uxpajournal.org/determining-what-individual-sus-scores-mean-adding-an-adjective-rating-scale/
2. Bogdanovych, A., Trescak, T.: Presented at the To Plan or Not to Plan: Lessons Learned from Building Large Scale Social Simulations (2017). https://doi.org/10.1007/978-3-319-67401-8_6
3. Brooke, J.: SUS: a quick and dirty usability scale. In: Jordan, P.W., Thomas, B., Weerdmeester, B.A., McClelland, I.L. (eds.) Usability Evaluation in Industry, pp. 189–194. Taylor & Francis (1996)
4. Brooke, J.: SUS: a retrospective. J. Usabil. Stud. **8**(2) (2013). https://doi.org/10.5555/2817912.2817913
5. Checa, D., Miguel-Alonso, I., Bustillo, A.: Immersive virtual-reality computer-assembly serious game to enhance autonomous learning. Virtual Reality 1–18 (2021). https://doi.org/10.1007/s10055-021-00607-1

6. Delamarre, A., Lisetti, C., Buche, C.: A cross-platform classroom training simulator: interaction design and evaluation. In: 2020 International Conference on Cyberworlds (CW), pp. 86–93. IEEE (2020). https://doi.org/10.1109/CW49994.2020.00020
7. Gratch, J., Rickel, J., Andre, E., Cassell, J., Petajan, E., Badler, N.: Creating interactive virtual humans: some assembly required. IEEE Intell. Syst. **17**(4), 54–63 (2002). https://doi.org/10.1109/MIS.2002.1024753
8. Hammady, R., Ma, M., Strathern, C., Mohamad, M.: Design and development of a spatial mixed reality touring guide to the Egyptian museum. Multim. Tools Appl. 3465–3494 (2019). https://doi.org/10.1007/s11042-019-08026-w
9. Hensen, B., Klamma, R.: VIAProMa: an agile project management framework for mixed reality. In: De Paolis, L.T., Arpaia, P., Bourdot, P. (eds.) AVR 2021. LNCS, vol. 12980, pp. 254–272. Springer, Cham (2021). https://doi.org/10.1007/978-3-030-87595-4_19
10. Holz, T., Campbell, A.G., O'Hare, G.M., Stafford, J.W., Martin, A., Dragone, M.: MiRA–mixed reality agents. Int. J. Hum.-Comput. Stud. **69**(4), 251–268 (2011). https://doi.org/10.1016/j.ijhcs.2010.10.001
11. Jia, T., Liu, Y.: Words in kitchen: an instance of leveraging virtual reality technology to learn vocabulary. In: Adjunct Proceedings of the 2019 IEEE International Symposium on Mixed and Augmented Reality. pp. 150–155. IEEE Computer Society, Conference Publishing Services, Los Alamitos, California (2019). https://doi.org/10.1109/ISMAR-Adjunct.2019.00-59
12. Klamma, R., et al.: Scaling mentoring support with distributed artificial intelligence. In: Kumar, V., Troussas, C. (eds.) ITS 2020. LNCS, vol. 12149, pp. 38–44. Springer, Cham (2020). https://doi.org/10.1007/978-3-030-49663-0_6
13. Lankoski, P., Björk, S.: Gameplay design patterns for believable non-player characters. In: DiGRA '07 - Proceedings of the 2007 DiGRA International Conference: Situated Play. The University of Tokyo (2007). http://www.digra.org/wp-content/uploads/digital-library/07315.46085.pdf
14. Marcotte, R., Hamilton, H.J.: Behavior trees for modelling artificial intelligence in Games: a tutorial. Computer Games J. **6**(3), 171–184 (2017). https://doi.org/10.1007/s40869-017-0040-9
15. Milgram, P., Kishino, F.: A taxonomy of mixed reality visual displays. IEICE Trans. Inf. Syst. **E77-D**(12), 1321–1329 (1994)
16. Paglis, L.L., Green, S.G., Bauer, T.N.: Does adviser mentoring add value? A longitudinal study of mentoring and doctoral student outcomes. Res. High. Educ. **47**(4), 451–476 (2006). https://doi.org/10.1007/s11162-005-9003-2
17. Palmas, F., Cichor, J., Plecher, D.A., Klinker, G.: Acceptance and effectiveness of a virtual reality public speaking training. In: 2019 IEEE International Symposium on Mixed and Augmented Reality (ISMAR), pp. 363–371. IEEE (2019). https://doi.org/10.1109/ISMAR.2019.00034

Asynchronous Manual Work in Mixed Reality Remote Collaboration

Anjela Mayer[1(✉)], Théo Combe[1,2], Jean-Rémy Chardonnet[2], and Jivka Ovtcharova[1]

[1] Institute for Information Management in Engineering, Karlsruhe Institute of Technology (KIT), Karlsruhe, Germany
anjela.mayer@kit.edu

[2] Arts et Metiers Institute of Technology, LISPEN, HESAM Université, Chalon-sur-Saône, France

Abstract. Research in Collaborative Virtual Environments (CVEs) is becoming more and more significant with increasing accessibility of Virtual Reality (VR) and Augmented Reality (AR) technology, additionally reinforced by the increasing demand for remote collaboration groupware. While the research is focusing on methods for synchronous remote collaboration, asynchronous remote collaboration remains a niche. Nevertheless, future CVEs should support both paradigms of collaborative work, since asynchronous collaboration has as well its benefits, for instance a more flexible time-coordination. In this paper we present a concept of recording and later playback of highly interactive collaborative tasks in Mixed Reality (MR). Furthermore, we apply the concept in an assembly training scenario from the manufacturing industry and test it during pilot user experiments. The pilot study compared two modalities, the first one with a manufacturing manual, and another using our concept and featuring a ghost avatar. First results revealed no significant differences between both modalities in terms of time completion, hand movements, cognitive workload and usability. Some differences were not expected, however, these results and the feedback brought by the participants provide insights to further develop our concept.

Keywords: Asynchronous remote collaboration · Collaborative Virtual Environments · Mixed Reality · Asymmetric collaboration

1 Introduction

Social collaboration is an important component in our daily work where the importance of remote collaboration systems is rapidly growing [9]. The work in companies, institutes and educational facilities increasingly involves stakeholders and interdisciplinary experts from all around the world. To address the effects of globalization, CVEs are required which the participants can virtually join from their remote locations and together conduct collaborative work within the

L. T. De Paolis et al. (Eds.): XR Salento 2022, LNCS 13446, pp. 17–33, 2022.
https://doi.org/10.1007/978-3-031-15553-6_2

shared virtual environment. In recent years, the covid-19 pandemic has boosted the transition of working from co-local to remote paradigms, especially during periods of social distancing and lockdowns [1]. As a positive side-effect CVEs help in minimizing travel. Since the stakeholders can simply meet in a shared virtual environment the need for travels to the remote locations of other collaborators decreases which results in a reduction of the carbon footprint. Global collaboration is characterized by spatial distribution of the participants. Additionally, the work force is time-distributed due to different time-zones. The need for CVEs supporting remote asynchronous collaboration increases with a growing global distribution of the collaborating teams. Asynchronous collaboration is required for a successful collaboration [33] and has several unique advantages over synchronous communication, such as: work parallelism, flexible time-coordination, reviewability, and reflection [3,13,15,27]. Nevertheless, CVEs should support synchronous as well as asynchronous collaboration and furthermore allow transition between both [3,9,21,23].

In application areas where the communication of spatial information is important, immersive CVEs are promising platforms to enable effective remote collaboration [15]. Because of advancements in MR technology, collaboration in immersive CVEs has become a research area [3,9,18]. De Belen et al. emphasize the need for asynchronous MR CVEs and discuss possible application areas [3].

The literature reviews [3,9,18] show an increasing interest in immersive collaboration approaches, in particular the number of publications addressing remote collaboration in MR is growing fast. Nevertheless, while the majority of publications is focusing on synchronous collaboration, the reviewers identified a gap in research of asynchronous collaboration. At the same time they emphasize the benefits of asynchronous CVEs and encourage further research in this area [3,7,9].

In this work we propose to follow the suggestions and research application concepts for asynchronous remote collaboration using MR technologies. In particular our main research question is: *How to relive manual work of a non-present collaborator in interactive CVEs?*

As main contribution of this paper we present a concept for the asynchronous record and replay of spatial motions of remote collaborators, in particular their hand motions and interactions with objects within a CVE. Furthermore, we show the application of this concept in an assembly training scenario from the manufacturing area and test it during pilot user experiments.

2 Related Work

This work mainly contributes to the research area of asynchronous CVEs, in particular immersive CVEs which are realized with MR technologies. In asynchronous collaboration scenarios the participants conduct their cooperative work at different times [7]. A key concept in asynchronous collaboration is to create and preserve digital information which can be reconstructed and consumed at another time [3]. In immersive CVEs this often involves the recording of users' actions within the virtual space and a later replay of these actions. To visualize spatial actions of the users within immersive virtual environments they are usually represented by 3D avatars. In this work we use the ghost metaphor as a representation method of non-present user actions.

2.1 Asynchronous Collaboration in MR

Asynchronous collaboration in MR is only slowly growing as a research topic, since most of the research in the CVE area is focusing on synchronous collaboration [3,7,9,15]. Ens et al. have reviewed 110 papers about collaboration in MR published between 1995 and 2018. They found that the vast majority of papers (106, or 95%) focus on synchronous collaboration [9]. Their findings are also backed up in the literature review of de Belen et al. [3] where a total of 259 papers between 2013 and 2018 were reviewed. Through this work, we aim at putting our stone to asynchronous collaboration.

Most of the papers about asynchronous collaboration in MR allow the creation and consumption of annotations, like virtual graffiti and photos which are placed at certain locations within the immersive environment and can be viewed and interacted with by other collaborators at another time [6,17,19,24,31]. Irlitti et al. [16] are researching combination methods for tangible markers and augmented annotations which can be left for the next worker. However, tasks in the engineering domain often involve continuous spatial information which is hard to communicate using static annotations and images.

Tseng et al. [36] present a system which not only preserves respectively correct annotations, but additionally visualizes the position and orientation of the recorded user's head and hands. This provides the minimum of continuous information to perceive the movements of the user's head and hands over time. In the work of Tsang et al. [35] an AR system is developed which can record multimodal streams of annotation data, including viewpoints, voice and gesture information. After a recording is complete, users can save or playback the annotation session.

While the majority of the literature focus on general concepts providing proof-of-concept prototypes, others show how to apply asynchronous collaboration methods to specific domains. A collaboration system for crime scene investigators with remote support from experts is presented by Poelman et al. [29]. Although the main focus is on synchronous collaboration during the investigation, the authors also discuss a record option to support a later review of the investigation research by judges. Marques et al. [21] present a collaboration system which enables remote experts to support on-site technicians with augmented annotations during synchronous as well as asynchronous sessions.

2.2 Spatial Capture and Replay of Body Motions

While the creation, preservation and later consumption of information in MR has been considered in existing research, the asynchronous combination of these actions has seldom been considered [15]. V-Mail [14] and MASSIVE-3 [11] are the most relevant approaches where the capture and replay of rich, multi-modal interactions were applied for asynchronous communication. Chow et al. [7] identified several application domains where this method was implemented for asynchronous collaboration: architectural review [12], creative feedback applications [25,35], training [4,38] and tele-communication [6,28,30]. In their work Chow et al. present a VR environment enabling asynchronous collaboration in spatial tasks by supporting multi-modal record and replay functionalities and several annotation methods. Other research groups focus on reliving virtual reality experiences and even support the recording and replaying of full body avatars [10,37]. Although, the literature presents methods for reliving experiences or collaborative planning sessions, further concepts have to be explored suited for the engineering domain, in particular involving tools and manual actions.

Lindlbauer and Wilson [20] propose several time manipulation methods for asynchronous sessions, including pause, loop and replay of a captured 3D environment as well as speed manipulation and jumping back to important moments during meetings. Their methods are useful for applications where users want to make temporal changes. Ogasaware and Shibata [26] developed a prototype CVE system which allows to record user editing to the scene and also to create snapshots of the scene state which can be preserved and operated like non-immersive version control systems such as git.

2.3 Representation of Non-present Collaborators

To address the loss of physicality in remote work and provide collaborators with awareness about what other collaborators are doing, groupware researchers are exploring user embodiment [9]. Embodiment must represent the functions within the CVE that a collaborator's body and hands would have during his work in the real environment, for instance his hand gestures. In immersive virtual environments users are usually represented by 3D avatars.

The ghost metaphor is a representation style for 3D avatars and was introduced as an intuitive and effective method for training within an immersive environment in the work of Yang and Kim [38]. As they describe, the motion of a trainer is visualized as a *ghost* moving out of the trainee's body in real-time. The trainee spectates the *ghost's* motion from the first-person view and tries to "follow" it as close as possible to imitate the trainer. This kind of interaction is only possible in MR and with additional algorithms the performance of the trainee can be evaluated. In a later work their method is extended with motion-retargeting which converts the recorded trainer data to different body sizes [2]. Their method was tested in experiments for training in fencing, dancing and calligraphy tasks and showed to be as effective as traditional learning methods despite a relatively low presence and problems with MR devices. The motion guidance system of Schönauer et al. [32] expands the *ghost* metaphor to multi-modal guidance feedback adding vibrotactile and pneumatic actuation. Their design space discussion can be used to guide developers of multimodal motion guidance systems. Further research explicitly focuses on arm and hand motion feedback utilizing the *ghost* metaphor [8,22,34].

2.4 Contribution

With our work we aim to contribute to the research area of MR asynchronous collaboration. In particular our concept includes a capture of the users actions to preserve their work process and thereby allows to relive this progress again at another time. Unlike past research, we propose a recording of continuous information in which the hands, head and manipulated objects' positions and rotations are kept, without however allowing users to record static information by placing annotations.

Furthermore, we applied our concept to a real use case in the engineering, extending the results in the related work by another application domain. The current study is a first step in the development of our collaborative application, aiming at enabling, for instance, experts to collaborate asynchronously with on-site technicians, or teachers with students.

In the scope of this work we focus on VR, although our concept also works in AR as our first tests with a Microsoft Hololens 2 have shown. Furthermore, our concept can support MR since the recordings of the user could be created in AR and played back in VR and vice versa. This is a first step towards a system which supports the transition between AR and VR as it is encouraged in the literature [9]. The adaptation of our concept to AR and MR will be evaluated in future work.

3 Asynchronous Capture and Replay of Spatial Work

In this work we present a MR concept for asynchronous capture and replay of manual work in remote collaboration. By visualizing former work processes of the collaborators, our concept enables communication through time which is a basic requirement in asynchronous collaboration.

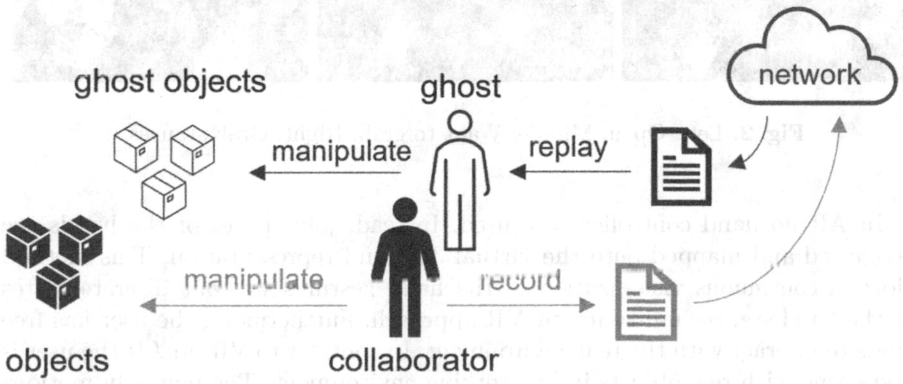

Fig. 1. Overview of the MR recording and replaying process in asynchronous collaboration from the perspective of one collaborator.

As depicted in Fig. 1, collaborators can capture their movements and interactions within their environment and send the resulting records to the other participants. Recorded interactions with virtual objects include information about the object's pose and appearance. Received recordings from others can be replayed visualising the non-present collaborators and their interacted objects as *ghosts*. During the MR replay process the collaborators are not restricted in their actions and are able to move and interact freely with their environment while observing the *ghosts*.

3.1 Representation of Collaborators and Their Manual Work

To visualize the manual work processes of the collaborators they are represented by 3D avatars. Because we focus on manual work, the representation of the hands and their actions is significant. Nevertheless, a minimal representation of the body is also needed to perceive the presence of the collaborators within the virtual environment.

In VR the hand poses and gestures are tracked via VR controllers. The gestures are visualized by predefined hand stances. In the current implementation three hand stances with the according transition animations are included: *open*, *grab* and *want to grab*, as depicted in Fig. 2. If the user moves his hand near a virtual object the virtual hand switches from the *open* to *wants to grab* state visualized by slightly bent fingers. By activating the grab button on the controller, near objects can be picked up with the virtual hand, which will switch to the *grab* state visualized by a closed hand holding the object. In follow-up work more hand gestures can be added with minimal effort.

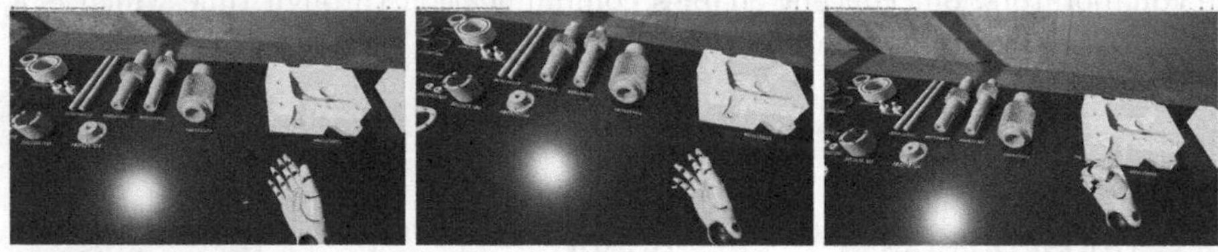

Fig. 2. Left: Open. Middle: Want to grab. Right: Grab stances.

In AR no hand controllers are used. Instead, joint poses of the hands are recognized and mapped onto the virtual 3D hand representation. This method allows a continuous visualization of the hand gestures without discrete states for the hand stances unlike in our VR approach. Furthermore, the user has free hands to interact with the real environment. In contrast to VR, in AR the user is interacting with real objects in his working environment. Thereby only motions of the hands are captured but not of the objects they are manipulating. In future work, image recognition could help to overlay the objects with their according virtual representations and allow recording of their movements in AR as well.

For the visualization of the work process of non-present users, record files are used to reconstruct their 3D avatars and their hand interactions with the virtual objects. To emphasize the absence of the collaborator and improve the visibility of the present environment, the ghost metaphor is utilized. Therefore, a transparent avatar is used for the visualization of the absent collaborator. If the absent user was interacting with virtual objects during the recording, they are represented by transparent duplicates during replay. By creating *ghost* duplicates of the objects, the present user can relive the changes the *ghost* has applied to the virtual environment without actually changing the present environment.

3.2 Record and Replay Process

In order to reproduce the work of non-present collaborators, the according information has to be collected and saved during their work sessions. The information is frequently collected and saved as a time-frame sequence per user within a record structure as depicted in Fig. 3.

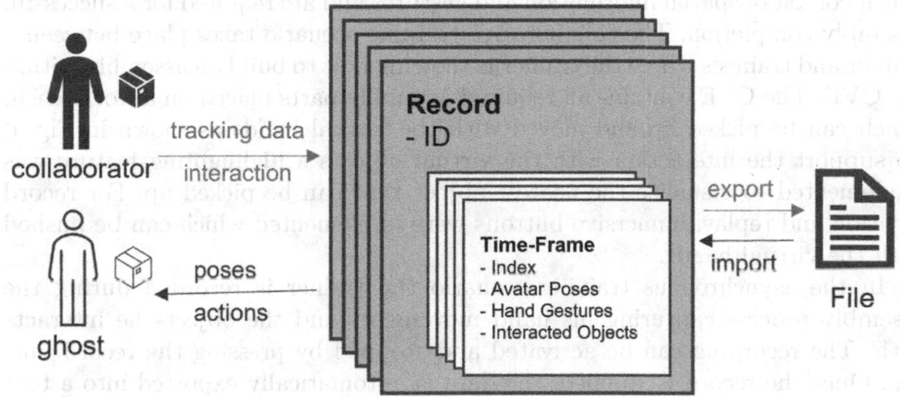

Fig. 3. A record contains sequential information about the collaborator's position, orientation, hand gestures and objects he interacted with. The records can be exported into files to be sent to remote collaborators. Received files can be imported into record data structures which are used to replay the remote collaborator's actions with *ghosts*.

Each time-frame includes information about the avatar poses, hand tracking and interacted objects. The avatar poses consist of the users head and hand positions and orientations within the CVE. Hand tracking information includes the hand states for the gesture representation if recorded in VR and 50 hand joint poses if recorded in AR. For each hand 25 joints are used to construct the gesture of the virtual 3D hand. For the interacted objects the time-frame includes information about the object orientation and position within the CVE as well as information about the appearance of the object, like the 3D model and scale factor.

During replay of a record the contained time-frame sequence is read frame by frame and the according information is applied on the *ghosts*. The avatar poses and hand gestures are applied on the *ghost avatar* representing the absent remote collaborator. If information about interacted objects is available *ghost objects* are created with the according appearance and placed at poses as specified in the record. When the replay is finished all *ghosts* are set to invisible.

For preservation and exchange the records are exported into files, which contain a textual representation of the information. The record files can be sent to the remote collaborators and played within the shared MR environment their local systems are connected to. Therefore, we store the files in a format which can be universally used either in VR and AR.

4 Application in Remote Assembly Training

The presented concept for asynchronous remote collaboration was implemented first in a VR assembly training application in manufacturing using the Unreal Engine 4 game engine. Manufacturing involves sequences of manual work steps which consist of spatial information and gestures and are required for a successful assembly completion. The collaborative training scenario takes place between a trainer and trainees where the trainer is showing how to build an assembly within the CVE. The CVE contains all required assembly parts placed on a workbench, which can be picked up and moved with the virtual hands as shown in Fig. 4. To support the interaction with the virtual objects a highlighting feature was implemented to visualize the nearest object that can be picked up. For record creation and replay, immersive buttons were implemented which can be pushed with the virtual hands.

In the asynchronous training scenario the trainer is recorded during the assembly process capturing his hand movements and the objects he interacts with. The recording can be activated and stopped by pressing the record button. Once the record is stopped, the data is automatically exported into a text file which can be shared with the trainees.

A trainee only receives the records of the trainer excluding his changes to the CVE with the finished assembly. Being in the initial CVE with the assembly pieces placed on the work bench the trainee can push the play button to view the recording of the trainer and see how to build the assembly as visualized in Fig. 4. During replay the ghost of the trainer and the assembly parts he has interacted with are visualized. By observing and imitating the *ghost* the trainee is guided through the assembly process without the simultaneous presence of a trainer. Furthermore, the trainee can record his assembly attempts and send it back to the trainer for review.

5 Pilot Experiment

This section presents a pilot study of our asynchronous collaboration application, considering the VR remote assembly training task detailed above. Thereby we

Fig. 4. VR implementation of the asynchronous collaboration concept in an assembly training scenario. The user can interact with the 3D assembly parts using his virtual hands (grey). During replay the *ghosts* (blue) of the trainer and the interacted objects can be viewed. (Color figure online)

considered a small sample size and we carried out the experiment using HMD devices, the AR mode being evaluated in a future study. The goal of this pilot study was to get a first insight on our application in a real use case, so that our concept could be enhanced with additional features and fully meet the actual participants' needs.

5.1 Experimental Design

10 participants (mean age= 24 ± 3, 1 female) were recruited inside the university, eight of them were familiar with VR devices. The experiment needed approximately thirty minutes to complete.

Upon arrival they were asked to fill in a short demographic questionnaire. Then we explained the purpose of the application, and we gave them the HMD. The HMD used was an *Oculus Quest 2*, which is a lightweight HMD (503g), with a 1832×1920 resolution per eye and a refresh rate 120 Hz.

Prior starting, we asked them to pick up a part on the workbench and to go through the steps without completing the assembly task, to ensure that they knew and understood how to use the application. Then, we requested them to start the assembly task. The assembly comprised ten steps to complete, and consisted in positioning parts with the others, including ball bearings, screws, circlips, rods and gears. During assembly, we recorded the time needed to complete the whole assembly task, and the hand positions. Once finished, participants were required to leave the application, and to complete three questionnaires: the NASA-TLX (Task load Index), the SUS (System Usability Scale) and a post-questionnaire including specific points about the application, such as the "ease of use", the "amount of time needed to complete the scenario" and the "satisfaction with the information given to complete the task". Last, participants were free to express themselves about the application, anything that they would improve, or if they were specifically satisfied about the features.

For this pilot study, two modalities were compared: one with the information provided by a *Manual* (M), and one with the information provided by a *Ghost* avatar (G), see Fig. 5. In each modality, buttons were displayed on the information panel, participants could push them to move to the next steps. Each participant had to complete one or the other modality, meaning that five of them conducted the M modality and the other five did the G modality.

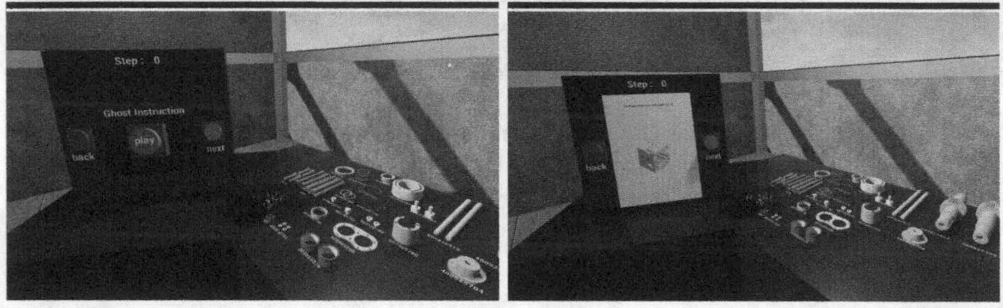

Fig. 5. Left: Ghost modality. Right: Manual modality.

We made the following hypotheses:

H1. The manual modality will induce higher cognitive workload than the ghost modality, because users will have to read the manual first and find the right part on the workbench.

H2. The ghost modality will lead to less hands movements, because users will not have to search for the right part on the table. Moreover participants will make less mistakes in the placement of the parts.

5.2 Results

The experiment led to a between-subject experiment. Each participant completed the application once with one modality, either *G* or *M*.

For all the data collected, we performed normality checks. When data were found normal, t-tests were run. On the contrary, when data were found not normal, Mann-Whitney tests were used. The significance threshold was set to .05.

Hand Movement: We recorded the positions of the hands at each frame, thus we were able to calculate the amount of movement in meters performed by each participant during the whole application. A t-test on the total distance done by the participant's hands showed no significant differences between both modalities

($t(8) = 1.869, p = .24$). Nonetheless, the ghost modality led to more movements than the manual modality ($M_G = 350, SD_G = 19.966, M_M = 317.291, SD_M = 40$), see Fig. 6 left. This result is unexpected and contradicts hypothesis H2, as we supposed that participants would stand still looking at the ghost and then reproduce the exact movement, while in the *Manual* modality they would have to search for the right part and the right position, which would involve more movements. Furthermore, we made the assumption that participants might imitate the ghost motion by motion, whereas the ghost might perform more movements than necessary, compared to the manual modality. Further investigation is needed to make this point clear.

Completion Time: No statistical difference was found in time completion ($t(8) = 1.859, p = .050$). However, since the p-value obtained is quasi-equal to the significance threshold, we could expect clearer results with more participants. Here, participants took in average more time to complete the assembly with the ghost modality, 13.30 min ($SD_G = 1.22$ min), than with the manual modality, 10.12 min ($SD_M = 1.12$ min), see Fig. 6 right. Time might be higher for the ghost modality, as participants had to wait for the ghost to accomplish each step, which, inherently, doubles the time needed, even though participants successfully accomplished the step at the first attempt. Thus, despite these results, we can assume that the manual modality may take in fact more time than with the ghost, from an absolute perspective.

SUS: A Mann-Whitney test did not reveal any significant difference between both modalities ($U = 6.5, p = .245$). The average scores for both modalities are above 75 ($M_G = 86, SD_G = 3.5, M_M = 78.5, SD_M = 5.624$), which is recognized to show high usability of the application. Only two participants rated under 75 for the manual modality. The scores for each item of the SUS questionnaire is depicted in Fig. 7. These results show that our application, whatever the modality, is usable, and none of the participants encountered major challenges when using it, which was one goal of this pilot study. Moreover, since improvements of our concept according to participants' feedback are already planned, the usability score should further increase.

Post-questionnaire: Three questions were asked: 1) *Overall, I am satisfied with the ease of completing the tasks in this scenario*, 2) *Overall, I am satisfied with the amount of time it took to complete the tasks in this scenario*, 3) *Overall, I am satisfied with the information media when completing the tasks.* Participants had to answer on a Likert scale ranging from 0-Strongly Disagree to 5-Strongly Agree. Although both modalities provided satisfaction to participants ($M_G = 4.4, SD_G = .163, M_M = 4.6, SD_M = 0.163$), no significant differences were found between each modality ($U = 8.5, p = .403$).

NASA-TLX: We asked participants to complete the NASA-TLX upon completion, no significanct difference could be highlighted ($t(10) = 1.814, p = .121$). If we look closely at each item of the NASA-TLX, we can observe that except for *Performance* and *Frustration*, each item has been rated higher for modality M, the higher difference being for *Mental Demand*, as depicted in Fig. 8. Although

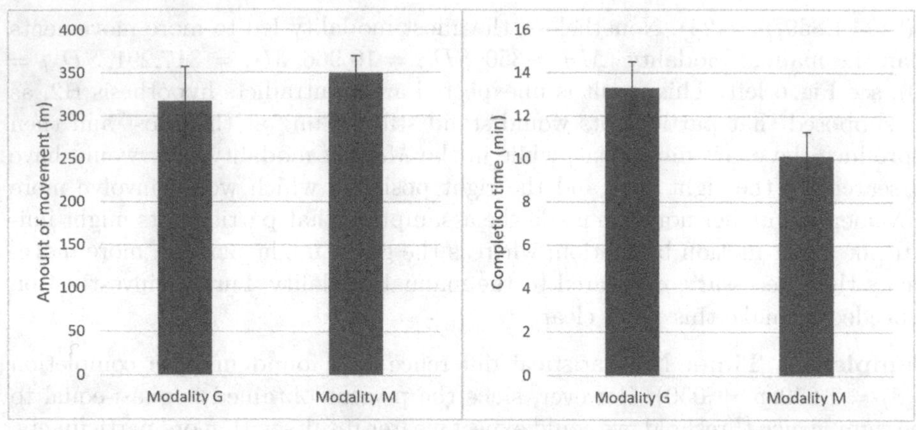

Fig. 6. Left: Hand movements. Right: completion time.

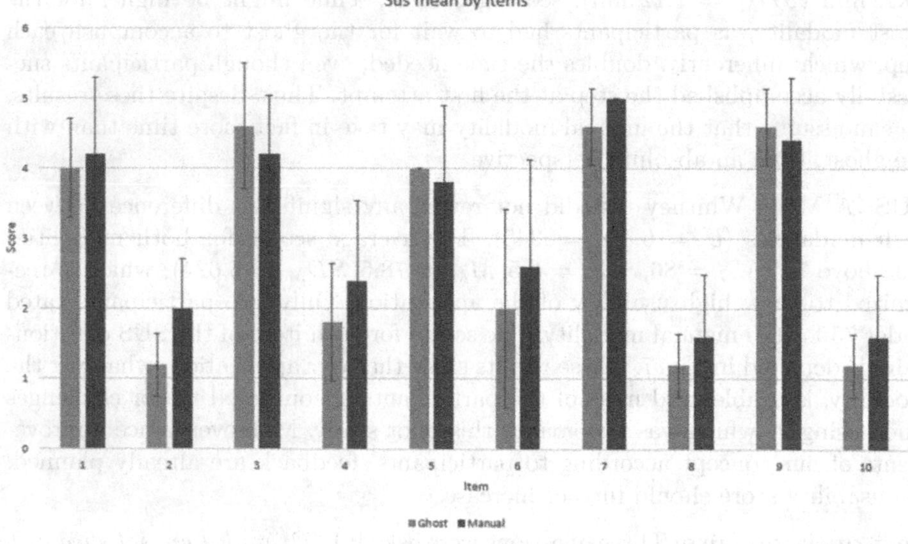

Fig. 7. SUS items results.

not significant, these observations tend to go in the same direction as hypothesis H1. Further investigation is however needed, as we took participants not coming from industry, for whom reading a manufacturing manual may be more cognitive demanding than for industrial operators.

Participant Feedback and Observation: During the experiment, we observed the participants, and after it we ask them to provide feedback. First of all, participants performing the manual modality tended to consider gravity and leave the parts directly on the workbench, even though it meant that they had to turn themselves to access a specific viewpoint, or they kept the part in

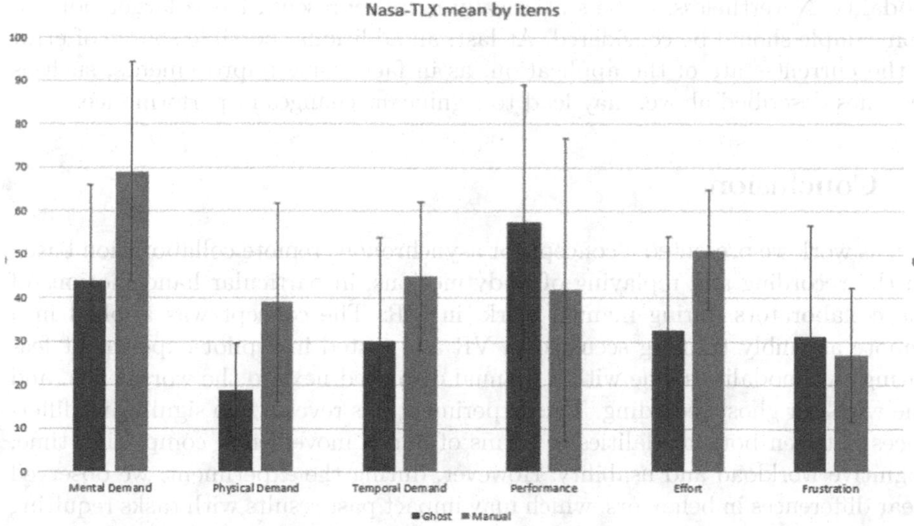

Fig. 8. NASA-TLX items results.

their hand during the whole process. Moreover, four of them used only one hand. On the contrary, users in the ghost modality used both hands and were more likely to ignore gravity and leave parts at their eyes' height. We may suppose that they took inspiration from what the ghost avatar did, which was to leave objects in the air and use his both hands. Participants gave advice on how to improve the application, such as having a time progression bar when the ghost performs a step, to know how much time left there would be before the ghost would stop, or adding physical feedback when a part is grabbed (currently the parts are highlighted in yellow when grabbed) or when they accurately place the part they are holding. Some steps require unnatural placement movements, such as placing screws which normally requires specific tools. For such steps, tools, such as screw drivers, could be added to enhance realism.

5.3 Limitations

Several limitations might have influenced the results obtained. First, except one participant, all participants were from our research institute, which activity focuses on MR, thus, they all had consequent experience with VR tools, which is not representative of final users. Furthermore, our results could be influenced by the novelty effect, which must be minimized in VR training applications [5]. Our post-questionnaire showed a slightly greater satisfaction of inexperienced participants compared to participants who had already spent more than 20 h in VR. Additionally, inexperienced subjects were more satisfied with the ghost modality compared to the manual. On the contrary, for experienced participants as well as in the overall results, a greater satisfaction was observed with the manual modality. Nevertheless, to be statistically more representative, a larger population sample should be considered. At last, an additional possible source of error is the current state of the application, as in fact, some improvements, such as the ones described above, may lead to significant changes in performance.

6 Conclusion

In this work we presented a concept for asynchronous remote collaboration based on the recording and replaying of body motions, in particular hand motions of the collaborators during manual work, in MR. The concept was applied in a remote assembly training scenario in VR and tested in a pilot experiment featuring two modalities: one with a manual displayed next to the workbench, and one with our ghost recording. This experiment has revealed no significant differences between both modalities in terms of hands movements, completion time, cognitive workload and usability. However, during the experiment, we observed clear differences in behaviors, which may impact past results with tasks requiring more steps. Moreover, we had only five participants for each modality, which may have impacted the results. We believe that more significant differences could be observed in a future experiment involving more steps to perform and integrating in the application the features proposed by the participants. Nonetheless, this pilot experiment provides insights to further develop the proposed concept.

For the evaluation of our concept a larger user study is planned as well as further experiments including AR. In the future work we aim to build a system for asynchronous MR collaboration including the presented record and replay of the collaborators as well as a synchronization of the shared CVE between all participants to exchange manipulations of the virtual environment along with the records. Additionally, we will work on multi-modal recordings, including verbal communication, pursue new concepts for time navigation through the recordings and implement our concepts in further application domains.

References

1. Almeida, F., Duarte Santos, J., Augusto Monteiro, J.: The challenges and opportunities in the digitalization of companies in a post-covid-19 world. IEEE Eng. Manage. Rev. **48**(3), 97–103 (2020). https://doi.org/10.1109/EMR.2020.3013206
2. Baek, S., Lee, S., Kim, G.J.: Motion retargeting and evaluation for VR-based training of free motions. Visual Comput. **19**(4), 222–242 (2003). https://doi.org/10.1007/s00371-003-0194-2
3. de Belen, R.A., Nguyen, H., Filonik, D., Favero, D., Bednarz, T.: A systematic review of the current state of collaborative mixed reality technologies: 2013–2018. AIMS Electronics and Electrical Engineering 3, 181–223 (2019). https://doi.org/10.3934/ElectrEng.2019.2.181
4. Chan, J.C., Leung, H., Tang, J.K., Komura, T.: A virtual reality dance training system using motion capture technology. IEEE Trans. Learn. Technol. **4**(2), 187–195 (2011). https://doi.org/10.1109/TLT.2010.27

5. Checa, D., Miguel-Alonso, I., Bustillo, A.: Immersive virtual-reality computer-assembly serious game to enhance autonomous learning. Virtual Reality (4), 1–18 (2021). https://doi.org/10.1007/s10055-021-00607-1
6. Chen, H., Lee, A.S., Swift, M., Tang, J.C.: 3d collaboration method over hololens and skype end points. In: Proceedings of the 3rd International Workshop on Immersive Media Experiences, ImmersiveME 2015, pp. 27–30. Association for Computing Machinery, New York (2015). https://doi.org/10.1145/2814347.2814350
7. Chow, K., Coyiuto, C., Nguyen, C., Yoon, D.: Challenges and design considerations for multimodal asynchronous collaboration in VR. In: Proceedings of the ACM on Human-Computer Interaction 3 (CSCW) (2019). https://doi.org/10.1145/3359142
8. Dürr, M., Kn, M.D., Weber, R., Pfeil, U., Reiterer, H.: EGuide: Investigating different Visual Appearances and Guidance Techniques for Egocentric Guidance Visualizations (2020). https://doi.org/10.1145/3374920.3374945
9. Ens, B., et al.: Revisiting collaboration through mixed reality: the evolution of groupware. Int. J. Human-Comput. Stud. **131**, 81–98 (2019). https://doi.org/10.1016/j.ijhcs.2019.05.011
10. Frécon, E., Nöu, A.A.: Building distributed virtual environments to support collaborative work. In: Proceedings of the ACM Symposium on Virtual Reality Software and Technology, VRST, pp. 105–114 (2019). https://doi.org/10.1145/293701.293715
11. Greenhalgh, C., Flintham, M., Purbrick, J., Benford, S.: Applications of temporal links: recording and replaying virtual environments. In: Proceedings IEEE Virtual Reality 2002, pp. 101–108 (2002). https://doi.org/10.1109/VR.2002.996512
12. Guerreiro, J., et al.: Beyond Post-It: Structured Multimedia Annotations for Collaborative VEs. In: Nojima, T., Reiners, D., Staadt, O. (eds.) ICAT-EGVE 2014 - International Conference on Artificial Reality and Telexistence and Eurographics Symposium on Virtual Environments. The Eurographics Association (2014). https://doi.org/10.2312/ve.20141365
13. Hollan, J., Stornetta, S.: Beyond being there. In: Proceedings of the SIGCHI Conference on Human Factors in Computing Systems, CHI 1992, p. 119–125. Association for Computing Machinery, New York (1992). https://doi.org/10.1145/142750.142769
14. Imai, T., Johnson, A., Leigh, J., Pape, D., DeFanti, T.: Supporting transoceanic collaborations in virtual environment, vol. 2, pp. 1059–1062 (1999). https://doi.org/10.1109/APCC.1999.820446
15. Irlitti, A., Smith, R.T., Itzstein, S.V., Billinghurst, M., Thomas, B.H.: Challenges for Asynchronous Collaboration in Augmented Reality. In: Adjunct Proceedings of the 2016 IEEE International Symposium on Mixed and Augmented Reality, ISMAR-Adjunct 2016, pp. 31–35 (2017). https://doi.org/10.1109/ISMAR-Adjunct.2016.0032
16. Irlitti, A., Von Itzstein, S., Alem, L., Thomas, B.: Tangible interaction techniques to support asynchronous collaboration. In: 2013 IEEE International Symposium on Mixed and Augmented Reality (ISMAR), pp. 1–6 (2013). https://doi.org/10.1109/ISMAR.2013.6671840
17. Kasahara, S., Heun, V., Lee, A.S., Ishii, H.: Second surface: multi-user spatial collaboration system based on augmented reality. In: SIGGRAPH Asia 2012 Emerging Technologies, SA 2012, p. 1–4. Association for Computing Machinery, New York (2012). https://doi.org/10.1145/2407707.2407727
18. Ladwig, P., Geiger, C.: A literature review on collaboration in mixed reality. In: Auer, M.E., Langmann, R. (eds.) REV 2018. LNNS, vol. 47, pp. 591–600. Springer, Cham (2019). https://doi.org/10.1007/978-3-319-95678-7_65

19. Langlotz, T., Grubert, J., Grasset, R.: Augmented reality browsers: Essential products or only gadgets? Commun. ACM 56(11), 34–36 (2013). https://doi.org/10.1145/2527190
20. Lindlbauer, D., Wilson, A.D.: Remixed Reality: Manipulating Space and Time in Augmented Reality, pp. 1–13. Association for Computing Machinery, New York (2018)
21. Marques, B., Silva, S., Rocha, A., Dias, P., Santos, B.S.: Remote asynchronous collaboration in maintenance scenarios using augmented reality and annotations. In: 2021 IEEE Conference on Virtual Reality and 3D User Interfaces Abstracts and Workshops (VRW), pp. 567–568 (2021). https://doi.org/10.1109/VRW52623.2021.00166
22. Matsas, E., Vosniakos, G.C., Batras, D.: Modelling simple human-robot collaborative manufacturing tasks in interactive virtual environments. In: Proceedings of the 2016 Virtual Reality International Conference, VRIC 2016. Association for Computing Machinery, New York (2016). https://doi.org/10.1145/2927929.2927948
23. Moloney, J., Amor, R.: Stringcve: advances in a game engine-based collaborative virtual environment for architectural design. In: Proceedings of CONVR 2003 Conference on Construction Applications of Virtual Reality, pp. 24–26 (2003)
24. Nassani, A., Bai, H., Lee, G., Billinghurst, M.: Tag it! ar annotation using wearable sensors. In: SIGGRAPH Asia 2015 Mobile Graphics and Interactive Applications, SA 2015. Association for Computing Machinery, New York (2015). https://doi.org/10.1145/2818427.2818438
25. Nguyen, C., DiVerdi, S., Hertzmann, A., Liu, F.: Collavr: collaborative in-headset review for vr video. In: Proceedings of the 30th Annual ACM Symposium on User Interface Software and Technology, UIST 2017 pp. 267–277. Association for Computing Machinery, New York (2017). https://doi.org/10.1145/3126594.3126659
26. Ogasawara, H., Shibata, Y.: Asynchronous collaborative support system by revision tree method. In: Proceedings - International Conference on Advanced Information Networking and Applications, AINA, pp. 564–569 (2009). https://doi.org/10.1109/WAINA.2009.180
27. Olson, G.M., Olson, J.S.: Distance matters. Human-Computer Interaction 15(2–3), 139–178 (2000). https://doi.org/10.1207/S15327051HCI1523_4
28. Orts-Escolano, S., et al.: Holoportation: virtual 3d teleportation in real-time. In: Proceedings of the 29th Annual Symposium on User Interface Software and Technology, UIST 2016, pp. 741–754, Association for Computing Machinery, New York (2016). https://doi.org/10.1145/2984511.2984517
29. Poelman, R., Akman, O., Lukosch, S., Jonker, P.: As if being there: mediated reality for crime scene investigation. In: Proceedings of the ACM 2012 Conference on Computer Supported Cooperative Work, CSCW 2012, pp. 1267–1276. Association for Computing Machinery, New York (2012). https://doi.org/10.1145/2145204.2145394
30. Regenbrecht, H., Meng, K., Reepen, A., Beck, S., Langlotz, T.: Mixed voxel reality: presence and embodiment in low fidelity, visually coherent, mixed reality environments, pp. 90–99 (2017). https://doi.org/10.1109/ISMAR.2017.26
31. Reisner-Kollmann, I., Aschauer, A.: Design and implementation of asynchronous remote support. CEUR Workshop Proc. **2618**, 9–11 (2020)
32. Schönauer, C., Fukushi, K., Olwal, A., Kaufmann, H., Raskar, R.: Multimodal motion guidance: Techniques for adaptive and dynamic feedback. In: ICMI 2012 - Proceedings of the ACM International Conference on Multimodal Interaction, pp. 133–140 (2012). https://doi.org/10.1145/2388676.2388706

33. Tam, J., Greenberg, S.: A framework for asynchronous change awareness in collaborative documents and workspaces. International Journal of Human-Computer Studies 64(7), 583–598 (2006). https://doi.org/10.1016/j.ijhcs.2006.02.004
34. Tecchia, F., Alem, L., Huang, W.: 3d helping hands: a gesture based mr system for remote collaboration. In: Proceedings of the 11th ACM SIGGRAPH International Conference on Virtual-Reality Continuum and Its Applications in Industry, VRCAI 2012, pp. 323–328. Association for Computing Machinery, New York (2012). https://doi.org/10.1145/2407516.2407590
35. Tsang, M., Fitzmzurice, G.W., Kurtenbach, G., Khan, A., Buxton, B.: Boom Chameleon: Simultaneous capture of 3D viewpoint, voice and gesture annotations on a spatially-aware display (2003)
36. Tseng, P.Y., Haraldsson, H., Belongie, S.: Annotate all ! A Perspective Preserved Asynchronous Annotation System for Collaborative Augmented Reality, pp. 1–3 (2019)
37. Wang, C.Y., Sakashita, M., Ehsan, U., Li, J., Won, A.S.: Again, Together: Socially Reliving Virtual Reality Experiences When Separated, pp. 1–12. Association for Computing Machinery, New York (2020)
38. Yang, U., Kim, G.J.: Implementation and evaluation of "just follow me": an immersive, vr-based, motion-training system. Presence: Teleoper. Virtual Environ. **11**(3), 304–323 (2002). https://doi.org/10.1162/105474602317473240

A Virtual Reality Serious Game for Children with Dyslexia: DixGame

Henar Guillen-Sanz[1(✉)], Bruno Rodríguez-Garcia[1], Kim Martinez[2], and María Consuelo Saiz Manzanares[3]

[1] Departamento de Ingeniería Informática, Universidad de Burgos, Burgos, Spain
{hguillen,brunorg}@ubu.es

[2] Departamento de Historia, Geografía y Comunicación, Universidad de Burgos, Burgos, Spain
kmartinez@ubu.es

[3] Departamento de Ciencias de la Salud, Universidad de Burgos, Burgos, Spain
mcsmanzanares@ubu.es

Abstract. Children with reading and writing difficulties, such as dyslexia, have been directly affected by the Covid-19 situation because they could not have the teacher's face-to-face support. Consequently, new devices and technological applications are being used in educational contexts to improve the interest of learning. This paper presents the design of a Virtual Reality Serious Game called DixGame. This game is a pedagogical tool specifically oriented to children between 8 and 12 years old with dyslexia. Two immersive mini-games are included in this game: a Whack-a-mole and a Memory, which try to improve different skills keeping the children focused on tasks. Whack-a-mole aims to work on the attention and visual and reading agility by recognizing correct letters and words. Memory aims to improve memory and attention ability by pairing letter-cards. The mini-game structure permits to incorporate new levels or games and the progressive increment of difficulty allows the autonomous treatment.

Keywords: Virtual reality · Serious game · Dyslexia · Education · Children

1 Introduction

Children with Specific learning difficulties (SpLDs) learn concepts more slowly for their age or educational level. Nevertheless, SpLDs are not related to the intelligence but to the rate of learning. People with this type of difficulties have oral and writing language problems and reading comprehension deficits. Some examples of SpLDs are dyslexia, dysgraphia, or dyscalculia. Special education is the most effective therapy for SpLDs, and it must be complementary to regular education for children with these conditions. Special education is provided by teachers specialized in the subject and can be done in a group or individually [1].

In recent years, the new devices and technology applications have become a necessity in the treatment of learning disorders. Crises such as COVID-19 have delayed children and adolescents with reading and writing difficulties. This situation has created a considerable disadvantage, especially to people who suffer from some learning disorder [2].

L. T. De Paolis et al. (Eds.): XR Salento 2022, LNCS 13446, pp. 34–43, 2022.
https://doi.org/10.1007/978-3-031-15553-6_3

Consequently, many teachers brought some applications and resources within reach to their students to intended to alleviate this delay. These applications would help them not to miss the pace of classes, even if they were at home. Currently, there are many applications for the treatment of learning disorders for the typical devices like tablets. Nevertheless, this type of technology is not immersive, and the lack of immersion can cause children to neglect interest in the application [3]. Children with reading and writing difficulties may be unattracted to educational content, therefore, immersion can support them because it is a positive component for emotional support [4].

This article will explain the design of a VR videogame called DixGame for the treatment of dyslexia in children between 8 and 12 years old. This game has educational content integrated with funny game mechanics for children to learn without realizing it. DixGame contains two games intended to deal with different reading and writing difficulties: Whack-a-mole and Memory.

The remaining sections of this paper will be organized as follows: in Sect. 2, the development of the immersive VR serious game for dyslexia treatment will be described. The conclusions and future lines of work will be presented in Sect. 3.

2 Related Work

Dyslexia is the most SpLDs known. Many dyslexic readers experience visual-perceptual problems, such as shifting and reversal of letters in a word. This causes words to appear to be moving, distorted, crowded, or overlapping [5, 6]. Dyslexic people, therefore, show more diffuse attention and have difficulties in tasks that require focused attention and visual search [7]. As a result, this condition entails a significant educational and occupational disadvantage throughout their lives [8].

Serious Games (SG), also known as games for learning, are activities designed to entertain users in an environment where they can also learn, educate, and train themselves in diverse areas and tasks. The main goals of a SG should be interaction, user engagement, immersion, and photorealism [9]. SG present a student-centered approach to education, unlike traditional teaching environments where the teacher controls the learning. This feeling facilitates active and critical learning [10]. Thus, to design an effective SG, it is necessary to incorporate gamified elements. Gamification can be defined as the use of game design elements in non-game contexts [11]. This technique looks for increasing usability and satisfaction and promoting more pleasant experiences to drive behaviours [12].

Nowadays, the way of learning of young people is changing and being adapted to the current technologies [13]. The use of these technologies, such as Virtual Reality (VR), aims to innovate and improve the educational field. This is intended to make the learning process flexible, collaborative, and individualized [14]. Numerous studies have tried to compare learning in VR and traditional learning with encouraging results [15, 16]. VR improves learning, and participants acquire greater commitment and more positive emotions. And a positive state of mind can also have favorable effects on learning.

VR offers two very important components for improving the rate of learning: presence and immersion [17]. Presence represents the feeling of "being there"; that is to say, the feeling of existing in the virtual environment [18]. Immersion is defined as the technological fidelity of VR that hardware and software can evoke [19]. Most people prefer and active learning than a passive one and 3D environments allow to view practical content in an active way [20]. Because of that, the VR interactivity and feedback are also useful to achieve high learning rates [21]. Moreover, VR offers a closed world where the users could feel more privacy, comfort and confidence than in a normal classroom [22]. Lastly, people have different ways of processing information. VR can bundle activities for different ways of learning and be adapted to a larger audience [16].

Several studies investigating SpLDs and videogames have been carried out. For example, Peters et al. analysed the visual training of dyslexia difficulties through action games [23]. They concluded that reading accuracy, speed, and comprehension were significantly improved. For this reason, action games were considered as a fun and engaging intervention for dyslexia. Other authors developed adaptative SG for different SpLDs [1]. The results showed positive feedback for the game ability to personalize to the needs of the player. They also defined a range of criteria for the development of serious games for children with SpLDs. In the first place, games should be geared toward children who can read and write. Moreover, the games must be easy to understand facilitating the children work. To conclude, it is necessary not to distract the children's attention in order to keep them focused on the main task.

Most of the studies that use video games as a treatment for dyslexia are focused on an audience between 5 and 14 years old. During these ages, the intervention may obtain the most significant benefits because children are undergoing rapid neural development and the attentional networks are still maturing [24]. Several reports ensure reading improvement using computerized games and applications that work with spatial and temporal attention [25]. Nevertheless, there are hardly any studies using an immersive VR-SG for the treatment of dyslexia. These studies have no significant results because they have no control group to compare the results, or the sample is formed for less than 30 people [26, 27].

3 Game Design: DixGame

DixGame is an immersive virtual reality serious game. The aim of this game is to work on the reading and writing needs of children with dyslexia. The chosen target audience for this game is children with dyslexia between 8 and 12 years old. This age range was decided to have some master language and the ability to learn to use the game without difficulty [24]. This game is constituted by two games: a whack-a-mole and a memory. The game's environment is a funfair; therefore, children may associate the game with favorable emotions. Gamification and positive reinforcement of this game are two key issues so that children do not get bored, frustrated, or feel evaluated. Therefore, a system of rewards and positive messages is offered throughout the game. The evaluation system is included in each game. Each of these levels has a progressively increased difficulty. It will be examined if the children are improving their reading and writing skills in case, they pass the proposed levels. DixGame was developed according to the flowchart proposed for the design and implementation of immersive VR-SG described in another paper of the researcher department [28].

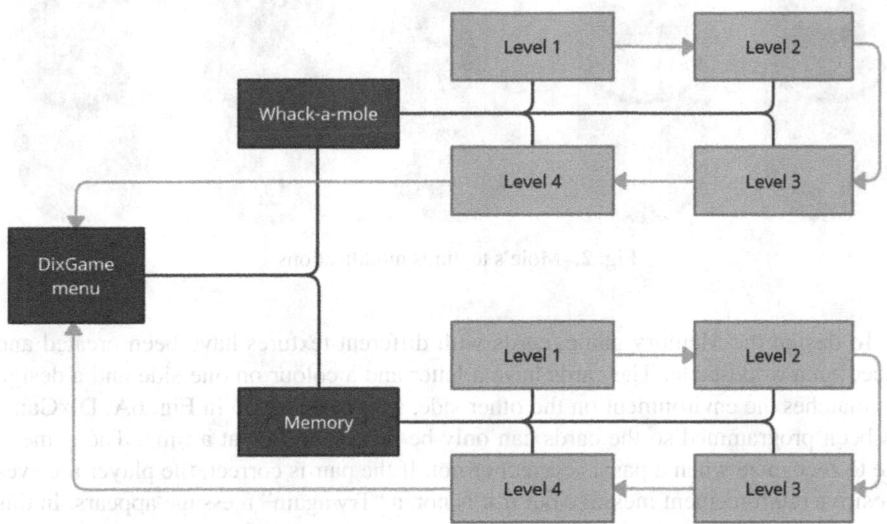

Fig. 1. DixGame flow chart for the recommended progressive learning (Color figure online)

In order to make possible an autonomous learning, Whack-a-mole and Memory games have got various levels of progressive difficulty. Figure 1 shows the diagram of the game. Blue rectangles indicate each of the games, and yellow rectangles show their levels. The recommended itinerary for progressive learning is indicated with yellow arrows. Nevertheless, the professional or the player are able to choose another game route.

3.1 Software

DixGame has been developed using the source code and the scenario of a game from Lightspeed Studios called Nvidia® Funhouse. These resources are available for developers for free on Steam platform. Mod Kit of the game can be reached via the Epic Games launcher. This game has been used as a tool to save time and resources using the environment and objects. Nevertheless, several modifications have been done to adapt the game to the requirements and objectives of DixGame.

The textures of the original moles in Whack a mole game have been replaced by colours, letters, or words to adapt this game (Fig. 2). The posters have also been changed to make the game more focussed on the educational field. Some messages have been included to explain how the game works, the task of each level, and to encourage the player. Furthermore, the game has been programmed to recognize the correct moles and to come out in pairs each time. Figure 3 shows some of the changes that have been made.

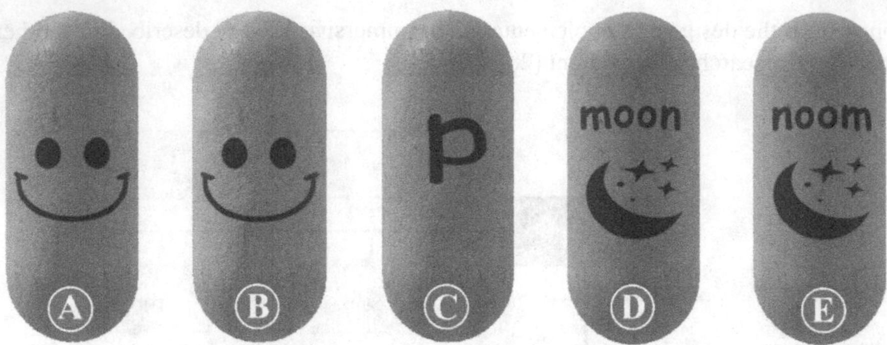

Fig. 2. Mole's textures modifications

To design the Memory game, cards with different textures have been created and placed on a wood-table. The cards have a letter and a colour on one side and a design that matches the environment on the other side, as it can be seen in Fig. 6A. DixGame has been programmed so the cards can only be picked up two at a time. The game is able to recognize when a pair is correct or not. If the pair is correct, the player receives a positive reinforcement message but if it is not, a "Try again" message appears. In this way, the child is encouraged to keep playing and learning with the game. In both games, different buttons have been created to allow to restart the levels if needed or to go back to the main menu and select another level (Fig. 4A, Fig. 6C).

Fig. 3. Modifications between the reference game and DixGame

The game engine used to develop DixGame was Unreal Engine with the 4.26 version. Unreal Engine is free and easy to use for people who do not know how to program with code because of its programming through nodes. Moreover, Unreal get realistic results, which is important to acquire a better level of immersion. The 3D models needed for the game have been created using Blender 2.91. Moreover, Adobe Photoshop has been used to produce the textures of these elements because of the knowledge of the program and its ease of use.

All these software have been chosen because of the previous and satisfactory experience of the researcher group in the development of educational applications [13, 21, 29].

3.2 Hardware

This game has been developed for any of the desktop Head Mounted Display (HMD) from Oculus. The user interacts with the game through the controllers that act as the user's hands in the virtual world. The right joystick is used to move around the scene and the left joystick to rotate the view. The user can grab the objects by pressing the side triggers as it simulates the movement of closing the hand. An Oculus Rift S headset was used for the beta test.

3.3 Whack-a-Mole

In the Whack-a-mole game, the player must hit different moles with a mallet (Fig. 4F). This game aims to work on the attention and visual and reading agility. The moles will appear in front of the child when the game is started (Fig. 4C). A series of challenges will be proposed to the player, and they must be completed to finish the game (Fig. 4D). The player will receive or lost five points each time a mole is hit correctly or incorrectly (Fig. 4E). The player wins the game when 150 points are attained. Furthermore, a series of light bulbs will indicate the remaining of time (Fig. 4B). If the correct moles are unhit, every two seconds, one of the bulbs will turn red. When every bulb is red, the player will lose the game.

Fig. 4. The appearance of DixGame's Whack-a-mole (Color figure online)

There are four levels of difficulty. The first one is a simple level where children must strike the moles with the colour that is requested (Fig. 2B). The simplicity of this level allows the child to adapt to the environment and understand how the game works in a visual way. Moreover, it provides a sense of fun because it hardly includes educational content. In the second level, the moles have different letters. The child is asked to hit only those moles with a specific letter. These letters are clearly identifiable for a child with dyslexia (Fig. 2C). In the third level, the challenges are similar to the previous one. The letters' identification is more complicated and different fonts, uppercase and lowercase are mixed. In the last level, each mole has a word or a pseudo-word, such as "moon" or "noom" (Fig. 2D and 2E). The challenge in this level is to hit just the words that are correctly written. As Fig. 5 shows, the speed of the moles will increase progressively in every level to increase the difficulty and encourage the player.

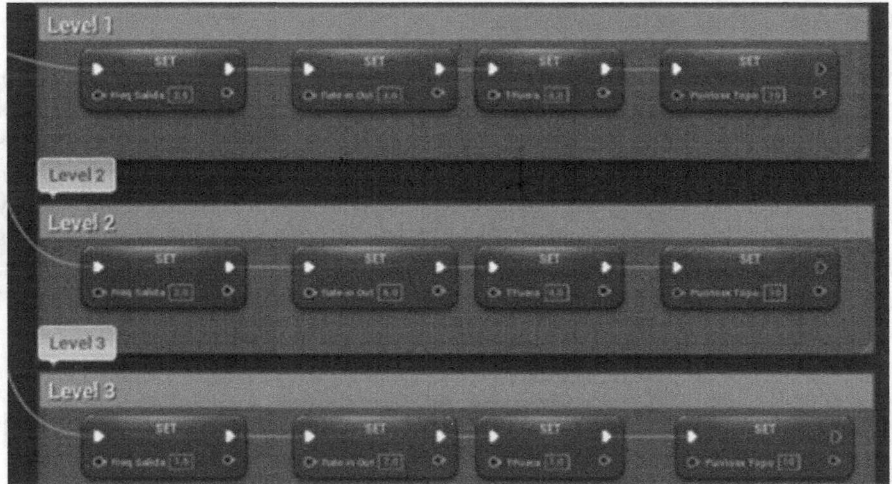

Fig. 5. Programming of level speed in Whack-a-mole game

3.4 Memory

The second game of DixGame is a memory where the player must pick up sixteen cards from a table to pair them off (Fig. 6A). These cards have different letters, colours, and fonts to make the player work on his reading and writing needs. Moreover, this game aims to improve memory and attention skills. A countdown has been included so that the child is aware of the passage of time and learns to manage it (Fig. 6B).

In the first level, a colour is assigned to each pair of cards to make easier for the child to match them up in a visual way. Furthermore, the letters in this level are very different between them to achieve this goal. This level wants to teach the player how the game works and show the playful component of this educational game. The second level is slightly difficult than the previous one. It has some duplicated colours without enlarging the similarity between the letters. In this way, the player could feel the increase

Fig. 6. The appearance of DixGame's Memory

of difficulty but without getting frustrated. Colours of the previous level are maintained in the third level; therefore, letters are more similar with each other. Finally, in the fourth level every card has the same colour, and the letters are very similar. For example, "p", "b", "q" and "d" are present in this level. In each level, the time that appears on the countdown is less than the previous one to increase the difficulty progressively. In order to progress through the recommended itinerary, the player must work on their difficulties and gradually improve with levels.

4 Conclusions and Future Work

DixGame has been created for the treatment of dyslexia for children between 8 and 12 years old. This is a virtual reality serious game that has two games inside: Whack-a-mole and Memory. These inner games pretend to improve some reading and learning skills of children with dyslexia. Whack-a-mole has been developed to recognize the letters and words depending on the proposed challenges in each level. Additionally, this game works on attention and visual and reading agility. However, Memory aims to improve memory and attention skills by pairing off letter-cards. To face these purposes, a game done was taken as a reference: Nvidia® Funhouse, to economize the resources. This open-code game had been modified to turn into this tool for dyslexia treatment.

It has not yet been possible to perform a proper usability test with a public target group. In the near future, DixGame will be tested by children between 8 and 12 years old with reading and writing difficulties to evaluate the performance of the already developed games. The children will try the game levels according to their needs for about twenty minutes. Subsequently, they will fill a satisfaction and usability questionnaire about the experience. Based on the answers obtained, the games will be modified so that they were able to obtain better results. In addition, it will be adapted to the needs observed in the experience according to the player's age, the game difficulty, the balance between fun and learning, etc. The update game pretends to be more useful for the treatment of dyslexia. The game will also be adapted so that it can be used on more HMD devices like HTC Vive so that more people can utilize it. Furthermore, they will be developed some more games that help to work on reading and writing skills through other types of exercises. For example, a game based on word formation through spelling.

Acknowledgements. This work was partially supported by the ACIS project (Reference Number INVESTUN/21/BU/0002) of the Consejería de Empleo e Industria of the Junta de Castilla y León (Spain) and the Erasmus+ RISKREAL Project (Reference Number 2020-1-ES01-KA204-081847) of the European Commission.

References

1. Yildirim, O., Surer, E.: Developing adaptive serious games for children with specific learning difficulties: a two-phase usability and technology acceptance study. JMIR Ser. Games **9**(2), e25997 (2021). https://doi.org/10.2196/25997
2. Asbury, K., Fox, L., Deniz, E., Code, A., Toseeb, U.: How is COVID-19 affecting the mental health of children with special educational needs and disabilities and their families? J. Autism Dev. Disord. **51**(5), 1772–1780 (2020). https://doi.org/10.1007/s10803-020-04577-2
3. Carreker, S., Birsh, J.R.: Multisensory Teaching of Basic Language Skills Activity Book. Paul H. Brookes Publishing, Baltimore (2011)
4. Villani, D., Carissoli, C., Triberti, S., Marchetti, A., Gilli, G., Riva, G.: Videogames for emotion regulation: a systematic review (2018). https://doi.org/10.1089/g4h.2017.0108
5. Boets, B., Wouters, J., van Wieringen, A., Ghesquière, P.: Auditory processing, speech perception and phonological ability in pre-school children at high-risk for dyslexia: a longitudinal study of the auditory temporal processing theory. Neuropsychologia. **45**(8), 1608–1620 (2007). https://doi.org/10.1016/j.neuropsychologia.2007.01.009
6. Facoetti, A., Luisa Lorusso, M., Paganoni, P., Umiltà, C., Gastone Mascetti, G.: The role of visuospatial attention in developmental dyslexia: evidence from a rehabilitation study. Cognit. Brain Res. **15**(2), 154–164 (2003). https://doi.org/10.1016/S0926-6410(02)00148-9
7. Franceschini, S., Gori, S., Ruffino, M., Pedrolli, K., Facoetti, A.: A causal link between visual spatial attention and reading acquisition. Curr. Biol. **22**(9), 814–819 (2012). https://doi.org/10.1016/j.cub.2012.03.013
8. Lyon, G.R., Shaywitz, S.E., Shaywitz, B.A.: A definition of dyslexia (2003). https://doi.org/10.1007/s11881-003-0001-9
9. Maria, R., Johnson, A., Moher, T., Leigh, J., Vasilakis, C., Barnes, C.: Learning and building together in an immersive virtual world. Presen. Teleoper. Virt. Environ. **8**(3), 247–263 (1999). https://doi.org/10.1162/105474699566215
10. Stapleton, A.J.: Serious games: serious opportunities. Health Care **1** (2004)
11. Deterding, S., Khaled, R., Nacke, L., Dixon, D.: Gamification: toward a definition. Chi 2011 (2011)
12. Baptista, G., Oliveira, T.: Gamification and serious games: a literature meta-analysis and integrative model. Comput. Hum. Behav. **92**, 306–315 (2019). https://doi.org/10.1016/j.chb.2018.11.030
13. Checa, D., Bustillo, A.: Advantages and limits of virtual reality in learning processes: Briviesca in the fifteenth century. Virtual Reality **24**(1), 151–161 (2019). https://doi.org/10.1007/s10055-019-00389-7
14. López Cabrera, M.V., Hernandez-Rangel, E., Mejía Mejía, G.P., Cerano Fuentes, J.L.: Factors that enable the adoption of educational technology in medical schools. Educ. Med. **20**, 3–9 (2019). https://doi.org/10.1016/j.edumed.2017.07.006

15. Webster, R.: Declarative knowledge acquisition in immersive virtual learning environments. Interact. Learn. Environ. **24**, 1319 (2016). https://doi.org/10.1080/10494820.2014.994533
16. Allcoat, D., von Mühlenen, A.: Learning in virtual reality: effects on performance, emotion and engagement. Res. Learn. Technol. **26** (2018). https://doi.org/10.25304/rlt.v26.2140
17. Mikropoulos, T.A., Natsis, A.: Educational virtual environments: a ten-year review of empirical research (1999–2009). Comput. Educ. **56** (2011). https://doi.org/10.1016/j.compedu.2010.10.020
18. Steuer, J.: Defining virtual reality: dimensions determining telepresence. J. Commun. **42**, 73–93 (1992). https://doi.org/10.1111/j.1460-2466.1992.tb00812.x
19. Bowman, D.A., McMahan, R.P.: Virtual reality: how much immersion is enough? Computer (Long Beach Calif). **40**, 36–43 (2007). https://doi.org/10.1109/MC.2007.257
20. Valdez, M.T., Ferreira, C.M., Martins, M.J.M., Barbosa, F.P.M.: 3D virtual reality experiments to promote electrical engineering education. In: 2015 International Conference on Information Technology Based Higher Education and Training, ITHET 2015 (2015). https://doi.org/10.1109/ITHET.2015.7217957
21. Checa, D., Miguel-Alonso, I., Bustillo, A.: Immersive virtual-reality computer-assembly serious game to enhance autonomous learning. Virtual Reality (2021). https://doi.org/10.1007/s10055-021-00607-1
22. Allcoat, D., Hatchard, T., Azmat, F., Stansfield, K., Watson, D., von Mühlenen, A.: Education in the digital age: learning experience in virtual and mixed realities. J. Educ. Comput. Res. **59** (2021). https://doi.org/10.1177/0735633120985120
23. Peters, J.L., Crewther, S.G., Murphy, M.J., Bavin, E.L.: Action video game training improves text reading accuracy, rate and comprehension in children with dyslexia: a randomized controlled trial. Sci. Rep. **11** (2021). https://doi.org/10.1038/s41598-021-98146-x
24. Klaver, P., Marcar, V., Martin, E.: Neurodevelopment of the visual system in typically developing children. In: Progress in Brain Research (2011). https://doi.org/10.1016/B978-0-444-53884-0.00021-X
25. Franceschini, S., Gori, S., Ruffino, M., Viola, S., Molteni, M., Facoetti, A.: Action video games make dyslexic children read better. Curr. Biol. **23** (2013). https://doi.org/10.1016/j.cub.2013.01.044
26. Kalyvioti, K., Mikropoulos, T.A.: A virtual reality test for the identification of memory strengths of dyslexic students in higher education. J. Universal Comput. Sci. **19** (2013)
27. Pedroli, E., Padula, P., Guala, A., Meardi, M.T., Riva, G., Albani, G.: A psychometric tool for a virtual reality rehabilitation approach for dyslexia. Comput. Math. Methods Med. **2017**, 1–6 (2017). https://doi.org/10.1155/2017/7048676
28. Checa, D., Bustillo, A.: A review of immersive virtual reality serious games to enhance learning and training. Multim. Tools Appl. **79**(9–10), 5501–5527 (2019). https://doi.org/10.1007/s11042-019-08348-9
29. Checa, D., Saucedo-Dorantes, J.J., Osornio-Rios, R.A., Antonino-Daviu, J.A., Bustillo, A.: Virtual reality training application for the condition-based maintenance of induction motors. Appl. Sci. **12**, 414 (2022). https://doi.org/10.3390/app12010414

Processing Physiological Sensor Data in Near Real-Time as Social Signals for Their Use on Social Virtual Reality Platforms

Fabio Genz[1(✉)], Clemens Hufeld[1], and Dieter Kranzlmüller[1,2]

[1] Ludwig-Maximilians-Universität München, Munich, Germany
fabio.genz@nm.ifi.lmu.de

[2] Leibniz Supercomputing Centre, Munich, Germany

Abstract. Social interactions increasingly shift to computer-mediated communication channels. Compared to face-to-face communication, their use suffers from a loss or distortion in the transmission of social signals, which are prerequisites of social interactions. Social virtual reality platforms offer users a variety of possibilities to express themselves verbally as well as non-verbally. Although these platforms take steps towards compensating the addressed communication gap, there is still high demand to ensure and further improve the correct transmission of social signals. To address this issue, we investigate the processing of physiological sensor data as social signals. This paper provides two major contributions: Firstly, a concept for processing physiological sensor data in near real-time as social signals. The concept enables the processing of physiological sensor data on an individual level as well as across all users. For both the individual user and the collective, single sensors or the data from the whole sensor cluster can be analysed, resulting in four ways of analysis. Secondly, we provide concrete suggestions for a software setup, based on an extensive analysis of available open source software, to support a potential future implementation of the proposed concept. The results of this work are highly relevant for social virtual reality platforms, especially since modern head-mounted displays are often already equipped with appropriate measurement sensors. Moreover, the results can also be transferred to numerous other media, applications and research fields concerned with processing physiological sensor data, which reinforces the provided added value.

Keywords: Physiological sensor data · Sensor networks · Streaming · Apache Kafka · Near real-time · Social signal processing · Social virtual reality platforms

L. T. De Paolis et al. (Eds.): XR Salento 2022, LNCS 13446, pp. 44–62, 2022.
https://doi.org/10.1007/978-3-031-15553-6_4

1 Introduction

Computer-mediated communication increasingly replace face-to-face social interactions [83]. While social media and the mass proliferation of smartphones increased this trend over the last decade [39], the global SARS-CoV-2 pandemic has further accelerated it [68]. The basis of social interactions are social signals, i.e. observable behaviours that - intentionally or unintentionally - cause noticeable changes in others which should in turn enable people to understand and reasonably predict the behaviour of their counterparts [83]. Previous research has shown that people respond to the same social signals in co-located meetings as they do when using computer-mediated communication technologies [69]. However, compared to face-to-face communication, their use suffers from the partial loss (e.g. missing facial expressions in the absence of a camera image) or distortion (e.g. artificial information channels as "likes") in the transmission of social signals [19].

Social virtual reality (VR) platforms enable web-based social interactions mediated by immersive technologies and take place in pre-built 3D virtual environments [28]. In February 2022, there are over 160 different platforms with an upward trend and increasing number of users [72]. Users are represented by avatars who can engage in collaborative activities and interpersonal conversations in real-time, with a variety of ways to communicate verbally (e.g. speech, text) as well as non-verbally (e.g. display and individualise avatars, natural reproductions of gestures with support of input devices for full body-, lip- and eye-tracking) [28,32]. Although social VR platforms take steps towards compensating the addressed communication gap, there is yet high need to ensure and further improve the correct transmission of social signals [85].

One research field that deals with questions concerning social signals in human-human and human-machine interactions is social signal processing (SSP). SSP is a computing domain aimed at three essential fields of research: modeling, analysis, and synthesis of social signals [67,81,82]. Researcher from the field of SSP already proposed the usage of physiological sensor data (PSD) as suitable social signals for a number of reasons [82]. Firstly, PSD offer more objective data in contrast to e.g. questionnaires or interviews [38]. Secondly, PSD expand the current spectrum of social signals, as humans perception is often limited and therefore not attributable [48,51]. Thirdly, PSD provides both supplementary and redundant information about the state of the user and thus enables a clearer interpretation of, for example, ambiguous social signals [82]. Fourthly, PSD offer potential ways of transmitting social signals for impaired people [19].

Although PSD as social signals are investigated in numerous papers (e.g. [15, 48,84]), also in the context of VR (e.g. [23,24,52,56,71]) there is still demand for work regarding the automatic synchronisation of different physiological sensors, especially in the context of the parallel analysis of several persons [19].

To bridge this gap, this paper provides two major contributions: Firstly, a concept for processing PSD near real-time as social signals. The concept enables the processing of PSD on the individual level as well as across all users. For both the individual user and the collective, single sensors or the data from the whole sensor cluster can be analysed, resulting in four ways of analysis. Secondly, we provide concrete suggestions for a software setup to implement the proposed concept based on an extensive analysis of available open source software.

Our paper is structured as follows. Section 2 gives an overview of relevant literature. Section 3 describes the concept, followed by Sect. 4 with concrete suggestions for a software setup to support a potential future implementation. In Sect. 5 we critically reflect on the results of this work and identify potential shortcomings. While Sect. 6 summarizes our approach and intentions, Sect. 7 recommends potential future work.

2 Related Work

The combination of several sensors with the intention of providing combined data that is more accurate and reliable than the evaluation of individual sensors is referred to as sensor fusion [90]. To put sensor fusion into a scalable environment this paper intersects and combines several areas of research. The first is research on sensor networks. Our concept assumes several sensors on one person, forming a network of sensors that needs management and proper analysis. The challenges associated with this are discussed in 2.1. Secondly, even though the amount of data produced by one or few sensors is small, the sensors of multiple users using an application at the same time produce large amounts of data very quickly. This pushes the topic of this paper into the area of databases, their management and how to deal with questions regarding big data analysis. In 2.2 previous work on the analysis of large quantities of data in the streaming world is outlined. While there is research on sensor networks and big data analysis the bridge between the sensor network and the analysis forms an integral part of this paper. This step is referred to as extract, transform, load (ETL) and is a main focus investigated in 2.3. The usefulness of sensors producing data after transfer and analysis is significantly impacted by its speed. There has been a great deal of research on the meaning and quality of real-time data analysis, which will be explicated in 2.4. After considering all these related areas of research, 2.5 explains how this paper fits into the existing literature and where it crosses the boundaries of existing research to make relevant contributions to the current state of research.

2.1 Processing Physiological Sensor Data

A sensor is a physical device that reacts to a physically detectable change in the environment around it to produce an analog signal. This analog signal is then converted to a digital one and either stored or emitted [27]. These sensors are not all singletons but rather connected to each other in a hierarchy of communication, a sensor network. A distinction has to be made between identical sensors that communicate with each other and multiple independent sensors used to measure different things each [14]. Body area networks, as in the present case, constitute the second kind where multiple types of sensors detect real life events independently from each other.

The medical field, similar to this paper, is interested in sensor networks measuring PSD. Thus, this is the most relevant field for the subject of sensor network studies. The medical sector has seen a strong use of sensor technology, which is still on the rise [1,2,25,50,66], creating fields such as telemedicine in the process.

One acknowledged benchmarking sensor data set for the area of human activity tracking is the PAMAP2 data set [70]. This data set serves as a useful sample in illustrating the diversity of PSD. Regardless of the data type produced, the most important part about the data sensors produce is the nature as log data which consists of tuples in the format "time stamp: event recorded". This log data allows a computational representation of the data as a directed acyclical graph [40].

In summary, physiological sensors measure real life events in, on or around the body as a network of independent devices, producing analysable log data.

2.2 Development of Database Technologies

Sensors do not produce data in chunks but as constant streams of data that are unbounded flows of information [86]. These data sources should be available to an arbitrary amount of data consumers. When considering how to make this data available to data consumers, a simple approach would be to create N-to-N connections between every sensor and every consumer. A more sophisticated solution allows for the separation of concerns. A middleware has to be introduced between data producers and data consumers that gathers data, performs actions on the data, passes the data on to consumers and provides services for the consumers that allow for completeness.

Traditional databases are made for bulk loading and bulk analysis of data in batches. These may reach a very large scale but the processing is of relatively low speed when compared to stream processing [74]. In the endeavour of combining the highly accurate batch processing techniques with the recency and high relevance of newly incoming data, a combination of batch architecture and pure stream processing was proposed. The general idea is to have a system in which the CAP theorem [17] is improved upon by providing a system that is both available and consistent in the presence of partitions. In an influential blog post by Nathan Marz called "How to beat the CAP theorem" he proposed a "batch layer + realtime layer" architecture [59], in which a distributed big data batch processing system such as Apache Hadoop [33] and Apache Storm [9] calculates results from data that is older than a specified batch size but the data after this point is analysed using a stream processing system such as Apache Storm [60].

Unlike batch systems that are built to analyse historical, fully available data at massive scales, streaming systems are built for unbounded data and for the inclusion of every incoming datum in real-time. There are several issues with this concerning fault tolerance of a streaming system [13,21,43,73,76], partitioning and buffering more specifically, correctness of the incoming data [77] and low latency [12,20,41,57,75,80]. In all of these areas, significant developments are to be expected. However, the current state of research does not allow any conclusive statements about what is"optimal" for an use case. The paper rather gives an assessment of the current state of technology with regard to the proposed concept in Sect. 3.

2.3 Transferring Physiological Sensor Data from Sensors into Streaming Software

ETL is a term which stems from the field of big data management and has been discussed under different terms such as data integration or bulk data loading [45,62]. Now, increasingly attention is paid to ETL with specific focus on the area of streaming. Mehmood et al. identify several issues the ETL research in the area of streaming is tackling, e.g. low latency, distributed computing, platform independence, scalability, fault tolerance, real-time processing and concurrent updates for moving objects [63]. Isah and Zulkernine propose an ETL pipeline that integrates Apache Kafka and Apache NiFi [45]. At the same time, Apache Kafka is the de facto industry standard in the area of streaming ETL [58]. Kafka offers a fault tolerant, highly scalable solution together with a large and active community that ensures a thriving ecosystem around the software solution. It offers exactly once delivery semantics and can buffer incoming and outgoing data almost indefinitely. It can take in data from any data store and Kafka Connect offers adapters for many devices available already. For any devices that produce data that is not portable to Kafka yet, an adapter can be created in code.

Beyond Kafka, streaming ETL is an active area of research. For example, Gözüacik et al. have proposed a parent aware routing mechanism [36] for data extraction, Marcu et al. have proposed a dynamic partitioning system that outperforms other ingestion systems five times in laboratory settings [58] on the load step. The transform step is the area where most research is located. Here, questions on fault tolerance [21], correctness of the data [77], windowing [62] and cleaning of the data are examined. Especially in the cleaning of data, there are multiple approaches, primarily using deep learning methods based on long short term memory artificial neural networks. The approaches differ between sequence-to-sequence imputation models [89], grid search method [37] or matrix factorization [42]. Most recently, a graph based method has been proposed [47].

2.4 Near Real-Time Processing

The term "real-time" is sometimes used by researchers like a self explanatory concept, without defining it (see e.g. [18,26]) but the concept requires closer scrutiny. The term can be separated into hard, firm and soft real-time systems. In a hard real-time system, there are severe consequences if the result of an analysis of events is not available at a specified deadline, for example for safety reasons. In a firm real-time system there might not be severe consequences if the analysis is not available at the deadline but the utility of the results drops sharply. In a soft real-time system, the utility is affected only slightly but a quick response would be desirable. This distinction affects the design of a system, depending on hard, firm or soft real-time requirements [49].

There are benchmarks for data streaming services. The most relevant benchmark for this paper is the RIoTBench [75], as it simulates sensor input data. It finds that latency greatly depends on the type of task and the way data is transferred. The mean latency should be in the sub-millisecond area but depending on the task, the latency can reach over 2 s, which can still be considered to be sufficient for human interaction. The ETL tasks for sensor data, specifically, were in the range of 25 milliseconds.

When processing PSD for use on social VR platforms, a strict sub-second deadline is neither necessary nor feasible for two reasons. Firstly, several human reactions of the body do not show in sub-second speeds (e.g. changes in heart rate or skin conductivity, take some time to show themselves) [46]. Secondly, human reaction speed is orders of magnitude larger than machine based latency requirements [49]. Therefore a response by the system under human reaction speeds is not necessary. Hence, a generous deadline of around two seconds response time to an event is still adequate for social VR platforms. This is not an absolute deadline of a hard real-time system but rather somewhere between a soft and firm real-time requirement. The usefulness of the information is not lost after the deadline. As a minimum requirement, the deadline should hence be the threshold of interactivity.

2.5 Research Gap and Contribution

We already mentioned the demand for works regarding the automatic synchronisation of different PSD, especially in the context of the parallel analysis of several persons [19]. In the area of sensor data streaming, the technical opportunity is there, but there is - as of yet - no contribution that combines the areas of physiological sensor networks and scalable streaming technology. Especially the combination of the analysis of individual users' sensor networks has not been done. Although the combination is a potent approach for SSP, the architecture is not limited to this field of research.

3 Concept

Figure 1 describes the concept proposed as a versatile architecture for sensor cluster analysis of multiple users. There are three stages to it and four different ways of analysing the resulting data. In the first stage, individuals wear at least one sensor. If there are at least two, they constitute a network, or sensor cluster. There is little restriction regarding these sensors. They can measure any physical activity in any way, as long as they produce loggable data. The data from these senors are introduced into a streaming ETL service, which takes the data, processes it and turns it into a stream. Importantly, the streaming ETL service should be able to filter the data and create multiple streams that data consumers can subscribe to. Namely one for each input sensor and also streams for combinations of different sensors, up to a stream combining the data from all sensors. These streams can now be passed into an analysis and visualisation software to display relevant PSD, such as heart rate or temperature in real-time, and analysis on data, such as development of electrodermal activity or analysed emotional state. This is what the boxes with number 1 and 2 on the top right represent.

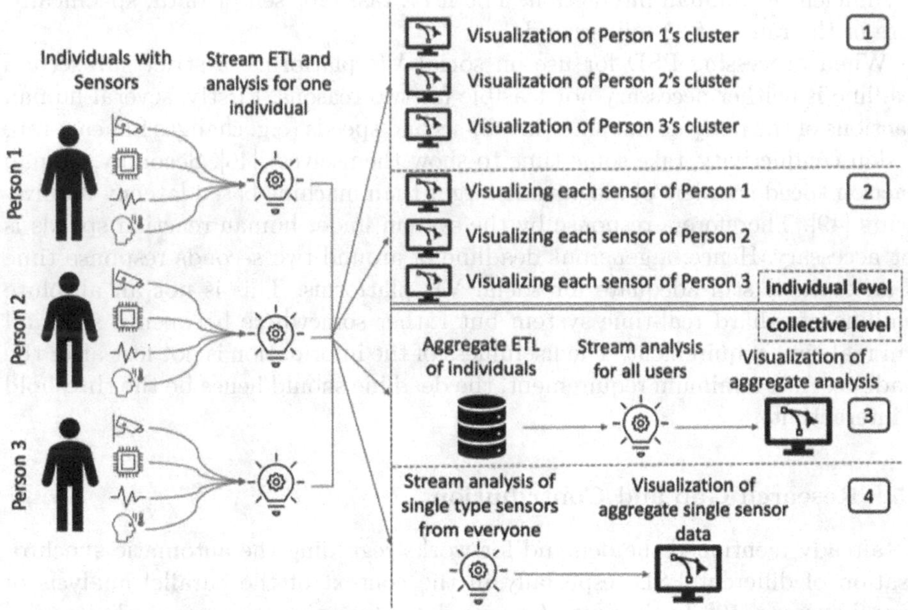

Fig. 1. Illustration of the proposed concept with four separate strains of analysis. Each person is monitored by a cluster of any sensors. The data is input to a streaming system, which outputs analysis of the streams for each individual (box 1) and single sensors for each individual (box 2), an aggregate analysis of all user clusters combined (box 3), and an analysis of all sensors of the same kind from all users (box 4).

In the third and fourth level, data from several users are aggregated and the users are analysed collectively, rather than individually. The third box with the number three shows an aggregate analysis of all individuals. This is relevant for system administrators but could also be made available to single users. The stream analyses from the stream analysis softwares are taken as input for another aggregate stream. This stream already contains analysed information from each individual. Once this information is gathered together in a new stream, it can be analysed as a stream again, this time for the whole system or any subset of the active users. Outliers and specific demographic groups of users can be analyzed in bulk this way. This analysis can, in turn, be visualised with another software and insights about the state and behavior of all users can be gathered.

The analysis with the number four follows the idea that while an aggregate analysis of all users may be very useful, it may not be able to reveal details about the state of individual sensor types in the whole system. Since the streaming

ETL service takes the sensor data and turns them into streams, this third step receives streams from every individual user split up by sensor type, e.g. heart rate stream, temperature stream, face camera stream etc.. Then, aggregate streams are created but rather than basing the aggregation on individuals, they are based on sensor type. This allows the comparison of users' sensor behavior and makes it easier to find outliers.

Even though the visualisation of PSD is an essential step in the usefulness of such an concept, this paper focuses on the steps before the visualisation. Therefore, this section outlines minimum requirements for such a concept and further list desirable qualities of the streaming ETL service and the stream analysis software. The basic idea of streaming is that data is more useful, the fresher it is. Therefore, the minimum requirements are modelled on the accuracy of data analysis when compared to batch processing.

The essential requirements - equally important and in no particular order - are:

- Scalability of the software
- Streaming capability of the software, rather than batch processing only. This includes lambda architectures
- The possibility of keeping the interactive real-time threshold for the entire system between data production and visualisation
- Fault tolerance of the streaming ingestion software
- Stream compatibility of the analysis software

The concept is designed so that any number of users may enter the system with any number of sensors each. Therefore, a scalable software is essential. To be able to outperform batch processing, this software has to be stream compatible, both in the way data is ingested and analysed. The requirement of fault tolerance is linked to the availability of the results. Without fault tolerance, a realization of the concept would be too fragile to guarantee the necessary reliability. Finally, the interactivity threshold is the lower bound to meet the set real-time requirement.

Over and above these basic requirements, there are further requirements that might not be strictly necessary for an implementation but allow a differentiation between different possible software solutions. Because not all of them have to be fulfilled, they are listed in order of importance.

The non-essential requirements - in order of importance - are:

- Delivery semantics guaranteeing exactly once processing
- Stateful application capabilities, i.e. some form of persistent buffering
- The software is embedded in a large, open source community
- There are mechanisms to ensure anonymity of the user data
- The software is compatible with many incoming data formats
- The streaming software and the stream analysis produce a data stream that is cross compatible between different tech stacks (no lock in effect)
- Data protection mechanisms are part of the software
- The software is energy efficient

– There are inbuilt possibilities of visualization

The delivery semantics play an important part for the accuracy of the results. There are three categories, namely at most once, at least once, and exactly once delivery. At most once delivery means the data at the source is sent once and lost forever afterwards. If it is not registered correctly at the streaming software, there is no way to recover the data. With lossy networks, this is unacceptable for analysis purposes. In at least once processing, data is sent from the source to the streaming software and is registered correctly, the streaming software sends an acknowledgement back to the data source. If this acknowledgement is lost, the source might send the data again. Under at least once delivery semantics, the streaming software would have no way to check, whether this data is a duplicate or new data, resulting in the analysis of duplicate data. With PSD, such duplicates are especially problematic, as the sequence is highly important and some measurements cannot be followed by others. This could be limited by a mechanism that seeks outliers in the incoming data stream, however this adds another layer of processing, which has an effect on the latency. In exactly once processing, the streaming software can check whether the incoming data is already present in the buffer or whether it is new data. This ensures that no duplicates are passed on to the analysis.

Persistent buffering is a feature that allows streaming software to be used as a basis of stateful applications. This is significant to create profiles for individual users and have checkpoints or dashboards of their past actions. This data could also be transferred to a persistent database outside of the streaming architecture, but a level of persistence is not only necessary for fault tolerance against short term outages of parts of the architecture but also for resistance against problems with low latency data transfer.

The open source community is not necessarily a metric of greater quality but an active community indicates several positive factors. Firstly, an avid adoption of the software shows that many people find it worthwhile and beneficial, indicating quality of the product. Secondly, a widespread adoption creates a community that generates network effects such as easier bug fixing for problems with the implementation, preexisting connections to other tech stacks, as well as a more thorough control of the source code for vulnerabilities. Thirdly, the open source aspect further means that the software can be used for free, rather than paying by server space or messages processed as with proprietary offers from Google [34], AWS [3] or Microsoft [65]. Therefore, the size of the community can be a strong argument for a software.

The anonymity and data protection mechanisms stem from the nature of the data envisioned in the present use case more than from the software setup itself. PSD is highly personalised, sensitive data and requires protection at the utmost level. Especially Art. 15 and 17 of the EU's General Data Protection Regulation require controllers of personal data to be able to give an account of each user's personal data and delete it if the user requests this. Beyond that, anonymity and data protection by design should not only be possible but a standard in the implementation.

The cross compatibility as a desirable requirement ensures the flexibility of future changes to the concept. Exchanging a part becomes more difficult, if there are limits to the compatibility of the new part with the other parts. If, for example, a streaming ETL software produces a stream that is tailor made for one specific tech stack but has to be transformed for another software environment, this would not be ideal.

4 Implementation

To implement the proposed concept, this section makes recommendations on the software setup to be used. This paper only takes into account open source software, as it assumes that this is both more accessible and ultimately provides a safer solution than proprietary software. Nevertheless, it is possible to fulfil the concept proposed here with either the AWS Kinesis [3], Microsoft Azure Streaming [65] or Google Dataflow [34] ecosystems. If a company is already embedded in these ecosystems and willing to invest more into it, these could work well to create the functionality the concept promises. It is theoretically also possible to create a pipeline with custom self-written code, however the resources needed to do this are only available to highly skilled specialists with a lot of time. The only reasons to do this would be to have maximum control over every step of the process or to create new proprietary software.

Table 1 lists possible software solutions that are capable of fulfilling at least one step in the implementation of the concept. Several of the listed software projects are only partially suitable. These should not be seen as competitors in the same niche but as building on top of and complimenting each other. For example, BookKeeper is a logging tool that is used as part of the implementation of other streaming solutions (e.g. Pulsar [87]). It could be used to implement a custom solution more quickly but is not capable of enabling streaming solutions by itself.

An optimal software setup for the proposed concept, e.g. how many levels the implementation has or how it is managed, is difficult to recommend without a specific use case in mind. This is because there are multiple possible software candidates in the area of creating stream production (e.g. Apache Kafka, Apache Pulsar), in the area of stream transformation and analysis engines (e.g. Apache Storm, Apache Spark Streaming, Apache Heron, Apache Flink) or in the area of real-time online analytical processing databases (e.g. Apache Druid, Apache Pinot). Of these software solutions, this paper recommends the combination of Apache Kafka for stream creation, Apache Flink as a data transformation as well as analysis engine and Apache Pinot as a real-time OLAP database. Apache Kafka appears to be the best option currently because of the strong position it has come to hold in the streaming environment. It is the *de facto* industry standard for stream creation and is compatible with almost every single other software in the streaming market. Additionally it offers exactly once delivery semantics and can be used almost like a persistent buffer. The most compelling argument is the strong open source community around Kafka that allows users

Table 1. Possible software solutions for any step of the streaming pipeline with which it is possible to reach the essential requirements. The "community" column lists the amount of stars on the respective GitHub repository.

Software name	Licence	Community	Source
Akka	Apache-2.0	12k	[16]
Apache AcitveMQ	Apache-2.0	2k	[4]
Apache Beam	Apache-2.0	5.3k	[11]
Apache Bookkeeper	Apache-2.0	1.5k	[10]
Apache Camel	Apache-2.0	4.1k	[5]
Apache Druid	Apache-2.0	11.5k	[64]
Apache Flink	Apache-2.0	18.2k	[6]
Apache Flume	Apache-2.0	2.2k	[8]
Apache Gobblin	Apache-2.0	2k	[55]
Apache Heron	Apache-2.0	3.6k	[78]
Apache Kafka	Apache-2.0	21.1k	[7]
Apache Pinot	Apache-2.0	3.8k	[35]
Apache Pulsar	Apache-2.0	10.4k	[87]
Apache Samza	Apache-2.0	700	[54]
Apache Spark Streaming	Apache-2.0	32k	[9]
Apache Storm	Apache-2.0	6.3k	[60]
AthenaX	Apache-2.0	1.2k	[79]
Logstash	Elastic	12.7k	[29]
Custom coded system	Any	No	N/A

to get help for their issues more quickly and reliably. Through Kafka Connect it is also possible to link almost any sensor into Kafka. Lastly, it is extremely scalable at low latency.

Apache Flink [18] is the best option as a stream analysis engine. It can take in multiple data sources, not just streams. When taking in batch data it follows what it calls a "kappa" architecture, which they see as a development of the lambda architecture. Instead of enabling streaming capabilities through micro-batching, Flink enables batch processing capabilities through streaming. This dual setup between streaming and batch processing is apt for sensor data, which does not lose its usefulness directly after production, e.g. in user dashboarding. It is a high throughput, low latency, fault tolerant cluster framework that can run in a YARN, Mesos or Kubernetes container. Additionally, it provides exactly once delivery semantics when reading from and writing to Kafka and offers a web based scheduling view. All of these, together with a strong community and widespread adoption that come with the same benefits as described for Kafka, Flink is a good option to realise the architecture.

Amongst the OLAP databases, Apache Druid [88] and Apache Pinot [44], it is difficult to find a relevant difference. They have been created in parallel, the former by Metamarket, the latter by LinkedIn with essentially the same functionality [53]. Both offer a powerful backend for GUIs that can query terabytes of data within real-time constraints and can take in streams of data. Druid has dependencies on Apache Zookeeper and a metadata store, such as any SQL database, while Pinot relies on the Apache Helix framework. Differences in performance have been found with Pinot outperforming Druid [31], however these are strictly use case based and depend on how the parameters are coded, so they should not be taken as absolute measurements [53]. Therefore, upon implementation, it is recommended to try both Pinot and Druid, as there will be differences in performance depending on the way data is taken in and the parameters are preferred.

Overall, this threefold architecture ensures exactly once delivery semantics all the way through and provides the lowest possible latency available on the market at the moment. It is not possible to express in milliseconds what the latency is going to be exactly, as this depends on the amount of data ingested, the tuning of parameters in Kafka, Flink and Druid/Pinot and the type of tasks Flink and Druid/Pinot perform on the data. For example, while some predictive tasks like interpolation can have a mean latency above 4 seconds, a sliding linear regression can be near instant [75].

5 Discussion

The present work contributes a concept that enables the bundled processing of PSD in near real-time, as well as software recommendations for a potential implementation. Since the results are all theoretical and the software recommendations are also based on purely literary research, it is difficult to have a concrete discussion about their validity and significance. With this in mind we would like to point out several limitations in our work, elaborate on the need and pitfalls of a potential implementation and take a brief and critical ethical perspective.

Regarding limitations, we briefly reiterate on the theoretical nature of our approach. In accordance to the V-model of software development [30], this paper takes the first steps of identifying criteria and providing a detailed plan for an implementation. If one or more of the assumptions from the literature review are incorrect or change due to other findings, certain elements might have to be updated. Hence our approach requires an implementation and subsequent testing, while keeping up to date with current research. Another limitation are the insufficient considerations regarding social VR platforms. Although at the beginning of the paper we refer to research that has already integrated PSD as social signals in VR, this requires further elaborations with potential derivations and adaptions for the concept and implementation. However, taking a closer look at current research gaps regarding the parallel processing of PSD for multiple users, it becomes clear that it is first necessary to find answers to the most pressing questions of this topic.

Referring to the recommendations for an implementation, they might already have to be changed at the time of reading this paper for three reasons. Firstly, streaming is an active area of research. Amongst others, new research is done on fault tolerance, windowing and delivery semantics. With new insights, the best options to chose for a setup might change significantly. Secondly, even without new research, new software projects could be created, better suited for the architecture. Time will inevitably bring improvements to common software issues in the existing open source projects or new ones will be created entirely. Thirdly, the use case might make different levels of analysis necessary. The concept is proposed for applications where users wear sensor networks each. However, the two tiered architecture where analysed data is aggregated and analysed again could be extended arbitrarily, if it is appropriate for a specific use case.

With respect to an ethical perspective, the present paper proposes an architecture and asks how it could be implemented. The question, whether it should be implemented is not presented. However, this ethical question is relevant, as the architecture might equally well be used for illegal and spurious activity in real life. Employers could control workers in a factory to measure productivity and punish slacking or regimes could maximize subjugation, down to an emotional level. With small progressions in the areas of emotional AI [61], the architecture could become a tool for mass control of people, be it by state actors or non state actors. This creates a shift towards Deleuze's Society of Control [22] in which prisons are obsolete, as control over people can be exacted everywhere. The architecture proposed here is a tool that can be used for good but in the wrong hands could also be used for reprehensible actions. Therefore, any implementation should be reflected against the surge of greater digital capabilities engendering further digital control and surveillance. This paper has tried to make at least a small step in that direction by talking about data protection and energy awareness, but this is without regard to many things left unsaid in the discussion on software use on a societal level.

6 Conclusion

The present work examined the processing of PSD in near real-time as social signals for their use on social VR platforms. A theoretical concept for processing PSD was developed based on an extensive literature review. The concept includes streaming, analysis and visualisation of PSD based on physiological sensor networks. Data from individual sensors or sensor clusters can be analysed both for individual users and across multiple users, resulting in a total of four ways of analysis. In addition to a graphical visualization and detailed explanation of the concept, both minimum as well as desirable requirements for the selection of suitable software for a potential implementation were defined. A detailed subsequent comparison of currently available open source software led to the recommendation to use Apache Kafka for streaming, Apache Flink for stream processing and Apache Druid or Pinot as OLAP data store for analysis and visualisation. This setup is versatile, and can be extended or parts of the pipeline replaced as needed.

Although the presented concept needs to be implemented first and the original goal of integrating PSD as social signals for their use on social VR platforms requires an additional intermediate step, as well as a separately associated validation, the present work creates valuable contributions. Taking into account the mentioned limitations and restrictions, it offers a promising starting point for further research and is of great importance for a variety of fields and applications which contain the processing of PSD.

7 Future Work

As mentioned, more research on social VR platforms is needed. User studies could be of particular interest here. In general, it must be taken into account that the quality of VR experiences depend on a number of factors, i.e. computing power, head-mounted displays, degree of immersion, internet connection [32]. Cybersickness caused by latencies would not only be reflected in PSD, but also have negative impact on social interactions.

Referring to our present work we suggest two main areas for future work. The first is on further theoretical development. A refinement or extension of our concept might deliver meaningful insights, e.g. including existing databases or creating a dual online-offline structure which compares users active at the moment to a database of previous users at the same checkpoint in an application. Other options are the optimisation of individual components of the streaming process. There are many open questions regarding windowing, transmission semantics, fault tolerance and the proper structuring of streaming data. Closely related to streaming, there are questions in the area of networking, e.g. scheduling and load balancing. Since currently only parts of a pipeline or individual elements, such as analysis engines, are benchmarked, more work on benchmarking the entire pipeline would be desirable. The second main area is rather practically orientated, although the most relevant approaches from our point of view are concerned with validating theoretical concepts. The implementation of our concept, or a revised version, could for example enable the analysis of cluster networks of individuals or tests regarding speed requirements. There are also opportunities to build on the present work outside the research areas we have considered. Since PSD provide largely objective quantitative data that are well suited for machine learning procedures [38], a potential implementation and the subsequent execution of user studies could set the scene for the development of PSD based machine learning algorithms.

Acknowledgement. We would like to thank Thomas Odaker, Elisabeth Mayer, Simone Müller and Daniel Kolb who supported this work with helpful discussions and feedback.

References

1. Acampora, G., Cook, D.J., Rashidi, P., Vasilakos, A.V.: A survey on ambient intelligence in healthcare. Proc. IEEE **101**(12), 2470–2494 (2013)
2. Albahri, A.S., et al.: Iot-based telemedicine for disease prevention and health promotion: state-of-the-art. J. Netw. Comput. Appl. **173**, 102873 (2021)
3. Amazon: Kinesis streams (2013). https://aws.amazon.com/de/kinesis/. (Accessed 21 Feb 2022)
4. Apache-Software-Foundation: Acitvemq (2007). https://github.com/apache/activemq. (Accessed 03 Mar 2022)
5. Apache-Software-Foundation: Camel (2007). https://github.com/apache/camel. (Accessed 22 Feb 2022)
6. Apache-Software-Foundation: Flink (2011). https://github.com/apache/flink. (Accessed 21 Feb 2022)
7. Apache-Software-Foundation: Kafka (2011). https://github.com/apache/kafka. (Accessed 21 Feb 2022)
8. Apache-Software-Foundation: Flume (2012). https://github.com/apache/flume. (Accessed 25 Feb 2022)
9. Apache-Software-Foundation: Spark streaming (2012). https://github.com/apache/spark/tree/master/streaming. (Accessed 21 Feb 2022)
10. Apache-Software-Foundation: Bookkeeper (2014). https://github.com/apache/bookkeeper. (Accessed 21 Feb 2022)
11. Apache-Software-Foundation: Beam (2016). https://github.com/apache/beam. (Accessed 21 Feb 2022)
12. Arasu, A., et al.: Linear road: a stream data management benchmark. In: Proceedings of the Thirtieth International Conference on Very Large Data Bases, vol. 30, pp. 480–491 (2004)
13. Balazinska, M., Balakrishnan, H., Madden, S., Stonebraker, M.: Fault-tolerance in the borealis distributed stream processing system. In: Proceedings of the 2005 ACM SIGMOD International Conference on Management of Data, pp. 13–24 (2005)
14. Bao, L., Intille, S.S.: Activity recognition from user-annotated acceleration data. In: Ferscha, A., Mattern, F. (eds.) Pervasive 2004. LNCS, vol. 3001, pp. 1–17. Springer, Heidelberg (2004). https://doi.org/10.1007/978-3-540-24646-6_1
15. Benssassi, E.M., Ye, J.: Investigating multisensory integration in emotion recognition through bio-inspired computational models. IEEE Trans. Affect. Comput. 1 (2021). https://doi.org/10.1109/taffc.2021.3106254
16. Bonér, J.: Akka (2009). https://github.com/akka/akka. (Accessed 24 Feb 2022)
17. Brewer, E.: Cap twelve years later: How the "rules" have changed. Computer **45**(2), 23–29 (2012)
18. Carbone, P., Katsifodimos, A., Ewen, S., Markl, V., Haridi, S., Tzoumas, K.: Apache flink: Stream and batch processing in a single engine. Bull. IEEE Comput. Soc. Tech. Committee Data Eng. **36**(4), 28–38 (2015)
19. Chanel, G., Mühl, C.: Connecting brains and bodies: applying physiological computing to support social interaction. Interact. Comput. **27**(5), 534–550 (2015). https://doi.org/10.1093/iwc/iwv013
20. Chintapalli, S., et al.: Benchmarking streaming computation engines: Storm, flink and spark streaming. In: 2016 IEEE International Parallel and Distributed Processing Symposium Workshops (IPDPSW), pp. 1789–1792. IEEE (2016)
21. Del Monte, B., Zeuch, S., Rabl, T., Markl, V.: Rhino: efficient management of very large distributed state for stream processing engines. In: Proceedings of the 2020

ACM SIGMOD International Conference on Management of Data, pp. 2471–2486 (2020)
22. Deleuze, G.: Postscript on the Societies of Control. Routledge (2017)
23. Desnoyers-Stewart, J., Stepanova, E., Pasquier, P., Riecke, B.E.: JeL: Connecting Through Breath in Virtual Reality (2019)
24. Dey, A., Chen, H., Hayati, A., Billinghurst, M., Lindeman, R.W.: Sharing manipulated heart rate feedback in collaborative virtual environments. In: 2019 IEEE International Symposium on Mixed and Augmented Reality (ISMAR). IEEE (2019). https://doi.org/10.1109/ismar.2019.00022
25. Dishongh, T.J., McGrath, M.: Wireless sensor networks for healthcare applications. Artech House (2010)
26. Doan, Q.T., Kayes, A., Rahayu, W., Nguyen, K.: Integration of iot streaming data with efficient indexing and storage optimization. IEEE Access **8**, 47456–47467 (2020)
27. Dumka, A., Chaurasiya, S.K., Biswas, A., Mandoria, H.L.: A Complete Guide to Wireless Sensor Networks: From Inception to Current Trends. CRC Press (2019)
28. Dzardanova, E., Kasapakis, V., Gavalas, D.: Social Virtual Reality. Encyclopedia of Computer Graphics and Games (2018)
29. Elastic: Logstash (2016). https://github.com/elastic/logstash. (Accessed 21 Feb 2022)
30. Forsberg, K., Mooz, H.: The relationship of system engineering to the project cycle. In: INCOSE International Symposium, vol. 1(1), 57–65 (1991). https://doi.org/10.1002/j.2334-5837.1991.tb01484.x
31. Fu, Y., Soman, C.: Real-time data infrastructure at uber. In: Proceedings of the 2021 International Conference on Management of Data, pp. 2503–2516 (2021)
32. Genz, F., Hufeld, C., Müller, S., Kolb, D., Starck, J., Kranzlmüller, D.: Replacing EEG sensors by AI based emulation. In: De Paolis, L.T., Arpaia, P., Bourdot, P. (eds.) AVR 2021. LNCS, vol. 12980, pp. 66–80. Springer, Cham (2021). https://doi.org/10.1007/978-3-030-87595-4_6
33. GitHub: Hadoop (2006). https://github.com/apache/hadoop, (Accessed 21 Feb 2022)
34. Google: Google cloud dataflow (2015). https://cloud.google.com/dataflow. (Accessed 21 Feb 2022)
35. Gopalakrishna, K., Fu, X.: Pinot (2014). https://github.com/apache/pinot. (Accessed 21 Feb 2022)
36. Gozuacik, N., Oktug, S.: Parent-aware routing for IoT networks. In: Balandin, S., Andreev, S., Koucheryavy, Y. (eds.) ruSMART 2015. LNCS, vol. 9247, pp. 23–33. Springer, Cham (2015). https://doi.org/10.1007/978-3-319-23126-6_3
37. Guzel, M., Kok, I., Akay, D., Ozdemir, S.: Anfis and deep learning based missing sensor data prediction in IoT. Concurrency Comput. Pract. Experience **32**(2), e5400 (2020)
38. Halbig, A., Latoschik, M.E.: A Systematic Review of Physiological Measurements, Factors, Methods, and Applications in Virtual Reality (2021)
39. Harper, R.: Human expression in the age of communications overload (2010)
40. He, P., Zhu, J., Xu, P., Zheng, Z., Lyu, M.R.: A directed acyclic graph approach to online log parsing. arXiv preprint arXiv:1806.04356 (2018)
41. Hesse, G., Matthies, C., Perscheid, M., Uflacker, M., Plattner, H.: Espbench: the enterprise stream processing benchmark. In: Proceedings of the ACM/SPEC International Conference on Performance Engineering, pp. 201–212 (2021)
42. Huang, X.Y., et al.: Multi-matrices factorization with application to missing sensor data imputation. Sensors **13**(11), 15172–15186 (2013)

43. Hwang, J.H., Balazinska, M., Rasin, A., Cetintemel, U., Stonebraker, M., Zdonik, S.: High-availability algorithms for distributed stream processing. In: 21st International Conference on Data Engineering (ICDE 2005), pp. 779–790. IEEE (2005)
44. Im, J.F., et al.: Pinot: realtime olap for 530 million users. In: Proceedings of the 2018 International Conference on Management of Data, pp. 583–594 (2018)
45. Isah, H., Zulkernine, F.: A scalable and robust framework for data stream ingestion. In: 2018 IEEE International Conference on Big Data (Big Data), pp. 2900–2905. IEEE (2018)
46. Jennings, J.R., Berg, W.K., Hutcheson, J.S., Obrist, P., Porges, S., Turpin, G.: Committee report. publication guidelines for heart rate studies in man. Psychophysiology **18**(3), 226–231 (1981). https://doi.org/10.1111/j.1469-8986.1981.tb03023.x
47. Jiang, X., Tian, Z., Li, K.: A graph-based approach for missing sensor data imputation. IEEE Sens. J. **21**(20), 23133–23144 (2021)
48. Jonell, P.: Using Social and Physiological Signals for User Adaptation in Conversational Agents (2019)
49. Kopetz, H.: The real-time environment. Real-Time Systems: Design Principles for Distributed Embedded Applications, pp. 1–28 (2011)
50. Korzun, D.G., Nikolaevskiy, I., Gurtov, A.: Service Intelligence support for medical sensor networks in personalized mobile health systems. In: Balandin, S., Andreev, S., Koucheryavy, Y. (eds.) ruSMART 2015. LNCS, vol. 9247, pp. 116–127. Springer, Cham (2015). https://doi.org/10.1007/978-3-319-23126-6_11
51. Lazer, D., et al.: Social science. computational social science. Science **323**(5915), 721–723 (2009). https://doi.org/10.1126/science.1167742
52. Lee, M., Kolkmeier, J., Heylen, D., IJsselsteijn, W.: Who Makes Your Heart Beat? What Makes You Sweat? Social Conflict in Virtual Reality for Educators (2021)
53. Leventov, R.: Comparison of the open source olap systems for big data: Clickhouse, druid, and pinot, Feb 2018. (Accessed 21 Feb 2022)
54. LinkedIn: Samza (2013). https://github.com/apache/samza. (Accessed 23 Feb 2022)
55. LinkedIn: Gobblin (2015). https://github.com/apache/gobblin. (Accessed 25 Feb 2022)
56. Lou, J., et al.: Realistic facial expression reconstruction for vr hmd users. IEEE Trans. Multimedia **22**(3), 730–743 (2020). https://doi.org/10.1109/tmm.2019.2933338
57. Lu, R., Wu, G., Xie, B., Hu, J.: Stream bench: Towards benchmarking modern distributed stream computing frameworks. In: 2014 IEEE/ACM 7th International Conference on Utility and Cloud Computing, pp. 69–78. IEEE (2014)
58. Marcu, O.C., et al.: Kera: Scalable data ingestion for stream processing. In: 2018 IEEE 38th International Conference on Distributed Computing Systems (ICDCS), pp. 1480–1485. IEEE (2018)
59. Marz, N.: How to beat the cap theorem, Oct 2011. http://nathanmarz.com/blog/how-to-beat-the-cap-theorem.html. (Accessed 21 Feb 2022)
60. Marz, N.: Storm (2011). https://github.com/apache/storm. (Accessed 25 Feb 2022)
61. McStay, A.: Emotional AI: The rise of empathic media. Sage (2018)
62. Meehan, J., Aslantas, C., Zdonik, S., Tatbul, N., Du, J.: Data ingestion for the connected world. In: CIDR (2017)
63. Mehmood, E., Anees, T.: Challenges and solutions for processing real-time big data stream: a systematic literature review. IEEE Access **8**, 119123–119143 (2020)

64. Metamarkets: Druid (2014). https://github.com/apache/druid. (Accessed 21 Feb 2022)
65. Microsoft: Azure stream analytics (2015). https://azure.microsoft.com/en-us/services/stream-analytics/. (Accessed 21 Feb 2022)
66. Mukhopadhyay, S.C.: Wearable sensors for human activity monitoring: a review. IEEE Sens. J. **15**(3), 1321–1330 (2014)
67. Pentland, A.: Social signal processing [exploratory dsp]. IEEE Signal Process. Mag. **24**(4), 108–111 (2007). https://doi.org/10.1109/msp.2007.4286569
68. Prokopowicz, D., Golebiowska, A., Matosek, M.: Growing importance of digitization of remote communication processes and the internetization of economic processes and the impact of the sars-cov-2 (covid-19) coronavirus pandemic on the economy. In: Socio-Economic and Legal Dimensions of Digital Transformation, pp. 221–250. SGSP, Warsaw (2021)
69. Reeves, B., Nass, C.: The media equation: How people treat computers, television, and new media like real people. Cambridge, UK. (1996)
70. Reiss, A., Stricker, D.: Introducing a new benchmarked dataset for activity monitoring. In: 2012 16th International Symposium on Wearable Computers, pp. 108–109. IEEE (2012)
71. Salminen, M.: Evoking physiological synchrony and empathy using social vr with biofeedback. IEEE Trans. Affect. Comput. **13**(2), 746–755 (2022). https://doi.org/10.1109/taffc.2019.2958657
72. Schultz, R.: Welcome to the metaverse: A comprehensive list of social vr/ar platforms and virtual worlds (2022). https://ryanschultz.com/list-of-social-vr-virtual-worlds/. (Accessed 21 Feb 2022)
73. Shah, M.A., Hellerstein, J.M., Brewer, E.: Highly available, fault-tolerant, parallel dataflows. In: Proceedings of the 2004 ACM SIGMOD International Conference on Management of Data, pp. 827–838 (2004)
74. Shahrivari, S.: Beyond batch processing: towards real-time and streaming big data. Computers **3**(4), 117–129 (2014)
75. Shukla, A., Chaturvedi, S., Simmhan, Y.: Riotbench: an iot benchmark for distributed stream processing systems. Concurrency Comput. Pract. Exp. **29**(21), e4257 (2017)
76. Silvestre, P.F., Fragkoulis, M., Spinellis, D., Katsifodimos, A.: Clonos: consistent causal recovery for highly-available streaming dataflows. In: Proceedings of the 2021 International Conference on Management of Data, pp. 1637–1650 (2021)
77. Stanford, C., Kallas, K., Alur, R.: Correctness in stream processing: Challenges and opportunities. In: Conference on Innovative Data Systems Research (CIDR) (2022)
78. Twitter: Heron (2015). https://github.com/apache/heron (Accessed 21 Feb 2022)
79. Uber: Athenax (2017). https://github.com/uber-archive/AthenaX. (Accessed 21 Feb 2022)
80. Van Dongen, G., Van den Poel, D.: Evaluation of stream processing frameworks. IEEE Trans. Parallel Distrib. Syst. **31**(8), 1845–1858 (2020)
81. Vinciarelli, A., et al.: Bridging the gap between social animal and unsocial machine: a survey of social signal processing. IEEE Trans. Affect. Comput. **3**(1), 69–87 (2012). https://doi.org/10.1109/T-AFFC.2011.27
82. Vinciarelli, A., Pantic, M., Bourlard, H.: Social signal processing: survey of an emerging domain. Image Vis. Comput. **27**(12), 1743–1759 (2009)
83. Vinciarelli, A., Pentland, A.S.: New social signals in a new interaction world: the next frontier for social signal processing. IEEE Syst. Man Cybern. Mag. **1**(2), 10–17 (2015). https://doi.org/10.1109/MSMC.2015.2441992

84. Wagner, J., Lingenfelser, F., Baur, T., Ionut, D., Kistler, F., André, E.: The social signal interpretation (SSI) framework: multimodal signal processing and recognition in real-time (2013)
85. Williamson, J., Li, J., Vinayagamoorthy, V., Shamma, D.A., Cesar, P.: Proxemics and social interactions in an instrumented virtual reality workshop. In: Proceedings of the 2021 CHI Conference on Human Factors in Computing Systems. ACM, New York (2021). https://doi.org/10.1145/3411764.3445729
86. Wingerath, W., Ritter, N., Gessert, F.: Real-Time & Stream Data Management. SCS, Springer, Cham (2019). https://doi.org/10.1007/978-3-030-10555-6
87. Yahoo: Pulsar (2016). https://github.com/apache/pulsar. (Accessed 22 Feb 2022)
88. Yang, F., Tschetter, E., Léauté, X., Ray, N., Merlino, G., Ganguli, D.: Druid: a real-time analytical data store. In: Proceedings of the 2014 ACM SIGMOD International Conference on Management of Data, pp. 157–168 (2014)
89. Zhang, Y.F., Thorburn, P.J., Xiang, W., Fitch, P.: Ssim-a deep learning approach for recovering missing time series sensor data. IEEE Internet Things J. **6**(4), 6618–6628 (2019)
90. Zimmermann, L.: Sensor Fusion in Human Activity Recognition and Occupancy Detection. Ph.D. thesis, Friedrich-Alexander-Universität Erlangen-Nürnberg (FAU) (2020)

Developing a Tutorial for Improving Usability and User Skills in an Immersive Virtual Reality Experience

Ines Miguel-Alonso[1(✉)], Bruno Rodriguez-Garcia[1(✉)], David Checa[1(✉)], and Lucio Tommaso De Paolis[2(✉)]

[1] Departamento Ingeniería Informática, Universidad de Burgos, Burgos, Spain
{imalonso,brunorg,dcheca}@ubu.es

[2] Department of Engineering for Innovation, University of Salento, Lecce, Italy
lucio.depaolis@unisalento.it

Abstract. The fast development and progressive price reduction of Virtual Reality (VR) devices open a broad range of VR applications. Especially interesting are those applications focused on educational objectives. However, before these VR applications can be extensively presented in the educational system, some main issues to optimize their efficiency in the student's autonomous learning process should be solved. While in non-VR games designers have consistently developed introductory tutorials to prepare new players for the game's mechanics, in the case of VR, the design of these tutorials is still an open issue. This research presents a tutorial for VR educational applications to help the users to become familiar with the virtual environment and to learn the use of the interaction devices and the different mechanics within the experiences. In addition, the usability of this tutorial was tested with final users to assure its effectiveness.

Keywords: Virtual reality · Tutorial · Education · E-learning · Novelty effect

1 Introduction

In recent years, Immersive Virtual Reality (iVR). This type of Virtual Reality (VR) allows the interaction in the environment versus the non-Immersive Virtual Reality (i.e. CAVE-type system [1]). Although virtual reality technologies have been around since the late 1950s, their mainstream adoption has been very limited due to the high cost of the equipment. Nowadays, the wide availability of affordable software and hardware tools on the market opens the door to a variety of new teaching and entertainment virtual reality experiences. Furthermore, several studies suggest that the use of immersive virtual reality in education or training can substantially improve interest in learning in these scenarios [2], as well as facilitate the understanding of complex concepts [3] and reduce misconceptions [4].

L. T. De Paolis et al. (Eds.): XR Salento 2022, LNCS 13446, pp. 63–78, 2022.
https://doi.org/10.1007/978-3-031-15553-6_5

This rapid growth is producing that many developers focus on developing new iVR experiences. Although, as iVR is still a novel technology, it is likely that most users have not used it before. The unfamiliar experience associated with the use of Head Mounted Displays (HMDs) and the novelty of using unnatural Virtual Reality interfaces could be a source of extraneous cognitive load [5]. This extra cognitive load can lead to lower satisfaction and learning rates in the case of iVR educational experiences. Slow and progressive familiarization, visual clues, and guidance incorporated in the educational iVR experiences can be used to help the user to overcome these limitations.

In non-VR games, game designers have consistently designed introductory tutorials to prepare new players for a game. Usually, these tutorials are the user's first exposure to a game. Therefore, it is crucial that tutorials are effective in order to engage and retain players [6]. Another objective of these introductory tutorials is the acquisition of basic skills. These tutorials should prepare players by providing basic instructions and allowing them to practice without a time limitation. By the end of the tutorial, the players' skills should match the challenges so that they can enjoy the game [7].

The design of these tutorials for iVR experiences poses different challenges than those of a conventional non-VR game. Players must use an HMD that fully immerses them in a strange environment while they must acquire the basic skills of the experience. When an introductory tutorial is not included in the iVR experience, players are likely to devote their initial attention to experimenting. Besides, they will begin to acquire interaction skills with the iVR environment during the game, rather than to concentrate on the content (narrative, objectives…). In this way, an introductory tutorial provides an opportunity for new players to acquire knowledge and skills before starting the virtual experience. Therefore, the objectives of these tutorials on iVR are to make the user familiar with the virtual environment, with the interaction devices and with the way to interact with the objects in the virtual world [8].

These tutorials play an essential role in any educational or training iVR applications, since their main purpose is to improve the learning or skills of the trainee. Typically, the most common experimental designs in these studies compare learning outcomes between a desktop solution and an iVR environment after testing for differences through pre- and post-testing within a group of participants. However, many of the virtual reality experiences found in the literature do not use an introductory tutorial and do not consider in their research the possible differences, in terms of acceptance of the technology, between the two digital approaches. Although a large variety of research literature points to the fact that the use of iVR experiences improves learning, it is also fair to highlight that some studies found no positive effects. Some studies reported negative effects of using iVR on learning even when learners were reporting very high satisfaction rates [9, 10] and some others presented no effects on learning outcomes [11–14]. Although inexperienced users may see their results compromised because they are not sufficiently proficient in the iVR environment, there is a lack of research on the effectiveness of using tutorials to bridge the gap responsible for these negative results. This fact only underscores the need for further research on the role of the design elements to explore the potential of iVR to enhance learning.

For this reason, this research focuses on the development and validation of an iVR tutorial to reduce the novelty effect in virtual reality environments. The conclusions obtained are intended to guide the design of iVR applications and maximize the potential of iVR in instruction.

The remaining sections of this paper will be organized as follows: Sect. 2 will present an analysis of the most recent work on the use of tutorials in iVR. In Sect. 3, the design of an iVR tutorial will be described. In Sect. 4, the usability evaluation will be analyzed with its procedure and results. Finally, in Sect. 5 the main conclusions of this research are highlighted, and future lines of work are established.

2 Related Work

For non-VR games, the influence and need for tutorials varies depending on how complex the game is. In a study with 45,000 players and 3 video games of varying complexity researchers found that tutorials were only justified in the most complex game when analyzing game's duration, levels completed, and return rate [6]. In addition, players who used tutorials played longer and completed more levels than those who did not have tutorials. This study implies that tutorials may not be necessary for simpler games because their game mechanics can be discovered through experimentation but are a must in complex games.

In commercial iVR games, it is common for the game to start with a tutorial teaching the player how to play [15]. They also come to the same conclusion that using a tutorial makes little difference in simple VR games. On the other hand, in complex VR commercial games, a tutorial can influence controls learnability, engagement-related outcomes, and performance [15].

With respect to iVR research experiences committed to improving learning or improving skills, the scenario is very different. Very few of these research experiences use or report the use of a tutorial. Based on an extensive literature review previously presented here [2], a re-analysis of the papers included in this investigation shows that only 10% of the total number of articles used a tutorial in their experiments. This disclosure becomes even more relevant since for inclusion in this review the articles had to include an evidence-based approach evaluation. Their conclusions about whether or not a virtual reality experience is effective in enhancing learning or skill acquisition may then be compromised on commitment-related outcomes and performance. Among the articles that do include a tutorial, it can be noticed that these tutorials are commonly used to make the players know what to do during the game. They are usually included as an initial level [9, 16–19]. However, other tutorials were used for accommodating users and making them get acclimatized to the VR environment. For instance, the tutorial used by Bhargava et al. [20] is used in a way that the user gets accustomed to select and manipulate elements. Shewaga et al. [21] uses the pre-created SteamVR Tutorial in order to let them learn how to handle the basis of the HTC Vive controllers. This group of tutorials, whose main objective is to introduce users to the VR environment, aims to familiarize the user with the virtual environment by teaching them how to use the interaction devices and interact with the objects in the virtual world. Consequently, the novelty effect is mitigated. This effect causes discomfort when users must perform specific VR video game tasks and do not feel sufficiently prepared or comfortable with the VR equipment because of its complexity [8]. In other research, users can choose whether or not to play the tutorial [22, 23] or do not specify how to use the tutorial [24].

Finally, other studies go beyond the introductory tutorial and use real-world tutorials [25]. This strategy increases people's sense of familiarity and confidence with a game. This study conducted an experiment in which players practice in a real or virtual environment before playing an iVR game. The study found that practicing in a familiar reality makes them feel as confident and familiar as someone who has practiced in VR. This implies that practicing indistinctly in the real world as well as in the virtual world has positive effects.

3 Designing an Effective and Engaging Tutorial

Before designing a tutorial, it is important to keep in mind that there is a lot of information to convey before players begin the iVR experience. For example, the context of the game, the goals, and different operations of the game's functions and its utilities. In an analysis of most successful commercial iVR games, the majority had in their introductory tutorials some form of text help (88%), diagrams or images (56%), and a small number of research use labels on those controllers to instruct the player (22%) [15]. The design of these games, according to their developers, rely on intuition, personal experience, existing examples, and user testing to create the tutorials [6].

The categorization of these tutorials can be established according to whether they are used to teach by instruction, teach by example, or teach by a carefully designed experience [26]. If taught by instructions, the tutorial should present a set of instructions explaining the rules of the game. In the case of teaching using examples, the tutorial should present demonstrations that demonstrate to the player what to do. Finally, in a carefully designed experience, the tutorial should be designed so that the player can explore and try out actions in an environment that should be easier to interact with without time constraints or attempts. In this research, the model of a carefully designed experience was chosen. This approach allows the user to practice in a quiet environment the different mechanics that will be used throughout the experience.

Likewise, this development is based on the cognitive theory of multimedia learning [27] which explores effective principles in designing multimedia experiences for learners. However, most of the literature investigating its application has been conducted on desktop 2D games, so certain principles need to be adapted for use in iVR. The principles followed or adapted from this model are:

- **Use Text and Graphics Together:** One of the principles of multimedia learning is that it is more effective to combine graphics with text, instead of presenting only words. It is recommended to use images that help the user to understand the material. In iVR, one of the main problems is learning how to operate the virtual controllers. Organizational graphics and diagrams that annotate different controller buttons with their purpose are commonly found in VR tutorials. In this research we chose to apply it in a way that the user could understand the use of the controllers through diagrams that use graphics and text together as illustrated in Fig. 1A. As well as a more novel and effective way by placing these texts directly on the controller as can be seen in Fig. 1B.

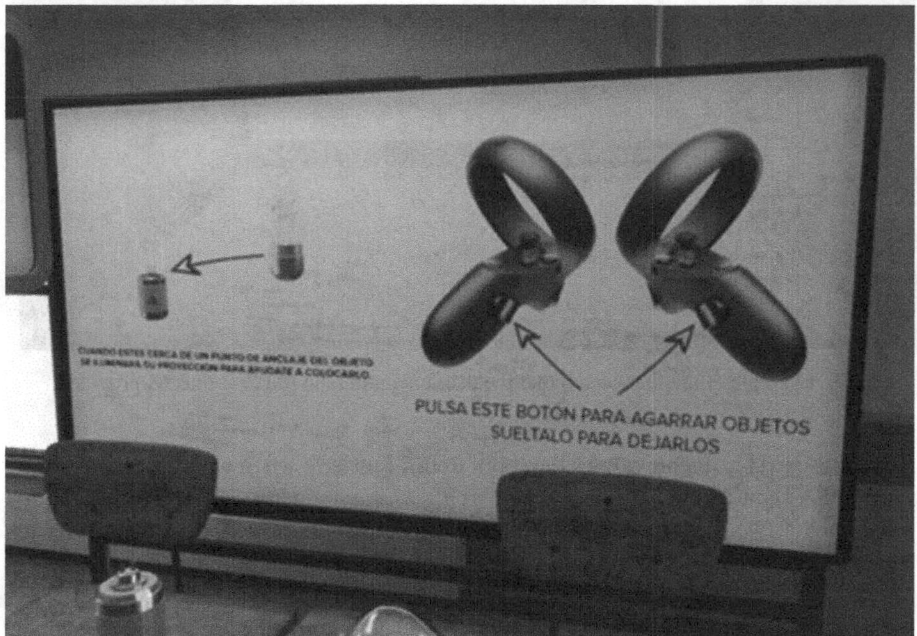

Fig. 1. (A) Diagram showing the user the different controller buttons used in this experience. (B) VR controllers with annotations anchored to the controller.

- **Coherence Principle:** According to this principle, extra material hurts learning. Therefore, any material that is unnecessary for the purpose of the instruction should be avoided [28]. This fact includes limiting the use of extraneous words and graphics as they can lead to distraction (directing the learner's attention to superfluous material), disruption (preventing the learner from constructing a mental model due to irrelevant material), and seduction (prioritizing an irrelevant knowledge domain). In this tutorial, as Fig. 2 shows, efforts have been made to limit any source of superfluous extra material that could distract the user. Likewise the environment has been designed to provide neutral colors with no distracting elements.

- **Signaling Principle:** This principle is based on using visual cues to direct the user's attention. Different research shows that the use of visual clues speed up the learning of information and improve learning efficacy [29], reduce cognitive load [30, 31], and improve the speed and accuracy of completing tasks [32]. These clues can be of different types. The most common forms are arrows, large text, bolded text, and color. In this research, the use of an assistant robot that guides the user through the tutorial

Fig. 2. Example of the first screen that the user encounters in the iVR tutorial provided.

is proposed. This feature allows the robot to offer its help when we look directly at it, as Fig. 3A shows, or to wait for our help's call, as shown in Fig. 3B. This functionality enables not overloading the environment with information, while offering relevant information to the user when is needed.

The development of a tutorial in iVR is a time and resort consuming task. To reduce this effort, a previously tested and validated framework was used [33]. This framework simplifies the development of iVR applications and allows researchers to focus on the design once the framework already solves the main technical issues of the iVR environment´s development. This framework has been developed in Unreal Engine™. This game engine stands out in its high capacity to create photorealistic environments and the ease of use. In addition, it is compatible with most iVR HMDs on the market. The framework includes tools for the most common tasks when it comes to creating iVR experiences: movement of the player, interactions with the scenario and objects, the creation of scene objectives and data collection.

The developed tutorial has been designed to be useful in a wide variety of applications. Firstly, this tutorial should help the user to become familiar with the virtual environment. Secondly, it should help to understand how to use the interaction devices and to learn how to interact with the objects in the virtual world. However, this goal can be difficult, as not all iVR applications use the same forms of interface or interaction. For this purpose, different modules have been developed that can be combined so that the tutorial can be adapted as much as possible to the user's subsequent experience and so that at the end of the tutorial the players' skills match the challenges they will face in the experience. The following phases are required for this purpose:

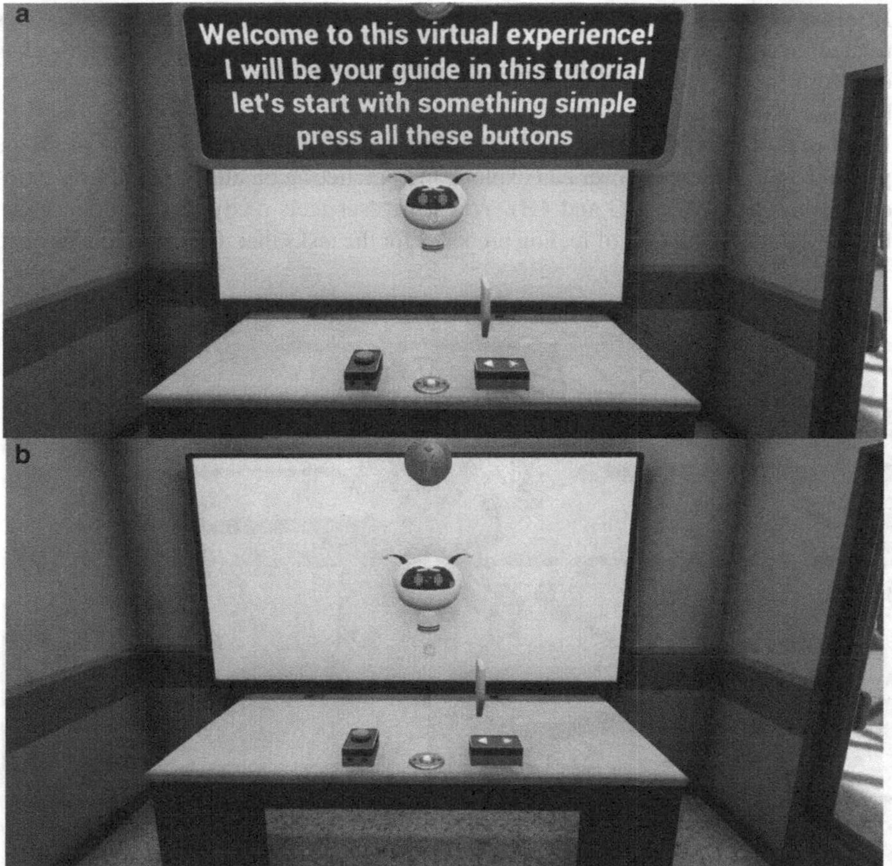

Fig. 3. (**A**) Robot assistant displaying information. (**B**) Robot assistant in standby mode.

- **Introduction:** This is a distraction-free space where the user can become familiar with the virtual environment. Also, following the principle of coherence, the use of extraneous words and graphics has been limited as they can lead to distraction.
- **Basic Interactions:** Once the user has settled into the virtual environment, in front of him, the button to start the tutorial can be pressed, as Fig. 4A shows. This interaction is very basic and accessible. Moreover, in this way, the user manages the pace of the tutorial on his own. The next module helps the user to deepen the basic button-pressing interaction (Fig. 4B).
- **Grab:** One of the most common interactions is grabbing objects. Usually, these objects fulfill a certain purpose and it is necessary to perform an attachment. As Fig. 4C and 4D show, in this module of the tutorial the user can learn to grab the objects as well as to attach them to other objects.
- **Complex Interactions:** Some experiences require more complex interactions than those already presented. This module aims to introduce some of them, such as interacting with levers (Fig. 5E).

- **Interact with User Interfaces:** Another important interaction to practice are the ones related to User Interfaces. This type of interface is often used to interact with menus or information screens. In Fig. 4F, an interaction with a complex user interface can be observed.
- **Explore and Play:** This final module has been conceived as an assembly of all the previous ones, where the user can explore and practice again all the previously introduced mechanics (Fig. 4G and 4H). When the user feels ready, the experience can begin, with the advantage of feeling prepared for the tasks that the user will face next.

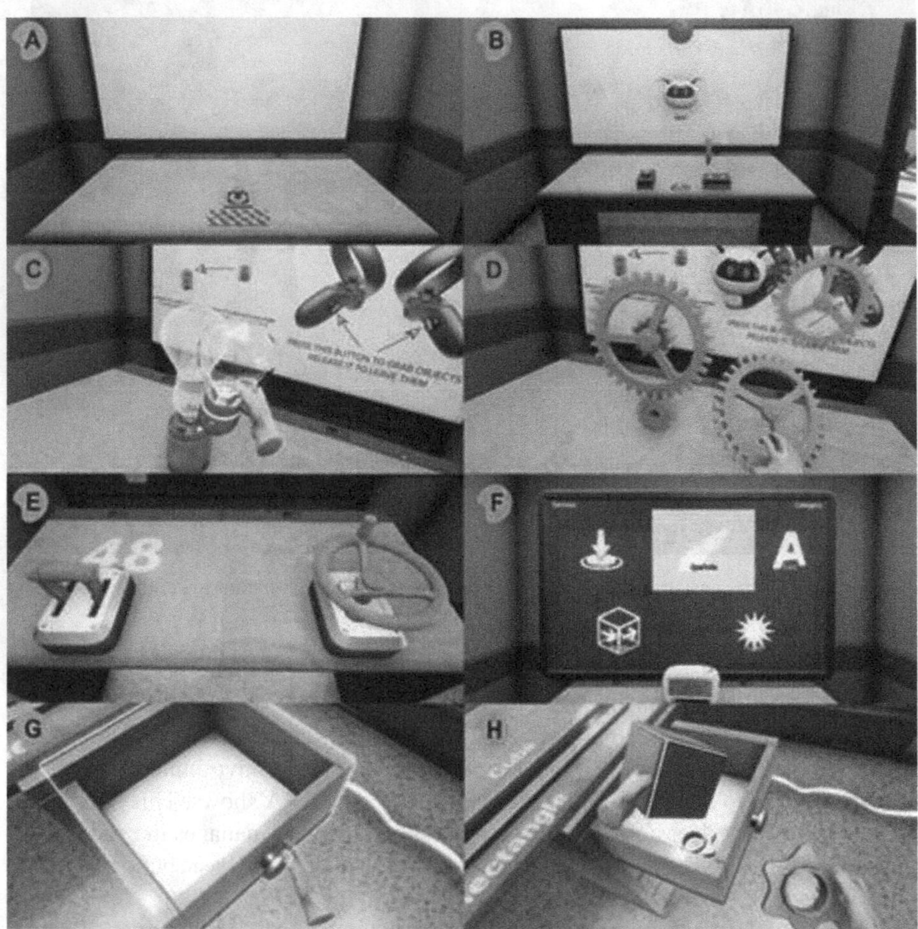

Fig. 4. Modules of the tutorial: **(A** and **B)** Basic interactions, **(C** and **D)** Grab, **(E)** Complex interactions, **(F)** Interact with User Interfaces and **(G** and **H)** Explore and play module.

4 Usability Evaluation

The usability of the iVR tutorial was tested as an introduction to the iVR experience "Computer Assembly VR" [34]. This VR experience was designed to study the enhancement of learning about computer assembly and its component parts. It seeks to reinforce users' knowledge of basic computer concepts such as cooling a desktop computer, identifying the parts of a motherboard or assembling a desktop computer with certain characteristics.

The tutorial was included at the beginning of this experience, in order to help the users become familiar with the virtual environment and to understand how to use the interaction devices and the different mechanics within the experience.

In order to study the effectiveness of the tutorial with those goals, an iVR experience was organized to measure the usability of the tutorial itself. The study sample consisted of 10 first-year students of Computing and Communications of a Vocational Education and Training (VET). Nine of them are men and one woman. Their mean age is 18.9 years old. The entire experience was executed following the security measures for the prevention of COVID-19 transmission. In addition, it complies with data protection regulations.

4.1 Preparation and Procedure

The setup of the experience consisted of three workstations equipped with Intel Core i7-10710U, 32 GB RAM, with NVIDIA GTX 2080 graphic cards connected to the HTC Vive Pro Eye HMDs.

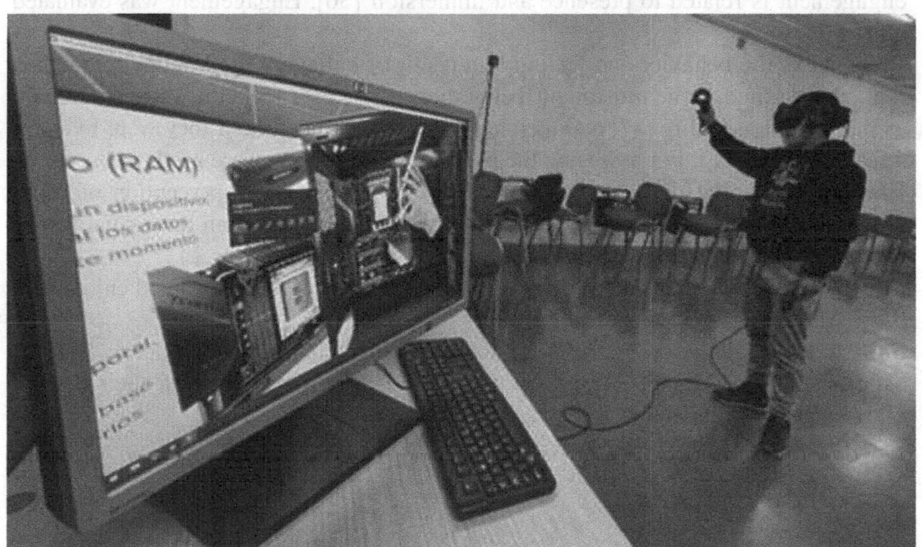

Fig. 5. User interacting with the iVR experience.

This iVR experience began with a brief explanation of the HMD and the experience itself. Then, 3 of the participants put on de HMDs and begin with the tutorial. In this particular event, and in order to test the usability of all the modules developed, the users tested all the modules. In addition, in the Explore and play module, the users were forced to stay for a certain amount of time, so that the total duration of the tutorial was never less than 5 min. The tutorial allowed the user to move all around the scenery and to squat to reach objects scattered on the virtual ground. The space was enabled to permit all the movements mentioned in dimensions of approximately 2 × 2 m.

Immediately after the iVR experience, the participants completed a satisfaction and usability survey. This test includes a question for cybersickness assessment, 22 Multiple-Choice Questions (MCQ) for usability rating each aspect with 1 to 5 points in a Likert scale and 3 open questions for giving their positive and negative aspects and suggestions of the iVR experience.

This Likert scale was converted to a scale of 1 to 9 to analyze more precisely the results of the survey. The conversion was done by making an equivalence between both of the scales. The 0 and 10 points were dismissed because the 0 means no data in this question.

The questions were divided into categories to evaluate 5 different aspects of a VR experience: engagement, presence, immersion, flow, and skill, as Tcha-Tokey et al. [35] proposed.

- **Engagement,** commonly known as involvement, is defined as the commitment that exists between the user and their actions in VR. If a user is not so motivated with the environment and the tasks to do in there, the engagement will be low. Also, engagement is related to presence and immersion [36]. Engagement was evaluated with 3 questions.
- **Presence** is the behavior and feeling as a result of believing the VR environment is real, also defined as the illusion of 'being there'. The user feels the VR environment as the dominant reality [37] and their behavior tends to be like if they were living in a real situation [38]. For assessing the presence, 5 questions were used.
- **Immersion** is related to the hardware. The immersion is the perception of being physically in the VR environment, as if all the stimuli came from the virtual world. For the evaluation of the immersion, 4 questions were asked.
- **Flow** is a psychological state that occurs when the user feels control and enjoyment. Flow was evaluated with 3 questions.
- **Skill** is the evolution of the user's knowledge in certain activities during the VR experience. To evaluate, 6 questions were used. The questions with their type of knowledge are collected in Table 1.

Table 1. Usability and satisfaction survey used.

Engagement	• This tutorial could be useful for learning • The information given by the tutorial was clear • The VR environment was realistic
Presence	• The interactions with the VR environment were natural • An objects' examination from diverse points of view and distances was possible • The interaction with VR controllers was natural • The VR controllers that monitor the interactions resulted distractive of doing the assigned tasks
Immersion	• The enjoyment of the experience was possible • The involvement in the VR environment was so high that the notion of time was lost • The VR experience provoked the sense of feeling physically good • The involvement in the VR environment was so high that what occurred around was not perceived
Flow	• The VR environment responded to the initiated actions by the user (e.g., taking an object was working well) • The actions were perceived as they can be controlled perfectly • In each proposed task, it was known what to do
Skill	• The VR controllers were easy to use • The VR interaction was fast to get accustomed to • At the beginning of the experience, the interaction with the VR environment felt well • At the end of the experience, the interaction with the VR environment felt well • The first time the computer components were collocated (first level), interacting with the VR environment, grabbing, and collocating objects was easy • The last time the computer components were collocated (last level), interacting with the VR environment, grabbing, and collocating objects was easy

4.2 Results

This section analyses the results of the usability and satisfaction survey. During the iVR experience, performance data was collected to measure the duration of the experience for each participant. The average duration of the tutorial was 456 s and the total time of the rest of the iVR experience was 648 s on average.

In comparison to a previous experience in which a tutorial was not included in the "Computer Assembly VR" [34], different performance was noticed, although no quantitative indicators were recorded to ground this result. The direct observation of the users' performance shows that the users demonstrate better and faster movements while they were interacting in "Computer Assembly VR" when they previously played the tutorial. The tutorial made them lose the novelty effect in the iVR environment. Participants were more confident and relaxed. Nevertheless, more experimentation and future research are required to corroborate it.

Furthermore, the usability and satisfaction with the tutorial provide useful conclusions. Participants reported high averaged rates of engagement (7.73), presence (7.34), flow (7.10), immersion (7.88) and skill (8.04). All these data and standard deviations are collected in Table 2.

Although three of the participants reported cybersickness, its level was very slight (rate 3 in a Likert scale in which 1 was a lot of cybersickness and 4 none at all). The experimented cybersickness by these three participants was considered for comparing the data between two groups: one with cybersickness and other without it. The difference between students with cybersickness and none is also collected in Table 2. The comparison between both groups shows that participants who experienced cybersickness had less skill, 7.86 versus 8.12. On the contrary, participants with cybersickness scored the rest of the questions' categories higher than the participants without cybersickness. This fact means that, despite the cybersickness, they got good experience satisfaction.

Table 2. Mean (M) and Standard Deviation (SD) of satisfaction and usability survey, and the difference with participants with cybersickness.

	All participants (N = 10)		Participants without cybersickness (N = 7)		Participants with cybersickness (N = 3)	
	M	SD	M	SD	M	SD
Engagement	7.73	1.38	7.67	1.30	7.89	1.35
Presence	7.34	1.77	7.21	1.76	7.63	1.59
Immersion	7.88	1.40	7.79	1.46	8.08	1.01
Flow	7.10	1.48	6.79	1.57	7.83	0.29
Skill	8.04	1.39	8.12	1.13	7.86	1.47

Participants commented in the open questions that the experience was realistic, easy to control, useful for learning and understanding a computer, it permitted good immersion and it was original. These results show high satisfaction with the experience. The participants who experienced cybersickness commented that, when they had to move too much their head, their vision was blurred, and they suffered from discomfort. They noticed some difficulties in grabbing objects, and they got distracted. The rest of the participants commented that the negative aspects are sporadic mistakes of not grabbing objects and punctual moments where the participants did not know what to do. These suggestions will serve to adjust the experience to make it easier to understand and give clearer instructions.

5 Conclusions

Tutorials can be considered as a lack of time for many users and developers, but they are required to make the users engaged in a video game or a VR application. The purpose of a tutorial is to familiarize users with the controls and the rules of the game. When the user is immersed in a VR environment for the first time, he will focus on learning the controls and paying attention to the details which involve him. Therefore, a lack of attention to the content of the game, for example history and learning tasks, will be experienced by the user. This means that a tutorial is required to make the user lose the novelty effect, and it is in which this research focuses on.

A tutorial was designed, developed, and tested for iVR educational experience. The tutorial is composed of different modules in order to adapt to the experience of the user who has to be capable of completing all the tasks in the experience at the end. This design solves the fact that previous research had demonstrated that the user can not feel prepared to do the tasks of the iVR experience because of its complexity. The users familiarize with the environment and learn how to interact with the elements. The actions they are meant to do are not specific, due to the fact that the tutorial can be used for more than one experience which does not need all the same actions. The tutorial was divided into 6 phases: introduction, basic interaction, grab, complex interactions, interact with User Interface and explore and play. An increasing complexity of the tasks is experimented as the user advances levels.

A framework in Unreal Engine was used to reduce the time of development of the tutorial, so that longer time could be invested in research. So, the production of the tutorial is based on the cognitive theory of multimedia learning. From this research, the tutorial includes text and graphics together in order to understand material and how to operate in the environment with the controls. In addition, it uses the coherence principle which explains that the minimum material it is required to not get users distracted. Finally, the signaling principles to improve learning of information and performing tasks without overloading the environment and being there when the user needs it.

The tutorial was tested in 10 Computing and Communications VET students. Firstly, participants completed the tutorial. Then they were immersed in "Computer Assembly VR" to improve their computer knowledge. Their performance was compared to a previous experience which was done without the tutorial. Participants who took the tutorial showed a better performance, more confident and relaxed than in the other experience. Finally, participants completed the satisfaction and usability survey composed by 22 MCQ to rate them from 1 to 5 in a Likert scale and 3 open questions. The questions were divided into 5 categories: engagement, presence, immersion, flow, and skill. The results showed that participants had a notable satisfaction.

Also, a cybersickness event was collected in the satisfaction and usability survey. 3 of the participants experience a little cybersickness. Therefore, the group with cybersickness and without it were compared. The analysis demonstrated that the group with cybersickness had less skill but a higher satisfaction than the group without cybersickness. In the open questions, participants commented that the application was easy to control, realistic and original. Contrary to this, the cybersickness group showed that they had blurred vision, discomfort suffered in their eyes and distraction.

While it is well accepted that tutorials affect game players in some contexts, there is a lack of research on the relative effectiveness of different tutorial modalities. Further research in this domain can help develop guidelines that will help game designers and researchers make more informed design decisions.

Acknowledgments. This work was partially supported by the ACIS project (Reference Number INVESTUN/21/BU/0002) of the Consejeria de Empleo e Industria of the Junta de Castilla y León (Spain), the Erasmus+ RISKREAL Project (Reference Number 2020-1-ES01-KA204-081847) of the European Commission and the FLEXIMEC20 project (Reference Number 10/18/BU/0012 of the Planes Estrategicos de I+D) of the Instituto para la Competitividad Empresarial de Castilla y León (Spain) cofinanced with European Union FEDER funds.

References

1. Lebiedz, J., Mazikowski, A.: Multiuser stereoscopic projection techniques for CAVE-type virtual reality systems. IEEE Trans. Human-Machine Syst. **51**(5), 535–543 (2021). https://doi.org/10.1109/THMS.2021.3102520
2. Checa, D., Bustillo, A.: A review of immersive virtual reality serious games to enhance learning and training. Multim. Tools Appl. **79**(9–10), 5501–5527 (2019). https://doi.org/10.1007/s11042-019-08348-9
3. Checa, D., Bustillo, A.: Advantages and limits of virtual reality in learning processes: Briviesca in the fifteenth century. Virtual Reality **24**(1), 151–161 (2019). https://doi.org/10.1007/s10055-019-00389-7
4. Mikropoulos, T.A., Natsis, A.: Educational virtual environments: a ten-year review of empirical research (1999–2009). Comput. Educ. **56**(3), 769–780 (2011). https://doi.org/10.1016/j.compedu.2010.10.020
5. Wu, H.-K., Lee, S.W.-Y., Chang, H.-Y., Liang, J.-C.: Current status, opportunities and challenges of augmented reality in education. Comput. Educ. **62**, 41–49 (2013). https://doi.org/10.1016/j.compedu.2012.10.024
6. Andersen, E., et al.: The impact of tutorials on games of varying complexity. In: Proceedings of the SIGCHI Conference on Human Factors in Computing Systems, May 2012, pp. 59–68 (2012). https://doi.org/10.1145/2207676.2207687
7. Buchanan, R., Csikszentmihalyi, M.: Flow: the psychology of optimal experience. Design Issues **8**(1), 80 (1991)
8. Fussell, S.G., et al.: Usability testing of a virtual reality tutorial. Proc. Hum. Factors Ergon. Soc. Annu. Meet. **63**(1), 2303–2307 (2019). https://doi.org/10.1177/1071181319631494
9. Makransky, G., Terkildsen, T.S., Mayer, R.E.: Adding immersive virtual reality to a science lab simulation causes more presence but less learning. Learn. Instr. **60**, 225–236 (2019). https://doi.org/10.1016/j.learninstruc.2017.12.007
10. Parong, J., Mayer, R.E.: Learning science in immersive virtual reality. J. Educ. Psychol. **110**(6), 785–797 (2018). https://doi.org/10.1037/edu0000241
11. Madden, J.H., et al.: Virtual reality as a teaching tool for moon phases and beyond (2019). https://doi.org/10.1119/perc.2018.pr.Madden
12. Meyer, O.A., Omdahl, M.K., Makransky, G.: Investigating the effect of pre-training when learning through immersive virtual reality and video: a media and methods experiment. Comput. Educ. **140**, 103603 (2019). https://doi.org/10.1016/j.compedu.2019.103603
13. Moro, C., Štromberga, Z., Raikos, A., Stirling, A.: The effectiveness of virtual and augmented reality in health sciences and medical anatomy. Anat. Sci. Educ. **10**(6), 549–559 (2017). https://doi.org/10.1002/ase.1696
14. Stepan, K., et al.: Immersive virtual reality as a teaching tool for neuroanatomy. Int. Forum Allergy Rhinol. **7**(10), 1006–1013 (2017). https://doi.org/10.1002/alr.21986
15. Kao, D., Magana, A.J., Mousas, C.: Evaluating tutorial-based instructions for controllers in virtual reality games. In: Proceedings of the ACM Human-Computer Interact, October 2021, vol. 5, no. CHI PLAY, pp. 1–28 (2021). https://doi.org/10.1145/3474661

16. Buttussi, F., Chittaro, L.: Effects of different types of virtual reality display on presence and learning in a safety training scenario. IEEE Trans. Vis. Comput. Graph. **24**(2), 1063–1076 (2018). https://doi.org/10.1109/TVCG.2017.2653117
17. Kleven, N.F., et al.: Training nurses and educating the public using a virtual operating room with Oculus Rift. In: 2014 International Conference on Virtual Systems & Multimedia (VSMM), December 2014, pp. 206–213 (2014). https://doi.org/10.1109/VSMM.2014.7136687
18. Khanal, P., et al.: Collaborative virtual reality based advanced cardiac life support training simulator using virtual reality principles. J. Biomed. Inform. **51**, 49–59 (2014). https://doi.org/10.1016/j.jbi.2014.04.005
19. Cheng, K.-H., Tsai, C.-C.: A case study of immersive virtual field trips in an elementary classroom: students' learning experience and teacher-student interaction behaviors. Comput. Educ. **140**, 103600 (2019). https://doi.org/10.1016/j.compedu.2019.103600
20. Bhargava, A., Bertrand, J.W., Gramopadhye, A.K., Madathil, K.C., Babu, S.V.: Evaluating multiple levels of an interaction fidelity continuum on performance and learning in near-field training simulations. IEEE Trans. Vis. Comput. Graph. **24**(4), 1418–1427 (2018). https://doi.org/10.1109/TVCG.2018.2794639
21. Shewaga, R., Uribe-Quevedo, A., Kapralos, B., Alam, F.: A comparison of seated and room-scale virtual reality in a serious game for epidural preparation. IEEE Trans. Emerg. Top. Comput. **8**(1), 218–232 (2020). https://doi.org/10.1109/TETC.2017.2746085
22. Janssen, D., Tummel, C., Richert, A., Isenhardt, I.: Virtual environments in higher education – immersion as a key construct for learning 4.0. Int. J. Adv. Corp. Learn. **9**(2), 20 (2016). https://doi.org/10.3991/ijac.v9i2.6000
23. Bucher, K., Blome, T., Rudolph, S., von Mammen, S.: VReanimate II: training first aid and reanimation in virtual reality. J. Comput. Educ. **6**(1), 53–78 (2018). https://doi.org/10.1007/s40692-018-0121-1
24. Ball, C., Johnsen, K.: An accessible platform for everyday educational virtual reality. In: 2016 IEEE 2nd Workshop on Everyday Virtual Reality (WEVR), March 2016, pp. 26–31 (2016). https://doi.org/10.1109/WEVR.2016.7859540
25. Ho, J.C.F.: Practice in reality for virtual reality games: making players familiar and confident with a game. In: Bernhaupt, R., Dalvi, G., Joshi, A., Balkrishan, D.K., O'Neill, J., Winckler, M. (eds.) INTERACT 2017. LNCS, vol. 10514, pp. 147–162. Springer, Cham (2017). https://doi.org/10.1007/978-3-319-67684-5_10
26. Green, M.C., Khalifa, A., Barros, G.A.B., Togelius, J.: 'Press Space To Fire': Automatic Video Game Tutorial Generation (2017)
27. Mayer, R.E.: Cognitive theory of multimedia learning. In: Mayer, R. (Ed.) The Cambridge Handbook of Multimedia Learning, pp. 43–71. Cambridge University Press, Cambridge (2005)
28. Clark, R.C., Mayer, R.E.: E-Learning and the Science of Instruction Important: Fourth Edition. Wiley, Hoboken (2016)
29. Lin, L., Atkinson, R.K.: Using animations and visual cueing to support learning of scientific concepts and processes. Comput. Educ. **56**(3), 650–658 (2011). https://doi.org/10.1016/j.compedu.2010.10.007
30. Wouters, P., Paas, F., van Merriënboer, J.J.G.: How to optimize learning from animated models: a review of guidelines based on cognitive load. Rev. Educ. Res. **78**(3), 645–675 (2008). https://doi.org/10.3102/0034654308320320
31. Mayer, R.E., Moreno, R.: Nine ways to reduce cognitive load in multimedia learning. Educ. Psychol. **38**(1), 43–52 (2003). https://doi.org/10.1207/S15326985EP3801_6
32. Kelleher, C., Pausch, R.: Stencils-Based Tutorials: Design and Evaluation (2005)

33. Checca, D., Gatto, C., Cisternino, D., De Paolis, L.T., Bustillo, A.: A framework for educational and training immersive virtual reality experiences. In: De Paolis, L.T., Bourdot, P. (eds.) AVR 2020. LNCS, vol. 12243, pp. 220–228. Springer, Cham (2020). https://doi.org/10.1007/978-3-030-58468-9_17
34. Checa, D., Miguel-Alonso, I., Bustillo, A.: Immersive virtual-reality computer-assembly serious game to enhance autonomous learning. Virtual Reality (2021). https://doi.org/10.1007/s10055-021-00607-1
35. Tcha-Tokey, K., Christmann, O., Loup-Escande, E., Richir, S.: Proposition and validation of a questionnaire to measure the user experience in immersive virtual environments. Int. J. Virtual Real. **16**(1), 33–48 (2016). https://doi.org/10.20870/IJVR.2016.16.1.2880
36. Jennett, C., et al.: Measuring and defining the experience of immersion in games. Int. J. Hum. Comput. Stud. **66**(9), 641–661 (2008). https://doi.org/10.1016/j.ijhcs.2008.04.004
37. Barfield, W., Zeltzer, D.: Presence and performance within virtual environments. In: Barfield, W., Zeltzer, D. (eds.) Virtual Environments and Advanced Interface Design. Oxford University Press, Oxford (1995). https://doi.org/10.1093/oso/9780195075557.003.0023
38. Ai-Lim Lee, E., Wong, K.W., Fung, C.C.: How does desktop virtual reality enhance learning outcomes? A structural equation modeling approach. Comput. Educ. **55**(4), 1424–1442 (2010). https://doi.org/10.1016/j.compedu.2010.06.006

Challenges in Virtual Reality Training for CRBN Events

Georg Regal[1(✉)], Helmut Schrom-Feiertag[1], Massimo Migliorini[2], Massimiliano Guarneri[3], Daniele Di Giovanni[4], Andrea D'Angelo[5], and Markus Murtinger[1]

[1] Center for Technology Experience, AIT Austrian Institute of Technology, Vienna, Austria
georg.regal@ait.ac.at
[2] Fondazione LINKS, Turin, Italy
[3] FSN-TECFIS DIM lab. at ENEA, Frascati Research Center, Frascati, Italy
[4] Industrial Engineering Department, University of Rome 'Tor Vergata', Rome, Italy
[5] Fondazione SAFE - Security and Freedom for Europe, Verona, Italy

Abstract. The re-emergence of chemical, biological, radioactive, and nuclear (CBRN) threats as a key area of focus for military (as well as civilian) actors, paired with the early stage of CBRN VR training, create a strong opportunity for future research. Improvement in-game engine technology and Virtual Reality hard and software can improve CBRN training and simulation for military and civilian responders to CBRN events. Therefore, in this work, we discussed the challenges of developing a European virtual reality-based CBRN training. By standardizing CBRN training on a European Level interoperability between different actors (military and civilian) and European nationalities shall be increased. We presented the main cornerstones for a VR CBRN training that shall be tackled in the VERTIgO project: (1) the Exercise Simulation Platform (2) Scenario Creator, and (3) a CBRN VR Mask.

Keywords: CBRN · Virtual Reality · Virtual environment · Training

1 Introduction

The contemporary geopolitical environment and strategic uncertainty shaped by asymmetric and hybrid threats coming from state and non-state actors urge future development of hands-on training in realistic environments. Training for eventual threats is a cornerstone to increasing EU preparedness and security, regardless of the end-users (military or civilian first responders). However, external factors like costs or danger for the trainees might prevent training as often as desired or needed.

Therefore Virtual Reality (VR) based training solutions have gained more and more attention in e.g. assembly training [19], medicine [5], police training [6, 18], military training [1,4], firefighters [16] and - especially interesting - training for chemical, biological, radioactive, nuclear (CBRN) events - e.g. [9,15,17].

L. T. De Paolis et al. (Eds.): XR Salento 2022, LNCS 13446, pp. 79–88, 2022.
https://doi.org/10.1007/978-3-031-15553-6_6

Interoperability issues with existing systems limit the possibility for different military and civilian responders to jointly train and test their capabilities. Throughout 2020, the re-emergence of major CBRN crisis situations (above all COVID-19, but also examples such as the dramatic chemical explosion which hit Beirut on the 4th of August), and the strong engagement of military (and civilian) actors in the response to the global crisis, underlined once again the importance of harmonized competences and skills in the field of CBRN preparedness and response, allowing coordinated deployment of expertise, within EU boundaries and beyond.

The re-emergence of CBRN as a key area of focus for military and civilian actors, paired with the early stage in which the development of CBRN VR simulation structures stands, creates a major opportunity for future research. The possibility of realistic 3D virtual environments, advancements in-game engine technology, and the (so-called) "second wave of VR" [3] may significantly improve CBRN training and simulation for military and civilian responders to CBRN events. By complementing already existing curricula and programs, training in VR will be more affordable and highly likely to solicit deeper and faster learning, due to the possibility to repeat training scenarios as often as needed, without the need to consider financial (e.g. material wear, no infrastructures functionality interruption) or hazardous (e.g. contaminated environments) aspect. Also, VR training provides strong possibilities for after-action review and thus provides more possibilities for (partially automatic-) evaluation of performance to trainers and more comprehensive feedback for trainees. Moreover, VR training can allow novel forms of collaborative/remote training where trainees and trainers are not co-located but joined virtually from different locations.

This on the one hand reduces costs but also increases possibilities for transnational and especially trans-European collaboration. Thus, an important aspect to consider is harmonization by providing an EU-wide standard for CBRN VR training inter-operability and joint training at the EU level could be increased in the future.

A proper training curriculum can be used to test and enhance: 1) individual technical skills; 2) the operational response; 3) the command structure; 4) cooperation among multiple teams in action.

The increased awareness of the potential of VR technology to support simulation and training procedures has led to several research initiatives, aimed at building application cases and delineating concrete advantages and limits. However, to date, no fully functional examples of VR simulation structure (i.e. simulators and their interconnections) for CBRN training exist in Europe.

2 Related Work

One of the key advantages of Virtual Reality is the ability to train in a virtual, therefore safe environment. This is ideal for applications in the CBRN sector, providing CBRN personnel with a practical solution to gain valuable experience in dangerous or life-threatening environments.

In this context, most applications exist in the Airforce and Navy environment [15], while few cases considered the CBRN and correlated procedures [9,14,17].

2.1 Virtual Training Environments

As outlined by [15] a large number of simulators using VR technology exists to train military personnel. Most prominent are training and simulation applications for aircraft personnel - e.g. Eurofighter Aircrew Synthetic Training Aids cf. [15] - due to the long history of training pilots in flight simulators. Similar driving simulators - e.g. for tanks like the Leopard Gunnery Skills Trainers cf. [15] - or ship simulators - e.g. Visual Bridge Simulator cf. [15] - are used. However, the transfer of concepts of flight, ship, and driving simulators to CBRN training is limited. Even though CBRN responders will reach the site of an event via car, tanks, hip, or flight (helicopter, airplane, etc.), the way to the site of the event is mostly not the focus of the CBRN training.

Examples of military and civilian training apart from driving/flight simulation are the PRODIGE project[1], VirtSim[2], the Blacksuit (Military), Redsuit (Firefighters) and Bluesuit (Policeforces) by re-lion[3] or the Refense Advanced Tactical Training Simulator for police, military and medical repsonders[4].

2.2 CBRN Training

In this work, we focus on dedicated training environments for CBRN responders. These training environments can either be non-immersive (e.g. Desktop computer-based) or fully immersive (e.g. virtual-reality-based training environments. A systematic review of scientific literature on disaster education for CBRN (published between 2004–2016) is provided by Kako et al. [12]. Their review includes non-immersive and immersive (VR) simulations for training.

Non-immersive An example of non-immersive training, mainly for civilian usage, is the Advanced Disaster Management Simulator[5]. It offers a wide range of possibilities for training. Target groups respectively use-cases are police, firefighters, medical responders, disaster management, and airports. Although the Advanced Disaster Management Simulator offers possibilities for flight and vehicle/driving simulation, most relevant in the context of CBRN training is the training and simulation for emergency management. Especially the training for command, control, coordination, and communication in critical disaster situations. Another example of a desktop-based training and simulation application

[1] http://www.pro-prodige.eu/-Last accessed 23.02.2022.

[2] https://www.motionreality.com/-Last accessed 23.02.2022.

[3] https://www.re-lion.com/-Last accessed 23.02.2022.

[4] https://www.refense.com/-Last accessed 23.02.2022.

[5] https://www.etcsimulation.com/adms-users-disaster-management.html-Last accessed 23.02.2022.

is virtual Battle Space[6]. The focus is on commander training (mission planning) and communication in the executing phase. Again mission planning and communication training are aspects that are highly relevant also for CBRN training, although the application is not directly targeted toward CBRN but claims to be an application that allows to "create and run any imaginable military training scenario".

Heinrichs et al. [11] proposed a simulator for training in acute-care medicine. The authors focus on three scenarios including one scenario for training emergency department teams and hospital staff to manage mass casualties after CBRN incidents.

Immersive Providing immersive training is important to feature a realistic training environment. Especially the feeling of presence [20] as well as representational fidelity and interactivity in such an environment is an important factor [7] that might contribute towards the learning experience and transfer to real-world situations. According to Göllner et al. [9] visual 3D immersion and navigation by natural walking are important factors for immersion and presence. Also perceived realism is an important factor to simulate stress and physical excitement which are important for experiencing realistic training scenarios and thus contribute toward the transfer from VR training to the real world.

One example of a training platform that can be used in the context of CBRN training is software by XVR Simulation[7]. The software addresses all kinds of first responder organizations, mostly firefighters and medical first responders. It is highly modular and customizable and allows for frontal training in classrooms to collaborative scenarios. Also, different aspects of emergency responders can be trained ranging e.g. operational skills, communication between teams, strategic decision and coordination, etc. Also, the XVR Platform allows for training on 2D screens as well as in fully immersive virtual environments.

Apart from commercial applications also research projects tackle CBRN-training in virtual reality. In cooperation with the technical university of Turin, the LINKS Foundation has successfully conducted two projects in this domain - VR4CBRN and VR4CBRN2. Both initiatives, funded by the Italian Military Airforce, were devoted to exploring the potential of Virtual Reality Simulation to train CBRN operators in intervening in the case of radiological and chemical contamination[8]. Different NATO procedures were simulated, and part of the work was presented during TOXIC TRIP 2019, an international NATO CBRN event.[9] The most relevant features of the VR simulations developed within VR4CBRN and VR4CBRN2 are (1) a virtual instructor - a virtual avatar guiding trainees in performing the CBRN procedures; (2) remote multi-user support to work with other trainees in task forces, in a real-time interactive digital environment); (3)

[6] https://bisimulations.com/products/vbs4-Last accessed 23.02.2022.

[7] https://www.xvrsim.com/ - Last accessed 23.02.2022.

[8] https://www.youtube.com/watch?v=Ut2h0_eqWOE&ab_channel=Massimo Migliorini-Last accessed 23.02.2022.

[9] https://vr.polito.it/news/toxic-aero-nato/-Last accessed 23.02.2022.

a library of NATO equipment - 3D models of NATO probes, tools, vehicles, etc. and (4) a user interface to support the instructors training assessment - constant tracking in time and space, reporting of errors, scoreboards, and statistics, debriefing, etc.

The Technical University Vienna has conducted successful projects towards investigating the feasibility of VR for CBRN responder training [9,15]. In the project *"Virtual Reality Training for CBRN-Defense and First Responders"* how VR can improve the *"quality of training, reduce costs and increase efficiency and effectiveness of CBRN defense training"*[10]. Güllner et al. [9, p.10 - Table 1] lists requirements for CBRN training that are important considerations when designing a novel CBNR training application: (1) Communication (2) Manipulation (3) specific manipulations (4) Movement, (5) Specific movement and (6) Customization of Scenario Content & Parameters. Lamberti et al. [13] describe a prototype of a VR platform for CBRN training. Altan et al. [2] describes serious games for CBRN-e training in mixed reality, virtual reality, and computer-based environments.

To the best of our knowledge, no immersive training applications for CBRN training of non-professional civilians in CBRN events exist.

3 Challenges for Virtual Reality CBRN Training

Based on the aforementioned related work we now present challenges for the future development of European VR training for CBRN responders that will be addressed in the EU-funded VERTIgO project.

The project's overall objective is the study, design, and validation (operational and in the laboratory) of a European Exercise Simulation Platform (EESP) for the application of Virtual Reality to CBRN training, complemented by the prototyping of an ad-hoc hardware solution that integrates a VR headset and CBRN mask.

VERTIgO aims to harmonize inter-operable CBRN VR training across the European Union, allowing military & civil European emergency-response bodies to create, customize, and use 3D virtual reality simulations for increased efficiency of training procedures in the CBRN sector. We envision covering scenarios from the strategic down to the tactical level of critical scenarios.

We foresee three important areas that need to be addressed in future VR CBRN training: (1) the training curricula that are implemented/provided by the *European Exercise Simulation Platform (EESP)* (2) content creation, authoring, and scenario development provided through a *scenario creator* and (3) realistic hardware for training by combining protective masks and head-mounted displays (HMD) into a *CBRN VR Mask*.

[10] https://www.ims.tuwien.ac.at/projects/vr-defensetraining-Last accessed 23.02.2022.

3.1 Exercise Simulation Platform

The Vertigo EESP shall enable trainees to train for CBRN events in a fully immersive, highly interactive environment with six degrees of freedom. We envision that trainees will be able to move and interact as naturally as possible within the training environments. Also to support the realistic performance of procedures and realistic usage of tools the question arises which equipment is important for CBRN responders, which equipment should be integrated physically and tangible into the VR environment and which equipment can be integrated virtually only.

The VERTIgO EESP would allow recreating fully interactive and adaptive simulation environments where the pace and the difficulty of the environment could be adapted based on the trainee's performance and individual/team training needs. The EESP will allow using pre-defined set-up for main CBRN procedures such as reconnaissance; sampling and identification of biological; chemical and radiological agents (SIBCRA), decontamination of vehicles and other gear; collective protection in a chemical, biological, radiological, and nuclear environment - conceptual communication area (COLPRO-CCA). An important asset is the ability to reproduce unpredictable elements with the use of Artificial intelligence (AI), including e.g. models for evolution and movement of fires or models for crowds movement.

We envision two main directions for developing training curricula: (1) the EESP will support training that is targeted towards training large groups of still untrained personnel in "simple" procedures. Hereby the target group is non-specialists, like firefighters, workers in chemical plants, etc., that are not regular responders to CBRN events but awareness and procedures training is still highly important. Also, this training shall be possible to be upscaled easily in terms of the number of participants and set up at different locations. Here the main benefit lies in training large groups of people that otherwise due to logistics of costs would have not received any or less training. (2) The EESP shall provide possibilities to train for highly complex scenarios that are hard to implement in current training curricula. For example, scenarios that involve large groups of people, complex environments e.g. airports, or other aspects that currently prevent training this scenario often in real-world training environments. These scenarios are targeted toward highly-educated and trained specialists to provide them with additional training possibilities that go beyond current possibilities.

The VERTIgO EESP will be designed, developed, tested, and demonstrated in full compliance with Military and Defence standards and requirements, encompassing an integrated and flexible VR environment, which would allow a combination of various devices, multi-user applications, as well as full-scale adaptability through its scenario builder functionality.

3.2 Scenarios and Scenario Creator

Building immersive 3D environments and scenarios is an important aspect when creating training curricula. To simplify the process authoring tools have been proposed that allow the creation and programming of 3D environments - e.g. FlowMatic [24]. Dörner et al. [8] give an overview of challenges that might arise for content creating and authoring for VR environments. Creating realistic virtual reality environments can be time-consuming and require computer science skills [10] and thus is often done by technical experts.

Therefore, related work has tried to bridge that gap by proposing tools that enable end-user and non-technical experts to author and create immersive environments. Examples are PolyVR [10], VR GREP [22,23], VREUD [21]. However - to the best of our knowledge - giving end-users from the CBRN sector the possibility to independently design immersive VR environments has not been done in related work so far.

Also, psychological well-being, e.g. realism of training (wounds, pain of victims) vs. realism of training, and o physical well-being - e.g.accidents with the MR system, simulator-induced discomfort, sickness or nausea, etc. need consideration. Moreover, when designing scenarios the overall objective of the VR CBRN training needs to be taken into account, e.g. is the CBRN training mainly targeted towards training procedures, skills, teamwork, communication, resource management, etc.

3.3 CBRN VR Mask

The VERTIgO EESP will be complemented by the development (prototyping and operational testing) of a hardware solution that aims at integrating an existing VR headset (e.g. Lynx-R1 headset[11]) with a fully functional CBRN mask.

Such a combination of a fully functional CBRN mask with a VR HMD will provide authenticity in training. Using such a fully functional VR CBRN mask will enable trainees to apply their understanding of the equipment (its limits and capacities) by training with the feeling of real equipment - e.g. breath flow, weight, pressure, etc. - in realistic virtual scenarios but without being exposed to a potentially dangerous environment.

Also in future scenarios, such an integrated mask can support virtual (VR) and augmented reality (AR) applications as well, which can go beyond training. For example, mission planning is a fruitful research direction for the usage of VR in CBRN events. Here, for example, unmanned aerial vehicles (UAVs) could be used to gather a 3D representation of the environment, which is then used for mission planning. By providing an immersive interactive 3D environment situation awareness and the quality of mission planning could be increased.

4 Conclusion

In this work, we discussed the challenges of developing a harmonized virtual reality-based CBRN training. By standardizing CBRN training on a European

[11] https://www.lynx-r.com/.

Level interoperability between different actors (military and civilian) and European nationalities shall be increased. Based on related work we presented challenges and future research directions for VR CBRN training that shall be tackled in the VERTIgO project: (1) the Exercise Simulation Platform (2) Scenario Creator, and (3) a CBRN VR Mask.

Acknowledgments. This work was partially funded through the project VERTIgO - Virtual Enhanced Reality for inTeroperable training of CBRN military and civilian Operators, which has received funding from the European Defence Industrial Development Program (EDIDP) under grant agreement EDIDP-SVTE-2020–047-VERTIgO. This publication reflects only the author's view and the Commission is not responsible for any use that may be made of the information it contains.

References

1. Ahir, K., Govani, K., Gajera, R., Shah, M.: Application on virtual reality for enhanced education learning, military training and sports. Augmented Human Res. **5**(1), 1–9 (2019). https://doi.org/10.1007/s41133-019-0025-2
2. Altan, B.: Developing serious games for CBRN-e training in mixed reality, virtual reality, and computer-based environments. Int. J. Disaster Risk Reduction **77**, 103022 (2022). https://doi.org/10.1016/j.ijdrr.2022.103022
3. Anthes, C., Wiedemann, M., Kranzlmüller, D.: State of the art of virtual reality technology. In: 2016 IEEE Aerospace Conference. pp. 1–19. IEEE, Big Sky, Montana, United States (2016). https://doi.org/10.1109/AERO.2016.7500674
4. Binsch, O., Bottenheft, C., Landman, A., Roijendijk, L., Vermetten, E.H.: Testing the applicability of a virtual reality simulation platform for stress training of first responders. Mil. Psychol. **33**(3), 182–196 (2021). https://doi.org/10.1080/08995605.2021.1897494
5. Bucher, K., Blome, T., Rudolph, S., von Mammen, S.: VReanimate II: training first aid and reanimation in virtual reality. J. Comput. Educ. **6**(1), 53–78 (2018). https://doi.org/10.1007/s40692-018-0121-1
6. Caserman, P., Cornel, M., Dieter, M., Göbel, S.: A concept of a training environment for police using VR game technology. In: Göbel, S. (ed.) JCSG 2018. LNCS, vol. 11243, pp. 175–181. Springer, Cham (2018). https://doi.org/10.1007/978-3-030-02762-9_18
7. Dalgarno, B., Lee, M.J.W.: What are the learning affordances of 3-D virtual environments? British J. Educ. Technol. **41**(1), 10–32 (2010). https://doi.org/10.1111/j.1467-8535.2009.01038.x
8. Dörner, R., Kallmann, M., Huang, Y.: Content creation and authoring challenges for virtual environments: from user interfaces to autonomous virtual characters. In: Brunnett, G., Coquillart, S., van Liere, R., Welch, G., Váša, L. (eds.) Virtual Realities. LNCS, vol. 8844, pp. 187–212. Springer, Cham (2015). https://doi.org/10.1007/978-3-319-17043-5_11
9. Göllner, J., et al.: Virtual reality cbrn defence. In: Meeting Proceedings of the Simulation and Modelling Group Symposium. vol. 171, pp. 1–25 (2019)
10. Haefner, V.: PolyVR - a virtual reality authoring system. In: EuroVR 2014 - Conference and Exhibition of the European Association of Virtual and Augmented Reality. The Eurographics Association (2014). https://doi.org/10.2312/eurovr.20141343

11. Heinrichs, W.L., Youngblood, P., Harter, P.M., Dev, P.: Simulation for team training and assessment: case studies of online training with virtual worlds. World J. Surg. **32**(2), 161–170 (2008). https://doi.org/10.1007/s00268-007-9354-2
12. Kako, M., Hammad, K., Mitani, S., Arbon, P.: Existing approaches to chemical, biological, radiological, and nuclear (CBRN) education and training for health professionals: Findings from an integrative literature review. Prehospital and Disaster Medicine 33, 1–9 (02 2018). https://doi.org/10.1017/S1049023X18000043
13. Lamberti, F., Lorenzis, F.D., Gabriele Pratticò, F., Migliorini, M.: An immersive virtual reality platform for training cbrn operators. In: 2021 IEEE 45th Annual Computers, Software, and Applications Conference (COMPSAC). pp. 133–137 (2021). /10.1109/COMPSAC51774.2021.00030
14. Maciejewski, P., Gawlik-Kobylińska, M., Lebiedź, J., Ostant, W., Aydın, D.: To survive in a CBRN hostile environment: Application of cave automatic virtual environments in first responder training. In: Proceedings of the 3rd International Conference on Applications of Intelligent Systems. pp. 1–5 (2020). https://doi.org/10.1145/3378184.3378212
15. Mossel, A., Peer, A., Göllner, J., Kaufmann, H.: Requirements analysis on a virtual reality training system for CBRN crisis preparedness. In: Proceedings of the 59th Annual Meeting of the ISSS. Inderscience Publisher (2015). https://doi.org/10.1109/VR.2017.7892324
16. Mossel, A., Schoenauer, C., Froeschl, M., Peer, A., Goellner, J., Kaufmann, H.: Immersive training of first responder squad leaders in untethered virtual reality. Virtual Reality **25**(3), 745–759 (2020). https://doi.org/10.1007/s10055-020-00487-x
17. Murtinger, M., Jaspaert, E., Schrom-Feiertag, H., Egger-Lampl, S.: CBRN training in virtual environments: SWOT analysis & practical guidelines. Int. J. Safety and Secur. Eng. **11**(4), 295–303 (2021). 10.18280/ijsse.110402
18. Nguyen, Q., Jaspaert, E., Murtinger, M., Schrom-Feiertag, H., Egger-Lampl, S., Tscheligi, M.: Stress out: translating real-world stressors into audio-visual stress cues in VR for police training. In: Ardito, C. (ed.) INTERACT 2021. LNCS, vol. 12933, pp. 551–561. Springer, Cham (2021). https://doi.org/10.1007/978-3-030-85616-8_32
19. Schwarz, S., Regal, G., Kempf, M., Schatz, R.: Learning Success in Immersive Virtual Reality Training Environments: Practical Evidence from Automotive Assembly. ACM, New York, USA (2020). https://doi.org/10.1145/3419249.3420182
20. Witmer, B.G., Singer, M.J.: Measuring presence in virtual environments: a presence questionnaire. Presence **7**(3), 225–240 (1998)
21. Yigitbas, E., Klauke, J., Gottschalk, S., Engels, G.: VREUD - an end-user development tool to simplify the creation of interactive VR scenes. In: 2021 IEEE Symposium on Visual Languages and Human-Centric Computing (VL/HCC). pp. 1–10 (2021). https://doi.org/10.1109/VL/HCC51201.2021.9576372
22. Zarraonandia, T., Díaz, P., Aedo, I., Montero, A.: Inmersive end user development for virtual reality. In: Proceedings of the International Working Conference on Advanced Visual Interfaces. p. 346–347. AVI '16, ACM, New York, USA (2016). https://doi.org/10.1145/2909132.2926067,https://doi.org/10.1145/2909132.2926067

23. Zarraonandia, T., Díaz, P., Montero, A., Aedo, I.: Exploring the benefits of immersive end user development for virtual reality. In: Ubiquitous Computing and Ambient Intelligence. pp. 450–462. Springer (2016). https://doi.org/10.1007/978-3-319-48746-5_46
24. Zhang, L., Oney, S.: FlowMatic: An Immersive Authoring Tool for Creating Interactive Scenes in Virtual Reality, pp. 342–353. ACM, New York, USA (2020). https://doi.org/10.1145/3379337.3415824

A Preliminary Study on the Teaching Mode of Interactive VR Painting Ability Cultivation

YanXiang Zhang(✉) and Yang Chen

Department of Communication of Science and Technology, University of Science and Technology of China, Hefei, Anhui, China

petrel@ustc.edu.cn, annandmax@mail.ustc.edu.cn

Abstract. This paper introduces the advantages and characteristics of VR painting compared with traditional painting and analyzes its application prospects. Based on the experience in interactive VR painting teaching, we initially explored the mode of training VR painting talents and summarized the current challenges VR painting faces.

Keywords: Virtual reality · VR painting · Art design · Ability training · Aesthetics

1 VR Painting and VR Painting Teaching

1.1 The Prospect of VR Painting

"Virtual Reality" is a technology, which allows a user to interact with a computer-simulated environment, be it a real or imagined one [1]. Since the 1990s, the technology of virtual reality (VR) has gone through a long stage of development and has achieved some results. In recent years, the technology of VR has been used in the military, industry, education, art, games, and other fields.

"The development of computer art has covered all applied art and traditional art fields" [2]. With the development of VR technology in art, one of the outstanding performances is the emergence of VR painting technology, which has realized the transformation from 2D to 3D. Users can create in three-dimensional space through VR head display and operating handle, a new form of digital media.

Fashion and technology can be mutually beneficial. VR technology also has great development space in the garment industry. VR painting can bring designers a new creative experience [3]. VR products represented by VR games will face colossal market demand in the future. Tilt Brush technology goes one step further, allowing the artist to create 3D images with a brush in hand while moving in the virtual world he creates [4].

In addition, many scholars have studied the role of VR painting in art psychotherapy. Scholars using qualitative research found that Till Brush has excellent potential in treatment practice. Participants said they gained some ability and insight by using this application in treatment [5]. But scholars who use quantitative research found no

L. T. De Paolis et al. (Eds.): XR Salento 2022, LNCS 13446, pp. 89–97, 2022.
https://doi.org/10.1007/978-3-031-15553-6_7

significant effect for the decrease of anxiety, depression, or stress across all participants. However, the study did see a general decrease in affect levels [6].

Some scholars have deployed interactive digital art applications on university campuses to investigate participants' initial experiences of bridging two realities through 3D artwork in a hybrid reality space. The underlying purpose of the installation is to bring liveliness and increased social interaction to both the virtual and the physical world [7].

1.2 Research Context of VR Painting Teaching

Since the advent of VR painting software, more and more VR painting artists and works have appeared on the network platform at home and abroad. However, due to the short time of technology, only a few colleges and universities in China have offered courses related to VR painting. The primary purpose is more inclined to experience and explore. There is no systematic and in-depth development of the teaching process. For example, in 2021, the University of Science and Technology of China offered an elective course, "VR/AR/MR Technology Creative Design and Application," for undergraduates, introducing Tilt Brush VR painting software and allowing students to complete VR paintings independently. We observed and experienced the course in-depth and got some inspiration from the teaching in this field.

The application of VR painting is more extensive in western countries. In Europe, some colleges and universities have carried out courses on VR painting, such as the London University of Art in the United Kingdom, which launched a VR painting workshop in 2019. However, due to the limitations of VR technology and human cognition at this stage, most VR painting courses at home and abroad are still in the stage of experience and exploration. In addition, the Cyprus University of Technology conducted a VR painting experiment to explore 3D art through virtual reality application in 2021. The experiment lasted for three days (three 75-min ESP courses). Students generally recognized the innovation of VR painting tools [8].

This paper will start with the characteristics of VR painting, summarize the teaching rules, and explore the mode of its ability training.

2 VR Painting Software

2.1 The Introduction of VR Painting Software

There is more and more VR painting software on the market. They have different emphases and painting experiences. The following is a comparison of three mainstream painting software:

Painting software	Main functions and features
Tilt Brush	Mainly three-dimensional painting, it has a wide range of applications (industrial design, clothing design, sculpture, painting, stage design, and other industries); its distinctive features are rich in brush styles and special effects (simulation brushes and dynamic special effects brushes, such as light, fire, stars, etc.)

(*continued*)

(*continued*)

Painting software	Main functions and features
Quill	Sketch creation; make and edit frame-by-frame animations; copy and reconstruct models; professional artistic creation. The VR animation tool in the software is easy to operate and can save a lot of time and cost for the creator [9]
Maya2022	Painting and modeling; include functions for creating curves, modeling NURBS surfaces, creating polygons, and more
Create VR	The software has just been launched in 2021 and currently has fewer functions. It can export and import files in FBX format for editing, but it cannot interact with Maya scenes in real-time

2.2 Advantages of VR Painting

Making the Creative Space More Realistic
The characteristic of VR painting is that it provides users with a virtual experience based on three-dimensional space. True 3D is a three-dimensional display technology based on the principle of three-dimensional technology, which can directly observe three-dimensional images with physical depth of field. This mode is more intuitive because there is no perspective distortion, and the results are more accurate. At the same time, the spatial relationship between the creator and the work has been dynamically adjusted from the single plane to 360° whole perspective.

Drawing Objects Can be Adjusted with a High Degree of Freedom
The most significant advantage of virtual objects is to give the creator a high degree of freedom. VR painting has a variety of unique material brushes for the creator. The high degree of freedom is also reflected in the arbitrary change of object size, spatial scale, scaling relationship, etc.

Assisting Design and Modeling
In VR painting, the creator can more easily depict the details, break through the creative inertia, and explore new creative modes.

At the same time, VR painting has instantaneity, which makes it possible to show the real-time process of creation without losing some basic features [10]. Cooperating with 3D software and importing the sketch obtained by VR painting as a reference can also provide some conveniences for modeling, which is more in line with the design intent.

3 The Main Points of the Construction of a VR Painting Talent Training Model

Some people without formal training expressed that thinking in 3D was complex or different from what they were used to when asked to describe their experience learning how to use the interface [11]. Therefore, it is essential to explore the VR painting teaching mode.

To study this field better, we opened an elective course, "creative design and application of VR/AR/MR technology," at the University of science and technology of China, taking VR painting experience as an essential course section (Fig. 1). We observed the students' whole VR painting practice process and summarized the talent training mode.

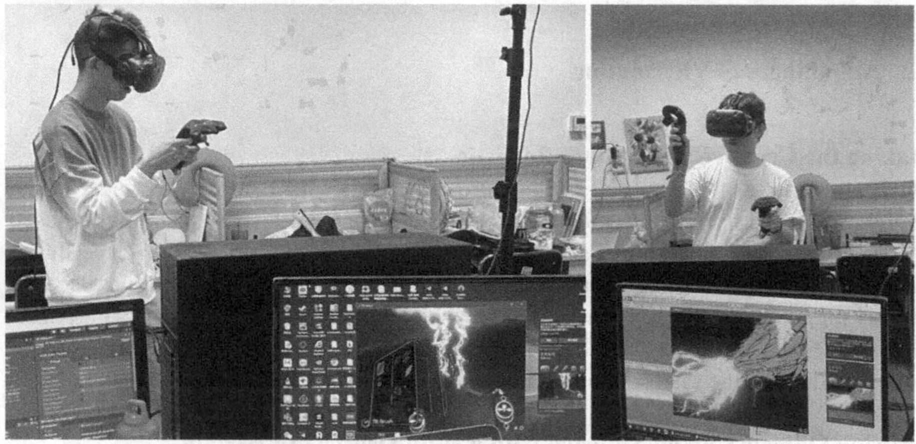

Fig. 1. VR painting course of University of science and technology of China

3.1 Building a Teaching System for VR Painting Tools

Exploring and mastering VR painting software is the first step in talent training. It is relatively easy to know a specific function. However, the painter can use it skillfully in the painting process still needs more training.

For example, in the experience class, we take tilt brush as the leading painting software. At the initial stage of the course, after we put on VR head display equipment for students, we let students understand various essential functions of VR painting software first, such as saving, deleting, mirroring, etc., and then let them try various brushes in tilt brush, which are timely. The strokes and effects are what you see in 3D space, so you can properly experience the different effects of different painting tools and materials in the training of VR painting skills. It is convenient for the painter to find the right feeling more quickly when painting, to find the similarities and differences between the natural brush and the virtual brush, to feel the changes brought by the material, and to get more possibilities for the divergence of thinking, the optimization of technology and the improvement of level. After trying all the brush effects, the students can freely choose the appropriate material and brush for painting.

3.2 Application of Traditional Art Skills in VR Painting

The cultivation of VR painting ability is inseparable from preparing traditional art foundations. Some of the most basic modeling skills and creative methods should become the basic abilities of digital painting artists [12]. Intuitively speaking, VR painting is the product of the development of traditional painting to a particular stage. Although the operation is simplified in many aspects, the essence is the progress of technology. During the experience of the VR painting course, we observed that there are still some differences in the painting level among students, which is mainly reflected in the fact that students interested in traditional art or who have a little art foundation can often submit better works.

In traditional three-dimensional modeling teaching, teachers mainly make students perceive the content of three-dimensional modeling through teaching and operation, but students may have a one-sided understanding. This kind of teaching is "fake" three-dimensional teaching [13]. VR painting is an actual three-dimensional experience, and students can enter the "virtual environment" experience. Therefore, in the process of ability building and talent training, it can combine with the teaching of sculpture to create three-dimensional objects in the virtual environment.

At the same time, students cannot ignore the study of perspective. The training of perspective perception helps control the relationship between the created objects, which is particularly important when creating large scenes. Although VR painting does not require perspective deformation, the theories and methods of expressing spatial relationships are the elements for systematically learning and understanding space and cultivating the ability to perceive space.

In addition, painters need to learn to use color and light. The artist needs to master the basic knowledge of color matching and use the functions of the software to adjust the parameters to change the inherent color, light source color, and ambient color of the picture. Some students do not understand color matching in the course practice. Usually, one color is painted until the end, resulting in their works not presenting better visual effects. Therefore, color processing is essential in the process of VR painting.

3.3 Develop Spatial Layout and Narrative Skills

In the paintings in the virtual space, every object can be fully displayed, getting rid of the limitations of the two-dimensional plane and showing a three-dimensional space composition. The amount of information is far more than the two-dimensional picture. Therefore, the painter needs to cultivate the ability of spatial layout, that is, to improve the ability to adjust the position of objects, grasp the hierarchical relationship between objects, and distinguish the primary and secondary components of the picture. The painter needs to enhance the guiding ability to view perspective and construct different visiting paths from the viewer's perspective. Therefore, the composition of VR painting not only needs to follow the formal beauty rules such as symmetry and balance, rhythm, change, and unity but also to explore the space [14].

In addition, the characteristics of VR painting determine that artists can skillfully use it for narrative creation, such as "Dear Angelica" and other VR movies produced through VR painting. However, due to the whole perspective of VR movies, the montage language has no place to be used, and the audience's perspective is challenging to control. Therefore, users cannot use the traditional lens language in the narrative.

3.4 Collaborative Creation with 3D Modeling Software

After preparing the relevant traditional art foundation and establishing a specific modeling ability and spatial layout ability, 3D modeling ability must also be cultivated when creating in the actual three-dimensional space. As an advanced technical application, we believe that VR painting needs to master 3D modeling software to exert its most significant value and better serve creation. In the process of VR painting, we can use various 3D software collaboratively. Taking Tilt Brush as an example, we can transfer the VR data to the holographic support by exporting the Tilt Brush project as a Filmbox (.fbx) file. Fbx is a format that allows to manipulation of digital content on various digital creation software [15]. Initially implemented in Tilt Brush to allow users to share their creations online, this function has proven to be an excellent tool for importing assets created in VR into game engines like Unity 3D. Similarly, we can import tilt Brush.fbx files into a 3D modeling software such as 3D Max for data processing [16].

In addition, VR devices are not very popular now. Due to various conditions, many people cannot access VR devices. Suppose images created in VR were to be turned into holograms. In that case, the three-dimensionality of these productions could be preserved and experienced without using a VR headset, making them accessible to a broader public [17]. This idea opens a new path for the development of VR painting.

3.5 Thinking Expansion and Material Accumulation

As a new artistic expression, VR painting inherits the essentials of traditional art to a certain extent and derives a new painting mode. The visual image formed in his mind by his previous visual experience and his imagination. It's a process of creating from the inherent concept of the pre-formed schema [18].

In the VR painting experience course, since the participating students choose the course out of their interests and hobbies, rather than majoring in art, we suggest that students start with their familiar things or store some relevant materials and imitation objects on their mobile phones to form a simple material library. Many students can draw works more easily after analyzing the reference object. Students will give free play to their inspiration based on the reference object in the painting process and often get unexpected works (Fig. 2). Therefore, we believe that in talent training, it is necessary to improve students' inspiration and imagination, open up students' creative ideas, and cultivate students' habit of accumulating creative materials to prepare for later painting creation.

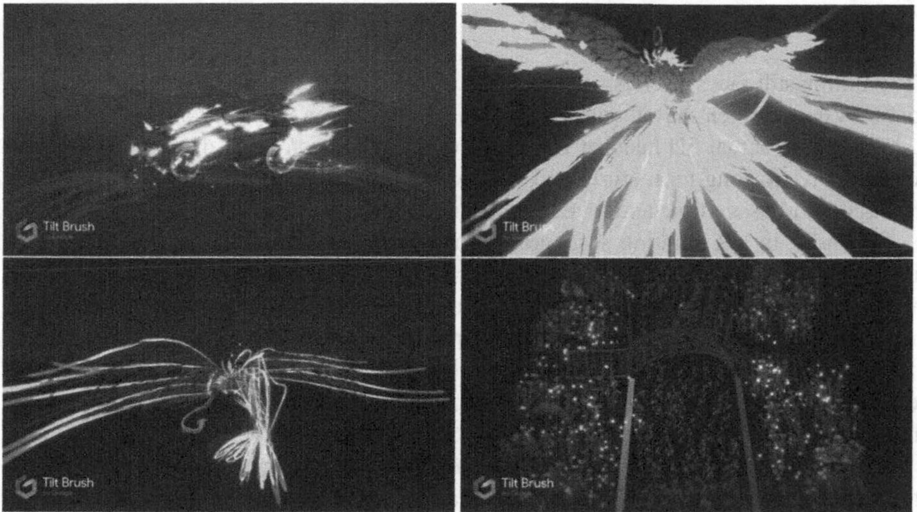

Fig. 2. Excellent VR paintings of students in this experiment

4 The Cultivation of Aesthetic Appreciation Ability Under the New Mode

"Artists are always dominated by the inherent logic system of the physical world and are inevitably bound by conventional concepts such as space, volume, and time. 'VR technology' is one of the most amazing technological achievements in digital technology. It provides the artist with the means to get free [19]." The many advantages of VR painting lay the foundation for the future direction of art development and, at the same time, will promote the development of new aesthetic methods. Virtual reality is likely to become the "Tenth art" in the future because it has boundless creative space, can trigger a variety of human senses, and let the audience become the subject of art [20].

Maurice Merleau-Ponty said that "the painting of the present does not deny the past to get rid of the past truly; the present painting only forgets the past while using the past [21]." The emerging painting model and its aesthetic paradigm is formed based on inheriting the tradition.

In VR painting, we not only focus on stimulating the subject's potential and strengthening the subject's feeling but also emphasize the personal interaction of the object and mobilize the various sensory organs of the creators and viewers, that is, to achieve "synesthesia." Compared with the pleasing experience of traditional painting, the ubiquitous "synesthetic" experience of VR painting has constructed a new aesthetic idea. "Art at this time is no longer based on the decisive aesthetics, but is shaped by new aesthetic experiences that embrace these unique digital properties…" [19]. This new aesthetic idea encourages users to innovate autonomously.

5 Challenges of VR Painting

VR painting still faces a series of challenges. First of all, in terms of hardware, the high cost of VR equipment has always been a significant reason why we cannot widely use it. Wearing an actual 3D headset for too long may cause physical discomfort and not be conducive to long-term study and homework. Students with Movement Disorders should control usage time and take appropriate breaks.

Secondly, in VR painting software, "visual space and intuition are the most basic elements in painting creation and play a crucial role" [22]. Because it directly establishes a virtual spatial relationship in three-dimensional space. After our experiment, we found that to master this new painting skill, spatial perception ability is the premise guarantee. In addition, the process of VR painting experience can only be carried out in "single person mode," which is challenging to realize the joint participation of many viewers simultaneously [23].

Finally, in terms of teaching, as a new technology, it has no teaching system at this stage and lacks the guidance of professional teachers; many art colleges or comprehensive universities have formed a specific mature teaching system. They don't want to break the conventions and try to use new technology.

6 Conclusion

Developing VR painting ability and forming a new teaching system is a rigorous and relatively long process, which requires step-by-step training steps. VR painting has excellent prospects in the industry and education, but for now, the specific teaching mode, curriculum system, teacher training, etc., still need to be explored. We believe that students can try out VR painting technology in the design discipline education of colleges and universities first. It is also the need for art education to adapt to the development of the times and industry changes. Using VR painting technology is a huge challenge, but it is an opportunity for progress.

References

1. Yoon, S.: Virtual reality in art education. Master's thesis, Virginia Commonwealth University (2010)
2. Meng, M.: A new field in the art world—digital painting. J. Jinzhong Norm. College **2**, 47–48 (2001)
3. Cheng, H.: Application of virtual reality technology in garment industry. In: 2017 3rd International Conference on Social Science and Management (2017)
4. Blazheva, S.: Tilt Brush. The new perspective of art. Cultural and history heritage: reservation, presentation, digitization (2021)
5. Haeyen, S.: The use of VR tilt brush in art and psychomotor therapy: an innovative perspective. The Arts in Psychotherapy (2021)
6. Schaaf, A.: Tilt Brush: The Utilization of a Virtual Reality Intervention for Evaluating Self-Reported Anxiety, Depression, & Stress (2019)
7. Pakanen, M.: Hybrid Campus Art: Bridging Two Realities through 3D Art (2017)

8. Christoforou, M., Boglou, D.: Exploring 3D artistry with the Virtual Reality application Tilt Brush: student perceptions. EuroCALL2021 (2021)
9. Da, M.: On the application and development of virtual reality painting software technology. Popular Color **1**, 77–78 (2019)
10. Pioaru, I.: Visualizing Virtual Reality Imagery through Digital Holography. In: International Conference on Cyberworlds (2017)
11. Ramsier, L.E.: Evaluating the usability and user experience of a virtual reality painting application (2019)
12. Ni, Y.: Analysis of VR painting technology in the field of digital painting art. Comedy World **9**, 116–117 (2021)
13. Wu, Z.: Design of experimental teaching system of 3D animation modeling based on VR technology. Anim. Res. 184–187 (2020)
14. Guo, Z.: Artistic exploration of virtual reality painting. Yunnan Arts Institute, MA thesis (2020)
15. https://www.autodesk.com/products/fbx/overview
16. Pioaru, I.: Visualizing virtual reality imagery through digital holography. In: International Conference on Cyberworlds (2017)
17. Pioaru, I.: Visualizing virtual reality imagery through digital holography. In: 2017 International Conference on Cyberworlds (2017)
18. Guan, Q.: The way of seeing: a study of painting style VR video works. Contemp. Films **7**, 171–176 (2020)
19. Li, H.: The end of the subject: the game experience of VR art. Sculpture **5**, 74–75 (2010)
20. Zhao, X., Wang, C.: The application of virtual reality technology (VR) in contemporary painting. Art Rev. **32**, 27–28+42 (2018)
21. Zhang, Y.: The Metaphorical Body—Merleau-Ponty's Phenomenological Research on the Body (PhD dissertation, Zhejiang University) (2004). https://kns.cnki.net/KCMS/detail/detail.aspx?dbname=CDFD9908&filename=2004082571.nh
22. Zhou, J.: Visual space and intuition in painting. Master's thesis, Liaoning Normal University (2016). https://kns.cnki.net/KCMS/detail/detail.aspx?dbname=CMFD201701&filename=1016237719.nh
23. Xu, J., Zhan, L.: VR painting research and design of "painting without fixed method." Res. Art Educ. **14**, 28–29 (2020)

eXtended Reality in Education

Factors in the Cognitive-Emotional Impact of Educational Environmental Narrative Videogames

Sofia Pescarin[1(✉)] and Delfina S. M. Pandiani[2]

[1] CNR ISPC, Florence, Italy
sofia.pescarin@cnr.it
[2] University of Bologna, Bologna, Italy

Abstract. This contribution describes an experiment carried out in 2020 with the goal of exploring factors affecting the cognitive-emotional impact of immersive VR Serious Games, and specifically of Educational Environmental Narrative Games. The experimental evaluation was aimed at better understanding three research questions: if passive or active interaction is preferable for users' factual and spatial knowledge acquisition; if meaningfulness could be considered as a relevant experience in a serious game (SG) context; and if distraction has an impact on knowledge acquisition and engagement in immersive VR educational games. Although the experiment involved only a limited number of participants, our results led to the identification of some relevant tendencies and factors which ought to be considered in the development of future SGs, and which reveal the need for further studies in HCI and game design.

Keywords: VR Serious Games · Cognition · Attention

1 Introduction

In 2019, the serious game (SG) "A Night in the Forum" (NiF) was published in Sony PlayStation store for Virtual Reality headsets. It was the second prototype of the H2020 European project REVEAL (Realizing Education through Virtual Environments and Augmented Locations); its design was based on the evaluation results of the first prototype, published in 2018 and titled "The Chantry" [1]. NiF is an Educational Environmental Narrative (EEN) videogame [2] dedicated to an archaeological site, the Forum of Augustus in Rome, whose remains are partially visible from the street, while other elements are conserved in the nearby museum (Museo dei Fori Imperiali). The game was developed taking into consideration two user scenarios: a) family home entertainment and b) schools or museums guided experience. The core educational goal of the game is to expand players' knowledge of Roman civilization, of the emperor Augustus and of his Forum. Therefore, comprehension and recall of historical facts and spatial information have been identified as key learning outcomes. A number of learning elements were identified and used in the development of a framework that connected the gameplay with

L. T. De Paolis et al. (Eds.): XR Salento 2022, LNCS 13446, pp. 101–108, 2022.
https://doi.org/10.1007/978-3-031-15553-6_8

the narrative of NiF, as described in [2]. To maximize success on the specified outcomes, cognitive and educational studies were considered and applied to the design, including on the positive effect on comprehension of a well-defined story structure [3–5, 7–9], on motivation and engagement [10] and on spatial memory [11–13]. Design insights were gathered from [4] (p.104), which found that recall was higher for high-level organizational story elements. Based on these studies, we designed the game so that it unfolds through a main story (the frame) and secondary stories (episodes), connected to in-game specific tasks and discoveries, following Thorndike's theory [4] (p.79). However, this theory was developed in regards to simple linear narratives, while NiF's is not linear, and is significantly more complex. Moreover, SGs are meant to involve players in engaging experiences. Thus, we wanted to understand *whether Thorndike's theory is also valid in the case of more complex and interactive narratives; whether game mechanics impact learning outcomes* and *what the role of meaningfulness might be.*

Following these questions, a first evaluation on "The Chantry" was initially conducted and described in [14]. To better understand how storytelling and game mechanics could reinforce factual and spatial knowledge acquisition in SGs without losing the sense of presence and engagement, we performed a further exploratory evaluation on NiF, with the goal of identifying factors potentially involved in the cognitive-emotional game experience and their effect on learning outcomes.

2 Research Questions and Procedure

NiF shares many characteristics with "The Chantry", but it also has some relevant differences that we took into consideration while planning the evaluation. NiF is more complex: the 3D scenario is wider (players move in a wider open space, such as the forum of Augustus); the scenario includes two versions of the site (current archaeological site and a re-constructed 1st century AD version); interaction is active and more complex (objects can be picked up, stored, etc.); game mechanics are strongly task-oriented. The narrative is more complex and developed in two levels: a higher level dedicated to the main explicit story (a tourist lost in time that has to play the role of the guardian of the forum for one night) and a lower level of a secondary narrative (Augustus emperor, his politics and life in imperial Rome).

First of all, we wanted to verify if results obtained in the previous evaluation were valid also for more complex games. Secondly, we extended the assessment to include conceptual knowledge acquisition, and to explore how engagement and meaningfulness are connected to knowledge acquisition and memorization. Finally, we included an exploratory analysis on further factors, such as distraction level and its impact. We therefore defined the three running questions we wanted to evaluate:

1) *Research Question 1 [RQ1]:* how passive/active interaction may affect factual/spatial knowledge acquisition and memorization in complex SG and nonlinear narratives;
2) *Research Question 2 [RQ2]* aimed at investigating the connection between conceptual knowledge and *meaningfulness* in SGs;
3) *Research Question 3 [RQ3]* focused on the impact of distraction/concentration on knowledge acquisition and recall in SGs.

3 Experiment Methodology

At the beginning of 2020, we set up an experiment to investigate the three mentioned aspects, with the goal of exploring the above mentioned impact factors and of defining new design requirements. We chose NiF and involved an homogeneous group of participants: 23 university students between 22–29 years of age, of various genders, and coming from 7 different countries were recruited and randomly assigned to a group (A to H) to participate in a series of tasks (reading, listening, playing), followed by questionnaires and drawing activities, for a total of between 60 and 180 min. The overall evaluation would have required three iterations (during February-May 2020 with 60 testers), but we have concluded only the first two, due to the unexpected worldwide pandemic. Below is a shortened version of the methodology, the full details will be published in an extended version in the near future.

In order to approach [RQ1], we performed a comparative analysis on the three main communication channels: active visual multimodal (playing the NiF game); passive reading of the story; and passive listening of the story. Regarding the written story, we decided to further develop two versions, to better get insights on the difference of knowledge acquisition in respect to the different communication styles.

To explore RQ2, we can *analyze user attention and interest* during the game, meaningfulness becoming a sort of filter in the experience [38], including by searching for repeated words [32], identifying causal links [33] or connections [37] among terms [33], and identifying similitudes or metaphors used [35]. Participants were asked, after they performed a task, to write short summary(s) of the experience, with what they recalled. Users who played the game, were also asked to sit with a facilitator and draw what they had experienced and mostly captured their attention.

In order to verify the impact of distraction on knowledge acquisition and recall [RQ3], we collected participants' average time spent on their smartphones in the previous two weeks, hypothesizing that a higher time spent on the phone would be connected with a higher distraction level. We then designed a priming "Focus exercise" by adapting a performance of the artist M. Abramovic, known as "Counting the Rice" [34], to be performed before the other tasks, with the goal of improving participants' concentration. Our assumption was that carrying out before other cognitive tasks, would increase performance in spatial and factual knowledge acquisition.

The performance of participants on the 28 + 22 questions of the 2 questionnaires was analyzed. First, each tester's responses were scored in terms of correctness and completeness on a scale from 0 to 3. Ssubsequently, results were aggregated by group (A-H), and each group was given two scores: a **BSP** (Binary Score Percentage): the percentage number of questions that were answered at least partially correct averaged over participants in the group; and a **CSA** (Correctness Score Average): the average correctness of answers, calculated by summing the score value (0–3) of each of the answers and averaging over participants in the group. The scores were further decomposed so as to obtain detailed information about performances of each group on each of the questionnaires. Given the reduced size of the groups, no independent statistical tests were performed, but rather score averages were calculated and are herein presented with no further independent analyses. Moreover the summaries were analyzed in terms of length, completeness, sequences of facts and wording, and the drawings were analyzed in terms of emergence of details and peculiarities. More details about data analysis and results can be found in an expanded publication in the near future.

4 Results and Conclusions

Although partial and with a limited of testers, the evaluation we present has highlighted some of the factors affecting the cognitive-emotional impact of immersive Serious Games and specifically EEN games, such as NiF.

Factor 1. The impact of story structure and its relation with game mechanics. Regarding the tendencies of linear narrative (and passive interaction) to contribute to better factual knowledge acquisition, the results obtained confirm the conclusions of the previous evaluation [14]. We observed that those involved in linear tasks, as reading and listening, better performed on recalling facts than did players. When we extended the analysis to spatial knowledge, however, we observed that players of SGs tended to perform better in the recall of *spatial* information. We should also highlight the low-performance overall results obtained in Q2d, which suggest the overall cognitive complexity of recognizing 3D reconstructed environments and locating them in real places, viewed from a different perspective. This investigation showed that the factual information that players best recalled corresponded to explicit knowledge in the main narrative of the game. On the other hand, players performed poorly on implicit knowledge and educational information in lower hierarchical nodes (i.e. the Roman legal system, life during Augustus time, etc.) and complex concepts (i.e. inequalities between Romans and foreigners, etc.), which required more reasoning, interpretation and reflection. It is likely that players were absorbed in the immersiveness of the spatial environment, with little possibility for interpretation or reflection. We can conclude that games should include appropriate game mechanics that explicitly support players' moments of reflection. Moreover, it would be beneficial to design story structure by aligning educational facts with high hierarchical narrative nodes.

Factor 2. Communication style and media channel's impact on knowledge acquisition. Reading a narrative story was shown to greatly outperform in the correctness and performance in Q2a, focused on spatial knowledge acquisition. The pattern changes in regards to Q2b, in which playing the game seems to be the best way to improve spatial knowledge, with reading and listening obtaining the worst results. As such, the experiment has highlighted how linear narrative (and specifically reading), can obtain better results in terms of factual knowledge acquisition and recalling. This result also in line with previous results [7], in which it was clarified how "adults […] are more critical to expository than narrative text recall". If linear narrative stories seem to be the best way to convey factual knowledge, we should further consider if these results could be obtained also by designing guided VR experiences and moderated SGs, or limiting the types and numbers of in-game interactions.

Factor 3. Meaningfulness' impact on SGs design and evaluation. RQ2 aimed at investigating the connection between conceptual knowledge and meaningfulness in SGs. The experiment did not lead to clear results on this question, although we did observe increased engagement and embodiment through the use of specific keywords and the use of the first person while summarizing the game experience (s). Other elements that enabled us to identify meaning-making elements were found in (s), anticipated by terms such as "like" "similar to" or "a kind of", that revealed personal cultural, cognitive and emotional context of the subject. Game-playing participants used the highest number of these expressions, thus indicating how game play could solicit meaningfulness. These results moreover suggest that SGs have the potential of becoming meaningful experiences, if they are designed accordingly. Meaning making as a process can be for instance included as a task in the gameplay and used to solicit reasoning and reflections, contributing to self-awareness and other positive effects, such as personal identity development [29, 30] or transformative contribution to support future choices or develop personal interpretations. The game design was not aimed at making players focus on concepts, thus preventing us to verify whether concept-oriented design could be a factor influencing personal reflection and meaning making. Although we have not observed significant emerging concepts, we explored potential new ways to evaluate them. The best methods have been the analysis of summaries, while the observations of drawings would need more structured and studied protocols on how to use psychogeography as an evaluation method to be adopted eventually to support both game designers in early stages as well as educators.

Factor 4. Concentration's impact on knowledge acquisition and engagement. RQ3 was focused on the impact of distraction on knowledge acquisition and recall in SGs. The experimental results show that distraction can substantially limit knowledge acquisition, not only when reading or listening to a story, but also when engaged in a VR immersive gaming experience. The results point towards a tendency towards higher performance for those who were "primed" by the attention-growing exercise. This tendency is especially strong for the players, while no specific connection with participants' time spent on their cell-phones was found. If this tendency is valid also beyond the tested category of users, it would mean that immersive VR per se is not sufficient as exercise to limit distraction and that SGs would need to seriously consider this potential issue to maintain players attention. A possible avenue of further research is the adoption of other approaches for attention-priming, such as persuasive technologies [23] (p. 66–69), as well as the inclusion of an analog exercise already within the first stages of design of SGs game mechanics.

All in all, the presented evaluation is a first step towards studying difficult matters regarding Serious Games (SG). One important caveat is that the chosen evaluation methods are mainly based on subjects' own observations—limiting the objectivity of the results. This initial study can and should be further expanded by expanding the subject pool to a more heterogeneous one, and considering also real-time tracking of biosignals which literature correlates to factors of attention and engagement.

Supplementary Materials. The trailer of the videogame is available online at https://www.youtube.com/watch?v=9AvCQexNbrU; the game is available at https://store.playstation.com/en-gb/product/EP2996-CUSA12481_00-THEIMPERIALFORUM/.

Acknowledgments. We acknowledge: the Museum of Imperial Forum in Rome (Lucrezia Ungaro and Paolo Vigliarolo) for their scientific contribution; Carlo Teo Pedretti and Mattia Spadoni (University of Bologna) for their contribution in the organization of the experiment.

Author Contributions. "Experiment Conceptualization, S. Pescarin; Experiment methodology, S. Pescarin, D. Pandiani; software, VRTRON; game assets, VR TRON, CNR ISPC (D. Ferdani, B. Fanini); general REVEAL project coordination, J. Habgood- Sheffield Hallam University. All authors have read and agreed to the published version of the manuscript."

Funding. "This research was funded by EU REVEAL H2020 project, grant number 732599": https://cordis.europa.eu/project/id/732599.

Abbreviations in Alphabetical Order:

CH	Cultural Heritage
d	Ask with participants drawing a map, eventually with details or comments
[Drawing]	Evaluation tool
EEN	Educational Environmental Narrative
ENViG	Environmental Narrative Videogames
f	Focusing or concentration exercise
l	Listening task
lSN	Listening a narrative version of the story task
NiF	Night in the Forum videogame
pG	Playing game task
PS VR	PlayStation VR
Q1	Questionnaire for personal data and background information;
Q2a	Questionnaire for factual and conceptual knowledge;
Q2b	Questionnaire for spatial knowledge evaluation;
Q2c	Questionnaire on spatial knowledge;
Q2d	Questionnaire on spatial knowledge;
r	Reading task
RQ1	Research Question 1
RQ2	Research Question 2
RQ3	Research Question 3
rSD	Reading a descriptive version of the story task
rSN	Reading a narrative version of the story task
s	Written short summary of the experience
SG	Serious Game

References

1. Habgood, J., Moore, D., Alapont, S., Ferguson, C., van Oostendorp, H.: The REVEAL educational environmental narrative framework for PlayStation VR. In: Proceedings of the 12th European Conference on Game-based Learning. ACPI, France, pp. 175–183 (2018)

2. Pescarin, S., Fanini, B., Ferdani, D., Mifsud, K., Hamilton, A.: Optimising environmental educational narrative videogames: The case of 'A night in the forum'. J. Comput. Cult. Heritage **13**(4) (2020). https://doi.org/10.1145/3424952
3. Mandler, J.M., Johnson, N.S.: Remembrance of things parsed: Story structure and recall. Cogn. Psychol. **9**(1), 111–151 (1977)
4. Thorndyke, P.W.: Cognitive structures in comprehension and memory of narrative discourse. Cogn. Psychol. **9**(1), 77–110 (1977)
5. Lorch, R.F., Lorch, E.P., Inman, W.E.: Effects of signaling topic structure on text recall. J. Educ. Psychol. **85**(2), 281–290 (1993)
6. Bashiri, A., Ghazisaeedi, M., Shahmoradi, L.: The opportunities of virtual reality in the rehabilitation of children with attention deficit hyperactivity disorder: a literature review. Korean J. Pediatr. **60**(11), 337 (2017)
7. Zabrucky, K.M., Moore, D.: Influence of text genre on adults' monitoring of understanding and recall". Educ. Gerontol. **25**(8), 691–710 (1999)
8. Norris, S.P., et al.: A theoretical framework for narrative explanation in science. Sci. Educ. **89**(4), 535–563 (2005)
9. Gustafsson, A., Katzeff, C., Bang, M.: Evaluation of a pervasive game for domestic energy engagement among teenagers. Comput. Entertainment (CIE) **7**(4), 1–19 (2010)
10. Wouters, P., van Oostendorp, H.: Overview of Instructional Techniques to Facilitate Learning and Motivation of Serious Games. In: Wouters, P., van Oostendorp, H. (eds) Instructional Techniques to Facilitate Learning and Motivation of Serious Games. Advances in Game-Based Learning. Springer, Cham, pp. 1–16 (2017). https://doi.org/10.1007/978-3-319-39298-1_1
11. Brooks, B.M.: The specificity of memory enhancement during interaction with a virtual environment. Memory **7**(1), 65–78 (1999)
12. Christou, C.G., Bülthoff, H.H.: View dependence in scene recognition after active learning. Mem. Cognit. **27**(6), 996–1007 (1999)
13. Conniff, A., Craig, T., Laing, R., Galán-Díaz, C.: A comparison of active navigation and passive observation of desktop models of future built environments. Des. Stud. **31**(5), 419–438 (2010)
14. Ferguson, C., Oostendorp, H.van., van den Broek, E.L.: The development and evaluation of the storyline scaffolding tool. In: Proceedings of the 2019 11th International Conference on Virtual Worlds and Games for Serious Applications (VS-Games), IEEE, pp. 1–8 (2019)
15. Berardone, F.: Videogame-induced tourism. Esperienze oltre lo schermo. Youcanprint (2017)
16. Dubois, L.-E., Gibbs, C.: Video game–induced tourism: a new frontier for destination marketers. Tourism Review (2018)
17. Lord, G.D.: The power of cultural tourism. Keynote Presentation, Wisconsin Heritage Tourism Conference. vol. 17(09) (1999)
18. Chen, H., Imran, R.: Cultural tourism: an analysis of engagement, cultural contact, memorable tourism experience and destination loyalty. Tourism Manag. Perspect. **26**, 153–163 (2018)
19. Katifori, A., et al.: The EMOTIVE Project-Emotive Virtual Cultural Experiences through Personalized Storytelling. Cira@ euromed (2018)
20. Perry, S.E.: The enchantment of the archaeological record. Eur. J. Archaeol. (2019)
21. Van Der Stigchel, S.: Concentration: staying focused in times of distraction. MIT Press (2020)
22. Clark, A., Chalmers, D.J.: The extended mind. Analysis **58**(1), 7–19 (1998)
23. Griffiths, M.D.: Adolescent social networking: how do social media operators facilitate habitual use? Educ. Health **36**(3), 66–69 (2018)
24. Pescarin, S.: Museums and virtual museums in Europe: reaching expectations. SCIRES-IT-Sci. Res. Inf. Technol. **4**(1), 131–140 (2014). https://doi.org/10.2423/i22394303v4n1p131

25. V-MUST. Terminology, definitions and types of Virtual Museums. (V-Must.net – Project Report: D2.1b): (2014). Accessible at https://www.academia.edu/6090456/Terminology_definitions_and_types_of_Virtual_Museums
26. Palombini, A.: Storytelling and telling history. Towards a grammar of narratives for Cultural Heritage dissemination in the Digital Era. J. Cult. Heritage **2,** 134–139 (2017)
27. Taylor, S.E.: Adjustment to threatening events: a theory of cognitive adaptation. Am. Psychol. **38**, 1161–1171 (1983)
28. Park, C.L.: Making sense of the meaning literature: an integrative review of meaning making and its effects on adjustment to stressful life events. Psychol. Bull. **136**(2), 257 (2010)
29. Baumeister, R.F., Wilson, B.: Life stories and the four need for meaning. Psychol. Inq. **7**(4), 322–325 (1996)
30. McAdams, D.P.: Personality, modernity, and the storied self: a contemporary framework for studying persons. Psychol. Inq. **7**(4), 295–321 (1996)
31. Roussou, M., et al.: Transformation through Provocation?. In: Proceedings of the 2019 CHI Conference on Human Factors in Computing Systems (2019)
32. Underwood, B.J., Schulz, R.W.: Meaningfulness and verbal learning (1960)
33. Pennebaker, J.W., Francis, M.E.: Cognitive, emotional, and language processes in disclosure. Cogn. Emot. **10**(6), 601–626 (1996)
34. Abramovic, M.: Walk Through Walls: A Memoir (2017)
35. Baumeister, R.F.: Meanings of life. Guilford press (1991)
36. Emmons, R.A.: Motives and life goals. Handbook of personality psychology. Academic Press, pp. 485–512 (1997)
37. Baumeister, R.F., Vohs, K.D.: The pursuit of meaningfulness in life. Handb. Positive Psychol. **1**, 608–618 (2002)
38. Park, C.L., Folkman, S.: Meaning in the context of stress and coping. Rev. Gen. Psychol. **1**(2), 115–144 (1997)
39. King, L.A., Pennebaker, J.W.: Thinking about goals, glue, and the meaning of life. Ruminative Thoughts **10**, 97–106 (1996)
40. Echavarria, K.R., et al.: Augmented Reality (AR) Maps for Experiencing Creative Narratives of Cultural Heritage. In: Proceedings of EUROGRAPHICS Workshop on Graphics and Cultural Heritage (2019)
41. Debord, G.: Introduction to a critique of urban geography. Praxis (e) press (2008)
42. Coverley, M.: Psychogeography. Pocket Essentials (2006)

Instinct-Based Decision-Making in Interactive Narratives

Tobías Palma Stade(✉)

Digital Creativity Lab, University of York, Heslington YO10 5GE, UK
tobias.palmastade@york.ac.uk

Abstract. This paper examines the expressive potential of instinct-based decision-making as a method to enhance narrative immersion in interactive storytelling. One of the key challenges to propose leaned-back interactive narratives lies in the methods through which users and system exchange inputs and outputs. While explicit interfaces tend to disrupt leaned-back participation – demanding a leaned-forward type of agency – and, thus, immersion in the narrative environment, this model proposes interactions based on diegetic stimuli that avoid interfaces and encourage instinctive and immediate reactions from the user in order to navigate a narrative immersive environment. The notion of instinct-based decision-making has been observed in three stages: (1) Conceptualization through previous practices and literature review, (2) Design and production of a Cinematic Virtual Reality (CVR) interactive prototype, and (3) system-testing of the model's key functional aspects.

Keywords: Interactive storytelling · Immersive environments · Instinctive decision-making · Cinematic virtual reality · Hands-off interactivity

1 Introduction

Post-broadcasting media – as it has been named by some media scholars [10] – is defined by the agency gained by audiences, by a much more hands-on approach to the curation of a variety of formats and contents. Yet, the consumption itself still remains mostly *leaned-back*: "TV viewing tends to be a more passive, 'lean back' experience, in contrast to the active involvement required of the 'lean forward' computer/Internet activity" [9]. In recent years, researchers and practitioners have started to attempt to merge these two approaches. Today we can see that in interactive television (SmartTVs, Netflix, Amazon Video, and many other On-demand platforms), once we select the content, the act of "watching the telly" remains mostly the same – sometimes complemented by side-consumption of complementing content through our mobile phones or other devices. While the content is accessible to be curated, it isn't by itself interactive. For now.

Technology has reached a point in which the exploration of interactive film and television content is possible, and imagining it in "the living room of the future" [1] seems feasible, if not immediately, in the short term. The fast development of immersive and haptic technology and its application into television devices might accelerate the

L. T. De Paolis et al. (Eds.): XR Salento 2022, LNCS 13446, pp. 109–127, 2022.
https://doi.org/10.1007/978-3-031-15553-6_9

leap into the next stage of interactive media in the following years. In the eventuality of this scenario, we have the possibility to explore and experiment with these technologies, in order to understand their potentially expressive means.

This paper focuses on the exploration of instinct-based interactions as a way to enhance leaned-back and hands-off interactive storytelling. The notion of interactivity has been for long related to lean-forward formats such as video games, that require explicit interaction through a device – usually a remote control of a certain kind – and always on a conscious level in which users are aware of the decisions they are making and their effects in the narrative. Instead, this project aimed to explore the possibilities of a leaned-back interaction defined by unconscious decision-making, through minimizing explicit interaction and focusing on implicit interaction and on the use of diegetic stimuli, enhanced by the characteristics of an immersive medium like Cinematic Virtual Reality (CVR).

2 Conceptualization

2.1 Immersion, Interactivity, and Agency

Generally, the definition of interactive storytelling is founded in the tension between the agency given to the user and the author's narrative intentions [3, 8, 11, 19] or a *Free Will versus Determinism* conflict, or a *Man versus Author* conflict. As in any interactive storytelling experience, the problem lies in the paradox of interactivity: "[T]he integration of the unpredictable, bottom-up input of the user into a sequence of events that fulfills the conditions of narrativity – conditions that presuppose a top-down design" [19]. Most of the revised literature discusses interactivity as the ability to affect the storyworld from *within* – considering that most of the authors refer to interactive storytelling mainly in video games or similar media.

According to Marie-Laure Ryan, "the combination of narrativity and interactivity oscillates between two forms: the *narrative game*, in which narrative meaning is subordinated to the player's actions, and the *playable story*, in which the player's actions are subordinated to narrative meaning" [19]. Especially nowadays, these two forms correspond more to a spectrum than to a binary categorization. Another way to understand this would be according to the objectives of a specific interactive story, which can oscillate between performing a series of tasks and accomplishing missions, to an intrinsically contemplative reception of the story.

Michael Mateas' more Aristotelian approach to interactivity distinguishes between *Interactive Drama* and *Interactive Storytelling*: "In interactive drama, the player assumes the role of a first-person character in a dramatic story. The player does not sit above the story, watching it as in a simulation, but is immersed in the story" [11]. On the other hand, Interactive Storytelling would not necessarily involve a *player*, but a user that, without being involved in the story – or *storyworld* – has the ability to manipulate elements of it.

Chris Crawford's definition of interactivity refers to it as a *conversation*: "A cyclic process between two or more agents in which each agent alternately listens, thinks, and speaks" [3]. According to this, in interactive storytelling the narration must contain several stimuli across its timespan to allow at least an equal amount of reactions from the user, where the term *reactions* summarizes Crawford's three steps of listening, thinking, and speaking, which he also clarifies are not to be taken literally, but rather as receiving the stimuli, processing it, and responding to it.

A more specific debate around interactivity is the paradox between narrative immersion and agency: "[A] distinction should be made between ludic and narrative immersion. Ludic immersion is a deep absorption in the performance of a task. Comparable to the intensity with which a mathematician concentrates on proving a theorem, or a soloist performs a concerto. (…) [N]arrative immersion is an engagement of the imagination in the construction and contemplation of a storyworld that relies on purely mental activity" [19]. TV audiences are not players and agency is not a condition for audiences to be immersed in stories. On the contrary, it is the inclusion of agency in storytelling that apparently affects narrative immersion.

This complicates the definition of agency. One perspective sees it as "the feeling of empowerment that comes from being able to take actions in the world whose effects relate to the player's intention" [11] a position that stresses that the user's agency must have effects on the storyworld [3]. Another, more dynamic vision observes that interactive narratives face the challenge of reconciling the tensions between immersion and agency, since the latter would affect the former [20]. As for immersion, Ermi and Mayra define it as "becoming physically or virtually a part of the experience itself" [4] a definition that is quite generous, as it can be applied to narrative and/or environmental immersion. They also distinguish three different types of immersion: Sensory, challenge-based, and imaginative. "Sensory immersion can be intensified with better graphics and sound; challenge-based by engaging gameplay […] and imaginative immersion as a 'game experience in which one becomes absorbed with the stories and the world'" [7].

Another dimension of the *agency vs immersion* problem is what Janet Murray approaches with the concept of *threshold objects*. These are devices that "take us across a symbolical and sometimes literal passageway" [13]. Murray and Ryan both criticize the real sense of immersion that these devices provide since, as a physical material object, they are also the material evidence and reminder that the storyworld is an illusion. They argue that interactivity which relies too much on the threshold device fails to provide an effective sense of immersion, since it would be the same object what pulls the user back from the story. While Murray refers specifically to physical devices – especially prosthetic devices, that are in any way attached to our bodies, such as controls or Head Mounted Displays (HMD) – on-screen non-diegetic interfaces have similar characteristics, in terms of, on the one hand, facilitating and allowing interactivity as they serve as a toolbox to affect the digital storyworld, since their usually non-diegetic and inorganic presence is a reminder of the nature of the immersion, and could even suppose a visual barrier as a sort of emerging fourth wall. Moreover, the counterintuitive usage of these devices and interfaces suppose a process of learning, adaptation, and acquisition of skills to properly perform the agency on the interactive narration. And yet, these same devices and interfaces are the ones that allow interactivity in the first place, which is the base for the paradox presented threshold objects.

This is one of the issues that leaned-back and hands-off interaction schemes aim to attack: How to provide interactivity with little-to-none friction in terms of immersion, aiming to reduce the explicit, non-diegetic, and inorganic, presence of threshold objects and interfaces. The current technological developments point to opening possibilities to this kind of interactivity, with technologies like eye-tracking, or motion-sensing input devices like haptics-based technology, that could allow interactivity with little effort from users and little friction in terms of crossing a physical threshold.

The challenge, in these hypothetical scenarios, would be to create strong narrative immersions based on story elements and not relying upon the consciousness of the devices. In this sense, amusement parks are usually referred as the best examples of spatial immersion with very restrained interactivity, but that doesn't necessarily affect the immersion [8, 13, 19]. This is based on the principle of *environmental storytelling,* which "creates the preconditions for an immersive narrative experience in at least one of four ways: spatial stories can evoke pre-existing narrative associations; they can provide a staging ground where narrative events are enacted; they may embed narrative information within their *mise-en-scéne*, or they provide resources for emergent narratives" [8]. Similarly, *spatial stories* are defined as "stories which respond to alternative aesthetic principles, privileging spatial exploration over plot development. Spatial stories are held together by broadly defined goals and conflicts and pushed forward by the character's movement across the map", where "the organization of the plot becomes a matter of designing the geography of imaginary worlds, so that obstacles thwart and affordances facilitate the protagonist's forward movement towards resolution" [8]. A practical approach to this proposed type of narrative is the application of Spatial Story Density (SSD) as the measurement of story elements that are arranged in the space of a scene simultaneously [23]. This means that spatial stories require a balance in the information contained in the spaces, in the same way, linear storytelling is founded on the principle of tension-and-release; the balance and dynamism of events taking place at a fast pace against moments of tension being built upon slower pace and moments of more reflexive contemplation. In other words, "with high temporal story density, narratives are fast paced, with high spatial story density, many narratives are happening simultaneously. Mental effort increases when temporal or spatial story density is high" [5].

2.2 Guidance

One of the key principles to consider in the engagement and interaction in immersive media is guidance, which refers to the methods used to establish a dialogical relation between system and user. Immersive environments present a particular challenge in terms of guidance because the surrounding space tends to be more stimulating and distracting than screen-based media, where attention can be more easily directed by the author. The dialogue between system an user should be subtle enough so the user doesn't feel that they are losing their agency. Guidance should feel like the system is suggesting decisions to the user, never imposing them.

Previous studies have explored the possibilities to provide guidance from within the narrative world in cinematic VR, [14, 22] in other words, encouraging diegetic guidance. For this, we can discriminate between explicit and implicit cues: "Implicit cues are likely, but no necessarily contingent upon bottom-up salience, whereas explicit cues are likely to cause voluntary, top-down shifts in attention" [14]. By this definition, most non-diegetic guidance corresponds to explicit cues, in the sense that attention is being explicitly called by the narrator.

Immersive spaces, by allowing the user more direct access to the diegetic storyworld, also allow more direct access to diegetic cues. Speicher et al. [22] specifically focused their research on how much attention do users pay to different types of stimuli, both visual and acoustic, diegetic and non-diegetic. One of their key findings is that users welcome guidance, as it facilitates participation, while Passmore et al. note that users tend to feel that navigation and exploration are facilitated by guidance: "The ability to look around is linked to the users' certainty about what they should be looking at, and their attention to, and concentration on, story" [15]. From then on, the question is what types of guidance are preferred. Gödde et al. identified five types of diegetic attentional cues in their study on cinematic conventions on CVR, which include: Gazes, Motion, Sound, Context (narrative elements like anticipation or suspense), and Perspective (the disposition of elements in the space by proximity, size, etc.) [5]. To these, Brillhart has added timing and rhythm [2]. She developed an editing technique she calls Probabilistic Experiential Editing, which aims to facilitate fluidity between cuts through the synchronic presence of relevant dramatic elements in the virtual space. This understanding of timing is considerably more subtle than what is broadly advised by other authors, "to give around at least 20 seconds per shot for the viewer to orientate to the new scene, unlike traditional TV, where shots can be much shorter" [15]. Brillhart's notion of timing and editing precisely aims to avoid the need for orientation through hopefully instant recognition of what she calls Point of Interest, or simply put, "places in a scene where a viewer is likely to be looking" [2]. Timing lies on a swift and organic cut cued by the visual elements and their role in their surrounding environment.

The conceptualization of these notions aimed to provide a theoretical, yet practical, framework to facilitate a type of interaction that relies on the user reacting to the diegetic elements strategically organized in an immersive environment through the application of SSD. While the proposed storyworld responds mainly to a top-down system which facilitates a series of diegetic stimuli, the prerendered nature of CVR makes the author concedes the narration to however the user reacts to these stimuli and whichever decisions they make from such reactions, ideally resulting in the self-editing of a unique and unrepeatable version of the story proposed by the author.

3 Methodology

The study followed a research-by-practice approach, with a strong interdisciplinary perspective that merged techniques from diverse expressive disciplines, mainly filmmaking and computer design, but also including theatre, screenwriting, and sound design. Its development consisted of three stages: Writing and Design, Production of a prototype (which in many ways resulted in an extension of the design), and a System-proof testing.

In the first stage, the processes of writing and design informed each other simultaneously in order to meet specific needs from one and the other. The second stage, the production of the prototype, prolonged the design of the model through the exploration of diverse expressive techniques in CVR. Despite its cinematic technical qualities, CVR presents a fertile ground for challenges and experimentation from multi and interdisciplinary approaches. There have been diverse experiences that have explored editing and montage in cinematic VR [2], adaptation of filmmaking practices into immersive narratives [12, 15], the properties of guidance [5, 14, 22], and that observe the feasibility of theatrical techniques in immersive spaces [16, 17].

This particular study added a somewhat more thorough and dramatic use of acoustic stimuli in immersive environments, exploring the potential of sounds as diegetic stimuli to provide guidance. This appears to be a novel approach to VR, since "[t]he technical literature exploring VR's potential is somewhat ocularcentric, focusing on two dominant visual techniques: computer-generated imagery (e.g. 3D environments) and 360° videography (a.k.a. "cinematic VR"). Yet VR also affords virtual soundscapes via ambisonic" [6]. Just like films make a dramatic use of sound, this study aimed to adapt some of the expressive acoustic techniques used in filmmaking into immersive narrative environments.

The final stage of system-proof consisted on a very basic demonstration of the prototype to a total of seven people, and focused on the functionality of the expressive concepts applied during the two previous stages. The sample involved in the evaluation, this was composed of: volunteers (4) – from here on referred to as participants – who got to watch the prototype and participate in a semi-guided focus group, experts (2) from academia and the industry, who watched to prototype and responded to a semi-structured interview designed for experts in the field, and crew members (2) who answered a survey at the end of the production process, and another (1), the sound designer, who watched the prototype and participated of a semi-structured interview.

It is worth noting that this consultations took place during the Covid-19 pandemic, particularly during the second lockdown, which affected the original planification for the system test. The consultations that took place consisted in simplified versions of this planification, in order to obtain sufficient data to evaluate the prototype and the key concepts behind its design.

4 Design and Production

4.1 Scriptwriting

The design and the scriptwriting processes informed each other simultaneously, taking into account that the conception of the story had to meet the requirements for an immersive and interactive model based on diegetic stimuli and instinct-based interactions. This stage aimed to apply the notion of Spatial Story Density, focusing on a) how actions and characters are distributed across the surrounding virtual environment, and b) how to use soundscape as an articulation between micronarratives and as a unifying element of the overall drama.

The idea for the technology is simpler than the architecture of the story. It consists of a virtual reality space divided into relatively similar angles, set from the perspective of a first-person viewer in the centre of the space. The surrounding sphere is then divided into as many acoustic environments as wished – in this case, three. In Fig. 1 we can see an example of a virtual space divided into four acoustic areas, so that the viewer, placed in the middle, has the ability to distinguish what's happening in each of these areas independently.

Applying this conception of the virtual space, the script consists of two parallel plots –one with its own main character: Ginny and the Grandmother– which we can see in the

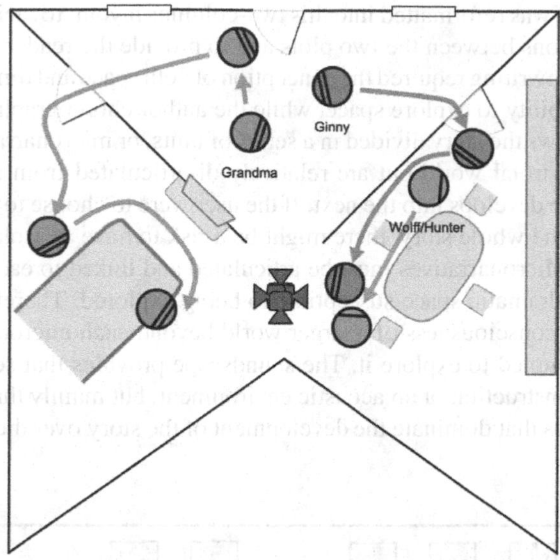

Fig. 1. Diagram of a virtual space divided in acoustic sub-spaces, where different micronarratives take place.

form of interlinked outlines in Fig. 2. Each plot consists of nine bullet-points that balance each other respectively, while they also mark the turning points and the moments when the characters meet and depart. Both plots are interdependent, influencing each other and forming part of one overall story. There are events in Ginny's plot that affect the Grandmother's and vice versa. There are also external events – embodied in secondary characters – that affect both protagonists, hopefully in a proportionate manner.

INTELINKED OUTLINE

Grandma and Wolff are cuddling	Ginny and Hunter are discussing on the phone
Wolff leaves	Hunter arrives by surprise
Grandma runs into Ginny while looking for Wolff	Ginny runs into Grandma while hiding Hunter
Grandma tries to hide her affair	Ginny she tries to hide Hunter
Grandma hears Hunter – she believes he's Wolff	Ginny kicks Hunter out
She flirts with Hunter	She finds Hunter's present
Ginny finds them	Ginny finds Hunter being courted by her Grandma
Hunter/Wolff leaves	Hunter/Wolff leaves
Grandma starts to believe she's delusional	Ginny realizes she's losing her boyfriend
She decides to deny it	She decides to take him back

Fig. 2. Interlinked Outline, we can see the two plots' bullet-points and how the keep the synchronicity and balance of the dramatic development of both plots.

The script itself was reformatted into this two-columns layout, to facilitate the choreography of the actions between the two plots and to provide the reader a good sense of simultaneity. Screenwriting required the conception of both space and time manipulation: To give users the ability to explore space, while the author choreographs time.

The outline shows the story divided in a series of units, or micronarratives [3]. These take place in one virtual world but are relatively disarticulated from each other until each micronarrative develops into the next. If the user were to choose to follow only one character through the whole story, there might be a risk to have an isolated plot and an incomplete story. Micronarratives must be articulated and linked to each other through their position in a dramatic space susceptible to being explored. Therefore, users must have some kind of consciousness of a larger world beyond each micronarrative, so that they would feel tempted to explore it. The soundscape provides that sense of a world, first through the construction of an acoustic environment, but mainly through the use of dramatic sound cues that dominate the development of the story over the interdependent micronarratives.

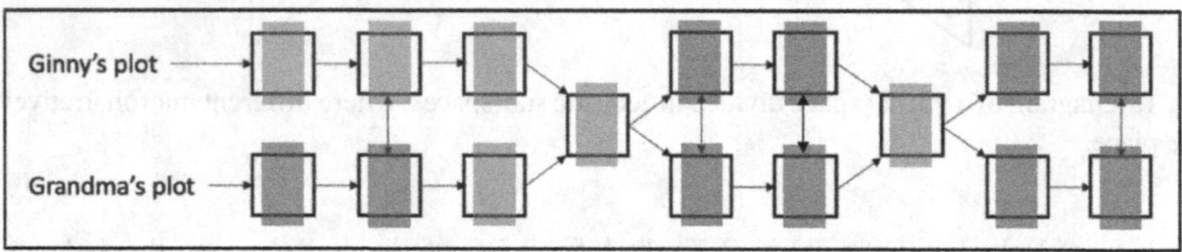

Fig. 3. Diagram of the narrative structure of The Hunter & the Wolff. Each square corresponds to a scene or micronarrative. The unidirectional arrows signal the linear temporal direction of the story, while the bidirectional arrows mark the points where sounds cues can be heard in all the immersive space.

Figure 3 shows how micronarratives articulate to each other linearly in time and in space, forming a narrative structure. While both plots unfold linearly, the simultaneity is illustrated by the parallel development. The merging micronarratives mark the points in the story when the plots merge both in time and space (which also divide the structure into thirds, following the three acts structure). The bidirectional arrows also mark the moments when sound cues can be heard in all of the immersive environment, linking parallel micronarratives together. While the medium allows the user to switch between spaces and plots at any time, and not necessarily in the points marked in the diagram, this illustration shows how narrative structures incorporated notions of interactivity and spatial storytelling.

In more practical terms, the overall, unifying soundscape is reflected in the script through *cue sounds*, which are very specific sounds related to the organic environment and that have direct dramatic influence over the characters. While each micronarrative is distinguished by its own soundtrack – which allows users to isolate the micronarrative from any other external disturbance and, therefore, focus on it – these cue sounds form part of the larger structure of the story and are omnipresent; users will hear them despite the micronarrative they're following at a given moment.

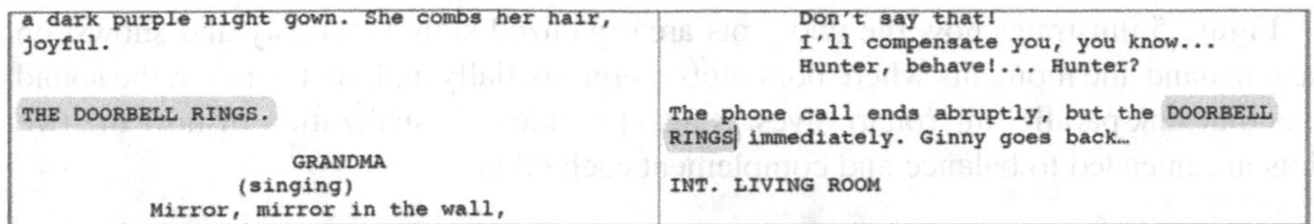

a dark purple night gown. She combs her hair, joyful. THE DOORBELL RINGS. GRANDMA (singing) Mirror, mirror in the wall,	Don't say that! I'll compensate you, you know... Hunter, behave!... Hunter? The phone call ends abruptly, but the DOORBELL RINGS immediately. Ginny goes back… INT. LIVING ROOM

Fig. 4. Cue sounds. In this excerpt we can see how an overall sound is present in both micronarratives, having dramatic influence in the two plots (Color figure online).

In Fig. 4 we see an example of this principle. Stressed in yellow and caps we can read the cue "DOORBELL RINGS" relatively in the same line of each plot (Ginny's on the left, Grandma's on the right). This is a very short excerpt.but long enough to notice that the actions going on are completely different for each character, yet the sound cue generates a reaction. These sounds have three key functionalities in the medium: dramatic, environmental, and interactivity-driver. They are dramatic because they generate reactions in the characters and keep the plots moving; environmental because they belong to the diegetic, organic world and hold the micronarratives together into one dramatic space; and they are the organic interactivity-drivers that are expected to stimulate users to *turn around* and *look the other way*. They are one of the main stimuli –apart from characters' movement and other visual elements of the blocking and *mise-en-scène*– that are supposed to generate organic, instinctive reactions on users.

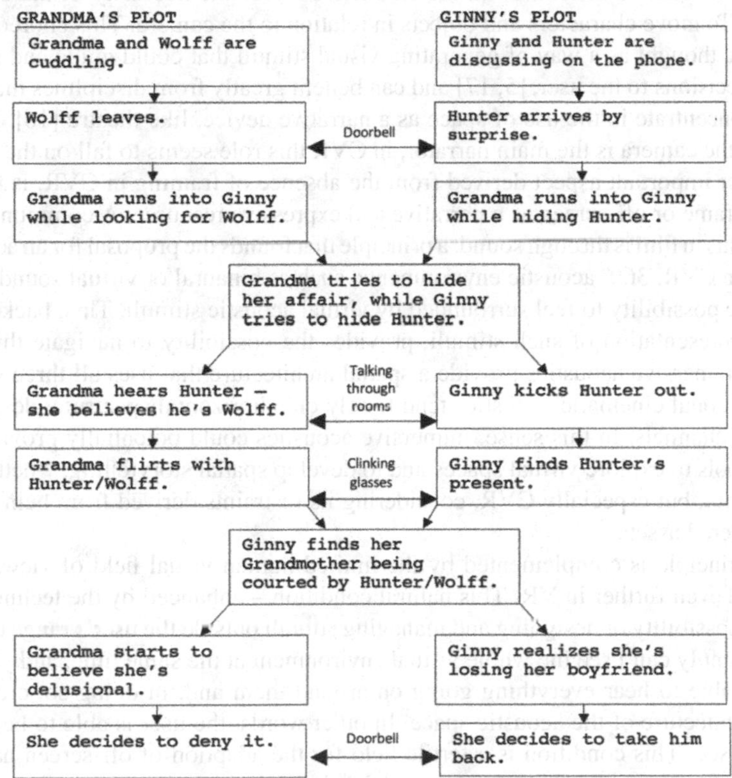

Fig. 5. Detailed diagram of the narrative structure of The Hunter & the Wolff. This merges Fig. 2 and Fig. 3, illustrating how the micronarratives are organized through the parallel timelines how these are interconnected with cue sounds.

Figure 5 illustrates how the two plots are organized simultaneously and shows, on the one hand, the moments where both plots merge spatially and, on the other, the sound cues that link parallel micronarratives. It also provides a visualization of how the two plots are intended to balance and complement each other.

4.2 Design

In this model, the virtual space is divided into three, which also has consistency with the environment: From left to right, the Grandmother's room, a Hall, and a Kitchen, which also provides a more instinctive and organic way to produce a mental map. In the script, the two main characters are relatively assigned one of the spaces, where most of their plots take place: Grandma's plot takes place mostly in her room, and Ginny's in the kitchen, while the hall serves as a transition area where characters meet each other and transit.

Spatial-narrative thinking greatly differs from traditional filmmaking; "it turned out that planning and shooting a film in 360° does not work the way it does in normal movies" [5]. Of the challenges for filming in CVR, the impossibility to frame is probably the easiest to spot. Of course, we lose the close-ups and, therefore, a very important tool to guide the spectator's attention to specific and sometimes small details. The impossibility place and move the camera in relation to the characters forces the necessity of the opposite approach: To move characters and objects in relation to the camera. This choreography ought to be thought as a way of generating visual stimuli that could guide and suggest possible decisions to the user, [5, 17] and can benefit greatly from disciplines that traditionally concentrate in the use of space as a narrative device, like theatre [16]. Indeed, if in films the camera is the main narrator, in CVR this role seems to fall on the space.

Another important aspect derived from the absence of framing in CVR, is the loss of out-of-frame or off-screen as a narrative and expressive resource. A common way to approach this in film is through sound, a principle that founds the proposal for an acoustic-guidance in CVR. 360º acoustic environments, such as binaural or virtual soundscapes, provide the possibility to feel surrounded by virtual acoustic stimuli. This, backed with a visual representation of such stimuli, provides the possibility to navigate this environment. Immersive acoustics provide a spatial architecture that uses all three vectors, while traditional cinematic acoustics tend to rely on a horizontal spectrum, despite the number of channels. In this sense, immersive acoustics could potentially provide very complex tools to explore virtual spaces and to develop spatial storytelling, whether cinematic or not, but especially CVR, considering its restraints derived from being based on prerendered assets.

This principle is complemented by the limited human visual field of view, which is hindered even further in VR. This natural condition – enhanced by the technology – offers the possibility of designing and managing stimuli outside the user's range of view. The user simply can't see the whole virtual environment at the same time, and yet, they should be able to hear everything going on around them and, in doing so, creating a mental architecture of the acoustic space. In other words, the user is able to hear what they don't see. This condition is a fertile field for the adaption of off-screen narrative in film language into an out-of-sight narrative in spatial storytelling: CVR provides the possibility to counterpoint visual and acoustic guidance, offering simultaneous and diverse stimuli to the user.

In CVR the camera becomes an embodiment of the user's presence, differently from film, where the camera is the narrator and a mediator between the spectator and the story, leaving them outside the storyworld. CVR requires the understanding that such mediation vanishes, facilitating the provision of agency to the user.

The user's narrative presence or embodiment has to be addressed as early as working in the script, since it affects the blocking and the relation actors, props, and scenery in the virtual environment have with the camera. We see that "in VR, framing and camera position correlate with each other even more than in normal film" [5], referring to the fact that camera position might have more drastic consequences for the user's immersion than those of the film camera to the film spectator, where the camera operates as a mediator instead of as a threshold [13].

The absence of mediation puts the user in a determining position from the start of the narrative, because the creation-of-sense of the world relies more on them than in a narrator that is now absence and has transferred their abilities to the user. The notion Initial Viewing Direction (IVD) is then crucial in immersive narratives, since they might determine the user's mental architecture of the narrative space for the rest of the story or, at the very least, the scene. Previous research shows that IVD is "accepted as the 'correct' viewing direction for both sitting and standing viewers, and the action is usually anticipated to begin there. Hence, the attention usually goes back to the IVD after the orientation phase, except when an attentional cue leads to a potential Point Of Interest (POI) somewhere else" [5]. In this proposal, which is based on the simultaneity of two plots with two main characters, the IVD might determine the perception that users have of the story. Considering there are two starting micronarratives taking place simultaneously at the very beginning of the piece, the IVD is assigned randomly by the system to provide equal chances of starting with one or the other character.

Once transported to the virtual environment, the user starts to make sensorial sense of the space. Immersive technologies so far have had a tendency to recreate naturalistic environments, particularly in the use of sound. On the contrary, this sound-based interactivity device challenged the naturalistic approach. To provide a more dramatic and interactive use of acoustic stimuli, sound mixes in each of the micronarratives are purposely manipulated to induce dramatic a reaction in the user, guiding them for narrative purposes. In other words, not only there are three independent acoustic spaces but also they are intervened to make them dramatically inter-dependent. The dramatic use of sound has a long history in screen-based media, and it makes sense that the acoustic aspect would play a significant role in immersive narratives, especially if we consider that "anecdotal reports indicate that sound has a highly significant impact on presence, and one study showed that spatialized sound was associated with higher reported presence than either no sound or non-spatialized sound" [21].

The conception of a dramatic and non-naturalistic approach to an acoustic landscape necessarily affects the design of the spaces, since sounds is one of the main perceptual accesses to the space. Considering that the story consists of two plots that take place in three spaces, one of the most relevant corrections was rethinking empty spaces. Throughout the overall story, at least one of the spaces always remains empty, either because one of the characters is absent or two of them are interacting in one of the rooms. This supposes many moments of wasted, undramatic spaces and the risk of having the user missing out part of the action(s) and, thus, being disoriented. Indeed, *Fear Of Missing Out* (FOMO, "a pervasive apprehension that others might be having rewarding experiences from which one is absent" [18]), which is usually understood as a risk and a liability of immersive drama, has been taken into consideration as an opportunity to enhance a dramatic engagement in the guidance device, a notion that can be summarized in the intention of users experiencing FOMO as a consequence of their own decisions – being forced to choose between two or more paths – and not because of the lack of guiding elements in the dramatic space.

This has been tackled with the notions of ON and OFF mixes. ON mixes correspond to the acoustic presence of elements and events that take place in the room where the gaze is centred at a specific moment – and any sound relevant to the actions according to the script – while OFF mixes correspond to the acoustic presence of sounds in the next room, primarily dialogues and other relevant sounds. In a way, this mechanic is related to the notion of *on-screen* and *off-screen* diegetic sounds frequently used in traditional filmmaking. Once again, this conception of the acoustic space doesn't respond at all to a naturalistic approach; ON and OFF mixes conveniently alternate in terms of functionality, requiring the OFF mix only when a room is empty, strongly suggesting the user, through sound, to move to the next room.

It is crucial to understand that OFF mixes are determined by the needs of each specific space. Each space is assigned ON and OFF mixes that are played continuously and simultaneously, but are mixed so they sound alternatively: They are always playing, but they turn quiet depending on the actions taking place in each room. For instance, when looking at the Bedroom when this is empty, then the Bedroom OFF mix would turn on, which corresponds to the sounds that come from the Hall, the room next door, guiding the user to assume that characters and actions are taking place in that room, as it can be seen in the bottom image of Fig. 6. Considering this prototype is still based on stereo mixing, this means that Bedroom OFF's sounds are concentrated on the right speaker – and also mixed according to spatial specifications, like lower volume and lower reverberation. This is why the Hall has two OFF mixes; one according to the room on each side. To illustrate in the top image of Fig. 6, when there are no actions taking place in the Hall, but there are in the other two rooms, if the user places their gaze in the Hall they will be able to hear the Hall OFF L mix on the left speaker (what is happening in the Bedroom) and the Hall OFF R mix on the right speaker (what is happening in Kitchen). In Fig. 7, we can see an illustration of how, while the Hall is empty, different actions are taking place in the other two rooms, which we could still hear through the OFF mixes.

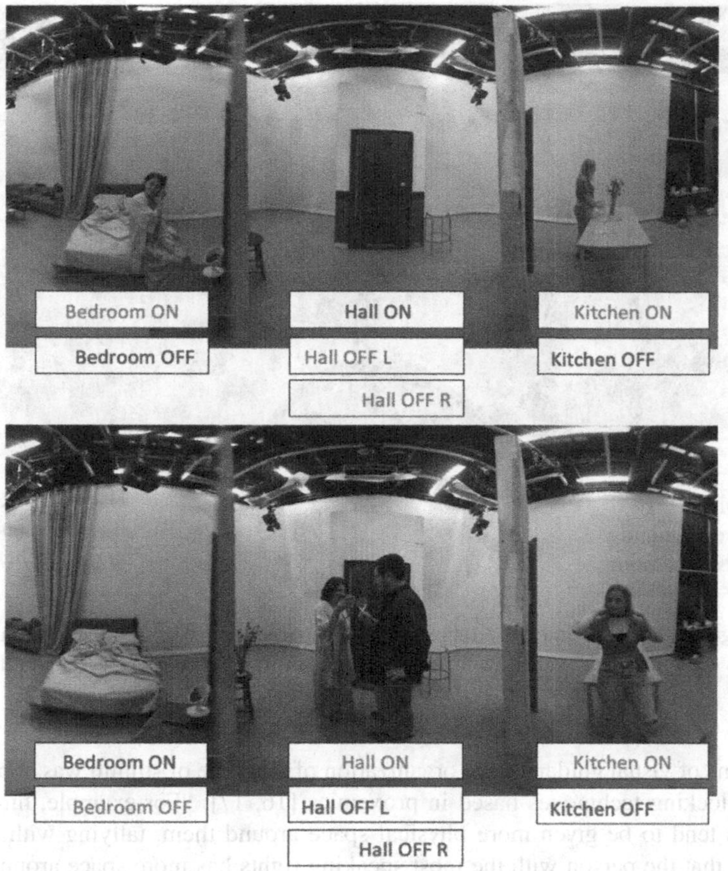

Fig. 6. Each of the three spaces contains a number of mixes (either 2 or 3). The figure shows how each mix "activates" depending on the actions taking place on each space.

If the acoustic dimension of this project has taken a particular prominence, it is because it is the main tool to provide guidance and facilitate hands-off reactions, the means through which the interactive environment and the user can establish a two-sided relation. In this specific type of interactivity guidance is a particularly delicate issue, since it has to be provided without breaking the illusion of freedom of agency nor the suspension-of-disbelief. Interactive narratives that rely on explicit and extra-diegetic guidance usually offer an interesting exploration experience but run the risk of attracting attention to the tool itself, undermining the immersion in the story. In this sense, extra-diegetic guidance, although sometimes fascinating by itself, can become an expression of the problem with threshold objects, which facilitates interaction while at the same time keeping the user from actually immersing [13].

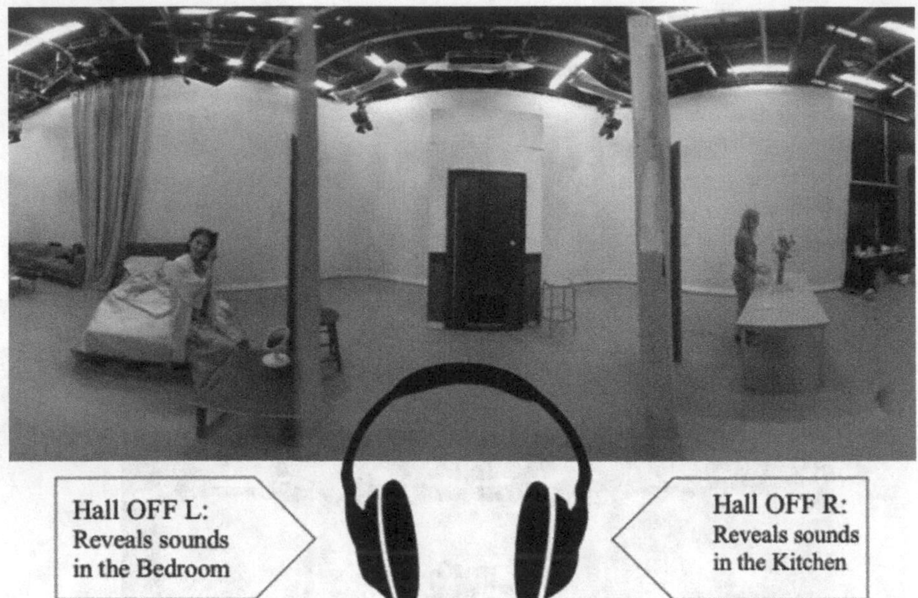

Fig. 7. Organization of sound deliverables: When a space is empty and no actions take place, OFF mixes come into play and allow users to become aware of what is happening in the spaces next door.

In terms of visual guidance, the organization of this type of stimuli was approached through blocking techniques based in proxemics [16, 17]: "For example, high status characters tend to be given more physical space around them, tallying with findings that show that the person with the most speaking rights has more space around them" and "rather than manipulating space in a fixed frame, such as close-ups and wide shots, actors can manipulate spatial relationships between one another in a way that is familiar in theatre and in everyday life" [16]. Positioning a character in a certain way can suggest they are to be followed, while still leaving an open option for other decisions.

Guidance through movement is mainly used as a device to track characters as they move from one room to other. For instance, when one character leaves one room to go to another, leaving another character alone in the first room. This movement supposes a decision the user must make between staying with one character or leave with the other. All these instances are specific points in the script that were conceived to propose a decision, and were brought into the blocking with this into consideration, but also in which most of the characters' own movements are driven by external factors and stimuli.

The main diegetic guidance methods used in this prototype were sound and movement. Through blocking, these elements were meant to motivate and potentiate each other – under the blocking principle that actions should always be motivated. For instance, sound cues and "off-sight" sounds (the immersive narrative equivalent to off-screen sounds) drive characters to move from one place to other. This is also the kind of stimuli that aims to suggest decision-making and to get the user's attention.

5 Results

The consultation process that served as a system-test consisted on observing how participants reacted to the prototype and focused on three main aspects: a) Perception and use of acoustic stimuli, b) perception and use of visual stimuli, and c) decision-making processes. It worth noting that participants weren't given a very detailed description of the prototype beforehand; they were only told to face forward until the end of an initial clock count as a way to have a referential starting point, and from then on they had the freedom to navigate as they wished.

Regarding the a) perception and use of acoustic stimuli, participants found that sound was a very important element within the narrative, that it helped them to place themselves within the immersive space, to re-orientate whenever they felt lost, to follow actions, and to make decisions. The system-test intended to see if the interdependent soundscapes would hinder the orientation process at the beginning of the film in any way. On the contrary, not only it didn't undermine this process; participants found it helpful to orientate themselves and to facilitate the immersion in the story.

In terms of b) perceptions and use of visual stimuli, initial observations show that movement caught the participants' attention, maybe even more than it was originally desired. In most of the cases, the secondary character was identified as the main one because of having a higher frequency in movement and his more frequent transits between the three rooms. This has several interesting implications. First, it undermines the original narrative intention of making the main characters the protagonists of their own interdependent plots, but that tended to move less and remain in one or two spaces precisely to keep the plots separated. It would become necessary to explore possible strategies to make the suggestion of these leading roles more emphatic, and develop blocking and directing strategies that would drive more attention to them. We know already that sound has proved to be very effective in this sense, so monologues, soliloquies, leitmotivs, extending the dialogues, or other dramatically relevant sounds could help. We also know that movement works in a very similar fashion, so making the characters move within the space they are already in could help to keep the attention focused on them. Finally, a more accurate and intended use of proxemics could be interesting to see how this affects the perception of the characters. Proximity has shown to be somewhat complicated, since some of the participants declared to feel discomfort when they felt that characters were too close to them, even when they weren't in an intimate space [16, 17]. The reasons for this were specially mentioned: invaded intimacy – in one or both directions – and losing field of vision, declaring that being too close to one character narrows the scope of vision.

For the most relevant aspect of this proposal, c) the decision-making process, participants of the consultation made a good part of their navigational decisions in a rather instinctive manner. On the one hand, the fact that they had to make decisions on the fly, without time to stop to think about them, generated a sense of urgency that made them feel more engaged not only with the environment but also with the story. Primarily, users indeed found themselves not stopping to consciously think about their decisions (instead, conscious decisions had to be made on the fly) but rather following the stimuli, in this case, mainly the acoustic ones, although not exclusively, as they were also driven by the characters. On the other hand, some of the participants described their decision-making process as more-or-less conscious, since they did realise they were making decisions but not necessarily *thinking* about them.

Participants weren't given a specific tutorial on the characteristics of the device before the test, which required of them to learn to use the system by themselves, which seemed to have taken a few seconds. The fact that participants didn't have any problem adapting themselves to the navigation method shows that the interactive device relies on instinctive reactions to stimuli more than on establishing a set of instructions for users to be followed. However, it is worth considering that these initial orientation moments could have been used for the sake of the story, and that this time could have been saved with a short set of instructions.

6 Conclusions

The overall design of an interactive story of this characteristics needs to consider the role and agency of the viewer, as well as the use and prioritization of different stimuli, both visual and acoustic. Participants confirmed what previous studies had found, that characters and elements that move tend to catch the viewers' attention, while more interestingly for this research, they also showed that acoustic stimuli not only helped to place themselves in the virtual environment, but also motivated them to explore the space, proving to be a very relevant tool for guidance. The adaptation of "off-screen" sounds into "off-sight" ones seems to have been proved successful in at least two dimensions: a) provides a dramatic spatial orientation, letting the user know that actions are taking place and where, and b) provides stimuli that motivate users to make decisions and navigate the dramatic space.

In terms of visual guidance, the use of theatrical blocking techniques proved to be very relevant not only to get the user's attention, but also to integrate the camera into the dramatic space, understanding, in the set, the camera is also a sort of and embodiment of the user. Even in the most passive treatment of the user, which is to assume them as a "fourth wall" type of spectator in which they don't integrate the dramatic space, the use of proxemics affects the hierarchy of visual stimulations that are intended to drive the user's decision-making. For instance, participants showed to be more inclined to follow characters that move, against those who are more anchored to one space. This is particularly relevant in a design like this, where following a character can drive you away from one action into another. This could suppose a grammar in which the relevance of characters and their actions might involve considering their movements and how they are presented in relation to the camera and other elements in the *mise-en-scène*.

Characters' movements are also relevant considering the importance of the Initial Viewing Direction (IVD), which tends to determine the user's initial choices. If in an IVD there's a character moving away, chances are that the user will probably follow this character. On the other hand, when the characters are still, users tend to make a quick exploration of the surrounding space, in the presumed safety that the character won't move yet. This also shows a sense of urgency that is quite determining in the decision-making process; when the story seems to be moving a little faster, users tend to make faster decisions, also motivated by fear-of-missing-out, in the conscience of the simultaneous actions.

It seems that the main aim of the CVR narrator would be to balance the stimuli directed to the user, in order to provide them with the moments and spaces to make narrative decisions. Despite being the elephant in the room, the incorporation of the user into the narrative is still the key challenge of immersive and interactive media, since creators can't longer hide behind a fourth wall and are being pushed to face the audience. Nevertheless, the adaptation and complementation of proved techniques from other expressive media are showing to be a fruitful enterprise.

7 Future Work

Precisely because the initial design for an instinct-based type of interactivity have had overall positive results, it is worth persisting in the exploration and experimentation of these methods for narrative purposes. The application of some of the key concepts related to diegetic stimuli to drive decision-making, hands-off interactivity, and the dramatic use of soundscaping, might be worth of further work not only in VR but in other immersive media as well. Considering the conditions proposed in this project, it doesn't seem impossible to apply them in MR or AR, as long as we count with suitable technology. For instance, one of the main conditions for the functionality of instinct-based decision-making is the absence of explicit interfaces that could generate a pull-back from diegetic immersion. With appropriate haptic devices, it seems feasible to imagine MR capable of providing such conditions, in which digitally generated diegetic elements blend with real environments. Similarly, dramatic soundscapes could be developed into a purely acoustic dimension, relying on binaural sound mixing or similar acoustic immersive means, as a way to provide a soundscape to a specific real location – in a museum, for instance – or simply as an independent sound-based storytelling medium. The main challenge for this would be, as it was for this project, to find the suitable technology that would gather inputs from the user(s) in order to generate the necessary dialogue for interactivity to exist. Either way, the conceptualization of these notions and a successful proof of concept, open the possibility to further explore them, and to test their resilience in other media.

On the other hand, due to the characteristics of the sample (and the disruptions generated by the global pandemic) it is important to acknowledge that these results do not intend to describe the behaviour of the audience, but to provide qualitative feedback on specific creative goals proposed for this prototype. In this sense, further research should also aim to obtain more conclusive evidence in regard of audience's behaviour towards these methods and this particular type of interactivity.

References

1. BBC R&D: StoryFormer: Building the Next Generation of Storytelling, 2 January 2019. https://www.bbc.co.uk/rd/blog/2018-10-object-based-media-tools-storyformer. Accessed 28 Feb 2022
2. Filmmaker Magazine: Look into the Cut: Jessica Brillhart on Editing VR. Online resource. https://filmmakermagazine.com/96090-look-into-the-cut/#.XVQAX5NKgWo. Accessed 28 Feb 2022

3. Crawford, C.: On Interactive Storytelling. New Riders, California (2005)
4. Ermi, L., Mäyrä, F.: Fundamental Components of the Gameplay Experience: Analysing Immersion. Digarec Series, vol. 06, pp. 88–115 (2011)
5. Gödde, M., Gabler, F., Siegmund, D., Braun, A.: Cinematic narration in VR – rethinking film conventions for 360 degrees. In: Chen, J.Y.C., Fragomeni, G. (eds.) VAMR 2018. LNCS, vol. 10910, pp. 184–201. Springer, Cham (2018). https://doi.org/10.1007/978-3-319-91584-5_15
6. Green, D., et al.: Using design fiction to explore the ethics of VR "in the wild". In: Proceedings of the 2019 ACM International Conference on Interactive Experiences for TV and Online Video, TVX 2019, Manchester, pp. 293–299 (2019). https://doi.org/10.1145/3317697.3323346
7. Haahr, M.: Creating location-based augmented-reality games for cultural heritage. In: Alcañiz, M., et al. (eds.) JCSG 2017. LNCS, vol. 10622, pp. 313–318. Springer, Cham (2017). https://doi.org/10.1007/978-3-319-70111-0_29
8. Jenkins, H.: Game design as narrative architecture. Computer **44** (2002)
9. Katz, H.: The Media Handbook: A Complete guide to Advertising Media Selection, Planning, Research, and Buying, 2nd edn. Taylor & Francis; Lawrence Erlbaum Associates, Publishers. Mahwah, New Jersey & London (2008)
10. Lotz, A.D.: The Television will be Revolutionized. New York University Press (2007)
11. Mateas, M.: A neo-aristotelian theory of interactive drama. In: Working Notes of the AAAI Spring Symposium on Artificial Intelligence and Interactive Entertainment. AAAI Press (2000)
12. Mateer, J.: Directing for cinematic virtual reality: how the traditional film director's craft applies to immersive environments and notions of presence. J. Media Pract. **18**(1), 14–25 (2017). https://doi.org/10.1080/14682753.2017.1305838
13. Murray, J.: Did it make you cry? Creating dramatic agency in immersive environments. In: Subsol, G. (ed.) ICVS 2005. LNCS, vol. 3805, pp. 83–94. Springer, Heidelberg (2005). https://doi.org/10.1007/11590361_10
14. Nielsen, L.T., et al.: Missing the point: an exploration on how to guide users' attention during cinematic virtual reality. In: Proceedings of the 2019 ACM International Conference on Interactive Experiences for TV and Online Video, TVX 2019, Manchester, pp. 229–232 (2019). https://doi.org/10.1145/2993369.2993405
15. Passmore, P., Glancy, M., Philpot, A., Fields, B.: 360 cinematic literacy: a case study. In: International Broadcasting Convention 2017, 14–18 September, Amsterdam (2017)
16. Pope, V.C., Dawest, R., Schweiger, F., Sheikh, A.: The geometry of storytelling: theatrical use of space for 360-degree videos and virtual reality. In: Proceedings of the 2017 CHI Conference on Human Factors in Computing Systems, CHI 2017, May 2017, pp. 4468–4478 (2017). https://doi.org/10.1145/3025453.3025581
17. Probst, P., Rothe, S., Hussmann, H.: Camera distances and shot sizes in cinematic virtual reality. In: ACM International Conference on Interactive Media Experiences, IMX 2021, 21–23 June 2021, Virtual Event, NY, USA, pp. 178–186. ACM, New York, NY, USA (2021). https://doi.org/10.1145/3452918.3458804
18. Przybylski, A.K., Murayama, K., DeHaan, C.R., Gladwell, V.: Motivational, emotional, and behavioral correlates of fear of missing out. Comput. Hum. Behav. **29**(4), 1841–1848 (2013). https://doi.org/10.1016/j.chb.2013.02.014(2013)
19. Ryan, M.L.: From narrative games to playable stories: towards a poetics of interactive narrative. Storyworlds J. Narrative Stud. **1**(2009), 43–59 (2009). University of Nebraska Press
20. Ryan, M.L.: The Interactive onion: layers of user participation in digital interactive texts. In: New Narratives: Stories and Storytelling in the Digital Age, pp. 43–59. University of Nebraska Press (2011)

21. Sanchez-Vives, M., Slater, M.: From Presence to consciousness through virtual reality. Nat. Rev. Neurosci. **6**, 332–339 (2005)
22. Speicher, M., Rosenberg, C., Degraen, D., Daiber, F., Krüger, A.: Exploring visual guiding in 360-degree videos. In: Proceedings of the 2019 ACM International Conference on Interactive Experiences for TV and Online Video, TVX 2019, Manchester, pp. 1–12 (2019). https://doi.org/10.1145/3317697.3323350
23. Unseld, S.: 5 Lessons Learned While Making Lost. Oculus Story Studio (2015). https://www.oculus.com/story-studio/blog/5-lessons-learned-while-making-lost/. Accessed 4 Feb 2020

The Application of Immersive Virtual Reality for Children's Road Education: Validation of a Pedestrian Crossing Scenario

Giulia De Cet[1,2](✉), Andrea Baldassa[2,3], Mariaelena Tagliabue[2,3,4], Riccardo Rossi[2,3], Chiara Vianello[1,3], and Massimiliano Gastaldi[2,3,4]

[1] Department of Industrial Engineering, University of Padua, 35131 Padua, Italy
{giulia.decet,chiara.vianello}@unipd.it

[2] Mobility and Behavior Research Center - MoBe, University of Padua, 35131 Padua, Italy
andrea.baldassa@dicea.unipd.it, {riccardo.rossi, massimiliano.gastaldi}@unipd.it

[3] Department of Civil, Environmental and Architectural Engineering, University of Padua, 35131 Padua, Italy

[4] Department of General Psychology, University of Padua, 35131 Padua, Italy
mariaelena.tagliabue@unipd.it

Abstract. Human beings face the matter of transportation and mobility from their early childhood, as vulnerable non-motorized users; besides, road injuries represent one of the leading causes of death for children. This work investigated the possibility of using virtual reality (VR) for educational purposes for road safety. Specifically, through the observation of children's behavior, a preliminary validation of an immersive virtual reality environment related to a pedestrian crossing scenario (signal and no signal-controlled), a critical component in road safety, was performed. An experiment was carried out, involving 46 middle school students aged between 11 and 13 years. Participants, wearing the headset, crossed the road in a virtual environment designed and implemented with Unity® software. The scenario consisted of training and trial sessions both one-way and two ways, with and without traffic signal. The goal of this preliminary work was to validate the pedestrian crossing scenario in order to use VR as a tool for Road Education. The results of this first analysis are promising: user's behavior in the experiment was rather consistent with that in the real world. 31 participants waited for the green light to cross, and 11 crossed with the red light matching what the participants declared in a previous survey. Besides, the analysis indicated that the average crossing speed recorded during the experiment was consistent with the one reported in the literature.

Keywords: Children · Virtual reality · Pedestrian crossing · Road safety · Human movement behavior

1 Introduction

Vulnerable road users are essentially pedestrians, cyclists and motorcyclists. They are considered as vulnerable due to the two drawbacks they face in potential accidents [1]:

L. T. De Paolis et al. (Eds.): XR Salento 2022, LNCS 13446, pp. 128–140, 2022.
https://doi.org/10.1007/978-3-031-15553-6_10

(a) except helmets, they do not have any protective shield in case of collision and (b) their mass, being significantly lower than the one of cars and trucks, is a major disadvantage in potential crashes. This is why their probability of being injured or killed in an accident is much higher than, for example, a car driver. Pedestrians and cyclists, as a category, encompass an extremely heterogeneous range of age. This allows the range of cognitive, visual and motor skills of the samples to be broadened.

The need for the Transportation Laboratory to open a research section dedicated to the vulnerable non-motorized users is also driven by the data on road accidents recently reported in the annual report of the National Institute of Statistics – ISTAT. In Italy in 2019, according to data published by ISTAT [2], road accidents were more than 450 per day. It was indicated that 8 people died every day in road accidents and that at least one of them was indeed a pedestrian. 3.5% of traffic crashes in Italy are caused by vehicles not giving right of way to pedestrians (21 per day).

Given the strong social impact of the phenomenon, numerous studies have focused on improving safety for pedestrians on the road environment. Innovative educational methodologies and possible operational or infrastructural interventions were proposed to increase safety in urban contexts.

1.1 Background

Noticeably, several studies in the literature tried to examine children's behavior in the road environment as pedestrians to prevent injury [3], to find a safe route for crossing the road [4] by using many methodologies and tools, e.g. virtual reality equipment.

The choice of virtual reality is dictated by the many advantages it presents, obviating all the pitfalls related to risk during field tests. VR simulators allow to collect variables describing road user's behavior in different hazard road situations, in a safe and controlled area, and save time and money. Regarding the study of pedestrian behavior, the set of observations that can be collected during a VR experiment makes it possible to carry out statistical analyses on the average crossing speed, on reaction times, on the choice of crossing gap, on influence of age and gender on the previous variables, etc.

However, it has to be noted that, in order to use data recorded within simulated scenarios, these technologies must be validated. What happens in a VR could be different from events occurring in real life (probably for lack of risk of the first). The validity of VR as a tool to measure road users' behavior is currently debated within the research community. Researches are trying to support VR (on different levels: immersive, semi-immersive, non-immersive) as an effective instrument to analyze users' behavior and for the design and execution of specific educational exercises. On condition that its validity is ascertained through appropriate validation, the general indication is that VR is a powerful tool for investigating road users' behavior (in particular for children).

Deb et al. [5] developed a pedestrian simulator and analyzed its effectiveness in reproducing a risky scenario where pedestrians had to cross an intersection. Bhagavathula et al. [6] also tried to demonstrate that user behavior in VR and the real world can be considered consistent, testing 16 participants crossing a real intersection subsequently reproduced in a virtual environment too. McComas et al. [7] tried to demonstrate the validity of using VR to educate children about good rules for crossing in real urban contexts. The goal was to reduce the accidents of children through training sessions that taught children the procedures to safely cross the road and minimize the risks associated with the maneuver. A total of 95 children, of different ages and background, were involved. Their behavior during the crossing phase was observed both before and after the training sessions, highlighting a significant improvement in performance from the point of view of the attention paid to the maneuver, especially for subjects in an extra-urban context.

Schwebel et al. [3] tried to demonstrate the validity of VR as a tool to understand the dynamics of vehicle-pedestrian (child) accidents and to prevent injuries. 102 children and 74 adults were recruited to complete the same crossing in both VR and the real world. This study, like those previously cited, indicates that it is possible to use VR to collect information with excellent reliability without resorting to field experiments.

Tzanavari et al. [8] built a VR experiment using CAVE with children who have to cross an intersection in an urban context. Also in this case VR proved to be a valid learning tool; their results indicated that immersion and traffic noise seem to affect children's performance.

The pedestrian-pedestrian interaction is another aspect to be taken into consideration, as reported in Nelson et al. [9]. A group of 18 subjects took part in a series of VR experiments with five different possible levels of pedestrian density: for the highest levels of crowding, a change in the participants' behavior was actually recorded, both in terms of speed (increases with the density) and trajectory followed (less linear as the density increases).

Reaction time (RT) is also a frequently investigated variable in the literature. The RTs of the young road users are influenced by disparate factors [10], such as gender, age and context complexity.

Virtual reality, inter alia, was also applied as a methodology to educate and train children to harmlessly cross the street. Indeed, McComas et al. [7] observed an increase in children's caution after the administration of VR trials. What was acquired in the virtual world was transferred to the real world.

The first aim of this study was to verify if the children's behavior observed at pedestrian crossings built-in virtual reality, can be considered similar to that observed at a real crosswalk. For this reason, in this paper a study that tries to validate a crossing scenario through the observation of children's behavior at traffic signals using immersive virtual reality is proposed.

The paper is organized as follows: Sect. 2 describes the methodology of the study; Sect. 3 presents the results obtained from the experiment; Sect. 4 discusses how these results are related to the goals declared and concludes with future developments.

1.2 Aims of the Study

The present study is part of the wider SID project "Safety of vulnerable road users: experiments in virtual environment" (2020–2022), funded by the University of Padua. This research embodies an opportunity to address the issue of mobility, with the aid of new technologies. At the moment, such technologies are, at least in Italy, rarely used in this research area and only few hours of Road Safety Education are taught during the school years. However, while this is an essential first step, students are unlikely to pay attention to the topic until they obtain a driving license. In this sense, this work proves to be innovative both in its educational objectives and in the means employed to achieve them. It is worth noticing that one of the goals of the Sustainable Development, within SDG 11, is to improve road safety by 2030 [11, 12]. In this respect, the project happens to be an opportunity to raise awareness about this crucial issue among young people. By creating a culture of safe and sustainable mobility, it will be possible to have careful road users, aware of changes, innovations in transportation modes and services, as well as environmental issues.

The goals of the above mentioned project include:

- Structuring a procedure for the creation of effective immersive virtual road scenarios for vulnerable road users' safety analysis;
- Creating and testing effective immersive virtual road scenarios for vulnerable road users' safety analysis;
- Identifying effective strategies to spread the culture of road safety (such as strategies for teaching children to cross roads safely, with the repeatability and risk-free advantages of virtual reality);
- Developing a procedure for the validation of virtual reality as a tool to prevent road accidents;
- Collecting data to design safer real-world infrastructures (e.g., traffic-calming interventions outside schools).

The present work aims at achieving the first two of the above-mentioned goals. Specifically, this work aims to validate immersive VR pedestrian crossing scenarios through the observation of children's behavior for future use of the tool for road safety educational purposes. In particular, one hypothesis was to observe performance parameter values (average crossing speed) coherent with the results provided by the literature. Second, we expected to find an overlap between the performance observed during the VR experience and the real behavior of the participants as measured in the questionnaire administered.

2 Procedure

Broadly speaking, the experiment examines children's behavior in a road environment. In the first part of the inquiry, participants were asked a series of general questions about mobility (e.g.: By what means do you go to school? How much do you walk per week?), and a questionnaire was administered to investigate their conduct as pedestrians [13]. In the second part, participants, wearing the headset, were asked to cross a street in a virtual environment.

2.1 Ethical Approval

The experiments were carried out in Trento (Italy), in a suitable space made available by the host organization (see Fig. 1). The study was conducted in compliance with the Code of Ethics of the World Medical Association (Declaration of Helsinki, Williams, 2008) and the experimental protocol was approved by the Ethical Committee for the Psychological Research of the University of Padua (protocol number 4307, 1/10/2021). From each participant, before the study, we obtained the written informed consent signed by parents.

Fig. 1. Experiment setting.

2.2 Simulator

The Pedestrian simulation device at the Transportation Laboratory (University of Padua) is a compact/portable wearable system produced by HP® (see Fig. 2). The apparatus is equipped with a backpack PC (HP Backpack VR G2) and a Reverb headset (HP Reverb VR Headset G2), delivering an immersive, comfortable, and compatible experience. The resolution is 2160 × 2160 LCD panels per eye, and a full RGB stripe. The headset also includes Valve speakers and sit off the ear by 10 mm. The simulation device allows a natural free-roam VR experience and the analysis of pedestrian behavior in road hazard situations. The strong point of this simulator is its compactness, the absence of cables as a connection to a fixed PC in the room allows a natural movement of the participants [9]. Not being a wireless device is also obviated the problem of latency, one of the causes of simulator sickness.

Fig. 2. Pedestrian simulator of Transportation Laboratory – University of Padua.

2.3 Participants

Forty-six voluntary participants (28 females, mean age 12.04) were recruited. They were: middle school students; all with normal or corrected to normal vision; aged between 11 and 13 years; naïve with the simulator. No participants dropped out of the study due to simulator sickness.

2.4 Scenario

After a careful analysis of the literature, an immersive road environment was designed and implemented, thanks to Unity® software (Unity LTS 2020.3.23f1). Scenario development in Unity is done through the use of C# scripts, which allow for scenario object management, positioning and logic management, as well as collecting data. The sampling frequency of the variables during each trial of the experiment was 10 Hz.

The environment was shaped considering realistic elements' dimensions. The guidelines for the design of crosswalks in Italy recommend a speed not exceeding 1 m/s in the design phase in order to include those with a slower gait. During the design phase this parameter has been taken as a reference. In the environment, no unevenness was created between road elements in order to prevent subjects from raising their legs as if to step onto the sidewalk and not finding a different thickness. For traffic lights setting and crossing design, measurements were taken in the real road environment.

The experiment consisted of 2 training sessions and 14 trials (see Table 1), the training sessions presenting two crosswalks (one 1-way and one 2-ways).

The 14 trials were then equally divided into 1-way (see Fig. 3) and 2-way (see Fig. 4). The following experimental situations were presented: no traffic signal, presence of green traffic signal, presence of red traffic signal, presence of traffic signal with a steady yellow light, presence of traffic signal that was off, presence of traffic signal with onset of yellow light when the participant was in the middle of the crossing, and presence of traffic signal with onset of yellow light when the participant stepped off the curb. The trials were introduced in random order.

Fig. 3. 1-way crosswalk in virtual environment. On the left without traffic signal, on the right with a traffic signal.

Fig. 4. 2-ways crosswalk in virtual environment. On the left without traffic signal, on the right with a traffic signal.

Participants were subdivided into two groups, counterbalanced by gender. The first one performed the 1-way training and trials first (see Fig. 5), whereas the second group the 2-ways training and trials first (see Fig. 6). Both Group 1 and Group 2 consisted of 14 females and 9 males.

Training 1 (1-way) → 7 trials (1-way) → Training 2 (2-ways) → 7 trials (2-ways)

Fig. 5. Sequence for group 1.

Fig. 6. Sequence for group 2.

Table 1. Description of training and trial sessions of the experiment.

Type	Ways	Traffic signal
Training	1	No
Trial	1	No
Trial	1	Turned off
Trial	1	Green
Trial	1	Red
Trial	1	Steady yellow light
Trial	1	Onset of yellow light when participant is in the middle of the crossing
Trial	1	Onset of yellow light when the participant steps off the curb
Training	2	No
Trial	2	No
Trial	2	Turned off
Trial	2	Green
Trial	2	Red
Trial	2	Steady yellow light
Trial	2	Onset of yellow light that when participant is in the middle of the crossing
Trial	2	Onset of yellow light when the participant steps off the curb

2.5 Variables

Considering the trials (1-way and 2-ways) with red light, the variables investigated were:

- The *reaction time* (s) from the moment of the light turning green to when the subject steps off the curb (for subject who have waited for the green light to cross);
- The *average crossing speed* (m/s) with the green light and with the red light (for subjects who have crossed with red light).

Considering the 2-ways trial with the green light, the variable investigated was the *average crossing speed* (m/s).

3 Analysis and Results

In this study, the behavior of children when facing a red and green light was examined. Data were analyzed with the aid of JASP Software [14].

With reference to the trials with red light, of the 46 participants:

- In both trials (1-way and 2-ways), 31 participants waited for the green light to cross;
- 11 participants crossed both times (1-way and 2-ways) with the red light;
- 1 participant crossed a single time on a red light;

- 3 participants were off the curb when the light was red (for this reason, RTs could not be calculated as defined).

3.1 Comparison of Behavior in Reality and in the Virtual Environment

The first analysis performed aims to investigate whether the behavior the user had during the experiment was consistent with the conduct as pedestrian stated during the administered surveys. For this reason, we focused on the particular case of the red light. Was their behavior consistent with their initial claims about crossing the road even with red light? In order to determine if this relationship exists, a contingency analysis was carried out between the two categorical variables. We categorized the 42 participants into those who claimed in the self-report that they crossed on red (11) and those who reported that they never did (31). χ^2 statistic with continuity correction ($\chi^2(1) = 8.144$, $p < 0.004$, $\varphi = 0.5$) suggested that there was a significant association between behavior and self-report questionnaire answer. Since the data set was a small sample and the table in one cell has an expected count of less than 5, continuity correction was applied to prevent overestimation of statistical significance [15]. This result showed that the children's behavior during the experiment was consistent with their behavior in real life for the road crossing scenario.

3.2 Reaction Time

The reaction time of the 31 participants that waited for the green light to cross was calculated. A repeated measure ANOVA was performed on RTs, with Trials (1st and 2sd trial with red light) as the within-participants factor. No significant effect was found ($p = 0.196$). This result indicates that there is no learning factor between the two trials due to familiarity. This result supports the use of VR simulator, as a safety tool; and it is important to note that the absence of a learning factor can be an excellent starting point for future developments.

3.3 Average Crossing Speed

The average crossing speed of the 11 participants crossing both trials with a red light, was calculated. Moreover, for the 11 the average crossing speed was calculated for the green light trials. A one-way ANOVA was performed to examine the effect of Kind of road (1-way and 2-ways) and Traffic signal colors (red/green) on crossing speed. No main effects of Kind of road ($p = 0.255$), colors ($p = 0.713$) and interaction ($p = 0.908$) were found. These results indicate that there is no difference in crossing speed between the two Kind of road (1-way and 2-ways) situations and no difference in crossing speed when the Traffic signal is red and when the Traffic signal is green (see Fig. 7).

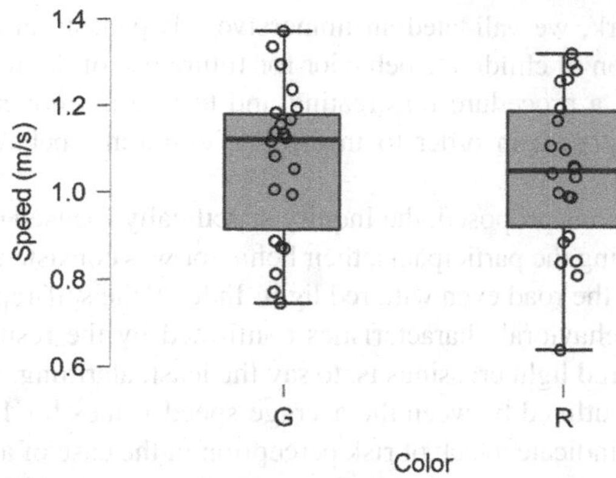

Fig. 7. Boxplot of crossing speed when the Traffic signal is red and green.

The average crossing speed of the 46 participants was calculated for the green light trial (2-ways). A one-sample t-test was performed, in order to verify if the speed obtained is consistent with other values in the literature. Comparing with the average walking speed (1.096 m/s) while crossing from the study by Deb et al. [5] (crosswalk's length ≈ 2-ways) under no-traffic conditions the one-sample t-test test showed no significant difference in speed compared to the design parameter ($t(45) = -1.475$, $p = 0.147$) (see Fig. 8).

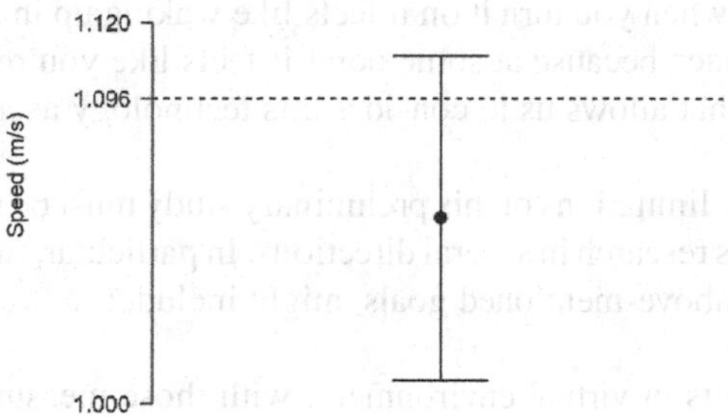

Fig. 8. Descriptive plot of one sample t-test comparing the average crossing speed of the 46 participants with literature value (1.096 m/s).

4 Conclusions and Future Developments

The usefulness of this work is supporting the use of VR simulators as reliable research tools to reproduce real pedestrian's behavior at crosswalks. This paper dealt with the issues above with specific reference to children's behavior at a pedestrian crossing.

One of the great advantages of VR consists in being able to study and stage risky situations that are not feasible in the real world (e.g. vehicle-pedestrian collision). The behavior of the participants was analyzed, highlighting a correspondence between the procedures they followed in VR and the common norms of the real world.

In the present work, we validated an immersive VR pedestrian crossing scenario through the observation of children's behavior for future use of the tool for road safety educational purposes: a procedure for creating and testing an immersive virtual road environment was proposed, in order to investigate children's behavior in crosswalk contexts.

Among the conditions proposed, the inquiry specifically focused on the case of red traffic signals. Regarding the participants, their behavior was consistent with their initial claims about crossing the road even with red light. Indeed, the self-report questionnaire allowed us to infer behavioral characteristics confirmed by the results obtained. The average speed during red light crossings is, to say the least, alarming. Indeed, no significant difference was outlined between the average speed values for 1-way and 2-ways crossings. This could indicate a lack of risk perception in the case of a 2-ways crossing: participants did not increase their speed; this needs further consideration. These first qualitative considerations certainly deserve future in-depth analysis; should these data be confirmed, a road safety education program will be necessary. Moreover, their crossing speed in the cases of green or red light does not change. Contrary to what one might imagine, children do not increase their speed (e.g. by running) in the case of red light.

Furthermore, the results found, in terms of crossing speed, are comparable to those of Deb et al. [5] and this also highlights the goodness of the scenario created.

In the end, the use of a VR seems to allow an adequate analysis of children's behavior at a pedestrian crossing. The experiment, here presented, confirmed that the children were completely involved in the virtual scenarios and behaved like in real-life situations.

It is also important to note that participants said they felt completely immersed in the scenario and "that when you turn it on it feels like waking up in a new world; it's so strange to be in that place because at some point it feels like you're really there." This is an important point that allows us to consider this technology as an excellent tool for road education.

Nevertheless, some limitations of this preliminary study must be noted and it appears necessary to extend this research in several directions. In particular, further developments to achieve the several above-mentioned goals, might include:

- Comparison of results in virtual environment, with those measured in real environment;
- Comparison of RTs results with a model to predict them; as in a study [16] conducted in Croatia, where a model for the prediction of reaction times of children in real traffic conditions was thus developed; we will implement models to predict children's RTs at crosswalks, calibrated using VR simulator data;
- Expansion of the sample of subjects both in terms of size and composition in order to better represent a real population of pedestrians; a replication of this study with a different sample of pedestrians (e.g., elderly people) will be conducted;
- Evaluate the effect of VR training at different time intervals (e.g., after one week, three months, one year, etc.) as in a study conducted in Iran [17] in which children's behaviors were observed respectively before, 1 week after, and 6 months after the intervention;
- Analysis of factors that could affect pedestrian behavior (speed and type of approaching vehicles on the main road, different visibility conditions);

- Further validation of other scenarios and the equipment;
- Presentation of results to the students involved and consequent reflections about road safety;
- Involvement of other schools to spread the culture of road safety through experiences with virtual reality (a new "Road Education");
- Analysis of road user interactions;
- The addition of eye-tracking instrumentations and the study of head movements;
- Design of new experiments enhancing the effective learning of correct pedestrian behaviors dynamically and entertainingly;
- Design a simulation environment with different soil thicknesses in order to make the experiment even more immersive.

Acknowledgments. The authors would like to thank Matteo Gardin for the support in designing the experiment; and Professor Tiziana Chiara Pasquini, head teacher of "Istituto Comprensivo Aldeno-Mattarello" and "Associazione Culturale Vogliam Cantare" for actively participating in the study during the data collection phase.

This study was financed by University of Padua (Project ID: BIRD200213/20 "Safety of vulnerable road user: experiments in virtual environment"). The work was carried out within the scope of the project "useinspired basic research" for which the Department of General Psychology of the University of Padua has been recognized as "Dipartimento di Eccellenza" by the Ministry of University and Research.

Author Contributions. The authors confirm contribution to the paper as follows: Conceptualization, G.D.C., M.T. and M.G; software, G.D.C.; formal analysis, G.D.C., M.T., and M.G; investigation, G.D.C.; data curation, G.D.C.; writing—original draft preparation, G.D.C. and A.B.; writing—review and editing, G.D.C., A.B., M.T., R.R., C.V. and M.G; supervision, M.G.; funding acquisition, M.G.. All authors have read and agreed to the published version of the manuscript.

References

1. Shinar, D.: Traffic Safety and Human Behavior (2017)
2. ISTAT: Incidenti stradali - Anno 2019 (2020)
3. Schwebel, D.C., Gaines, J., Severson, J.: Validation of virtual reality as a tool to understand and prevent child pedestrian injury. Accid. Anal. Prev. (2008). https://doi.org/10.1016/j.aap.2008.03.005
4. Ampofo-Boateng, K., Thomson, J.A., Grieve, R., Pitcainr, T., Lee, D.N., Demetre, J.D.: A developmental and training study of children's ability to find safe routes to cross the road. Br. J. Dev. Psychol. (1993). https://doi.org/10.1111/j.2044-835x.1993.tb00586.x
5. Deb, S., Carruth, D.W., Sween, R., Strawderman, L., Garrison, T.M.: Efficacy of virtual reality in pedestrian safety research. Appl. Ergon. (2017). https://doi.org/10.1016/j.apergo.2017.03.007
6. Bhagavathula, R., Williams, B., Owens, J., Gibbons, R.: The reality of virtual reality: a comparison of pedestrian behavior in real and virtual environments. In: Proceedings of the Human Factors and Ergonomics Society (2018)
7. McComas, J., MacKay, M., Pivik, J.: Effectiveness of virtual reality for teaching pedestrian safety. In: Cyberpsychology and Behavior (2002)

8. Tzanavari, A., Matsentidou, S., Christou, C.G., Poullis, C.: User experience observations on factors that affect performance in a road-crossing training application for children using the CAVE. In: Zaphiris, P., Ioannou, A. (eds.) LCT 2014. LNCS, vol. 8524, pp. 91–101. Springer, Cham (2014). https://doi.org/10.1007/978-3-319-07485-6_10
9. Nelson, M.G., Koilias, A., Gubbi, S., Mousas, C.: Within a virtual crowd: exploring human movement behavior during immersive virtual crowd interaction. In: Proceedings - VRCAI 2019: 17th ACM SIGGRAPH International Conference on Virtual-Reality Continuum and Its Applications in Industry (2019)
10. Hillier, L.M., Morrongiello, B.A.: Age and gender differences in school-age children's appraisals of injury risk. J. Pediatr. Psychol. (1998). https://doi.org/10.1093/jpepsy/23.4.229
11. Agbedahin, A.V.: Sustainable development, Education for Sustainable Development, and the 2030 Agenda for Sustainable Development: emergence, efficacy, eminence, and future. Sustain. Dev. (2019). https://doi.org/10.1002/sd.1931
12. Wismans, J., Thynell, M., Lindberg, G.: Economics of road safety – what does it imply under the 2030 agenda for sustainable development? In: Intergovernmental Tenth Regional Environmentally Sustainable Transport (EST) Forum in Asia, Vientiane, Lao PDR, 14–16 March 2017 (2017)
13. Granié, M.A., Pannetier, M., Guého, L.: Developing a self-reporting method to measure pedestrian behaviors at all ages. Accid. Anal. Prev. (2013). https://doi.org/10.1016/j.aap.2012.07.009
14. Love, J., et al.: JASP: graphical statistical software for common statistical designs. J. Stat. Softw. (2019). https://doi.org/10.18637/jss.v088.i02
15. Goss-Sampson, M.A.: Statistical analysis in JASP: a guide for students (2019)
16. Otkovia, I.I.: A model to predict children's reaction time at signalized intersections. Safety (2020). https://doi.org/10.3390/safety6020022
17. Zare, H., Niknami, S., Heidarnia, A., Fallah, M.H.: Improving safe street-crossing behaviors among primary school students: a randomized controlled trial. Heal. Promot. Perspect. (2018). https://doi.org/10.15171/hpp.2018.44

Collaborative VR Scene Broadcasting for Geometry Education

YanXiang Zhang(✉) and JiaYu Wang

Department of Communication of Science and Technology, University of Science and Technology of China, Hefei, Anhui, China
Petrel@ustc.edu.cn, Jiayu0909@mail.ustc.edu.cn

Abstract. Virtual reality (VR) is promising for future education, and teachers need student management to improve class effectiveness. The authors absorb the broadcasting advantages of video teaching, put forward a VR scene broadcasting (VRSB) for geometry education. VRSB includes a database (DB) and an active server page (ASP) and a distributed database (DDB), which enables teachers and students to enjoy different permissions and statuses to satisfy teachers' teaching management and stimulate students' creativity through interactive collaboration and independent exploration.

Keywords: Virtual reality · Scene broadcast · Geometry education · Mechanic education

1 Introduction

Constructivism focuses on the importance of learners actively constructing their knowledge through a more experiential model. Kolb's learning cycle is one of the better known, which defines learning in four steps—concrete experience, reflective observation, abstract conceptualization, and active experimentation [1]. In current education, abstract geometry, the invisible surface of the stars in the universe, microstructure, and so on lack concrete experience and direct observation. A virtual learning environment (VLE) allows learners to explore environments and situations that would be rare to visit in the real world [2], which is beneficial to the current situation. Schunk defines Social Cognitive Theory as learning that occurs within a social environment through observation and emulation of others. That means we learn by observing others and validating our outcomes by their reactions [3]. VLE allows learners to collaborate at different scales [4] or in different spaces [5]. That shows VLE can realize greater possibilities for collaboration in digital mediums, like remote participation and innovative multiuser interactions.

Due to its immersive and interactive nature, VR has the advantage of understanding abstract concepts. For individuals, users can observe objects from various angles and pick them up for close observation by wearing VR devices. However, the individual scene of VR experience is not enough for teaching scenes, and it is common for teachers to teach many students. In broadcasting video teaching, many online teaching platforms assist

L. T. De Paolis et al. (Eds.): XR Salento 2022, LNCS 13446, pp. 141–149, 2022.
https://doi.org/10.1007/978-3-031-15553-6_11

teachers in managing students and courses, which helps improve teaching efficiency. The authors think it can draw lessons from broadcasting video teaching to form VR scene broadcast mode when teaching applied VR. As for teaching in VR, which is not enough to manage students' check-in and online duration, and the interaction is not only dialogue but more cooperation in action. Assessment may also change from filling in and correcting to observing students' operation, which is more personalized and teachers cannot handle in batches. Thus, this article aims to design a system that aids teachers in managing the class efficiently and promotes cooperation among students at the same time. The system is mainly applied to practice teaching, making students do experiments on their initiative to gain experience and knowledge, which gives full play to the maximum benefit of VR education.

2 Related Work

2.1 Development of VR in Geometry Education

Geometry exists in people's daily lives, and one critical aspect is the ability to understand and convey spatial relationships. Spatial understanding is not an ability that people are born with, and it requires practice to develop [6]. Leopold showed that the students could mainly improve spatial visualization abilities in two ways. The first is sketching and drawing 3D objects, and the second is creating and working on 3D models [7]. It is difficult for students to understand geometry, particularly abstract geometry, through 2D pictures or videos in traditional video teaching because they have few opportunities to experiment and observe. The results of N. K. Andreasen et al.'s study show a significant interaction between media and methods in process knowledge presentation, with VR groups having the highest performance [8]. VR can provide a virtual space for users to manipulate 3D objects, allowing students to generate experiential knowledge and strengthen memory in geometry.

2.2 Possible Solutions to Facilitate VR Collaboration

Individual VR experiences do an excellent job of enhancing understanding of abstract concepts. It is also vital to promote multi-person interaction for teaching based on social cognition theory. Collaborative virtual reality (CVR) provides different users with a flexible perspective, emphasizing a shared environment and content-centric to drive collaboration [9]. Kaufmann et al. designed a 3D geometric construction tool, Construct3D, which realizes multi-view interaction in multi-person real-time scenes through a decentralized network [10]. In Construct3D, any changes in data will synchronize with everyone else, which may create chaos. In addition to CVR, social games and social VR can also enrich interaction and collaboration. Lai C et al. create a game about manipulating the volumes of the shapes in a VR environment. Students who complete the geometry tasks earn points and rankings [11]. The game rules make the class more exciting but risk making teaching over-entertaining.

Both CVR and social VR lack management, which results in inefficient teaching [12] and shifts the students' focus out of the teaching content. Therefore, the authors propose the VRSB, which applies to the scene of one teacher facing a group of students. VRSB Promotes collaboration through VR interactive experience and teaching plan design. Teachers and students have different permissions, aiming to achieve management, control, collaboration, interaction, and other behaviors required for the application scenes of teaching collaboration. This article will take geometry education as an example to expound on the design and implementation of VRSB and illustrate the flexibility of VRSB in different cases.

3 Design

3.1 Infrastructure of VRSB

The infrastructure of VRSB includes Distribution Network (D-Web), DDB, DB, and ASP. Based on web VR, VRSB allows users to create and search for information on the Internet. It can realize the one-to-many online teaching scene by expanding the users' creation to virtual environments for other users' interactions. However, each user's hardware and network systems are heterogeneous [13]. First of all, VRSB uses D-Web to change the data transmission mode from centralized to distributed, reducing the possibility of a single node failure and the delay value in the VR framework [14]. Besides, DDB is used to store and update information, which has the advantages of shortening the service time and enhancing security. It includes Gun DB and Orbit DB, and it utilizes the Collision Free Replication Data Type (CRDT) to synchronize data [15]. VRSB uses Gun DB as storage for shared state and its updates. Gun DB uses a state-based CRDT for solid consistency and communicates the system's state at any time among its peers without centralized authorization [16]. Finally, VRSB introduces a general DB to manage users and set up user permissions, and it achieves dynamic access to DDB through Active Server Pages (ASP) [17]. The application of web VR and DDB forms Distributed virtual environment (DVE), which makes the virtual display platform more extensible and collaborative. Due to its cost-effectiveness, reproducibility, and security, DVE applied in education can enable teachers and students to share information through VR equipment, meet the needs of teachers for scene editing, and promote the improvement of teaching efficiency.

3.2 Independent Expanding Space and Shared Space

Demonstration and collaboration in the teaching process need unified focus and shared space. In VRSB, all students and teachers have the same immersive teaching space. They also have their own independent expanding space to complete real-time interaction and an independent learning environment. The authors construct a framework for broadcast teaching called VRSB to realize that. VRSB includes basic data and derived data [18]. All users' basic data in VRSB is the same, mainly basic teaching data. It is stored in DDB and synchronized between all students and teachers. Due to independent expanding space, each operation will generate derived data, which is asynchronous and has different extensions in shared space [19]. VRSB uses DDB to store and publish the basic data and manage the derived data, effectively dealing with the basic and derived data [20]. Figure 1 shows the data flow of the proposed architecture.

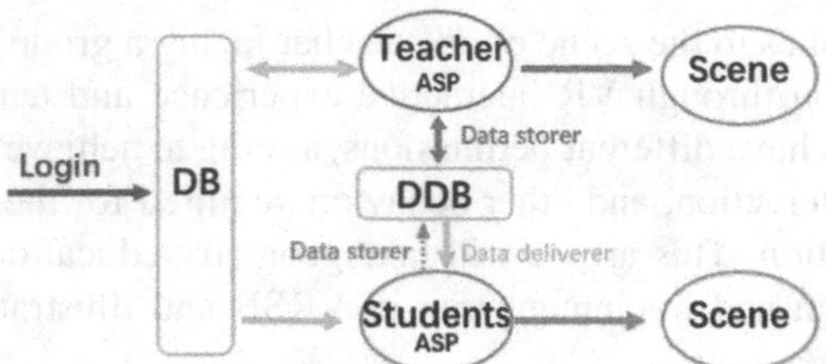

Fig. 1. Data flow of the proposed architecture

3.3 Publish Side and Subscribe Sides

VRSB manages the teaching by allowing teachers to modify scenes but limits students to modify. VRSB uses DB for user management and permission authentication [21]. All users must input their accounts and roles when they subscribe to the VR teaching scene. The system judges the user's role when a user modifies a scenario. If the user is a teacher, he/she can modify the scene, view students, manage students and perform the modification. If the user is a student, he/she only can view the scene, and VRSB limits his/her modification. Teachers have the authority to manage basic data. They can give the modification authority to the student who wants to modify the scenario. After the student modifies, VRSB makes every subscriber update his/her modification synchronously. Table 1 shows user roles and permission assignments.

Table 1. User type and permission assignment

User type	Group	Authority
Teacher	M	All
Students have the permission	S1	View, Modify
Students have no permission	S2	View

When the teacher modifies the scene, the subscribe side sends the file to the webserver to request to modify the data in the DDB, and the student side updates the view in real-time through the ASP [22]. When students demonstrate or experiment, the teacher should change the permission status of the student in DB [23]. The teacher can change the role of students from S2 to S1, who will obtain view and modification permission. Then they can modify and publish the data, and each subscriber update and view the page in real-time through the dynamic server. All students use the base data updated in real-time through the derived data to extend the personal DVE on the subscribe side. It's worth noting that other subscribers can selectively synchronize modifications made by the student who publishes content. At the same time, the teacher can view the results of students' modifications through a synchronous page to understand students' levels and the class's progress.

4 Implementation

VRSB supports students in observing and practicing scenarios independently and supports teachers in managing teaching scenarios. It has high application value and flexibility to match different types of teaching content through teaching plan design. In this article, the authors take two teaching contents of geometry as cases to illustrate the application of VRSB in the teaching process. They are related to the practical application of geometry and are suitable for middle school students to think deeply and recognize the combination of geometry in application with mechanics. Figure 2 shows the implementation overview of VRSB for education.

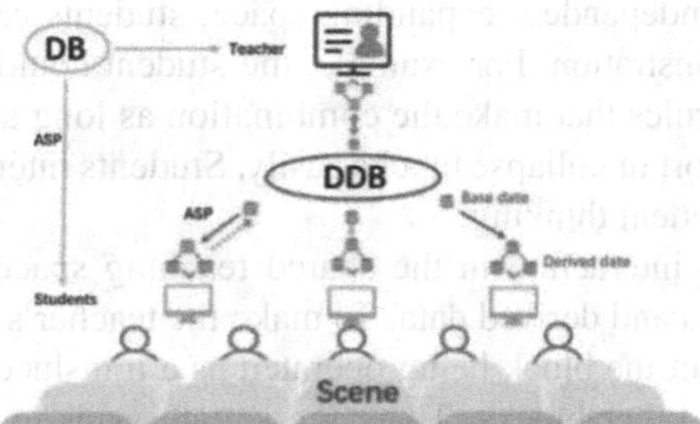

Fig. 2. The implementation overview of VRSB for education

4.1 A Case Study of the Lira Leaning Tower

A classic geometry case known as the Leaning Tower of the Lira tells us using Harmonic functions can extend stacking blocks to infinity [24]. In reality, it isn't easy to control precision of less than 1mm when people stack the blocks, and a slight external force may cause structural problems and collapse. In addition, the number of planks required for the extension length increases dramatically in the experiment. For example, people need 227 pieces of blocks if they want to extend five times the blocks' length. Due to the difficulty of the experiment, the teacher only presents pictures and formulas in a traditional class. In that situation, the students could not acquire experiential knowledge, have difficulty understanding, and forget easily.

VRSB supports students to stack blocks in the shared VR scenes and supports teachers in achieving the teaching objective. The teaching objective usually includes understanding the geometry case, mastering the calculating methods, and acquainting Harmonic functions. Students may have different computing ways and attempt paths. They can verify the method's feasibility through their experiments in VR scenes. The key is that students can explore the process of stacking blocks under ideal conditions and find the law that extends blocks to the longest distance in practice.

For one thing, every student has independent expanding spaces that extend from the shared space. Students can observe the model presented by teachers from different angles, which simulates the actual blocks in the classroom. Multiple views can convey different intuitive information in the expanding spaces. For example, students need the top view to obverse the overlap part of many blocks, but they are accustomed to observing the overall state of blocks from the front view. Different perspectives can meet the different purposes of students' observation. It's worth noting that the view position of each subscriber is derived data, which allows each student to view and learn from the view angle he needs during the learning process.

For another, the basic data synchronization between teachers and students is necessary for the teaching process. The construction scheme is that VRSB limits the permission of students to modify data when teachers demonstrate teaching. The teacher stores data in the Gun DB and publishes the scene. The student side receives data and updates. Then, the students synchronize the data at each extension and view the change in the scene from their extended perspective. The modification permissions that students can share are limited, but in the independent expanding space, students can try on their minds after the teacher's demonstration. For example, the student could stack several blocks to explore the stacking rules that make the combination as long as possible. They may extend the blocks too short or collapse blocks easily. Students interact with those blocks to promote their independent thinking.

Students experience interaction in the shared teaching space, which expands the space by using basic data and derived data. To make the teacher's operation focus clear to the students, VRSB set the block being operated as a translucent block in this case, which is different from other blocks. There are square grids to assist students when placing new blocks for ease of operation. And the blocks generated in the virtual hand are always parallel to the ground to assist students and teachers with aligning other blocks, as shown in Fig. 3.

Fig. 3. Assist the interactive design of VR teaching content

Besides, Students without permission cannot modify the scene, but their virtual hands are visible with different colors, as shown in Fig. 4. The practice in a VR scene can avoid the deviation of manual placement and collapse caused by other external forces, like wind and voice in reality.

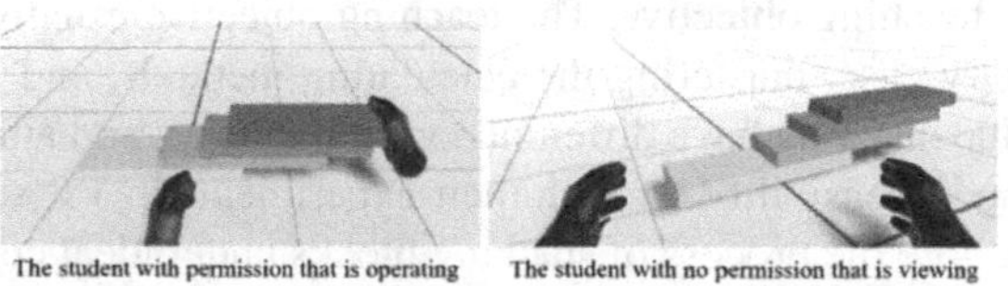

The student with permission that is operating
The student with no permission that is viewing

Fig. 4. Virtual hands with different permissions

The teachers can view the operation progress of the students and modify the student permissions in the DB user management module based on the teaching needs. They can synchronize the operation of the student to each subscriber. The synchronous process is like a student show. Teachers or other students selected them to present their ideas, facilitating discussion between students and teachers and improving enthusiasm. In addition, teachers can also design the contests or points rules to encourage students to apply for accessing permission of their own accord. At the class end, the teacher can share the correct conclusion and give the algebraic formula according to the intuitive demonstration of geometry to complete the teaching goal.

4.2 A Case Study of the Building Bridges

The case of Lira Leaning Tower tends to cultivate students' independent thinking and practice. In contrast, the case of bridge construction tends to team collaboration and emphasizes the cultivation of collective sense and innovation ability. This case is often used to train new engineering students.They always use solid materials that make by rolling paper to save cost but waste a lot of time rolling paper repeatedly in reality.

The case sets up solid or hollow, round or square tubes to simulate authentic bridge design. Students can choose one of the four kinds of components, and different kinds of components of the same size have different bearing forces. Teachers use Gun DB to build the basic components of the bridge structure synchronously and demonstrate the combination method of foundation construction in the shared space. Then, students are free to team up and brainstorm possible structures, either through instant messaging or in person. They attempt in expanded space, and the changes of the trying times will not publish. Virtual components can reduce the waste of authentic materials and the impact of different material sources on the structure. Besides, it can save time used to replicate the same components or structure. In the teaching process, VRSB allows teachers to observe student groups' real-time works and give detailed guidance. They can specify student groups to share their ideas at the same time. VRSB allows the teacher to revise the authority to let the student groups share their achievements, achieving teaching management. The group's works presented in the shared space will encourage students to innovate actively and collaborate, which will realize the teaching goal of increasing students' thinking on geometrics in collaboration and innovation.

5 User Feedback

Large-scale user studies were not possible due to the epidemic environment and quantity of VR equipment. The authors invited one middle school teacher and four middle school students to experience it and paid 8 dollars per participant. The system has received positive reviews and encouragement, and some suggestions are worth following. After experiencing the first case of Leaning Tower, the teacher said, "Restricting students' revision authority during my demonstration helps them focus on the following tasks." His teaching management experience believes that this mode will be very efficient for at most 12 students. One of the Students said, "Teachers modify permissions as a spot check in class, and we can't copy others…There are computer records, and we have to do it independently." That proves the advantages of the system for cultivating students' independence. for the second case, called bridge-building, a student commented, "The teacher gave me the authority to show my creation in the scene is an approval, which is similar to asking me to show myself in front of the classroom in a traditional class." That illustrates the need for VRSB's emphasis on teaching management.

The author also found some problems from observations and interviews. Some students shifted attention due to the changing perspectives during the operation, which means it's vital to have an optimal perspective and locking mechanism to prevent the perspective change triggered by some actions. Besides, one student said, "The freedom of grasping and moving objects needs to be limited. I always failed to align the blocks." Due to the high degree of freedom of VR, the teacher suggested that "The system built the new block can be generated directly above the existing block. That means students only need to drag in the direction of extension and control the length rather than align it to the existing block." That is an actionable proposal. He also said, "VR has richer operations, so it poses a higher challenge to focus on each student for me." More research needs to reduce teachers' management pressure by strengthening students' self-exploration and mutual supervision.

6 Discussion and Conclusion

The authors propose a VRSB framework suitable for one-to-many broadcast teaching in a VR environment. It inherits VR education's advantages and breaks through the limitation of graphic media teaching. In geometry education, it can avoid the impact of external forces and material factors in the real world and improve efficiency. But the more important innovation is that the system emphasizes the design of teaching management. VRSB uses DB to manage users to divide users into teacher roles and student roles. It uses DDB to store and share real-time data, eliminates centralized server control, shortens service time, and provides changeable features. And it uses ASP for each DB and DDB for dynamic access, which is helpful for remote participants.

VRSB has not yet conducted tests on actual teaching sizes, and the possible problems of application in large-scale teaching are unknown at present. It still needs to be supplemented to accommodate a broader range of teaching needs, like adding a dialogue window with classmates or teachers, annotation of knowledge, class records, and notes at any time. In the future, the authors will optimize the framework of VRSB based on the results of small-scale user studies and with further reference to broader user studies and expert evaluations. The authors also make efforts to expand application areas, like microscopic chemical structures.

Acknowledgements. The work is supported by Ministry of Education (China) Humanities and Social Sciences Research Foundation under Grant No.: 19A10358002.

References

1. Kolb, D.A.: Experiential Learning: Experience as the Source of Learning and Development. FT Press, New Jersey (2014)
2. Scavarelli, A., Arya, A., Teather, R.J.: Virtual reality and augmented reality in social learning spaces: a literature review. Virtual Real. **25**, 257–277 (2021)

3. Schunk, D.H.: Learning Theories, vol. 53. Printice Hall Inc., New Jersey (1996)
4. Irawati, S., Ahn, S., Kim, J., Ko, H.: VARU framework: enabling rapid prototyping of VR, AR and ubiquitous applications. IEEE (2008)
5. Grasset, R., Looser, J., Billinghurst, M.: Transitional interface: concept, issues and framework. IEEE (2006)
6. Ben-Haim, D., Lappan, G., Houang, R.T.: Visualizing rectangular solids made of small cubes: analyzing and effecting students' performance. Educ. Stud. Math. **16**(4), 389–409 (1985)
7. Leopold, C.: Geometry education for developing spatial visualisation abilities of engineering students. J. Biuletyn Polish Soc. Geom. Eng. Graph. **15**, 39–45 (2005)
8. Andreasen, N.K., Baceviciute, S., Pande, P., Makransky, G.: Virtual reality instruction followed by enactment can increase procedural knowledge in a science lesson. IEEE (2019)
9. Churchill, E.F., Snowdon, D.: Collaborative virtual environments: an introductory review of issues and systems. Virtual Real. **3**(1), 3–15 (1998)
10. Kaufmann, H., Schmalstieg, D.: Mathematics and geometry education with collaborative augmented reality (2002)
11. Lai, C., McMahan, R.P., Kitagawa, M., Connolly, I.: Geometry Explorer: Facilitating Geometry Education with Virtual Reality. Springer, Toronto (2016)
12. Faure, C., Limballe, A., Bideau, B., Perrin, T., Kulpa, R.: Acting together, acting stronger? Interference between participants during face-to-face cooperative interception task. IEEE (2019)
13. Lv, Z., Yin, T., Han, Y., Chen, Y., Chen, G.: WebVR-web virtual reality engine based on P2P network. J. Netw. **6**(7), 990 (2011)
14. Zhu, M., et al.: Distributed network system architecture for collaborative computing (2006)
15. Deftu, A., Griebsch, J.: A scalable conflict-free replicated set data type. IEEE (2013)
16. Huh, S., Muralidharan, S., Ko, H., Yoo, B.: XR collaboration architecture based on decentralized web (2019)
17. Andersen, T.: Database access using active server pages (2002)
18. Kelly, J.W., Beall, A.C., Loomis, J.M.: Perception of shared visual space: establishing common ground in real and virtual environments. Presence **13**(4), 442–450 (2004)
19. Chaudhuri, S., Dayal, U.: An overview of data warehousing and OLAP technology. ACM SIGMOD Rec. **26**(1), 65–74 (1997)
20. Mohan, C., Lindsay, B., Obermarck, R.: Transaction management in the R* distributed database management system. ACM Trans. Database Syst. (TODS) **11**(4), 378–396 (1986)
21. Haake, J.M., Haake, A., Schümmer, T., Bourimi, M., Landgraf, B.: End-user controlled group formation and access rights management in a shared workspace system (2004)
22. Esposito, D.: Building web solutions with ASP. NET and ADO. NET. Microsoft Press, Redmond (2002)
23. Wong, L.C., Aggarwal, S.M., Beebee, P.L.: Methods and systems for controlling access to presence information according to a variety of different access permission types (2005)
24. Kifowit, S.J., Stamps, T.A.: The harmonic series diverges again and again, 1. (2006, To appear in The AMATYC Review)

Collaborative Mixed Reality Annotations System for Science and History Education Based on UWB Positioning and Low-Cost AR Glasses

YanXiang Zhang(✉) and LiTing Tang

Department of Communication of Science and Technology, University of Science and Technology of China, Hefei, Anhui, China
petrel@ustc.edu.cn, nino3@mail.ustc.edu.cn

Abstract. In this research, the authors designed a low-cost mixed reality (MR) collaborative annotations system for science and history education based on Ultra-wideband (UWB) communication technology. The position of the user is provided by the gyroscope in AR Glasses and the UWB antenna tag which is carried with users. The system is suitable for science education in developing countries that lack quality science teaching resources. It can provide comparably sized things or scenes that may be difficult to see clearly or do not exist in daily life for users to observe and experience. While using the system, the users can interact with each other. The system has some unique advantages, such as low-cost, accurate positioning in areas where GPS signal is weak, virtuality, and reality combination in large indoor spaces.

Keywords: Mixed reality · AR glasses · Ultra-wideband positioning · Developing country

1 Introduction

Science education is an essential topic in all countries nowadays. But there are many barriers to advancing science education. Science teachers and science classrooms are scarce in many developing countries like China. K. E. Cordova and O. M. Yaghi showed that financial and economic problem is the number one issue of science education in Vietnam [1]. Desta Berhe Sbhatu from Ethiopia pro-poses the lack of input and professional teachers is a vital problem [7]. The high cost of teaching and the lack of quality teaching resources are problems faced by many countries.

The authors designed a low-cost collaborative mixed reality (MR) system for science and history education. It's based on Ultra-wideband (UWB) technology and AR glasses. The system can be used in large indoor spaces. It enables real-time interaction between users and the system. Users can also communicate with each other. The design is low-cost, so less developed countries and areas can afford it. Developed countries and areas can invest more in scenario modeling to optimize the experience.

L. T. De Paolis et al. (Eds.): XR Salento 2022, LNCS 13446, pp. 150–158, 2022.
https://doi.org/10.1007/978-3-031-15553-6_12

2 Relative Work

2.1 The Superiority of Applying MR in Education

"MR" is mixed reality which has both "virtual space" and "reality". It can realize the integration of virtual and reality [2]. MR has many advantages over traditional media and is popular in education now. There are many studies on the application of MR technology in primary and secondary education. Research by N. Pel-las, I. Kazanidis and G. Palaigeorgiou found that comparing to students learning by the traditional method, most students using MR had significantly better learning performance [6]. J. G. Kovoor, A. K. Gupta, and M. A. Gladman demonstrated the effectiveness of AR in education through a statistical review of existing studies [4].

2.2 Status Quo of AR Glasses

J. Garzon studied the applications of AR in education in the past 25 years and believed that AR glasses might affect our life like smartphones in the future [4]. And it would bring convenience to special education. It's a good idea, but many AR glasses are still costly. The most popular AR glasses on the market nowadays are HoloLens, SLAMS, Magic Leap One, Action One, and EPSON BT-300. HoloLens, Magic Leap One, and Action One have many functions. They can achieve more accurate gesture recognition and spatial positioning, but they are expensive [3]. EPSON BT-300 is inexpensive and can be controlled with the controller but cannot realize positioning. Therefore, based on EPSON BT-300, the authors use UWB positioning technology to make EPSON BT-300 have the function of large indoor space positioning.

Fig. 1. EPSON BT-300, the picture is from the website

2.3 Equivalent Systems

HoloLens and Magic Leap are based on depth cameras for environmental measurement tracking. HoloLens' scan range is 0.8 ~ 3.1 m [10]. But the space mapping may turn wrong when users leave away. Simultaneous localization and mapping (SLAM) reconstruct the actual environment by acquiring data from the environment [11–13]. However, in large space, the data to build the environment is too huge, and the system can't run for a long time [14]. There is also an approach combining SLAM and UWB to spatially register multiple SLAM devices without sharing maps or involving external tracking infrastructures. The positioning could be quite accurate [13, 14]. But SLAM is still considered quite expensive to be widely used.

GPS and ultrasonic are commonly used for spatial positioning. But in indoor environments, GPS signals are often blocked. Frequently used indoor positioning systems include RFID, Ultra-wideband (UWB) communication technology, Wi-Fi, Bluetooth, etc. UWB positioning technology is cheaper, and its accuracy is much higher than other technologies, which can reach centimeter level. The signal power of the UWB positioning system is distributed over a wide band, enabling it to coexist with conventional radios without compromising their link quality. Therefore, in the case of multiple devices, the congestion problem of the common frequency band can be effectively solved. UWB positioning is suitable for large and medium-sized indoor scenarios. Studies have verified the feasibility of UWB as a solution for AR and VR positioning. Researchers used UWB to track actors' movements on the stage [8].

Therefore, the authors proposed a mixed reality system in a large indoor space. The system obtains 3d positioning of users based on the UWB positioning system and gyroscope angle provided by EPSON BT-300.

3 System Design

This is an application based on EPSON BT-300. It's Sci-MR. This system includes user module, positioning module, and scene module. The consistency of user location information and virtual camera location information is the basic principle of this design. The system is developed by Unity. Figure 2 shows how the system works.

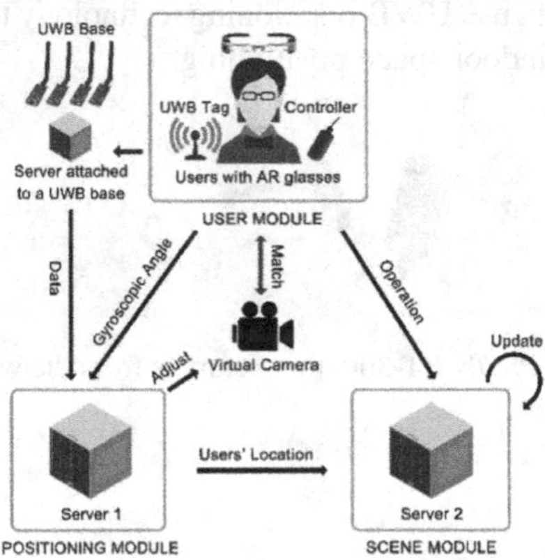

Fig. 2. System flow chart

3.1 Introduction of Three Modules

User Module

The user module generates data and transmits it to the positioning module and scene module. To use Sci-MR, the user should carry a UWB label and wear an EPSON BT-300

AR glasses. The gyroscope in AR Glasses provides the perspective of the users. The user can use the controller, which generates and transmits the operation type's data to the scene module. There are two kinds of operations: to see more information about the annotations on a page and to close the page.

Positioning Module

The positioning module processes the transmitted data, including data from the UWB positioning system and gyroscopic data provided by EPSON BT-300. The data from the UWB positioning system will be converted to users' coordinates. The positioning module can determine the user's perspective through these data and then adjust the virtual camera's position to make it coincide with the user's perspective.

Scene Module

The scene module presents and updates scenes. The system provides over ten scenes, including a blue whale skeleton, a rocket, a dinosaur, the Terracotta Warriors, the twelve animal zodiacs of China, and so on. The scenes are huge or hard to see in people's daily life. By presenting them in a space people are familiar with, Sci-MR can help users to better understand the size and to learn in a more interesting way. When users perform operations on the scene, the scene module modifies the scene based on the users' location provided by the positioning module and the operation type provided by the user module. Uses can use Sci-MR alone or in a group of users connected through WIFI. The update can be shared with users in the same group.

Fig. 3. Some of the Terracotta Warriors and a blue whale skeleton

3.2 Principle of Space Positioning

The authors use the UWB Mini3sPlus development board developed by YCHIOT, a company in Wenzhou, Zhejiang, China.

The positioning system uses four base stations and multiple tags. The two-way time-of-flight method can obtain tag coordinate values and the modified four-point ranging method. This method is provided in the article " Approach for 3D Localization Based on RSSI of 4 Nodes [9]. The two-way flight can measure the distance between the tags and each base station. Each module generates an independent time stamp from the start. The module's transmitter transmits a pulse signal of the requested nature at Ta1 on its time stamp, and module B transmits a signal of a reactive nature at time Tb2, which module A receives at its time stamp Ta2. From this, the flight time of the pulse signal between the two modules can be calculated to determine the flight distance(S). Where (Cx) represents the speed of light.

$$S = C_x \frac{[(T_{a2} - T_{a1}) - (T_{b2} - T_{b1})]}{2}$$

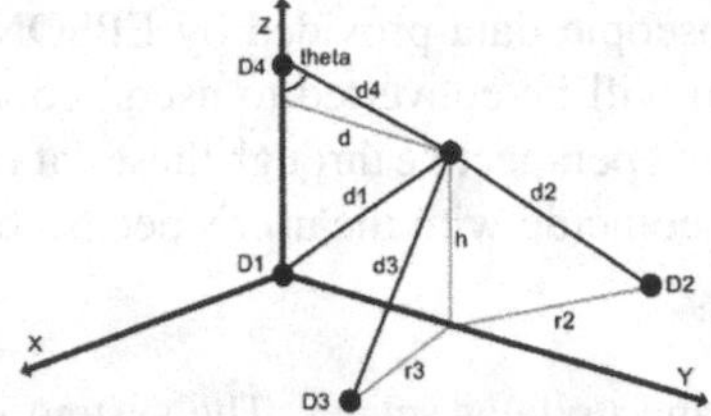

Fig. 4. 3D localization based on RSSI of 4 Nodes

In the revised four-point ranging method, it is necessary to place a base station in a Cartesian coordinate system, as shown in the figure. The relative positions of the four base stations are fixed. Define coordinates as Di = (xi, yi, zi) D1 = (0, 0, 0).

Finally, the calculation formula is:

(x-x1)2 + (y-y1)2 = r12.
(x-x2)2 + (y-y2)2 = r22.
(x-x3)2 + (y-y3)2 = r32.
z = h = d-(d42-d12 + d2)/2d.

In solving the triangular centroid method, there are cases where the three circles cannot be crossed by two due to the distance error. At this time, the imaginary solution is ignored, and only the real solution with x $\geq$ 0 is used as the positioning result.

3.3 Measurement and Positioning of Physical Space

In this design, the authors used an indoor gymnasium. It has a size of about 40 * 60 square m. The stadium has entrances on all sides. The long side is east-west. Many schools have such gyms. Based on the actual physical space, we built a proxy 3D model (as shown in Fig. 5). We put the UWB base stations D1, D2, D3, and D4 in the stadium's four corners. D1, D2, and D3 are 1m above the ground, and D4 is 2m above that. The UWB tag is stuck onto the user's clothes. Then we create a Cartesian coordinate system with D1 as the source. Since Unity uses a left-handed coordinate system to ensure physical space coincides with virtual space, we also use the UWB positioning system to define the coordinate system as the same as Unity.

3.4 Acquisition, Calculation, and Propagation of Positioning Coordinates

As shown in Fig. 5, using the UWB positioning system, we set up four base stations to determine the coordinate positions of the UWB tags. We need to connect one of the base stations to a server that can compute the distance measurement information

Fig. 5. Picture of the gym and the 3D model of the gym

as position coordinates (x, y, z). In addition to computing coordinates, the server has location propagation capabilities. Users' AR glasses can receive location data from the server over Wi-Fi so real-time location data can be transmitted to AR glasses. This makes it possible to write scripts to retrieve location data.

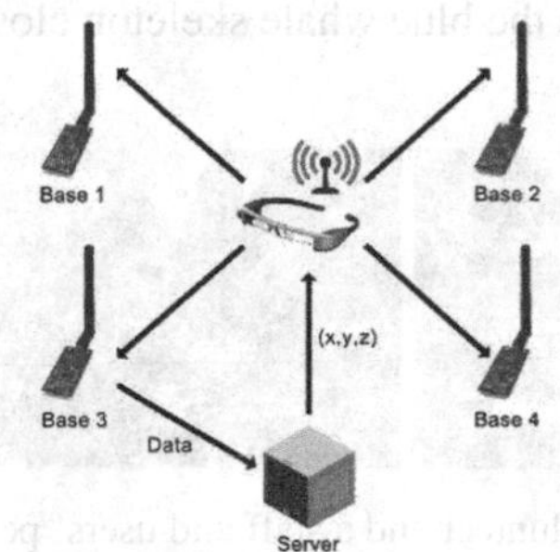

Fig. 6. Location data acquisition model

3.5 Alignment of Virtual Space with Real Space

To ensure that annotations are not misplaced, the orientation of the virtual space axis needs to be the same as that of the actual space. Unlike augmented reality (AR), which does not reflect perspective relationship, MR with perspective function needs to correct the direction of the virtual space coordinate axis in real-time.

The output data format for the gyroscope in the AR glasses is AdcGyroXZ. It's the angle of the projection of the direction of the AR glasses in the XZ and YZ planes. After retrieving the two data, the system takes a negative value of AdcGyroXZ and adds it as an action command script to the virtual space axis built for Unity to rotate the virtual space. This correction process needs to be performed in real-time.

Based on the above, the script is called to transfer the UWB location information, which he transmitted to the AR glasses to Unity and binds it to the virtual camera as an action command. At the same time, we also need to retrieve the angle data measured by the gyroscope in real-time to get the direction of the AR glasses. Then, the virtual camera can be synchronized with the user's perspective.

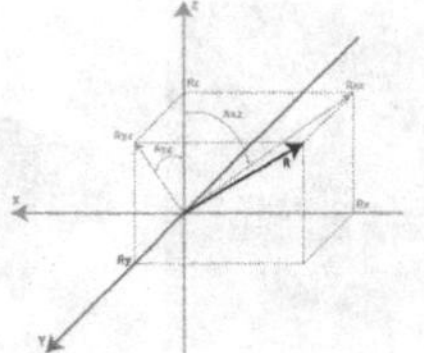

Fig. 7. Gyroscope Angle

4 User Study

We conducted a user study by offering an "Observing the blue whale skeleton" program. The blue whale skeleton is one of the scenes provided by Sci-MR. Blue whales are largest mammal and can grow to over 30 m in length. They are hard to get close to in everyday life. In this study, users can see the blue whale skeleton closely.

Fig. 8. A volunteer and a staff and users' perspective

We invited ten volunteers to experience the system. They had 20 min to experience it in the company of a staff who also wears a pair of AR glasses. The volunteer and the staff were in the same group so that they could share the same scene. The staff would interact with the volunteers and help them find the annotations. After volunteers had experienced the system, we interviewed them to find out what they thought about it. An interview lasts for 10 to 20 min. Volunteers were also asked to score the system in some aspects shown in Fig. 9. Volunteers are paid $10 an h.

volunteer	gender	age	used AR/VR before	Comfort	Education	Interest
1	female	23	No	2/5	3/5	5/5
2	male	23	No	3/5	4/5	4/5
3	male	19	Yes	3/5	4/5	3/5
4	male	18	Yes	5/5	5/5	4/5
5	female	20	Yes	4/5	4/5	4/5
6	female	21	Yes	3/5	3/5	4/5
7	male	20	No	3/5	5/5	4/5
8	male	19	Yes	4/5	5/5	5/5
9	male	20	Yes	4/5	4/5	5/5
10	female	20	Yes	5/5	4/5	3/5

Fig. 9. Volunteers' basic information and scores

We found that all the volunteers gave positive feedback. The system was mainly praised for the following reasons. First, the scene was impressive. Second, the science education form was creative. Third, the annotations were helpful. Finally, the strong sense of engagement was exciting. There are some typical comments:

Comment A: I'm totally shocked to see a 1:1 whale skeleton in the gym. It's an impressive experience to use the system.

Comment B: It's very interesting to learn science knowledge like this. I hope this could be applied in our school for some lessons in the future.

Comment C: I have no concept of large numbers, so it's hard for me to realize how giant a blue whale is. But now I get it.

Comment D: The design of annotation is surprising, but it's hard to notice because the scene is too big.

Comment E: It's very interesting that only we can see the blue whale skeleton! Some people play badminton in the gym, but they can't see the shocking scene. It's like a secret between us. That makes me quite exciting and engaged.

5 Conclusions and Discussion

This system is suitable for wide indoor spaces. It can achieve MR at a low cost. Based on EPSON BT-300 AR Glasses and UWB, large-scale MR can be realized.

We compared other schemes to prove that this system can meet the needs of low-cost science and history education in school gyms. First, we compared the price of this system to other AR/MR devices. The system consists of four base stations, UWB tags, and EPSON BT-300 AR glasses. Four base stations are $380, a UWB tag is $90, and the BT-300 is $780. Four base stations can support approximately ten location tags. So, the system with only one user costs $1,250, but with ten users, it costs only $908 per person. HoloLens costs $3,000 each person. Magic Leap costs about $2,295 each person. Moreover, this system is relatively simple and needs low maintenance costs. This design has a large price advantage, so it's easy to promote. UWB-based positioning method has higher accuracy, lower cost, and can support more users. In addition, the UWB is perfect for remote areas and areas without GPS signals.

The system provides comparably sized scientific things for users to observe and experience. It makes science and history education more immersive and impressive. It eliminates the limitations of time and space. It can carry out science and history education activities in any large indoor space. Moreover, it saves the materials for building natural scenes. And it can even realize magical landscapes that are difficult to see. The combination of virtuality and reality in a large space is a highlight of this research. This system also has high interactivity. The interaction between users and the system enables users to obtain further information, and the interaction between users can increase their interest. Based on the interaction ritual chain theory, interaction symbols, shared emotions, live gatherings, and shared attention can form an interaction ritual chain between people, making people more connected [16]. Users in the same space and share the same virtual scene may help them feel mentally pleasant.

There are still some problems and defects. First, UWB positioning still has a positioning error of less than 5 cm. It will occur when the distance is too close. Second, 3D modeling needs to be more realistic. Third, users may go across the 3D model. Therefore, this system is not suitable for small space.

Acknowledgements. The work is supported by National Social Science Foundation of China, under grand number: 21VSZ124.

This paper is also supported by Ministry of Education (China) Humanities and Social Sciences Research Foundation under Grant No.: 19A10358002.

References

1. JCordova, K..E.., Yaghi, O..M.: Buil+ding a global culture of science the Vietnam experience. Angewandte Chemie-Int. Ed. **58**(6), 1552–1560 (2019). https://doi.org/10.1002/anie.201812076
2. Milgram, P., Kishino, F.: A taxonomy of mixed reality visual displays. IEICE Trans. Inf. Syst. **77**(12), 1321–1329 (1994)
3. Fan, L., Ma, J., Zhang, K., Miao, X., Li, J.: The development status and the prospect of the augmented reality hardware industry. Sci. Technol. Rev. **37**(15), 114–124 (2019). https://doi.org/10.3981/j.issn.1000-7857.2019.15.017
4. Garzon, J.: An overview of twenty-five years of augmented reality in education. Multimod. Technol. Interact. **5**(7), Article 37 (2021). https://doi.org/10.3390/mti5070037
5. Oguntala, G., Abd-Alhameed, R., Jones, S., Noras, J., Patwary, M., Rodriguez, J.: Indoor location identification technologies for real-time IoT-based applications: an inclusive survey. Comput. Sci. Rev. **30**, 55–79 (2018). https://doi.org/10.1016/j.cosrev.2018.09.001
6. Pellas, N., Kazanidis, I., Palaigeorgiou, G.: A systematic literature review of mixed reality environments in K-12 education. Educ. Inf. Technol. **25**(4), 2481–2520 (2019). https://doi.org/10.1007/s10639-019-10076-4
7. Sbhatu, D.B.: Challenges of 20th century Ethiopian Science education. Heliyon **7**(6), Article e07157 (2021). https://doi.org/10.1016/j.heliyon.2021.e07157
8. Zhang, H., Zhang, Z.H., Gao, N., Xiao, Y.J., Meng, Z.Z., Li, Z.: Cost-Effective wearable indoor localization and motion analysis via the integration of UWB and IMU. Sensors, 20(2), Article 344 (2020). https://doi.org/10.3390/s20020344
9. Dai, C., Song, L., Yan, D.: Three-dimensional spatial localization algorithm based on four-node RSSI. Computer Measur. Control 24(1), 229232 (2016). (in Chinese). https://kns.cnki.net/KCMS/detail/detail.aspx?dbcode=CJFQ&dbname=CJFDLAST2016&filename=JZCK201601065
10. Tuliper, A.: Introduction to the HoloLens, Part 2: Spatial Mapping. https://docs.microsoft.com/en-us/archive/msdn-magazine/2017/january/hololens-introduction-to-the-hololens-part-2-spatial-mapping
11. Borrmann, D., et al.: A mobile robot-based system for fully automated thermal 3D mapping. Adv. Eng. Inform. **28**(4), 425--440 (2014)
12. Fraundorfer, F., et al.: Vision-based autonomous mapping and expLoRation using a quadrotor MAV. Proc. IROS **2012**, 4557–4564 (2012)
13. Shin, T., Roh, B.H.: Component mapping method for indoor localization system based on mixed reality. In: 2019 Eleventh International Conference on Ubiquitous and Future Networks (ICUFN) (pp. 379–383). IEEE, July 2019
14. Bae, H., GolparvarFard, M., White, J.: High-precision vision-based mobile augmented reality system for context-aware architectural engineering construction and facility management (AEC/FM) applications. Vis. Eng. **1**(1), 113 (2013)
15. Huo, K., et al.: Scenarios: spatially mapping smart things within augmented reality scenes. In: Proceedings of the CHI Conference on Human Factors in Computing Systems (CHI), Montreal, Canada, 21–26 Apr 2018 (2018)
16. Collins, R.: Interaction Ritual Chains. Princeton University Press, Oxford (2004)

Artificial Intelligence and Machine Learning for eXtended Reality

Can AI Replace Conventional Markerless Tracking? A Comparative Performance Study for Mobile Augmented Reality Based on Artificial Intelligence

Roberto Pierdicca[1](✉), Flavio Tonetto[2], Marco Mameli[3], Riccardo Rosati[3], and Primo Zingaretti[3]

[1] Dipartimento di Ingegneria Civile Edile e dell'Architettura (DICEA), Università Politecnica delle Marche, Via Brecce Bianche, 60131 Ancona, Italy
r.pierdicca@staff.univpm.it

[2] Sinergia Consulenze Srl, Viale Goffredo Mameli 44, 61121 Pesaro, Italy
ftonetto@sinergia.it

[3] Dipartimento di Ingegneria dell'Informazione (DII), Università Politecnica delle Marche, Via Brecce Bianche, 60131 Ancona, Italy
{m.mameli,r.rosati}@pm.univpm.it, p.zingaretti@staff.univpm.it

Abstract. AR is struggling to achieve its maturity for the mass market. Indeed, there are still many challenging issues that are waiting to be discovered and improved in AR related fields. Artificial Intelligence seems the more promising solution to overcome these limitations; indeed, they can be combined to obtain unique and immersive experiences. Thus, in this work, we focus on integrating DL models into the pipeline of AR development. This paper describes an experiment performed as comparative study, to evaluate if classification and/or object detection can be used an alternative way to track objects in AR. In other words, we implemented a mobile application that is capable of exploiting AI based model for classification and object detection and, at the same time, project the results in AR environment. Several off-the-shelf devices have been used, in order to make the comparison consistent, and to provide the community with useful insights over the opportunity to integrate AI models in AR environment and to what extent this can be convenient or not. Performance tests have been made in terms of both memory consumption and processing time, as well as for Android and iOS based applications.

Keywords: Augmented reality · Object detection · Deep learning · Tracking · AI4XR

1 Introduction

The increase of eXtended Reality (XR) applications is due to their use in almost every domain of day life [1]. Thanks to the technological advances, companies and research centres are investing and acting to spread XR applications, whilst

L. T. De Paolis et al. (Eds.): XR Salento 2022, LNCS 13446, pp. 161–177, 2022.
https://doi.org/10.1007/978-3-031-15553-6_13

the end users are growing their interest given the irrefutable usefulness to facilitate daily tasks [37]. XR proved its benefit in education [13,28], industry [27], cultural heritage [4,10,26], medicine [40], assistive technology in elderly care [25], prototyping [19] and many more.

Among them, AR is struggling to achieve its maturity for the mass market. Indeed, there are still many challenging issues that are waiting to be discovered and improved in AR related fields. One of the major difficulties is that there are several AR markers on the market, each with its own unique encoded information algorithm [23]. They usually require the users to modify their original material contents in some way, either partially or completely. Another problem is the marker identification process, which utilises the standard computer vision-based feature extraction approaches, such as scale-invariant feature transformations or histograms of oriented gradients [17], for classification tasks. These mathematical methods are vulnerable to unanticipated real-world lighting, marker orientation and unexpected noises [7]. Deep learning (DL) approaches that use Convolutional Neural Networks (CNNs) models are a useful tool to overcome the standard computer vision difficulties in the AR marker identification process as in [11,24,29]. The review presented in [12] highlights that the functionality of AR increases using DL based approaches. To facilitate the development of AR experiences by overcoming the above-mentioned limitations, we started from the following assumption: AR and AI are disruptive technologies that, albeit being two distinct technologies, can be combined to obtain unique and immersive experiences. Thus, in this work, we focus on integrating DL models into the pipeline of AR development.

Considering this due premise, to facilitate the reader understanding the main technologies used in our experiments, we performed a comparative study to evaluate if classification and/or object detection can be used an alternative way to track objects in AR. In other words, we implemented a mobile application that is capable of exploiting AI based model for classification and object detection and, at the same time, project the results in AR environment. Several off-the-shelf devices have been used, in order to make the comparison consistent, and to provide the community with useful insights over the opportunity to integrate AI models in AR environment and to what extent this can be convenient or not. Performance tests have been made in terms of both memory consumption and processing time, as well as for Android and iOS based applications.

The remainder of the paper is organised as follows. In Sect. 2, the most recent paper that use deep learning approaches for mobile phone application. Section 3 describes the specific objectives, the problems encountered and the techniques adopted. The results obtained are described in Sect. 4. Finally, Sect. 5 describes the degree of achievement of the objectives and the ideas for future developments.

2 Related Works

Several approaches have been proposed in literature that exploit DL to produce different application for mobile devices. In this section we present most recent application for smartphones based on deep learning for classifciation and object detection tasks in different sector. For example, in agricultural sector there are several applications for mobile devices able to classify and detect objects acquired by the camera and using deep learning method. The work of [36] proposes a mobile phone application based on Inceptionv3 [39] network that aims to support smallholder farmers in Tanzania to early detect banana diseases. Once the image of the leaf is acquired, the mobile application was able to detect in real time and with good performance two possible diseases. This study is important since allows to prevent serious damage to crops through a common and inexpensive tool, by avoiding major damage in poor regions. In the same context the work of [6] proposes a smartphone application based on a deep learning approach able to identify disease on tomatoes leaves. The authors implement an application based on MobilNet [9] model that is able to identify 10 common diseases of tomatoes. The choice of MobilNet depends on the fact that this model works on mobile phone with acceptable speed and perform high classification accuracy. The work of [22] aims to increase performances in the identification of diseases in the tomatoes leaves. They implemented a novel mobile phone application based on Convolutional Neural Network by performing automatic background subtraction for leaf, since this task enhances disease recognition accuracy. Once the user captures the image of the leaf, the segmentation app removes the background features so that only the target leaf remains. Also in the recent work of [3] an application for smartphone is presented, with the aim to prevent damage to crops. The authors do not only identify the pest but unlike all other works are able to also recognise the scale insects. A complex architecture consisted of Faster region-based convolutional networks (Faster R-CNNs) [32], single-shot multibox detectors (SSDs) [16], and You Only Look Once v4 (YOLO v4) [30], is implemented to identify and locate scale pests in the image acquired by the camera of the smartphone.

In the ambit of healthcare, the work that deals with the support tool for impaired and blind persons is presented by [21]. The authors proposes an application based on YOLO that detects and recognises the objects in the image acquired by the camera. After recognising the objects in the scene, a browser based voice library narrates to the person what's in front of them. Similar is the mobile application proposed by [34], that describes an android app that in real time helps visually impaired people in understanding their surrounding environment. As in the previous work, the camera of the smartphone captures the images, but a Tensorflow's object detection API detects the objects. Then the objects are converted into an audio output through android's text-to-speech library.

Following we present some application for smartphone that also implement an augmented reality method to add information to the reality. In food and beverages sector there are several applications for mobile devices that combine object detection tasks and augmented reality contents. Interesting is the "HealthCAM" application proposed by [2] that combines augmented reality and machine learning techniques, in particular Mobilenet SSD model. From an image acquired by the phone's camera the app identifies a snack and in real time presents a visual warning on the camera that indicates the degree of sugar, sodium and fat of the snack. Similar is the work of [20] that proposes a mobile application that recognises fruits and vegetable and gives information, searched in the web, about nutritional property of the detected object. Unlike the previous approach, this application uses the object recognition model in Tensorflow API to be embedded in the devices. Another interesting paper is presented in [38], where AI is used to perform the object detection task. The authors develop an iOS application, which combines AR with the object detection and recognition tasks. The purpose is to verify if the combination of these fields is possible with the modern tools available. The application must be an alternative option to traditional furniture assembly manuals.

The literature already briefly reviewed demonstrates the interest in blending AI models into AR applications; none of the existing papers, however, perform a comparative analysis over the real performances of such integration. Our work cover this gap.

3 Materials and Methods

3.1 Classification Task

The architecture used for the classification task is the MobileNetV2 [35]. It is a family of lightweight CNN architectures suitable for image classification within embedded device. Despite its relatively small architecture, what makes this model widely used is the much lower computing power required to perform real-time inferences. The number of parameters and weight storage consumption of the MobilenetV2 model compared to other state-of-the-art classification methods are reported in Table 1. Thereby, this aspect allowed this network to be established as the reference model for mobile devices, embedded systems, and more. MobileNet uses depthwise separable convolutions, significantly reducing the number of parameters compared to CNNs with regular convolutions with the same depth. A depthwise separable convolution is a factorised convolution constituted by two operations:

- depthwise convolution: this convolution is originated from the idea that a filter's depth and spatial dimension can be separated;
- pointwise convolution: convolution with a kernel size of 1×1 that simply combines the features created by the depthwise convolution.

Essentially, depthwise separable convolutions splits kernel into two separate kernels, one for filtering (the depthwise one) and the other for combining (the pointwise one). Moreover, MobileNetV2 presents the addition of another two basic structures, which are the linear bottle-neck layer and the reverse residual structure: these features contribute to speed up model convergence and prevent from vanishing gradient. The overall architecture is describe in [35]. In our case, we use MobileNetV2 trained on the well-known ImageNet dataset [5], that is an image database in which each node of the hierarchy is depicted by hundreds and thousands of images. The network takes as input a tensor with shape [224, 224, 3] (corresponding to height, width and number of channel of the image respectively) and return as output a tensor with shape [1, 1, 1000] with the probability that the image represents a specific class among the 1000 classes of the entire dataset.

Table 1. Number of parameters and weight storage of state-of-the-art classification models.

Classification models	Parameter (Million)	Weight storage (MB)
DenseNet	8.1	33
VGG-16	138.3	528
AlexNet	60	220
InceptionV3	23.8	92
ResNet-101	44	171
MobileNetV2	3.5	14

3.2 Object Detection Task

The state-of-the-art object detection approaches include objectness detection (OD), salient object detection (SOD) and category-specific object detection (COD) [8]. The task the plugin aims to perform is the COD one, where the goal is to detect multiple predefined object categories from each given image, identifying at the same time the image regions that may contain the objects of interest but also the specific object category of each region. In particular, according to the literature ([15,41]), there are generally two main categories of COD methods: region proposal-based or two-stage approaches (e.g., Faster R-CNN [33]) and regression/classification-based or one-stage approaches (e.g. YOLO [30] and SSD [16]). The former first generate a set of proposal bounding-boxes by using region proposal methods and then pass the detected object proposals to the CNN classifiers; the latter work dividing the region proposals into categories at the moment of generation. One-stage detectors are preferred for embedded real-time application since they are highly efficient: the entire detection task runs in real-time with acceptable memory and storage demands, which is a key aspect for mobile/wearable devices that have limited computational capabilities and storage space. Table 2 shows speed (measured as frames per second [FPS]) and storage consumption comparison on COCO [14] test set. The reported computational cost comparison suggests that regression-based COD methods are much faster than region proposal-based methods, showing that one-stage approaches are the most promising COD direction for real-time application.

For this reason, the architecture we used for object detection task is the Tiny YOLOv2 [31], which belongs to the family of regression-based one stage detectors. The network is constituted by convolutional layers with a 3×3 kernel and max-pooling layers with a 2×2 kernel. The number of layers is reduced compared to the traditional YOLOv2 architecture: it presents only 9 convolutional layers and 6 pooling layers. We use Tiny YOLOv2 trained on UEC-Food100 benchmark dataset [18], which contains 100 categories of dishes. For this network, the input layer expects a tensor with shape $[3, 416, 416]$, while the output layer generates a $[525, 13, 13]$ tensor. The output divides the image into a 13x13 grid, where each cell in the grid consisting of 525 values. Each grid cell contains 5 potential object bounding boxes, and each bounding box is represented by the following 105 elements:

- x: the x position of the bounding box center relative to the grid cell it's associated with;
- y: the y position of the bounding box center relative to the grid cell it's associated with;
- w: the width of the bounding box;
- h: the height of the bounding box;
- o: the confidence value that an object exists within the bounding box, also known as "objectness score";
- $p1$–$p100$: class probabilities for each of the 100 classes predicted by the model for the considered dataset.

Table 2. Frame per second (FPS) performed on a Pascal Titan X and weight storage of principal state-of-the-art object detection models.

Object detection models	FPS	Weight storage (MB)
Faster R-CNN	4	168
Retinanet-101	11	228
SSD500	19	77
YOLOv1	45	190
Tiny YOLOv1	155	58
YOLOv2	40	202
Tiny YOLOv2	244	43
YOLOv3	35	237
Tiny YOLOv3	220	34

4 Experimental Processing

In this section, performance analysis of the devices listed in Tables 3 and 4 are reported. This analysis focuses on the model execution performance of the two DL models Mobilenet v2 and TinyYolo v2. In this section we will analyse the motivation for this analysis, the configurations and the motivations that led to the choice of the employed devices and finally an examples of the results of the execution of the models are showed in Fig. 1.

Table 3. List of Apple devices used for the test execution. The GPU for the AX SOC series the GPU has the same name of the chip.

Model (model number)	Processor	GPU Execution Units
iPad Air 64 GB (iPad13,1)	A14 Bionic	4 EU
iPhone 11 128 GB (iPhone12,1)	A13 Bionic	4 EU
iPhone SE 2 256 GB (iPhone12,8)	A13 Bionic	4 EU

Table 4. List of Android devices from different manufactures, with different SOC configuration.

Model (model number)	Processor	GPU model and Execution Unit (EU)
Xiaomi Mi 10T (M2007J3SY)	Snapdragon 888	Adreno 660 - 2 EU
Xiaomi RedMi Note 9 Pro	Snapdragon 750G	Adreno 619 - 2 EU
Xiaomi RedMi Note 9T (M2007J22G)	Mediatek Dimensity 800U	Mali G57 - 3 EU
Samung Galaxy Note 20 (SM-N981B)	Exinos 990	Mali G77 - 11 EU
Motorola One Fusion+	Snapdragon 730	Adreno 618 - 2 EU

The used indicator for the tests are:

- **Model Processing Time**: the time needed by the physical devices to obtain the inference result from model;
- **System Memory Size**: the total amount of RAM of the devices;
- **Managed Total Memory**: The total amount of RAM used by the application during the execution;

4.1 Motivation for the Choice of Devices

For the Apple models the selected devices are representative of a range of devices currently available on the market, in fact at the time of writing the article it is possible to buy the iPhone SE 2, iPhone 11, iPhone 12 and iPhone 13 models, for the choice of the iPad model we based on a choice of popularity as the iPad Air 4th generation was among the best selling models. For this reason these devices have been selected in order to approximate the tests carried out on devices that are on the market and that are owned by a wide audience of people and possible users of final products made with the workflow presented here.

For the Android models, since there is a wide choice of possible configurations, the choice was made by considering, at present, the terminals of the best-selling manufacturers and interweaving this information with the 3 possible SOC configurations that can be found on the market. In this case, find configurations based on Mediatek SOC in Italy is very complex, so we used only one device based on this SOC, for the Snapdragon configurations the choice fell on the top model at the (time of testing), i.e. the SOC Snapdragon 888, while the terminals with SOC Snapdragon 750G and 730 are terminals with performance and features comparable with the chip Mediatek Dimensity 800U and therefore have been included in the list of devices. In addition, a Samsung terminal from the Note 20 series based on the Exynos 990 chip has also been included, thus enabling a comparison with a different SOC, which from a conceptual point of view is similar to the Snapdragon 888 chips, differing in two aspects such as the manufacturing technology (7 nm vs 5 nm) and the GPU model. Tablets were not selected for the Android segment as they use identical SOCs to smartphones but have less RAM.

4.2 Test Configuration and Description

The aim of the tests carried out on these devices was to provide information on the inference times of the two models and the amount of memory used during execution. For this reason, two applications were created, using the framework presented, in order to simulate the real use of the framework. In particular, these applications, once started, loaded the model in memory and loaded ready-to-use images directly from the application assets. For each model, images were selected from the test dataset belonging to the dataset used for the training of the model itself. From each test dataset 4000 images were selected and loaded into the application, which simulated their acquisition by the device's camera. In this way, the tests were conducted in parallel on all the devices, connected to a power source to keep the battery charged throughout the duration of the test. Moreover, thanks to this configuration, the tests carried out used images of the same resolution for all the devices, which on the one hand undermines the specialisation of the test on the resolutions of the cameras inside the smartphones, but also allows us to understand how different hardware levels can affect the same amount of data to be analysed, providing more useful data for the purpose of the test, namely to understand the behaviour of the devices currently on the market for the use of neural network models within augmented reality. Precisely from this point of view, as previously mentioned, the studies carried out are based on the inference times of the two models and on the amount of memory used to obtain the results. In order to obtain the graphs that will be analysed in Sect. 4.4, a system of data collection from the terminals based on logging was used; in fact, at the end of the model inference, the collected data are sent to a collection server. The data collected for each inference are: inference time, memory occupied, smartphone model, SOC model, operating system version.

4.3 Test Application Execution

In addition to the model performance tests, the execution test was carried out on mobile devices, the results of which are shown in Fig. 1. In particular, in Fig. 1a there is the execution of the YOLO network trained on the food dataset, the result displays in the top left corner the class of the recognised object and the bounding box around the object projected in reality through the use of Unity's ARFoundation. Figure 1b shows the result of the execution of the MobileNet network trained on ImageNet, the model correctly recognizes the visualized object, a mouse, and projects in reality the name of the same for the visualization in the centre of the object. Other examples of real object detected and projected in AR mode are depicted in Fig. 2.

(a) (b)

Fig. 1. Example of classification running.

Following, the performance graphs are presented and analyzed based on the inference times and the memory used by the app during the processing phase.

4.4 Graph Analysis

The behaviour of the various terminals with the various models are analysed. The analysis is be performed separately based on the software platform.

The inference time is a parameter of fundamental importance for a neural network model and it becomes even more important considering the purpose of using these models in the context of AR applications. In fact, when using a smartphone for augmented reality, we expect to obtain a visual response in a few tenths of a second for the application to be engaging and usable by the user and the user does not decide to abandon its use. Considering that using neural networks within an app, not only do we have to wait for the calculation times necessary for the network to return a result, but there are also times necessary for the pre-processing of the data and for the post-processing of the results for the visualisation. Assuming constant pre-processing and post-processing times, a hypothesis that is possible and plausible thanks to software optimisation and

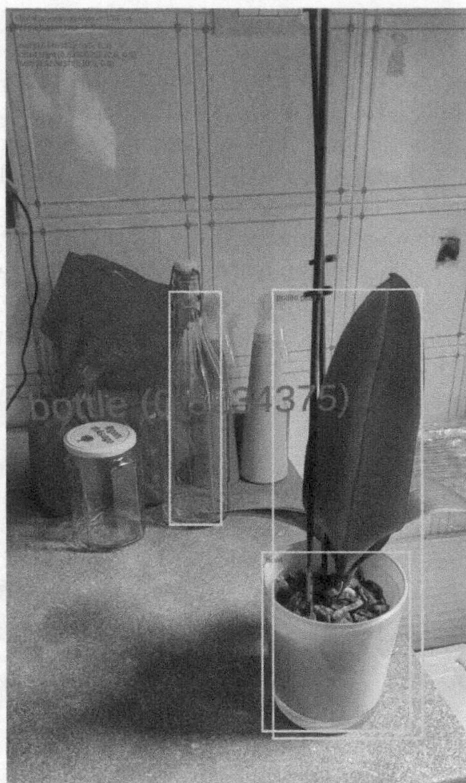

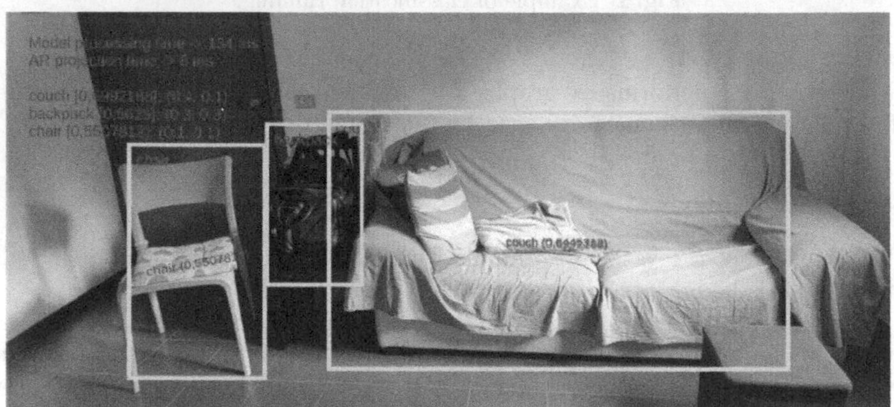

Fig. 2. Examples of detection and labelling running.

today's SOCs, which for these tasks have performances that differ by hundreds of thousandths of a second between the various categories under examination, it can be stated that the latency time that has the greatest impact on usability is precisely the network inference time.

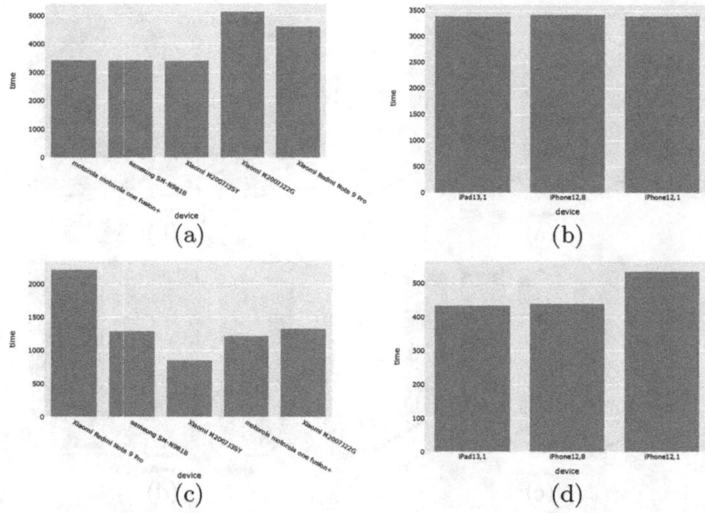

Fig. 3. Graphs of the average inference time of the models under analysis. Figure 3a and Fig. 3b show the average execution time of MobileNet for Android and iOS respectively. Figure 3c and Fig. 3d show the average execution time of Tiny-YOLO for Android and iOS respectively. For the name of the smartphone models see Table 4 and Table 3

On the devices available for testing, considering the average latency time over the whole test and excluding possible outliers outside the 99% quartile, we obtained the average times in Fig. 3 for both software platforms most used in mobile today.

Observing Fig. 3a and Fig. 3c inherent to the Android system, it can be seen that MobileNet requires on average more time for inference than Tiny-YOLO.

Observing the network architectures, it can be seen that MobileNet has skip-connections which require more computational time than a model with only consecutive connections and no skip-connections such as YOLO, and it is for this reason that MobileNet, despite being a model with fewer parameters (as demonstrated also by the amount of memory occupied Fig. 4) requires more computation time than YOLO.

Continuing on the graphs of Android devices we can see how the model of the SOC can influence, in fact considering the smartphones Xiaomi Mi 10T and Samsung Galaxy Note 20 that contain the top of the range SOCs in the execution of the MobileNet model present the best time. The Xiaomi Mi 10T, and consequently the Snapdragon 888 SOC, are also confirmed to be the best for running the YOLO model. It is precisely the execution of the YOLO model that allows us to understand how the configuration of the SOC also influences this, as the two top-of-the-range models (Xiaomi and Samsung) use SOCs that have similar architectures but differ in terms of resource management and GPU, and this with models that are more robust in terms of the number of parameters (such as the tiny-YOLO architecture) leads to a difference in inference times.

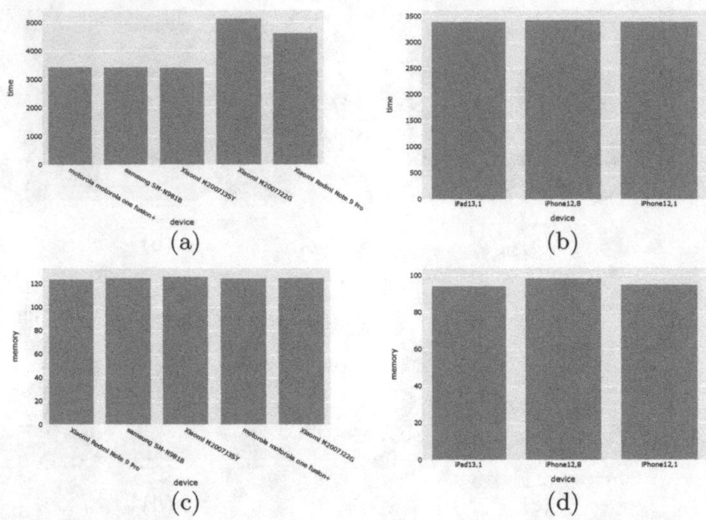

Fig. 4. In Fig. 4a and Fig. 4b there is the average memory usage during the execution of MobileNet for Android and iOS respectively. Figure 4c and Fig. 4d show the average memory usage while running Tiny-YOLO for Android and iOS respectively. For the name of the smartphone models see Table 4 and Table 3

Furthermore, focusing on mid-range smartphones shows that it is no longer just the SOC that makes a difference but also the software customisations. These can affect runtimes so much so that the Motorola One Fusion+ with pure Android and no customisations, which has a lower capacity SOC, runs faster than the Xiaomi Redmi Note 9T, a difference that is even more noticeable in the graph in Fig. 3c compared to the MobileNet graph in Fig. 3a.

Considering now iOS terminals, with iPhone and iPad, and analysing the MobileNet graph in Fig. 3b the execution does not show substantial differences in execution time. While the execution of the tiny-YOLO model of iPhone 11 requires a longer time to perform the inference, this difference with respect to iPhone SE 2 is due to the need of iPhone 11 to manage a terminal with a more advanced screen and sensors (which, even if the smartphone is not in use, generate data and require processing) and this can cause delays in the inference of the model, as visible in Fig. 3d.

In the case of the memory graphs, Fig. 4, it can be seen that for both software platforms there is a constant use of the amount of memory, although in different amounts. As a matter of fact, in the case of MobileNet Fig. 4a and Fig. 4b we can see that the amount of memory is less than the amount required by the tiny-YOLO model Fig. 4c and Fig. 4d. In addition to this by comparing the amount required per platform it can be seen that iOS based devices require less memory to load the model. This less exorbitant request is due to the software optimization in the compilation phase realized through the request and the obligation to use X-Code to obtain the apps for iOS, which applies software optimizations on the

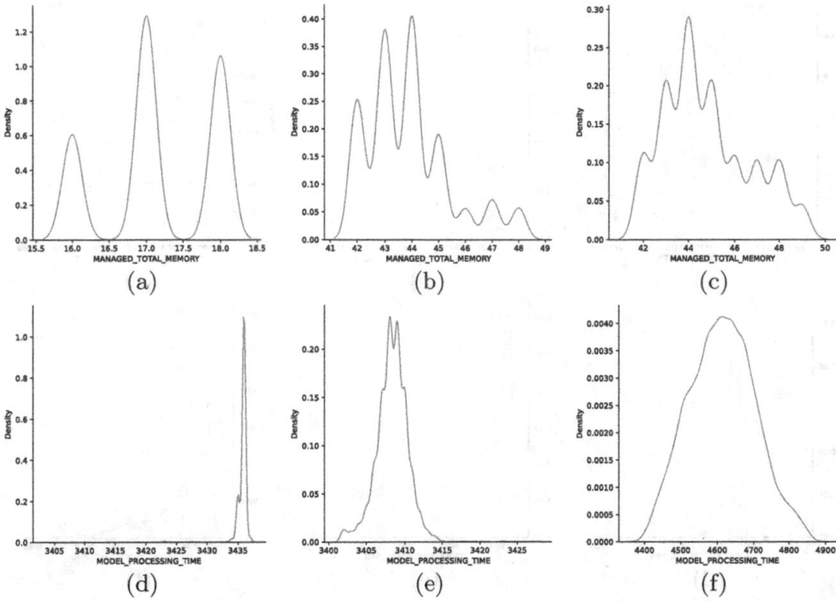

Fig. 5. The distribution plot of three terminal, two from the Table 4 and one from the Table 3 for the MobileNet architecture. In Fig. 5a and Fig. 5d was depicted the distribution, respectively, of the memory usage and processing time for the execution of the MobileNet on the iPhone 12,8. In Fig. 5b and Fig. 5e the memory and the processing time for the Xiaomi Mi 10T. In Fig. 5c and Fig. 5f the memory and processing time distribution for the Xiaomi RedMi Note 9 Pro

computational side that allow to obtain both lower inference times and lower memory usage and make the application realized using these models allow a realtime use unlike android devices that, despite being realtime, have higher latency times that in some cases could result in a frustration of use by the end user.

This analysis is also confirmed by the graphs in Fig. 5 and Fig. 6. In fact, from them we can see that on iOS, despite the presence of three peaks for the amount of memory used, its variation is narrow in terms of absolute values for the MobileNet (in Fig. 5a and Fig. 5d we considered iPhone 12.8). While in the case of Android terminals we find a high variation of memory usage for both terminals. Continuing on the memory analysis for the YOLO architecture, Fig. 6a, Fig. 6b and Fig. 6d, we see that the memory occupied is always lower than the Android terminals but this time, although the amounts used are lower on iOS, the range of variation is similar for all three terminals under analysis. Analysing again the execution times, the previous hypotheses are also confirmed by the way the execution time peaks are presented: on iOS, even though YOLO values are outside the central peak, they define very narrow ranges, confirming that the optimisation applied by X-Code affects the execution of the models. While on Android terminals it is immediately noticeable that the SOC 888 presents narrow

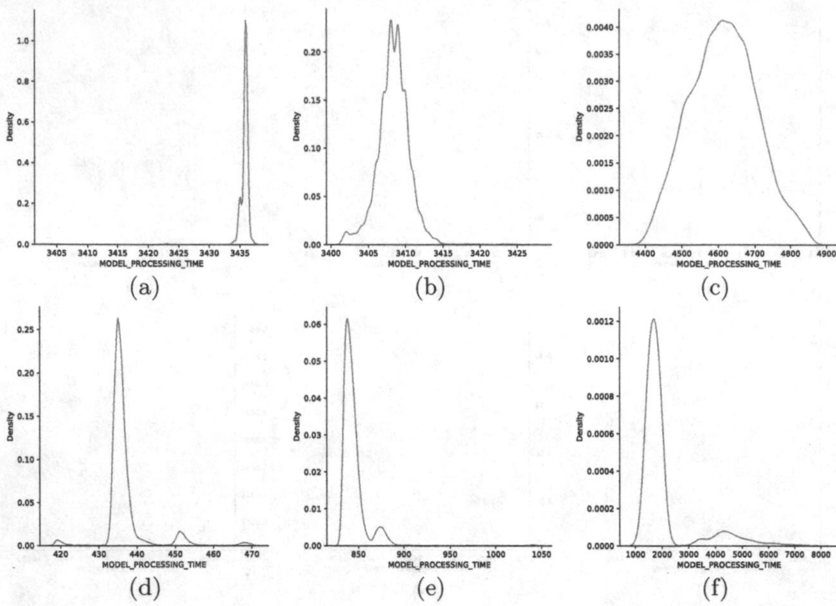

Fig. 6. The distribution plot of three terminal, two from the Table 4 and one from the Table 3 for the YOLO architecture. In Fig. 5a and Fig. 5d was depicted the distribution, respectively, of the memory usage and processing time for the execution of the YOLO on the iPhone 12,8. In Fig. 5b and Fig. 5e the memory and the processing time for the Xiaomi Mi 10T. In Fig. 5c and Fig. 5f the memory and processing time distribution for the Xiaomi RedMi Note 9 Pro

peaks even if the high complexity of the MobileNet (the skip connections) cause the presence of a wider range than on iOS. While the SOC 750G in the case of MobileNet presents a bell with a wide variance that makes us immediately understand how its performance is strongly influenced by the presence of a more complex architecture in terms of connections. While in the case of YOLO, a linear model in terms of connections, it also presents a narrow peak on higher execution values, although there are some values that, even if they are out of scale, suggest that this SOC has difficulties to manage neural models in conjunction with the use of augmented reality.

5 Conclusions and Future Works

In this study, a comparative analysis for the integration of AI-models into AR environments was performed. Two test applications have been developed and the execution time and memory usage data have been analysed, demonstrating the feasibility and possibility of integrating and using neural network models in mobile applications for augmented reality. The applications have been developed for both classification and object detection tasks with state of the art neural networks, specifically integrated to be run on mobile devices. Given the statistics here presented, we can state that the models run in real time even in medium-low level devices, demonstrating that the integration is in its maturity. Several limitations still exixts, and our future work will push on the following directions. First of all, performances are based on the automatic management by the SoCs, which manage the memory occupation between GPU and CPU. By developing a native solution, it will be possible to integrate AI models that better fits with the devices' architectures.

More in general, our group is working on the release of a dedicate framework, integrated in Unity, that will enable the user to integrate AI models directly with Barracuda, overcoming all the limitations described in this work. The corpus of the main idea, the source code end demos can be found at (https://github.com/SinergiaGit/DeepReality) and (https://assetstore.unity.com/packages/tools/integration/deepreality-201076).

Acknowledgment. This project has received funding from the European Union's Horizon 2020 research and innovation programme through the XR4ALL project with grant agreement No 825545.

References

1. Bekele, M.K., Pierdicca, R., Frontoni, E., Malinverni, E.S., Gain, J.: A survey of augmented, virtual, and mixed reality for cultural heritage. J. Comput. Cul. Herit. (JOCCH) **11**(2), 1–36 (2018)
2. Cantillo, D., Cervantes, B., Cardona, J.: HealthCam: machine learning models on mobile devices for unhealthy packaged food detection and classification. In: 2020 IEEE International Conference on E-health Networking, Application & Services (HEALTHCOM), pp. 1–6. IEEE (2021)
3. Chen, J.W., Lin, W.J., Cheng, H.J., Hung, C.L., Lin, C.Y., Chen, S.P.: A smartphone-based application for scale pest detection using multiple-object detection methods. Electronics **10**(4), 372 (2021)
4. Clini, P., Frontoni, E., Quattrini, R., Pierdicca, R.: Augmented reality experience: from high-resolution acquisition to real time augmented contents. Adv. Multimedia **2014**, 1–9 (2014)
5. Deng, J., Dong, W., Socher, R., Li, L.J., Li, K., Fei-Fei, L.: ImageNet: a large-scale hierarchical image database. In: 2009 IEEE Conference on Computer Vision and Pattern Recognition, pp. 248–255. IEEE (2009)
6. Elhassouny, A., Smarandache, F.: Smart mobile application to recognize tomato leaf diseases using convolutional neural networks. In: 2019 International Conference of Computer Science and Renewable Energies (ICCSRE), pp. 1–4. IEEE (2019)
7. Gammeter, S., Gassmann, A., Bossard, L., Quack, T., Van Gool, L.: Server-side object recognition and client-side object tracking for mobile augmented reality. In: 2010 IEEE Computer Society Conference on Computer Vision and Pattern Recognition-Workshops, pp. 1–8. IEEE (2010)
8. Han, J., Zhang, D., Cheng, G., Liu, N., Xu, D.: Advanced deep-learning techniques for salient and category-specific object detection: a survey. IEEE Sig. Process. Mag. **35**(1), 84–100 (2018)

9. Howard, A.G., et al.: MobileNets: efficient convolutional neural networks for mobile vision applications. arXiv preprint arXiv:1704.04861 (2017)
10. Khan, M.A., Israr, S., Almogren, A.S., Din, I.U., Almogren, A., Rodrigues, J.J.: Using augmented reality and deep learning to enhance Taxila Museum experience. J. Real-Time Image Proc. **18**(2), 321–332 (2021). https://doi.org/10.1007/s11554-020-01038-y
11. Lalonde, J.F.: Deep learning for augmented reality. In: 2018 17th Workshop on Information Optics (WIO), pp. 1–3. IEEE (2018)
12. Lampropoulos, G., Keramopoulos, E., Diamantaras, K.: Enhancing the functionality of augmented reality using deep learning, semantic web and knowledge graphs: a review. Vis. Inf. **4**(1), 32–42 (2020)
13. Lin, P.H., Chen, S.Y.: Design and evaluation of a deep learning recommendation based augmented reality system for teaching programming and computational thinking. IEEE Access **8**, 45689–45699 (2020)
14. Lin, T.-Y., et al.: Microsoft COCO: common objects in context. In: Fleet, D., Pajdla, T., Schiele, B., Tuytelaars, T. (eds.) ECCV 2014. LNCS, vol. 8693, pp. 740–755. Springer, Cham (2014). https://doi.org/10.1007/978-3-319-10602-1_48
15. Liu, L., et al.: Deep learning for generic object detection: a survey. Int. J. Comput. Vis. **128**(2), 261–318 (2020)
16. Liu, W., et al.: SSD: single shot multibox detector. In: Leibe, B., Matas, J., Sebe, N., Welling, M. (eds.) ECCV 2016. LNCS, vol. 9905, pp. 21–37. Springer, Cham (2016). https://doi.org/10.1007/978-3-319-46448-0_2
17. Lowe, D.G.: Object recognition from local scale-invariant features. In: Proceedings of the 7th IEEE International Conference on Computer Vision, vol. 2, pp. 1150–1157. IEEE (1999)
18. Matsuda, Y., Hoashi, H., Yanai, K.: Recognition of multiple-food images by detecting candidate regions. In: 2012 IEEE International Conference on Multimedia and Expo, pp. 25–30. IEEE (2012)
19. Monteiro, P., Gonçalves, G., Coelho, H., Melo, M., Bessa, M.: Hands-free interaction in immersive virtual reality: a systematic review. IEEE Trans. Vis. Comput. Graph. **27**(5), 2702–2713 (2021)
20. Muñoz Bocanegra, R., et al.: Aprendizaje profundo en dispositivo portable para el reconocimiento de frutas y verduras (2019)
21. Nasreen, J., Arif, W., Shaikh, A.A., Muhammad, Y., Abdullah, M.: Object detection and narrator for visually impaired people. In: 2019 IEEE 6th International Conference on Engineering Technologies and Applied Sciences (ICETAS), pp. 1–4. IEEE (2019)
22. Ngugi, L.C., Abdelwahab, M., Abo-Zahhad, M.: Tomato leaf segmentation algorithms for mobile phone applications using deep learning. Comput. Electron. Agric. **178**, 105788 (2020)
23. Nguyen, M., Tran, H., Le, H., Yan, W.Q.: A tile based colour picture with hidden QR code for augmented reality and beyond. In: Proceedings of the 23rd ACM Symposium on Virtual Reality Software and Technology, pp. 1–4 (2017)
24. Park, K.B., Kim, M., Choi, S.H., Lee, J.Y.: Deep learning-based smart task assistance in wearable augmented reality. Robot. Comput. Integr. Manuf. **63**, 101887 (2020)
25. Park, Y.J., Ro, H., Lee, N.K., Han, T.D.: Deep-care: projection-based home care augmented reality system with deep learning for elderly. Appl. Sci. **9**(18), 3897 (2019)
26. Pescarin, S.: Digital heritage into practice. SCIRES-IT Sci. Res. Inf. Technol. **6**(1), 1–4 (2016)

27. Pierdicca, R., Frontoni, E., Pollini, R., Trani, M., Verdini, L.: The use of augmented reality glasses for the application in industry 4.0. In: De Paolis, L.T., Bourdot, P., Mongelli, A. (eds.) AVR 2017. LNCS, vol. 10324, pp. 389–401. Springer, Cham (2017). https://doi.org/10.1007/978-3-319-60922-5_30
28. Puggioni, M., Frontoni, E., Paolanti, M., Pierdicca, R.: ScoolAR: an educational platform to improve students' learning through virtual reality. IEEE Access **9**, 21059–21070 (2021)
29. Rao, J., Qiao, Y., Ren, F., Wang, J., Du, Q.: A mobile outdoor augmented reality method combining deep learning object detection and spatial relationships for geovisualization. Sensors **17**(9), 1951 (2017)
30. Redmon, J., Divvala, S., Girshick, R., Farhadi, A.: You only look once: unified, real-time object detection. In: Proceedings of the IEEE Conference on Computer Vision and Pattern Recognition, pp. 779–788 (2016)
31. Redmon, J., Farhadi, A.: YOLO9000: better, faster, stronger. In: Proceedings of the IEEE Conference on Computer Vision and Pattern Recognition, pp. 7263–7271 (2017)
32. Ren, S., He, K., Girshick, R., Sun, J.: Faster R-CNN: towards real-time object detection with region proposal networks. In: Advances in Neural Information Processing Systems, vol. 28 (2015)
33. Ren, S., He, K., Girshick, R., Sun, J.: Faster R-CNN: towards real-time object detection with region proposal networks. IEEE Trans. Pattern Anal. Mach. Intell. **39**(6), 1137–1149 (2016)
34. Salunkhe, A., Raut, M., Santra, S., Bhagwat, S.: Android-based object recognition application for visually impaired. In: ITM Web of Conferences, vol. 40, p. 03001. EDP Sciences (2021)
35. Sandler, M., Howard, A., Zhu, M., Zhmoginov, A., Chen, L.C.: MobileNetV2: inverted residuals and linear bottlenecks. In: Proceedings of the IEEE Conference on Computer Vision and Pattern Recognition, pp. 4510–4520 (2018)
36. Sanga, S., Mero, V., Machuve, D., Mwanganda, D.: Mobile-based deep learning models for banana diseases detection. arXiv preprint arXiv:2004.03718 (2020)
37. Sereno, M., Wang, X., Besançon, L., McGuffin, M.J., Isenberg, T.: Collaborative work in augmented reality: a survey. IEEE Trans. Vis. Comput. Graph. **28**, 2530–2549 (2020)
38. Svensson, J., Atles, J.: Object detection in augmented reality. Master's Theses in Mathematical Sciences (2018)
39. Szegedy, C., Vanhoucke, V., Ioffe, S., Shlens, J., Wojna, Z.: Rethinking the inception architecture for computer vision. In: Proceedings of the IEEE Conference on Computer Vision and Pattern Recognition, pp. 2818–2826 (2016)
40. Tanzi, L., Piazzolla, P., Porpiglia, F., Vezzetti, E.: Real-time deep learning semantic segmentation during intra-operative surgery for 3d augmented reality assistance. Int. J. Comput. Assist. Radiol. Surg. **16**(9), 1435–1445 (2021)
41. Zhao, Z.Q., Zheng, P., Xu, S., Wu, X.: Object detection with deep learning a review. IEEE Trans. Neural Netw. Learn. Syst. **30**(11), 3212–3232 (2019)

Find, Fuse, Fight: Genetic Algorithms to Provide Engaging Content for Multiplayer Augmented Reality Games

Federico Aliprandi, Renato Avellar Nobre, Laura Anna Ripamonti(✉), Davide Gadia, and Dario Maggiorini

Computer Science Department, University of Milano, Milan, Italy
{federico.aliprandi,renato.avellarnobre}@studenti.unimi.it,
ripamonti@di.unimi.it, {davide.gadia,dario.maggiorini}@unimi.it

Abstract. In Augmented Reality (AR) mobile games, several technical aspects are still partially under-explored, thus limiting the creativity of game designers and the spectrum of possible uses of AR. As a result, too often AR is used only to superimpose in a static way predefined digital content to real scenarios. In the present work, we have started to tackle this issue by designing a game to overcome the limited interactivity among players and the somewhat static use of AR on resource-limited devices (i.e., cell phones). In particular, we have designed and prototyped FFF: Find, Fuse, Fight, a game that supports multiplayer mode, offers a more creative use of AR, and demonstrates that Procedural Content Generation (PCG) techniques could be effectively exploited for introducing a higher degree of variability both in the content and in the gameplay, even on devices far less performing than a standard PC. In particular, we developed a prototype that exploits Genetic Algorithms (GAs) to create new content and apply meshes deformation to 3D models in real-time. We have used such content to prototype a mobile game that features AR battles among creatures in an online multiplayer environment. The prototypes have undergone a performance test to evaluate the feasibility of AR multiplayer games with generated content, collecting encouraging preliminary outcomes.

Keywords: Alternate reality games · Genetic Algorithms · Game design

1 Introduction

Researchers have been studying Augmented Reality (AR) since the early 1990s, but it was not until the 2010s that we saw a considerable boost in research and development on this subject [1]. The market success of smartphones was the factor that significantly impacted this trend. Having always connected pocket devices with cameras and significant computational power widespread among the population created the perfect platform for such applications [1]. In the

L. T. De Paolis et al. (Eds.): XR Salento 2022, LNCS 13446, pp. 178–197, 2022.
https://doi.org/10.1007/978-3-031-15553-6_14

mid-2010s, Apple and Google also released their framework for developing AR applications for their platforms (i.e., iOS and Android): ARKit and ARCore, thus attracting developers that started working on AR applications, aided by the availability of high-level solutions, which promptly supported these frameworks right after their release, such as the Unity3D game engine [23]. While early studies on AR mainly proposed applications to support training and manufacturing, more recent works have focused also on entertainment and edutainment (i.e., the use of entertainment methods finalized to teach something to the end-user), [10]. Nowadays, one popular AR application for mobile devices is games, e.g., the very well-known Pokémon Go by Niantic. Consequently, more innovative approaches are emerging, especially from the entertainment perspective.

Nevertheless, several technical aspects are still partially under-explored, thus limiting the creativity of game designers and - more in general - the type and finality of AR applications. Among those aspects, one that, in our opinion, is both relevant and intriguing is the possibility to have interactive content that is dynamically generated on the fly, thus allowing for more complex game mechanics and more flexible AR applications. As a matter of fact, one of the current limitations of AR games for mobile devices is a certain repetitiveness of the gameplay: the most diffused games exploit AR at best to superimpose some pre-defined digital content (e.g., a game character like in the case of Pokémon Go or Pikmin Bloom - released in 2016 and 2021 by Niantic) to real scenarios, with a minimal possibility to interact with it and to use the AR content in the context of the interaction among users, as it happens for example in a multiplayer game.

Starting from this observation, we have tried to tackle the problem by investigating the possibility of designing and developing a multi-user AR application for mobile devices that uses content dynamically generated on the fly. This implied dealing with different categories of issues, such as designing a prototypal game, defining an approach to the Procedural Content Generation (PCG) able to couple with the limited resources of a mobile device, as well as dealing with the issue of designing and implementing an appropriate client-server application able to support the multiplayer mode of the game. As a proof of concept, we have designed and prototyped "FFF: Find, Fuse, Fight" (FFF for brevity from now on), a game that exploits Artificial Intelligence (AI) techniques to sustain a gameplay that includes a turn-based battle system and the procedural generation of the majority of the content that will be enjoyed in AR. Its gameplay is based on three main aspects:

- **Find**(ing) eggs which contain procedural generated Creatures (i.e., characters controlled by players during battles);
- **Fuse**(ing) pairs of Creatures to generate a new one that inherits characteristics from both its parents;
- **Fight**(ing) against another player's Creatures in online multiplayer, turn-based battles.

FFF relies on Genetic Algorithms (GAs) for the generation of contents. In time, GAs have been used in many fields, particularly in AI and operations research, to generate high-quality optimization and search problems solutions

[9,12,14]. Nevertheless, they have also been successfully used in commercial video games, and they are still the object of academic research in this field [5,18]. The evolutionary crossover and mutation concepts are the foundation of GAs [8], whose structure borrows from the biological sexual reproduction process, during which parents chromosomes are mixed and recombined to generate one or more offspring [19]. Thus, the use of GAs provides an intriguing approach to the Fuse aspect of the game. The chromosomes representing a couple of "parent" Creatures are combined to produce a new one that inherits characteristics from them (and may also have some mutations). Therefore, the chromosome of the offspring contains a set of genes representing its battle-related skills (such as type of attacks, life points, etc.) and another set that defines its appearance. The 3D model of the creature is a combination of the parents' model to mimic the inheritance of the physical traits. Last but not least, certain physical traits can affect some specific features of the Creature: e.g., having a large body produces an increase in its life points. While the recombination of the Creature skills only requires some bit-switching in the chromosome representation, the model morphing is a bit more complex and its outcome may impact both some gene subsets, as said before, and the complexity of the generated mesh of the model, thus possibly affecting the performance of the application on a mobile device.

The remaining of this paper is organized as follows. Section 2 outlines the related works in the field, analyzing the relevant approaches by commercial and academic research works about applying AR and GAs to video games. Section 3 describes the concept of FFF, the mobile AR game that makes use of ideas inspired by GAs, along with an overview and description of the architecture and implementations details in the development of the prototypes. In Sect. 4, the results of a performance test done on a mobile device are given. Finally, in Sect. 5, the result of the work produced for this paper is discussed together with an overview of possible future developments.

2 Related Works

We believe that one of the main limitations of AR games for mobile devices is the repetitiveness of their gameplay and a certain lack of engaging mechanics. Therefore, this section briefly presents a selection of recent state-of-the-art studies and commercial approaches in video games that use AR techniques or GAs for the Procedural Generation of Content (PGC).

2.1 AR Video Games

The Eye of Judgment (Sony Computer Entertainment, 2007) is one of the first successful commercial AR games [26]. It is a turn-based card battle game that uses PlayStation Eye camera to recognize cards on a game board and augment the view on the TV screen. In a similar vein, the gameplay of Invizimals for PlayStation Portable (Sony Computer Entertainment, 2009) consists of hunting and capturing creatures visible in AR through the device camera and then using them to fight against other creatures. Invizimals has seen many sequels, including mobile AR games. Another example of Sony efforts on AR is Wonderbook (2012), an AR book designed to be used in many games, such as the Book of Spells, based on the Harry Potter franchise.

An early approach by Niantic to location-based mobile AR games is Ingress (2013). The gameplay involves capturing portals at physical places of interest, such as monuments, and linking them to create virtual control fields over geographical areas. This game laid the foundations for the studio's most successful release: Pokémon Go (2016). In Pokémon Go the player must find and catch creatures. When a Pokémon is located, the player can see it in the actual environment through the device camera and can try to capture it. Pokémon Go is probably the most successful commercial AR game released so far, and it has had a significant impact on media all over the world [6]. After the success of their previous two AR games, in 2019, Niantic released Harry Potter: Wizards Unite, another mobile AR game themed after the renowned franchise, and - in October 2021 - Pikmin Bloom, based on the successful Pikmin trilogy by Nintendo.

After observing the massive success of Pokémon Go, Tong *et al.* [24] designed an online survey to better understand why players spend so much time playing the game. In particular, they tried to understand the player's primary motivations, when and how they play the game, and what potential changes in physical activity Pokémon Go may elicit. The goal of this survey was to better understand the motivation behind the game's success to derive some guidelines about crucial success features to introduce in applied games aimed at promoting physical activity. According to the participants' answers, the main reasons for playing the game are collecting Pokémon and socializing with other players. The main reason for stopping playing, instead, is because all Pokémons have been collected, followed by the fact that the game requires too much time and energy. The features most liked by participants are catching Pokémon in an AR environment, finding special areas mapped into real-world locations, and battling. However, the most disliked aspects are the too simple core mechanic and some hardware and software issues (currently mainly fixed). Another relevant example of AR games for mobile devices is Star Wars: Jedi Challenges (Disney, 2017). To function the game needs to use, besides the app, a Lenovo Mirage AR headset, a Lightsaber controller, and a tracking beacon. The game allows the player to engage in battles either single-player or against another player and play Holochess, a turn-based strategy game.

Besides commercial games, AR in entertainment applications has also been studied by scholars. For example, an AR Chinese Checkers video game has been developed to investigate user interface issues for tabletop projected AR entertainment applications [2]. The authors state that the advantages of playing games on a digital device rather than on a physical board include introducing animations and other multimedia presentations, which add excitement to the gameplay while also being helpful for players to learn the rules and understand invalid moves. The AR Chinese Checkers application is based on the Passive Detection Framework [20], which supports a variety of displays and interaction modalities to track marked objects in space. Additionally, the approach uses markers to define the game board and to allow players to place their pawns. Another system for AR for board games has been used by Molla *et al.* [13] for the popular Monopoly™game. In this case, the developers did not create a virtual board, but instead they augment the experience over an existing physical board and pawns. The physical objects act as a tangible interface. The experience is improved by applying visual effects over these objects and letting game logic be performed automatically by the computer. Another example of the use of AR has been developed by Vera *et al.* in SituAR [25]. Their work propose a prototype platform that enables users to craft AR experiences directly through their smartphone, place them at specific points of interest and share them with other users. Therefore, SituAR encourages users to visualize, create and share location-based stories, thus allowing potential visitors to learn more about the area they are visiting while at the same time sustaining and promoting physical exercise. In a similar vein, AR has been used in edutainment: Explorez [15] is a quest-based, AR mobile game that promotes learning French as a foreign language. Using GPS, Explorez transforms a University campus into a virtual francophone world, where students interact with characters, items, and media as they improve their French language skills and discover their campus.

From the previous example, it appears evident that a certain number of AR games rely on external equipment to enhance the game experience, such as Star Wars: Jedi Challenges or the Wonderbook. When AR is used solely on mobile devices for gaming purposes, Tong *et al.* [24] and Zubair *et al.* [28] note that many games have issues with oversimplified game mechanics and hardware and software problems. With this in mind, FFF tries to propose an approach to AR games able to leverage enjoyable multiplayer-based game mechanics that include content procedurally generated according to the Experience-Driven Procedural Content Generation (EDPCG) approach [27] (see Sect. 2.2).

2.2 GAs for PCG in Games

There are few commercial video games known to make use of GAs. At the same time, academic research is still exploring new effective ways to exploit them for entertainment applications [4,5,7,18].

Grand *et al.* [4] propose Creatures, a life simulation video game in which the player can interact with synthetic agents. The internal architecture of the creatures is inspired by animal biology. Each creature has a neural network responsible for sensory-motor coordination and behavior selection, plus artificial biochemistry, which models a simple metabolism and a hormonal system. Additionally, a variable-length genetic encoding specifies both the network architecture and the creature's biochemistry details, allowing for evolutionary adaptation through reproduction. The creature's structure and function are determined by its genes. Grand has used Binary Encoding for the creatures' chromosomes. A similar approach is that of Galactic Arms Race (GAR) [7], a space shooter video game that includes elements typical of action-Role Playing Games (RPGs). GAR was developed as an experiment during the 2010 Indie Game Challenge and then became a commercial product. It uses a custom version of the NeuroEvolution of Augmenting Topologies (NEAT) [21] to implement a system that evolves unique weapons according to players' preferences, based on their weapons usage statistics. In the work Generator Of Life Embedded into MMOs (GOLEM) [5], the authors propose the use of an adaptation of GAs to populate with creatures the vast environments of Massive Multiplayer Online Role-Playing Games (MMORPGs), thus providing diversity across the population and consequently more varied gameplay. GOLEM creatures are modeled on the characteristics of those used in the paper-and-pen RPG Dungeon & Dragons. In particular, a chromosome composed of 53 genes represents their physical traits, magic abilities, and skills. The Diversity Regulated Adaptive Generator ONline (DRAGON) [18] further evolves GOLEM capabilities. The work proposes multiple improvements to the GOLEM algorithm, among which the most notable aspect is that DRAGON has been designed in the framework of the Experience-Driven Procedural Content Generation (EDPCG) [27] approach. This means putting the experience lived by the player while playing the game as the guiding principle for evolving monsters, whose "fitness" is directly linked to the quality of their interaction with the player.

Both GOLEM and DRAGON have a limitation: since they have been designed as multi-purpose support tools for game designers (in the sense that can produce literally any type of monster for any possible setting) they only provide "archetypal" descriptions of the generated creatures, but not their actual representation in terms of game assets (3D models, animations, etc.). FFF tries to overcome such limitations by applying a GA that causes visual changes in the 3D models of creatures by deforming their mesh.

3 FFF: Find, Fuse, Fight

As stated before, mobile AR games have seen a considerable growth, but the possibilities they could offer are still mainly under explored from many perspectives. Generally, they are primarily focused on single-player interactions, in which the AR does not add much, playing the role, in many cases, of a mere cosmetic add-on [28]. In our opinion, for example, seeing digital characters of a multiplayer AR game moving around and performing their attacks within the actual world environment could represent a much more exciting experience. Especially if we consider that, for a large number of players, AR is still a new experience, and even well-known games, such as Checkers, when played in AR, can provide a completely new experience [2].

To address this gap in AR games, we have decided to tackle two major under-explored features: the multiplayer mode and the dynamic adaptation of content. To this extent, we have devised and prototyped the game "FFF: Find, Fuse, Fight", which adds the AR feature to the turn-based battle system classical of dozens of Japanese Role-Playing Games (JRPGs) such as the Pokémon (by Nintendo) and Final Fantasy (by Square Enix) series. In particular, FFF implements Player-versus-Player (PvP) features, which are very popular among gamers but too often under-used in mobile AR games. Moreover, in FFF, the characters used by players to compete can evolve thanks to content procedurally generated by GAs, thus introducing a reasonable degree of variability and making the game less predictable, more strategical and more compelling. Nevertheless, the "rules of good game design" underline the importance of putting the user experience of the player at the center of the design process [3], and the automatic creation of content is no exception, in the sense that it should try to fit the player expectations and desires, as demonstrated by [27]. For this reason, we have included in the design process of FFF, and more specifically in the Fuse phase, the main principles of EDPCG [27] by enabling the player to impact directly on the PCG process. We think that the overall approach we have devised could be exploited, e.g., to address the notorious players' retention issue so common among AR mobile games [28], but could as well become a feature able to support and enrich AR-based educational content or business applications.

3.1 Overview of FFF

Basically, in FFF, the players' goal is to collect Creatures, fuse them or use them to play PvP battles against other players. Consequently, the gameplay consists of three different moments, as suggested by the game's title:

1. *Find*: players must collect eggs. Eggs are hidden in locations in the actual world and can be located using a map. Once players are close enough to an egg, they can tap on an icon on the device's screen to get it and put it in their bag (i.e., the in-game player's inventory). This phase is a kind of egg hunt inspired by the classical game played by American children on Easter day. After some time has elapsed, the egg will hatch, rewarding players with a Creature. The longer time an egg needs to hatch, the higher the resulting Creature's stats will be.
2. *Fuse*: players can combine a couple of their Creatures to obtain a new one that inherits some characteristics from both. This process, in the game, is referred to as *fusion*, and it is implemented using an *ad hoc* GA.
3. *Fight*: players choose two of their Creatures to engage in a battle against another - human or synthetic - player. The gameplay consists of a traditional turn-based battle system. The match occurs in the augmented real world: the device camera detects a planar surface (such as a table) to place the virtual battlefield, where the animated Creatures' 3D models are rendered. Players can see the 3D Creatures fighting inside the real world, making the user experience much more immersive.

Since the purpose of our work was not to create a commercial product but to explore whether AR games for mobile devices could become more complex (and probably also more engaging), we have fully prototyped only the Fuse and Fight game mechanics. We adopted Unity 3D [23] as game engine, since it has built-in support for the AR SDK Vuforia Engine [16] and for Google ARCore and Apple ARKit frameworks.

3.2 Fuse: Generation of New Creatures

During this phase, players select a couple of their Creatures to perform a "fusion". The fusion process uses GAs to produce a new Creature starting from the selected "parents". The resulting Creature combines the parents' characteristics, both physical appearance and battle statistics and attacks. Since a Fusion forces players to lose the fused Creatures, a preview of the resulting offspring is shown, and - according to the EDPCG principles - they can decide whether to confirm it. Furthermore, a particular *bonus* or *malus* can be added to one or more of the offspring skills, depending on some traits of its physical appearance. For instance, if a Creature is very tall, it would receive a *bonus* on its life points but a *malus* on its agility value.

The proposed approach introduces a certain complexity in the strategy the player has to develop. Firstly, it ensures that some skill values are improved at the expense of others: players should preview the fusion of a certain number of Creatures before finding the combination that provides them the result they were hoping for. Additionally, it adds a correlation between physical appearance and intrinsic characteristics, thus allowing expert players to guess "at first sight" which strengths and weaknesses the offspring (or an opposing Creature during a Fight) probably has.

Creatures Customization Prototype. A Creatures Customization prototype has been developed to test the Fuse process. It allows users to produce a new Creature, customize its characteristics, or fuse existing Creatures into new ones. The prototype finality is twofold: on the one hand, it has been used to test the feasibility (also in terms of performance) of applying meshes deformation to 3D models on the fly, and on the other, to verify the effectiveness of the GA approach we have devised.

The prototype is based on Unity Multipurpose Avatar (UMA), which supports developers in creating avatar customization systems for games or other multimedia interactive applications. The main reasons for which, among the different alternatives available in the Unity Asset store, we picked UMA are its support of morphing, its high-performance optimization and high flexibility, and the fact that it has an active community of maintainers. Actually, it allows applying modifiers to individual parts of a model, such as changing arms length, head size, ears position, or eyes rotation. Additionally, it is optimized: when baking an avatar, it generates a single skinned mesh, allowing for less intensive rendering, hence being a suitable solution for less powerful devices such as mobile phones.

As shown in Fig. 1, the Edit Creature screen of our prototype shows the Creature being edited on the right, while on the left side there are some tabs and sliders through which it is possible to modify the value assumed by various genes. In particular, it is possible to customize the Creature's appearance by changing the values of over 50 body modifiers. Moreover, it is also possible to edit combat statistics, Creature's type, and attacks type. For the sake of testing, only humanoid Creatures have been prototyped; nonetheless, UMA is a general-purpose framework that is not limited to humanoid models, but can manage

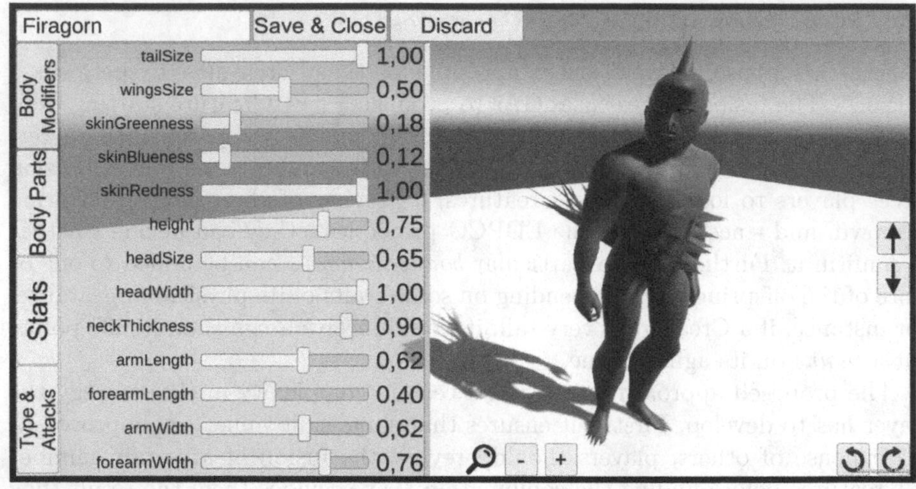

Fig. 1. Creatures customization prototype edit screen.

quite any kind of skeleton. Hence our approach could quite easily be generalized to any creature type.

Once at least two Creatures have been created, users can select them to perform a Fusion, thus generating a new Creature (see Fig. 2). Users can perform a Fusion between two creatures as many times as they wish: the interface will always allow them to compare the actual numeric value of each characteristic between the parents and the resulting child.

How the Fuse Phase Exploits GAs. GAs are a particular class of algorithms used in many fields, especially in AI and Operations Research (OR), to generate high-quality solutions to optimization and search problems [9,12,14]. They are inspired by Darwin's Theory of Evolution and rely on bio-inspired operators such as Selection, Crossover, and Mutation. They were conceived by John Holland, who stated that "computer programs that evolve in ways that resemble natural selection could solve complex problems even their creators do not fully understand" [8]. In the "classical" version of GAs, a candidate solution to a complex problem is represented by a chromosome (also called an "individual"). It contains a set of genes [12], that, following the biological similitude, are recombined through *crossover* and *mutation* with another chromosome to produce a new solution [8], whose "goodness" is then measured by an appropriate *fitness function.* Different types of crossover can be applied, and how they are implemented depends on how the genes are represented [19] (e.g., they can be bit sequences [8]). FFF implements an *ad hoc* version of a GA to procedurally generate creatures during the Fuse process. In particular, we use chromosomes, crossover, and mutation, but no fitness function, since our goal is to create diversity, not to find an "optimal monster" for the game (which, by the way, would disrupt the fun for

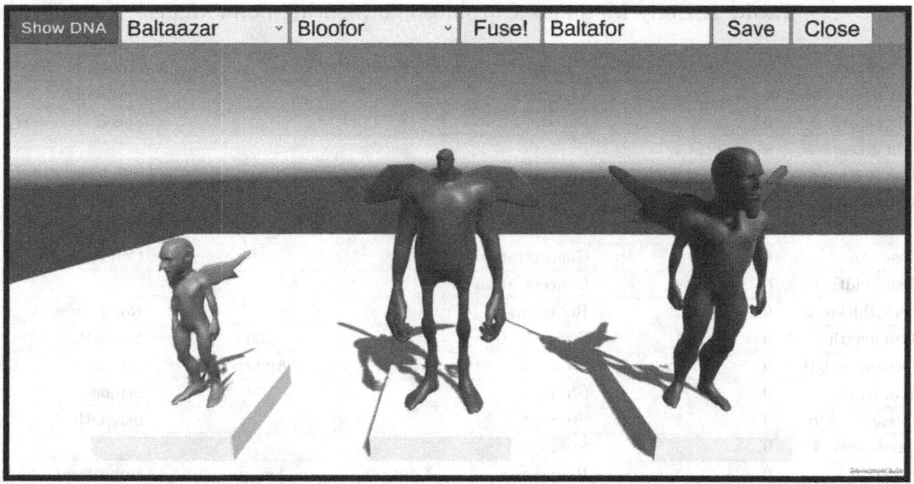

Fig. 2. Creatures Customization prototype fusion screen. Left and center creature are the parents, offspring on the right.

the players, being too though for any opponent). In GAs, a set of chromosomes for the same individual is called DNA [12]. In FFF, Creatures DNA is composed by the following chromosomes:

- **Body Modifiers:** represents the exact configuration of the different body parts of the creature model. Table 1 lists the genes and the *bonus* or *malus* that a variation in their value produces;
- **Body Parts:** indicates which mesh(es) to use for each body parts, as summarized in Table 2;
- **Parts Presence:** two genes that define whether the creature has wings or tail;
- **Stats:** represent the Creature's Stats (i.e., the value assumed for the various creature skills, such as strength or life point - see Table 3), which affect its fighting performance;
- **Type:** defines the creature's type, which can be either Water, Fire, Wood, Electricity, or any combination of two of these;
- **Attacks:** consists of a list of attack types available for the creature.

In FFF, the DNA to be mixed is picked by the player when he or she selects the couple of parents. Then FFF applies on them two different crossover techniques: (i) Uniform Crossover, in which the genes of the offspring chromosome are copied from the corresponding gene of the chromosome of one of the parents chosen randomly [22]; and (ii) Arithmetic Crossover, in which, for each couple of genes, an arithmetic operation (such as AND or OR for bitwise operations) is performed to determine the value of the corresponding gene in the offspring [11]. Hence, during the Fuse phase, the crossover is performed in the following way:

Table 1. Body Modifiers Chromosome (floating point values)

Gene name	Min value	Max value	High value bonus	High value malus	Low value bonus	Low value malus
Tail size	0	1	Technique			Technique
Wing size	0	1	Speed			Speed
Skin greenness	0	1				
Skin bluenness	0	1				
Skin redness	0	1				
Height	0	1	Max HP	Agility	Agility	Max HP
Head size	0	1	Concentration			Concentration
Head width	0	1	Concentration			
Neck thickness	0	1	Robustness			Robustness
Arm length	0	1	Strength	Agility	Agility	Strength
Forearm length	0	1	Strength	Agility	Agility	Strength
Arm width	0	1	Strength			Strength
Forearm width	0	1	Strength			Strength
Hands size	0	1	Strength			
Feet size	0	1	Robustness	Agility	Agility	Robustness
Leg separation	0	1				Speed
Upper muscle	0	1	Strength			Strength
Lower muscle	0	1	Strength			Strength
Upper weight	0	1	Robustness	Agility	Agility	Robustness
Lower weight	0	1	Robustness	Speed	Speed	Robustness
Legs size	0	1	Speed	Agility	Agility	Speed
Belly	0	1	Max HP	Speed		
Waist	0	1			Agility	
Gluteus size	0	1	Max HP	Speed		
Ears size	0	1	Accuracy			Accuracy
Ears position	0	1				
Ears rotation	0	1	Accuracy			Accuracy
Nose size	0	1	Technique			Technique
Nose curve	0	1				
Nose width	0	1	Technique			
Nose inclination	0	1	Accuracy	Technique	Technique	Accuracy
Nose position	0	1				
Nose pronounced	0	1	Technique			Technique
Nose flatten	0	1	Technique		Accuracy	
Chin size	0	1	Technique		Accuracy	
Chin pronounced	0	1	Technique			
Chin position	0	1				
Mandible size	0	1	Robustness			Robustness
Jaws Size	0	1	Max HP			
Jaws position	0	1				
Forehead size	0	1	Concentration			
Eye size	0	1	Accuracy			Accuracy
Breast size	0	1	Strength			Strength

Table 2. Body parts chromosome (integer values).

Gene name	Min value	Max value
Head type	1	5
Torso type	1	3
Hands type	1	3
Legs type	1	2
Feet type	1	3
Tail type	1	4
Wings type	1	3
Skin texture	1	1

Table 3. Stats chromosome (integer values).

Gene name	Min value	Max value
Max HP	1	10000
Concentration	1	100
Strength	1	1000
Robustness	1	1000
Speed	1	1000
Agility	1	1000
Accuracy	1	1000
Technique	1	1000

1. *Uniform Crossover* is performed on Body Modifiers, Body Parts, and Parts Presence chromosomes;
2. *Arithmetic Crossover* is performed on the Stats chromosomes, using the Maximum arithmetic operation, thus selecting the best value for each stat;
3. *Arithmetic Crossover* is performed on the Type chromosome, using the Boolean AND operation. If the resulting type does not contain any valid value, a valid combination is randomly chosen among all the possible combinations the offspring could inherit from parents. Moreover, since the number of attacks is fixed, an exceeding number of attacks are randomly deleted, or a new attack is randomly added in case of need.

After the conclusion of the crossover, the FFF algorithm performs some mutation operations as follows:

- each gene of Body Modifiers is mutated with a 20% probability. The value of the random mutation must not exceed 10% of the current value;
- each gene of Body Parts is mutated with a 5% probability to increase or decrease its value of 1 (up to its minimum or maximum value);

- each gene of Stats can get a random *bonus* or *malus*, depending on the values of Body Modifiers, thus adjusting the stats based on the physical appearance of the creature;
- the attacks lists of parents are merged, removing duplicates and attacks which are not compatible with the Type of the offspring, to create its attack list. This list is then mutated (probability 20%) by replacing one attack with another compatible one.

3.3 Fight: The AR Fighting System

FFF uses a classic, strategic turn-based Battle System, typical of the JRPG genre. At the beginning of the match, players choose up to two Creatures to use in battle. During each turn, the player secretly chooses an attack for each of his/her Creatures. When both have finished choosing, each Creature performs the selected attack. During the battle, players can choose between letting the Creature recover or performing an attack action. By performing an attack, the Creature's energy is reduced by a certain amount. In contrast, during recovery, its energy increases, and its robustness is temporarily powered up, enabling the Creature to defend itself. The probability for an attack to deal damage depends on the combination of the attack characteristics (e.g., power, cast time, hit chance) and the stats of the attacking and target Creatures (see Table 3). The actual damage inflicted is influenced by the attack's type and the target Creature's type (e.g., Fire attacks are weak against Water Creatures). Some attacks might also have one or more particular effects (such as stun, interruption, healing, blinding), and each effect has a certain probability of being effective. Turns follow each other until a player defeats all his/her opponent's Creatures.

Battle Prototype. The Battle prototype has been developed with the following goals:

- testing the effectiveness of using AR to render characters' 3D models in a classic multiplayer turn-based Battle System;
- testing the implementation of a fully authoritative server infrastructure to support online multiplayer battles;
- testing the designed Battle System in terms of effectiveness.

The Battle Prototype consists of two applications: a server-side application, which manages communication with clients and processes gameplay logic, and a client-side cross-platform mobile AR app for iOS and Android, which connects to the server and allows the player to challenge another player in a battle. It implements the multiplayer session using a fully authoritative server architecture: this centralized approach allows to "keep-alive" the match even when both connected devices temporarily lose connectivity for a few seconds. The server application keeps listening for client connections, and when two clients have connected, it manages a match between them. We used the Unity3D networking (UNet) APIs to support the application necessities. UNet has been chosen over other solutions because of the availability of a low-level API such as a transport layer, which fits very well with developing a networked turn-based Battle System like that of FFF. Actually, the UNet's API is very flexible, allowing for better optimization of the amount of data sent over time.

The client application receives the players' input and renders 3D Creatures in AR. Additionally, it uses the UNet library to communicate with the server by sending players' actions choices and receiving updates on the battle state, triggering the appropriate animations and user interfaces.

To incorporate the AR component, FFF uses Vuforia Engine [16], a framework for developing AR applications. It supports mobile devices running iOS, Android, or Windows and some wearable devices such as HoloLens. Vuforia has been chosen because of its broad range of supported devices, maturity, and deep integration with Unity3D. Additionally, it can work with iOS devices that do not support ARKit and Android devices that do not support ARCore. However, if a device supports either of them, Vuforia uses those libraries to provide a better AR experience. Using Vuforia, a set of "detectable targets" can be created using a web interface dedicated to developers and then downloaded (in a format readable by the Vuforia engine) to be included within the application under development. Vuforia can detect Image Targets, like photos or pictures, and Model Targets, like toys or action figures. Furthermore, it also supports the detection of horizontal surfaces with a feature known as Ground Plane, which enables marker-less AR experiences. For the development of the FFF prototype, Image Targets have been used (Fig. 3).

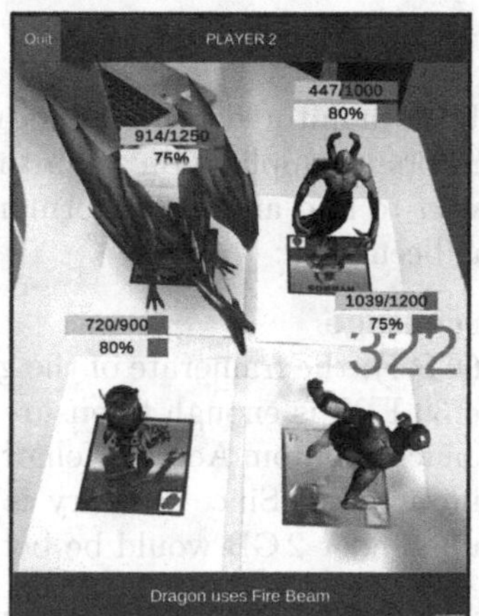

Fig. 3. The Battle Prototype. A Red Dragon is attacking an opponent using a Fire Beam, dealing to it a damage of 322 points (Color figure online).

4 Performance Test

The main critical point of FFF is the use of procedurally generated 3D models (hence that could become quite "cumbersome") on devices that have limited computational power. Hence, to evaluate the actual feasibility of AR multi-player games with generated content, the FFF prototypes have undergone a performance test that has been conducted using a mid-tier smartphone released in 2016, whose technical specifications are listed in Table 4. We have chosen a mid-tier device to verify the application performance on less powerful and older devices. Moreover, when we experimented, that phone did not support Google ARCore.

Table 4. Asus Zenfone 3 (ZE520KL) technical specification.

Model:	Asus Zenfone 3 (ZE520KL)
Display:	5.2″
Resolution:	1080 × 1920
CPU:	Octa-core 2.0 GHz Cortex-A53
GPU:	Adreno 506
RAM:	3 GB
OS:	Android 8.0 (Oreo)
Main camera:	16 MP, f/2.0, 4 axis OIS
Battery capacity:	2600 mAh

The performance has been monitored using Snapdragon Profiler developed by Qualcomm [17]. It monitors an application's run-time performance on multiple metrics, making it easier to find and fix performance bottlenecks [17]. The following metric subset has been used:

- **CPU Utilization Percentage**
- **Frames Per Second (FPS):** the framerate of the game. For a mobile game, usually anywhere above 30 FPS is enough to ensure smooth gameplay;
- **Memory Usage:** how much Random Access Memory (RAM) the application is occupying in a specific instant. Since memory is quite limited on smartphones, keeping this value under 2 GB would be better.

We set up two different battle tests: one using a sample 3D model of a Dragon optimized for its intended use and another using a Firagorn, a creature generated by FFF. Table 5 summarizes the characteristics of the two models, and it is evident that the generated "Firagorn" model is much more complex than that of the Dragon. The number of vertices in Firagorn is higher, and Unity3D standard shader is notoriously quite "heavy" (the Dragon model's material uses the Unlit/Texture shader, which is more lightweight, making it a better choice for a mobile game). Additionally, the Firagorn model's texture is rather big, with its 512 × 4096 size, whereas the dragon's texture is 1024 × 1024. Finally, the Dragon's texture image format uses the Ericsson Texture Compression algorithm, while the UMA-generated model's texture image is uncompressed. The lack of compression combined with the significant texture size results in a texture weight of 10.7 MB for Firagorn against a much lower 1.3 MB for the Dragon.

Table 5. Common Dragon and Firagorn UMA-generated attributes.

	Dragon model	Firagorn UMA model
# of vertices	3,785	4,006
# of triangles	4,832	6,812
Material's shader	Unlit/Texture	Standard
Texture size	1024 × 1024	512 × 4096
Texture image format	RGBA Compressed ETC2 8 bits	ARGB32
Texture weight	1.3 MB	10.7 MB

The results of the first test, performed using four identical Dragons (two for each player) all equipped with the same attach so to have exactly the same animation, are shown in Fig. 4. The performance test is pretty satisfying. The CPU Utilization Percentage is around 50%, with peak values of 68%, which is a good result for a real-time interactive multimedia application that uses AR. The FPS is excellent for a mobile application with a value of around 60 FPS, except for some drops that correspond to drops of CPU Utilization Percentage. However, the Memory usage is not very good: memory rises progressively until stabilizing at 2.24 GB. Even if this is not an exceptionally high value for an application of this kind, it would be better to keep Memory Usage below 2 GB. A possible way to reduce memory usage could be by minimizing the textures resolution and the sampling of sound effects.

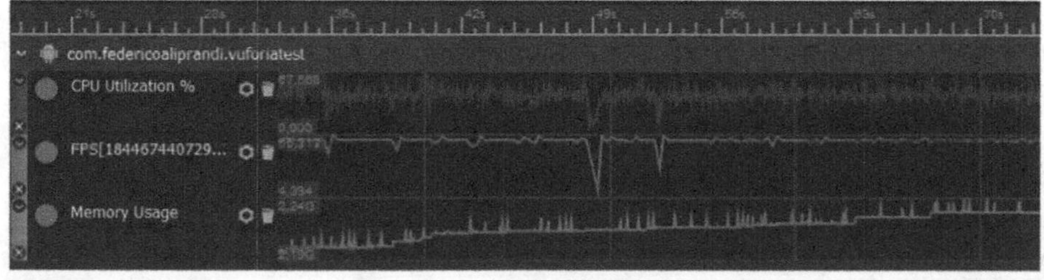

Fig. 4. Profiling of the Battle Prototype with the Dragon. Segment of 40 s of the profiling session during actual gameplay.

The results of the second test, performed on a version of the Battle Prototype in which models have been generated with the creatures Customization application, are shown in Fig. 5. Like the previous test, we have used four identical Firagorns, each equipped with the same attack animation. The results of this test are not as good as the results of the previous one, in particular as far as FPS are considered. The CPU utilization percentage is good, even a little better than before, with values around 50% and peaks reaching almost 60%. However, FPS is much lower than in the previous test (around 30 FPS, which is about half of the previous result). Nonetheless, it is still a value which allows for a smooth gameplay. Memory usage is still the primary concern, since it constantly stays at 2.72 GB, too high for a mobile game.

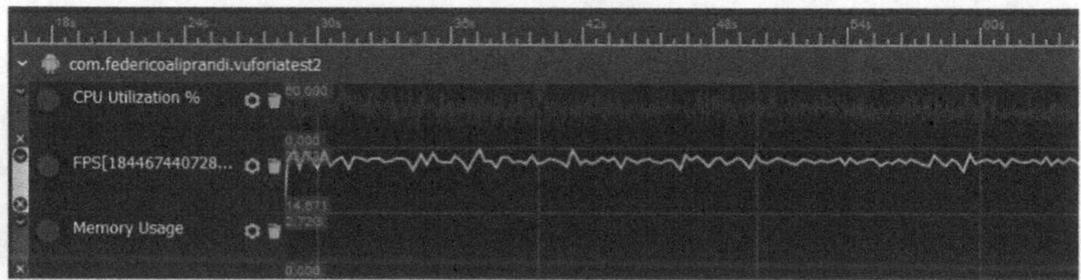

Fig. 5. Profiling of the Battle Prototype with Firagorn. Segment of 40 s of the profiling session during gameplay.

Observing the results, we can infer some interesting conclusions. First of all, the Battle Prototype has a good overall performance that achieves at most 68% CPU usage and supports 60 FPS. However, even with simpler models (like the Dragon), the memory usage is higher than expected. This problem could be mitigated, e.g., by limiting the texture resolution or the sampling of sound effects. By analyzing the outcome of the second experiment, we can notice the impact of generated sub-optimized 3D models that intrinsically have a higher resolution and a more cumbersome mesh size. These characteristics are likely the reason behind the drop in FPS and in Memory performance. Therefore, further improvements in the Creatures Customization prototype are essential to integrate it with the battle system and allow for a fluid AR mobile gaming experience.

5 Conclusion and Future Works

Among many relevant current limitations of AR games for mobile devices, there is the minimal interactivity among players, the under exploitation of the possibility offered by AR, and the repetitiveness of the gameplay. In this work, we have tried to investigate whether it would be possible to envisage some solution to these issues. In particular, we have designed and prototyped FFF, an AR game for mobile devices that supports the multiplayer mode, offers a bit more creative use of AR, and demonstrates that PCG techniques, sometimes applied in video games released for much more powerful platforms (such as personal computers or gaming consoles), could be effectively exploited for introducing a higher degree of variability both in the content and in the gameplay, even on devices far less performing than a standard PC. FFF is divided into three distinct phases: Find, Fuse and Fight. We have focused on prototyping the second and third phases since they are the real core of the game that implements both PCG and AR multiplayer mode.

The Creatures Customization prototype, corresponding to the Fuse phase of the game, had the objective to build an application able to produce some procedurally generated content (Creatures) that can be delivered in AR in a game for mobile devices. It has been designed following the principles of EDPCG [27] and exploits the GAs paradigm to automatically deliver contents that are then tuned to the desire and expectations of the player. Our main concern was to generate Creatures that are both believable (in terms of physical appearance, animations, etc.) and not too cumbersome to be managed by a device with limited resources like a cell phone. We have developed our prototype starting from UMA because of its mesh deformation system's high quality and flexibility. We have obtained convincing offspring in terms of both the model's quality and resemblance to the parents' couple.

The Battle Prototype goals were two-folded: on the one hand, we wanted to implement and test the feasibility of multiplayer real-time matches in which the procedurally generated Creatures combat in AR, and on the other, we wanted to make sure that the generated Creature models had the necessary characteristics (in terms of resource consumption) to be used in that way on a mobile device (not necessarily belonging to the last generation). The prototype implemented the multiplayer session using a fully authoritative server architecture: this centralized approach allows to "keep-alive" the match even when both connected devices temporarily lose connectivity for a few seconds.

The performance of the Battle Prototype is relatively good when standard 3D models for AR are used in the game. However, memory use is a bit high, and it needs some optimization in future further development. The prototype performance deteriorates - as we expected - when procedurally generated Creatures are used, since UMA generates higher-quality models not fully optimized for being used in AR. We presume this is just a minor problem that could be easily fixed by fine-tuning the generation process. The Creature model depends on the base and the material associated with the custom Creature template on which a character is based in UMA. If either the base model, its material definition, or the alternative body parts meshes are not optimized, the derived characters will not be optimized. Hence, it should be possible to improve the application's performance that uses UMA-generated models by using, e.g., low-poly base meshes and a more lightweight shader.

An interesting future development of FFF would be including non-humanoid Creatures in the Fuse phase. This will add a layer of complexity from the perspective of mesh morphing since, for example, problems would arise when trying to fuse the skeletons of a humanoid and a quadruped creature. A straightforward solution could be allowing fusion only between a creature that is similar enough in terms of physical appearance. Otherwise, the fusion algorithm should be modified to manage a couple of Creatures with different skeleton structures and different DNA. A possible solution would be to set some chromosomes common among all the species, plus some specie-specific chromosomes. Therefore, a Fusion could be performed by applying the existing algorithm to the common chromosomes and then completing the DNA by randomly including the species-specific chromosomes of one of the two species of the parents. Last but not least, extensive testing of a complete prototype should be done with real players to validate the results in terms of user experience. Unfortunately, this has not yet been done, mainly due to the current restrictions deriving from the ongoing pandemic.

References

1. Arth, C., Grasset, R., Gruber, L., Langlotz, T., Mulloni, A., Wagner, D.: The history of mobile augmented reality. arXiv preprint arXiv:1505.01319 (2015)
2. Cooper, N., et al.: Augmented reality Chinese checkers. In: Proceedings of the 2004 ACM SIGCHI International Conference on Advances in Computer Entertainment Technology, pp. 117–126 (2004)
3. Fullerton, T.: Game Design Workshop: A Playcentric Approach to Creating Innovative Games. AK Peters/CRC Press (2018)
4. Grand, S., Cliff, D., Malhotra, A.: Creatures: artificial life autonomous software agents for home entertainment. In: Proceedings of the 1st International Conference on Autonomous Agents, pp. 22–29 (1997)
5. Guarneri, A., Maggiorini, D., Ripamonti, L., Trubian, M.: GOLEM: generator of life embedded into MMOs. In: The 12th European Conference on Artificial Life, ECAL 2013, pp. 585–592. MIT Press (2013)
6. Hamari, J., Malik, A., Koski, J., Johri, A.: Uses and gratifications of Pokémon Go: why do people play mobile location-based augmented reality games? Int. J. Hum.-Comput. Interact. **35**(9), 804–819 (2019)
7. Hastings, E.J., Guha, R.K., Stanley, K.O.: Evolving content in the galactic arms race video game. In: 2009 IEEE Symposium on Computational Intelligence and Games, pp. 241–248. IEEE (2009)
8. Holland, J.H.: Genetic algorithms. Sci. Am. **267**(1), 66–72 (1992)
9. Khuri, S., Bäck, T., Heitkötter, J.: The zero/one multiple knapsack problem and genetic algorithms. In: Proceedings of the 1994 ACM Symposium on Applied Computing, pp. 188–193 (1994)
10. Klopfer, E., Squire, K.: Environmental detectives-the development of an augmented reality platform for environmental simulations. Educ. Tech. Res. Dev. **56**(2), 203–228 (2008)
11. Kora, P., Yadlapalli, P.: Crossover operators in genetic algorithms: a review. Int. J. Comput. Appl. **162**(10), 34–36 (2017)
12. Mitchell, M.: An Introduction to Genetic Algorithms. MIT Press (1998)
13. Molla, E., Lepetit, V.: Augmented reality for board games. In: 2010 IEEE International Symposium on Mixed and Augmented Reality, pp. 253–254. IEEE (2010)
14. Montana, D.J., Davis, L., et al.: Training feedforward neural networks using genetic algorithms. In: IJCAI, vol. 89, pp. 762–767 (1989)

15. Perry, B.: Gamifying French language learning: a case study examining a quest-based, augmented reality mobile learning-tool. Procedia. Soc. Behav. Sci. **174**, 2308–2315 (2015)
16. PTC Inc.: Vuforia engine. https://developer.vuforia.com. Accessed 04 Apr 2022
17. Qualcomm Technologies Inc.: Snapdragon profiler. https://developer.qualcomm.com/software/snapdragon-profiler. Accessed 01 Apr 2022
18. Ripamonti, L.A., Distefano, F., Trubian, M., Maggiorini, D., Gadia, D.: DRAGON: diversity regulated adaptive generator online. Multimedia Tools Appl. **80**(26), 34933–34969 (2021)
19. Sivanandam, S., Deepa, S.: Genetic algorithms. In: Introduction to Genetic Algorithms. Springer, Heidelberg (2008). https://doi.org/10.1007/978-3-540-73190-0_2
20. Slay, H., Thomas, B., Vernik, R.: Using ARToolkit for passive tracking and presentation in ubiquitous workspaces. In: 2003 IEEE International Augmented Reality Toolkit Workshop, pp. 46–53. IEEE (2003)
21. Stanley, K.O., Miikkulainen, R.: Evolving neural networks through augmenting topologies. Evol. Comput. **10**(2), 99–127 (2002)
22. Syswerda, G., et al.: Uniform crossover in genetic algorithms. In: ICGA, vol. 3, pp. 2–9 (1989)
23. Unity Technologies: Unity3D. https://unity.com. Accessed 01 Apr 2022
24. Tong, X., Gupta, A., Gromala, D., Shaw, C.D.: Players' experience of an augmented reality game, *Pokémon Go*: inspirations and implications for designing pervasive health gamified applications. In: Streitz, N., Markopoulos, P. (eds.) DAPI 2017. LNCS, vol. 10291, pp. 675–683. Springer, Cham (2017). https://doi.org/10.1007/978-3-319-58697-7_50
25. Vera, F., Sánchez, J.A.: A model for in-situ augmented reality content creation based on storytelling and gamification. In: Proceedings of the 6th Mexican Conference on Human-Computer Interaction, pp. 39–42 (2016)
26. Wetzel, R., McCall, R., Braun, A.K., Broll, W.: Guidelines for designing augmented reality games. In: Proceedings of the 2008 Conference on Future Play: Research, Play, Share, pp. 173–180 (2008)
27. Yannakakis, G.N., Togelius, J.: Experience-driven procedural content generation. IEEE Trans. Affect. Comput. **2**(3), 147–161 (2011)
28. Zubair, M.S.: What do mobile AR game players complain about?: a qualitative analysis of mobile AR game reviews. In: 34th British HCI Conference, vol. 34, pp. 23–35 (2021)

Synthetic Data Generation for Surface Defect Detection

Déborah Lebert[1(✉)], Jérémy Plouzeau[1(✉)], Jean-Philippe Farrugia[2(✉)], Florence Danglade[1(✉)], and Frédéric Merienne[1(✉)]

[1] Arts et métiers, LISPEN, Institut Image, Chalon sur Saône, France
{deborah.lebert,Jeremy.PLOUZEAU,Florence.Danglade, frederic.merienne}@ensam.eu

[2] LIRIS, Lyon, France
jean-philippe.farrugia@univ-lyon1.fr

Abstract. Ensuring continued quality is challenging, especially when customer satisfaction is the provided service. It seems to become easier with new technologies like Artificial Intelligence. However, field data are necessary to design an intelligent assistant but are not always available. Synthetic data are used mainly to replace real data. Made with a Generative Adversarial Network or a rendering engine, they aim to be as efficient as real ones in training a Neural Network. When synthetic data generation meets the challenge of object detection, its capacity to deal with the defect detection challenge is unknown. Here we demonstrate how to generate these synthetic data to detect defects. Through iterations, we apply different methods from literature to generate synthetic data for object detection, from how to extract a defect from the few data we have to how to organize the scene before data synthesis. Our study suggests that defect detection may be performed by training an object detector neural network with synthetic data and gives a protocol to do so even if at this point, no field experiments have been conducted to verify our detector performances under real conditions. This experiment is the starting point for developing a mobile and automatic defect detector that might be adapted to ensure new product quality.

Keywords: Database generation · Synthetic data · Defect detection

1 Introduction

When customer satisfaction is the main objective of a product, constant improvement in quality control during its production and all along its life circle becomes essential. Our study focuses on ensuring continued cosmetic quality during the product's life through periodic inspection of all products. Then the inspection goal is to index visual defects on plastic and metal parts. However, these inspections are time-consuming and limited by product uptime. The challenge here is developing an assistant for inspectors to detect and differentiate defects from

Supported by organization Arts et métiers.

L. T. De Paolis et al. (Eds.): XR Salento 2022, LNCS 13446, pp. 198–208, 2022.
https://doi.org/10.1007/978-3-031-15553-6_15

normal wear. Our assistant must then be based on visual features like detectors using Neural Network (NN) are. However, data collection for deep learning is time-consuming. Therefore, our assistant must be trained using generated data [1]. Our assistant should be able to detect each defect, no matter the shape. Thus during our study, we will see how to generate synthetic data in order to train a NN.

This paper starts with state of the art on object detection using synthetic data in Sect. 2. Section 3 aims to contextualize our project by highlighting its scientific issues, Sect. 4 presents the generation and customization process. Finally, Sect. 5 presents the first results on real data. To finish, we will conclude and introduce our future development on this topic in Sect. 6.

In the following, the term "SD" will be used to designate Synthetic Data.

2 Background in Defect Detection Using Synthetic Data

To satisfy the increasing need for ensured quality, companies include more validation processes from random inspection to computer vision solutions to get a global idea of the quality of all pieces. For example, computer vision can be used to detect structure defects by comparing the actual piece with its digital twin [2] which is a digital representation of the part designed and modified according to the part evolution. It can also be used to detect surface defects using a NN trained with a set of real pictures of defects as in [3].

Our project requires the creation of an original dataset, but it can become time-consuming, especially when dealing with new classes such as "wearing a mask" [1] or specific ones such as chemical classification. In addition, deep learning requires a large quantity of data that must be annotated which is usually manually performed. Then SD appears to be a possible solution to these problems. So we choose to generate our dataset using previous work on SD generation.

SD plays an important role when data are nonexistent or unavailable for privacy reasons. First used in the economic field in the form of de-identified data [4], SD is now used to face NN challenges. In his book [4], K. El Emam highlights the main difficulty when dealing with SD, which is "showing that the results from the SD are similar to the results from the real data". This study will try to fit this definition with our SD.

Through studies, we identify two ways to generate SD. The first is Generative Adversarial Network (GAN), first introduced in 2014 by Goodfellow et al. [5]. GAN is already used for defect detection as in [6]. It can be considered as synthetic data augmentation using one generative and one discriminant network. The generative part creates new images based on provided dataset then the discriminant one checks if the generated image is plausible. Then it needs a large amount of real data, as seen in [6] where S. Jain and co. used 5400 images to train their GAN.

In our context, approximately fifty pictures of defects are available. Therefore a GAN cannot be used.

Unlike the first method, the second one does not need real pictures of the target but a digital representation. Indeed in industry 4.0 it is easy to get our digital target twin directly or to build it using some pictures. Then it is possible to use any rendering engine to generate data as in [8]. For instance, M. Johnson-Roberson et al. used a video game (GTA V) to generate a traffic dataset in [7], and J. Cohen used a CAD software to do so in [8]. In our context, we choose to focus on this second methodology since 3D models of our targets are directly available, and defect generation can be done from images or mathematical models.

As highlighted in [9] and [16], SD generation strategy depends on features we want to detect. Thus realism requirement seems to be a determinant for synthetic data effectiveness, as emphasized in most studies about SD generation [10,11]. Since our data aim to be used to train a NN, their realism i.e. their ability to appear to people as real pictures instead of generated ones [12] will not be studied here. Indeed, as highlighted in [13], the plausibility of the images is more important than the global realism when generated synthetic data are used for training. But when GAN is creating realistic data thanks to real ones, manual generation of SD has to simulate it through environment randomization and 3D model precision.

That is why we will consider realism as "the accurate, detailed, unembellished depiction" [1] of our real object.

Consequently, when identifying an object from its texture, it is necessary to get an accurate capture of it. As seen in [11] it is possible to use real images to "cut and paste" real objects from pictures to synthetic images or to directly use a textured 3D scan [15]. Moreover some studies proved SD realism is important for NN training, first regarding the environment in [17] and [18], then concerning the targeted object in [13] and [19]. Additionally, some studies worked on photorealism in SD as in [8,10] and [14] in which teams enhanced it by adding noise. Besides, J. Hodapp et al. [11] demonstrated that a good real/synthetic data distribution could improve NN performances: their best distribution is 5% of real data, 47,5% of SD, and 47,5% of "mixed" data or "cut-and-paste" data. They generated SD with CAD software without any photorealism requirement, whereas the "cut-and-paste" dataset is created with realistic details extracted from pictures and integrated into another SD set.

3 Scientific Issues

We saw that defect detection with NN was becoming common. However, the use of SD in this field stays limited to GAN-generated ones. Our designed detector is supposed to take part in maintenance procedures. However, in our case, taking pictures of parts would be time-consuming (collecting pictures, performing pre-processing procedures to de-identify data and annotating data). Moreover, an important challenge is to differentiate real defects from regular attrition. A defect can be defined as an unexpected difference of color on a homogeneous

[1] Definition from https://www.britannica.com/.

surface. Here we consider only two different surface defects: cracks and spots that occur mainly on plastic surfaces. The purpose of our work is then to determine how to generate an effective synthetic database. Since cracks and spots are surface defects, they can be projected on a plane. This association may then be manipulated as an object. Therefore we choose to generate SD using methods from literature seen in Sect. 2. Breaks could be added to the defect list, but they will not be studied here since detecting breaks cannot be compared with object detection and should be done using 3D comparison as in [2].

4 Our Synthetic Data Generator and Training

We decided to generate SD as in [8] and [7] where both teams were using SD to train an object detector but to detect cracks and spots. Some examples of defects we want to detect are given in Fig. 1.

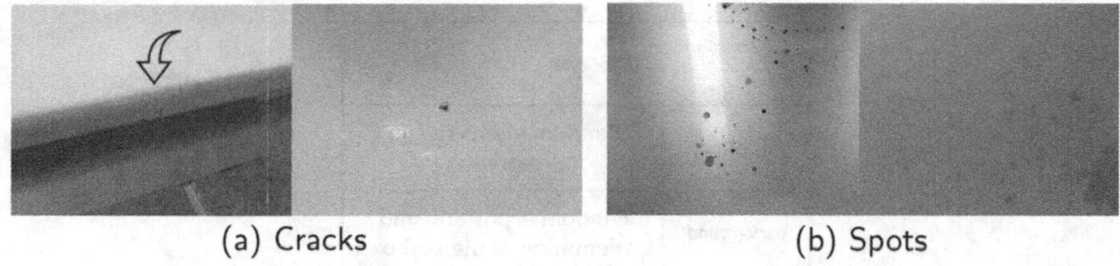

(a) Cracks (b) Spots

Fig. 1. Example of defects

Our first step is to define a workflow to generate SD. We design our generation process using previous work on SD generation results [8,11], given in Fig. 2. The scene is composed of our targeted defect and may include some other 3D object as distractors. Then we decide to simulate a real environment by varying lighting parameters (nature of sources, orientation and light color), background and post-processing parameters.

Our scene design aims to meet realism requirements previously defined i.e. to get an accurate, detailed and unembellished depiction of the targeted object in a realistic and plausible environment. In order to do so, we decide to use Unity3D[2], a game development platform as in [7] with its Universal Renderer Pipeline to get access to more post-processing parameters and high definition materials. Our scene parameters can be divided into two groups: extrinsic parameters and intrinsic ones. Extrinsic parameters are not modifying the defect but are essential for the scene plausibility: the architecture of the scene and environment conditions. In contrast, intrinsic parameters are directly related to the aspect of the defect: its shape, to meet the environment realism requirement regarding extrinsic parameters, the targeted object is located in a space surrounded by a High Dynamic Range Image (HDRI). A HDRI is either a panoramic picture or a cubemap containing a large amount of data like brightness, which can be used to

[2] https://unity.com version 2020.1.15f1.

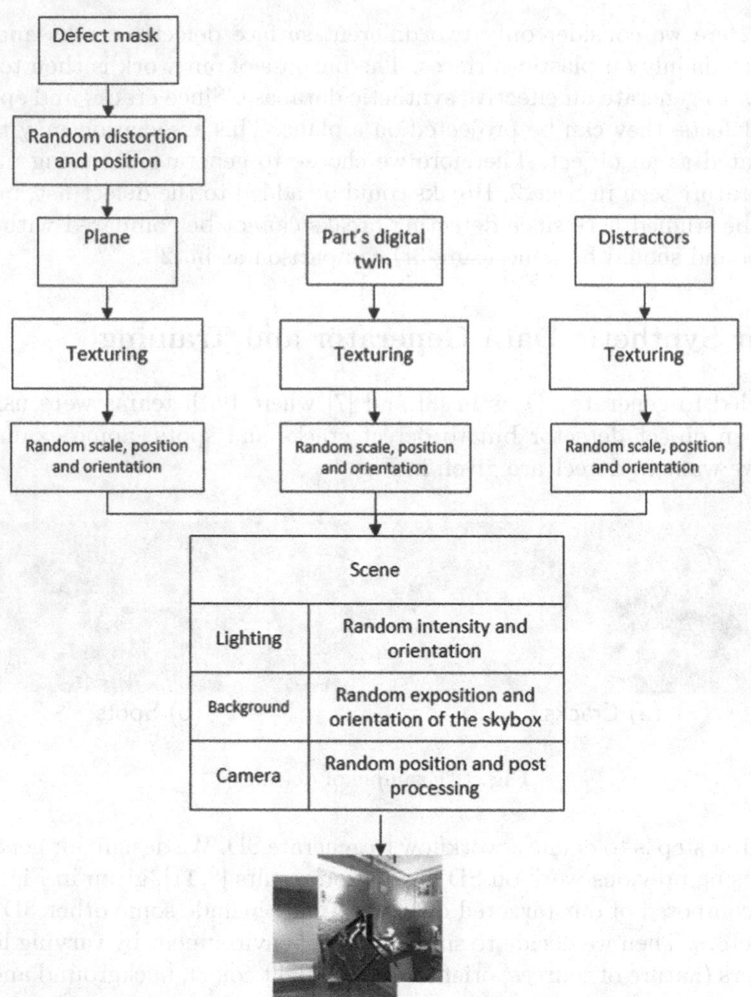

Fig. 2. Adopted workflow for synthetic data generation based on 3D Model

illuminate a virtual scene. The environment variability is simulated by rotating this skybox. The lightning environment is simulated by varying exposure of the skybox from 1 to 3, rotating an extra light source and randomizing its intensity from 1 to 10. Finally, random noises are added as a post-processing effect, to simulate the user impact on the picture quality as motion blur (intensity between 0 and 0.2) or unmanageable environmental conditions as dust simulated with a grain (intensity between 0 and 1).

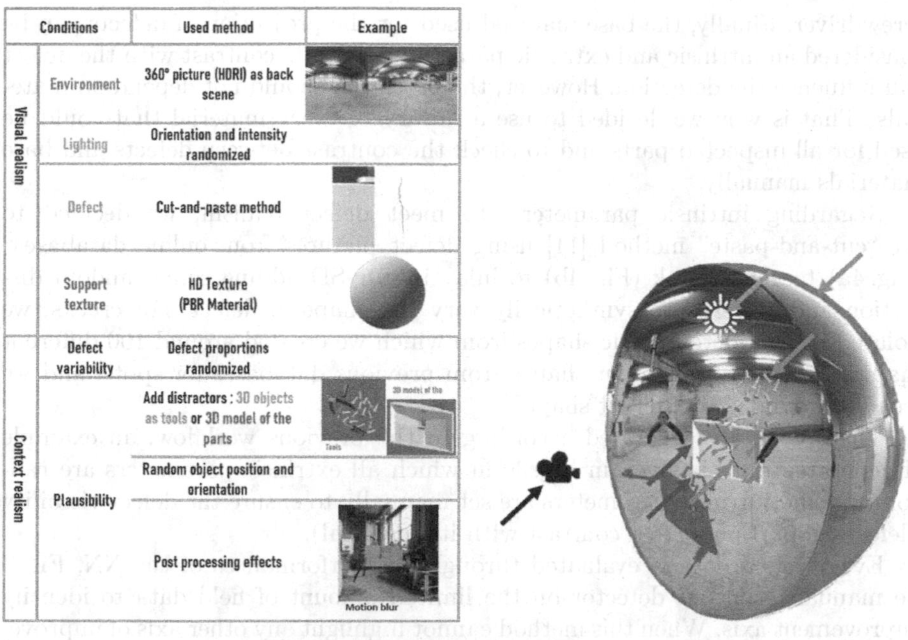

Conditions
Used method
Example
Visual realism
Environment
360° picture (HDRI) as back scene
Lighting
Orientation and intensity randomized
Defect
Cut-and-paste method
Support texture
HD Texture (PBR Material)
Context realism
Defect variability
Defect proportions randomized
Add distractors : 3D objects as tools or 3D model of the parts
Plausibility
Random object position and orientation
Post processing effects
Motion blur

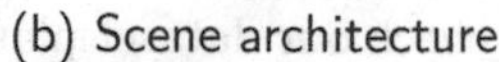

(a) Scene details, and fig.3b legend (b) Scene architecture

(c) Resulting picture

Fig. 3. Scene details

However, to ensure scene plausibility, some distractors must be added. These 3D objects are used to prevent misclassification during detection by adding common geometry to the training dataset. Since the detector would be used during maintenance sessions, we picked around 20 distractors, mostly tools such as a screwdriver. Finally, the base material used for the projection of defects can be considered an intrinsic and extrinsic parameter since its contrast with the defect will influence the detection. However, the detection should not depend on materials. That is why we decided to use a library of every material that could be used for all inspected parts and to check the contrast between defects and base materials manually.

Regarding intrinsic parameters, to meet defect realism, we decided to use "cut-and-paste" method [11] using defect pictures from online databases[3] (Fig. 4a) to get a mask (Fig. 4b) to inlay in our SD adding some random distortion and material to synthetically vary the shape of defect. For cracks, we isolated eight different basic shapes from which we created around 100 different shapes. We got ten different shapes from previous databases for spots, and we created around 150 different shapes.

Then, data are generated according to the previous workflow, an example of generated data is given in Fig. 3c in which all extrinsic parameters are randomized and intrinsic parameters are set manually to ensure the defect visibility (defect proportion, defect contrast with its material).

Every set of data is evaluated through the performances of the NN. First, we manually run our detector on the limited amount of field data to identify improvement axis. When this method cannot highlight any other axis of improvement, we check our dataset plausibility by measuring the mean average precision and the Intersection over Union (IoU) score of each NN trained with our sets. Here the IoU loss we use is presented in [20] as the "computing process [that] will trigger the calculation of the four coordinate points of the bounding box by executing IoU with the ground truth". In order to do so, we create a test set of real data to get around 70 real pictures. Finally, the verified dataset is used to train the final multiple class detector, adding some multiple class generated pictures. Then performances of the final detector are checked in every class thanks to the previous test-set. The final test will be to check the performance of our detector in real conditions i.e. handled by the final operator in a real environment. Since our work does not aim to improve existing NN architecture, we set up supervised training for object and defect detection reusing the well-known regression-based architecture: YOLO v4[4] [20] trained in Darknet environment [21]. Studies do not agree on a fixed number of images required for training. Thus we use 5,000 pictures for training with 80% for training (4 000 pictures) and 20% for testing (1 000 pictures) as seen in "training YOLO v4 on custom dataset" project[5]. We decided to fine-tune our model using weights pre-trained for object detection to speed up the training process. In our case, we decided to generate 1,000 pictures at first per class and increase the set at each iteration depending on the deficiencies of NN trained with the previous generation. To identify it quickly, we chose

[3] http://defectsdatabase.npl.co.uk/defectsdb/defects_query.php and https://www.kaggle.com/yidazhang07/bridge-cracks-image.

[4] YOLO is a real-time object detector, previous work [1,14,16] used different version of this NN to perform object detection.

[5] https://github.com/AlexeyAB/darknet.

to work on each class independently before mixing training to generate our final detector. Our final dataset comprises 2 000 pictures of cracks, 1 500 images of spots, and 1 500 images of spots and cracks.

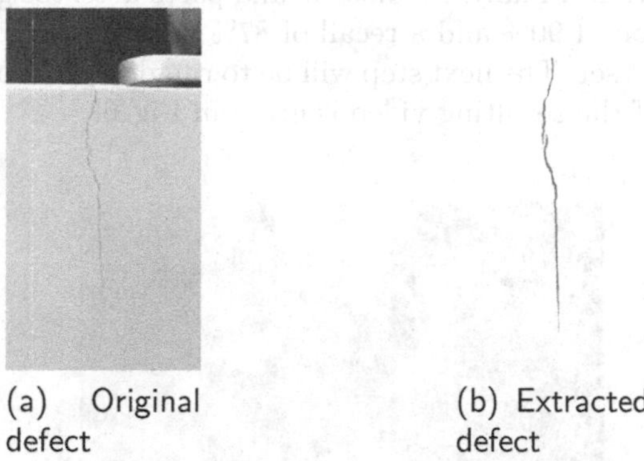

(a) Original defect (b) Extracted defect

Fig. 4. "Cut-and-paste" defect

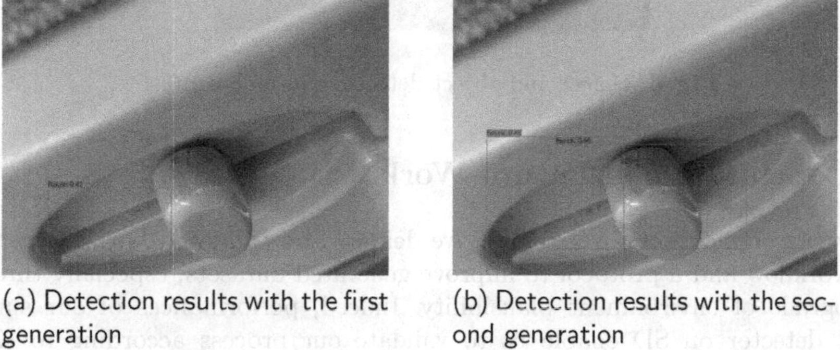

(a) Detection results with the first generation (b) Detection results with the second generation

Fig. 5. Results obtained after 3 iterations of our improvement process

5 Results

Our evaluation process is divided into three steps: first, we check our detector result on a set of SD, then we use a limited amount of real pictures we retrieved to identify axis of improvement, and finally, we run the detection on in field video. This improvement process focused on defect detection since the part detection gets an average accuracy of 98% for eight different parts.

Regarding defect, the first generation of SD shows defects on a big planar surface, we can directly see on the result on real data that the NN does not detect the defect (Fig. 5a), but it detects a false positive defect. Our objective was then to detect the defect and reduce this false positive detection. Thus, we decided to add some distractors and reduce the plane size in our scene, even if our false positive detection is mainly related to the scene composition and shadows. We choose distractors related to maintenance operations to prevent false positive detection. Finally, our defects and parts detector gets a F1-score of 88% with a precision of 90% and a recall of 87% when testing its performances on the synthetic test set. The next step will be to run detection on an on-the-field video, an extract of the resulting video is given in Fig. 6.

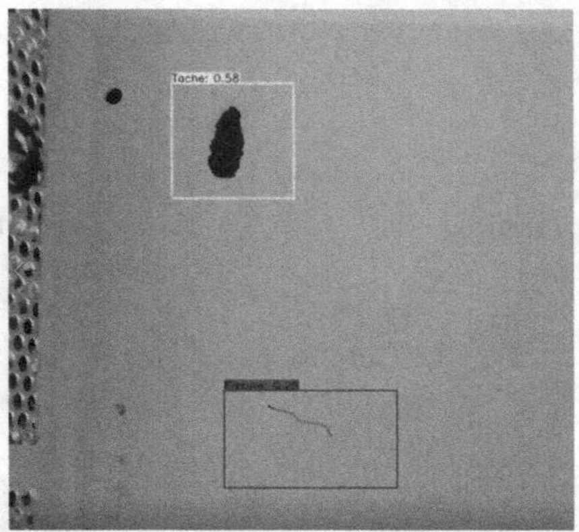

Fig. 6. Defect and object detection on real armrest

6 Conclusion and Future Work

Regarding application development, we defined and validated both SD generation workflow and a protocol to improve generated datasets, especially through an upgrade of environment plausibility. Indeed, performances of our surface defect detector on SD enable us to validate our process according to K. El Emam's definition of SD [4]. We must measure our detector performances with a proper protocol to qualitatively check our synthetic data efficiency and ensure that our device becomes effective assistance for inspection. It implies studying our application's impact on inspection preparation, inspection and its results compilation, and the user's impact on the detector's performance. Furthermore, some extra work can be done during the training stage, indeed recent studies show good performances in detecting surface defects using unsupervised learning [22]. Thus, comparing both training strategies using SD must help design an accurate surface defect detector.

References

1. Yu, J., Zhang, W.: Face Mask Wearing Detection Algorithm Based on Improved YOLO-v4. https://doi.org/10.3390/s21093263

2. Jovančević, I., Orteu, J.J., Sentenac, T., Gilblas, R.: Inspection d'un aéronef à partir d'un système multi-capteurs porté par un robot mobile", 14ème Colloque Méthodes et Techniques Optiques pour l'Industrie (2015). https://hal.archives-ouvertes.fr/hal-01350898
3. Tabernik, D., Šela, S., Skvarč, J., Skočaj, D.: Segmentation-based deep-learning approach for surface-defect detection. J. Intell. Manuf. **31**, 759–776 (2019). https://doi.org/10.1007/s10845-019-01476-x
4. El Emam, K.: Accelerating AI with Synthetic Datan (2020). https://www.nvidia.com/fr-fr/deep-learning-ai/resources/accelerating-ai-with-synthetic-data-ebook/ebook link, ch.1&2
5. Goodfellow, I., Pouget-Abadie, J., Mirza, M., Ozai, S., Courville, A., Bengio, Y.: Generative adversarial networks. In: Advances in Neural Information Processing Systems 27, vol. 63, pp. 139–144 (2014). https://doi.org/10.1145/3422622
6. Jain, S., Seth, G., Paruthi, A., Soni, U., Kumar, G.: Synthetic data augmentation for surface defect detection and classification using deep learning. J. Intell. Manuf. 1–14 (2020). https://doi.org/10.1007/s10845-020-01710-x
7. Johnson-Roberson, M., Barto, C., Mehta, R., Sridhar, S.N., Rosaen, K., Vasudevan, R.: Driving in the Matrix: Can virtual worlds replace human-generated annotations for real world tasks?. In: 2017 IEEE International Conference on Robotics and Automation (ICRA), pp. 746–753 (2017). https://doi.org/10.1109/ICRA.2017.7989092
8. Cohen, J., Crispim-Junior, C., Grange-Faivre, C., Tougne, L.: CAD-based Learning for Egocentric Object Detection in Industrial Context. In: 5th International Conference on Computer Vision Theory and Applications, pp. 644–651 (2020). https://doi.org/10.5220/0008975506440651
9. Tremblay, J., Prakash, A., Acuna, D., Brophy, M., Jampani, V.: Training Deep Networks with Synthetic Data: Bridging the Reality Gap by Domain Randomization. In: 2018 IEEE/CVF Conference on Computer Vision and Pattern Recognition Workshops (CVPRW), pp. 1082–10828 (2018). https://doi.org/10.1109/CVPRW.2018.00143
10. Proença, P.F., Gao, Y.: Deep Learning for Spacecraft Pose Estimation from Photorealistic Rendering. In: 2020 IEEE International Conference on Robotics and Automation (ICRA), pp. 6007–6013 (2020). https://doi.org/10.1109/ICRA40945.2020.9197244
11. Hodapp, J., Schiemann, M., Arcidiacono, C., Reichenbach, M., Bilous, V.: Advances in automated generation of convolutional neural networks from synthetic data in industrial environments. In: Hawaii International Conference on System Sciences, pp. 1278–1286 (2020). https://doi.org/10.24251/HICSS.2020.565
12. Fan, S., Ng, T.T., Herberg, J.S., Koenig, B.L., Tan, C.Y.-C., Wang, R.: An Automated estimator of image visual realism based on human cognition. In: 2014 IEEE Conference on Computer Vision and Pattern Recognition, pp. 4201–4208 (2014). https://doi.org/10.1109/CVPR.2014.535
13. Hodan, T., et al.: Photorealistic Image Synthesis for Object Instance Detection. arXiv 1902.03334 (2019)
14. Huh, J., Lee, K., Lee, I., Lee, S.: A simple method on generating synthetic data for training real-time object detection networks. In: 2018 Asia-Pacific Signal and Information Processing Association Annual Summit and Conference (APSIPA ASC), pp. 1518–1522 (2015). https://doi.org/10.23919/APSIPA.2018.8659778
15. Wong, M.Z., Kunii, K., Baylis, M., Ong, W.H., Kroupa, P., Koller, S.: Synthetic dataset generation for object-to-model deep learning in industrial applications Peer J. Comput. Sci. **5**, e222 (2019). https://doi.org/10.7717/peerj-cs.222

16. Jing, J., Zhuo, D., Zhang, H., Liangm Y., Zheng, M.: Fabric defect detection using the improved YOLOv3 model. J. Eng. Fibers Fabrics **15** (2020). https://doi.org/10.1177/1558925020908268
17. Peng, X., Sun, B., Ali, K., Saenko, K.: Learning deep object detectors from 3D models. In: 2015 IEEE International Conference on Computer Vision (ICCV), pp. 1278–1286 (2015). https://doi.org/10.1109/ICCV.2015.151
18. Sarkar, K., Varanasi, K., Stricker, D.: Trained 3D Models for CNN based object recognition. In: Proceedings of the 12th International Joint Conference on Computer Vision, Imaging and Computer Graphics Theory and Applications - VISAPP, (VISIGRAPP 2017), vol. 5. https://doi.org/10.5220/0006272901300137
19. de Melo, C.M., Rothrock, B., Gurram, P., Ulutan, O., Manjunath, B.S.: Vision-based gesture recognition in human-robot teams using synthetic data. In: 2020 IEEE/RSJ International Conference on Intelligent Robots and Systems (IROS), pp. 10278–10284 (2020). https://doi.org/10.1109/IROS45743.2020.9340728
20. Bochkovskiy, A., Wang, C.-Y., Mark Liao, H.-Y.: YOLOv4: Optimal Speed and Accuracy of Object Detection. arXiv 2004.10934 (2020)
21. Redmon, J.: Darknet: Open Source Neural Networks in C (2013–2016). https://pjreddie.com/darknet/
22. Roth, K., Pemula, L., Zepeda, J., Schölkopf, B., Brox, T., Gehler, P.V.: Towards Total Recall in Industrial Anomaly Detection. CoRR - Volume abs/2106.08265 (2021). https://arxiv.org/abs/2106.08265

eXtended Reality in Geo-information Sciences

ARtefact: A Conceptual Framework for the Integrated Information Management of Archaeological Excavations

Damianos Gavalas[1(✉)], Vlasios Kasapakis[2], Evangelia Kavakli[2], Panayiotis Koutsabasis[1], Despina Catapoti[2], and Spyros Vosinakis[1]

[1] Department of Product and Systems Design Engineering, University of the Aegean, Syros, Greece
{dgavalas,kgp,spyrosv}@aegean.gr

[2] Department of Cultural Technology and Communication, University of the Aegean, Lesvos, Greece
{v.kasapakis,kavakli,dcatapoti}@aegean.gr

Abstract. The information management of archaeological excavations (and the follow-up conservation and restoration of excavated objects) is complex, time consuming and laborious in practice. Currently available technological aids in the broader area of digital archaeology are limited in scope, while most are not interoperable. Herein, we propose ARtefact, a conceptual framework which encompasses an integrated technological toolset supporting the digital documentation, knowledge management and interactive presentation of digital resources produced throughout the archaeological excavation and the study/conservation of Artefacts. ARtefact accounts for several end-products: a mobile digital documentation application (executed on mobile devices with built-in depth sensors) which addresses the needs of all stakeholders involved in the documentation of the excavation process and its findings (mainly field archeologists and conservators); a web-based knowledge management tool which enables archaeologists to specify semantic relationships between digital resources; authoring tools used by curators and archaeologists without any technical expertise to create custom AR/VR applications which allow users to retrieve and interact with the ARtefact digital resources, thus enhancing the experience of -physical and virtual- visits in archaeological sites and museum exhibitions. A prototype implementation of ARtefact will be validated in pilot studies conducted in an active archeological excavation site and an archeological museum in Greece.

Keywords: Archaeology · Excavation · Conservation · Artefact · Digital documentation · Metadata · Knowledge management · Semantic linking · Mobile application · Authoring tool · Augmented reality · Virtual reality

1 Introduction

Digital data play an increasingly important role in our perception of the present and the past. The challenges inherent in understanding and using digital data are as intellectually

L. T. De Paolis et al. (Eds.): XR Salento 2022, LNCS 13446, pp. 211–223, 2022.
https://doi.org/10.1007/978-3-031-15553-6_16

demanding as any other archaeological research endeavor. For data to be meaningfully preserved and used in intellectually rigorous ways, they need to be integrated fully into all aspects of archaeological practice, including documentation, publishing and teaching [11].

The management of data generated during archaeological excavations require careful planning and organization, and are complex, time consuming and laborious in practice. In the recent years, the emergence of new technologies has stimulated the development of methods and tools for the digital documentation of the excavation, offering greater flexibility compared to conventional methods (excavation calendars, catalogs, topographic plans, photographs, etc.) traditionally used by archaeologists and conservators. However, the use of new technologies in archaeological information management so far has indicated significant weaknesses:

- At the level **digital documentation** of excavations, existing technological tools address the requirements for documenting excavations in a fragmentary way. Where web systems and mobile applications are used, these typically include necessary but limited functionality such as: digital excavation calendars, metadata and photo processing features, etc. [29]. Where geographic systems (GIS) are utilized, the emphasis is on mapping and management of spatial and descriptive archaeological data, with no direct semantic links between the individual finds. Also, where 3D scanning technologies are utilized, the 3D modelling of excavation fields and finds involves specialized personnel.
- At the level of **knowledge management**, several digital applications are used separately for individual tasks (excavation, conservation, research), often not adhering to established documentation standards, thus impeding the effective use of produced digital resources in the archaeological research. The proposed technological solutions (metadata standards, controlled vocabularies, term treasures, etc.) mostly focus on digital resource management and not so much on methods for supporting the interpretive approach of excavation information. The latter requires the documentation not only of the structure but also of data semantics, therefore, corresponding extensions of the existing metadata standards through a suitable knowledge management system.
- At the level of -interactive- **presentation** of digital assets, this is limited to Artefacts finally exhibited in a museum or generally accessible to the general public (e.g., in an archaeological site). Unfortunately, a substantial proportion of archaeological findings, although documented, remain "in storage" (e.g., due to limited space availability in museums). In addition, where state-of-the-art technologies (mobile and pervasive computing, AR/VR, etc.) are utilized for the presentation of digital assets, this often involves the development of proprietary applications with rigidly defined content and features, which are tailored to specific archeological sites or museum exhibitions, therefore, cannot be extended or ported elsewhere.

This article proposes ARtefact, a conceptual framework for the integrated information management of archaeological excavations, which addresses the abovementioned challenges. ARtefact comprises a technological ecosystem which encompasses the digital documentation, knowledge management and interactive presentation of digital resources produced throughout archaeological excavations and the study/conservation process of excavated items.

ARtefact accounts for the following end-products: (1) Digital documentation - mobile- application, which provides a range of features, such as: 3D scanning and modelling of the excavation field and relevant findings (along with automated measurements of their spatial dimensions); capability to insert photos, comments and metadata; spatiotemporal annotation of findings. (2) Knowledge management tool that provides access to ontology, database and digital resources with a wealth of relevant information and semantic relationships, to enable search and presentation of digital assets from external applications. (3) An authoring tool for custom augmented reality applications (AR editor), which present interpretive content related to Artefacts and museum exhibitions, but also to the excavation field itself, thus enhancing the experience of visiting the archeological site and the museum. (4) An authoring tool for custom virtual reality applications (VR editor), which allow users to immerse and experience a virtual tour in the excavation field, locate findings at the exact locations where they were found, study and interact with the corresponding digital resources.

The remainder of this article is structured as follows: Section 2 discusses the key principles and objectives of our framework's design. Section 3 reviews related research. Section 4 presents the ARtefact architecture, while Sect. 5 describes the envisioned end-products and usage scenarios. Section 6 argues on the innovative character of ARtefact from a scientific and technological viewpoint. Finally, Sect. 7 concludes our work.

2 Principles and Objectives

The ARtefact framework addresses the above analyzed challenges in a holistic way, providing an integrated environment for the documentation, management and presentation of digital resources derived on the process of archaeological excavations (Fig. 1). ARtefact aims at providing a conceptual basis for the design, development and pilot implementation of an integrated platform which encompasses state-of-the-art technological tools to manage the whole life cycle of digital resources related to archaeological excavations, particularly the:

- digital documentation of the excavation and conservation of the findings, through a mobile application,
- knowledge management for each finding through a web information system,
- creation of interactive VR and AR applications through authoring tools (VR/AR editors).

As regards *digital documentation*, ARtefact aims to integrate the existing technological means of digital documentation in a *single* application that holistically meets the needs of archaeological documentation, both in the field (including the conservation workspace where findings are sorted, studied and restored), and in the museum exhibition, providing features like:

- 3D scanning and modelling of both the excavation field and selected findings.
- Recording of topographic measurements.
- Annotation of movable and immovable findings in the field, through intuitive interfaces.

- Metadata logging for each finding/Artefact.
- Taking timestamped and geotagged photos.

As regards *knowledge management*, ARtefact involves:

- Creation of an ARtefact ontology, which is based on established standards and extends them to cover the whole lifecycle of the excavation fieldwork and its findings.
- Formulation of queries that are necessary to search and present digital resources.
- Creation of a linked data DB to define the semantics of each resource.
- Identification of semantic connections between different data sets.
- Publication of semantic data of archaeological findings on the web.

As regards the *presentation & promotion* of digital assets, the framework design aims at the:

- Implementation of two innovative tools for the automated creation of AR/VR applications with custom (i.e., defined by a content editor) and extensible content (AR/VR application editors or authoring tools); those tools should be usable by non-specialized users (archaeologists, conservators, curators, educators).
- Integration of the tools with the knowledge management infrastructure for the selection of the presented digital resources.
- Pilot execution and empirical evaluation of the tools by representatives of the above-mentioned user groups (archaeologists, etc.), as well as of the authored interactive applications by end-users of their target audience (visitors of archeological sites and museum exhibitions).

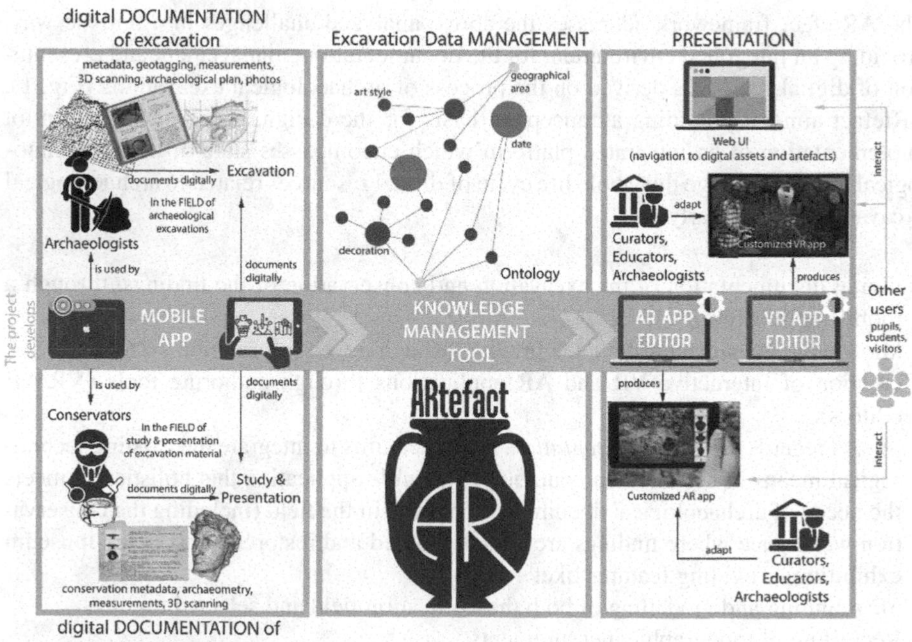

Fig. 1. The conceptual model of ARtefact.

The framework contributes to the more effective interpretation of the archaeological excavation, and also supports the archaeological research, the digital documentation and the education. Therefore, the target audience (beneficiaries) of the project includes the whole range of scientists, professionals and stakeholders involved in the excavation (archaeologists, conservators, art historians, curators, museologists, etc.); students and educators in relevant scientific subjects; the general public.

3 Scientific and Technological State-of-the-Art

3.1 Technologies and Applications for the Digital Documentation of Excavations, Documentation Study and Conservation

The data collected during a field excavation or conservation is complex and of different types and formats. Digital technologies offer reliable solutions in recording and managing data with various tools tailored to the needs and facts of archaeological excavations. The digitization of the excavation field and objects is based on modern techniques, such as laser scanners, photogrammetry and precision topographic instruments (total stations) [5]. Archaeometric data can be generated for the findings using analysis tools, such as XRF fluorometry [9], while semi-automated tools have been developed for the digital reconstruction of fragments [23]. All digital annotation data referring to the field and objects can be geographically referenced through GIS technologies, making it easy to locate correlations between them as well as the wider environment [14]. Documents and notes produced during an excavation (such as archaeological data, conservation data and archaeometric data) have traditionally been recorded in handwritten bulletins, while now are manually entered through specialized mobile/web applications [31]. Recently, there has been a trend of transition from 2D recording data to 3D, due to lower costs and the proliferation of available technical solutions (hardware and software) [26]. In addition, portable devices are increasingly utilized during the excavation [29], as they easier to use in the field; however, integrated solutions are still lacking. The ARtefact framework incorporates the above trends in a single mobile application supporting 3D scanning of the excavation, georeferencing of findings and digital documentation.

3.2 Semantic Linking of Archaeological Data with the Use of Ontologies

The organization of archaeological data is a problem of defining the appropriate entities used by researchers to classify the microworld of excavation. The subjectivity of the classifications makes it difficult to link the data recorded by the excavation application to cultural management systems. A possible solution lies in understanding the semantics of the microworld of excavation, and the correlation of its different models in standardized ontologies [17]. The research applications of ontologies in archeology mainly focus on the interoperability of different systems and the semantic interconnection of data [12]. One such example is the dating of excavation finds (e.g., pottery fragments), which can be deduced from the added materials. Information on impurities is obtained from the conservation process. Therefore, there should be some sort of logical connection between the excavation database (DB) and the conservation DB. Such rules codify the researcher's knowledge and are not incorporated in generic ontologies such as CIDOC-CRM [1], making their extension necessary to meet the specific requirements of the excavation. The ARtefact framework focuses on codifying the rules that describe the interpretive process of excavation with the aim, apart from the semantic linking of data, their enrichment through information, which is logically inferred through the ontology.

3.3 Applications for the Interactive Presentation of Cultural Heritage and Excavation Findings

In the recent years, the use of state-of-the-art interactive systems in museums and archeological sites allows visitors to access digital cultural content on the field. Such systems utilize a diverse set of technologies, such as: mobile apps, augmented reality [13, 27], large public displays and multi-touch tables [19, 20], virtual reality [25, 30], voice interfaces [10], soundscapes [18], and kinesthetic interaction [16, 24]. At present, we are not aware of any applications that highlight the entire life cycle of archaeological finds (from discovery to exhibition) [2], but only applications that address certain aspects [7]. Also, cultural promotion applications often overlook the historical accuracy as regards the edited content [15]. It is stated that "the design of interactive exhibitions should be guided by a main concept around stories, topics, objects and experiences that the exhibition aims to communicate" [14]. In ARtefact, the key concept is to shed light on the lifecycle of archaeological finds. An additional problem is that AR/VR application development is costly, and such applications can only be produced/customized by specialized application designers & developers. ARtefact accounts for user-friendly tools facilitating the development of AR/VR applications that will promote archeological sites (or museum exhibitions) with available digital documentation.

3.4 Digital Archaeology Projects

Since the early 2000s a large number of research and development projects have applied digital technologies to assist and improve traditional archaeological practices. Early projects focused mainly on the digital recording and 3D visualization of archeological data (3D MURALE [3]), as well as the virtual reconstructions of historic and cultural sites aiming at the enhancement of visitor experience by imaging the relation of archaeological ruins with historical data (Archeoguide [34], Lifeplus [22], ARAC Maps [6]). More recent projects focus on the excavation process itself and the facilitation of the documentation, storage and analysis of field data directly in the excavation field using hand held and mobile devices (iDig [33], REVEAL [28], ArchAIDE [8]). In addition, they propose the use of 3D maps and mixed reality tools for offsite visualization of the archaeological dig providing useful insights during the interpretation process (VITA [2, 32]). Finally, in order to facilitate the codification, access and sharing of archaeological excavation data, the ARIADNE project [21] has developed a reference model for the documentation of the archaeological excavation process. Despite the remarkable growth of related projects, they mostly focus specific aspects of the digital archaeology workflow. ARtefact aims to address this limitation by providing an integrated platform which encompasses the whole life cycle of digital resources related to archaeological excavation.

4 The ARtefact Architecture

The proposed ARtefact system architecture comprises 3 layers: the digital resources layer, the digital documentation data layer, and the semantics layer (see Fig. 2).

The digital resources layer stores heterogeneous data related to the excavation lifecycle and may include images, videos, 3D models, spatial vector data, textual notes, bibliographic sources, etc.) which refer to a specific time and location in relation to the excavation. Examples of such resources are the 3D scan of the excavation field (at a specific phase of the excavation process) and photographs of findings.

Due to resource heterogeneity, current practices involve the use of different digital documentation systems, which adopt different metadata schemas to characterize resources. This is done on the digital documentation layer which involves the characterization of resources in some structured form (relational database). Examples include a DB of excavation findings or a DB of an archaeological collection that includes Artefacts of different types.

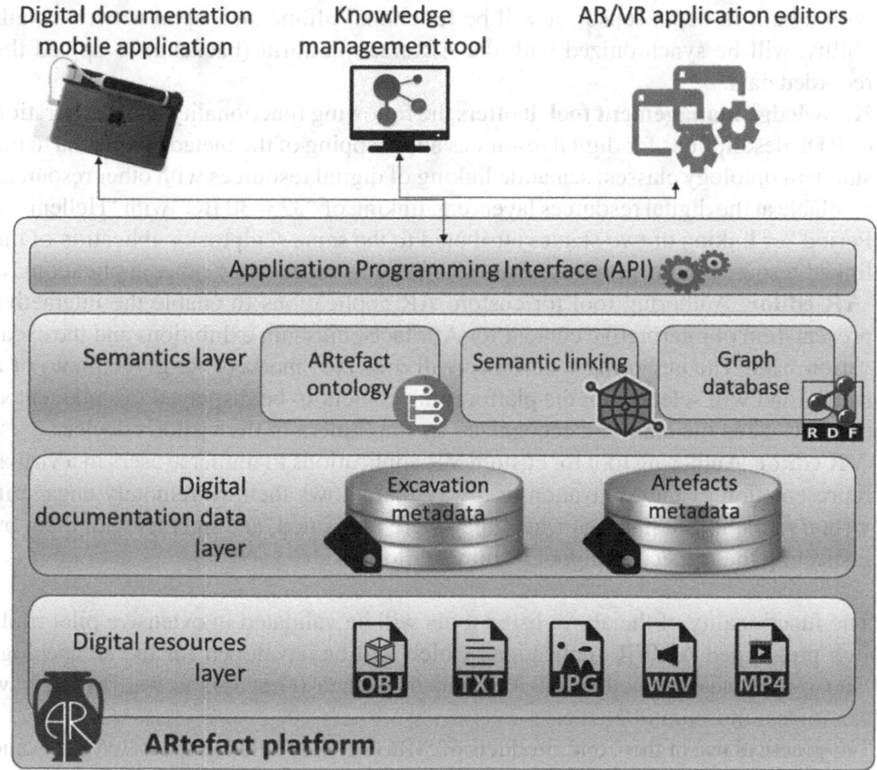

Fig. 2. Software architecture of the ARtefact platform.

The integration of the above resources takes place at the upper, semantics layer, wherein heterogeneous resources are transformed into RDF descriptions, based on the

ARtefact ontology. In addition, semantic relationships between resources are established. The semantically linked data is published in a graph DB, which enables semantic search upon data.

The above subsystems will be accessible from other applications through a programming interface (API), which, as part of the platform, will be used to interface the ARtefact platform with the 4 envisioned end-products.

5 End Products and Usage Scenarios

The end products of ARtefact include:

1. **Digital documentation -mobile- application**. The application features a broad range of functions such as: 3D scanning and modelling of both the excavation field and selected findings; capacity to insert photos, comments and annotations, automated measurements, markup (e.g., spatiotemporal data) for findings and items on the excavation field; metadata recording. The application will be executed on a device with a built-in depth sensor. It will be functional offline and, upon network availability, will be synchronized with the ARtefact platform (backend) to upload the recorded data.
2. **Knowledge management tool**. It offers the following functionality: auto-generation of RDF descriptions for digital resources and mapping of the metadata schema to the standard ontology classes; semantic linking of digital resources with other resources available at the digital resources layer (e.g. linking of "323–30 BC" with "Hellenistic Period" or linking of two statues attributed to the same sculptor); publication of the linked resource in the graph database to enable its retrieval by other applications.
3. **AR editor**. Authoring tool for custom AR applications to enable the interactive presentation of interpretive content for Artefacts, museum exhibitions and the excavation field. The authoring tool's user will indicate "markers" (e.g. the photo of a statue) and will select from the platform the content to be displayed (as augmented content) when the marker is recognized by the camera of the visitor's device.
4. **VR editor**. Authoring tool for custom VR applications to immerse users in a virtual representation of the excavation in a way that allows them to remotely engage in virtual tours, locate findings where they were excavated, and interact with them by inspecting the respective digital documentation.

The functionality of the above listed tools will be validated in extensive pilot trials through prototyped AR/VR applications which will be developed for the archaeological site (Mycenaean cemetery) of Aidonia, in Nemea (Greece), as well as the new archaeological museum of Nemea.

The practical use of the 4 end-products of ARtefact is detailed in the following usage scenario:

- A field archaeologist involved in an active excavation uses the *mobile digital documentation application* to: scan and create a 3D model of the excavation field where he recently discovered a stone-made domed tomb with a human skeleton and a bronze sword; take a geo/timestamped photo of the tomb, in the exact condition it was found; operate the depth sensor through the mobile app to measure the tomb's dimensions and mark the exact position where the sward was found in the tomb's interior; annotate the tomb as "unplundered Mycenaean tomb"; enter metadata for immovable finds (e.g., excavation sector and altitude at which they were found).

- The movable excavation findings are transferred to the conservation workspace for sorting and further study. Therein, the conservator uses a different view (i.e., features) of the same *mobile app* to: scan and create a 3D model of the sword, and measure its dimensions; record the conservation & restoration work performed on the Artefact; record the space (room/shelf /box) wherein the artefact will be temporarily stored.
- The archaeologist uses the *knowledge management tool* to search for and link the Artefact to others found in the same tomb as well as to others of a similar type, style, dating or decoration.
- The curator of the museum where the sword will be exhibited uses the *AR editor* to create a custom AR application that will promote the most important exhibits of the collection (including the sword). The museum's visitor: installs the AR application on his smartphone; while walking through the museum, her camera tracks and sword, and superimposes the augmented content (3D model, conservation metadata, semantically linked Artefacts, etc.).
- An archeology professor at a US university uses the *VR editor* to create a custom VR application for presenting the excavation to her audience. Her student: wears a VR head-mounted display (HMD) to be immersed (transported) to the excavation site; has a virtual walkthrough in the site and approaches the tomb labeled "unplundered Mycenaean tomb", which initially appears empty; interacts with a virtual interface to visualize the sword and access its corresponding metadata; interacts with the 3D model of the sword (rotation, magnification, etc.).

6 Scientific and Technological Innovation

The ARtefact framework is innovative from a scientific perspective:

- Integration of all functions related to the digital documentation of an excavation (including its findings) into a single mobile application, addressing the requirements to all involved stakeholders (field archaeologist, curator, exhibition curator, etc.). No integrated solution is available today in the broader area of digital archaeology, although separate aids and tools are available to address specific requirements. The ARtefact's approach integrates this fragmented technological landscape, producing innovation from a requirements engineering, methodology and design standpoint.
- Specification of an ontology that will codify the excavation process both in terms of recording and interpretation of excavation findings throughout their life cycle. In order to ensure the extensibility and interoperability of the approach, ARtefact proposes revisions/extensions of existing metadata schemes.
- Development of usable, intuitive interfaces for VR environments to easily manipulate and interact with excavation findings.

- Provisioning of tools that open opportunities for creating engaging educational experiences; in particular, the VR applications will complement traditional education methods enabling students to have a fully immersive 3D reasoning from the beginning and throughout the whole archaeological process, which is recognized as an open challenge in archaeology education [4].

ARtefact is also innovative from a technical point of view:

- Combined use of state-of-the-art mobile devices equipped with built-in (or connected) depth cameras and a multitude of sensors for 3D scanning/modelling and annotation.
- Application of ontologies and semantic data linking technologies to create a scalable excavation knowledge base.
- Utilization of AR and VR technologies (authored by archeologists and curators without any technical expertise) to promote cultural assets and evoke compelling experiences during -physical or virtual- visits to archeological sites or museum exhibitions.

7 Conclusions

This article introduced ARtefact, a conceptual framework which holistically addresses the requirements related to the digital documentation, knowledge management and interactive presentation of digital resources produced throughout the archaeological excavation and the study/conservation of Artefacts.

The end-products planned in ARtefact are: (1) A -mobile- digital documentation application (operated on mobile devices with built-in depth sensors) which offers a broad range of features, such as: 3D scanning and modelling of the excavation field and its findings; geo/timestamping of findings; capacity to take and store photos, comments and annotations. (2) Web-based knowledge management tool that enables access to ontology, database and semantically linked digital resources and facilitates efficient search and retrieval of digital assets from external applications. (3) An authoring tool for creating custom AR applications, which promote interpretive content related to Artefacts and museum exhibitions, but also to the excavation field itself, thus enhancing the experience of visiting the archeological and museum site. (4) An authoring tool for creating custom VR applications, which enable -remote- immersed users to pursue virtual tours in the excavation field, discovering findings at the precise location where they were found, and also to study and interact with the corresponding digital resources.

Overall, ARtefact specifies the necessary technological substrate for the documentation, management and promotion of the "biography" of archaeological excavations and Artefacts. The scientific and technological approach of the project goes far beyond the current state-of-the-art of existing technological solutions employed in the excavation and preservation of Artefacts. The framework contributes to the interpretation of archaeological excavations, as well as to the archaeological research, digital documentation and education. The target audience of ARtefact includes the whole range of scientists, professionals and bodies involved in archaeological excavations (field archaeologists, conservators, art historians, curators, museologists, etc.), students and educators in relevant scientific subjects, as well as the wide public (visitors of cultural heritage sites).

In the near future, we aim at concluding a prototype implementation of ARtefact, which we plan to validate in the context of two complementary pilot studies: an active archeological excavation site in Greece and an archeological museum which features several Artefacts excavated from the archeological site.

Acknowledgement. This research was funded by the Research e-Infrastructure "Interregional Digital Transformation for Culture and Tourism in Aegean Archipelagos" {Code Number MIS 5047046} which is implemented within the framework of the "Regional Excellence" Action of the Operational Program "Competitiveness, Entrepreneurship and Innovation". The action was co-funded by the European Regional Development Fund (ERDF) and the Greek State [Partnership Agreement 2014–2020].

References

1. CIDOC CRM (2015): Definition of the CIDOC Conceptual Reference Model. Version 6.1, February (2015)
2. Benko, H., Ishak, E., Feiner, S.: Collaborative visualization of an archaeological excavation. In NSF Lake Tahoe Workshop on Collaborative Virtual Reality and Visualization (CVRV 2003), pp. 26–28 (2003)
3. Cosmas, J. et al.: 3D MURALE: A multimedia system for archaeology. In: Proceedings of the 2001 Conference on Virtual Reality, Archeology, and Cultural Heritage, pp. 297–306 (2001)
4. Derudas, P., Berggren, Å.: Expanding field-archaeology education: the integration of 3D technology into archaeological training. Open Archaeol. **7**(1), 556–573 (2021)
5. Doneus, M., Verhoeven, G., Fera, M., Briese, C., Kucera, M, Neubauer, W.: From deposit to point cloud–a study of low-cost computer vision approaches for the straightforward documentation of archaeological excavations. Geoinformatics FCE CTU **6**, 81–88 (2011)
6. Eggert, D., Hücker, D., Paelke, V.: Augmented reality visualization of archeological data. In: Cartography from Pole to Pole, pp. 203–216 (2014)
7. Georgiadi, N., et al.: A pervasive role-playing game for introducing elementary school students to archaeology. In: Workshop on Mobile Cultural Heritage, Mobile HCI 2016 (18th International Conference on Human-Computer Interaction with Mobile Devices and Services) (2016)
8. Gualandi, M.L., et al.: ArchAIDE-archaeological automatic interpretation and documentation of cEramics. In: EUROGRAPHICS Workshop on Graphics and Cultural Heritage The Eurographics Association, pp. 1–4 (2016)
9. Janssens, K., et al.: Use of microscopic XRF for non-destructive analysis in art and archaeometry. X-Ray Spectrom. **29**(1), 73–91 (2000)
10. Jylhä, A., Hsieh, Y.T., Orso, V., Andolina, S., Gamberini, L., Jacucci, G.: A wearable multimodal interface for exploring POIs. In: Proceedings of the 2015 ACM on International Conference on Multimodal Interaction, ACM, pp. 175–182 (2015)
11. Kansa, E., Kansa, S.W.: Digital data and data literacy in archaeology now and in the new decade. Adv. Archaeol. Pract. **9**(1), 81–85 (2021)
12. Karmacharya, A., Cruz, C., Boochs, F., Marzani, F.: ArchaeoKM: managing archaeological data through archaeological knowledge. Comput. Appl. Quant. Methods Archeol. CAA, 6–9 (2010)

13. Kasapakis, V., Gavalas, D., Galatis, P.: Augmented reality in cultural heritage: field of view awareness in an archaeological site mobile guide. J. Ambient Intell. Smart Environ. **8**(5), 501–514 (2016)
14. Katsianis, M., Tsipidis, S., Kotsakis, K., Kousoulakou, A.: A 3D digital workflow for archaeological intra-site research using GIS. J. Archaeol. Sci. **35**(3), 655–667 (2008)
15. Koutsabasis, P.: Empirical evaluations of interactive systems in cultural heritage: a review. Int. J. Comput. Methods Heritage Sci. **1**(1), 100–122 (2017)
16. Koutsabasis, P., Vosinakis, S.: Kinesthetic interactions in museums: conveying cultural heritage by making use of ancient tools and (re-) constructing artworks. Virtual Reality **22**(2), 103–118 (2017). https://doi.org/10.1007/s10055-017-0325-0
17. Lombardo, V., Damiano, R., Karatas, T., Mattutino, C.: Linking ontological classes and archaeological forms. In: International Semantic Web Conference, pp. 700–715 (2020)
18. Marshall, M.T., et al.: Audio-based narratives for the trenches of World War I: intertwining stories, places and interaction for an evocative experience. Int. J. Hum Comput Stud. **85**, 27–39 (2016)
19. Marton, F., Rodriguez, M.B., Bettio, F., Agus, M., Villanueva, A.J., Gobbetti, E.: IsoCam: interactive visual exploration of massive cultural heritage models on large projection setups. J. Comput. Cult. Heritage **7**(2), 12 (2014)
20. Maye, L.A., McDermott, F.E., Ciolfi, L., Avram, G.: Interactive exhibitions design: what can we learn from cultural heritage professionals?. In: Proceedings of the 8th Nordic Conference on Human-Computer Interaction: Fun, Fast, Foundational, ACM, pp. 598–607 (2014)
21. Niccolucci, F., Richards, J.D.: ARIADNE: Advanced research infrastructures for archaeological dataset networking in Europe. Int. J. Humanit. Arts Comput. **7**(1–2), 70–88 (2013)
22. Papagiannakis, G.: Lifeplus: revival of life in ancient pompeii. In: Proceedings of the 8th International Conference on Virtual Systems and Multimedia (VSMM 02), pp. 25–27 (2002)
23. Papaioannou, G., Karabassi, E.A., Theoharis, T.: Virtual archaeologist: assembling the past. IEEE Comput. Graphics Appl. **21**(2), 53–59 (2001)
24. Pietroni, E., Adami, A.: Interacting with virtual reconstructions in museums: the etruscanning project. J. Comput. Cult. Heritage **7**(2), 9 (2014)
25. Reunanen, M., Díaz, L., Horttana, T.: A holistic user-centered approach to immersive digital cultural heritage installations: case vrouw maria. J. Comput. Cult. Heritage **7**(4), 24 (2015)
26. Roosevelt, C.H., Cobb, P., Moss, E., Olson, B.R., Ünlüsoy, S.: Excavation is destruction digitization: advances in archaeological practice. J. Field Archaeol. **40**(3), 325–346 (2015)
27. Rubino, I., Barberis, C., Xhembulla, J., Malnati, G.: Integrating a location-based mobile game in the museum visit: evaluating visitors' behaviour and learning. J. Comput. Cult. Heritage **8**(3), 15 (2015)
28. Sanders, D.H.: Enabling archaeological hypothesis testing in real time using the REVEAL documentation and display system. Virtual Archaeol. Rev. **2**(4), 89–94 (2011)
29. Styliaras, G.: Towards a web-based archaeological excavation platform for smartphones: review and potentials. Springerplus **4**(1), 1–14 (2015). https://doi.org/10.1186/s40064-015-1115-3
30. Sylaiou, S., Kasapakis, V., Dzardanova, E., Gavalas, D.: Leveraging mixed reality technologies to enhance museum visitor experiences. In: 2018 International Conference on Intelligent Systems (IS), pp. 595–601 (2018)
31. Tsiafakis, D., Tsirliganis, N., Pavlidis, G., Evangelidis, V., Chamzas, C.: Karabournaki-recording the past: the digitization of an archaeological site. In: International Conference on Electronic Imaging & the Visual Arts EVA (2004)
32. Tsipidis, S., Koussoulakou, A., Kotsakis, K.: Geovisualization and archaeology: supporting excavation site research. In: Advances in Cartography and GIScience, Springer, Heidelberg, vol. 2, pp. 85–107 (2011)

33. Uildriks, M.: iDig-recording archaeology: a review. Internet Archaeol. **42** (2016)
34. Vlahakis, V., et al.: Archeoguide: an augmented reality guide for archaeological sites. IEEE Comput. Graphics Appl. **22**(5), 52–60 (2002)

Geomatics Meets XR: A Brief Overview of the Synergy Between Geospatial Data and Augmented Visualization

Roberto Pierdicca[1(✉)], Maurizio Mulliri[2], Matteo Lucesoli[2], Fabio Piccinini[1], and Eva Savina Malinverni[1]

[1] Dipartimento di Ingegneria Civile Edile e dell'Architettura (DICEA), Università Politecnica delle Marche, Via Brecce Bianche, 60131 Ancona, Italy
{r.pierdicca,f.piccinini,e.s.malinverni}@staff.univpm.it

[2] Microgeo s.r.l., Via Campi Bisenzio, 50013 Firenze, Italy
{m.mulliri,m.lucesoli}@microgeo.it

Abstract. Extended Reality (XR) is an extension of the real world obtained thanks to the increase of innovative features that allow users to perceive the surrounding reality in a different and enhanced way, combining it with virtual elements. XR is declined through three different technologies that help change the perception of reality: Virtual Reality (VR), Augmented Reality (AR), Mixed Reality (MR). The latter combines VR and AR creating a more complex experience, generating a new reality resulting from the union between real and virtual allows the user to interact simultaneously with the real world and the virtual environment. In the last years XR technology has been employed in several fields of application, except in geomatics, that is the less explored field. Given the extreme complexity of heterogeneous geomatics data, the visualization is complex, and there is the need to better understand the potential of MR for both users and experts. Considering the potentiality of this technology in geomatics, in this paper we present GEOLENS, an MR application in an eXtended environment. With GEOLENS it is possible to visualize digitally produced objects and information in the field and superimpose them on reality. The advantages of this solution in the field of surveying, architectural design and Geographical Information System (GIS), are the interaction of digital design with reality for greater decision control, time saving and office-field sharing. This paper reports over the development of a cloud-based platform which acts as a repository of geomatics data, ready to use in the real environment. The features described prove the suitability of the solution for multiple purposes.

Keywords: Geomatic · eXtended reality · Geo spatial information systems · Miscrosoft holoLens

1 Introduction

The terms Virtual, Augmented, and Mixed Reality (VR, AR, MR) refer to technologies and conceptual propositions of spatial interfaces studied by engineering,

L. T. De Paolis et al. (Eds.): XR Salento 2022, LNCS 13446, pp. 224–235, 2022.
https://doi.org/10.1007/978-3-031-15553-6_17

computer science, and human-computer-interaction (HCI) researchers over several decades. Recently, the term 'extended reality' (or XR) has been adopted as an umbrella term for VR/MR/AR technologies [5,6]. The AR is usually interactive and created three-dimensionally, so to harmonise with the real world. The theory of the Reality-Virtuality continuum is explained by Paul Milgram and Fumio Kishino [16] as a continuum between the real and the virtual environment, by overlapping objects in real-time. Through technology, in fact, all five senses can theoretically be enhanced: the AR can in fact be used to replace or enrich the missing senses of the user as through the correction of sight or the improvement of hearing [13]. Virtual objects add information that would otherwise not be directly perceptible to the user [18]. The information can help the user to carry out everyday work activities, such as the maintenance of electrical cables of an aircraft thanks to an optical device. The information can also have pure entertainment purpose. Over the years, with the development of the necessary technology and the very popular diffusion of smartphones and tablets, the research regarding AR has increased greatly [9]: not only for the improvement of hardware and software, but also for the study of possible uses. According to [18], it is the second generation AR, characterised by the current season of desktop and mobile applications: from road navigators to video games. The AR for navigators allows the user who has installed the correct application on the smartphone, to follow the graphic indications both by displaying them on typical road maps, directly, and interactively, on the video shooting of the urban environment. As for gaming applications, these are variations of the typical tests of reflexes and skills, but can be carried out on the screen of a personal computer to which a webcam is connected (or on the display of the smartphone equipped with a camera). Interaction with graphics and three-dimensional characters is no longer limited within pre-established scenarios, but can take place on any media within the camera's acquisition field. For the correct functioning of an application, there are two key elements that characterise the AR experience.

- The application must be able to recognise the physical world in which it is used and at the same time understand the virtual world of reference;
- The application must be able to synchronise the physical and virtual world, so as to add virtual elements to the user's vision of reality.

There are three main components of an AR system to support this process, involving a part of hardware and a part of software. They include sensors, processors and displays. To understand and interact correctly and quickly with the real world, sensors are critical to the AR system. The three main categories of sensors needed to activate this technology are: sensors for tracking, cameras, Global Positioning System (GPS), gyroscopes, accelerometers and other sensors. The heart of any AR system lies in the processor [7], which coordinates and analyses input from sensors. It stores and retrieves data, performs the tasks of the AR application and generates appropriate signals on the display. In all situations the computer must have enough power to be able to perform its tasks in real time, providing an appropriate and useful AR experience [21]. The scene needs to be updated quickly depending on user requests and environment shift.

In AR, it is particularly important that the objects represented virtually match as much as possible with the physical world that is displayed through the display (virtual mirror and smartphones) or directly by the human eye (smart glasses) otherwise the user cannot benefit from the usefulness of the application fully [12]. Finally, the main displays used for AR are: head mounted displays (HMD), hand held displays, spatial displays [15]. Thanks to the creation of dedicated software, the areas in which AR can be used are many and varied. Everything can be increased with digital content, so infinite can be the possible applications of this technology. The largest production concerns the video game and entertainment industry, then the other sectors are tourism, education, cultural heritage, industry and many more. In the last decade, MR became more and more practised, and industry shed the light to this amazing opportunity which can replace conventional AR products [17]. MR is a refined and powerful technology, able to affect perceptions, in particular sight and hearing, increasing them in terms of sensitivity and experience [20]. Digital contents can be provided to the user through different types of platforms, being both commercial or open-source. MR is defined as the direct or indirect vision of the real world improved or increased through the addition of virtual information designed on the computer [10,22]. MR combines VR and AR creating a more complex experience, generating a new reality resulting from the union between real and virtual. It requires the use of a specific MR device and allows the user to interact simultaneously with the real world and the virtual environment.

In the last years, in these sectors also XR technology has been employed, since it is able to create in a completely unique way experiences in which users interacting with the environment acquire spatial information [6]. Thanks to the recent advancements, spatial computing is an useful tool that allows users to map the environment and interact with its in real time. According to [6], in traditional spatial analysis, further cognitive processing is required to relate the data product and space. Whereas mobile technologies, including smartphones, tablets and HMD, allow the connection of data and space through a process called real-time reification. One of the domains in which XR is less exploited is Geomatics. The visualisation of complex and spatial data is still entrusted on web platform or, worthily, on paper support. The main reason is that Geomatics data are complex, really heavy to manipulate, and can be useful to several users. However, XR interfaces allow to view, perceive and interact with spatial data and perform spatial operations by promoting the transfer of spatial knowledge and reducing the distance between traditional analysis environment and the ones where GIS analyses are generally performed [6]. Moreover, considering some experiments presented in [2], the use of XR in Geomatics is possible, but it is justified weather high accuracy and precision can be ensured in the localisation of virtual objects on the screen. Up to know, the visualisation of Geomatics data is only partially explored. For this reason, this article aims to push over this interesting issue, by proposing GEOLENS. GEOLENS is a Mixed Reality (MR) application based on interactive glasses for a combined vision of digital geo-located contents with reality. Our solution, through the use of special three-dimensional glasses, allows to operate in the field even hands-free, being able to view our design idea directly in the field and evaluate the activities to be done. The paper aims to open the debate on how Geomatic applications and data can be improved with a Mixed Visualisation, making the field work more intuitive in both indoor and outdoor scenario. The proposed solution was developed by the cooperation between Microgeo s.r.l.[1] and the academic research lab GAP[2] (Geomatics Application and Processing @UNIVPM), attempting to fill the gap between the market and the research community.

2 Related Works

In the field of 3D modeling and Geomatics, thanks to AR, projects can be viewed three-dimensionally, entering the preview directly in the chosen urban context before the actual completion. The AR can also be exploited in a design workspace, offering the ability to view 3D models from their 2D drawing. A successful case in this regard is the English architecture firm LSI [8]. The primary objective is to create sustainable and innovative structures and AR facilitates the communication of ideas for construction. Leveraging on continuous improvements to the accuracy of GPS and other location systems, companies are able to use AR to visualise geo-referenced models of construction sites, underground structures, cables and pipes using mobile devices. For example, after the New Zealand earthquake in 2011, the University of Canterbury released CityViewAR [14], which allowed city designers and engineers to view buildings that were destroyed by the earthquake. In the field of logistics and maintenance, thanks to dedicated smart glasses or tablets, employees can have in real time useful information to improve the quality and speed of activities, even in critical situations. The use of AR visors in logistics has the potential to significantly reduce storage costs and improve the management process [4]. In the application of visors for maintenance, an application for the new BT-200 glasses [3] has been developed. The technician can adjust a sensor by acting with his hands on its mechanical positioning and simultaneously see superimposed on the scene, the information provided by the diagnostic software. The use of glasses and safety information that can be obtained thanks to AR reduces the risk of dangerous operations, because every critical point is highlighted by signals that appear superimposed through the glasses.

Following we propose some works of recent literature that present XR applications. XR is used in the field of Digital Cultural Heritage (DHC) in the work of [1]. The authors aim to demonstrate how it is possible to promote the architectural heritage by integrating Building Information Modeling (BIM) and XR through the use of entertainment software and gaming. For this purpose they propose a case study, by collecting data of historical records of a church in Milan and using 3D survey create a XR experience that allows an innovative interaction for expert and non-expert users and for different typologies of devices.

[1] https://www.prontomicrogeo.com.
[2] https://www.gapgeomatica.it.

Also in cultural heritage field is placed the work of [19] that describes a case study in Serralves Museum and Coa Archeologic Park with the aims to create a more involving and engaging but also high culture experience. They propose an XR platform based on an engine that has core experiences functions and can be applied to create, process, and deliver immersive and interactive content for multiple experiences for CH field.

A notable recent application is an interactive XR toolkit, named BlocklyXR [11]. The authors provide users a visual programming environment to create XR applications for digital storytelling. The contextual design was generated from real-world map data retrieved from Mapbox GL. The application has been tested to replicate the PalmitoAR and the results have demonstrated that the design and the task fit technology had positive effects on the perceived ease of use and usefulness.

For our application we make use of Microsoft hololenses, that are the next generation of AR headsets and are far removed from other glasses by the different and much more advanced features. In the following section we describe specific features of Microsoft holoLens used in our mixed reality project.

2.1 Microsoft HoloLens

Microsoft hololens is the first fully independent holographic computer that allows the interaction with digital content and holograms displayed in the world around the wearer. The hololens were developed by Microsoft in collaboration with NASA and work independently, as they do not require any connection with a smartphone or other device. It is a real wearable holographic computer equipped with motion sensors, depth sensors, video cameras, microphone and audio with spatial sound. They present content in mixed reality and allow to view multimedia content and stay with the gaze perpetually anchored to the real world that becomes an integral part of the user experience. In addition, the system is also able to handle the prospect. Approaching or moving away from objects, the entire context is correctly scaled accordingly. Such a viewer has aroused a lot of interest to companies who see in such technology a valuable tool thanks to its autonomy, ease of use, portability and the ability to make available information leaving hands free.

Sensors and accessories, including cameras and processors, are located in the front. The visor is coloured and inside there is a pair of transparent lenses combined, on which the projected images are displayed in the lower half. The hololens must be calibrated according to the user's inter-pupillary distance to ensure the correct display of the virtual elements. Along the lower edges, located close to users' ears, are a pair of small red speakers for 3D audio. On the top edge there are two pairs of buttons: display brightness and volume. The hololens features an inertial measuring unit (IMU) that includes an accelerometer, gyroscope, and a magnetometer, four room tracking sensors, a depth camera, a video camera, a microphone and an ambient light sensor.

3 Description of GEOLENS Solution

3.1 Device and Web Platform

The mixed reality solution allows to operate hands-free wearing a helmet hololens and then transporting our project, our realisation, our cad model directly in the field and then walk inside it. To do this, it is always necessary having a topographic survey that allows to anchor our project, our CAD model and our 3D object in the context of reality. All this is possible to run it directly in the field by identifying objects, characteristic points that we know are present on site or we could use the GPS to be able to identify, on the moment, the point that is part of our design. Table 1 shows the technical specifications of the glasses used for the GEOLENS application.

Table 1. Technical specifications of GEOLENS glasses

Display	
Optical	Transparent holographic lenses
Resolution	2000 lighting devices 3:2
Holographic density	<2500 rad (radiant light points)
Eye-based rendering	Display optimization for 3D eye position
Sensors	
Head tracking	4 cameras with visible light
Eye tracking	2 infrared cameras
Depth	1MP flight time depth sensor
IMU	Accelerometer, gyroscope, magnetometer
Camera	8MP images, video 1080p30

A very common, issue when working in the field with Geomatics data, is the necessity to have the project always updated, even remotely by the insiders. To solve this issue, a specific web platform was designed, that allows to load our project starting from three-dimensional objects (obj transformed into a glTF format suitable for the glasses) or dxf or from points of known coordinates. The web-platform is then queried by the operator in the field, which finds the updated file from the cloud service. The web-platform is depicted in (Fig. 1).

3.2 Georeferencing the Project

The main issue concerning the use of Hololens in outdoor settings is the lack of marker points recognizable by the device. This is due to the illumination issues, that hamper a proper markerless recognition by the device. To overcome this issue, the exploitation of a reference system is essential.

The project, in the case of this example, exploits three landmarks previously computed via GNSS receiver. Afterwards, the user can use the geo-location functionality to set the reference system directly on the working site. It is also

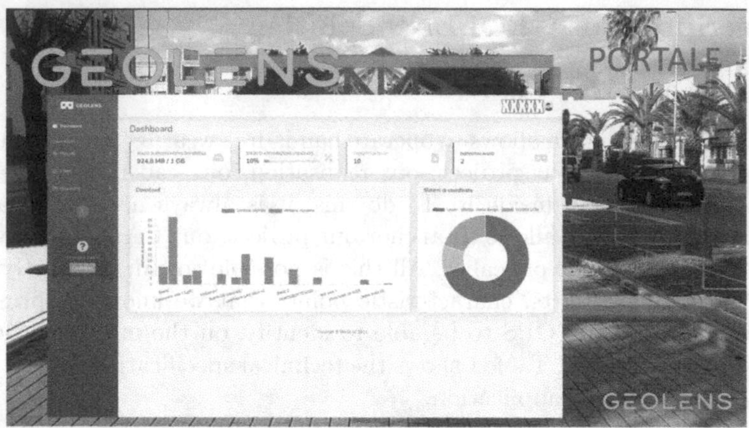

Fig. 1. Dashboard of GEOLENS platform, where the user can load the updated models in the field.

(a) (b)

Fig. 2. Manual positioning of signal for the proper geolocation of the project.

possible to interact with the site choosing a reference point with the command "get marker". As the Fig. 2 shows, the signal that appears can be positioned manually, then confirming the position. In this way, all the points that we have decided to be fundamental elements to anchor our design can be manually selected. After the project can be perfectly overlapped, it is possible to load the entire 3D model from the platform. In this example, we propose the mixed visualization of pipes, underground services and fountains in urban streets. The Fig. 3 shows the visualization of the project directly on site.

It has a three-dimensional design, and interesting is that being hands-free you can have other equipment that we can use to take measurements or make other assessments.

What you see helps to better understand the positions of objects and especially the perspective, so in this case you see the tree that is inside its flowerbed

Fig. 3. The visualised project using GEOLENS glasses

with the various pipes in various depths (Fig. 4) and the fountain above the ground with the various pipes that go to connect to the most important ones (Fig. 5).

Fig. 4. Visualization of the tree inside its flowerbed.

Finally, our project could be composed of wireframe models coming from a cad dxf drawing, or three-dimensional objects from cad Edwin, So the solution is projected through our view and this view will be enriched precisely by the ability of our eye to appreciate the three-dimensionality. What we see is a direct recording of the glasses that does not evaluate what our brain is visualising but actually we visualise our pipes, our infrastructures and the solutions that we wanted to represent in our project.

Fig. 5. Visualization of the fountain above the ground

3.3 Examples of Possible Applications Domains

As one can guess, this solution opens up to countless applications where a user need to visualise, on the site work, the paper based projects. A good example is given by the archaeological excavations. Indeed, once the operator get to the working site for an inspections, he/she generally cannot find the reference system. By overlapping the paper based project with the one uploaded with Geolens platform, the user can easily visualize the cad data, increasing the awareness thanks to the mixed location based service. An example of this application can be found in Fig. 6.

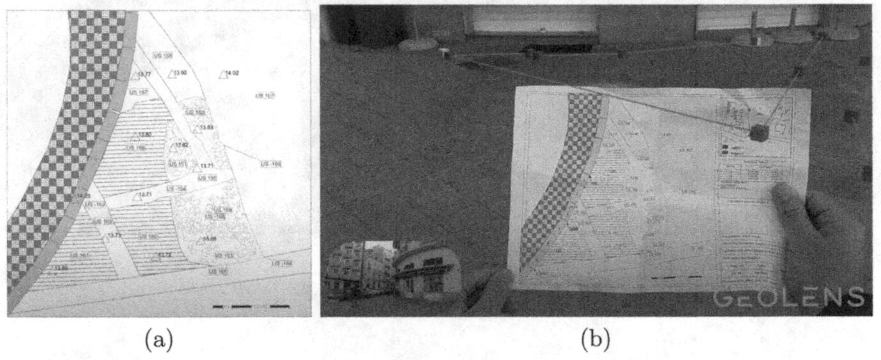

(a) (b)

Fig. 6. Example of archaeological project with landmarks for excavations.

In the field of urban furniture, but more in general dealing with urban environment, it is essential for designers, as well as for the client committing the project, to have a sight of the output of the design phase. With location based services, aided with the Mixed visualization of the 3D objects. An example can be seen in Fig. 7.

Fig. 7. Visualization of the urban forniture above the ground.

4 Conclusions and Future Works

The aim of this paper is to present our MR solution that helps designers, stylists, architects, and private individuals to see in advance and create their own project. GEOLENS is a user-friendly application that uses an helmet hololens to explore the scene with hands-free. With GEOLENS it is possible to visualize digitally produced objects and information in the field and superimpose them on reality. This information is projected directly into the field in addition to the natural view of the operator. The advantages of this solution in the field of surveying, architectural design and Geographical Information System (GIS), are the interaction of digital design with reality for greater decision control, time saving and office-field sharing. Thanks to the cloud based service, the user can directly download updated projects. The advantages for the Geomatic domain are many, which can be summarized as follows:

- reducing the complexity of heterogeneous data with a smart visualization for maintainance and/or design purposes;
- possibility to exploit georeferenced data (e.g. with GNSS coordinates), for a more precise overlapping of 2D/3D data;
- increasing the awareness by experts, making the visualization of object otherwise invisible to the naked eye;
- reducing the error of transferring the data from the map to the ground, thanks to the location based service

Despite being a PoC, this solution will be expanded by making the interchange of data and the interoperability more efficient. In the future we even foresee to perform a usability test between experts and non experts to verify, with the broader public, the effectiveness of this solution.

References

1. Banfi, F., Brumana, R., Stanga, C.: Extended reality and informative models for the architectural heritage: from scan-to-bim process to virtual and augmented reality (2019)
2. Bednarczyk, M.: The use of augmented reality in geomatics. In: Environmental Engineering. In: Proceedings of the International Conference on Environmental Engineering. ICEE. vol. 10, pp. 1–7. Vilnius Gediminas Technical University, Department of Construction Economics (2017)
3. Blattgerste, J., Strenge, B., Renner, P., Pfeiffer, T., Essig, K.: Comparing conventional and augmented reality instructions for manual assembly tasks. In: Proceedings of the 10th international conference on pervasive technologies related to assistive environments, pp. 75–82 (2017)
4. Cirulis, A., Ginters, E.: Augmented reality logistics. Proc. Comput. Sci. **26**, 14–20 (2013)
5. Ç, A., et al.: Geospatial information visualization and extended reality displays. In: Guo, H., Goodchild, M.F., Annoni, A. (eds.) Manual of Digital Earth, pp. 229–277. Springer, Singapore (2020). https://doi.org/10.1007/978-981-32-9915-3_7
6. Ç, A., et al.: Extended reality in spatial sciences: A review of research challenges and future directions. ISPRS Int. J. Geo-Inf. **9**(7), 439 (2020)
7. Craig, A.B.: Understanding augmented reality: Concepts and applications. Newnes (2013)
8. Estrada, O.E.S., Urbina, M.G., Ocaña, R.: Augmented reality for evaluating low environmental impact 3d concepts in industrial design. In: Augmented Reality for Enhanced Learning Environments, pp. 222–245. IGI Global (2018)
9. Flavián, C., Ibáñez-Sánchez, S., Orús, C.: The impact of virtual, augmented and mixed reality technologies on the customer experience. J. Bus. Res. **100**, 547–560 (2019)
10. Gregory, I., Murrieta-Flores, P.: Doing digital humanities: Practice, training, research (2016)
11. Jung, K., Nguyen, V.T., Lee, J.: Blocklyxr: an interactive extended reality toolkit for digital storytelling. Appl. Sci. **11**(3), 1073 (2021)
12. Kim, D., Choi, Y.: Applications of smart glasses in applied sciences: a systematic review. Appl. Sci. **11**(11), 4956 (2021)
13. Lampropoulos, G., Keramopoulos, E., Diamantaras, K.: Enhancing the functionality of augmented reality using deep learning, semantic web and knowledge graphs: a review. Vis. Inf. **4**(1), 32–42 (2020)
14. Lee, G.A., Dünser, A., Kim, S., Billinghurst, M.: Cityviewar: A mobile outdoor AR application for city visualization. In: 2012 IEEE international symposium on mixed and augmented reality-arts, media, and humanities (ISMAR-AMH), pp. 57–64, IEEE (2012)
15. Masotti, N., De Crescenzio, F., Bagassi, S.: Augmented reality in the control tower: a rendering pipeline for multiple head-tracked head-up displays. In: De Paolis, L. T., Mongelli, A. (eds.) AVR 2016. LNCS, vol. 9768, pp. 321–338. Springer, Cham (2016). https://doi.org/10.1007/978-3-319-40621-3_23
16. Milgram, P., Takemura, H., Utsumi, A., Kishino, F.: Augmented reality: a class of displays on the reality-virtuality continuum. In: Telemanipulator and telepresence technologies, International Society for Optics and Photonics, vol. 2351, pp. 282–292 (1995)

17. Rokhsaritalemi, S., Sadeghi-Niaraki, A., Choi, S.M.: A review on mixed reality: current trends, challenges and prospects. Appl. Sci. **10**(2), 636 (2020)
18. Sartal, A., Carou, D., Davim, J.P.: Enabling technologies for the successful deployment of industry 4.0. CRC Press (2020)
19. Silva, M., Teixeira, L.: Developing an extended reality platform for immersive and interactive experiences for cultural heritage: Serralves museum and coa archeologic park. In: 2020 IEEE International Symposium on Mixed and Augmented Reality Adjunct (ISMAR-Adjunct), pp. 300–302, IEEE (2020)
20. Steffen, J.H., Gaskin, J.E., Meservy, T.O., Jenkins, J.L., Wolman, I.: Framework of affordances for virtual reality and augmented reality. J. Manage. Inf. Syst. **36**(3), 683–729 (2019)
21. Thomas, T., Alex, J.: Investigating the implementation of augmented reality in logistics (2020)
22. Wang, P., Wu, P., Wang, J., Chi, H.L., Wang, X.: A critical review of the use of virtual reality in construction engineering education and training. Int. J. Environ. Res. Publ. Health **15**(6), 1204 (2018)

Utilization of Geographic Data for the Creation of Occlusion Models in the Context of Mixed Reality Applications

Christoph Praschl[1(✉)], Erik Thiele[2], and Oliver Krauss[1]

[1] Research Group Advanced Information Systems and Technology, Research and Development Department, University of Applied Sciences Upper Austria, Softwarepark 11, 4232 Hagenberg i. M., Austria
{christoph.praschl,oliver.krauss}@fh-hagenberg.at

[2] Research and Development, Realsim, Softwarepark 21, 4232 Hagenberg i. M., Austria
erik.thiele@realsim.at

Abstract. Emergency responder training can benefit from outdoor use of Mixed Reality (MR) devices to make trainings more realistic and allow simulations that would otherwise not be possible due to safety risks or cost-effectiveness. But outdoor use of MR requires knowledge of the topography and objects in the area to enable accurate interaction of the real world trainees experience and the virtual elements that are placed in them. An approach utilizing elevation data and geographic information systems to create effective occlusion models is shown, that can be used in such outdoor training simulations. The initial results show that this approach enables accurate occlusion and placement of virtual objects within an urban environment. This improves immersion and spatial perception for trainees. In the future, improvements of the approach are planned with on the fly updates to outdated information in the occlusion models.

Keywords: Occlusion · Geographic information service · Elevation data · Mixed Reality

1 Introduction

This work deals with simulating outdoor training scenarios for emergency response. Mixed reality technology can be applied in such scenarios to enable new trainings and accurately convey information to trainees. To do so, occlusion models are used to more accurately simulate what emergency responders can/should see when training outdoors. As an example trainers can use such occlusion to hide virtual safety hazards behind corners of real world buildings.

The training of outdoor emergency response or disaster operations is often a requirement for emergency response teams such as police, ambulance services, fire brigades or even the military. Another outdoor training situation that affects the general population is driving courses. These trainings are done as close as

L. T. De Paolis et al. (Eds.): XR Salento 2022, LNCS 13446, pp. 236–253, 2022.
https://doi.org/10.1007/978-3-031-15553-6_18

possible to real operations to accurately prepare the trainees to respond correctly in case a real emergency happens. Training is however often restricted by keeping the trainees safety in mind, such as trainers acting as crash victims, or just explaining where a fire is happening instead of setting a real one. Often the costs of accurate simulation would be too excessive for emergency training, such as simulating destructive entry into vehicles or buildings.

While the training of many indoor areas as e.g. product maintenance and assembly [7,10,22,46] or medical fields of application [20,29,41,43] are digitalized successively using Augmented (AR) or Mixed Reality (MR), the field of emergency trainings remains largely unaffected. Especially, when it comes to outdoor training situations, current approaches face their limitations, due to the missing link of available Augmented and Mixed Reality devices to the global real world position and orientation. This problem was already tackled in Anonym et al. [35], but have not considered the user's environment so far. This leads to the situation that outdoor trainings can be done using state-of-the-art AR and MR devices via our previous approach, but the correct occlusion of virtual objects based on distant, real-world objects is still missing. That discrepancy of the blended virtual world and the real counterpart has a negative impact on the user's immersion and therefore may affect the training.

2 Problem Statement

With the recent improvements of Augmented and Mixed Reality hardware in the form of head mounted displays like the Microsoft HoloLens 2 [42], outdoor applications become feasible in many areas as guided working or trainings. One crucial aspect of these technologies refers to the possibility to combine real world objects with virtual counterparts by smoothly mixing both worlds in at least a visual way using occlusions [37]. This issue seems to be solved for indoor applications due to the availability of depth and visual sensors, as well as accurate reconstruction paradigms, creating a virtual model of an user's close environment. In the context of outdoor applications, current technologies still face their limitations [27]. Devices as the Microsoft HoloLens 2 are restricted to working distances up to 3.5 m [19]. When it comes to long distance applications those devices are not capable of recognizing real world objects as buildings, trees or terrain like hills and mountains. For this reason, virtual objects are not occluded at all, or at least not correctly. Figure 1 shows a situation where a virtual car should be spatially behind a real house, but is not occluded at all, because the MR device lacks the information of the position and size of the example house. Because of that, the user can unintentionally see the complete car and may not even be able to accurately gauge their distance to the car. In a different scenario, Fig. 2 shows a virtual skyscraper that should be placed behind a hill and is not covered correctly, so again the complete building is visible for the user. Currently, this problem can't be tackled using on-device sensors, but different external data sources can be utilized to enrich the virtual model of the real world and for this provide bases for object coverage.

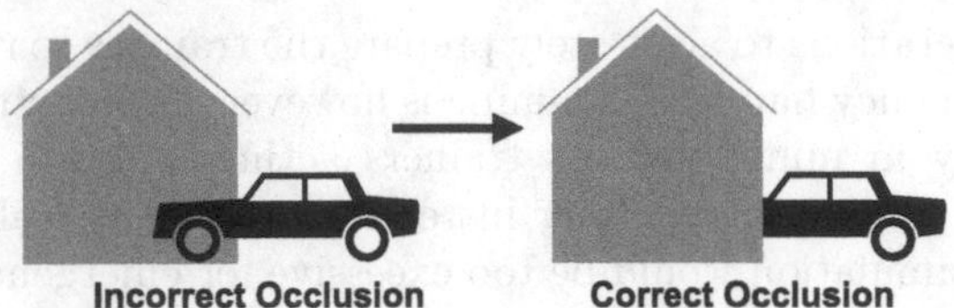

Fig. 1. Incorrect occlusion due to unknown spatial information of the affected objects, where a virtual car should be positioned behind a real world house.

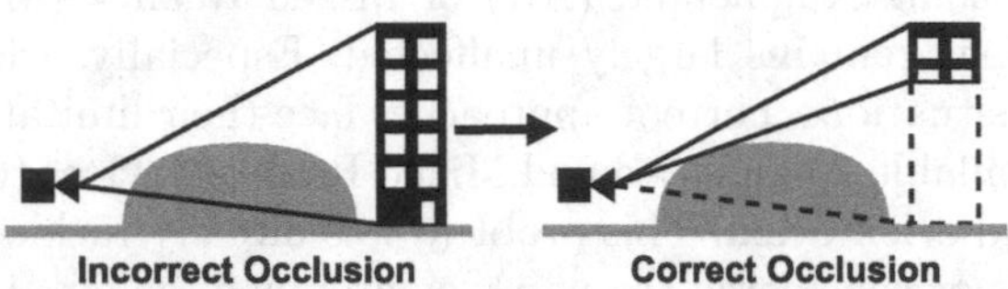

Fig. 2. A virtual building should be place behind a real world hill, which is not possible if there is a lack of elevation information of the surrounding environment.

3 State of the Art

In the context of creating virtual counterparts of the real world environment different state-of-the-art approaches exist. Especially, in the field of Computer Vision and Robotics, there are multiple algorithms that can be utilized to perform a 3D reconstruction based on monocular images, as well as videos like the Visual-SLAM algorithm [40]. As input for such algorithms, recordings of e.g. robots or unmanned aerial vehicles (UAV) like drones can be used to reconstruct the landscape of the region of interest [38].

In addition to those visual methods, also the utilization of depth information from depth cameras [21], Time-of-Flight [31] or LiDAR sensors [39] is suitable. Combining both worlds, also deep learning models can be applied for the approximation of depth information from RGB images [44]. Unfortunately, those approaches are often limited in their spatial range and are hardly useable for outdoor applications.

Next to the near-field sensors, there are also satellite or airborne based approaches [17] that are used to map elevations of local or even global regions of the world from a bird's eye view. While, the last approaches have the advantage that they are applicable for long distances and large areas, they come with the disadvantage being highly expensive in terms of costs and time and are not suitable for real-time applications. Fortunately, such aerial photographs and surface models are available from different public domains in form of e.g. elevation data sets [13], with the advantage of an easily available basis for occlusion models, but with the disadvantage of partly outdated data or a resolution of multiple meters. For the representation of such geographic data the GeoTIFF standard [36] is widespread and allows for example exchanging geo-referenced elevation information for a spatial region.

Next to such digital surface models, there are also many geographic information services (GIS) in the form of enriched maps containing objects of interest as streets, buildings, but compared to that also smaller entities as trees or even park benches. Such providers as Google Maps [30], OpenStreetMap [16], Bing Maps [34] or many others, often offer an application programming interface (API) to get information of real world objects for a certain position. These providers differ in the accuracy of the data, as well as the types of provided objects, but also according to the license and usage conditions [6]. For example OpenStreetMaps provides not only the information of road networks, but also the geo-referenced position of buildings, park benches, trees, fountains and many other elements for free under the "Open Data Commons Open Database" License. Next to the longitude and latitude position, there is often also additional metadata provided by users as e.g. for trees the species, the height, the circumference or even the crown diameter [33].

Holynski and Kopf [18] present an approach based on Computer Vision algorithms as SLAM and optical flow to calculate depth edges, which allow the authors to apply occlusion-aware AR video effects. The shown examples are limited to low distances of a few meters and are too small scale, compared to the targeted area of application of this work.

Kido et al. [24] show a real-time semantic segmentation approach using the ICNet [47] neural network to detect individual object instances from monocular images. Based on the segmented objects, a mask image is created that is used as basis for the occlusion. The authors use an interactive, virtual map to place the augmented objects. As in this work, the presented system is separated in a client-server architecture, where the segmentation is done on the server-side, as well as the arrangement of the virtual objects. The client device is then only used to display the final scene. In contrast to the present approach, Kido et al. don't use geo-referenced positions for the virtual objects, but only relative distances from the statically positioned camera. The approach also shows limitations in the occlusion process based on dynamic re-orientations of the camera due to pan and/or tilt adaptions.

Next to the previous publications, Chalumattu et al. [5] present a process for creating augmented outdoor scenes in urban scenarios. This is done based on a three-dimensional city model that is used as basis for the occlusion of virtual objects. The used city model includes virtual spatial anchors, that are the basis for the positioning of the occlusion model. In contrast to this work, Chalumattu et al. do not incorporate real world coordinates from the Global Positioning System (GPS) [23] for the localization of the objects and also do not create the occlusion models dynamically based on neither geographic information systems (GIS), nor on elevation data sets.

Multiple studies show AR applications in combination with GIS for the purpose of positioning virtual objects at given real world positions. Ghadirian and Bishop [14] present an approach for combining AR applications with GIS. The shown methods are used to place virtual objects in a real world scene based on historical data to provide a source of comparison of the change of the local vegetation. In contrast to the present approach, they don't use the geographic data as basis for occlusion, but only as source for augmented objects.

Capece et al. [4] use geographic information in combination with virtual objects to develop an outdoor AR system, that allows to present the position and distance of infrastructural points of interests in the context of electrical power lines and hydrogeological risks. Like Ghadirian and Bishop, Capece et al. use the geographic data only as basis to display virtual objects for long-distanced real world counterparts, but not for the task to create occlusion models.

Kiliman et al. [25] also present a GIS based method in combination with Computer Vision approaches to visualize planned real world objects at their actual geographic location. In a first step virtual objects like wind turbines or power poles are placed at given GPS positions, which are occluded in a second step based on a k-means segmentation approach. The segmentation technique is used to separate the image into its foreground and background based on the pixel colors of the sky, which is in turn used as occlusion mask for the virtual objects. In contrast to the present work, they are using GIS information only for the positioning of objects, but not for the occlusion.

Maurer et al. [28] present an approach for creating geo-referenced 3D reconstructions, based on public available elevation data, as well as aerial images. Like the present approach, the authors are utilizing the elevation information to enrich a model. In contrast to the present work, the resulting model is not used for occlusion purposes in the context of AR, but for localization or change detection of the reconstructed environment.

4 Material

The developed system for creating occlusion models based on geographic data in the context of Mixed Reality applications, is tested using different types of data sources. For this, multiple configurations of GIS as Google Maps, Bing Maps and OpenStreetMap considering the different license conditions of these providers were evaluated. Especially, OpenStreetMap and its open and rich information of different real world objects as trees is an important source of information. In the context of elevation data different national and international sources in the form of GeoTIFF data sets with different raster resolutions are used. To create geo-referenced occlusion models of land forms the global ASTER data set with a resolution of 30 m [9], the US American NED data set with a resolution of 30 m and partially 10 m [12], the European EU-DEM data set with a resolution of 25 m [3], as well as the national Austrian digital elevation model with a resolution of 10 m [11] and the elevation data set of the Upper Austrian capital Linz with a resolution of 0.5 m [26] are used. Two of the used data sets are shown for reference in Fig. 3. The system is also prepared according to the incorporation of 3D reconstructed models from different sources of information as LiDARs, cameras or airborne recordings from e.g. drones, as shown in Fig. 4. This third pillar of the system is currently not included in the present tests.

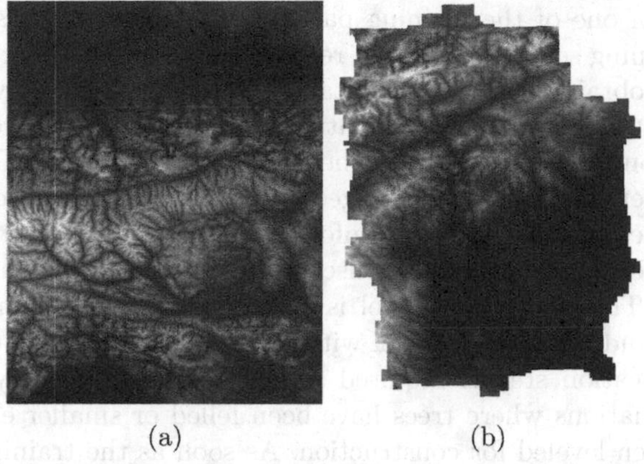

Fig. 3. Two of the used elevation data sets with (a) a clipping of the E40N20 tile from the EU-DEM data set [3] and (b) a clipping of the Austrian digital elevation model for the region of Styria [1].

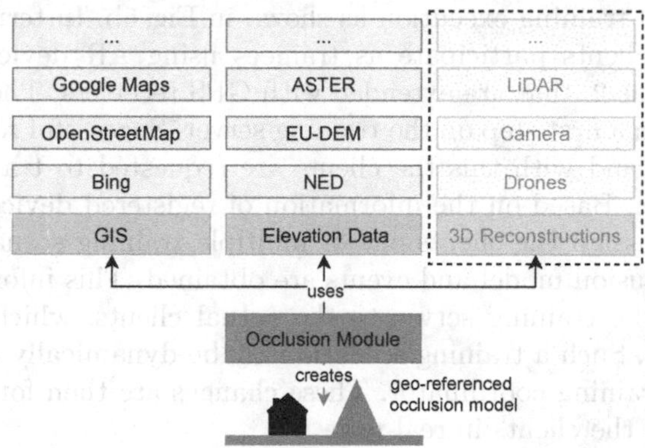

Fig. 4. Data sources used in the developed system for creating occlusion models based on geographic data from different sources as geographic information services as OpenStreetMap and multiple elevation data sets as the EU-DEM data. Next to these sources, also the usage of 3D reconstructed models from e.g. drones is planned, but is not part of the presented evaluation.

5 Methodology

The present approach is part of a two-step process for the creation of AR-supported, outdoor trainings in the context of emergency services or driving safety. In a first step, a training coordinator uses the application to create training scenarios for a selected region of interest (ROI) like a fire brigade training area or a driving safety center. For such a scenario the coordinator defines virtual objects and sequences of events like spreading fires based on geo-referenced coordinates. The defined events are either triggered by time or by the spatial approximation of one of the training participants. This virtual scenario is forwarded to a training server, which will request the different geographic information services to obtain the required data for the surrounding environment. For this purpose, on the one hand the elevation information is acquired from one or multiple elevation data sets. On the other hand one or multiple GIS are used to request supplementary information of geo referenced objects as houses and trees and like that to extend the elevation information. The elevation data, as well as the geo referenced objects, are then used to create an occlusion model on the training server. This occlusion model is then sent to the training coordinator, who will check and adapt the model with an AR device on site of the training area. This verification step is required since the used data may be outdated. For example situations where trees have been felled or smaller elevations, such as hills, have been leveled for construction. As soon as the training coordinator approves the occlusion model, it is combined with the remaining training scenario and persisted into a database. The described first part of the application is shown in Fig. 5a.

Next to the training creation, the second part of the application is situated in the actual training execution as shown in Fig. 5b. In terms of this part, one or multiple clients participate as trainees using AR devices such as the Microsoft HoloLens 2, that are extended with GPS receivers. These devices register themselves in a first step on the training server. Successful registrations will be acknowledged and with this the clients are requested to transfer their current GPS position. Based on the information of registered devices, the training coordinator will assign the clients one or multiple training scenarios, for which the prepared occlusion model and events are obtained. This information is then forwarded from the training server to the actual clients, which will load and start the scenario. Such a training scenario may be dynamically adapted during runtime by the training coordinator. These changes are then forwarded via the training server to the clients in real-time.

5.1 Elevation Data

An elevation data server is used during the training scenario creation as shown in Fig. 5a. This server is used as source of information for elevation data sets as the EU-DEM or the NED data set. To make use of the elevation information, this server provides multiple functionalities to obtain the data for a given georeferenced position. For this, longitude and latitude coordinates are used, that are translated to the pixel coordinates of the used GeoTIFF files.

Next to the possibility of accessing individual coordinates, the elevation server also provides the functionality to obtain elevation data for a bounding box based region. This region is defined by a bottom left and a top right GPS coordinate. Combined with a desired resolution, this information is used to create an $n \times m$ elevation grid. This grid is in turn used as the basis for the landscape occlusion model and is for this reason transformed to a three-dimensional mesh as shown in Fig. 6.

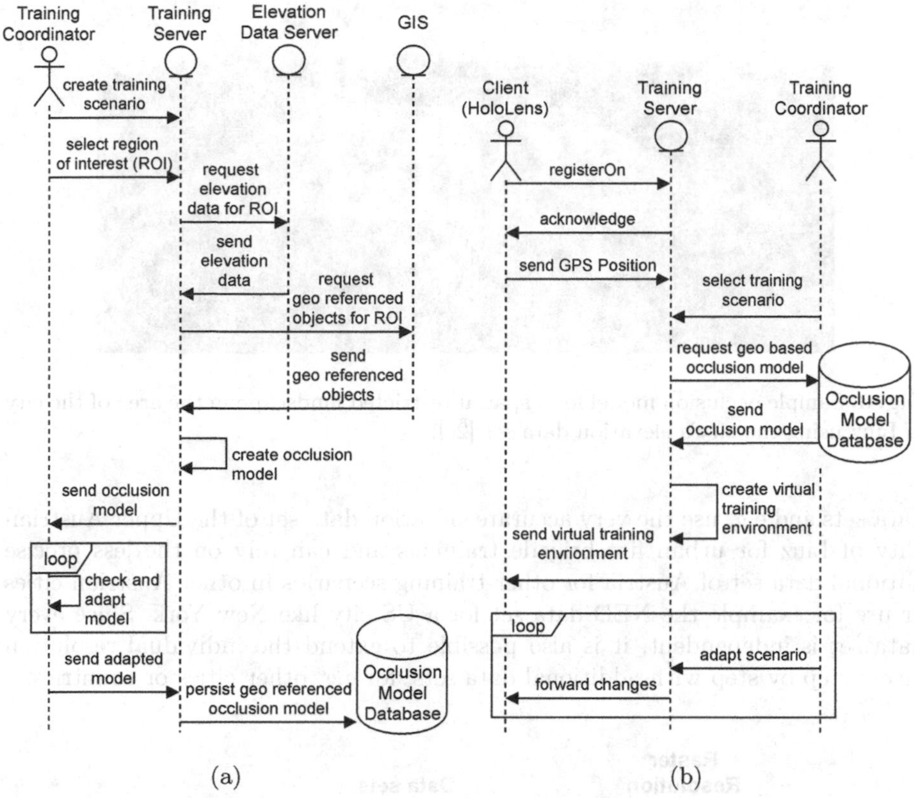

Fig. 5. (a) Process overview for the creation of an AR training scenario. The scenario loads an occlusion model based on geo-referenced information as elevation data or virtual objects from one or multiple GIS. (b) Sequence of events for an actual AR training using the presented approach with one or multiple clients performing the training and a coordinator, who is responsible for dynamic events. Next to the human participants, the system also consists of a training server with configured training scenarios and prepared occlusion models.

As using multiple elevation data sets with partially overlapping areas and different raster resolutions are used, the most accurate result for the given GPS coordinate, respectively bounding box has to be found. For this reason, all data sets are grouped in the form of an inverted resolution pyramid as shown in Fig. 7 and checked if the currently received GPS coordinate is part of one of the data sets in the lowest layer. If this is the case, the elevation data from this layer is taken, otherwise the next top layer is proofed. This process is repeated, until the global and thus most imprecise data sets is reached. In the case of multiple matching elevation data sets, that are equal according to the raster resolution, the retrieved information is interpolated between the sources to improve the result. Based on this approach, it is possible to dynamically switch between the

Fig. 6. Sample occlusion model for a spatial-restricted landscape in the area of the city of Linz using the city's elevation data set [26].

data sets and e.g. use the very accurate elevation data set of the Upper Austrian City of Linz for urban fire brigade trainings and can rely on the less precise national data set of Austria for other training scenarios in other Austrian cities or use for example the NED data set for a US city like New York. Since every data set is independent, it is also possible to extend the individual resolution layers step by step with additional data sets, for e.g. other cities or countries.

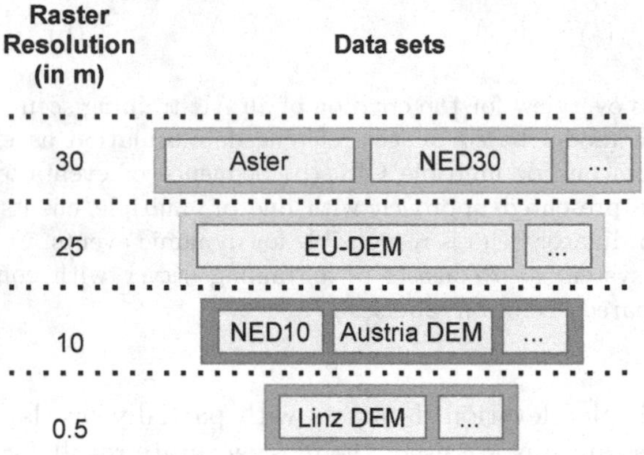

Raster Resolution (in m)	Data sets
30	Aster, NED30, ...
25	EU-DEM, ...
10	NED10, Austria DEM, ...
0.5	Linz DEM, ...

Fig. 7. Inverted data set pyramid with the local elevation sources with the lowest raster resolution and for this the highest accuracy in the bottom area, to the global ones with the highest resolution in the top layer.

5.2 Geographic Information Services

In addition to the elevation data sets, the presented approach is also based on geographic information services as source of information. In most applications these services are used to retrieve insights about geo-referenced real-world infrastructures as streets, country borders or the position of cities for navigation systems. Since streets, except of bridges and similar special occurrences, are normally on the same level as the ground, they are not that relevant for the occlusion of raised virtual objects. This is also already considered using the elevation information.

However, many GIS also provide additional information of inhomogeneous real-world objects that are actually relevant for the correct occlusion and therefore have to be considered. For this reason, sample types of geo-referenced objects are selected, that are available through such services such as buildings and trees for the proof of concept of the present system. In addition to the GPS position, these objects also come with type related meta information according to their spatial expression, that can be utilized for the occlusion. In the case of buildings you can not only retrieve the exact position of the floor space, but also the height of the building. In the context of trees, some GIS services provide additional data such as the circumference of the log or the diameter of the tree's crown. Incorporating this information, the system is able to create geo-referenced occlusion objects. Since such virtual counter-parts of distant, real-world objects are only used to cover virtual ones and are not visualized at all, the level of detail is not that relevant to the user's experience of immersion. For this reason, simple shapes for the occlusion as the extruded base area for buildings as well as cubes for tree logs and the trees' crowns are used. Such an occlusion model is shown in Fig. 8. While this approach has the advantage that it is simple and therefore does not need that much computational power, it comes with the disadvantage that the level of detail may become relevant the closer objects are to the user. Additionally, it also has the disadvantage that the system is dependent on the retrieved data. For example, if a building is demolished, its virtual counterpart could continue to exist in the used GIS and like that would be mistakenly used for occlusions in the present system.

6 Implementation

The presented system is created for the Microsoft HoloLens 2 as target platform. For this reason it is mainly developed using the Unity game engine [32] in version 2019.4.19f1. In the context of the elevation server, a Python 3.7.9 application is used based on the "Open Topo Data" project [2] in version 1.5.1, which is based on RasterIO [15], that is in turn a Python wrapper for one of the most common C++ libraries in the context of processing spatial raster formats the Geospatial Data Abstraction Library (GDAL) [45]. "Open Topo Data" consists of a configurable server implementation for elevation data sets, that allows to get elevation information for given GPS coordinates using RESTful [8] API calls. As "Open Topo Data" only supports the access of individual coordinates and for this also requires the definition of the source data set to be used, the implementation is extended. This extension allows to access the elevation data for a given region using a bounding box and an expected resolution in number of coordinates per kilometer for all configured data sets with one API call. Next

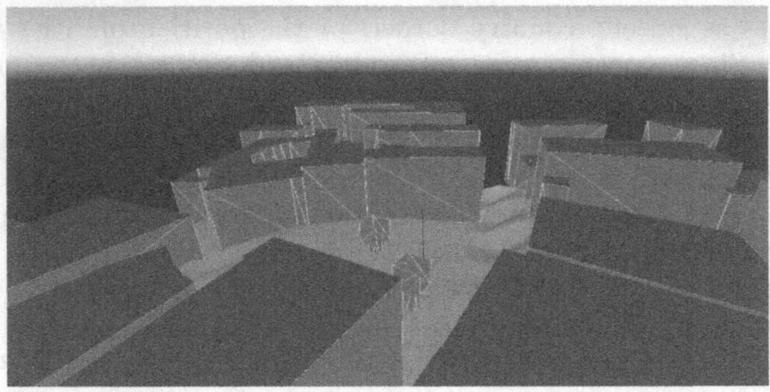

Fig. 8. Occlusion model based on geo-referenced objects in the form of buildings and trees obtained from OpenStreetMap in combination with the landscape model for a spatial restricted region of the city of Linz.

to that, this functionality is also extended using the inverted resolution pyramid as described in Sect. 5.1, which allows us to find the best matching data sets for a given GPS position or bounding box. In some cases, multiple, matching data sets are equal according to their raster resolution. To further improve the landscape model, the information of such data sets is combined by using the average elevation value.

For the utilization of geographic information services OpenStreetMaps is selected to retrieve geo-referenced objects and additional meta information for buildings, as well as trees. This is achieved via OpenStreetMaps's open RESTful API. In combination with the API of the extended "Open Topo Data" server, it is possible to create occlusion models for a given training area. These models are distributed via an additional server for the training execution to all participating trainees, respectively the used head-mounted displays. Thus the models are only created once per training and are reusable. This allows us to reduce the required computational power, as well as time.

7 Results

The presented approach is evaluated using a test setup based on a virtual and a real-world cube with the dimensions of 1 m × 0.52 m × 1 m that are placed near a building's corner at the GPS position (48.368512, 14.513185). Specifically, the cube has a distance of 0.5 m towards the east, as well as the south from the corner, as shown in Fig. 9b. Next to this, a Microsoft HoloLens 2 is placed with 5 m distance to the corner, towards West using a tripod (c.f. Fig. 9a). To decouple the system from external influences, the static GPS position (48.368509, 14.513117) is used for the MR device as start position. The distances between the real world cube and building are ensured using a laser based device.

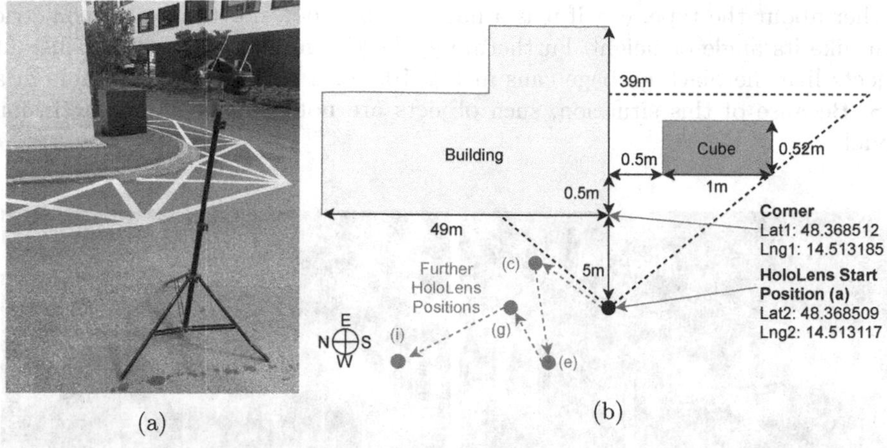

(a) (b)

Fig. 9. (a) Shows the initial position of the HoloLens on a tripod and the cube near the building. In addition to that, (b) shows the test setup with the geo-referenced building, the initial as well as further positions (compare positions (a), (c), (e), (g), (i) with respective sub-figures of Fig. 12) of the HoloLens during the test, as well as the test cube.

Based on this setup, the virtual box is placed at the same position as its real-world counterpart and an occlusion model is dynamically created using the proposed methodology using the extended "Open Topo Data" server with the Austrian digital elevation model, together with OpenStreetMap as GIS. Like this, the approach can be evaluated using pixel overlaps and offsets from the real-world building's corner. After the initial setup, the HoloLens can be moved to different perspectives to show the influence of the occlusion model. Figure 12 in the Appendix shows the mentioned setup from multiple perspectives. For the shown examples, binary masks have been manually created, highlighting occlusion errors. The binary masks shown in Fig. 11b and 12b are empty, signaling that the virtual occlusion perfectly matches the real-world situation. Compared to that, the remaining binary masks show minimal errors, such as Fig. 11d with an offset of 507 pixels, Fig. 12d with 210 pixels and Fig. 12f with 206 pixels.

Next to the evaluation setup, Fig. 10a shows the utilization of the method in a real-world urban scenario for the city of Linz in the area of the so called Tummelplatz within the GPS coordinates (48.30491, 14.28383) and (48.30592, 14.28523). For comparison, Fig. 10b shows the same scenery with a geo-referenced virtual object, but without the usage of the occlusion model. All in all, this sample shows that the utilization of geographic data for the creation of occlusion models in the context of Mixed Reality applications is basically applicable. Because the present method only relies on external data without any visual check or post-processing, the spatial accordance of the virtual occlusion model and the real world objects is not met in all details. For example, the used geographic information services do not provide any information about roofs, neither about the type, e.g. if it is a flat or gable roof, nor the exact geometric form like its angle or height. Furthermore, there is no knowledge about distant objects like the black garbage cans in Fig. 10, since they are not available in a GIS. Because of this situation, such objects are not included in the occlusion model.

(a) (b)

Fig. 10. (a) Utilization of the occlusion model from Fig. 8 for merging both, the virtual and the real world created with geographic data and for comparison (b) using only the HoloLens internal occlusion model of the surrounding environment without additional information.

8 Conclusion

Combining of elevation data and geospatial information in an approach to create occlusion models shows promise. The results show that such occlusion models can be created in an outdoor scenario in an urban environment.

As the approach is static, and pre-calculates the occlusion models it is only as good as its data. Creating occlusion models from outdated information will provide models that are incorrect. An example is occlusion for buildings that have been demolished, or missing occlusion for buildings constructed after the data was generated. Using the presented data set pyramid can help with such occlusion models and can in the future be expanded to also consider up-to-dateness of information in addition to its raster resolution. State of the art MR devices such as the Microsoft Hololens 2 can use the presented occlusion models, as they are kept simple and do not consist of many polygons, since the approach does server side processing.

9 Outlook

Due to the promising results, creating geo-referenced occlusion models based on external geographic information services as OpenStreetMap and elevation information from GeoTIFFs as the EU-DEM or the Austrian digital elevation model, it is planned to also incorporate 3D reconstructions from Microsoft's

HoloLens 2 or alternatively from camera images and/or drones to tackle the problem of outdated data as well as small or not fixed positioned objects such as boxes or barrels in training areas. Especially, in the area of task force training for the police or fire departments, this additional source of data will allow creating dynamic training scenarios. In addition to that, it is also planned to expand the tests to other cities and even in rural training scenarios in the context of emergency service trainings.

Acknowledgment. The authors thank their project partners of the Austrian Mixed Reality company Realsim®, especially Thomas Peterseil and Mario Voithofer, for their efforts.

Funding. Our thanks to the Austrian Research Promotion Agency FFG for facilitating the project *MRCC* (program number: 883742) with the Small Scale Project funding program, with research budget provided by the Federal Republic of Austria

Appendix

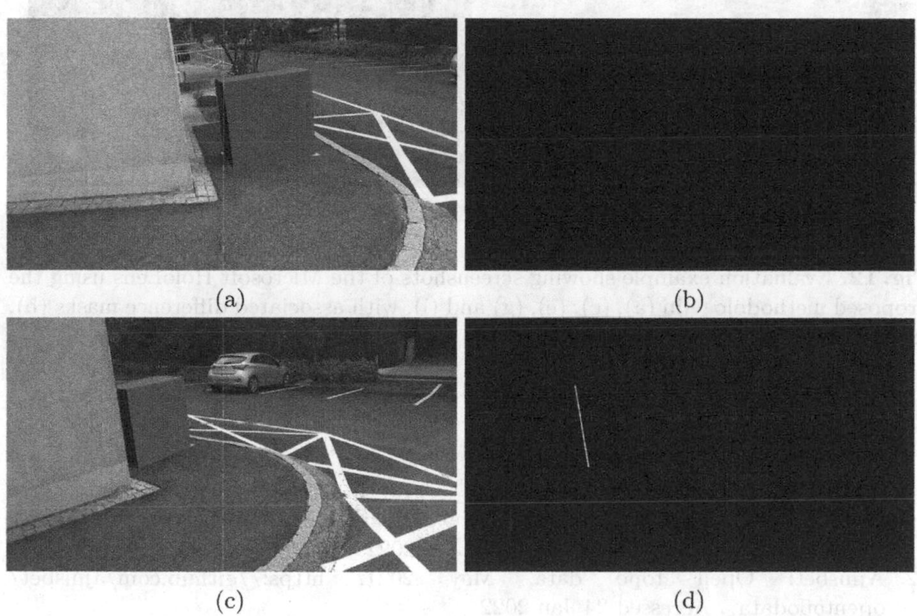

(a) (b) (c) (d)

Fig. 11. Evaluation example showing screenshots of the Microsoft HoloLens using the proposed methodology in (a), (c), (e), (g) and (i), with associated difference masks (b), (d), (f), (h) and (j).

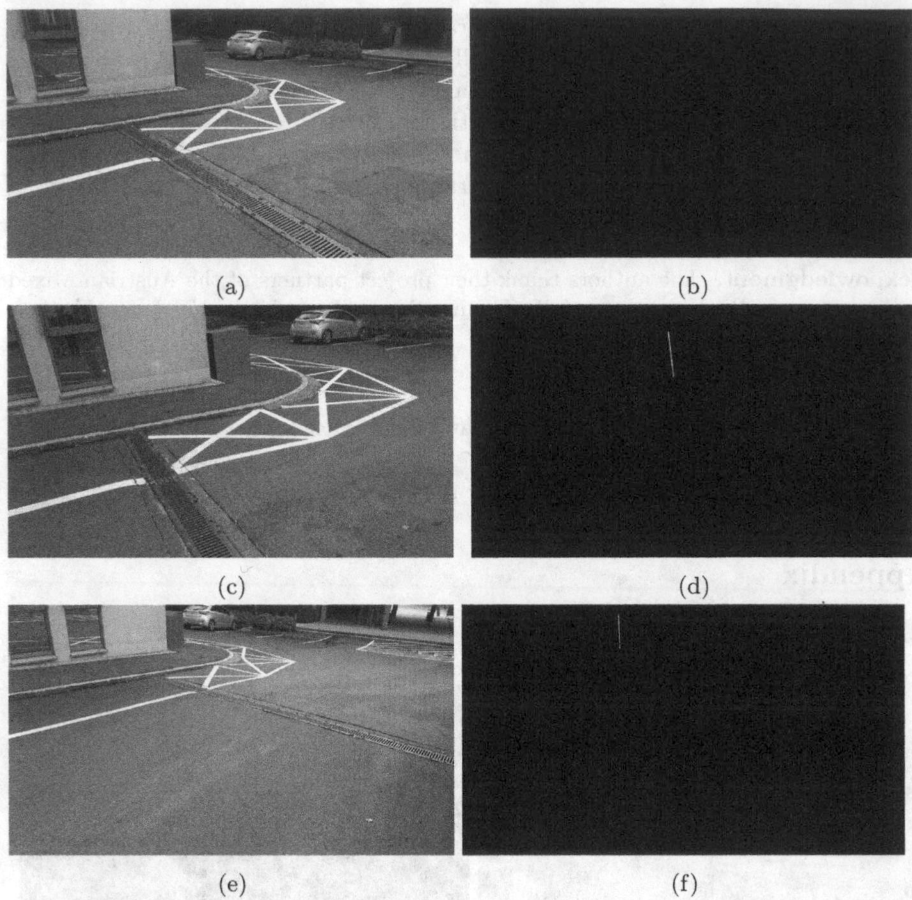

Fig. 12. Evaluation example showing screenshots of the Microsoft HoloLens using the proposed methodology in (a), (c), (e), (g) and (i), with associated difference masks (b), (d), (f), (h) and (j).

References

1. A17 GIS: Digitales Geländemodell - 10 m - steiermark - datensätze - data.gv.at, May 2021. https://www.data.gv.at/katalog/dataset/land-stmk_digitalesgelndemodell10m. Accessed 24 Jan 2022
2. Ajnisbet: Open topo data, May 2021. https://github.com/ajnisbet/opentopodata/. Accessed 24 Jan 2022
3. Bashfield, A., Keim, A.: Continent-wide DEM creation for the European union. In: 34th International Symposium on Remote Sensing of Environment. The GEOSS Era: Towards Operational Environmental Monitoring, Sydney, Australia, pp. 10–15. Citeseer (2011)

4. Capece, N., Agatiello, R., Erra, U.: A client-server framework for the design of geolocation based augmented reality applications. In: 2016 20th International Conference Information Visualisation (IV), pp. 130–135 (2016). https://doi.org/10.1109/IV.2016.20
5. Chalumattu, R., Schaub-Meyer, S., Wiethuchter, R., Klingler, S., Gross, M.: Simplifying the process of creating augmented outdoor scenes. In: 2020 IEEE International Conference on Multimedia Expo Workshops (ICMEW), pp. 1–6 (2020). https://doi.org/10.1109/ICMEW46912.2020.9106030
6. Ciepłuch, B., Jacob, R., Mooney, P., Winstanley, A.C.: Comparison of the accuracy of OpenStreetMap for Ireland with Google maps and Bing maps. In: Proceedings of the Ninth International Symposium on Spatial Accuracy Assessment in Natural Resources and Environmental Sciences, 20–23rd July 2010, p. 337. University of Leicester (2010)
7. De Crescenzio, F., Fantini, M., Persiani, F., Di Stefano, L., Azzari, P., Salti, S.: Augmented reality for aircraft maintenance training and operations support. IEEE Comput. Graph. Appl. **31**(1), 96–101 (2011). https://doi.org/10.1109/MCG.2011.4
8. Fielding, R.T.: Architectural Styles and the Design of Network-Based Software Architectures, vol. 7. University of California, Irvine Irvine (2000)
9. Fujisada, H., Urai, M., Iwasaki, A.: Technical methodology for ASTER global DEM. IEEE Trans. Geosci. Remote Sens. **50**(10), 3725–3736 (2012)
10. Gavish, N., et al.: Evaluating virtual reality and augmented reality training for industrial maintenance and assembly tasks. Interact. Learn. Environ. **23**(6), 778–798 (2015). https://doi.org/10.1080/10494820.2013.815221
11. geoland.at: Digitales Geländemodell (DGM) österreich - data.gv.at, April 2021. https://www.data.gv.at/katalog/dataset/d88a1246-9684-480b-a480-ff63286b35b7. Accessed 24 Jan 2022
12. Gesch, D., Oimoen, M., Greenlee, S., Nelson, C., Steuck, M., Tyler, D.: The national elevation dataset. Photogramm. Eng. Remote Sens. **68**(1), 5–32 (2002)
13. Gesch, D.B., Oimoen, M.J., Evans, G.A., et al.: Accuracy assessment of the US Geological Survey National Elevation Dataset, and comparison with other large-area elevation datasets: SRTM and ASTER, vol. 1008. US Department of the Interior, US Geological Survey (2014)
14. Ghadirian, P., Bishop, I.D.: Integration of augmented reality and GIS: a new approach to realistic landscape visualisation. Landscape Urban Planning **86**(3), 226–232 (2008). https://doi.org/10.1016/j.landurbplan.2008.03.004, https://www.sciencedirect.com/science/article/pii/S0169204608000479
15. Gillies, S.: Rasterio documentation. MapBox, 23 July 2019
16. Haklay, M., Weber, P.: OpenStreetMap: user-generated street maps. IEEE Pervasive Comput. **7**(4), 12–18 (2008)
17. Hodgson, M.E., Bresnahan, P.: Accuracy of airborne lidar-derived elevation. Photogramm. Eng. Remote Sens. **70**(3), 331–339 (2004)
18. Holynski, A., Kopf, J.: Fast depth densification for occlusion-aware augmented reality. ACM Trans. Graph. **37**(6), 1–11 (2019). https://doi.org/10.1145/3272127.3275083
19. Hübner, P., Clintworth, K., Liu, Q., Weinmann, M., Wursthorn, S.: Evaluation of HoloLens tracking and depth sensing for indoor mapping applications. Sensors **20**(4), 1021 (2020)
20. Ingrassia, P.L., et al.: Augmented reality learning environment for basic life support and defibrillation training: usability study. J. Med. Internet Res. **22**(5), e14910 (2020). https://doi.org/10.2196/14910

21. Izadi, S., et al.: KinectFusion: real-time 3D reconstruction and interaction using a moving depth camera. In: Proceedings of the 24th Annual ACM Symposium on User Interface Software and Technology, pp. 559–568 (2011)
22. Kaplan, A.D., Cruit, J., Endsley, M., Beers, S.M., Sawyer, B.D., Hancock, P.: The effects of virtual reality, augmented reality, and mixed reality as training enhancement methods: a meta-analysis. In: Human Factors, p. 0018720820904229 (2020)
23. Kaplan, E., Hegarty, C.: Understanding GPS: Principles and Applications. Artech House, London (2005)
24. Kido, D., Fukuda, T., Yabuki, N.: Development of a semantic segmentation system for dynamic occlusion handling in mixed reality for landscape simulation. In: Blucher Design Proceedings (2019)
25. Kilimann, J.E., Heitkamp, D., Lensing, P.: An augmented reality application for mobile visualization of GIS-referenced landscape planning projects. In: The 17th International Conference on Virtual-Reality Continuum and its Applications in Industry, pp. 1–5 (2019)
26. Land Oberösterreich: Land Oberösterreich - Digitales Geländemodell 50 cm / 1 m (XYZ), December 2018. https://www.land-oberoesterreich.gv.at. Accessed 24 Jan 2022
27. Liu, Y., Dong, H., Zhang, L., El Saddik, A.: Technical evaluation of HoloLens for multimedia: a first look. IEEE MultiMedia **25**(4), 8–18 (2018)
28. Maurer, M., Rumpler, M., Wendel, A., Hoppe, C., Irschara, A., Bischof, H.: Georeferenced 3D reconstruction: fusing public geographic data and aerial imagery. In: 2012 IEEE International Conference on Robotics and Automation, pp. 3557–3558. IEEE (2012)
29. McKnight, R.R., Pean, C.A., Buck, J.S., Hwang, J.S., Hsu, J.R., Pierrie, S.N.: Virtual reality and augmented reality-translating surgical training into surgical technique. Curr. Rev. Musculoskelet. Med. **13**(6), 663–674 (2020)
30. Miller, C.C.: A beast in the field: the Google maps mashup as GIS/2. Cartographica Int. J. Geogr. Inf. Geovisualization **41**(3), 187–199 (2006)
31. Nguyen, T.N., Huynh, H.H., Meunier, J.: 3D reconstruction with time-of-flight depth camera and multiple mirrors. IEEE Access **6**, 38106–38114 (2018)
32. Nicoll, B., Keogh, B.: The Unity Game Engine and the Circuits of Cultural Software, pp. 1–21. Springer, Cham (2019). https://doi.org/10.1007/978-3-030-25012-6_1
33. OpenStreetMap: OpenStreetMap Wiki - Tag:natural=tree - Tag:natural%3Dtree. Open Street Map, May 2021. https://wiki.openstreetmap.org/wiki/
34. Pendleton, C.: The world according to Bing. IEEE Comput. Graph. Appl. **30**(4), 15–17 (2010)
35. Praschl, C., Krauss, O., Zwettler, G.A.: Enabling outdoor MR capabilities for head mounted displays: a case study. Int. J. Simul. Process Model. **15**(6), 512–523 (2020)
36. Ritter, N., Ruth, M.: The GeoTiff data interchange standard for raster geographic images. Int. J. Remote Sens. **18**(7), 1637–1647 (1997)
37. Shah, M.M., Arshad, H., Sulaiman, R.: Occlusion in augmented reality. In: 2012 8th International Conference on Information Science and Digital Content Technology (ICIDT2012), vol. 2, pp. 372–378. IEEE (2012)
38. Sumikura, S., Shibuya, M., Sakurada, K.: OpenVSLAM: a versatile visual slam framework. In: Proceedings of the 27th ACM International Conference on Multimedia, pp. 2292–2295 (2019)
39. Tachella, J., et al.: Real-time 3D reconstruction from single-photon lidar data using plug-and-play point cloud denoisers. Nat. Commun. **10**(1), 1–6 (2019)

40. Taketomi, T., Uchiyama, H., Ikeda, S.: Visual slam algorithms: a survey from 2010 to 2016. IPSJ Trans. Comput. Vis. Appl. **9**(1), 1–11 (2017)
41. Thøgersen, M., Andoh, J., Milde, C., Graven-Nielsen, T., Flor, H., Petrini, L.: Individualized augmented reality training reduces phantom pain and cortical reorganization in amputees: a proof of concept study. J. Pain **21**(11), 1257–1269 (2020)
42. Ungureanu, D., et al.: HoloLens 2 research mode as a tool for computer vision research. arXiv preprint arXiv:2008.11239 (2020)
43. Vergel, R.S., Tena, P.M., Yrurzum, S.C., Cruz-Neira, C.: A comparative evaluation of a virtual reality table and a HoloLENS-based augmented reality system for anatomy training. IEEE Trans. Hum.-Mach. Syst. **50**(4), 337–348 (2020)
44. Wang, K., Shen, S.: MVDepthNet: real-time multiview depth estimation neural network. In: 2018 International Conference on 3D Vision (3DV), pp. 248–257. IEEE (2018)
45. Warmerdam, F.: The geospatial data abstraction library. In: Hall, G.B., Leahy, M.G. (eds.) Open Source Approaches in Spatial Data Handling. Advances in Geographic Information Science, vol. 2, pp. 87–104. Springer, Heidelberg (2008). https://doi.org/10.1007/978-3-540-74831-1_5
46. Westerfield, G., Mitrovic, A., Billinghurst, M.: Intelligent augmented reality training for motherboard assembly. Int. J. Artif. Intell. Educ. **25**(1), 157–172 (2014). https://doi.org/10.1007/s40593-014-0032-x
47. Zhao, H., Qi, X., Shen, X., Shi, J., Jia, J.: ICNet for real-time semantic segmentation on high-resolution images. In: Ferrari, V., Hebert, M., Sminchisescu, C., Weiss, Y. (eds.) ECCV 2018. LNCS, vol. 11207, pp. 418–434. Springer, Cham (2018). https://doi.org/10.1007/978-3-030-01219-9_25

Development of an Open-Source 3D WebGIS Framework to Promote Cultural Heritage Dissemination

Alessandra Capolupo(✉), Cristina Monterisi, and Eufemia Tarantino

Department of Civil, Environmental, Land, Construction and Chemistry (DICATECh), Politecnico di Bari, via Orabona 4, 70125 Bari, Italy
{alessandra.capolupo,cristina.monterisi, eufemia.tarantino}@poliba.it

Abstract. Italian territory is characterized by a conspicuous number of cultural heritage sites to be promoted and preserved. Therefore, regional, and local authorities feel the need to identify an economic and efficient solution to monitor their status and encourage their knowledge among heritage and environmental agencies and the business communities. Usually, Geographical Information Systems have been introduced to store and manage data concerning cultural heritage sites albeit, just in the last few years, its role is becoming more and more important thanks to the development of web applications. These ones allow helping cultural heritage dissemination as well as providing a relevant tool to data treatment. Therefore, in this study, an interactive WebGIS platform aimed at supporting cultural heritage management and enhancement has been developed. In accordance with the standards proposed by the Open Geospatial Consortium and EU directive INSPIRE, Free and Open-Source Software for Geographic information systems were applied to develop proper codes aimed at implementing the whole three-tier configuration. Moreover, a user-friendly interactive interface was also programmed to help IT and non-IT users in stored data management. Although the proposed WebGIS appears as the optimal tool to meet research purposes, further improvements are still needed to handle multiple contacts simultaneously and increase the real-time processing options.

Keywords: Web mapping · IoT · Cultural heritage · 3D visualization mode · Remotely Piloted Aircraft Systems (RPAS)

1 Introduction

The landscape is the product of the synergic combination of the influence of anthropogenic and geogenic activities that occurred on a specific area [1, 2], and, thus, investigating its dynamic evolution implies understanding the identity of a population [3–5]. Among the various elements, Cultural Heritage (CH) sites represents a relevant source of information required for meeting such purposes. Therefore, adequate management

L. T. De Paolis et al. (Eds.): XR Salento 2022, LNCS 13446, pp. 254–268, 2022.
https://doi.org/10.1007/978-3-031-15553-6_19

strategies are needed to preserve their physical status and hand down them to further generations. Additionally, CH dissemination and their monitoring may encourage tourism and, consequently, result in economic investment.

Over the years, Geographical Information System (GIS) has become a key tool to handle geospatial big data concerning CH sites and, thanks to the internet coming, to disseminate information too. In fact, the Web Geographic Information System (WebGIS) provides the possibility to integrate base maps, such as Microsoft Bing Maps or Google Maps, with public or own layers produced to tackle a specific problem [6]. Moreover, thanks to technological advancement, such applications give the opportunity to the users to interact with both two-dimensional (2D) and three-dimensional (3D) data directly and process them in real-time [7].

WebGIS architecture, based on a typical client-server structure, involves a three-tier configuration aimed at managing all components into three logical and physical levels [8]. In fact, it consists of hardware elements (e.g., Web server) as well as software parts, such as geospatial data management and DataBase Management System (DBMS) software and proper libraries [9, 10]. A user-friendly interface is commonly introduced too to help end-users in visualizing and handling such data [11]. Both proprietary and open-source software can be applied to develop and customize the different elements of the platform. These last ones are usually preferred since they are extremely adaptable and, consequently, easily customizable to meet authors' needs [12, 13]. In addition, Free Open-Source Software (FOSS) show also competitive performance compared to the proprietary ones [14] without forgetting that they observe the indications provided by the Infrastructure for Spatial InfoRmation in the European Community (INSPIRE) completely.

This research aims at describing the procedures adopted to design and implement a WebGIS platform devoted to disseminating the information of CH sites. Therefore, after detecting potential users' requirements and needed data to meet such purposes, available information provided by open-source datasets were gathered and the remaining ones were obtained by carrying out proper field data campaigns and processing the acquired data. An intuitive interface was also programmed to help IT and non-IT users to access the platform and handle the stored information. Both 2D and 3D viewers were integrated in such interface in order to manage 2D and 3D formats. 3D visualization was essential to integrate metric reconstructions of the CH assets and, thus, facilitate their status monitoring. Detailed 3D models were produced by adopting Remotely Piloted Aircraft Systems (RPAS)-based photogrammetric techniques. All application components were realized using Free and Open-Source Software for Geospatial Applications (FOSS4G) software.

The paper is organized into three main sections. Section 2 "Material and methods" illustrates i) the methodology adopted to design and implement the webGIS platform (Sect. 2.1); ii) data required to meet users' needs and geodatabase construction (Sect. 2.2); and, lastly, iii) the approaches adopted to generate detailed 3D textured models of pre-selected pilot sites. Conversely, Sect. 3 "Results" and Sect. 4 "Discussion and conclusion" describe the generated outcomes in terms of performance, quality, and utility of the produced application beyond to summarize the conclusion. Platform strengths and weaknesses are also reported in the "Discussion and Conclusion" Section (Sect. 4).

2 Material and Methods

In this study, the operative pipeline proposed by Huxhold and Levinsohm [15] (Fig. 1) was adopted as a baseline to the WebGIS framework development, aimed at supporting cultural heritage promotion. As reported in Fig. 1, such a workflow consists of six main steps, each of which should be considered as an interactive and iterative process. Firstly, the potential end-users and required data to meet the research purpose were identified. This information, thus, was used to design the WebGIS application configuration and structure, subsequently implemented in a pilot project, whose quality and performance were further evaluated. Lastly, the real framework was launched.

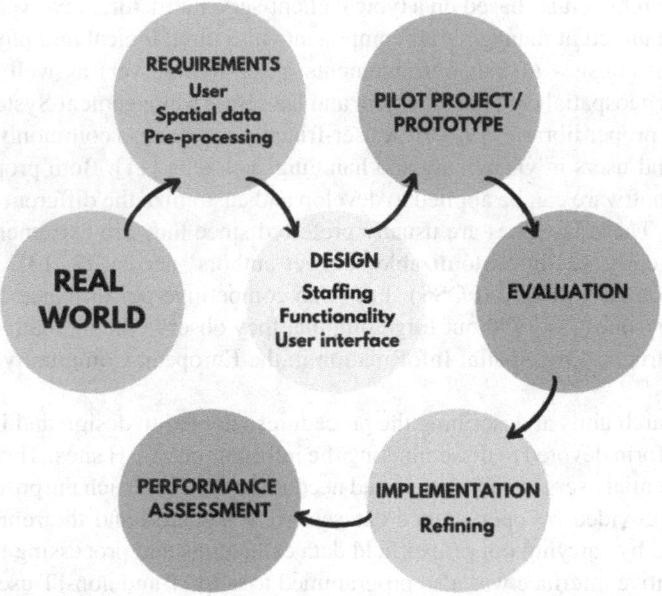

Fig. 1. Operative pipeline applied to develop and implement WebGIS application

2.1 WebGIS Application Design and Implementation

The WebGIS application was designed on the basis of three main perspectives: i) pinpointing the potential consumers and their expectations and requirements; ii) outlining the needed data, the available sources, and datasets to collect; and, lastly, iii) setting the optimal hardware and software configuration.

Different target groups, such as the national/regional/local heritage and environmental agencies and the business communities (e.g., tourism agencies, cultural and creative entities) could benefit from the proposed framework since CH preservation brings clear economic benefits (e.g., higher rates of employment, investments). Similarly, individual citizens could take advantage of the provided information. Indeed, location and path to achieve them as well as site description and historical details will be provided in such a platform. The scientific community may be also interested in the gathered information since they can use them as input data for further processing algorithms or to validate their results.

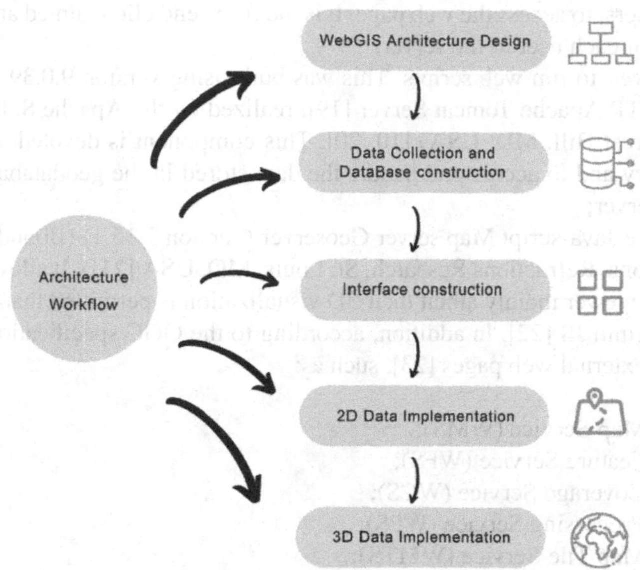

Fig. 2. Architecture operative workflow.

The most appropriate data, such as base maps, open datasets describing the CH sites, and that one needed to reproduce a physical asset with "precision" were selected and collected from available external sources or that one produced by handling data acquired during the proper field campaigns. Therefore, a large volume of geospatial big data in different formats should be integrated and processed into the platform. This characteristic together with users' expectations has to be taken into account to define the processing system capabilities. Thus, the design step started by implementing the procedure proposed by [16] consisting of five phases detailed in Fig. 2. Firstly, WebGIS architecture was built by defining the platforms and the corresponding software and, then, raster and vector data, point clouds, and 3D models were gathered. Thus, both 2D and 3D viewers were implemented in the interface, created to be easily manageable by expert and not-skilled users.

All WebGIS components were structured in three tiers (Fig. 3): the first level (interface) was dedicated to data presentation, while the second one was devoted to the analysis module and, lastly, the third tier was aimed at storing and handling the data. An adequate infrastructure was developed for each of them. This allowed generating three independent modules by using FOSS4G, as suggested by the standards and best practices established by the Open Geospatial Consortium (OGC) and EU directive INSPIRE [17]. OGC standards outline all the technical details required to program interfaces and encoding required to use spatial data via web pages. Although standards are similar for different spatial data, service parameters, data types, request URL and interfaces should be adapted to their formats [18]. Those standards and the corresponding applications could be freely downloaded from OGC web site.

The architecture was organized by combining:

1. Web browsers, to access the web page. It is the front-end client aimed at transferring the query of each user to the server;
2. HTTP Server, to run web scripts. This was built using version 9.0.39 of the open-source HTTP Apache Tomcat Server [19], realized by the Apache Software Foundation (Forest Hill, MD, USA) [10, 20]. This component is devoted at translating users' query and to access and handle the data stored in the geodatabase thanks to the Map server;
3. open-source Java-script Map server Geoserver (version 2.15.1) (Boundless Spatial, GeoSolutions, Refractions Research, St. Louis, MO, USA [21]). It allows managing data in 2D viewer mainly albeit their 3D visualization is permitted thanks the adoption of Cesium JS [22]. In addition, according to the OGC specifications, it allows involving external web pages [23], such as:

   (a) Web Map Service (WMS);
   (b) Web Feature Service (WFS);
   (c) Web Coverage Service (WCS);
   (d) Web Processing Service (WPS);
   (e) Web Map Tile Service (WMTS);

4. Additional libraries (e.g., OpenLayers - version 6.4.3, OSGEO, (Boundless Spatial, GeoSolutions, Refractions Research, St. Louis, MO, USA) [24] and Cesium JavaScript (Cesium JS, version 1.75; Analytic Graphics, Exton, PA, United States [22]). Those libraries are detailed in [25–27];
5. An open DataBase Management System (DBMS), designed by applying version 12.0 of the PostGre Structured Query Language (PostGreSQL) database system (PostgreSQL Global Development Group [28]).

HTML language was used to create the interface whose style was improved by applying version 4.5.0 and 4.7.0 of the Bootstrap [29] and version 4 of W3 [30] libraries as well as a CSS style file, generated to introduce additional variations. HTML and JS codes were integrated in a single script which was used to program specific menus in the 2D interface where data were imported directly [31]. Conversely, data were uploaded in the 3D viewer using CESIUM Ion Web interface [22, 32]. A detail of the developed code is reported in the Fig. 4.

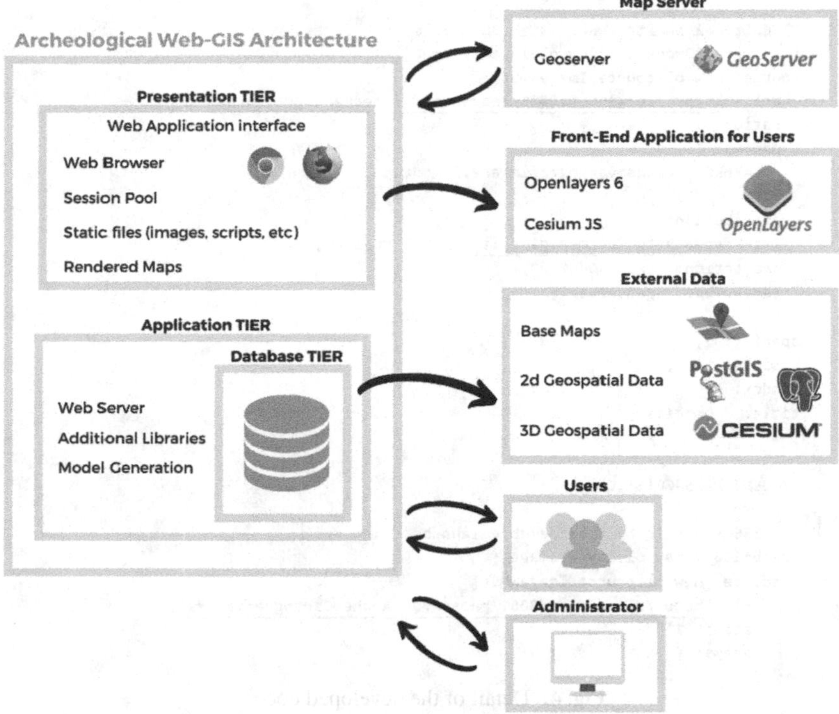

Fig. 3. Detailed of the implemented WebGIS configuration

2.2 Data Collection and Geodatabase Building

After defining data needed to georeference and describe cultural heritage sites in Puglia Region, available open datasets were checked and gathered. Specifically, National Geoportal [33] and Territorial Information System of Apulian Region (SIT Puglia [34]) were investigated. Such data were uploaded in PostGreSQL, through the application of PostGIS extension, using the external web services. Additionally, proper 3D models were generated by processing own photogrammetric pictures. The approach adopted to obtain accurate textured 3D models is detailed in the next paragraph.

Once all collected data together with the corresponding web services url, reference system and style were stored, they were reprojected by applying the WGS84 UTM 33N (EPSG: 32633) reference system. Data style was created in QGIS environment. Such data were grouped together in three main categories: i) basemaps layers, including OpenStreeMap, Satellite Big Map Aerial and Stamen Terrain; ii) Base layers, aimed at describing Apulian region morphology and landform mapping; iii) Archeological layers, comprising all maps concerning archeological sites positions and features as well as 3D models.

```

  // Cultural heritage Size with 3D Models
var Cultural3Dmodels = new ol.layer.Image({
  source: new ol.source.ImageWMS({
    url: "http://localhost:8081/geoserver/ArcheoCartografia/wms",
    ratio: '1',
    params: {
      LAYERS: "ArcheoCartografia:area3dmodels",
    },
    attributions:
    "<a href = http://sit.puglia.it/> © SIT Puglia",
    projection: "EPSG:4040000",
    serverType: "geoserver",
  }),
  opacity: 1,
  visible: true,
  zIndex: 6,
  title: "3Dmodels",
});

  // BENI PAESAGGISTICI

  //bp136 - assets of considerable landscape interest
  var bp136 = new ol.layer.Image({
    source: new ol.source.ImageWMS({
      url: "http://localhost:8081/geoserver/ArcheoCartografia/wms",
      ratio: '1',
      params: {
```

Fig. 4. Detail of the developed code

Concerning data visualization, IT and non-IT users can access them in both 2D and 3D viewers directly. A proper JS code based on the above-mentioned libraries was developed to implement each data in the most adequate menus of the 2D viewer directly [31]. As already specified, instead, 3D models and point clouds were uploaded using CESIUM Ion Web interface [22]. That application generates a JS script, suitable for implementing the data in the viewer, automatically [27, 31].

2.3 3D Model Produced by RPAS-Photogrammetry

Detailed 3D models were produced using the RPAS photogrammetry. Such a technique was selected because of its great number of advantages. Indeed, thanks to the introduction of the structure from motion (SfM) approach and multiview stereo (MVS) algorithms, photogrammetry allows obtaining textured 3D models with a comparable accuracy of that one generated by applying traditional techniques, e.g., Terrestrial Laser Scanner (TLS) [35–37]. In addition, RPAS introduction allows to program the flight campaigns in flexible dates and achieve areas difficult to reach [38].

As suggested by [39], RPAS-photogrammetry is based on five main steps: i) planning and performing of flight missions; ii) dataset creation and its quality assessment; iii) block orientation; iv) filtering and georeferencing of pre-processed images; v) photogrammetric outcomes generation (Fig. 5).

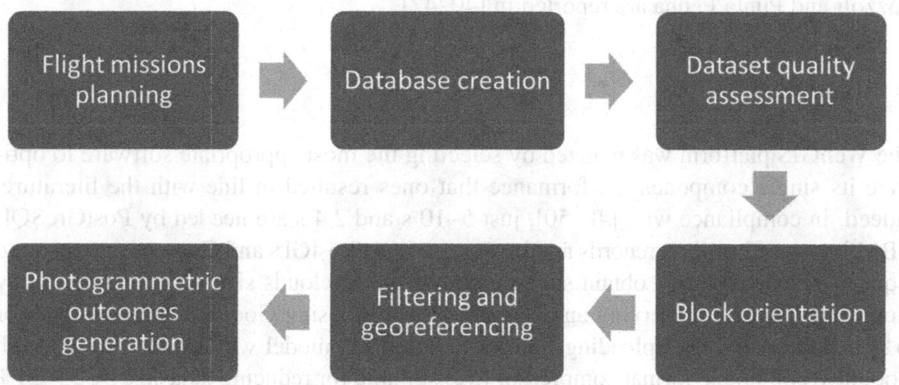

Fig. 5. Operative photogrammetric workflow

Firstly, flight campaigns were planned and carried out using a commercial quadcopter DJI Inspire 1, equipped with the DJI ZenMuse X3 camera. Flight height and speed was programmed according to the desired Ground Sample Distance (GSD). Simultaneously, a topographic survey was carried out to acquire Ground Control Points (GCPs), homogeneously distributed over the study area, subsequently introduced into the software to georeference the resultant model. Such points were surveyed using a network Real Time Kinematic (nRTK) mode. GCPs number was defined according to study area size and heterogeneity, as described in [40–42].

Then, all collected images were grouped together in a dataset and their quality was evaluated both qualitative (just inspecting them and cleaning out all blurry pictures) and quantitative (using the "Estimate Image Quality" tool, implemented in Agisoft environment) points of view [43]. The "Estimate Image Quality" tool assigns a value between 0 and 1 according to the image quality. A threshold of 0.8 was set to select the satisfying image [47].

After selecting the adequate images and setting Agisoft software workspace, the accuracy of the on-board UAV equipment and GCPs coordinates were fixed. Indeed, Camera Accuracy (m), Camera Accuracy (deg) and Marker Accuracy (m) parameters were set equal to 0.05 m, 10 degrees and 0.01 m, respectively. Additionally, to allow camera correction increment proportionally to the photogrammetric block adjustments, the camera correction option was enabled. Thus, the image block orientation step started by adopting the "High mode option", and the pre-processed photos were aligned [45, 46] and, then, filtered to remove the useless pictures characterized by a Reprojection Error value higher than 0.4 [47]. Sparse point clouds were extracted and the committed systematic error estimated to improve model reliability, as proposed by [37]. To further improve the accuracy of the final outcome, GCPs, were introduced in Agisoft environment and used to re-orient the clouds. Lastly, dense point clouds and detailed 3D models were produced. Their accuracy was evaluated through the computation of Root Mean Square Error (RMSE).

More details about the metric reconstruction of the Chiesa di Ognissanti, Torre Zozzoli and Punta Penna are reported in [40–42].

3 Results

The WebGIS platform was realized by selecting the most appropriate software to optimize its single component performance that ones resulted in line with the literature. Indeed, in compliance with [48–50], just 5–10 s and 2.4 s are needed by PostGreSQL DBMS to run 12 million records and by PostgreSQL/PostGIS and Geoserver to respond a query, respectively. To obtain such outcomes, point clouds size was compressed by more than 7 times, preserving an accuracy of 1 mm, using Google Draco compressor [51]. Additionally, the uploading time of detailed 3D model was speeded up through Google WebP image format compressor [52] suitable for reducing data size by 25–34% [53]. Lastly, scripts running speed was further incremented by splitting the main page into several JS files. This resulted in programming errors reduction too.

Fig. 6. 2D viewer interface: A) archeological sites with 3D models; B) baseline maps; C) 2D layers stored in the database and set in the more adapted menu; D) export tools; E) zoom in/zoom out widgets; F) frame visualization; G) scale and H) viewer window.

To speed up data catalogue consultation as well as help potential end-users in accessing it, an interactive interface, shown in Fig. 6, was programmed. This is split into two windows by the "div" tags. The former, commonly called Table of Contents (TOC), is located on the left and consists of layers to be activated or deactivated and tools aimed at drawing and export polygons. Conversely, the latter, set on the right, includes both 2D and 3D view maps as well as an overview map and a scale bar at the bottom-left and a vertical toolbar at the top-left. This involves navigation tools, such as zoom in, zoom out, slide zoom, zoom to layer extension and full screen. Lastly, coordinates of the mouse pointer are shown on the top-right. 3D viewer is activated just clicking on the layers correlated by the 3D models.

Accessing to the main page, the Standard Open Street Map (OSM) layer is visualized in the 2D viewer and, when active, the data stored in the database will be overlaid to it. Such data are grouped together in various drop-down menu according to the information that they provide and, for each of them, legend and metadata can be pictured by clicking on the correct button (Fig. 7). Base layers can be visualized in the 3D viewer too, selecting the optimal ones from the toolbar. In this case, the reference DTM is that one available in Cesium environment.

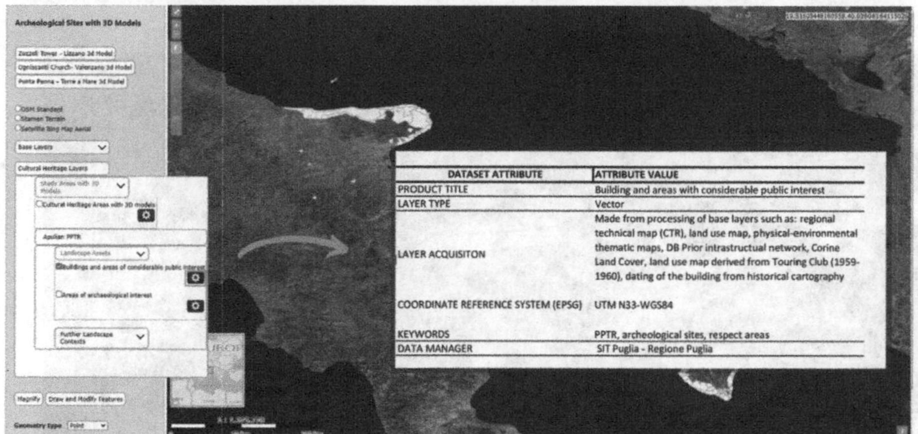

Fig. 7. Metadata example

Therefore, 3D viewer allows displaying DEM and points clouds as well as detailed 3D models. Figure 8 reports an example of the own 3D models generated by applying RPAS-photogrammetry and available in the developed platform. Specifically, the metric reconstruction of Torre Zozzoli (Taranto, Puglia Region) and Chiesa di Ognissanti (Valenzano - BA, Puglia Region) are depicted in Fig. 8.

Fig. 8. Examples of 3D models visualized in the 3D viewers: A) Torre Zozzoli (Taranto, Puglia Region); B) Chiesa di Ognissanti (Valenzano - BA, Puglia Region)

4 Discussion and Conclusion

In this paper, the procedure required to produce a 3D open-source WebGIS aimed at promoting CH dissemination was reported. Its potentialities in meeting research purposes were explored too.

Supporting CH sites is essential in order to encourage tourism development as well as to protect and preserve their physical status, often compromised by the lack of both investment and knowledge. As previously outlined, a WebGIS application appears as the optimal tool to highlight the relevance of such resources. Nevertheless, several constraints, mainly linked to the possibility to i) be used by different users simultaneously, ii) realize an interactive platform, and iii) handle heavy geospatial big data in a short time, were faced in its implementation. To solve these issues, a big effort was made in detecting the optimal software and hardware tools during the design phase and used, subsequently, to build such an application. In compliance with OGC and EU directive INSPIRE, FOSS4G were picked up and used. This ensures that any browser may access the developed platform. The selected FOSS4G were not the only potential solutions to be adopted to meet research purposes. For instance, thanks to their simple and intuitive interfaces, the combination of QGIS Desktop, QGIS Server and Lizmap Web Client could be a valid alternative albeit they are not customizable. Nevertheless, FOSS4G are preferable to proprietary softwires, such as StoryMap by ESRI, GeoMedia Web Map, etc., since they are less versatile, and their structure is not open.

Nevertheless, more work is needed to extend the number of contact points that can simultaneously access the database and interact with them. For this, additional improvements concerning system interactive ability have been devised and, they will be set in the further steps. Specifically, real-time processing tools capable of combining the diverse layers stored in the platform have been programmed to allow customizing the elaborations in accordance with users' needs. This may cause target audience enlargement implying an increment of users interested in consulting the developed application. Therefore, a large volume of geospatial data should be collected and processed, and proper field data campaigns should be planned to fill the lack of data. In this research, indeed, several photogrammetric flights and/or TLS surveys were carried out to acquire the pictures adapt to reconstruct 3D models, able to reproduce a physical asset "with precision".

In conclusion, although some limitations have been detected, the integration of accurate 3D textured models in a WebGIS tool seems to be the optimal solution to encourage CH dissemination and monitor their status. Indeed, it allows to provide reliable information about cultural heritage position and reconstruction. However, in contrast to the virtual reality, in this case, the world is reproduced exactly and, therefore, not replaced with a synthetic context. Moreover, the implemented 3D tiled models are correlated with additional data, such as graphic and textual information as well as geolocated data. Consequently, this could be considered as a rough example of Augmented reality. In the next future, it will be further improved by introducing visual and multimedia elements too.

Acknowledgments. This research was conducted within the project "Programma Operativo Nazionale Ricerca e Innovazione 2014-2020—Fondo Sociale Europeo, Azione I.2 "Attrazione e Mobilità Internazionale dei Ricercatori"—Avviso D.D. n 407 del 27/02/2018" CUP: D94I18000220007—cod. AIM1895471—2.

References

1. UNESCO–World Heritage Center: Operational Guidelines for the Implementation of the World Heritage Convention. UNESCO, Paris (2017)
2. Capolupo, A., Boccia, L.: Innovative method for linking anthropisation process to vulnerability. World Rev. Sci. Technol. Sustain. Dev. **17**(1), 4–22 (2021)
3. Boccia, L., Capolupo, A., Rigillo, M., Russo, V.: Terrace abandonment hazards in a Mediterranean cultural landscape. J. Hazard. Toxic Radioact. Waste **24**(1), 04019034 (2020)

4. Capolupo, A., Saponaro, M., Fratino, U., Tarantino, E.: Detection of spatio-temporal changes of vegetation in coastal areas subjected to soil erosion issue. Aquat. Ecosyst. Health Manage. **23**(4), 491–499 (2020)
5. Palladino, M., Nasta, P., Capolupo, A., Romano, N.: Monitoring and modelling the role of phytoremediation to mitigate non-point source cadmium pollution and groundwater contamination at field scale. Ital. J. Agron. **13**(s1), 59–68 (2018)
6. De Amicis, R., Conti, G., Girardi, G., Andreolli, M.: 3D WebGIS and visualization issues for architectures and large sites. In: 4th International Workshop "3D-ARCH 2011": Virtual Reconstruction and Visualization of Complex Architectures (2011)
7. Capolupo, A., et al.: An interactive WebGIS framework for coastal erosion risk management. J. Mar. Sci. Eng. **9**(6), 567 (2021)
8. Alesheikh, A.A., Helali, H., Behroz, H.A.: Web GIS: technologies and its applications. In: Symposium on Geospatial Theory, Processing and Applications, ISPRS, Ottawa, ON, Canada (2002)
9. Soto-Garcia, M., Del-Amor-Saavedra, P., Martin-Gorriz, B., Martínez-Alvarez, V.: The role of information and communication technologies in the modernisation of water user associations' management. Comput. Electron. Agric. **98**, 121–130 (2013)
10. Kuria, E., Kimani, S., Mindila, A.: A framework for web GIS development: a review. Int. J. Comput. Appl. **178**, 6–10 (2019). ISSN: 0975-8887
11. Caradonna, G., Novelli, A., Tarantino, E., Cefalo, R., Fratino, U.: A WebGIS framework for disseminating processed remotely sensed on land cover transformations. Rep. Geod. Geoinf. **100**, 27–38 (2016)
12. Caradonna, G., Tarantino, E., Novelli, A., Figorito, B., Fratino, U.: Un WebGIS per la divulgazione delle analisi dei processi di desertificazione del territorio della Puglia. In: Proceedings of the Atti Conferenza Nazionale Asita, Lecco, Italy, 29 September–1 October 2015, pp. 217–223 (2015)
13. Kitsiou, D., Patera, A., Tsegas, G., Nitis, T.: A webGIS application to assess seawater quality: a case study in a coastal area in the Northern Aegean Sea. J. Mar. Sci. Eng. **9**, 33 (2021)
14. Wheeler, D.A.: Why Open Source Software/Free Software (OSS/FS) (2007). http://www.dwheeler.com/oss_fs_why.html. Accessed 18 Jan 2020
15. Huxhold, W.E., Levinsohn, A.G.: Managing geographic information system projects. Cartographica **32**, 63 (1995)
16. Caradonna, G., Figorito, B., Tarantino, E.: Sharing environmental geospatial data through an open source WebGIS. In: Gervasi, O., et al. (eds.) ICCSA 2015. LNCS, vol. 9157, pp. 556–565. Springer, Cham (2015). https://doi.org/10.1007/978-3-319-21470-2_40
17. Caprioli, M., Scognamiglio, A., Strisciuglio, G., Tarantino, E.: Rules and standards for spatial data quality in GIS environments. In: Proceedings of 21st International Cartographic Conference, Durban, South Africa, 10–16 August 2003
18. Sample, J.T., Shaw, K., Tu, S., Abdelguerfi, M.: Geospatial Services and Applications for the Internet. Springer, Cham (2008). https://doi.org/10.1007/978-0-387-74674-6_1. ISBN-13: 978-0-387-74673-9
19. Apache Tomcat. http://tomcat.apache.org/. Accessed 10 Mar 2020
20. Carter, B.: HTML Architecture, a Novel Development System (HANDS). An approach for web development. In: Proceedings of the 2014 Annual Global Online Conference on Information and Computer Technology, Louisville, KY, USA, 3–5 December 2014
21. Geoserver. http://geoserver.org/. Accessed 3 Mar 2020
22. Cesium, J.S. https://cesium.com. Accessed 4 Mar 2020
23. Agrawal, S., Dev Gupta, R.: Development and comparison of open source based web GIS frameworks on WAMP and Apache Tomcat Web Servers. In: Proceedings of the International Archives of the Photogrammetry, Remote Sensing and Spatial Information Sciences, Suzhou, China, 14–16 May 2014, vol. XL-4 (2014)

24. Openlayers. https://openlayers.org/. Accessed 3 Mar 2020
25. Fustes, D., Cantorna, D., Dafonte, C., Arcay, B., Iglesias, A., Manteiga, M.: A cloud-integrated web platform for marine monitoring using GIS and remote sensing. Application to oil spill detection through SAR images. Future Gener. Comput. Syst. **34**, 155–160 (2013)
26. Huang, Z., Xu, Z.: A method of using GeoServer to publish economy geographical information. In: Proceedings of the 2011 International Conference on Control, Automation and Systems Engineering (CASE), Singapore, 30–31 July 2011, pp. 1–4. IEEE, Piscataway (2011)
27. Brovelli, M.A., et al.: Urban geo big data. In: Proceedings of the International Archives of the Photogrammetry, Remote Sensing and Spatial Information Sciences, Bucharest, Romania, 26–30 August 2019, vol. XLII-4/W14 (2019)
28. PostgreSQL: The World's Most Advanced Open Source Relational Database. https://www.postgresql.org/. Accessed 22 Apr 2020
29. Getbootstrap. https://getbootstrap.com/. Accessed 21 Oct 2019
30. W3.CSS. https://www.w3schools.com/w3css/. Accessed 20 Oct 2019
31. Kommana, K.: Implementation of a Geoserver application for GIS data distribution and manipulation. Master's thesis, Physical Geography and Quaternary Geology, Department of Physical Geography and Quaternary Geology, Stockholm University, Stockholm, Sweden (2013)
32. Caradonna, G., Frigorito, B., Novelli, A., Tarantino, E., Fratino, U.: Geomatic techniques for disseminating processed remotely sensed open data in an interactive WebGIS. Plurimondi (2017). http://193.204.49.18/index.php/Plurimondi/article/view/47. Accessed 19 May 2021
33. Geoportale Nazionale. http://www.pcn.minambiente.it/mattm/. Accessed 3 Jan 2020
34. SIT Puglia. http://www.sit.puglia.it/. Accessed 16 Dec 2019
35. Rieke-Zapp, D.H., Wegmann, H., Santel, F., Nearing, M.A.: Digital photogrammetry for measuring soil surface roughness. In: Proceedings of the American Society of Photogrammetry & Remote Sensing 2001 Conference Gateway to the New Millennium', St. Louis, MO, USA, 23–27 April 2001. American Society of Photogrammetry & Remote Sensing, Bethesda (2001)
36. Colomina, I., Molina, P.: Unmanned aerial systems for photogrammetry and remote sensing: a review. ISPRS J. Photogramm. Remote Sens. **92**, 79–97 (2014)
37. Saponaro, M., Tarantino, E., Fratino, U.: Generation of 3D surface models from UAV imagery varying flight patterns and processing parameters. In: AIP Conference Proceedings, vol. 2116, no. 1, p. 280009. AIP Publishing LLC, July 2019
38. Nex, F., Remondino, F.: UAV for 3D mapping applications: a review. Appl. Geomat. **6**(1), 1–15 (2013). https://doi.org/10.1007/s12518-013-0120-x
39. Manfreda, S., et al.: On the use of unmanned aerial systems for environmental monitoring. Remote Sens. **10**, 641 (2018). https://doi.org/10.3390/rs10040641
40. Saponaro, M., Capolupo, A., Caporusso, G., Borgogno Mondino, E., Tarantino, E.: Predicting the accuracy of photogrammetric 3D reconstruction from camera calibration parameters through a multivariate statistical approach. In: XXIV ISPRS Congress, vol. 43, pp. 479–486. ISPRS (2020)
41. Capolupo, A., Maltese, A., Saponaro, M., Costantino, D.: Integration of terrestrial laser scanning and UAV-SFM technique to generate a detailed 3D textured model of a heritage building. In: Proceedings SPIE 11534, Earth Resources and Environmental Remote Sensing/GIS Applications XI, 115340Z, 20 September 2020. https://doi.org/10.1117/12.2574034
42. Saponaro, M., Capolupo, A., Turso, A., Tarantino, E.: Cloud-to-cloud assessment of UAV and TLS 3D reconstructions of cultural heritage monuments: the case of Torre Zozzoli. In: Proceedings SPIE 11524, Eighth International Conference on Remote Sensing and Geoinformation of the Environment (RSCy2020), 1152408, 26 August 2020. https://doi.org/10.1117/12.2570771

43. James, M.R., Robson, S., d'Oleire-Oltmanns, S., Niethammer, U.: Optimizing UAV topographic surveys processed with structure-from-motion: ground control quality, quantity and bundle adjustment. Geomorphology **280**, 51–66 (2017)
44. Agisoft, L.L.C.: Agisoft PhotoScan User Manual: Professional Edition, Petersburg, Russia (2014). https://www.agisoft.com/pdf/photoscan-pro_1_4_en.pdf. Accessed 12 Dec 2021
45. Gruen, A., Beyer, H.A.: System calibration through self calibration. In: Gruen, A., Huang, T.S. (eds.) Calibration and Orientation of Cameras in Computer Vision, pp. 163–194. Springer, Heidelberg (2001). https://doi.org/10.1007/978-3-662-04567-1_7
46. Triggs, B., McLauchlan, P.F., Hartley, R.I., Fitzgibbon, A.W.: Bundle adjustment — a modern synthesis. In: Triggs, B., Zisserman, A., Szeliski, R. (eds.) IWVA 1999. LNCS, vol. 1883, pp. 298–372. Springer, Heidelberg (2000). https://doi.org/10.1007/3-540-44480-7_21
47. Saponaro, M., Capolupo, A., Tarantino, E., Fratino, U.: Comparative analysis of different UAV-based photogrammetric processes to improve product accuracies. In: Misra, S., et al. (eds.) ICCSA 2019. LNCS, vol. 11622, pp. 225–238. Springer, Cham (2019). https://doi.org/10.1007/978-3-030-24305-0_18
48. Haynes, D., Ray, S., Manson, S.M., Soni, A.: High performance analysis of big spatial data. In: Proceedings of the 2015 IEEE International Conference on Big Data, Santa Clara, CA, USA, 29 October–1 November 2015
49. Ružicka, J.: Comparing speed of Web Map Service with GeoServer on ESRI Shapefile and PostGIS. Geoinformatics **15**, 3–9 (2016)
50. Geoext3. http://geoext.github.io/geoext3/. Accessed 16 May 2020
51. Github. https://github.com/google/draco. Accessed 16 May 2020
52. WebP. https://developers.google.com/speed/webp. Accessed 16 May 2020
53. Shehata, O.: Faster and Smaller 3D Tiles with WebP Image Compression. Cesium Blog (2019). https://cesium.com/blog/2019/02/12/faster-3d-tiles-streaming-webp/. Accessed 12 Sept 2019

Industrial eXtended Reality

A Framework for Developing XR Applications Including Multiple Sensorial Media

M. Bordegoni[1], M. Carulli[1](✉), and E. Spadoni[2]

[1] Mechanical Engineering Department, Politecnico di Milano, Milan, Italy
{Monica.bordegoni,Marina.carulli}@polimi.it
[2] Design Department, Politecnico di Milano, Milan, Italy
Elena.spadoni@polimi.it

Abstract. eXtended Reality applications include multiple sensorial media to increase the quality of the User Experience. In addition to traditional media, video, and sound, two other senses are typically integrated: touch and smell. The development of applications that integrate multiple sensorial media requires a framework for properly managing their activation and synchronization. The paper describes a framework for the development of eXtended Reality mulsemedia applications and presents some applications based on the integration of smells developed using the framework.

1 Introduction

Multimedia is a term used since the 90s to address the combination of two or more media delivered by a computer, including text, graphics, sound, animation, and video. Multimedia contents are delivered by multimedia devices, which typically are smartphones and tablet PCs.

eXtended Reality (XR) is a term recently introduced and commonly used for addressing interactive systems combining real and virtual environments. XR includes Virtual Reality, Mixed Reality and Augmented Reality and can be referred to as the reality-virtuality continuum proposed by Milgram [1]. In Milgram's spectrum, the levels of the virtuality of the User Experience range from being fully real to being immersive virtual. XR can be considered one of the key technologies for the next generation of the Human-Computer Interaction (HCI).

Multimedia can be viewed as an essential component of an eXtended Reality system. In fact, it is a necessary element of the user's experience in systems simulating visual, audio and physical models of the real world.

Technological advances in computing have allowed the implementation of more immersive and engaging experiences for users. These experiences provide high-quality visualizations and sounds, eliciting the two senses that have been traditionally investigated in the HCI domain, which are the senses of sight and hearing. In recent years, applications started introducing smell and touch, which have been proven effective for enhancing the quality of the User's Experience.

The concept of multimedia has evolved into the one of mulsemedia, intended as multiple sensorial media [2]. Mulsemedia systems use heterogeneous technologies to

L. T. De Paolis et al. (Eds.): XR Salento 2022, LNCS 13446, pp. 271–286, 2022.
https://doi.org/10.1007/978-3-031-15553-6_20

deliver a variety of sensory effects, including smell, taste, vibration and touch, lighting, and wind [3]. Multimedia aims at stimulating sight and hearing, while mulsemedia typically combines the former plus at least one more sense among touch, smell, and taste. This new notion is a consequence of the observation that most humans perceive the world through a combination of the five traditional senses (as defined by Aristotle). Coherently, computer-based applications should also engage human senses beyond sight and hearing.

An updated view of eXtended Reality systems includes computer-generated environments enriched with multimedia and mulsemedia components (Fig. 1). For example, in an immersive virtual environment, we can see a virtual world, hear computer-generated sounds and voices, and smell computer-generated fragrances.

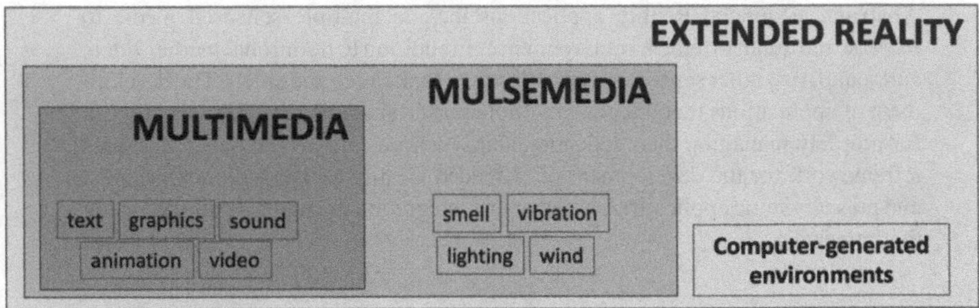

Fig. 1. Multimedia, mulsemedia and eXtended Reality.

Recently, the research into mulsemedia and XR has focused on including the sense of smell, which has been neglected in HCI until recently. The sense of smell has great importance in our daily life because it is devoted to acquiring and interpreting chemical signals in the environment and supports some basic biological functions, such as danger recognition, location and identification of food, and social communication. People react quickly and emotionally to odors, and they recall smell memories with greater accuracy than visual or auditory sensations.

The inability to smell is called anosmia and is a serious handicap [4]. People with anosmia cannot sense the presence of odor-related danger signals such as smoke, toxic chemical smells, or rotten food.

The integration of the sense of smell in XR and mulsemedia applications is in its infancy and requires the development of methodologies for designing smell-augmented applications, technologies for delivering aromas, case studies and scenarios to demonstrate the feasibility and evaluate performances.

This paper proposes a framework to design smell-augmented applications and presents some case studies of smell augmentation in eXtended Reality applications.

2 Main Issues Concerning the Sense of Smell

To well manage issues underpinning the design and implementation of XR applications including smells, it is useful to understand some basics of olfaction and smells.

Olfaction is a chemical sense, different from the visual and the auditory ones that are based on physical stimuli. Consequently, one of its characteristics is the nonlinearity, which means that a change in the intensity of the stimulus can result in a qualitative change in the subjective sensation [5].

Correlated to that, are two conditions, which are relevant for the generation of smell-based interaction: the *detection threshold*, and the *recognition threshold*. The *detection threshold* is the minimum amount of olfaction stimulus needed to provide a person with a sensory sensation. The *recognition threshold* is the minimum physical intensity of a stimulus required to allow a person to recognize a smell each time it is presented. Both conditions are subjective, as they depend on the biological characteristics of individuals, and also on the context and situation when a person has the olfactory experience.

Adaptation is another parameter to consider. This is related to the reduction over time of a person's ability to detect smells. When a smell is present in an environment continuously, an individual perceives it initially, but becomes addicted after a certain period, and no longer recognizes it. In fact, human sensitivity to a surrounding smell diminishes with the duration of exposure, and people gradually adapt to common smells. For example, a person may cease to notice the odor of a perfume applied a few hours earlier while others still do.

All this suggests that smells must be diffused with sufficient intensity and for a proper time to be perceived as intended. The continuous diffusion of a smell in an XR application must be avoided for two reasons. First to avoid user addiction, and second to limit the problem of removing a smell in the environment in case we want to release another smell, which may not be perceptible due to the presence of the previous one.

For what concerns the classification of smells, scientists and fragrance professionals have tried to establish standards for the description and measurement of odor quality characteristics. So far, a consensus has not been reached on a classification of "primary" smells. It is an open question how many fundamental types of odor qualities there are. Odor qualities have often been assessed by perception-based ratings. Traditionally, odor classification systems have been based on the individual expertise of botanists, chemists, or perfumers. Because of that, odor classification schemes are often developed for specific applications. Odor wheels have been constructed for a variety of odor classification applications, such as for wine, coffee, and perfume. For example, the perfume fragrance wheel proposed by Edwards is a circular diagram showing the inferred relationships among olfactory groups based upon similarities and differences in their odor [6].

A question still open is whether there is a basic set of smells that, when mixed, can yield all detectable smells. It would be possible to combine various chemicals, representing one odor each, to generate a specific smell (for example, vanilla smell). In practice, real chemicals generally stimulate more than one receptor. People have hundreds of olfactory receptor molecules. Therefore, it would be difficult to generate a specific smell by combining primary chemicals. In addition, the mix of scent receptors differs between people. So, chemicals can be perceived differently by people. For these reasons, smells are mostly defined and included individually in mulsemedia applications-for example, smell of chocolate, smell of rose, smell of smoke.

The next question is how to refer to a smell. The name of a smell is often that one of the objects or material generating that smell. For example, the orange smell refers to the orange fruit, the rose smell refers to the rose flower, and the chocolate smell refers to chocolate confectionery products. Besides, names of smells can also be evocative and consist of descriptions of places, situations, thoughts, and memories. Some examples are "the smell of grass on a rainy day", and "the fragrance of the apple pie cooked by my grandmother".

Smell quality and *smell sources* are other parameters that can be used for describing smells. Smell qualities are described through adjectives like floral, fresh, light, wispy, airy, musty, stale, putrid, faint, rancid, and acrid.

Smell sources can be described through adjectives, like skunky, floral, leathery smell, or through verbs, like baking, frying, digging, sweating, burning, and rotting.

Smells can be generated through chemical techniques and distributed into different media, including oils, liquids, and powders. For example, smells used in XR applications can be generated by essential oils extracted from plant materials like flowers, leaves, fruit, and seeds.

Smell, as well as taste, is often termed "gatekeeping sense" that is, sensations created because of the interaction with molecules being assimilated into the body. For this reason, gatekeeping senses are linked to biological and emotional processes, and this property can be properly exploited in XR applications.

All the issues discussed above affect the design of applications and also of devices for the generation of smells, as discussed in the following section.

3 Framework for Smell Augmented XR Applications

In this section, it is proposed a framework to use for developing XR applications, including mulsemedia. The framework is general and can be used for managing any sensorial media effects. The focus here is on the generation and management of smell effects (Fig. 2).

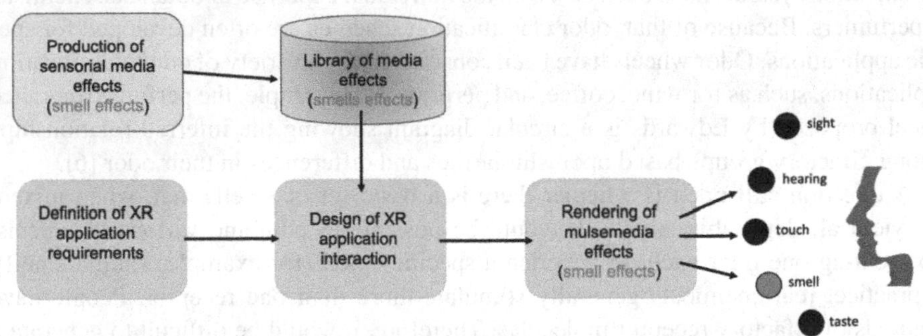

Fig. 2. Framework for the generation and management of smell effects.

First it is necessary to create a library of smell effects that can be used in the XR application. The smell effects can be described by using the properties and adjectives described in the previous section. The description includes metadata that allow retrieving the kind of smell to associate with environments, situations, and events in the XR application. A smell effect is described by a name, quality, source, and the media storing it (Table 1).

Table 1. Smells library including the description of smell effects.

Smells library			
Name	*Quality*	*Source*	*Medium*
Rose	Floral	Floral	Oil
Apple pie	Yummy	Baking	Liquid
Smog	Acrid	Burning	Powder

According to the XR application we intend to develop, a set of requirements are defined. It includes the description of users, the type of experience we intend to provide (i.e., immersive), the mulsemedia that need to be included and how they are interconnected.

Starting from the requirements, the interaction for the XR application is designed, and the most appropriate technology for rendering the media effects are selected. The following sections describe both activities, focusing on smells effects.

3.1 Designing XR Interaction Including Smell Effects

An eXtended Reality application typically consists of a virtual environment and a combination of sensorial media effects. When designing multi-sensorial experiences, smells shall not be simply added but must be holistically designed and integrated with the other sensory experiences.

A sensorial media effect can be present in an application continuously or discreetly. Continuous sensorial media effects are delivered continuously. An example is a background sound that can be heard while navigating a virtual scenario.

Instead, discrete sensorial media effects are delivered for a limited period. The duration of the effect can be predefined, or the effect can be terminated by another event. For example, one can start hearing music when she turns on a virtual radio; the music ends when the radio is turned off.

Smell effects are typically discrete media in an interactive XR application. This is mainly due to humans' adaptation to smells, which would prevent them from the recognition of the smell present in the environment after a while, as previously discussed.

The sensorial media effects are activated by triggers which can be the following events (Fig. 3):

- events occurring in the XR environment;
- events generated by the external environment and managed by the XR environment, i.e., user's input, sensors' input;
- events generated by other media.

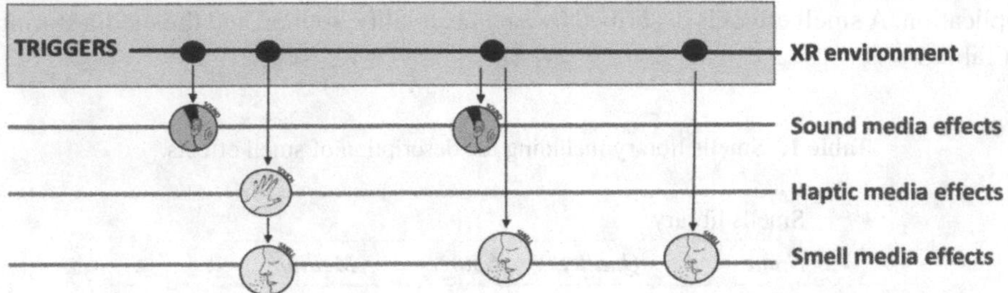

Fig. 3. Sensorial media effects activated by triggers.

Examples of the three types are as follows: two virtual objects collide emitting a sound; a user turns a virtual radio on, and the music starts playing; a user touches a virtual flower, which consequently emits a smell.

The smell effects to integrate in the XR application can be described including the following items of information:

- Number of smells: how many to use in the application;
- Smells: name of the smell, and eventually the medium to store it (oil, liquid, powder)
- Intensity of smell: intensity variation according to the user, the context, and the environment. Since the detection and recognition thresholds are subjective, the intensity should be customized for each user.
- Duration of smell effects: variation of the duration of smell delivery according to user, context, and environment. Customization for each user should also be applied to this parameter for the smell to be properly perceived.

The next step concerns the selection of the technology for rendering the smell effects and is described in the following section.

3.2 Rendering Smell Effects

In the domain of XR and simulation, several studies have recently addressed technology for including smells in XR environments. This is done by Olfactory Displays (OD), which are devices controlled by a computer that generates scented air.

Since people smell by using their noses, odorants should be vaporized and delivered to the nose. Olfactory Display consists of two main components, each performing a task [7].

The first is the *smell generation* component, which produces scented air from the stocked form of odor materials with the desired components and concentrations. Techniques for smell generation are many and include heating, airflow-based vaporization, airflow-based atomization, and ultrasonic vaporization.

The second is the *smell delivering* component, which has the task of conveying scented air from the smell generation component to the human olfactory organ by enabling spatial and temporal control of the olfactory stimuli. Many are the techniques proposed for smell delivery, consisting of natural diffusion, airflow, vortex ring, and tubes going from the smell generation component to the person's nose.

Olfactory Displays developed so far are often cumbersome or very limited for what concerns performances and airflow control. Therefore, researchers keep on proposing new solutions and developing new prototypes to better understand the phenomena related to olfaction and test the technical solutions with users.

When developing a new OD, the following parameters and issues must be considered.

First, the Olfactory Display can be wearable or placed in the environment.

Wearable Olfactory Display should have the typical features of personal wearable devices. They must be small and light, comfortable to wear and non-intrusive, discreet and not embarrass the wearer, connected to a software application controlling its functioning, and sustainable in terms of energy consumption.

Olfactory Displays placed in the environment have fewer design constraints than the wearable display. Still, they have a main issue concerning the position of the display with respect to the user who must perceive the delivered smell. In fact, the distance that the scented air can cover, and the airflow direction are two main issues to consider when designing OD for the environment.

Wearable displays have the advantage that minimum amounts of scent stimuli can be presented, as they are by their nature close to the users' olfactory field. On the contrary, they can be cumbersome and intrusive for the user.

When using Olfactory Displays placed in the environment, a positive property is that the users may not be aware of the display until their olfactory sense is stimulated by the smell effects. Conversely, the delivery of the olfaction is heavily affected by the context and by the users' movement in the environment.

The *number of scents* that can be stored and generated is an important parameter, which is related to the XR application requirements. The number of scents influences the shape, dimension, and weight of the device.

Another parameter influencing the shape, and also the technological solutions used for implementing the smell generation and delivery components, is the *medium* used for stoking the smell material.

Other two functions to consider are the *intensity of smell* and the *duration of the delivery*. The Olfactory Display must include a mechanism for controlling the quantity and duration of smell during the delivery task.

Many Olfactory Displays reported in the literature consist of prototypes integrating the various components and testing the functions and performances. A method for testing some solutions and solving some problems more rapidly and efficiently is using virtual prototyping before developing the real prototype. We experimented with the use of Computational Fluid Dynamics (CFD) analysis and simulation for the development of new Olfactory Displays, which allowed us to optimize the architecture of the device, the position, and the type of the components [8].

4 Case Studies

The case studies and experimental setups developed and presented in this section aim at increasing the realism of the XR experience and at improving the User Experience of XR environments, taking advantage of the demonstrated impacts of smells on people's physiological and psychological states. In fact, smell augmentation in XR applications in areas such as marketing, healthcare, medical rehabilitation, driving [9], learning [10], training [11], entertainment [12], product design [13], and cultural heritage [14, 15] can be particularly effective for improving the quality of the User Experience.

4.1 Olfaction-Augmentation for Training

The first application described is an XR application developed for training operators to use a lathe machine. A lathe is a machine tool used for shaping pieces of metal, wood, or other materials by causing the workpiece to be held and rotated by the lathe while a tool bit is advanced into the work causing the cutting action.

Before starting using the machine, the operators must learn what personal protective equipment (PPE) to wear and use and how to operate the machine safely. The use of XR applications has been shown to be effective in allowing operators to train and practice safely [11].

The XR application we have developed consists of a Virtual Reality application in which a virtual machine simulates a real lathe. The application can be experienced using a Head Mounted Display (HMD) and two Controllers. Some buttons allow the operator to switch the machine on/off and increase or decrease the speed. Smells are delivered by a wearable Olfactory Display integrated into the HMD. They have been included in the XR application for two purposes. The first purpose is to send the operator notifications, and the second is to improve the quality of the experience and the realism of the situation that is experienced.

Vanilla has been selected as the smell to notify the operator that everything is going fine and the task has been accomplished correctly. For the second purpose, the smell of coolant is used to create a realistic effect of the machine while operating and cutting a piece of metal.

The interaction flow is shown in Fig. 4. Before starting to operate the machine, the user selects the PPEs. If the selection is correct, the smell of vanilla is delivered for 3 s to acknowledge the user about the appropriate selection. The user starts the machine, and a sound is emitted; then, he/she sets the tool speed, and a second sound is emitted. When the metal piece starts being cut, the smell of coolant is delivered for 3 s.

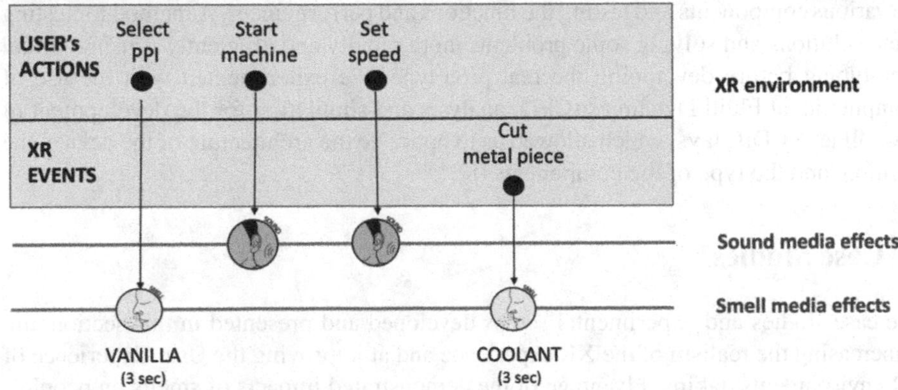

Fig. 4. Sensorial media effects used in the virtual training application

The wearable Olfactory Display used in this XR application consists of two modules attached on the two sides of the HMD (an Oculus Rift). Each module uses two fans as smell generation components (Fig. 5). The fans are connected to containers that contain the perfumed liquids used in the application. The two liquids are vanilla and coolant, which are delivered when triggered by the XR application described before. Each fan is activated by the user's action performed in the virtual environment.

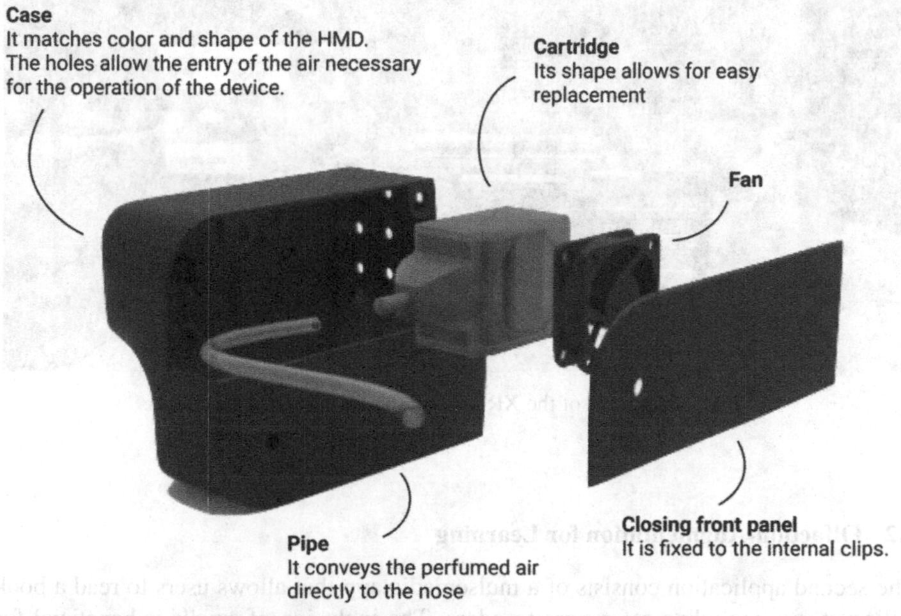
Case
It matches color and shape of the HMD.
The holes allow the entry of the air necessary for the operation of the device.
Cartridge
Its shape allows for easy replacement
Fan
Closing front panel
It is fixed to the internal clips.
Pipe
It conveys the perfumed air directly to the nose

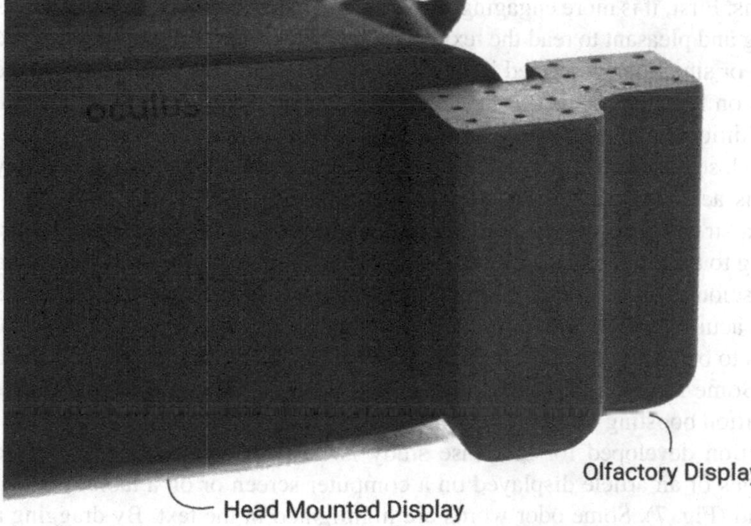
Olfactory Display
Head Mounted Display

Fig. 5. Wearable Olfactory Display using a smell generation technology based on airflow

The XR training application is shown in Fig. 6. The virtual environment, including the lathe machine, is shown on the HDM screens. The Olfactory Display is attached to the HMD so that the airflow directly reaches the user's nose.

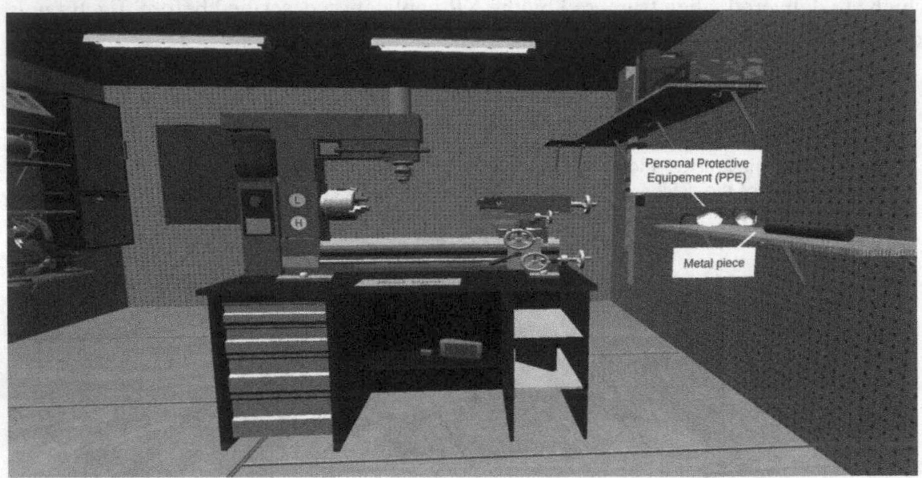

Fig. 6. Screenshot of the XR application including smell effects.

4.2 Olfaction-Augmentation for Learning

The second application consists of a mulsemedia app that allows users to read a book telling stories including references to odors. The inclusion of smells is beneficial for two main reasons. First, it is more engaging and amusing than traditional reading. Users find it surprising and pleasant to read the text and at the same time feel the smell related to some objects or situations described in the story. The second reason is related to the effect of smells on learning. In fact, it has been demonstrated in previous studies that odors add an additional component to learning [10]. It incorporates another sense, i.e., the sense of smell, so the brain is activated by an emotional and biological stimulus. Any time our brain is activated in multiple ways, learning seems affected. Memory recall is triggered by a strong unconscious reaction to a smell. This is known as the "Proust Effect," referring to the author Marcel Proust who wrote about memory recall as having a strong unconscious connection to certain smells. It also seems that certain smells improve mental acuity by their nature. In fact, essential oils have been used as a natural aid for centuries to boost cognitive performance. At present days, this practice is named aromatherapy. Some research has found that some essential oils can have significant mood and cognition boosting effects, possibly affecting attention and learning.

The application developed for this case study is desktop-type and consists of a sequence of pages of an article displayed on a computer screen or on a tablet PC that the user can read (Fig. 7). Some odor words are highlighted in the text. By dragging a nose icon over these words, an Olfactory Display emits the corresponding odor. Figure 7 shows a page of the article quoting the sentence "l'odore delle mandorle amare gli ricordava sempre il destino degli amori contrastati" ("the smell of bitter almonds always reminded him of the fate of thwarted loves"). The word "mandorle amare" triggers the delivery of the smell of bitter almonds.

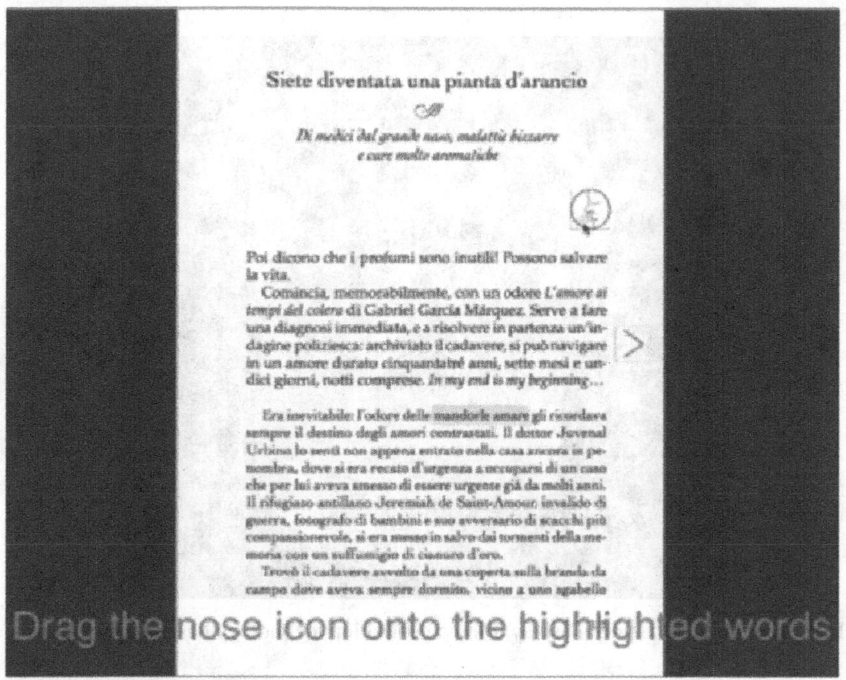

Siete diventata una pianta d'arancio

Di medici dal grande naso, malattie bizzarre e cure molto aromatiche

Poi dicono che i profumi sono inutili! Possono salvare la vita.

Comincia, memorabilmente, con un odore *L'amore ai tempi del colera* di Gabriel García Márquez. Serve a fare una diagnosi immediata, e a risolvere in partenza un'indagine poliziesca: archiviato il cadavere, si può navigare in un amore durato cinquantatré anni, sette mesi e undici giorni, notti comprese. *In my end is my beginning...*

Era inevitabile: l'odore delle mandorle amare gli ricordava sempre il destino degli amori contrastati. Il dottor Juvenal Urbino lo sentì non appena entrato nella casa ancora in penombra, dove si era recato d'urgenza a occuparsi di un caso che per lui aveva smesso di essere urgente già da molti anni. Il rifugiato antillano Jeremiah de Saint-Amour, invalido di guerra, fotografo di bambini e suo avversario di scacchi più compassionevole, si era messo in salvo dai tormenti della memoria con un suffumigio di cianuro d'oro.

Trovò il cadavere avvolto da una coperta sulla branda da campo dove aveva sempre dormito, vicino a uno sgabello

una diagnosi immediata, e a risolvere in partenza un'indagine poliziesca: archiviato il cadavere, si può navigare in un amore durato cinquantatré anni, sette mesi e undici giorni, notti comprese. *In my end is my beginning...*

Era inevitabile: l'odore delle mandorle a... gli ricordava sempre il destino degli amori contrastati. Il dottor Juvenal Urbino lo sentì non appena entrato nella casa ancora in penombra, dove si era recato d'urgenza a occuparsi di un caso che per lui aveva smesso di essere urgente già da molti anni. Il rifugiato antillano Jeremiah de Saint-Amour, invalido di guerra, fotografo di bambini e suo avversario di scacchi più compassionevole, si era messo in salvo dai tormenti della memoria con un suffumigio di cianuro d'oro.

Trovò il cadavere avvolto da una coperta sulla branda da campo dove aveva sempre dormito, vicino a uno sgabello

125

Fig. 7. Images of the mulsemedia application, including smell effects.

The Olfactory Display integrated into this application uses twelve air cannons as smell generation components. Each air cannon is connected to a case containing a scented liquid (bitter almonds, orange, cyanide, …) and is activated by the user's action in the XR application. In addition, a fan is placed at the center of the device to create a cleaning airflow after each generation of scented mist (Fig. 8).

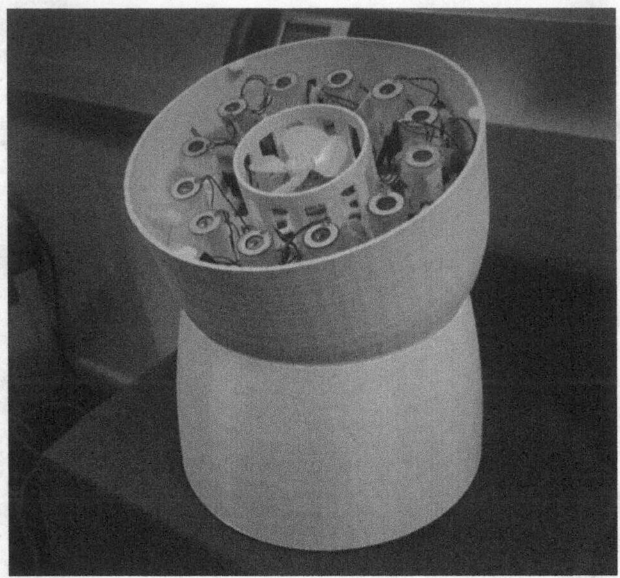

Fig. 8. Desktop Olfactory Display using a generation technology based on air cannons.

The smells are released for 3 s also in this application, so as to be perceivable but not pervasive (Fig. 9).

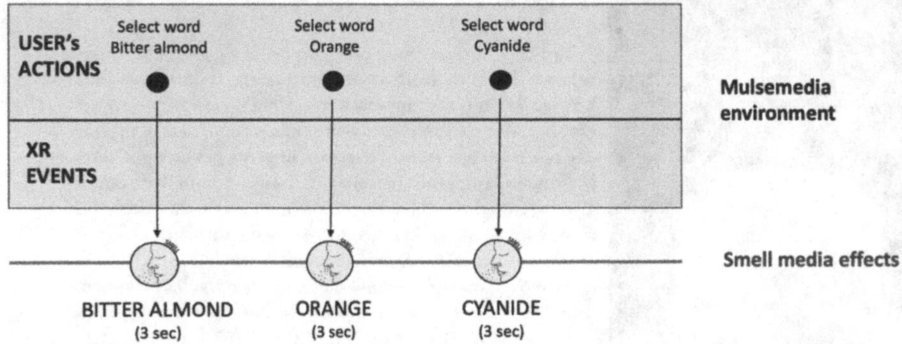

Fig. 9. Sensorial media effects used in the learning application.

4.3 Olfaction-Augmentation in Museums

This last application consists of a multisensory AR application developed to improve the User Experience and the learning performances in museum exhibitions. In particular, the purpose of the application is to increase user engagement and to improve the learning process through user's active interaction and sensorial stimulation.

This experience concerns a hypothetical Vermeer's paintings exhibition where visitors can play the multisensory AR application directly on their smartphones. The application proposes game-like interactions enriched with augmented contents to engage the user during the experience. During the interaction, smells are delivered through a wearable Olfactory Display that is worn as a necklace (see Fig. 10).

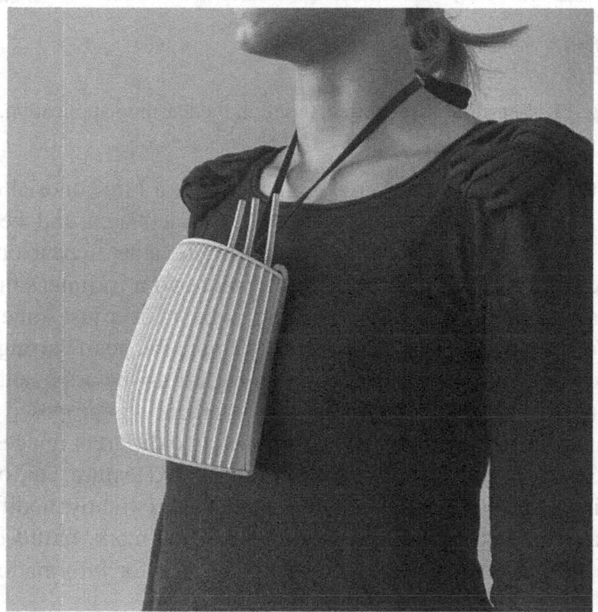

Fig. 10. Wearable Olfactory Display used for the multisensory AR application.

The smells have been included in the experience for two main purposes. The first one consists in making the user more engaged and entertained than in traditional museum experiences. The second purpose is related to the effect of smell on learning performances. In fact, as stated before, the stimulation of the sense of smell can activate memory, making learning and later recalling items of information more accessible.

The interaction flow is shown in Fig. 11.

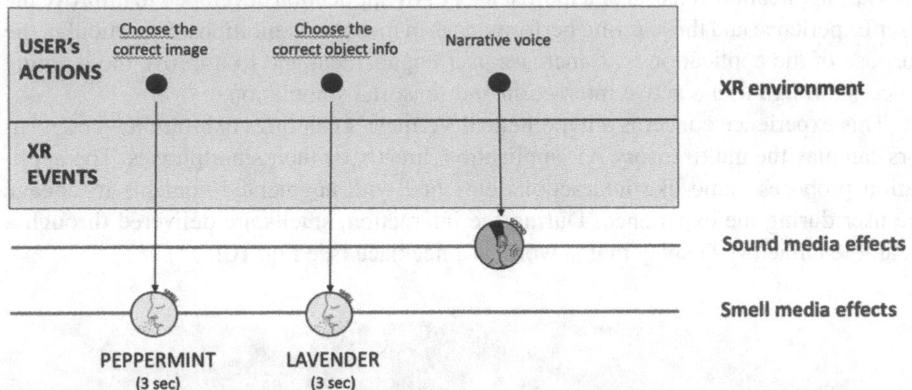

Fig. 11. Sensorial media effects used in the learning application.

At first, the user can select the language and watch a brief tutorial explaining the steps of the experience. Then, the smartphone camera is activated, and the user is invited to frame one of Vermeer's paintings. Some digital elements appear on the painting, covering specific parts of it with a checkered texture and a tridimensional box with a question mark on it (see Fig. 12). These elements, which cover just some iconic objects represented in Vermeer's paintings, such as for example the pearl earring, are clickable and allow the user to discover more information regarding the artist and his paintings. After clicking on these elements, the game-like interaction is proposed to the user by introducing a quiz game model (see Fig. 12). In fact, two different images related to the covered element are displayed by clicking on the checkered texture. One of the images is original (belonging to the painting), while the other is false (slightly modified). The same interaction modality is used for the box with the question mark. In this case, an image representing the hidden object appears and asks the user for information about itself.

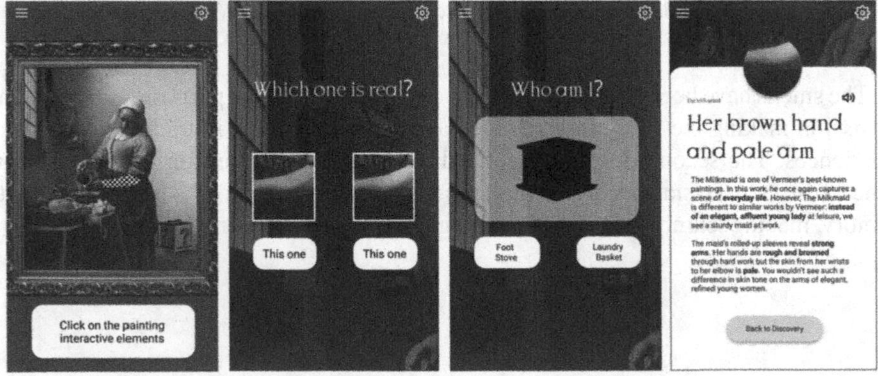

Fig. 12. Application screens presenting the AR contents, the Quiz game (in the two modalities), and the Information

The user is asked to select the correct answer for removing the covers from the painting and watching it entirely. If the user answers correctly, text and images describing the element are displayed. In addition, an audio guide reads the information displayed. If the user gives the wrong answer, he/she is invited to repeat the quiz until he/she gives the correct answer.

Smells are delivered as feedback to the user when he/she gives the correct answers. Smells are released for 3 s by the Wearable Olfactory Display, allowing the users to easier memorize the correct information. Two smells have been used: peppermint smell is used to give feedback in association with the checkered texture, and the scent of lavender is used in relation to the tridimensional box contents.

5 Conclusions

The culture regarding eXtended Reality is spreading more and more rapidly. Today, many applications based on Virtual Reality and Augmented Reality technologies are proposed in various application contexts. Even ordinary people are familiar with terminology and technologies and have used XR applications.

The reasons for this growth are many and are mainly related to the availability of technologies that are increasingly performing at low and accessible costs and that have-high level of usability. XR applications are extensively used in many domains. For example, video games, maintenance, training, cultural heritage, and medical sectors.

Research invests heavily in the development of new XR technologies and of applications that make use of them. In recent years, the focus has been on creating environments where people can have sensory experiences that are highly engaging. The possibility of interacting with virtual worlds not only through the sense of vision and hearing but also through the other senses, such as touch and smell, is now considered an essential aspect of a satisfying, memorable, and effective experience, whatever it is the application context.

The inclusion of the sense of smell in XR applications is particularly relevant, given its importance in our daily life. Studies have shown that the sense of smell enriches the quality of human experiences even in virtual worlds. However, the development of multisensory XR applications adds complexity, given the many aspects that must be considered. This new paradigm shift poses many challenges, mainly related to mulsemedia integration, delay, responsiveness, sensory effects intensities, and the development of wearable and other heterogeneous devices for delivering sensory effects.

Therefore, it is necessary to develop multisensory devices, which can be integrated together, methodologies for the development of multisensory XR applications, and also applications that demonstrate their effectiveness through tests performed with users.

This paper aims to contribute to the field of multisensory XR applications that include olfaction, proposing a framework for the development of such applications. Three case studies are presented that demonstrate the use of the framework. The applications were developed by students of the Virtual and Physical Prototyping course of the School of Design at Politecnico di Milano and preliminarily validated by the students themselves. More systematic tests will be performed to demonstrate the effectiveness of the framework, of the Olfactory Devices, and of the multisensory XR applications.

References

1. Milgram, P., Takemura, H., Utsumi, A., Kishino, F.: Augmented reality: a class of displays on the reality-virtuality continuum. In: Proceedings of SPIE, Telemanipulator and Telepresence Technologies, vol. 2351, pp. 282–292 (1994)
2. Ghinea, G., Timmerer, C., Li, W., Gulliver, S.R.: Mulsemedia: state of the art, perspectives, and challenges. ACM Trans. Multimed. Comput. Commun. Appl. **11**(1s), 17:1–17:23 (2014). https://doi.org/10.1145/2617994
3. Covaci, A., Zou, L., Tal, I., Muntean, G.M., Ghinea, G.: Is multimedia multisensorial? - a review of mulsemedia systems. ACM Comput. Surv. (CSUR) **51**(5), 1–35 (2018)
4. Boesveldt, S., et al.: Anosmia-a clinical review. Chem. Senses **42**(7), 513–523 (2017)
5. Nakamoto, T.: Human Olfactory Displays and Interfaces: Odor Sensing and Presentation. Information Science Reference (2013)
6. Edwards, M.: Fragrances of the World: 2012 Edition, 28th edn. Sydney (2012)
7. Yanagida, Y., Tomono, A.: Basics for olfactory display. In: Nakamoto, T. (ed.) Human Olfactory Displays and Interfaces, Odor Sensing and Presentation. IGI Global (2012)
8. Rossoni, M., Carulli, M., Bordegoni, M, Colombo, G.: Prototyping of an olfactory display supported by CFD simulations. In: CAD2022 Conference (2022)
9. Bordegoni, M., Carulli, M., Shi, Y.: Demonstrating the effectiveness of olfactory stimuli on drivers' attention. In: Chakrabarti, A., Chakrabarti, D. (eds.) ICoRD 2017. SIST, vol. 65, pp. 513–523. Springer, Singapore (2017). https://doi.org/10.1007/978-981-10-3518-0_45
10. Bordegoni, M., Carulli, M., Shi, Y., Ruscio, D.: Investigating the effects of odour integration in reading and learning experiences. Interact. Des. Archit. **32**, 104–125 (2017)
11. Bordegoni, M., Carulli, M., Spadoni, E.: Multisensory virtual reality for delivering training content to machinery operators. J. Comput. Inf. Sci. Eng. **22**(3), 031003 (2022)
12. Carulli, M., Bordegoni, M., Bernecich, F., Spadoni, E., Bolzan, P.: A multisensory virtual reality system for astronauts' entertainment and relaxation. In: Proceedings of the ASME 2019 International Design Engineering Technical Conferences & Computers and Information in Engineering Conference, IDETC/CIE 2019 (2019)
13. Bordegoni, M., Carulli, M.: Evaluating industrial products in an innovative visual-olfactory environment. ASME-JCISE (2016). https://doi.org/10.1115/1.4033229
14. Carulli, M., Bordegoni, M.: Multisensory augmented reality experiences for cultural heritage exhibitions. In: Rizzi, C., Andrisano, A.O., Leali, F., Gherardini, F., Pini, F., Vergnano, A. (eds.) ADM 2019. LNME, pp. 140–151. Springer, Cham (2020). https://doi.org/10.1007/978-3-030-31154-4_13
15. Carulli, M., Bordegoni, M.: Wearable olfactory display museum exhibition. In: ISOEN Conference, Fukuoka, 26–29 May 2019

Augmented Reality Remote Maintenance in Industry: A Systematic Literature Review

David Breitkreuz[1,2](✉), Maike Müller[1,2], Dirk Stegelmeyer[2], and Rakesh Mishra[1]

[1] School of Computing and Engineering, University of Huddersfield, Huddersfield, UK
david.breitkreuz@hud.ac.uk

[2] Institut für Interdisziplinäre Technik, Frankfurt University of Applied Sciences, Frankfurt am Main, Germany

Abstract. Augmented reality (AR) is a promising technology for supporting industrial maintenance applications. Two major types of AR technology are used for maintenance applications. One of those is AR remote maintenance, a technology that connects remote experts to on-site technicians to work collaboratively on industrial maintenance applications. This seems especially valuable for non-standardized tasks. Although several recent systematic literature reviews (SLRs) on AR for maintenance applications have been published, the growing body of literature calls for an ever-differentiated view of the knowledge base of AR remote maintenance. Therefore, this paper aims to map AR remote maintenance literature by conducting an SLR, characterizing the literature, describing applications in industry, and making suggestions for further research. Based on the analysis of 89 articles from the last two decades, this paper contributes the following findings: 1) the research field has a strong engineering focus on system development. 2) scholars share a common understanding of AR remote maintenance, despite using heterogeneous terminology; 3) the prevailing study design only allows for limited comparison of prototypes and applications; 4) transferability to industrial maintenance professionals is limited, due to the study design; 5) AR remote maintenance appears to raise business model opportunities for product-service systems; and 6) the diversity of AR remote maintenance applications indicates the technology's industrial versatility. Overall, the maturity of the research field is increasing; however, it is still at an early stage. Based on these findings, we made two proposals for advancing the AR remote maintenance research field.

Keywords: Augmented reality · Remote maintenance · Tele-assistance · Mobile collaboration · Product-service system

1 Introduction

Augmented reality (AR) can be used in various industrial applications, such as design, quality management, logistics, production, training, and maintenance [1–3]. One of the most popular fields of application is industrial maintenance [1, 4, 5]. For industrial maintenance, two major types of AR have been distinguished in the literature: 1) automatic single-user AR, and 2) AR remote maintenance [6].

L. T. De Paolis et al. (Eds.): XR Salento 2022, LNCS 13446, pp. 287–305, 2022.
https://doi.org/10.1007/978-3-031-15553-6_21

The first type, which is the automatic single-user AR (e.g., AR-based step-by-step guide [7–9]) is suitable for well-defined maintenance tasks, where a predetermined work plan is available [6, 10, 11]. However, the effort to dynamically adapt this AR type to undefined maintenance tasks is disproportionate, for example, during fault diagnosis, where a work plan is not available [10].

The second type, AR remote maintenance, is particularly suitable for undefined maintenance tasks [11]. AR remote maintenance enables at least two physically separated users (remote experts and on-site technicians) to share an AR experience to collaboratively perform a maintenance task [6, 12, 13]. These collaborative maintenance tasks include inspection [14], fault diagnosis [15], and the complex replacement of components [16]. In the literature, AR remote maintenance is sometimes also referred to as "remote collaboration" [e.g., 17, 18], "tele-assistance" [e.g., 19, 20], or "mobile collaborative augmented reality" [e.g., 21, 22].

Recently, scholars have published systematic literature reviews (SLRs) on AR for maintenance applications [e.g., 23, 24]. Generally, SLRs play a central role in research by contributing to the effective use of the existing knowledge base [25]. Previous SLRs investigated both types of AR but focused strongly on automatic single-user AR for defined maintenance tasks. In practice, maintenance tasks are often undefined, therefore, the industry is particularly interested in support tools, such as AR remote maintenance. Consequently, we are interested in analyzing the growing body of AR remote maintenance literature to make the existing knowledge base accessible to academics and practitioners.

This paper aims to map the literature to contribute to the AR remote maintenance research field. To this end, an SLR on AR remote maintenance was conducted to answer the following research questions (RQs):

RQ 1: What are the characteristics of the relevant literature addressing AR remote maintenance?
RQ 2: What examples of AR remote maintenance applications and industry sectors can be found in literature?
RQ 3: What suggestions for further research can be derived from the body of literature?

The remainder of the paper is structured as follows: Sect. 2 provides definitions to facilitate the understanding of this paper. Section 3 describes the methodological approach of the SLR. Section 4 presents the results regarding RQ 1 and RQ 2, while Sect. 5 addresses RQ 3. This paper concludes with Sect. 6.

2 Definitions

To facilitate the understanding of this paper, we provide the following definitions. *Maintenance tasks* are pieces of maintenance works, such as inspections, preventive maintenances, replacements of wearing parts, fault diagnoses, and repairs using spare parts. *Configuration is* defined as a specific technical implementation of software (e.g., tracking algorithm, rendering, data interfaces) and hardware components (e.g., head-mounted display, tablet, network architecture). A *prototype,* is a specific configuration proposed in the literature, such as Vishnu [26], ARTab [27], 3DGAM [28], ARAMS [29], CARM^2-PSS [30]. Maintenance application means using a prototype for a specific maintenance task, for example, using CARM^2-PSS for valve lubrication of a machine tool [30].

3 Methodology

To map AR remote maintenance literature and answer the RQs, an SLR was conducted following the guidelines proposed by vom Brocke et al. [25].

Table 1. Search results by database from 2000-01-01–2020-12-31.

Database			Articles
Scopus	Search string	TITLE-ABS-KEY ((“augmented reality” OR “mixed reality”) AND (tele* OR remote OR collaborat*) AND (maintenance OR service* OR assembly OR repair OR training))	1507
	Filter	Language: English or German; Publication year: ≥2000; Publication stage: final;	
WoS – All databases	Search string	TS = (“augmented reality” OR “mixed reality”) AND TS = (tele* OR remote OR collaborat*) AND TS = (maintenance OR service* OR assembly OR repair OR training)	503
	Filter	Language: English or German; Timespan: 2000–2020	
ACM – Guide to Computing Literature	Search string	Title: ((“augmented reality” OR “mixed reality”) AND (remote OR tele* OR collaborat*) AND (service* OR assembly OR maintenance OR training OR repair)) OR Abstract: ((“augmented reality” OR “mixed reality”) AND (remote OR tele* OR collaborat*) AND (service* OR assembly OR maintenance OR training OR repair)) OR Keyword: ((“augmented reality” OR “mixed reality”) AND (remote OR tele* OR collaborat*) AND (service* OR assembly OR maintenance OR training OR repair))	260
	Filter	Publication date: 2000–2020	
		Duplicates removed	450
		Corrected articles	1
		Total	1819

As the research field of AR remote maintenance lacks homogenous terminology, the topic of this SLR has been conceptualized using the following three themes: 1) 'Augmented reality' describes the technology used for AR remote maintenance; 2) 'Remote collaboration' characterizes the interaction between at least two physically separated users during AR remote maintenance sessions; and 3) 'Maintenance context' outlines the industrial application of the technology. Based on these themes, we derived the following keywords: 'augmented reality', 'mixed reality', 'tele', 'remote', 'collaboration', 'assembly', 'maintenance', 'repair', 'service', and 'training'. Using these keywords, we developed search strings which were applied to the Association for Computing Machinery Digital Library (ACM), Scopus and Web of Science (WoS) databases (cf. Table 1). These databases were chosen because they sufficiently covered the topic addressed in this SLR. This research field is still in its infancy, therefore, conference and journal articles published from 2000 to 2020 were considered.

The database search yielded a total of 1819 articles after removing duplicates. Relevant articles were identified through a title and abstract screening, followed by a full-text screening (cf. Fig. 1), applying appropriate inclusion and exclusion criteria (cf. Table 2). The abstract screening resulted in a total of 168 articles. After applying the inclusion criteria for full-text screening, a total of 89 articles were identified as the relevant body of literature for analysis.

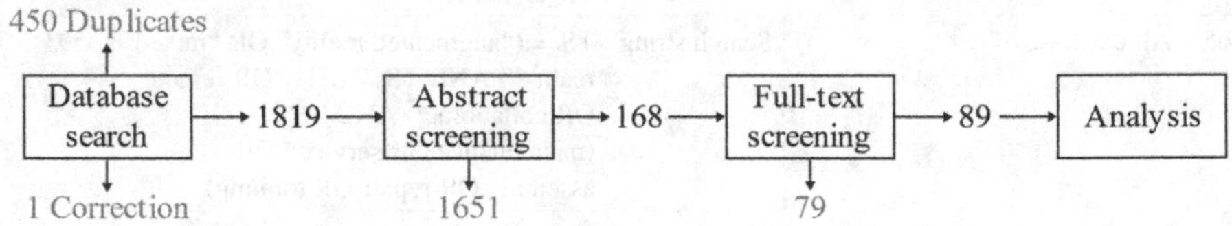

Fig. 1. SLR phases with numbers of included and excluded articles.

Table 2. Screening criteria for abstract and full-text screening.

Screening	Type	Statement
Abstract	Inclusion	Mentioning AR technology referencing collaboration between at least two physically separated users
	Exclusion	Referencing non-industrial sectors such as civil engineering, medical, library, education, tourism
Full-text	Inclusion	Description of AR remote maintenance
	Inclusion	Description of a maintenance application

The analysis of this SLR consisted of the extraction of relevant data and the classification of the articles. The RQs were used as a framework for the analysis. In this context, similarities, and differences between the articles regarding the applied study type, applications of AR remote maintenance and industrial sectors were identified. Terminology describing AR remote maintenance and corresponding definitions were also analyzed. Based on this analysis, the predetermined RQs were answered.

4 Results and Discussion

4.1 Temporal Distribution

Before 2011, articles on AR remote maintenance were only occasionally published, with two or fewer publications per year (cf. Fig. 2). By 2011, interest in the research field has grown with four or more publications per year, and reaching a peak in 2020 with 19 publications. Conference publications and journal articles are distributed in a ratio of 74%:26%. This indicates a low maturity of the research field, although the distribution of publications over time shows a clear increase in journal publications from 2018 onwards (cf. Fig. 2). While only 17% of publications were published in journals before 2018, 38% of articles were already published in journals as of 2018.

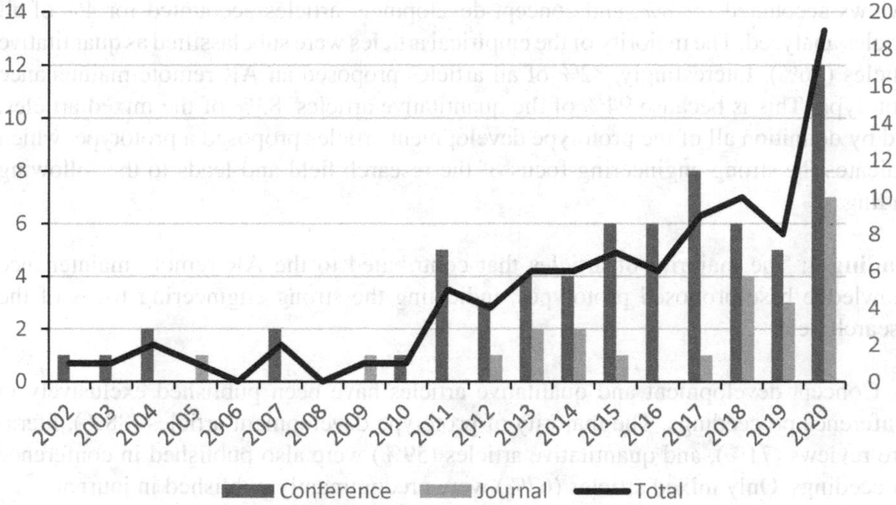

Fig. 2. Number of conference and journal articles per year.

All articles within our sample were classified according to their methodological approach (i.e., theoretical vs. empirical) and subclassified further specifying the research methods used. Theoretical articles were subclassified as prototype development, concept development, and literature review. Prototype development articles introduce prototypes developed by the team of authors lacking empirical evaluation. Concept development articles merely propose a conceptual idea without having developed a prototype. Literature reviews, on the other hand, summarize, and synthesize previous studies from a specific viewpoint without using additional empirical data to answer RQs.

Empirical articles were further subclassified as qualitative, quantitative, and mixed. Articles in the qualitative subcategory used empirical research methods such as industrial case studies, interviews, and focus groups, while articles in the quantitative subcategory used research methods such as surveys and user studies. Articles were classified as mixed when qualitative and quantitative research methods were combined.

Half of the articles (49%) were classified as theoretical articles, most of which were subclassified as prototype development articles (37%) (cf. Table 3). Literature

Table 3. Number of articles per article type with percentages of proposed prototypes.

Methodology		Articles (%)	Proposed prototypes (%)
Theoretical	Prototype development	33 (37%)	33 (100%)
	Literature review	7 (8%)	–
	Concept development	4 (4%)	–
Empirical	Quantitative	32 (36%)	30 (94%)
	Qualitative	7 (8%)	5 (71%)
	Mixed	6 (7%)	5 (83%)
	Total	**89 (100%)**	**73 (82%)**

reviews accounted for 8%, and concept development articles accounted for 4% of all articles analyzed. The majority of the empirical articles were subclassified as quantitative articles (36%). Interestingly, 82% of all articles proposed an AR remote maintenance prototype. This is because 94% of the quantitative articles, 83% of the mixed articles, and by definition all of the prototype development articles proposed a prototype, which indicates the strong engineering focus of the research field and leads to the following finding:

Finding 1: The majority of articles that contributed to the AR remote maintenance knowledge base proposed prototypes, indicating the strong engineering focus of the research field.

Concept development and qualitative articles have been published exclusively in conference proceedings. The majority of prototype development articles (88%), literature reviews (71%), and quantitative articles (59%) were also published in conference proceedings. Only mixed articles (67%) were predominantly published in journals.

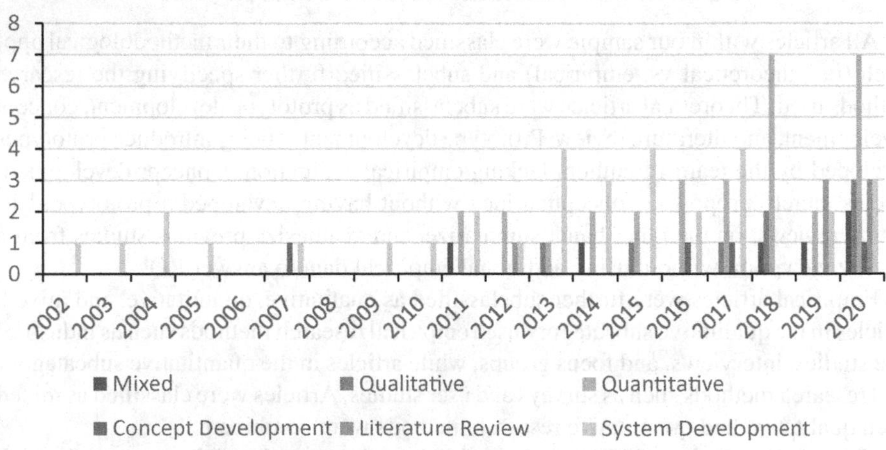

Fig. 3. Number of articles by article type per year.

Before 2011, exclusively theoretical articles (i.e., system, and concept development) were published (cf. Fig. 3). This changed in 2011 with the publication of the first empirical articles. Those empirical articles evaluated system latency [31], or conducted user studies comparing their proposed prototype to a baseline condition, namely, audio-only support [32], and a combination of audio support and snapshot exchange [11]. Empirical articles peaked in 2020, with a total of 12 publications.

In 2012, the concept of AR remote maintenance (referred to as AR-assisted maintenance system) was mentioned for the first time in a literature review as a field of application [33]. In 2019 and 2020, a total of six literature reviews (three per year) that mention AR remote maintenance have been published indicating the increasing attention on this type of AR [4, 34–38].

4.2 Definitions and Terminology

Based on our analysis, we observe a great deal of heterogeneity in the field of AR remote maintenance terminology, as reflected in the number of different terms used. Of the 89 articles analyzed, 49 different terms for AR remote maintenance were identified. In some articles (8%), the authors use the term 'AR remote maintenance' [e.g., 12, 30] or the variant 'remote maintenance' (3%) [e.g., 39, 40]. However, other terms such as 'mobile collaborative augmented reality' (7%) [e.g., 41–43], and 'remote collaboration' (9%) [e.g., 44–46] are also used frequently. Variants of the terms 'tele-maintenance' (8%) [e.g., 4, 47] are commonly used among German-speaking authors.

Although the terminology varies greatly, the authors share a common understanding of AR remote maintenance. Only 16 (18%) articles provided definitions for AR remote maintenance, and the analysis showed that those definitions were largely consistent, despite authors emphasizing different aspects.

Within their definition, some authors highlighted the application aspect of AR remote maintenance in industry [e.g., 4, 15, 48], while others emphasized the configuration aspect [e.g., 20, 49]. Those who focused on the configuration aspect within their definition, for example, described an audio-video stream that was augmented by virtual objects and communication cues [e.g., 20, 22, 43, 50], or derived their definition from various established technical concepts, such as AR, mobile computing, and computer-supported cooperative work [21, 41, 51]. Those authors who focused on the application aspect, emphasized a physical separation of the collaborating users [e.g., 52], that is, remote experts and on-site technicians, or the maintenance application [e.g., 12, 15, 48].

Finding 2: Despite the heterogeneous terminology used, scholars in the research field share a common understanding of AR remote maintenance.

Based on our analysis, we suggest that a definition of the technology should include three components: 1) digital cues to enhance communication and object awareness between the collaborating users through AR, e.g., drawing tool, 3D virtual objects, and eye gaze visualization; 2) a shared view to enhance communication and situation awareness between the collaborating users, that is enabled through suitable remote technologies, e.g., video links, images, or immersive environments; 3) the maintenance application itself. Therefore, we propose AR remote maintenance as the most suitable term. Based on the definitions provided by Mourtzis et al. [12], Fang et al. [52] and Fleck et al. [20] we propose the following definition:

AR remote maintenance is defined as a technology that enables two or more users (remote experts and on-site technicians) who are not in the same physical space to create a shared view that is enhanced with AR-based communication cues to collaboratively accomplish maintenance tasks.

4.3 Empirical Study Type

All empirical articles in our sample were further classified according to their study types. Articles were classified as lab experiments, when the studies were conducted under laboratory conditions, and as field experiments, when conducted outside the laboratory in an industrial setting with industrial professionals. In contrast with field experiments, articles were classified as industrial case studies when the investigation took place outside the laboratory in an industrial setting and the unit of analysis was organizational rather than individual (e.g., value of the technology for a manufacturer's service unit). Articles were classified as industrial interview studies when industrial experts (e.g., field service technicians) were interviewed, and the unit of analysis was individual rather than organizational (e.g., usability of technology).

Table 4. Number of empirical articles per study type.

Study type	Articles (%)
Lab Experiment	31 (69%)
Industrial Case Study	8 (18%)
Industrial Interview Study	3 (7%)
Field Experiment	2 (4%)
Industrial Interview Study & Lab Experiment	1 (2%)
Total	**45 (100%)**

Lab experiments are the prevailing evaluation method with 69% of the empirical articles classified in this category (cf. Table 4). Many authors have conducted laboratory user studies comparing their prototype to a baseline condition (e.g., audio/video-only support, paper-based instructions) in terms of performance indicators, such as task completion time, accuracy, or usability [e.g., 28, 39, 45]. In accordance with Aschenbrenner et al. [39], the analysis of the lab experiment articles shows that these user studies often prove the relative advantage of the prototype compared to the baseline condition [e.g., 53–56]. Nevertheless, this study design does not allow comparison of one prototype with another, since configurations found in literature vary greatly. To enable shared views, live video links augmented with virtual content often are the remedy of choice [e.g., 52, 57–59], whereas others developed highly sophisticated protypes combining AR and VR technology [e.g., 28, 45, 53, 60]. In addition, the prototypes also vary greatly in terms of communication cues and augmented virtual content provided. Communication cues and virtual content can be provided in different forms: 2D objects, such as cursors, arrows, and circles [e.g., 56, 61]; 3D objects, such as CAD images of machine components [e.g., 28, 62]; freehand drawing tools [e.g., 17, 52]; or sophisticated communication cues, such as hand gestures and head and/or gaze rays [e.g., 26, 58]. Another option for configuration decisions are the AR devices used for prototype development, such as smartphones [e.g., 45, 56], binocular video see-through head-mounted displays [e.g., 26, 53], monocular orthoscopic video see-through head-mounted displays [e.g., 46, 59], helmets with camera and near-eye displays [e.g., 42, 58], or binocular optical see-through devices [e.g., 16, 52, 63]. Binocular optical see-through devices such as the Microsoft HoloLens might be powerful devices and a regular choice in prototype development [e.g., 15, 20, 44, 60, 64]; however, their real-life suitability for maintenance applications is uncertain, since such devices considerably impair the field of view [15, 28, 52, 60]. Thus, such devices might impair on-site technicians' ability to perform physical maintenance tasks and negatively affect work safety [57]. Consequently, Aschenbrenner et al. called for comparative studies of different prototypes on the same maintenance application to allow for comparability [39].

In our view, it would be equally beneficial to evaluate the same prototype in various maintenance applications to identify the most useful prototype for a specific maintenance application. This is because different maintenance applications vary greatly in complexity, from simple tasks such as inspection and testing to more complex tasks such as diagnosis of malfunctions [65]. These different applications may benefit from different configurations. For example, Fang et al. showed that the increasing task complexity negatively influences the performance of their prototype [52]. This suggests that different task complexity levels may require different configurations. Besides that, users' skill levels may influence the performance of the prototype. Vorraber et al., for example, found that their prototype is especially useful for inexperienced on-site technicians performing complex and difficult tasks [57]. Inexperience, however, is not only a problem with junior maintenance professionals, but also a common issue with maintenance and field service delivery, since workforces consist of technicians with different skill profiles and expertise backgrounds (e.g., mechanics, electrics, automation, software, and application technology). Yet, the technician available is often not the most suitable in terms of skill level and profile [66]. Thus, to identify the most useful prototype configuration for a specific maintenance application, it is necessary to consider task complexity, user skill levels and skill profiles when conducting user studies. This means that, to consider task complexity, user skill levels and skill profiles in these studies, it is essential to recruit industrial maintenance professionals as study participants. As complex tasks are too demanding for students [39], different task complexity levels cannot be considered in studies with student participants.

Yet, students represent the majority of participants in user studies, as the recruiting is convenient and they are suitable subjects for early usability tests [e.g., 19, 27]. This holds true especially when standardized measurement tools such as NASA-TLX are used [e.g., 20, 67]. However, transferability of the results to industrial maintenance professionals in terms of performance indicators is limited, as students lack experience regarding maintenance tasks and are less diverse in their skill levels and profiles. Thus, the complexity level of maintenance tasks in those studies must be adapted to students instead of representing the diversity of real-life maintenance tasks.

Only two articles (5%) were assigned to the field experiment category. Since, per definition, the studies' participants were industrial maintenance professionals and the studies' setups were in industrial environments, the applicability of the prototype for specific real-life maintenance applications is assessable. He et al. showed that their prototype could reduce complexity and improve the first-time fix rate in a specific data center inspection application [14]. Vorraber et al. showed the applicability of their prototype for a 5-axis processing machine maintenance application in the automotive industry [57]. Even though these studies suggest industrial applicability, more studies are needed following the criteria for comparability mentioned above to allow for generalization of the results. Our analysis leads to the following findings:

Finding 3: The prevailing user study design neither allows for comparison of proposed AR remote maintenance prototypes against each other nor assesses their usefulness for specific maintenance applications.
Finding 4: Using students as participants allows only a limited transfer of the results to industrial maintenance professionals.

In our sample, eight (18%) articles were classified as industrial case studies, thus forming the second-largest group within the sample. Interestingly, all articles in the industrial case study category deal with AR remote maintenance in the context of Product-Service Systems (PSS) [12, 13, 16, 22, 30, 42, 49, 68]. This suggests that the industry is particularly interested in using AR remote maintenance in PSS.

PSS are understood as coherent offerings of products, software, and service components that extend the traditional products of machinery and industrial equipment manufacturers to provide additional value to their customers [69, 70]. PSSs are widespread in industry [71, 72]. In the context of PSS, AR remote maintenance might reduce the duration and costs of service interventions as well as increase first-time-fix-rates [10, 16, 30, 42]. Therefore, AR remote maintenance seems to be a promising pathway for improving PSS in industry.

4.4 Industrial Sectors and Applications

The analysis of industrial sectors and applications shows that most studies (54%) did not address a particular industry (cf. Fig. 4). When the industrial sector was not specified, often the prototype was also not evaluated on a maintenance task. Some authors tested their prototype on entirely different tasks, such as LEGO part localization [44] and LEGO gear box assembly [73]. Others have tested aspects of the AR remote maintenance prototype, such as the general improvement in the interaction between remote experts and on-site technicians [26, 46, 74]. Complex industry-like tasks were replicated in a few laboratory user studies, for example, car engine repair [67], 3D printer and robot manipulator maintenance [45].

The most popular industrial sectors for which AR remote maintenance prototypes were developed and/or evaluated are machinery and industrial equipment (15%), aerospace (9%), and robotics (8%).

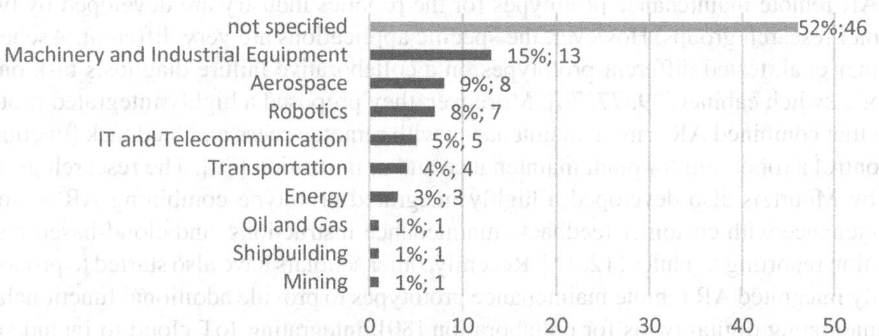

Fig. 4. Number of articles specifying an industrial sector.

Machinery and industrial equipment comprise (capital goods) manufacturing industries, such as machine tools [e.g., 10, 68], industrial printers [42], coating machines, and vacuum technology, among others [49]. Some case studies highlighted the opportunity to leverage AR remote maintenance for value co-creation with customers by providing assistance for self-service [22, 30]. For example, Mourtzis et al. presented a case study in which an equipment manufacturer supported a customer's machine operator instead of deploying its own field service technician to perform a machine tool valve lubrication maintenance [30]. Others described cases where the equipment manufacturer's field service technicians were supported by their remote expert colleagues during customer visits to avoid second deployments [10, 42]. This indicates the possibility of supporting two different use case logics, supporting own field service technicians as distinct from supporting customer's operators. Both use cases were also described by Ohlig et al., who explored impacts on the service business model of machinery and equipment manufacturers, utilizing insights from focus groups with executives in strategic service positions in twelve German manufacturing firms [49]. They found that the impact on the business model depends on the use case. The analysis of the aforementioned case leads to the following finding:

Finding 5: AR remote maintenance appears to raise opportunities for novel remote service offerings and business models in the context of PSS delivery.

For the aerospace industry—a highly regulated industry—early AR remote maintenance applications have been described even before 2010 [75, 76]. In contrast to the above-mentioned machinery and equipment articles, where usually one on-site technician is supported by a remote expert, prototypes for aerospace enable several aircraft technicians to collaboratively work on one aircraft, while being supported by remote experts from several engineering disciplines. Another application in the aircraft industry is a remote approval procedure, where multiple experts join a remote session with an external civil flying authority to gain clearance to fly after repair [76]. This shows that AR remote maintenance is an inter-organizational technology that is not only limited to the collaboration of manufacturers and their customers but also enables the inclusion of other external organizations of the maintenance value-creation network.

AR remote maintenance prototypes for the robotics industry are developed by two distinct research groups. However, the specific applications are very different. Aschenbrenner et al. tested different prototypes on a collaborative failure diagnosis task on a robotic switch cabinet [39, 77, 78]. Moreover, they proposed a highly integrated prototype that combined AR remote maintenance with remote access and feedback functions to control a robot arm for plant maintenance and optimization [79]. The research group led by Mourtzis also developed a highly integrated prototype combining AR remote maintenance with customer feedback, maintenance instructions, and cloud-based malfunction reporting modules [12, 16]. Recently, other scholars have also started to propose highly integrated AR remote maintenance prototypes to provide additional functionality by integrating digital twins for collaboration [80], integrating IoT cloud to include an automatic alert system [63], integrating 3D–CAD data and gesture control to further reduce misunderstandings in collaboration [28] among others.

The industrial sectors and applications analysis allow us to formulate the following finding:

Finding 6: The diversity of industrial sectors and the variety of applications referenced in the literature suggest the versatility of AR remote maintenance for various maintenance applications.

5 Further Research and Limitations

Overall, the analysis allows us to formulate the following concluding findings: the maturity of the AR remote maintenance research field is increasing. The indicators for this are the growing number of: 1) publications, especially journal articles; 2) references in literature reviews; 3) empirical studies of proposed prototypes; 4) industrial case studies; and 5) more sophisticated highly integrated prototypes. Yet, the research field is still at an early stage of development due to the strong engineering focus on prototype development. Based on our findings, we make two proposals for advancing the AR remote maintenance research field.

1. AR remote maintenance research study designs should allow comparability of prototypes and maintenance applications.

   The engineering research community should adopt comparative study designs in terms of unified maintenance applications or prototypes considering task complexity, skill levels, and skill profiles, rather than merely testing for relative advantages of prototypes toward a baseline condition. Indeed, laboratory experiments are indispensable, as they allow us to retain control over the experimental setup and conditions. However, comparability and repeatability of the studies must be assured. Therefore, we encourage the AR engineering research community to adopt study designs that fulfill the criterion to keep either the maintenance application or the prototype variable constant while using standardized measurement tools (e.g., NASA-TLX). To advance the research field, we call for user acceptance studies with industrial maintenance professionals, such as that conducted by Rapaccini et al. [42]. Therefore, in our view, research should turn toward the following topics:

a. Further enhancing communication by developing advanced digital communication cues and shared views and evaluating those developments in user acceptance studies with maintenance professionals.
b. Further developing novel integrated AR remote maintenance prototypes and evaluating those prototypes in user acceptance studies with industrial maintenance professionals.

2. AR remote maintenance research should engage in industrial adoption studies. Other research communities should address AR remote maintenance from an organizational perspective, since the engineering research community has solved the most limiting technical issues (e.g., processing power [59] and wearing comport [42] of head-mounted displays, or tracking accuracy for virtual content alignment [10, 19, 29]) of AR remote maintenance, and the technology is already on the verge of industrial adoption. In line with Masoni et al., we encourage other research communities to solve the practical challenges of AR remote maintenance in industry [40]. This is all the more relevant, as the COVID-19 pandemic has forced manufacturers to adopt AR remote maintenance, since the strict travel restrictions made field service technician deployment, a key pillar of PSS provision, challenging [81–83]. In our view, research should therefore turn toward the following topics:

a. Conducting organizational technology adoption studies to identify the success factors and challenges of AR remote maintenance adoption.
b. Developing and evaluating PSS offerings and business model opportunities based on AR remote maintenance to assess the value of the technology.

Despite our efforts to apply a rigorous methodology, this study has some limitations. Since we did not conduct a forward and backward search following the database searches, it is possible that we did not identify the entire body of relevant literature. Moreover, articles published from January 2021 onwards are not included in this SLR. Therefore, possible recent developments in this research field could not be analyzed.

6 Conclusion

Although several SLRs on AR for maintenance were recently published, AR remote maintenance has not yet been reviewed in a differentiated manner to make the existing knowledge base accessible to academics and practitioners. Therefore, this paper aims to map the literature on AR remote maintenance. To this end, an SLR was conducted, analyzing 89 relevant articles.

Based on the analysis, we were able to answer the three predetermined research questions: RQ 1) What are the characteristics of the relevant literature addressing AR remote maintenance? RQ 2) What examples of AR remote maintenance applications and industry sectors can be found in the literature? RQ 3) What suggestions for further research can be derived from the body of literature?

In terms of RQ 1, our analysis shows that the AR remote maintenance research community uses heterogeneous terminology while scholars within the community share a common understanding. We also observe a strong engineering focus of the research field, which is reflected by the high number of conference publications, prototype development articles and few empirical studies. Furthermore, the prevailing research design does not allow assessment of the superiority of certain AR remote maintenance prototypes compared to others. Although the research field has been gaining momentum as a result of the recent increase in the number of journal publications and empirical studies, it is still in its infancy.

Regarding RQ 2, our analysis shows that the diversity of the industrial sectors referenced in the literature illustrates the versatility of AR remote maintenance for various maintenance applications. In addition, AR remote maintenance appears to raise opportunities for novel remote service offerings and business models in the context of PSS delivery.

Referring to RQ 3, we call for research on two broad areas. First, the engineering research community should apply AR remote maintenance research designs that allow for the comparability of prototypes and maintenance applications. In particular, we suggest further developing and evaluating advanced digital communication cues and shared views, as well as novel integrated AR remote maintenance prototypes. Second, other research communities should turn toward AR remote maintenance adoption studies. In particular, we suggest conducting industrial adoption studies from an organizational perspective and developing and evaluating PSS offerings and business model opportunities based on AR remote maintenance systems.

References

1. Bottani, E., Vignali, G.: Augmented reality technology in the manufacturing industry: a review of the last decade. IISE Trans. (2019). https://doi.org/10.1080/24725854.2018.1493244
2. Dini, G., Dalle Mura, D.: Application of augmented reality techniques in through-life engineering services. Procedia CIRP (2015). https://doi.org/10.1016/j.procir.2015.07.044
3. Fernández del Amo, I., Erkoyuncu, J.A., Roy, R., Palmarini, R., Onoufriou, D.: A systematic review of Augmented Reality content-related techniques for knowledge transfer in maintenance applications. Comput. Indust. (2018). https://doi.org/10.1016/j.compind.2018.08.007
4. Egger, J., Masood, T.: Augmented reality in support of intelligent manufacturing – a systematic literature review. Comput. Ind. Eng. (2020). https://doi.org/10.1016/j.cie.2019.106195
5. de Souza Cardoso, L.F., Mariano, F.C.M.Q., Zorzal, E.R.: A survey of industrial augmented reality. Comput. Indust. Eng. (2020). https://doi.org/10.1016/j.cie.2019.106159
6. Porcelli, I., Rapaccini, M., Espíndola, D.B., Pereira, C.E.: Innovating product-service systems through augmented reality: a selection model. In: Shimomura, Y., Kimita, K. (eds.) The Philosopher's Stone for Sustainability, pp. 137–142. Springer, Heidelberg (2013). https://doi.org/10.1007/978-3-642-32847-3_23
7. Schlagowski, R., Merkel, L., Meitinger, C.: Design of an assistant system for industrial maintenance tasks and implementation of a prototype using augmented reality. In: 2017 IEEE International Conference on Industrial Engineering & Engineering Management, pp. 294–298. IEEE, Piscataway (2017). https://doi.org/10.1109/IEEM.2017.8289899

8. Gao, L., Wu, F., Liu, L., Wan, X.: Construction of equipment maintenance guiding system and research on key technologies based on augmented reality. In: Wang, Y., Martinsen, K., Yu, T., Wang, K. (eds.) IWAMA 2019. LNEE, vol. 634, pp. 275–282. Springer, Singapore (2020). https://doi.org/10.1007/978-981-15-2341-0_34
9. Blattgerste, J., Renner, P., Strenge, B., Pfeiffer, T.: In-situ instructions exceed side-by-side instructions in augmented reality assisted assembly. In: PETRA 2018, pp. 133–140. ACM, New York (2018). https://doi.org/10.1145/3197768.3197778
10. Lamberti, F., Manuri, F., Sanna, A., Paravati, G., Pezzolla, P., Montuschi, P.: Challenges, opportunities, and future trends of emerging techniques for augmented reality-based maintenance. IEEE Trans. Emerg. Top. Comput. (2014). https://doi.org/10.1109/TETC.2014.2368833
11. Kleiber, M., Alexander, T.: Evaluation of a mobile AR tele-maintenance system. In: Stephanidis, C. (ed.) UAHCI 2011. LNCS, vol. 6768, pp. 253–262. Springer, Heidelberg (2011). https://doi.org/10.1007/978-3-642-21657-2_27
12. Mourtzis, D., Vlachou, E., Zogopoulos, V.: Mobile apps for providing product-service systems and retrieving feedback throughout their lifecycle: a robotics use case. Int. J. Prod. Lifecycle Manag. (2018). https://doi.org/10.1504/IJPLM.2018.092821
13. Mourtzis, D., Siatras, V., Angelopoulos, J.: Real-time remote maintenance support based on augmented reality (AR). Appl. Sci. (Switzerland) (2020). https://doi.org/10.3390/app10051855
14. He, C., Song, X., Rao, Y., Wu, C., Zhang, B.: An AR operation and maintenance system for data center. In: 2018 International Conference on Computer Science and Software Engineering (CSSE 2018), pp. 165–177. DEStech Publications, Inc., Lancaster (2018). https://doi.org/10.12783/dtcse/csse2018/24494
15. Fernández del Amo, I., Erkoyuncu, J., Vrabič, R., Frayssinet, R., Vazquez Reynel, C., Roy, R.: Structured authoring for AR-based communication to enhance efficiency in remote diagnosis for complex equipment. Adv. Eng. Inf. (2020). https://doi.org/10.1016/j.aei.2020.101096
16. Mourtzis, D., Zogopoulos, V., Vlachou, E.: Augmented reality application to support remote maintenance as a service in the robotics industry. Procedia CIRP (2017). https://doi.org/10.1016/j.procir.2017.03.154
17. Aleksy, M., Vartiainen, E., Domova, V., Naedele, M.: Augmented reality for improved service delivery. In: Barolli, L., Li, K.F., Enokido, T., Xhafa, F., Takizawa, M. (eds.) IEEE AINA2014. 28th International Conference on Advanced Information Networking and Applications. IEEE (2014). https://doi.org/10.1109/AINA.2014.146
18. Hadar, E., Shtok, J., Cohen, B., Tzur, Y., Karlinsky, L.: Hybrid remote expert - an emerging pattern of industrial remote support. In: Franch, X., Wieringa, R., Ralyte, J., Matulevicius, R., Salinesi, C. (eds.) CEUR Workshop Proceedings. CEUR-WS (2017)
19. Ferrise, F., Caruso, G., Bordegoni, M.: Multimodal training and tele-assistance systems for the maintenance of industrial products. Virtual Phys. Prototyping (2013). https://doi.org/10.1080/17452759.2013.798764
20. Fleck, P., Reyes-Aviles, F., Pirchheim, C., Arth, C., Schmalstieg, D.: Maui: tele-assistance for maintenance of cyber-physical systems. In: Bouatouch, K., Sousa, A.A., Braz, J. (eds.) Proceedings ofthe 15th International Joint Conference on Computer Vision, Imaging and Computer Graphics Theory and Applications. SciTePress, Setúbal (2020)
21. Boulanger, P., Geoganas, N., Zhong, X., Liu, P.: A real-time augmented reality system for industrial tele training. In: El Hakim, S.F., Gruen, A., Walton, J.S. (eds.) Proceedings of SPIE 5013. Videometrics VII. SPIE (2003). https://doi.org/10.1117/12.473350
22. Rapaccini, M., Porcelli, I.: How advances of ICT will impact on service systems and on the delivering of product-related services. In: Prabhu, V., Taisch, M., Kiritsis, D. (eds.) APMS 2013. IAICT, vol. 415, pp. 57–64. Springer, Heidelberg (2013). https://doi.org/10.1007/978-3-642-41263-9_8

23. Bertele, M., Lucke, D., Jooste, J.L.: A framework to establish an assistance system by using reality technology in maintenance. Procedia CIRP (2021). https://doi.org/10.1016/j.procir.2021.11.103
24. Palmarini, R., Erkoyuncu, J.A., Roy, R., Torabmostaedi, H.: A systematic review of augmented reality applications in maintenance. Robot. Comput.-Integrat. Manuf. (2018). https://doi.org/10.1016/j.rcim.2017.06.002
25. vom Brocke, J., et al.: Reconstructing the giant: on the importance of rigour in documenting the literature search process. In: ECIS 2009 Proceedings (2009)
26. Le Chenechal, M., Duval, T., Gouranton, V., Royan, J., Arnaldi, B.: Vishnu: virtual immersive support for HelpiNg users an interaction paradigm for collaborative remote guiding in mixed reality. In: 2016 IEEE Third VR International Workshop on Collaborative Virtual Environments. 3DCVE. IEEE (2016). https://doi.org/10.1109/3DCVE.2016.7563559
27. Aschenbrenner, D., Maltry, N., Kimmel, J., Albert, M., Scharnagl, J., Schilling, K.: ARTab - using virtual and augmented reality methods for an improved situation awareness for telemaintenance. IFAC-PapersOnLine (2016). https://doi.org/10.1016/j.ifacol.2016.11.168
28. Wang, P., et al.: 3DGAM: using 3D gesture and CAD models for training on mixed reality remote collaboration. Multim. Tools Appl. **80**(20), 31059–31084 (2020). https://doi.org/10.1007/s11042-020-09731-7
29. Ong, S.K., Zhu, J.: A novel maintenance system for equipment serviceability improvement. CIRP Ann. Manuf. Technol. (2013). https://doi.org/10.1016/j.cirp.2013.03.091
30. Mourtzis, D., Vlachou, A., Zogopoulos, V.: Cloud-based augmented reality remote maintenance through shop-floor monitoring: a product-service system approach. J. Manuf. Sci. Eng. (2017). https://doi.org/10.1115/1.4035721
31. Fukayama, A., Takamiya, S., Nakagawa, J., Arakawa, N., Kanamaru, N., Uchida, N.: Architecture and prototype of augmented reality videophone service. In: 2011 15th International Conference on Intelligence in Next Generation Networks. IEEE (2011). https://doi.org/10.1109/ICIN.2011.6081108
32. Zhu, J., Nee, A.Y.C., Ong, S.K.: Online authoring for augmented reality remote maintenance. In: Hamza, M.H., Zhang, J.J. (eds.) Proceedings of the 12th IASTED International Conference on Computer Graphics and Imaging, CGIM 2011. ACTA Press, Calgary (2011). https://doi.org/10.2316/P.2011.722-004
33. Nee, A.Y.C., Ong, S.K., Chryssolouris, G., Mourtzis, D.: Augmented reality applications in design and manufacturing. CIRP Ann. Manuf. Technol. (2012). https://doi.org/10.1016/j.cirp.2012.05.010
34. Alavikia, Z., Shabro, M.: Pragmatic industrial augmented reality in electric power industry. In: 34th International Power System Conference. PSC 2019, pp. 25–32. IEEE (2019). https://doi.org/10.1109/PSC49016.2019.9081538
35. Gallala, A., Hichri, B., Plapper, P.: Survey: the evolution of the usage of augmented reality in Industry 4.0. IOP Conf. Ser. Mater. Sci. Eng. (2019). https://doi.org/10.1088/1757-899X/521/1/012017
36. Ifrim, A.-C., Moldoveanu, F., Moldoveanu, A., Morar, A., Butean, A.: Collaborative augmented reality – a survey. In: Roceanu, I. (ed.) eLearning sustainment for never-ending learning. Proceedings of the 16th International Scientific Conference "eLearning and Software for Education". Editura Universitara (2020). https://doi.org/10.12753/2066-026X-20-107
37. Ladwig, P., Geiger, C.: A literature review on collaboration in mixed reality. In: Auer, M.E., Langmann, R. (eds.) REV 2018. LNNS, vol. 47, pp. 591–600. Springer, Cham (2019). https://doi.org/10.1007/978-3-319-95678-7_65
38. Vargas, D., Vijayan, K.K., Mork, O.J.: Augmented reality for future research opportunities and challenges in the shipbuilding industry: a literature review. Procedia Manuf. (2020). https://doi.org/10.1016/j.promfg.2020.04.063

39. Aschenbrenner, D., et al.: Comparing human factors for augmented reality supported single-user and collaborative repair operations of industrial robots. Front. Robot. AI (2019). https://doi.org/10.3389/frobt.2019.00037
40. Masoni, R., et al.: Supporting remote maintenance in Industry 4.0 through augmented reality. Procedia Manuf. (2017). https://doi.org/10.1016/j.promfg.2017.07.257
41. Boulanger, P.: Application of augmented reality to industrial tele-training. In: Proceedings - 1st Canadian Conference on Computer and Robot Vision. IEEE Computer Society, Washington (2004). https://doi.org/10.1109/CCCRV.2004.1301462
42. Rapaccini, M., Porcelli, I., Espíndola, D.B., Pereira, C.E.: Evaluating the use of mobile collaborative augmented reality within field service networks: the case of Océ Italia – Canon Group. Prod. Manuf. Res. (2014). https://doi.org/10.1080/21693277.2014.943430
43. Müller, M., Stegelmeyer, D., Mishra, R.: Introducing a field service platform. In: Ball, A., Gelman, L., Rao, B.K.N. (eds.) Advances in Asset Management and Condition Monitoring. SIST, vol. 166, pp. 195–205. Springer, Cham (2020). https://doi.org/10.1007/978-3-030-57745-2_17
44. Hoppe, A.H., Westerkamp, K., Maier, S., van de Camp, F., Stiefelhagen, R.: Multi-user collaboration on complex data in virtual and augmented reality. In: Stephanidis, C. (ed.) HCI 2018. CCIS, vol. 851, pp. 258–265. Springer, Cham (2018). https://doi.org/10.1007/978-3-319-92279-9_35
45. Choi, S.H., Kim, M., Lee, J.Y.: Situation-dependent remote AR collaborations: image-based collaboration using a 3D perspective map and live video-based collaboration with a synchronized VR mode. Comput. Ind. (2018). https://doi.org/10.1016/j.compind.2018.06.006
46. Bottecchia, S., Cieutat, J.-M., Jessel, J.-P.: T.A.C.: Augmented reality system for collaborative tele-assistance in the field of maintenance through internet. In: ACM International Conference Proceeding Series. 1st Augmented Human International Conference, AH2010. ACM (2010). https://doi.org/10.1145/1785455.1785469
47. Kleiber, M., Alexander, T., Winkelholz, C., Schlick, C.M.: User-centered design and evaluation of an integrated AR-VR system for tele-maintenance. In: 2012 IEEE International Conference on Systems, Man and Cybernetics. IEEE (2012). https://doi.org/10.1109/ICSMC.2012.6377938
48. Schneider, M., Rambach, J., Stricker, D.: Augmented reality based on edge computing using the example of remote live support. In: 2017 IEEE International Conference on Industrial Technology (ICIT), pp. 1277–1282. IEEE (2017). https://doi.org/10.1109/ICIT.2017.7915547
49. Ohlig, S., Stegelmeyer, D., Mishra, R., Müller, M.: Exploring the impacts of using mobile collaborative augmented reality on the field service business model of capital goods manufacturing companies. In: Ball, A., Gelman, L., Rao, B.K.N. (eds.) Advances in Asset Management and Condition Monitoring. SIST, vol. 166, pp. 473–484. Springer, Cham (2020). https://doi.org/10.1007/978-3-030-57745-2_40
50. Kim, J., Lorenz, M., Knopp, S., Klimant, P.: Industrial Augmented Reality: Concepts and User Interface Designs for Augmented Reality Maintenance Worker Support Systems, pp. 67–69 (2020). https://doi.org/10.1109/ISMAR-Adjunct51615.2020.00032
51. Reitmayr, G., Schmalstieg, D.: Mobile collaborative augmented reality. In: IEEE and ACM International Symposium on Augmented Reality, pp. 114–123. IEEE Computer Society, Los Alamitos (2001). https://doi.org/10.1109/ISAR.2001.970521
52. Fang, D., Xu, H., Yang, X., Bian, M.: An augmented reality-based method for remote collaborative real-time assistance: from a system perspective. Mobile Netw. Appl. **25**(2), 412–425 (2019). https://doi.org/10.1007/s11036-019-01244-4
53. Le Chenechal, M., Duval, T., Gouranton, V., Royan, J., Arnaldi, B.: Help! I need a remote guide in my mixed reality collaborative environment. Front. Robot. AI (2019). https://doi.org/10.3389/frobt.2019.00106

54. Plopski, A., Fuvattanasilp, V., Poldi, J., Taketomi, T., Sandor, C., Kato, H.: Efficient in-situ creation of augmented reality tutorials. In: 2018 Workshop on Metrology for Industry 4.0 and IoT. IEEE (2018). https://doi.org/10.1109/METROI4.2018.8428320
55. Rios, H., García, G., Gonzalez, E., Martínez, B.N., Neira, L.: Improving maintenance & troubleshooting process through AR for grinding operations in the tooling industry. In: Hussain, A.I.M. (ed.) Electronics, Communications and Networks IV - Proceedings of the 4th International Conference on Electronics, Communications and Networks. CECNet2014 (2015)
56. Obermair, F., et al.: Maintenance with augmented reality remote support in comparison to paper-based instructions: experiment and analysis. In: 2020 IEEE 7th International Conference on Industrial Engineering and Applications. ICIEA 2020. IEEE (2020). https://doi.org/10.1109/ICIEA49774.2020.9102078
57. Vorraber, W., Gasser, J., Webb, H., Neubacher, D., Url, P.: Assessing augmented reality in production: remote-assisted maintenance with HoloLens. Procedia CIRP (2020). https://doi.org/10.1016/j.procir.2020.05.025
58. Alem, L., Huang, W.: Developing mobile remote collaboration systems for industrial use: some design challenges. In: Campos, P., Graham, N., Jorge, J., Nunes, N., Palanque, P., Winckler, M. (eds.) INTERACT 2011. LNCS, vol. 6949, pp. 442–445. Springer, Heidelberg (2011). https://doi.org/10.1007/978-3-642-23768-3_53
59. Bottecchia, S., Cieutat, J.-M., Merlo, C., Jessel, J.-P.: A new AR interaction paradigm for collaborative teleassistance system: the POA. Int. J. Interact. Des. Manuf. (2009). https://doi.org/10.1007/s12008-008-0051-7
60. De Pace, F., Manuri, F., Sanna, A., Zappia, D.: A comparison between two different approaches for a collaborative mixed-virtual environment in industrial maintenance. Front. Robot. AI (2019). https://doi.org/10.3389/frobt.2019.00018
61. Wang, J., Feng, Y., Zeng, C., Li, S.: An augmented reality based system for remote collaborative maintenance instruction of complex products. IEEE Int. Conf. Automat. Sci. Eng. (2014). https://doi.org/10.1109/CoASE.2014.6899343
62. Oda, O., Elvezio, C., Sukan, M., Feiner, S., Tversky, B.: Virtual replicas for remote assistance in virtual and augmented reality. UIST 2015 - Proceedings of the 28th Annual ACM Symposium on User Interface Software and Technology (2015). https://doi.org/10.1145/2807442.2807497
63. Pierdicca, R., et al.: Augmented reality smart glasses in the workplace: safety and security in the fourth industrial revolution era. In: De Paolis, L.T., Bourdot, P. (eds.) AVR 2020. LNCS, vol. 12243, pp. 231–247. Springer, Cham (2020). https://doi.org/10.1007/978-3-030-58468-9_18
64. Funk, M., Kritzler, M., Michahelles, F.: HoloCollab: a shared virtual platform for physical assembly training using spatially-aware head-mounted displays. ACM Int. Conf. Proc. Ser. (2017). https://doi.org/10.1145/3131542.3131559
65. Woyte, A., Goy, S.: Large grid-connected photovoltaic power plants. In: The Performance of Photovoltaic (PV) Systems, pp. 321–337. Elsevier (2017). https://doi.org/10.1016/B978-1-78242-336-2.00011-2
66. Küssel, R., Liestmann, V., Spiess, M., Stich, V.: "TeleService" a customer-oriented and efficient service? J. Mater. Process. Technol. (2000). https://doi.org/10.1016/S0924-0136(00)00727-5
67. Alexander, T., Ripkens, A., Westhoven, M., Kleiber, M., Pfendler, C.: Virtual tele-cooperation: applying AR and VR for cooperative tele-maintenance and advanced distance learning. In: Andre, T. (ed.) AHFE 2017. AISC, vol. 596, pp. 234–244. Springer, Cham (2018). https://doi.org/10.1007/978-3-319-60018-5_23

68. Mourtzis, D., Vlachou, E., Zogopoulos, V., Fotini, X.: Integrated production and maintenance scheduling through machine monitoring and augmented reality: an Industry 4.0 approach. In: Lödding, H., Riedel, R., Thoben, K.-D., von Cieminski, G., Kiritsis, D. (eds.) APMS 2017. IAICT, vol. 513, pp. 354–362. Springer, Cham (2017). https://doi.org/10.1007/978-3-319-66923-6_42
69. Baines, T.S., et al.: State-of-the-art in product-service systems. Proc. Inst. Mech. Eng. B: J. Eng. Manuf. (2007). https://doi.org/10.1243/09544054JEM858
70. Meier, H., Roy, R., Seliger, G.: Industrial product-service systems—IPS 2. CIRP Ann. Manuf. Technol. (2010). https://doi.org/10.1016/j.cirp.2010.05.004
71. Mastrogiacomo, L., Barravecchia, F., Franceschini, F.: A worldwide survey on manufacturing servitization. Int. J. Adv. Manuf. Technol. **103**(9–12), 3927–3942 (2019). https://doi.org/10.1007/s00170-019-03740-z
72. Neely, A.: Servitization in Germany: An International Comparison (2013). https://cambridgeservicealliance.eng.cam.ac.uk/system/files/documents/2013November_ServitizationinGermany.pdf
73. Li, D., Mattsson, S., Fast-Berglund, Å., Åkerman, M.: Testing operator support tools for a global production strategy. Procedia CIRP (2016). https://doi.org/10.1016/j.procir.2016.02.089
74. Zenati-Henda, N., Bellarbi, A., Benbelkacem, S., Belhocine, M.: Augmented reality system based on hand gestures for remote maintenance. In: Proceedings of 2014 International Conference on Multimedia Computing and Systems (ICMCS), pp. 5–8. IEEE Computer Society (2014). https://doi.org/10.1109/ICMCS.2014.6911258
75. de Bonnefoy, N., Moussa, W.A., Jessel, J.-P.: Intuitive and adaptive mixed reality system to support nomadic maintenance collaborative activities. In: 2007 IEEE International Technology Management Conference (ITMC) (2007)
76. Gautier, G., et al.: Collaborative workspace for aircraft maintenance. In: Proceedings of 3rd International Conference on Virtual and Rapid Manufacturing. Advanced Research in Virtual and Rapid Prototyping 2007, pp. 689–693 (2007)
77. Aschenbrenner, D., et al.: Comparing different augmented reality support applications for cooperative repair of an industrial robot. In: 2018 IEEE International Symposium on Mixed and Augmented Reality Adjunct (ISMAR-Adjunct), pp. 69–74. IEEE (2018). https://doi.org/10.1109/ISMAR-Adjunct.2018.00036
78. Leutert, F., Schilling, K.: Projector-based augmented reality for telemaintenance support. IFAC-PapersOnLine (2018). https://doi.org/10.1016/j.ifacol.2018.08.368
79. Sittner, F., Aschenbrenner, D., Fritscher, M., Kheirkhah, A., Krauß, M., Schilling, K.: Maintenance and telematics for robots (MainTelRob). In: IFAC Proceedings Volumes (IFAC-PapersOnline) (2013). https://doi.org/10.3182/20131111-3-KR-2043.00010
80. Utzig, S., Kaps, R., Azeem, S.M., Gerndt, A.: Augmented reality for remote collaboration in aircraft maintenance tasks. In: 2019 IEEE Conference on Aerospace. IEEE Computer Society (2019). https://doi.org/10.1109/AERO.2019.8742228
81. Agrawal, M., Eloot, K., Mancini, M., Patel, A.: Industry 4.0. In: Reimagining Manufacturing Operations after COVID-19. McKinsey & Company (2020)
82. Cavaleri, J., Tolentino, R., Swales, B., Kirschbaum, L.: Remote video collaboration during COVID-19. In: 2021 32nd Annual SEMI Advanced Semiconductor Manufacturing Conference (ASMC) 10–12 May 2021, pp. 177–182. IEEE, Piscataway (2021). https://doi.org/10.1109/ASMC51741.2021.9435703
83. Li, X., Voorneveld, M., de Koster, R.: Business transformation in an age of turbulence – lessons learned from COVID-19. Technol. Forecast. Soc. Change (2022). https://doi.org/10.1016/j.techfore.2021.121452

Virtual Teleoperation Setup for a Bimanual Bartending Robot

Sara Buonocore(✉), Stanislao Grazioso, and Giuseppe Di Gironimo

Department of Industrial Engineering, University of Naples Federico II, Piazzale Vincenzo Tecchio, 80, 80125 Napoli, Italy
sara.buonocore2@studenti.unina.it

Abstract. This paper presents the preliminary design of a teleoperation system for a bimanual bartending robot, with reference to the BRILLO (Bartending Robot for Interactive Long Lasting Operations) project. The aim is to simulate the remote control of the robotic bartender by the human operator in an intuitive manner, using Virtual Reality technologies. The proposed Virtual Reality architecture is based on the use of commercial Head Mounted Display with a pair of hand controllers and the virtual simulation of the remote environment of the robot, with the robotic simulator CoppeliaSim. Originally, virtual simulations of the robot environment have allowed to identify the possible scenarios and interactions between the customers and the different robotic systems inside the automatized bar: the totem for the selection and payment of the order, the robotic bartender to prepare the cocktail and the mobile robot for the cocktail serving at the table. Secondly, focusing on a sequence of main tasks that the robotic bartender must perform for the cocktails preparation, the operator's control on the simulated robotic system has been reproduced. In fact, the aim of this first experimental phase is to test the interaction between the human operator and the simulated immersive environment for the remote control of the robotic system. Two use cases have been reproduced: the first is related to the recovery from a failure situation such as the fall of a glass, while the second refers to the trajectory training to perform some repeating actions. Six operators (three males and three females), who already knew the taks, with an age between 25 and 40 years and a minimum experience with VR technology for personal entertainment, have been involved in the test phase. For this reason, the paper will finally discuss the perception of the involved operators about the use of the proposed VR architecture in terms of usability and mental workload.

Keywords: Virtual Reality · Teleoperation · Remote control · CoppeliaSim · HTC VIVE Pro

L. T. De Paolis et al. (Eds.): XR Salento 2022, LNCS 13446, pp. 306–325, 2022.
https://doi.org/10.1007/978-3-031-15553-6_22

1 Introduction

A robotic teleoperation system has the aim of enabling the operator's remote control on the robot. The need of developing teleoperated systems is pushed by the fact that in some applications, as in unknown environments, building a completely autonomous robot would be complex or even not feasible. In these scenarios, a teleoperation system is more convenient, as the robot itself can be directly controlled and supervised by a human operator in the execution of a task.

During the last two decades, the use of Virtual Reality (VR) technology, which was originally limited to entertainment, is increasingly spreading also in the industrial field [1]. The combined use of Virtual Reality and robotic teleoperation allows the human operator to be immersed in a 3D virtual world and to perform a complex task interacting with a digital twin of the robotic system, while receiving visual and (eventually) haptic/cutaneous feedback from the environment [2]. The VR teleoperation provides the operator with a sense of depth and immersion and allows to explore the scenario recreated on the computer from the inside and to move within it without constraints. The use of controllers with position and orientation tracking offer a more natural and intuitive interaction with 3D objects than the one that can be provided by keyboard and mouse [3,4].

In this paper we describe the use of Virtual Reality technology within a teleoperation framework for a bimanual bartender robotic system. Virtual simulation have been conducted to reproduce the possible scenarios and evaluate the different interactions of the customer with three different robotic systems: a totem for the selection of the cocktail and payment, the bimanual bartender for the preparation of the cocktail and the mobile robot for the orders serving.
The proposed VR architecture is based on an immersive Head Mounted Display (HMD) with a pair of hand controller and the robotic simulator CoppeliaSim, aiming to allow the human operator to perform manipulation tasks which are typical of a bar scenario, through a remotely teleoperated virtual bimanual bartending robot. In particular, two use cases have been reproduced: in the first one, the remote control for the recovery from a failure situation such as the fall of a glass is simulated; in the second one, the operator teaches the robot a given task, to train the trajectories for an autonomous operation.

In the light of this, the present work describes in the second chapter the state of the art about the most used Virtual Reality devices and evaluation metrics for teleoperation systems, further to a comparison between the most common simulators for robotic applications. The third chapter is dedicated to simulations of BRILLO use cases, related to the interactions between the user and some elements of the scenario. The fourth and fifth chapter address respectively the software/hardware architecture adopted for the implementation of the remote control system and the experiments with related results about the defined use cases of teleoperation. Six operators (three males and three females) aged between 25 and 40 have been involved in the test phase, to evaluate their perception about the use of the proposed VR architecture in terms of usability and mental workload. Finally, the last chapter is devoted to conclusions and future developments.

2 State-of-the-Art

In this section we present an overview of the state-of-the-art related to: (i) teleoperation systems in Virtual Reality; (ii) input devices and tracking systems for virtual reality and teleoperation; (iii) simulators classically used for robotic systems.

Virtual Reality Teleoperation Architecture. In the robotics field and beyond [5], the use digital twins [6] is a common trend of the last years. By using robotic digital twins, the realization of a real system can be anticipated by the design and programming of the robot and environment in a simulated scenario. Later, the robotic digital twins can also be used during the teleoperation.

Typically, Virtual teleoperation systems can be divided into two parts, a local (master) and a remote (slave) part that communicate via a communication channel [7]. In the first part we find the operator and the devices used for interacting and giving commands to the virtual teleoperated system. The second part of the framework instead includes the virtual robot that receives commands and acts within the simulation environment.

Virtual Reality Teleoperation Applications. Whitney et al. in [8] have teleoperated the Baxter robot to grab objects and stack them on top of each other. Baxter robot is used in many teleoperation applications, as it is an easily available robot and it is human–like. In [9], the master side is not represented by a human operator but by a Franka Emika Panda robot identical to the slave robot. In [10], the operator remotely controls the mobile robot Pioneer P3AT movements via a graphical human-robot communication interface, with the help of an intermediary client PC.

Due to the high degree of interaction with the user, teleoperation systems are often designed according to the needs and tasks to be performed. In particular, it is possible to define a level of autonomy of the robot, in order to have teleoperation systems in which the robot is completely teleoperated and others in which only some degrees of freedom are teleoperated, as done by Mohsen et al. in [11] where only the links along axis 1 and 2 of a SCARA robot are controlled.

The most common simulated tasks in VR teleoperation are pick and place tasks as in [12] but also tasks that simulate surgical operations as in [13].

Virtual Reality Teleoperation Evaluation. A teleoperation system must be intuitive, simple and pleasant to use for the operator. The evaluation is based on: performance measures or objective workload, physiological measures (postural or bio-mechanical analysis, heart rate variability, direction of pupil gaze) and subjective measures (such as Instantaneous Self Assessment (ISA), the Bedford

Rating Scale (BFRS)). In [8], the effectiveness of the teleoperation system is measured by monitoring how many times the user completes the task correctly and the time spent doing it. In [14], in addition to the objective measurements, carried out by measuring the time taken to perform a task and the percentage of errors committed by the operator, subjective measurements are also carried out, subjecting the participants to a questionnaire to evaluate the experience of teleoperation. The most used questionnaires are the System Usability Scale (SUS) Questionnaire, which measures the usability of the system and the NASA Task Load Index (TLX) Questionnaire, which measures the workload by making a weighted average (Eq. 1) between different factors such as Mental Demand, Physics, Temporal Demand, Performance, Effort and Frustration [4].

Input Devices and Tracking Systems. Classical systems used as input devices for teleoperation and navigation within virtual environments are keyboard and mouses. There are few applications in which the teleoperation is performed with mouse and keyboard through dedicated interfaces, such as in [15], where the operator remotely grasp objects through a robotic system, modifying the position and orientation of the end effector through an interface point and click. However, such systems do not provide an engaging operator experience.

To provide the operator with a sense of immersion in the virtual environment, the involvement of as many senses as possible is necessary. The most important are sight and touch. Head Mounted Displays (such as HTC VIVE and Oculus Rift [16]) are wearable helmets, generally combined with a pair of hand controllers, that allow the operator to view the 3D environment reproduced on the computer, giving the feeling of being part of the scenario. Since their usage is limited to simple tasks such as opening and closing of the gripper, gloves (such as Manus VR [17], VRFree Glove [18]) are introduced to substitute the controllers to perform more complex manipulation tasks [19,20] but show significant difficulties in the calibration process. Manus VR, from this point of view, is not very precise, especially for the estimation of the position of the thumb, making it unsuitable for right-hand manipulations and more suitable for recognizing simple movements [21]. LEAP Motion Controller [22] is another very intuitive tracking device. Indeed, it tracks the movements of the operator's bare hand so the user can teleoperate a robot without using a joystick or glove. However, its lack of accuracy and not reproducibility of the measurements make it difficult to use this device in effective applications. Jang et al. in [23] through Leap Motion have controlled the Robotiq gripper and the position and orientation of the Ur5 end effector through the movement of the hand.

Simulators. Simulation software is a safe and cost-effective tool for validating complex systems, platforms or prototypes. The use of simulators, in fact, brings with it some advantages such as lower development costs, lower risk of accidents and damage to things and people. For this reason, software and virtual reality are increasingly used also in the industrial field and beyond.

	CoppeliaSim	Gazebo	Unity
Physics Engine	- Bullet - ODE - Vortex - Newton	- Bullet - ODE - Sim-body - Dart	- PhysX
Supported Languages	- remote API - ROS nodes - BlueZero nodes - Plugins - Add-ons - Embedded Scripts	- Plugins C++ - API C++	- C#
Utility and Usability	- High	- Medium	- Low
VR Compatibility	- VR devices (HTC Vive and Oculus Rift)	- VR/AR devices (HTC Vive, Oculus Rift, Microsoft HoloLens, Gear VR...)	- VR/AR devices (HTC Vive, Oculus Rift, Microsoft HoloLens, Gear VR...)

Fig. 1. Comparison among CoppeliaSim, Gazebo and Unity.

Currently there are several robotic simulators available: CoppeliaSim, Gazebo, OpenHRP [24], Unity [25], Webots, SimSpark. Among these, the most used are CoppeliaSim, Gazebo and Unity, followed by Webots and ARgOS.

Depending on the application, it may be more convenient to use one simulator rather than another. Figure 1 shows the comparison about supported physics engines, supported languages, usability and VR compatibility between the first three software that, according to the literature, are most used.

As can be seen from Fig. 1, CoppeliaSim turns out to be the most suitable software for robotic simulation than Gazebo or Unity. The results obtainable with CoppeliaSim can also be obtained with the others two software but are more complex for algorithm development, interfacing with other software and object modeling. Gazebo offers a limited choice for modeling and editing of the scene, presenting some limitations for meshes modeling that cannot be optimized and for this reason it may require the support of external software. CoppeliaSim, on the other hand, allows to import, modify and simplify the meshes within the simulator and also has an intuitive and user-friendly interface.

3 Virtual Simulations for the Identification of the Possible Scenarios and Use Cases

This section illustrates the virtual simulations of the automized bar within CoppeliaSim software to identify the possible scenarios and customer interactions with the different robotic systems. These simulations have been propaedeutic to the development of the teleoperation framework.

CoppeliaSim is a 3D robot simulation software developed by Coppelia Robotics, with an integrated development environment, that allows to model, edit, program and simulate any robot or robotic system. It offers a multitude of functionality that can be integrated and combined through an exhaustive

API and script functionality. CoppeliaSim supports two different physics engines (Bullet and ODE), the handling of inverse/forward kinematics of any type of mechanism, the simulation of proximity and cameras sensors, path planning.

Each object/model can be controlled through an embedded script. Controllers can be written in C/C++, Python, Java, Lua, Matlab, Octave or Urbi. The Lua [26] script interpreter is embedded in CoppeliaSim, and extended with specific commands. CoppeliaSim scripts are the main control mechanism for a simulation. Each scene has a non-threaded main-script that manages all the functions of the simulator and child scripts that can be associated with each object and manage a specific part of the simulation.

CoppeliaSim uses IK groups and IK elements to solve inverse and forward kinematics tasks. A human operator wears a commercial headset (Vive Pro, HTC, Taiwan) whose position/orientation corresponds to the position/orientation of the head of the virtual bimanual robot. Each arm of the robot consists of a KUKA LBR iiwa 14 R820 [27]. The human teleoperates the robotic system in inverse kinematics mode, as the position/orientation of each hand controller corresponds to the position/orientation of the two end effectors of the robot. The virtual scenario is recreated in CoppeliaSim (Coppelia Robotics AG, Zurich, Switzerland), where the 3D models of the robot and environment are imported.

3.1 The Implementation of Virtual Simulations

Step 1: Import the 3D Models and Reduce the Geometry Complexity. The first action to construct the virtual simulation is the import of 3D models within CoppeliaSim, starting from the robotic bartender. It is necessary to outline that each created link is made up of two shapes, of which only one is visible during the simulation. Fact, a simplified and dynamic copy of each imported shape has been created as dynamic model that the CoppeliaSim physical engine will use to simulate the robot's behaviour. This shapes' visibility is turned on only during the construction of the virtual environment, with the aim of reducing the computational burden required to work on complex shapes. On the other side, these latter are employed as pure visualization shapes, to confer a higher quality of rendering and realism to the simulation.

Another strategy adopted to reduce the complexity of the imported 3D models, also employed for the import of the selected gripper (Shunk EGL 90 PN) is the use of CoppeliaSim Decimate mesh function, which allows to reduce the number of triangles that compose the mesh. This technique is illustrated in Fig. 2 for the KUKA LBR iiwa 14 R820 robot.

Step 2: Create the Tip-Target Relationship. After importing and modifying the model of the robot and the gripper, the CoppeliaSim Inverse Kinematics module has been employed for the creation of the robot's kinematic chain. In particular: the joints have been enabled in "IK mode" and the Target pose has been created and the respective Tip has been added to the end effector. Secondly, the necessary limits on each joint have been introduced to simulate a realistic robot's behaviour. At this point, the robot's trajectory planning to make the Tip reach

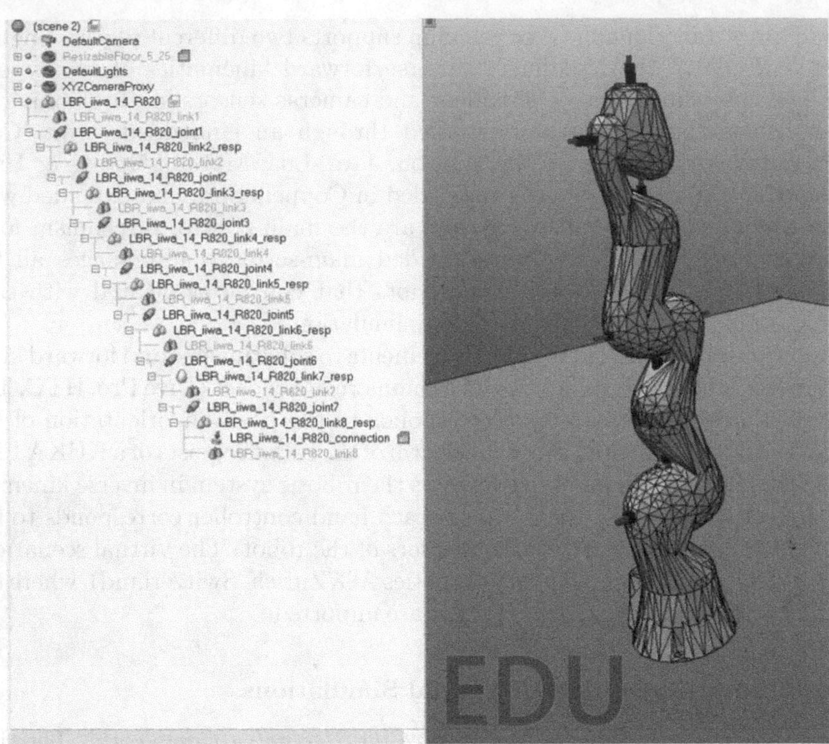

Fig. 2. Hierarchy scene of the LBR iiwa 14 R820 robot imported into CoppeliaSim. The robot is divided into seven shapes and the joints are positioned to move the robot appropriately

the Target pose has been defined via script and associated to the respective objects in the hierarchy.

Step 3: Create the Bar Environment. At this point, the bartender scenario has been created in CoppeliaSim (Fig. 3), importing 3D models of the bartender. Most of the objects were imported as ".stl" files from CATIA V5 software, following the same steps previously described.

Further to the bimanual bartender in charge of preparing the required cocktail, in the perspective of a fully-automated bar, an additional robotic system for the selection, payment and eventual service of the order to the table was necessary. For this reason, a totem for creating, modifying and paying the order and a mobile robot that serves the customers directly at the table were included. Figure 4 shows the final configuration of virtual representation of the automated bar within CoppeliaSim. The displayed dummies were already provided by CoppeliaSim 3D models database. Vision sensors have been added for the customer recognition in every robotic site: totem, bartender, mobile robot. In addition, the CoppeliaSim XML Plugin has been used to create, through scripting, the

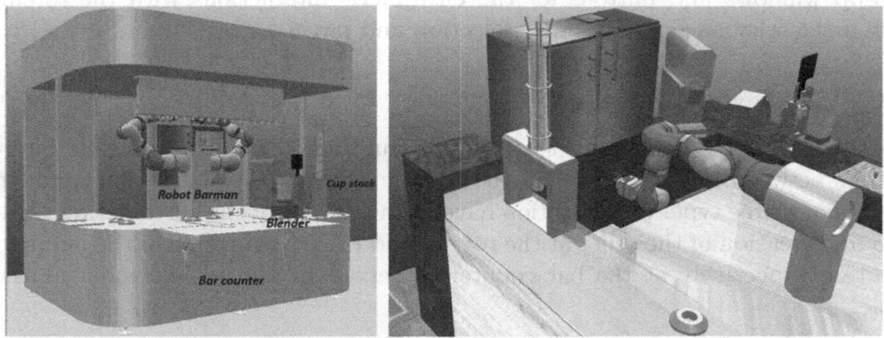

Fig. 3. The scenario recreated in CoppeliaSim: the bartender robot consists of two KUKA lbr 14 R820 and two Schunk EGL 90 PN grippers.

Fig. 4. Top and side view of the scenario reconstructed in CoppeliaSim

pop-up windows and buttons for the customer's interactions with the totem, such as identity recognition, order selection and payment.

3.2 The Customer Journey

Starting from this configuration of all the automated bar, the possible interactions between the customer and the robotic systems have been simulated. In particular, three types of interaction have been addressed: the customer registration and creation of the order at the totem, and the consumption of the required cocktail respectively at the bar counter or served by the mobile robot at the table.

Interaction 1: Customer-Totem. Registration and Order Selection. The customer enters the bar and goes to the totem to select the order. As illustrated in Fig. 5, the totem firstly asks for the recognition or registration of the customer, having at disposition a database of registered users with name and surname, email, telephone and other info. In case of a new customer, the registration is necessary to proceed. Secondly, it is possible to insert the order and pay for it. At this point, the customer can choose to consume the cocktail at the bar counter or at the table: these two situations have been addressed separately.

Interaction 2: Customer-Robotic Bartender. Consumption of the Cocktail at the Bar Counter. The customer goes to the bar counter and, after the recognition process, decides to confirm or modify the order; consequently, the robotic bartender proceeds to prepare the cocktail (Fig. 6). After the consumption, the customer leaves the bar.

Interaction 3: Customer-Mobile Robot. Consumption of the Cocktail at the Table. Alternatively to the previous case, the customer may prefer to consume the cocktail comfortably at the table, without any direct interaction with the robotic bartender. The customer, in fact, after having concluded the order request at the totem, is free to confirm or modify it at the table through the mobile robot, further to the possibility of paying the bill. In case of confirm, when the cocktail is ready, the mobile robot serves the customer at the table.

3.3 Identification of the Robotic Bartender's Tasks

Consistently with the identified scenarios and possible requests by the customer, some common tasks to be performed by the bimanual robotic system have been outlined. The Fig. 7 illustrates the succession of fundamental actions that the robot must perform to prepare a cocktail in general, such as: open the fridge, switch on and off the blender and pour its content into a glass.

The simulation within the software CoppeliaSim allowed to virtualize and visualize the tasks for the evaluation of the robot's movements feasibility. In fact, the simulation has demonstrated that all the listed actions are feasible for the robot with respect to its encumbrance and kinematic configuration, without detecting any unwanted collision.

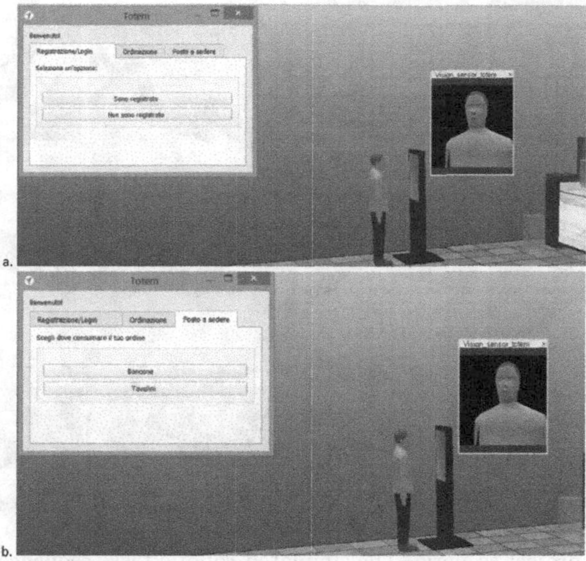

Fig. 5. a. The customer enters the bar and goes to the totem. The vision sensor scans the customer, who will log-in or register on the platform. Then, the customer proceeds to the order selection; b. The customer pays for the order and decides to consume it at the bar counter or at the table.

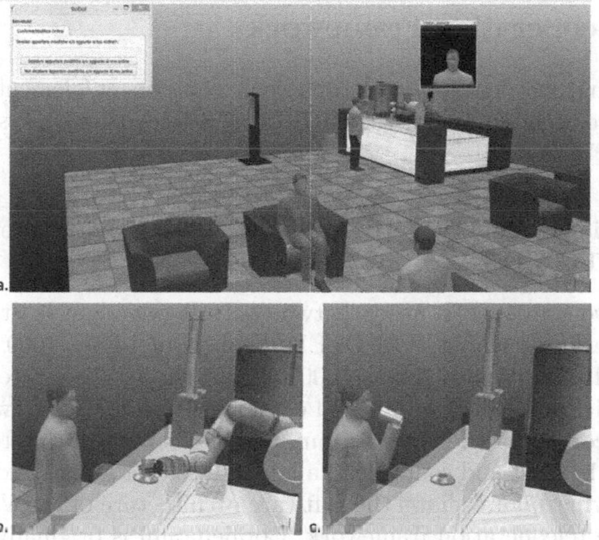

Fig. 6. a. The customer goes to the bar counter. The vision sensor recognises the customer; b. The robotic bartender prepares the cocktail; c. The customer consumes the cocktail, then leaves the bar.

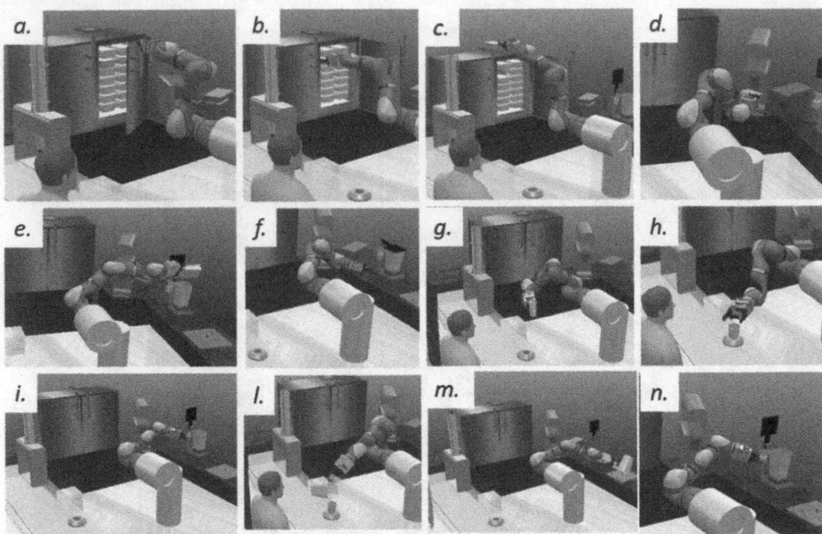

Fig. 7. BRILLO project scenario. The simulated robot's tasks sequence consists in: a. open the freezer; b. take a box; c. place the box on a support on the top of the freezer; d. close the freezer and take the box under the juice dispenser; e. pour the content of the box; f. switch on the blender; g. take a glass; h. put the glass on the bar counter grab the blender; l. pour its content into the glass; m. wash the blender; n. put the blender back in its place.

4 VR Teleoperation Framework

In the following, we describe in details each component/element of the Software/Hardware architecture for the BRILLO VR teleoperation system, which is illustrated in Fig. 8.

4.1 CoppeliaSim and VR Toolbox: An Immersive Experience with HTC VIVE Pro System

HTC VIVE Pro consists of a headset, two controllers and, at least, two infrared camera. The headset mounts two OLED displays of 1400×1600 pixels at 615 ppi, for a total resolution of 2800×1600 pixels with a refresh rate 90 Hz, which avoids cyber-sickness. The two infrared cameras (Base Stations), which must be placed in the corners of the virtual room, emit invisible light intercepted by the sensors on the headset and controllers, allowing the user's head and hands tracking. The following Figure shows the software architecture of the Virtual Reality system for the teleoperation framework. CoppeliaSim is originally designed for a desktop interaction. Despite this, it is possible to visualize in immersive mode the scenario previously developed in CoppeliaSim desktop mode thanks to the VR toolbox [28] from Bogaerts et al. [29] was used. This interface, compatible with HTC Vive, contains an application that visualizes the CoppeliaSim scene

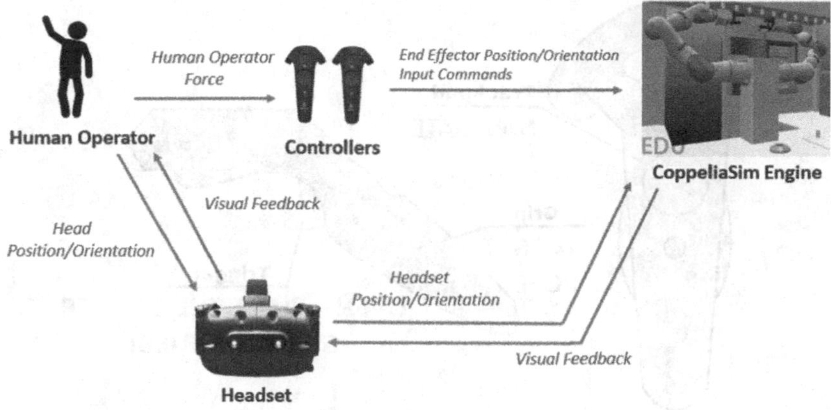

Fig. 8. system architecture.

in openVR compatible devices, and returns user interactions. The VR Toolbox links CoppeliaSim to the Visualization Toolkit (VTK) and allows to return the actions performed by the operator through the devices and to provide visual feedback to the operator.

4.2 User's Interaction

With the aim of enabling the interaction of the user within the virtual environment via VIVE controller, the following main actions have been implemented and then associated to a specific button of the controller, in the so-called "binding operation" (Fig. 9):

- navigate within the immersive environment;
- command a Target pose for the robot;
- open and close the gripper;
- grasp, move and release an object.

First of all, further to the possibility of physically walking inside the "play area", which reflects in a walk within the virtual environment, a navigation mode for wider movements is necessary. For this reason, the user is also able to walk only inside the virtual environment, staying still in the "play area", by touching the trackpad. By scrolling up or down on the trackpad, is possible to move quickly forward or backward in the virtual environment.

The controller's grip button is employed to command a Target pose to the robot's end effector. Once it is pressed, the target of the end effector becomes the child of the controller (and the controller itself becomes the further object). Therefore, when the operators moves the hand, the movement of the controller causes the respective movement of the target. The tip object, which is in the

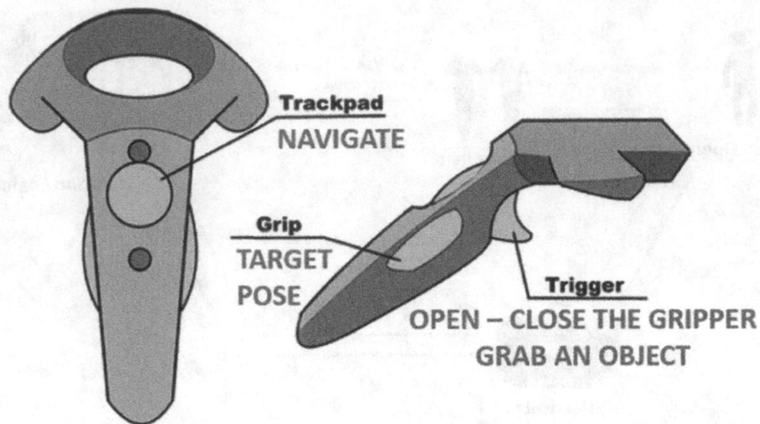

Fig. 9. Vive Controllers' bindings for user's interaction within CoppeliaSim immersive environment.

robot's end effector, will move to reach the target pose, making the robot move in inverse kinematics.

The opening and closing of the virtual gripper, instead, are associated respectively with the pressure and the release of the trigger button.

For manipulating objects present in the scenario, since the physic engine offered by CoppeliaSim is not accurate in replicating the friction, the grip of the objects was little stable and precise. To ensure a stable grip, proximity sensors were placed in correspondence with the objects to be grasped. To obtain a more stable grip, two conditions must occur simultaneously: if the sensor detects the gripper and the trigger button is pressed, the object to be grasped becomes a child of the gripper (parent object). By releasing the trigger button, however, the gripper opens and the gripped object falls.

5 Tests and Results

In this section we report the experimental setup, the performed experiments and the achieved results about an effective use of the simulated scenario within CoppeliaSim for the teleoperation purpose. Two use cases were selected to evaluate the effective contribute of Virtual simulation to the teleoperation framework, requiring the operator to conduct the defined tasks, immersed within the virtual environment.

5.1 Use Cases

Use Case 1: Remote Control of the Bimanual Robot for Recovery from a Failure Situation. This use case is referred to what could happen if an unexpected situation occurs. The operator can help the robot to manage a new unexpected task remotely through teleoperation. In particular, we have chosen to simulate the case in which the robot on the left, after having grabbed the cup, drops it in a point of the counter that it cannot reach. Therefore, the operator locates the fallen cup and teleoperates the other robotic arm to grab and reposition the cup in the correct position, re-establishing a configuration that allows the interrupted task to continue.

Use Case 2: Remote Control of the Bimanual Robot for Trajectory Training. The technique that is most used to teach the robot a trajectory is the kinesthetic teaching, in which the operator physically moves the robot from one point to another in the operating space. This technique cannot be put into practice if the operator is not close to the robot or where the workspace doesn't allow the operator to move it easily. In these cases, teleoperation is a valid alternative.

For this use case, we have chosen to simulate the tasks related to gripping the blender jug, pouring its contents into the glass, washing and repositioning the jug in its starting point.

5.2 Experiments

The experimental setup is shown in Fig. 10, comprising all the components described in Sect. 4. It was recreated in the MARTE laboratory at CESMA Center, University of Naples Federico II.

The aim of these experiments was to evaluate specifically the designed VR architecture's usability and the required users' mental workload, aiming to reduce the presence of disturbance factors. For this reason, six mixed participants in term of genre (three males and three females respectively), who already knew the simulated tasks, have been involved in the experiments. In addition, their age is in the range of 25–40 years, and all of them has a basic experience of Virtual Reality technology, even if only for personal entertainment.

Figure 11 and Fig. 12 show the principal frames of the experiments relative to use case 1 and 2. As can be seen in the Fig. 12, the operator controls the simulated robot to teach the trajectory, which is subsequently reproduced by the robot autonomously.

For the evaluation of the VR teleoperation system, two questionnaires have been used, in order to evaluate both the usability and the workload provided by the system. These questionnaires were submitted after the execution of the tasks relating only to use case 1, as the tasks of use case 2 are already included in the previous one. Furthermore, use case 1 is more significant as it is more demanding from the point of view of the duration and complexity of the manipulation.

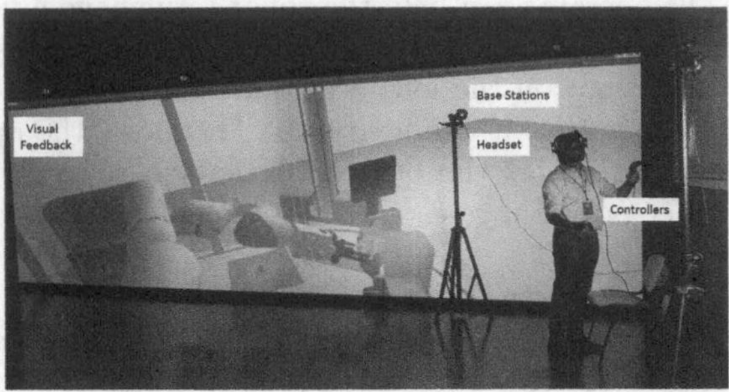

Fig. 10. The experimental setup in the MARTE laboratory. The operator is controlling the simulated robot to grasp the jug, using the hand controllers. The visual feedback is also displayed in the background screen.

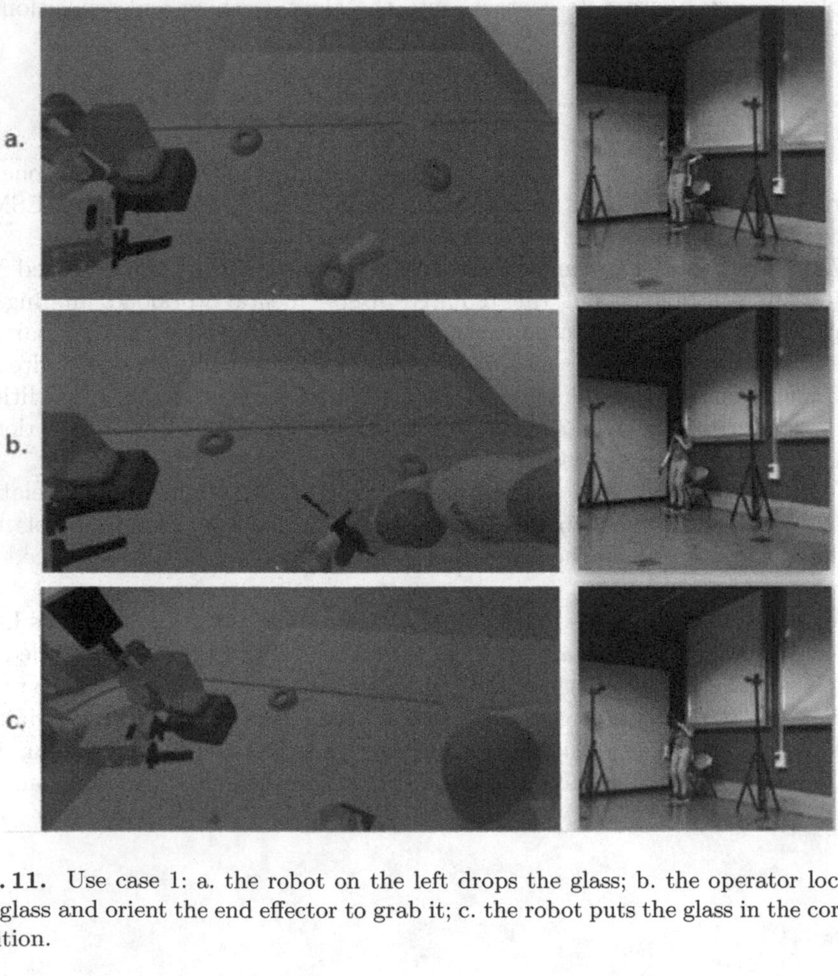

Fig. 11. Use case 1: a. the robot on the left drops the glass; b. the operator locates the glass and orient the end effector to grab it; c. the robot puts the glass in the correct position.

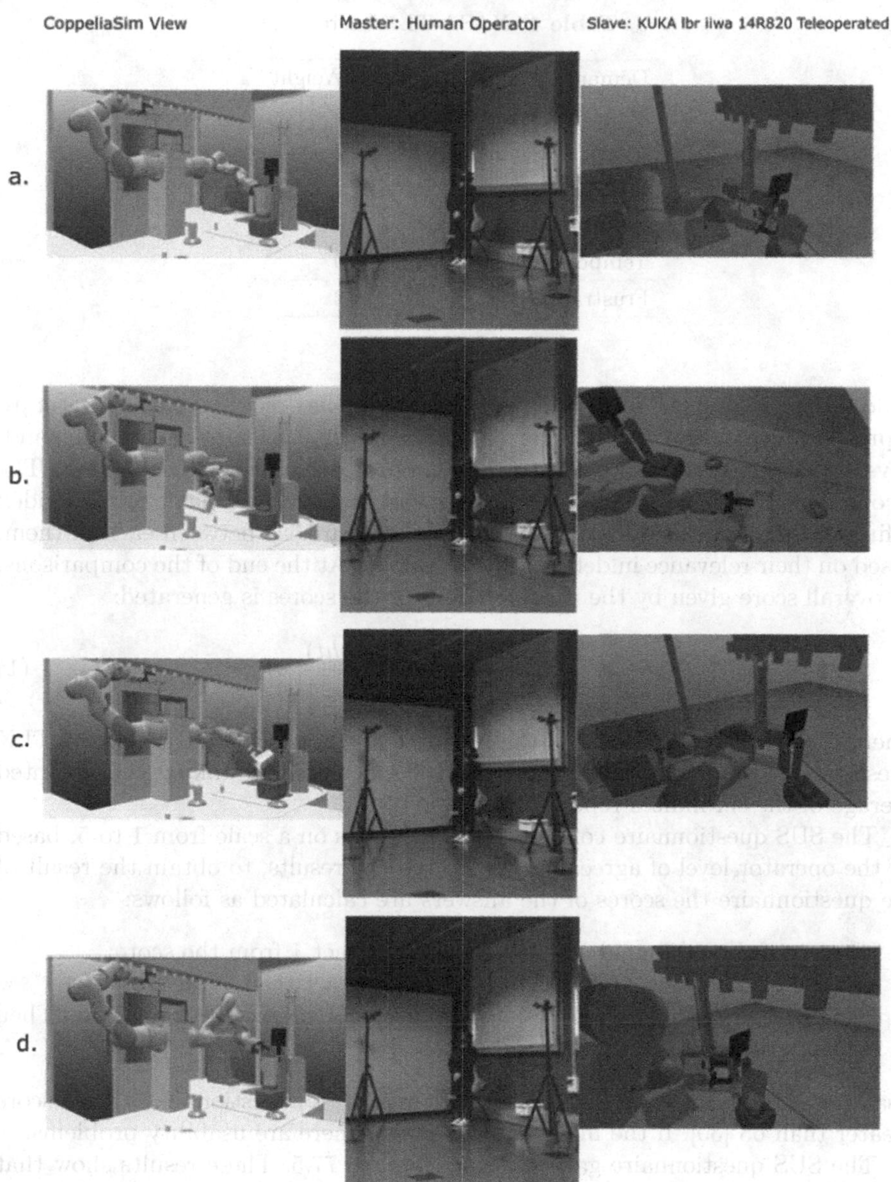

Fig. 12. Use case 2: a. grabbing blender; b. pouring in the glass; c. blender cleaning; d. blender positioning.

5.3 Result and Discussion

The NASA Task Load Index (NASA TLX) is a multidimensional tool measure of the mental workload which, on this scale, is defined like the cost that a human operator has to pay to reach a specific level of performance. The NASA Task

Table 1. NASA-TLX score.

Demand	Rating	Weight
Mental demand	50	5
Physical demand	31	2
Effort	6	2
Performance	6	5
Temporal demand	1	0
Frustration	1	2

Load Index is divided into two parts: the first one requires the operator to express an evaluation by replying to six items that refer to mental demand, physical demand, effort, performance, temporal demand and frustration. The second part of the questionnaire intends to assign a relative weight to each index defined by making the operator do pairwise comparisons between each of them, based on their relevance in defining the workload. At the end of the comparisons, an overall score given by the weighted sum of the scores is generated:

$$\alpha = \sum \frac{(Rating \cdot Weight)}{\sum Weight} \tag{1}$$

where α is the Overall Rating, β the Rating and γ the Weight. The NASA-TLX questionnaire gave a result equal to 25/100 calculated by taking the weighted average of the six indices reported in Table 1.

The SUS questionnaire consists of 10 questions on a scale from 1 to 5, based on the operator level of agreement. Collected the results, to obtain the result of the questionnaire the scores of the answers are calculated as follows:

- for each of the odd numbered questions, subtract 1 from the score;
- for each of the even numbered questions, subtract their value from 5;
- take these new values which you have found, and add up the total score. Then multiply this by 2.5.

Usability is to be considered valid if the average of the questionnaires has a score greater than 68 [30]. If the mean is lower, then, there are usability problems.

The SUS questionnaire gave a result equal to 77.5. These results show that the operator is not only subjected to a low workload, which does not require particular cognitive or ergonomic efforts, but, by comparing the result obtained in the SUS with the scale in Table 2, it appears that the system has a good degree of usability. Therefore, it has been demonstrated that the operator does not consider the proposed teleoperation system difficult-to-use and evaluates its pleasant experience to the point of not excluding a more frequent use.

Table 2. SUS score.

SUS score	Grade	Adjective rating
>80.3	A	Excellent
68–80.3	B	Good
68	C	Okay
51–68	D	Poor
<51	E	Awful

6 Conclusions and Future Works

In this work, a first design review of the teleoperation framework for the BRILLO project has been conducted. Thanks to the adoption of Virtual Reality technology, without the aid of any physical prototype, it has been possible to evaluate the possible scenarios with the specific request of the customers and the main tasks that the bimanual bartender should carry out. Secondly, the virtual simulations inside CoppeliaSim in immersive mode have allowed to verify the feasibility of the remote control of the defined tasks with reference to the overall system encumbrance and usability of the VR architecture.

The remote control on the simulated system has been tested and validated on two use cases: the recovery from a failure situation such as the fall of a glass and the teaching of the tasks related to the blender to the robot. Three male and three female operators with a basic experience of VR devices have been involved in the test phase. It has resulted that the use of such devices is easy and intuitive: the tasks were completed within a reasonable time without causing neither particular cognitive and muscular efforts or long-term fatigue after several consecutive hours of use in the development phase.

It must be outlined that the selected operators already had experience of the tasks and a basic knowledge of the employed VR devices before the start of the test phase: therefore, a preliminary training stage was not necessary in this case. Anyway, in general, an introduction for the user's familiarization with such complex manipulation tasks, especially for a first time interaction, must be planned.

After the experimental phase, as done in [14] and [9], two questionnaires have been subjected to the operators, to evaluate the usability of the system with respect to the tasks performed and the required mental workload. It can be said that the positive results obtained in this work pave the way to graft the developed Virtual teleoperation framework with the real system setup, focusing on two main criticalities: the real-virtual objects' mapping and the latency in communication between the robot and the remote operator site. In fact, deep studies are already in progress to confirm (or not) CoppeliaSim software's suitability to communicate with well-structured frameworks for robotic systems' control, as Robot Operating System (ROS).

Acknowledgement. This work has been supported by the BRILLO project (Bartending Robot for Interactive Long-Lasting Operations) which has received funding from the PON I&C 2014-2020 MISE. The authors are solely responsible for the content of this manuscript.

References

1. Di Gironimo, G., Lanzotti, A.: Designing in VR. Int. J. Interact. Des. Manuf. **3**(2), 51–53 (2009)
2. Gammieri, L., Schumann, M., Pelliccia, L., Di Gironimo, G., Klimant, P.: Coupling of a redundant manipulator with a virtual reality environment to enhance human-robot cooperation. Procedia CIRP **62**, 618–623 (2017)
3. Kuan, C., Young, K.: VR-based teleoperation for robot compliance control. J. Intell. Robot. Syst. Theor. Appl. **30**(4), 377–398 (2001)
4. Ke, S., Xiang, F., Zhang, Z., Zuo, Y.: A enhanced interaction framework based on VR, AR and MR in digital twin. Procedia CIRP **83**, 753–758 (2019)
5. Rosen, R., Von Wichert, G., Lo, G., Bettenhausen, K.D.: About the importance of autonomy and digital twins for the future of manufacturing. IFAC-PapersOnLine **28**, 567–572 (2015)
6. Cichon, T., Rossmann, J.: Simulation-based user interfaces for digital twins: pre-, in-, or post-operational analysis and exploration of virtual testbeds. In: 31st Annual European Simulation and Modelling Conference 2017, ESM 2017, pp. 365–372 (2017)
7. Bugalia, N., Sen, A., Kalra, P., Kumar, S.: Immersive environment for robotic teleoperation. In: ACM International Conference Proceeding Series, 02–04 July 2015 (2015)
8. Lipton, J.I., Fay, A.J., Rus, D.: Baxter's homunculus: virtual reality spaces for teleoperation in manufacturing. IEEE Robot. Autom. Lett. **3**(1), 179–186 (2018)
9. Singh, J., Srinivasan, A.R., Neumann, G., Kucukyilmaz, A.: Haptic-guided teleoperation of a 7-DoF collaborative robot arm with an identical twin master. IEEE Trans. Haptics **13**(1), 246–252 (2020)
10. Mostefa, M., Lahouari, K.E.B., Loukil, A., Mohamed, K., Amine, D.: Design of mobile robot teleoperation system based on virtual reality. In: 3rd International Conference on Control, Engineering and Information Technology, CEIT 2015 (2015)
11. Mohsen, M., Ibrahim, K., Mohamed, A.M.: Design and control of a two degree of freedom teleoperated manipulator. In: IOP Conference Series: Materials Science and Engineering, vol. 435 (2018)
12. Whitney, D., Rosen, E., Phillips, E., Konidaris, G., Tellex, S.: Comparing robot grasping teleoperation across desktop and virtual reality with ROS reality. In: Amato, N.M., Hager, G., Thomas, S., Torres-Torriti, M. (eds.) Robotics Research. SPAR, vol. 10, pp. 335–350. Springer, Cham (2020). https://doi.org/10.1007/978-3-030-28619-4_28
13. Laaki, H., Miche, Y., Tammi, K.: Prototyping a digital twin for real time remote control over mobile networks: application of remote surgery. IEEE Access **7**, 20235–20336 (2019)
14. De Pace, F., Gorjup, G., Bai, H., Sanna, A., Liarokapis, M., Billinghurst, M.: Assessing the suitability and effectiveness of mixed reality interfaces for accurate robot teleoperation. In: Proceedings of the ACM Symposium on Virtual Reality Software and Technology, VRST (2020)

15. Leeper, A.E., Hsiao, K., Ciocarlie, M., Takayama, L., Gossow, D.: Strategies for human-in-the-loop robotic grasping. In: Proceedings of the 7th Annual ACM/IEEE International Conference on Human-Robot Interaction, HRI 2012, pp. 1–8 (2012)
16. Oculus Rift. http://www.oculus.com/rift/
17. Manus VR. https://www.manus-meta.com/
18. VR Free Glove. https://www.sensoryx.com/product/vrfree-glove-system-cv/
19. Kobayashi, F., Ikai, G., Fukui, W., Kojima, F.: Two-fingered haptic device for robot hand teleoperation. J. Robot. **2011**, 1–8 (2011)
20. Fischer, M., van der Smagt, P, Hirzinger, G.: Learning techniques in a dataglove based telemanipulation system for the DLR hand (1998)
21. Mizera, C., Delrieu, T., Weistroffer, V., Andriot, C., Decatoire, A., Gazeau, J.-P.: Evaluation of hand-tracking systems in teleoperation and virtual dexterous manipulation. IEEE Sens. J. **20**(3), 1642–1655 (2020)
22. Leap Motion. https://www.ultraleap.com/product/leap-motion-controller/
23. Jang, I., Carrasco, J., Weightman, A., Lennox, B.: Intuitive bare-hand teleoperation of a robotic manipulator using virtual reality and leap motion. In: Althoefer, K., Konstantinova, J., Zhang, K. (eds.) TAROS 2019. LNCS (LNAI), vol. 11650, pp. 283–294. Springer, Cham (2019). https://doi.org/10.1007/978-3-030-25332-5_25
24. Sian, N.E., Yokoi, K., Kajita, S., Kanehiro, F., Tanie, K.: Whole body teleoperation of a humanoid robot - a method of integrating operator's intention and robot's autonomy. In: Proceedings of the IEEE International Conference on Robotics and Automation, vol. 2, pp. 1613–1619 (2003)
25. Rosen, E., Whitney, D., Phillips, E., Ullman, D., Tellex, S.: Testing robot teleoperation using a virtual reality interface with ROS reality. In: Proceedings of the 1st International Workshop on Virtual, Augmented, and Mixed Reality for HRI (VAM-HRI), pp. 1–4 (2018)
26. LUA Reference Manual. http://www.lua.org/manual/5.3/
27. KUKA LBR iiwa brochure. https://www.kuka.com/-/media/kuka-downloads/imported/9cb8e311bfd744b4b0eab25ca883f6d3/kuka_lbr_iiwa_brochure_en.pdf?rev=46b7f50a907d44c29dd2c12cae2f92cf&hash=4985B631C9AD8F95387870213AB5D614
28. CoppeliaSim VR Toolbox. http://github.com/BorisBogaerts/CoppeliaSim-VR-Toolbox
29. Bogaerts, B., Sels, S., Vanlanduit, S., Penne, R.: Connecting the coppeliasim robotics simulator to virtual reality. SoftwareX **11**, 100426 (2020)
30. Sauro, J.: Sustisfied? Little-known system usability scale facts. https://uxpamagazine.org/sustified/

eXtended Reality in the Digital Transformation of Museums

Virtualization and Vice Versa: A New Procedural Model of the Reverse Virtualization for the User Behavior Tracking in the Virtual Museums

Iva Vasic[1(✉)], Aleksandra Pauls[1(✉)], Adriano Mancini[1(✉)], Ramona Quattrini[1(✉)], Roberto Pierdicca[1(✉)], Renato Angeloni[1(✉)], Eva S. Malinverni[1(✉)], Emanuele Frontoni[1,2(✉)], Paolo Clini[1(✉)], and Bata Vasic[3(✉)]

[1] Università Politecnica delle Marche, Ancona, Italy
{i.vasic,a.pauls}@pm.univpm.it, {a.mancini,r.quattrini, r.pierdicca,r.angeloni,e.s.malinverni,e.frontoni, p.clini}@staff.univpm.it

[2] Università di Macerata, Macerata, Italy
emanuele.frontoni@unimc.it

[3] Faculty of Electronic Engineering, University of Nis, Nis, Serbia
bata.vasic@ppf.edu.rs

Abstract. In this paper we present a method of the user behavior (UB) tracking by capturing and measuring user activities through the defined procedural model of the reverse virtualization process, implementing a proof of concept on a real case scenario: the Civic Gallery of Ascoli. In order to define the universal model of such "vice versa" virtual reality (VR) experience, we assigned particular descriptive functions (descriptors) to each interactive feature of the virtual user space. In this virtualization phase we store user interaction information locally using the web-socket streams protocol, ensuring complete control and manipulation of monitored functions. Our algorithm firstly collects the user interaction data and extracts the descriptors' arguments into the indexed vector of corresponding variables. The next step determines UB pattern by solving the inverse descriptive functions in combination with an appropriate statistical analysis of gathered data. The final result of the proposed method is the repository of salient data that is used in the further user experience improvement, as well as to enable the museums to distinguish the most important points of the visitor interest in the virtual web tours. Our approach also offers a potential benefit of obtained results in an automatic calculation and prediction of UB patterns using artificial intelligence (AI).

Keywords: Cultural Heritage · User behavior (UB) tracking · Virtual Museum · Virtual reality

L. T. De Paolis et al. (Eds.): XR Salento 2022, LNCS 13446, pp. 329–340, 2022.
https://doi.org/10.1007/978-3-031-15553-6_23

1 Introduction

The modern era of significant technological achievements focuses initiatives of all spheres of museology on creating digital assets for exploiting Cultural Heritage (CH) in many important domains including education [1, 2], science [3], as well as humanities and arts [4]. Accelerated transition from on-place to remote exploration of museums suddenly became necessary amid unpredictable development of pandemic in the last two years [5].

Museum institutions are continuously seizing the opportunities of the advanced technology used for digitization of their collections [6] and exploiting the rapid development of the immersive algorithms such as eXtended Reality (XR) and emerging networks of three-dimensional (3D) virtual environment such as metaverse [7] and its significant user experience. Comprehensive research studies related to the user experience in the museum's settings [8] caused the need for User Behavior (UB) tracking and also measuring their interest. The development of intuitive algorithms that would be able to deal with this large semantic and spatial data becomes an imperative.

UB tracking in Virtual Reality (VR) and/or Augmented Reality (AR) environments relies mostly on the software tools developed by the leader providers in statistical data analysis such as Google Analytic, eye tracking, Global Positioning system that uses the statistical computations, and artificial intelligence (AI). However, in our knowledge there are a few proposed studies that consider virtual tours of museum settings and even less related to the UB prediction based on its interactions on the Web.

This paper proposes a novel approach for the UB tracking by capturing and measuring user activities through the defined procedural model of the reverse virtualization.

This paper is organized as follows. The Sect. 2 gives an overview of the prior works using techniques that addressed UB tracking and predictive UB environments. Notations and concepts employed for our study are described in the Sect. 3. Our algorithm is explained in the Sect. 4. The conclusion is given in the Sect. 5 including the potential improvement of proposed method and discussion for the future work.

2 Prior Work

A systematic approach in behavior prediction and control, so called Behaviorism, was claimed as a purely directive experimental branch of natural science that has been formally established in [9] by psychologist John B. Watson in 1913. Nowadays, UB tracking is still a common subject even in CH contexts and it is assessed especially through virtual platforms on the Web.

The good example of the user interaction observing in the museology field, using analytics tools such as Google Analytics and eye tracking is presented in [10]. Also, the question of behavior and learning in a virtual environment can be considered in terms of user experience. This model was proposed by Katy Tcha-Tokey et al. [11], where is described using the ten components that are extracted from existing models (i.e., presence, engagement, immersion, flow, usability, skill, emotion, experience, consequence, judgment, and technology adoption). The user interface is an important component that we should pay special attention to. Sara de FreitasTim and Neumann in their paper [12] suggest the idea of extended Kolb's experiential learning mode to adapt the use of 3D applications and to exemplify how the model works in practice.

Analysis of various metrics of UB [13, 14] will improve certain aspects of the museum environment. The article [15] suggests using software in combination with hardware, i.e., cameras and computer vision algorithms and use a distributed video sensor network for detecting.

Previous research works of UB pattern definition were proposed both for the real and virtual environments. Respectively, [16] proposes trajectory prediction using Long Short-Term Memory and Generative Adversarial Network architectures, and [17] introduced VRAI deep learning application that captures UB using three convolutional neural networks from a single RGB-D video flow with nearly real-time performances.

Our approach is comprehensive and involves all previously achieved results and knowledge to define UB pattern that will be further subjected to statistical analysis, but also as a training set in AI learning.

3 Preliminaries

In this section, we describe the case study and introduce the notation and concepts used through the paper. We start with the discussion about the Civic Art Gallery situated in Ascoli Piceno in the central part of Italy. Then, we briefly describe the basic workflow of the virtualization process accompanied with most important geometrical and procedural features that will be used in calculations. Finally, at the end of this section we introduce the definitions of all segments of the reverse virtualization process.

3.1 Case Study - Pinacoteca Civica Museum

The Civic Art Gallery of Ascoli was officially established on August 4, 1861 by two artists from Ascoli, Giorgio Paci (1820–1914) and Giulio Gabrielli (1832–1910). The imposing artistic collection, now amounting to over 800 exhibits, has been housed in the halls of the Palazzo dell'Arengo since its origins.

Among the precious works of art, the most important of the thirteenth century, of English manufacture, donated in 1288 to the Cathedral of Ascoli by Pope Niccolò IV, the paintings of Carlo Crivelli (the two triptychs of Valle Castellana XV sec.), Cola dell'Amatrice (La salita al Calvario,1527), Tiziano (San Francesco riceve le stigmate, XVI sec.), Guido Reni (Annunciazione, 1575), Strozzi, De Ferrari, Magnasco, Mancini, Morelli, Palizzi e Pellizza da Volpedo (Passeggiata amorosa, 1901). The highlights reported here also constitute a thematic tab of the developed Virtual Museum, as will be detailed in the Sect. 4.1.

The Civic Art Gallery has been chosen as a case study for the Virtual Museum analyzing because it is a common example of an exhibition gallery where the rooms cannot be separated from the host collection. Being immersed in environments so dense with meanings and values, both in the real and virtual experience can be a challenge for the user, and the observation of UB could give rise to unexpected or non-trivial results.

3.2 Terminology

We will use the term *panorama* to refer to a 360-degree full-view panoramic image. In our case, it is taken with the Nikon D90 camera equipped with an 8 mm fisheye lens. The term *descriptor* will be used for each of interactive functions with inputs of countable user actions as their arguments. The *Virtual tour* will denote an interactive virtual web environment supplied with visual interactive features.

3.3 Virtualization Process Notations

The flowchart of the virtualization process flow is shown on Fig. 1.

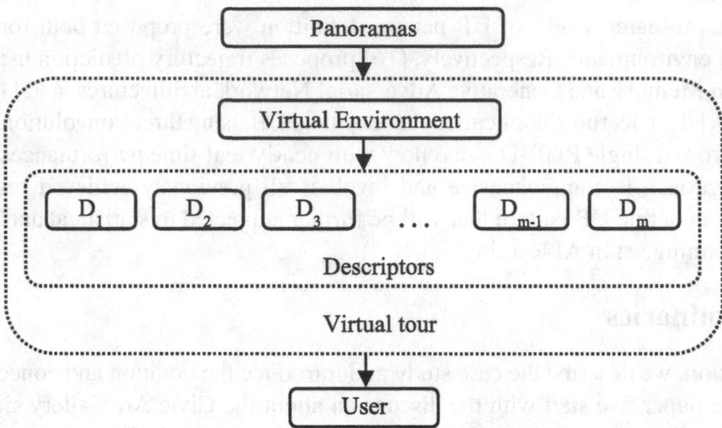

Fig. 1. VR visualization process flow

The technique for the distortion-free panorama view creation includes the usage of a tripod and a spherical head designed for panoramic imaging, as well as the software that is able to compensate both: the radial distortion, and residual horizontal and vertical shift [18]. Interactive virtual environment contains a set $\mathbf{D} = [\mathrm{D}_1, \mathrm{D}_2, \ldots, \mathrm{D}_\mathrm{m}]$ of m descriptors i.e., functions $\mathrm{D}_\mathrm{i} = f_\mathrm{i}(t_1, t_2, \ldots, t_n)$, whose n arguments are obtained from the interactive input and form a vector of UB *trackers* $\mathbf{T} = [t_1, t_2, \ldots, t_n]$, where n is a total number of input tracking values.

3.4 Panoramic Equirectangular Projection

In order to precisely and uniformly describe our proposed algorithm for calculating panoramas in equirectangular projection, here we introduce all notations and definitions that will be used further in the paper. The Fig. 2(a) illustrates the spherical equirectangular projection in two-dimensional (2D) space. Since the panorama covers 360° (2π) field of view horizontally and 180° (π) field of view vertically, its resolution is defined as $\mathrm{W} \times \mathrm{H}$ pixels where $\mathrm{W} = 2\mathrm{H}$, and the focal length is $\mathrm{r}_f = \mathrm{W}/2\pi$ pixels. The horizontal vanishing line of the ground plane is at the image coordinates $[-\mathrm{W}/2, \mathrm{W}/2] \times \lfloor -\mathrm{H}/2, \mathrm{H}/2 \rfloor$.

Let $\mathbf{P}(x, y)$ be the point on the panorama plane given in $\mathbb{R}^2$ space, where x and y are the pixel values along the horizontal width (W) and vertical height (H) of panorama axes respectively. The point $\mathbf{P}(\mathrm{x}, \mathrm{y})$ is a mapping of the point $\mathbf{P}(\mathrm{X}, \mathrm{Y}, \mathrm{Z})$ in the $\mathbb{R}^3$ space, where $\mathrm{Y} = 0$ since it is supposed to be positioned on the ground plane. Using simple and trivial proportions $\theta_x : \theta_{x_{max}} = x : W$; $\theta_y : \theta_{y_{max}} = y : \mathrm{H}$, and as we know $\mathrm{W} = 2\mathrm{H}$, we can explicitly express following angles:

$$\theta_x = \frac{2\pi}{\mathrm{W}}x;\ \theta_y = \frac{\pi}{\mathrm{H}}y,\ \text{or}\ \theta_x = \frac{\pi}{\mathrm{H}}x;\ \theta_y = \frac{\pi}{\mathrm{H}}y \tag{1}$$

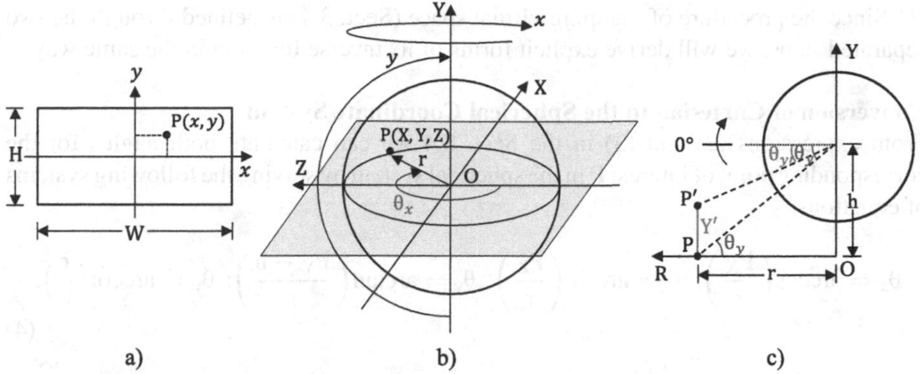

Fig. 2. Geometry derivation [19]: a) 2D representation of panorama plane where x and y are respectively horizontal and vertical axis of its equirectangular projection, b) the point **P**(X, Y, Z) in the ground plane (Y = 0) with the assigned values of radius r and angle θ_x, b) slice of 3D sphere at the h = 1.7 m from the ground plane and angles θ_y and $\theta_y^{'}$ that build points **P** and **P**$'$ respectively.

In the most common virtualization case, the vertical position of the camera is h = 1.7 m above the ground plane. Then we can calculate coordinates of the point **P**(Y = 0) and its corresponding radius to the circular projection of the panorama width W as:

$$P_X = r\cos\theta_x;\ \ P_Z = r\sin\theta_x;\ \ r = h|\cot\theta_y| \tag{2}$$

For the point $\mathbf{P}^{'}$ ($Y \neq 0$) above the ground plane, its projection to the vertical axis is $P_Y^{'} \neq 0$. With the slight approximation of notation from Fig. 2(c), for any point **P** we will have:

$$P_Y = h + r\tan\theta_y. \tag{3}$$

3.5 Reverse VR Process Definitions

Assume that the result of the UB tracking is a captured position of the 3D point $\mathbf{P}^{'}(X, Y, Z)$ in the interactive virtual space $\mathbb{R}^3$. Then we can define the vector of its equirectangular projections $\mathbf{P}^{'} = \left[P_X^{'}, P_Y^{'}, P_Z^{'}\right)]$. If the function $f(x, y)$ is defined as mapping the $\mathbb{R}^2$ space of panorama onto the $\mathbb{R}^3$ spherical space, then we introduce a function $g(\mathbf{P}')$ that maps the point $\mathbf{P}^{'}(X, Y, Z)$ to the point $\mathbf{P}(x, y)$ as an inverse function of $f(x, y)$. Then, $g\left(\mathbf{P}^{'}\right) = f^{-1}(x, y)$.

Since the procedure of mapping virtual space (Sect. 3.4) is defined through the two separated steps, we will derive explicit forms of its inverse function in the same way.

Conversion of Cartesian to the Spherical Coordinate System
From expressions (2) and (3) in the Sect. 3.4 we can calculate both angles for the corresponding point of interest **P** in the spherical system by solving the following systems of equations:

$$\theta_x = \arccos\left(\frac{\mathrm{P_X}}{\mathrm{r}}\right);\ \theta_x = \arcsin\left(\frac{\mathrm{P_Z}}{\mathrm{r}}\right);\ \theta_y = \arctan\left(\frac{\mathrm{P_Y - h}}{\mathrm{r}}\right);\ \theta_y = \mathrm{arccot}\left(\frac{\mathrm{r}}{\mathrm{h}}\right), \tag{4}$$

where h = 1.7 m is the constant value, and radius r is given by the focal length of the virtualization system.

The Point Position in the Panorama Image
Combining the results of solving the previous system of equations and expressions (1) in the Sect. 3.4 we can calculate horizontal and vertical pixel values of the point of interest **P**:

$$x = \frac{\theta_x \mathrm{H}}{\pi};\ y = \frac{\theta_y \mathrm{H}}{\pi} \tag{5}$$

where H is obtained as a result of JavaScript function for detecting original dimensions of the panorama image, or priory defined within the virtualization process code.

4 Methodology

The essence of our approach is reflected in a parallel consideration of the problem of the most important panorama regions determination observed by visitors, and in UB tracking and measurement in digital virtual solutions that both can improve the presentation of museum offerings. Such the streamlined and optimally reduced tracking functions, and shortened calculation procedure ensure fast and effective way to achieve numerous information of UB.

The primary focus of the developed methodology is able to connect high-resolution (HR) resources and digital tools to help both historians and visitors and thus the analysis of heterogeneous data collected directly from users by monitoring of user preferences and needs.

The flowchart of proposed procedure is presented in the figure Fig. 3, whereas the explanations of the most important steps are included in following subsections.

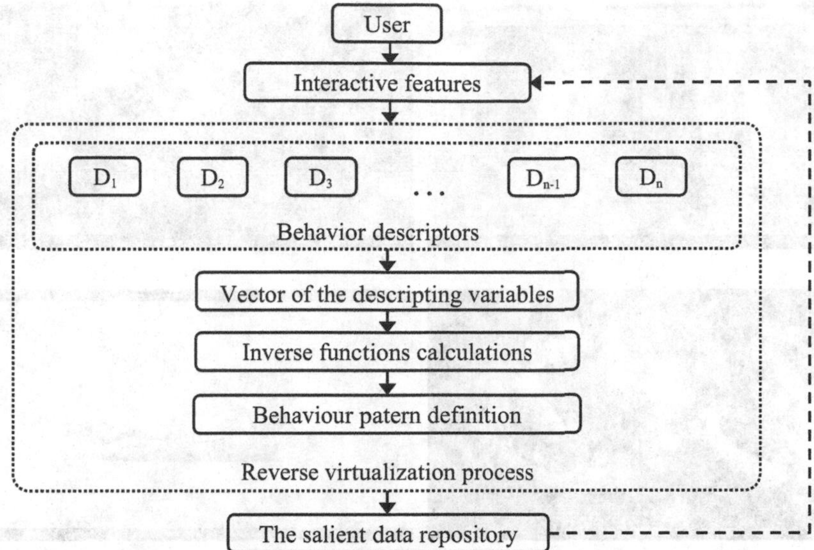

Fig. 3. The flowchart of the operations within our algorithm.

4.1 Interactive Virtual Web Museum

Our developed application [20] presents a case study of virtual museum with 84 panoramas and various descriptive features such as information about the artefacts, 3D models and HR painting representations, as well as building information. Intuitive interface that consists of visually comprehensive buttons is designed for different groups of people including even the stuff of the museum.

Interactive elements such buttons, menus and the interactive popups are incorporated in the executable web application within the used software tool functionality and improved by inserting the additional JavaScript codes that additionally ensure the rich user experience and also availability of UB tracking, measurement, and useful statistic analyze.

The Fig. 4 illustrates some of interactive functionalities of our virtual application including at the same time the richness of perceptual historical and artistic details that undoubtedly show the superiority of used digitization technique.

4.2 User Behavior Descriptors

The concept of defining the user descriptive functions aims to follow and capture the interaction of various events such as movement, view, perceptive field, video, 2D and 3D representations, zoom and VR functionalities. These functions are executed by clicking on specific buttons and allow tracking the most important parameters of UB for further collection of statistics.

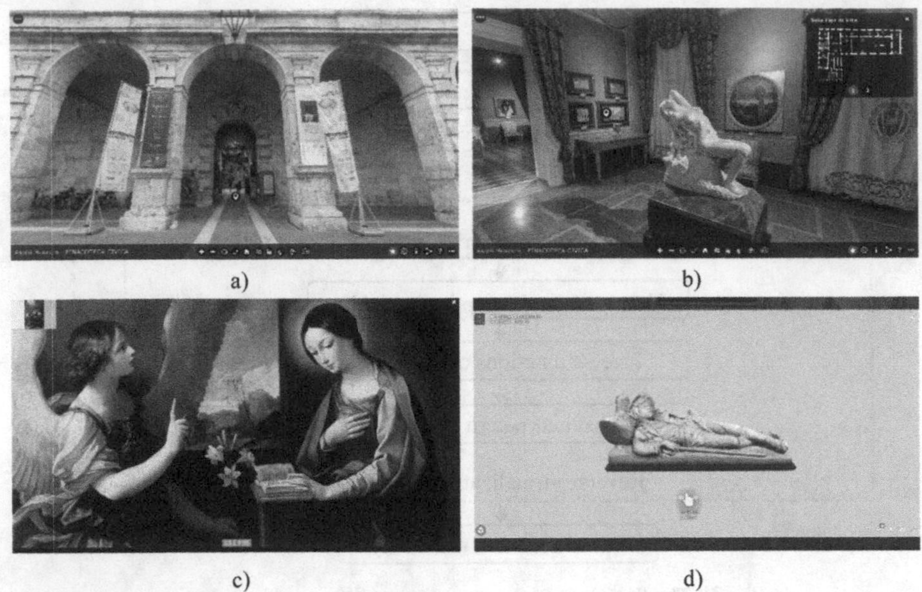

Fig. 4. The virtual tour interface of Civic Art Gallery: a) the main entrance, b) Sala Fior di Vita, c) HD painting “Annunciazione”, d) interactive 3D model “Pastorello”

We first defined the highest-priority functions including: D1) changing a position by clicking on the node feature positioned in the space; D2) full-screen mode; D3) opening the list of exhibition rooms; D4) opening the map of the museum; D5) opening the building's description panel; D6) viewing the HD paintings from the thumbnail “Exhibition Rooms”; D7) opening the list of 3D models by mouse click to “3dmodels” button; D8) clicking on the 3D model for detailed information; D9) entering to VR mode; D10) returning to the main page; and D11) viewing and interacting with the selected model in Sketchfab.

We also include in our calculation the secondary functions such as: D12) clicking on HD painting model for detailed information; D13) selecting specific images in “HD-paintings” panel; D14) opening the information about the room from the room's title on the map; D15) viewing an HD painting by zooming. The selected functions with related JavaScript codes are listed in Table 1.

Table 1. The list of descriptors and corresponding JavaScript codes from the virtual tour

D_i	Function description	JavaScript code
D_1	Change the viewing position	`me._ht_node.onclick=function (e)`
D_2	Full Screen	`me._button_fullscreen.onclick=function (e)`
D_3	Open the "thumbnail" to see Exhibition Rooms	`me._thumbnail_show_button.onclick=function (e)`
D_4	Open Map	`me._button_open_map.onclick=function (e)`
D_5	Open building description panel	`me._button_building.onclick=function (e)`
D_6	Click on HD Paintings button	`me._button_hdpainting.onclick=function (e)`
D_7	Click on "3dmodels" button to see the list of 3D models	`me._button_3dmodels.onclick=function (e)`
D_8	Click on the 3D object to obtain detailed information	`me._polygon_hotspot_container_3d.onclick= function (e)`
D_9	Enter to VR mode	`me._enter_vr.onclick=function (e)`
D_{10}	Click on home button	`me._button_home.onclick=function (e)`
D_{11}	Click on "Pastorello" 3D model	`me._button_3d.onclick=function (e)`
D_{12}	Click on the HD painting to obtain detailed information	`me._polygon_hotspot_container_hd.onclick= function (e)`
D_{13}	Choose one among four HD paintings in HD Painting panel	`me._imageicon_1.onclick=function(e)` `me._imageicon_2.onclick=function(e)` `me._imageicon_3.onclick=function (e)` `me._imageicon_4.onclick=function (e)`
D_{14}	Click on the room title on the map	`me._title_room_1st_floor.onclick=function (e)`
D_{15}	Click on "button_look closer" to view HD model	`me._button_look_closer.onclick=function (e)`

4.3 Inverse Functions Calculations

The whole tracking process targets two goals: i) Tracking the direct user interactivity using *click events* in JavaScript, and ii) capturing the user view and the region importance analysis.

The Direct User Interactivity
In order to track the inputs and consequently obtain UB pattern, we embedded short JavaScript commands in each function in the main output file of our virtual tour application which can be seen down below.

```
function UBTracking(){let arr = []; arr = [...arr, "Di"]}
```

The variable denoted with *arr* is defined as an empty array of string values, and the inputs are added and stored on every iteration of the corresponding function execution.

Table 2 lists a statistically calculated pattern of ten experimental user behaviors that is recorded in the virtual tour locally in the browser. The patterns show the chronology and frequency of certain actions listed in Table 1. For example, we notice that the User 6 performed only one function (D1) repeatedly and we define such behavior as an *error*. User 10 did not perform any action from the list and our application writes 0 values for this case which can be either an *error* or the interest for other functions that we have not included in the list of descriptors (Fig. 5).

Table 2. The output of UB tracking by storing the descriptors into input arrays

User	UB descriptors pattern tracking
1	['D3', 'D1', 'D1', 'D5', 'D6', 'D13', 'D12', 'D15', 'D9', 'D4', 'D14', 'D7', 'D8', 'D11']
2	['D4', 'D1', 'D1', 'D1', 'D1', 'D1', 'D1', 'D1', 'D1', 'D1', 'D1', 'D5', 'D3', 'D2', 'D1', 'D1', 'D1']
3	['D5', 'D7', 'D1', 'D1', 'D6', 'D13', 'D12', 'D15', 'D7', 'D8', 'D11']
4	['D4', 'D14', 'D4', 'D1', 'D14', 'D3', 'D7', 'D1', 'D1', 'D5', 'D6', 'D13', 'D1', 'D1', 'D1', 'D1', 'D1', 'D1', 'D1']
5	['D1', 'D4', 'D5', 'D2', 'D4', 'D6', 'D13', 'D12', 'D15', 'D9', 'D1', 'D1', 'D4', 'D14']
6	['D1', 'D1', 'D1', 'D1', 'D1', 'D1', 'D1', 'D1', 'D1']
7	['D10', 'D6', 'D13', 'D12', 'D15', 'D3', 'D1', 'D1', 'D1', 'D1', 'D1', 'D1', 'D1', 'D1', 'D7', 'D8', 'D11']
8	['D4', 'D14', 'D5', 'D6', 'D13', 'D1', 'D1', 'D1', 'D1', 'D1', 'D3', 'D1', 'D1', 'D1', 'D1']
9	['D1', 'D1', 'D5', 'D6', 'D1', 'D3', 'D4', 'D14', 'D6', 'D13', 'D12', 'D12', 'D15', 'D1', 'D1', 'D8']
10	0

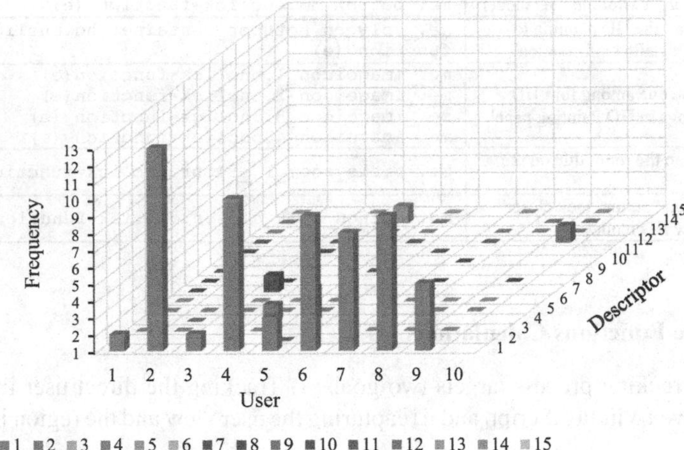

Fig. 5. Histogram of UB patterns performed by 10 users. The frequency axis values represent the number of times that functions (D_i) are executed by each user in one virtual tour session.

Capturing the User Selected Panorama Regions

According to the notations and definitions in Sect. 3.5 this step calculates pixel coordinates of each user point of interest allowing the measurement and the statistical analyse of the most visited HR artefact within the virtual gallery. Capturing the user current resolution denoted with *w_s* and *h_s,* we can calculate the scale ratio of the natural resolution of the source panorama image denoted as *#panorama.*

```
function getResolution() {
  var w_s = screen.width;
  var h_s = screen.height;
  var myImg = document.querySelector("#panorama");
  var W = myImg.naturalWidth;
  var H = myImg.naturalHeight; }
```

The retrieved values are sufficient for the further calculations of the desired exact values of the panorama regions using expressions (4) and (5) from the Sect. 3.5.

5 Conclusion and Future Works

In this paper we presented a novel approach to UB tracking in the virtual museum settings achieving the strategic objective to develop a prototype of virtual museum designed for society and under the several terms, democratizing, accessible, inclusive, and participatory spaces as well as "driver" of justice, equality, and social wellbeing. Our method ensures fast and efficient calculations of the inverse virtual functions by tracking the inputs in the virtual tour of Civic Art Gallery. We proved that the locally stored results obtained from the direct user interactivity may predict the UB patterns and determine the most important panorama regions related to the most interesting CH artifact within the presented museum collection.

The direction of our future research will be guided by the state-of-the-art technological achievement and the needs of visitors and museums with the clear goal to determine the most common UB pattern and its employment as a training set for the AI learning. In this way we could determine unusual behaviors in the virtual tours in order to prevent misuse and malicious behaviors in real and online museum environments.

Acknowledgments. The authors acknowledge the research presented here is part of Project V.I.T.A. (Virtual Immersion in Territorial Arts), funded by the Marche region and object of the grants among the Dep. DICEA and the cooperatives PULCHRA, TOGHETER WE CARE and GREEN PARK. The authors would like to thank also to the Director of the Civic Gallery of Ascoli, Prof. Stefano Papetti.

The panoramic acquisition and processing were carried out by Luigi Sagone and the TLS acquisition by Floriano Capponi.

References

1. Mortara, M., Eva Catalano, C., Bellotti, F., Fiucci, G., Houry-Panchetti, M., Petridis, P.: Learning cultural heritage by serious games. J. Cult. Herit. **15**, 318–325 (2014). https://doi.org/10.1016/j.culher.2013.04.004
2. Gaitatzes, A., Christopoulos, D., Roussou, M.: Reviving the past. In: Proceedings of the 2001 Conference on Virtual Reality, Archeology, and Cultural Heritage – VAST 2001, p. 103. ACM Press, New York, New York, USA (2001)
3. Fuhrmann, S., Langguth, F., Moehrle, N., Waechter, M., Goesele, M.: MVE - an image-based reconstruction environment. Comput. Graph. (Pergamon) **53**, 44–53 (2015). https://doi.org/10.1016/j.cag.2015.09.003
4. Garau, C.: From territory to smartphone: smart fruition of cultural heritage for dynamic tourism development. Plann. Pract. Res. **29**, 238–255 (2014). https://doi.org/10.1080/02697459.2014.929837
5. Samaroudi, M., Echavarria, K.R., Perry, L.: Heritage in lockdown: digital provision of memory institutions in the UK and US of America during the COVID-19 pandemic. Museum Manage. Curatorship **35**, 337–361 (2020). https://doi.org/10.1080/09647775.2020.1810483

6. Garlandini, A.: Museums and Heritage in the digital age. The challenge of cultural change and technological innovation. SCIRES-IT – Sci. Res. Inf. Technol. **11**, 11–18 (2021). https://doi.org/10.2423/I22394303V11N1P11
7. Forte, M., Lercari, N., Galeazzi, F., Borra, D.: Metaverse communities and archaeology: the case of Teramo. Digital heritage. In: Third International Conference EuroMed 2010 Dedicated on Digital Heritage. Short Papers. Limassol, Cyprus, 8–13 November 2010 (2010)
8. Sylaiou, S., Pavlidis, G., Giannini, T., Bowen, J.P.: Museums and digital culture: from reality to digitality in the age of COVID-19. Heritage **5**, 192–214 (2022). https://doi.org/10.3390/heritage5010011
9. Watson, J.B.: Psychology as the behaviourist views it. Psychol. Rev. **20**, 158–177 (1913). https://doi.org/10.1037/h0074428
10. Bekele, M.K., Pierdicca, R., Frontoni, E., Malinverni, E.S., Gain, J.: A survey of augmented, virtual, and mixed reality for cultural heritage. J. Comput. Cult. Heritage **11**, 1–36 (2018). https://doi.org/10.1145/3145534
11. Tcha-Tokey, K., Christmann, O., Loup-Escande, E., Loup, G., Richir, S.: Towards a model of user experience in immersive virtual environments. Adv. Human-Comput. Interact. **2018**, 1–10 (2018). https://doi.org/10.1155/2018/7827286
12. de Freitas, S., Neumann, T.: The use of "exploratory learning" for supporting immersive learning in virtual environments. Comput. Educ. **52**, 343–352 (2009). https://doi.org/10.1016/j.compedu.2008.09.010
13. Pierdicca, R., Sasso, M., Tonetto, F., Bonelli, F., Felicetti, A., Paolanti, M.: Immersive insights: virtual tour analytics system for understanding visitor behavior. In: De Paolis, L.T., Arpaia, P., Bourdot, P. (eds.) AVR 2021. LNCS, vol. 12980, pp. 135–155. Springer, Cham (2021). https://doi.org/10.1007/978-3-030-87595-4_11
14. Angeloni, R., Pierdicca, R., Mancini, A., Paolanti, M., Tonelli, A.: Measuring and evaluating visitors' behaviors inside museums: the Co.ME. project. SCIRES-IT – Sci. Res. Inf. Technol. **11**, 167–178 (2021). https://doi.org/10.2423/I22394303V11N1P167
15. Quattrini, R., Pierdicca, R., Paolanti, M., Clini, P., Nespeca, R., Frontoni, E.: Digital interaction with 3D archaeological artefacts: evaluating user's behaviours at different representation scales. Digital Appl. Archaeol. Cult. Heritage. **18**, e00148 (2020). https://doi.org/10.1016/j.daach.2020.e00148
16. Rossi, L., Paolanti, M., Pierdicca, R., Frontoni, E.: Human trajectory prediction and generation using LSTM models and GANs. Pattern Recogn. **120**, 108136 (2021). https://doi.org/10.1016/J.PATCOG.2021.108136
17. Paolanti, M., Pietrini, R., Mancini, A., Frontoni, E., Zingaretti, P.: Deep understanding of shopper behaviours and interactions using RGB-D vision. Mach. Vis. Appl. **31**(7–8), 1–21 (2020). https://doi.org/10.1007/s00138-020-01118-w
18. Fangi, G., Nardinocchi, C.: Photogrammetric processing of spherical panoramas. Photogram. Rec. **28**, 293–311 (2013). https://doi.org/10.1111/phor.12031
19. Xiao, J., Ehinger, K.A., Oliva, A., Torralba, A.: Recognizing scene viewpoint using panoramic place representation. In: Proceedings of the IEEE Computer Society Conference on Computer Vision and Pattern Recognition (2012)
20. Vasic, I.: Virtual Tour of Civic Art Gallery in Ascoli Piceno. https://dhekalos.it/tour/ascoli/index.html

"You Can Tell a Man by the Emotion He Feels": How Emotions Influence Visual Inspection of Abstract Art in Immersive Virtual Reality

Marta Pizzolante(✉) and Alice Chirico

Department of Psychology, Research Center in Communication Psychology, Universitá Cattolica del Sacro Cuore, Largo Gemelli 1, 20123 Milan, Italy
marta.pizzolante@unicatt.it

Abstract. Art is a complex subject of analysis. Nonetheless, Empirical Aesthetics has proved that the interaction between some bottom-up and top-down mechanisms shapes individuals' perception of a work of art. Recently, the *Vienna Integrated Model for Art Perception* [1] added that, during the observation of an artwork, the emotional state of the observer, as a top-down component, could influence the visual perception of the artwork, as a bottom-up one. Positive emotions can influence visual exploration, by broadening the attention focus during the observation of a normal stimulus [2]. However, whether this mechanism applies also for peculiar objects, i.e., abstract paintings, is still unexplored. In this study, we investigated how the emotional state of the subject influenced his/her following visual exploration of abstract works of art, featured in an immersive format. Thirty participants (20 males, 10 females) had been emotionally primed by either a positive (condition 1), negative (condition 2) or neutral affect (condition 3), as a control condition, before they observed 11 abstract paintings displayed in an immersive° format. Participants' eyes gazes were measured during the view of artistic stimuli through an eye-tracking device integrated in a virtual reality viewer (HTC VIVE Pro-eye). Analyses of eye-tracking metrics from participants - fixations and saccades- showed that individuals experiencing an induced positive mood broadened their visual attention, thus exploring more each painting, while participants in a negative mood explore generally less each work of art. This study confirmed that positive emotions pushed subjects to visually explore more the paintings presented in a virtual environment and confirmed the influence of the emotional state of the observer, as a top-down component, also in the visual exploration of an artwork.

Keywords: Psychology of aesthetic · Virtual reality · Emotion · Visual perception

1 Introduction

Artistic images are the result of a complex process that starts from the eye. The information provided by the retinal image is translated into nerve impulses; these, are transmitted

L. T. De Paolis et al. (Eds.): XR Salento 2022, LNCS 13446, pp. 341–359, 2022.
https://doi.org/10.1007/978-3-031-15553-6_24

to the brain and processed in various parts of the visual cortex. Zeki et al. in 1991 identified areas of the visual cortex that are activated by the perception of both color and movement [3]. These foci were bilateral and located in the most anterior and inferior regions of the occipital lobe. However, the investigation of the modalities through which the visual exploration of an artwork takes place does not rely only on the identification of those parts of the brain that are thought to be activated when observing an artwork. Aesthetic experience involves the creation of a relationship between the art product and the observer since it implies the establishment of some relational dynamics that are bidirectional and observable from a behavioral point of view [4]. The debate around their definition is very controversial. Literature referred to those components as *top down* and *bottom-up* processes but what some theories argue about is the dominance of *bottom-up* processes on *top-down* ones and vice versa. In particular, *top-down* processes concern factors such as the characteristics of the spectator as his cultural background, his level of education, the emotional state in which he is: these elements can interact with each other and therefore could influence the *bottom-up* ones. *Bottom-up*, hence, are generated by the pure sensorial coding of the stimulus and therefore, in this case, of the perception of the artistic elaborate. Different theoretical frames emphasize one or the other for the construction of a model of the aesthetic experience. Models may focus on only certain processing aspects—vision, artwork features, or basic fluency. The work of Berlyne highlighted the relevance of bottom-up components above top-down components [5]. The author stated that the interest evoked by a stimulus is activated by a number of properties possessed by the stimulus itself. Also, Kreitler and Kreitler affirmed that artwork content and its structure are the first features from which the observer begins to build multiple meanings that can stimulate understanding and emotion [6]. On the other hand, Martindale put more emphasis on top-down dynamics, especially on cognition: he tried to correlate the possible schema the spectator created when observing the stimulus, proposing that, for example, prototypicality is a key determinant for positive appraisal or affective response [7]. Indeed, it is more likely that when an observer is looking at a work of art, the aesthetic experience emerges from the interaction between the two processes, top-down and bottom-up, which operate in different ways on the various levels of experience of the spectator. One of the most recent models attempting this, the "Vienna Integrated Model of top-down and bottom-up processes in Art Perception" (VIMAP) by Pelowski and colleagues [1] posits also that, in the earlier stage of the aesthetic experience, top-down components, such as the emotional state of the observer, can have relapses on the bottom-up ones, influencing the visual elaboration of the stimulus such as where the gaze of the observer will focus when exploring the artwork.

1.1 The Potential Role of Emotions, as a Top-Down Component, During Aesthetic Experience: A Brief State of the Art

Aesthetic experience is initially produced by the action of different top-down processes which can be schematically classified as cognitive and affective [8]. Historically, the various theories of emotion have considered the relationship between cognition and emotion through different perspectives. A first group of theories considered emotion and cognition as substantially different [9]. A second group of theories on emotions focused the attention on the central role that cognitive processes play during the emotional experience. These theories' roots can be traced back to the tradition started by James and Cannon [10, 11] with later developments in the theory proposed by Schachter and Singer [12].

However, according to the most current psychological perspective, emotion can be better studied and understood through a multi-componential approach in which the emotional episode consists of a consequential and coordinated series of modifications in the various components. But is it possible to adopt the same model also for the "aesthetic" emotions? In Scherer's "Component Process Theory" [13], emotion is described as a rapid organization of all the major functioning systems of the organism (central nervous system, autonomic nervous system, somatic nervous system, neuro-endocrine system) in response to the evaluation of an external or internal stimulus, relevant to the organism itself.

Another scientist, Barbara Fredrickson, agreeing with this approach, defining emotions as "*multicomponent response tendencies that develop over relatively short periods of time*". The author also underlined the necessity to apply this perspective, that studied negative emotions such as fear, anger, disgust (i.e., negative emotions), also on the positive ones. For this purpose, she developed the so-called "Broaden-and-Build theory", starting from 1998, and commonly associated with positive psychology [2]. The theory claimed that positive emotions seem to broaden an individual's momentary thought-action repertoire while negative emotions are generally involved in the opposite mechanism, a kind of "shrinking" process, resulting in a "narrow-minded mechanism". Decades ago, Easterbrook [14] suggested indeed that states of anxiety narrow attentional focus by reducing the ability to process peripheral information. Indeed, negative emotional states and traits have been linked to narrowed attentional scope [15, 16].

To conclude, as emerged from the previous studies, positive emotions, on the long period, could help to develop higher levels of creativity, resilience, and self-confidence during the life span of an individual but what we aim at demonstrating in this study is that, potentially, they could have relapses on where subjects, on a short-term, focused their gaze during the aesthetic perception and so how they explore a visual stimulus.

1.2 Visual Attention, as a Bottom-Up Component, Influenced by Emotion

Gaze represents an important topic in both art history/visual studies and cognitive neuroscience.

Studies that have been conducted to affirm this, are based on the analysis of the behavior of the eyes of some subjects, using tools such as eye tracking, a research method that uses a device to track the point of gaze or eye movement of a person, during a task. Most common eye-tracking metrics used are represented by two different parameters: fixations and saccades. The former is defined as the period of time where the eye is kept aligned with the target for a certain duration, allowing for the image details to be processed; and the latter are the type of eye movement used to move the fovea rapidly, from one point of interest of the image to another, without the visual processing of the image. It was demonstrated that these types of metrics might be used to define observer's pattern of visual exploration of a stimulus [17]. One of the most useful methods to analyze the above-mentioned eye-movements on images is the evaluation of AOIs,

Areas of Interest(s). An Area of Interest is a high importance part of stimulus, usually defined and based on the semantic information of the stimulus.

Currently, also the domain of aesthetic, trying to determine the visual pattern of exploration of paintings or artworks, is progressively making more use of those eye-movements parameters [18,19].

In 2015, Koide used eye-tracking, measuring eye fixations, to detect differences in eye movement parameters and patterns between art experts and novices during the free viewing of various abstract paintings [20]. The authors compared the distribution of their fixations for each painting, with a topological attentional map that quantifies the conspicuity of low-level features in the painting through a saliency map - an indicator of stimulus-driven visual selection - used to quantify whether fixations were knowledge-based or not. They found out that the fixations' distribution of artists was more distinguishable from the saliency map than that of novices. In viewing representational images, artists' fixations have been shown to be attracted less to the semantic objects than those of novices. This implies that artists' fixations are attracted more to non-semantic visual patterns than those of novices. Furthermore, this study gave evidence of superiority of artists to recognize visual patterns compared to novices.

2 The Present Study

Previous evidence showed that i) emotions, as a top-down component, present within a pre-classification stage of aesthetic experience, can also influence the visual exploration of an artwork following a logic, and not by chance, according to the Broaden and Built Theory [1, 2]; ii) aesthetic experience, as a set of highly complex cognitive-emotional processes involving attentional mechanisms, could be the result of the reciprocal influence between top-down components (e.g., emotional state of the observer) and bottom-up ones (e.g., visual perception/exploration of the artwork) [1].

In line with this evidence, we hypothesized that individuals' emotional state induced before (and lasting during) the observation of a visual artwork, could influence the way the observer directed his/her gazes during the following observation of each artistic stimulus. Therefore, when observing the same work of art, depending on the emotional state induced, the viewer's gaze could focus on different elements. To test this hypothesis, we examined the impact of positive vs. negative emotional states on participants' visual exploration patterns of abstract paintings. Specifically, according to Fredrickson's "Broaden-and-Build theory", it was plausible to expect a positive mood to expand participants' exploration patterns during the observation of an artwork (i.e., finding a visual pattern of exploration of the stimulus characterized by several fixation points, equally distributed over the entire surface of the picture, covering also, for example, the perimeters of the painting). On the contrary, it is assumed that an opposite mood, sadness for example, will diminish the exploratory behavior of the subject, limiting the fixation points and grouping them in a few areas of the painting. To test this hypothesis, we expose participants to the observation of several abstract paintings displayed in an immersive format (360° videos) and we measured how their gazes changed in relation to their previous emotional state (positive vs. negative), as a priming condition. Their eye movements were monitored through an eye-tracking system, integrated into the virtual reality device, to understand which parts of the work the viewer's gaze focuses on, depending on the emotional state in which the subject is. The induction of the chosen emotional state takes place before the presentation in virtual reality of the artistic works through the viewing of 360° videos. The two videos to be presented were chosen from a public database compiled by Stanford which contains 350 videos associated with various levels of arousal and valence.

3 Methods

3.1 Participants

Thirty participants (20 males, 10 females) between the ages of 18 and 40 took part in this study ($M_{age} = 26.4$, $S.D_{age} = 3.090$). They gave their written informed consent to the experimental procedure. Only participants without vision, vestibular or neurological disorders that could interfere with the eye-tracking technique, were included.

3.2 Research Design

In order to be tested, each participant was assigned randomly - using an online randomizer[1] - only to one of the three priming conditions: positive affect (Condition 1), negative affect (Condition 2) neutral condition (Condition 3). Each Condition (*between-subject variable*) differed in terms of the type of affect induced: in Condition 1, a positive mood was induced, in Condition 2, a negative mood was elicited, while in Condition 3, which acted as the control condition, no specific affect was induced. After the emotion-induction phase, all participants explored 11 abstract paintings through a virtual reality viewer (HTC VIVE Pro-eye) while their eye-gaze was monitored.

3.3 Abstract Paintings Selection

Eleven different art paintings were selected to be presented to participants (i.e., *Catrame*, Alberto Burri - 1949; *Superficie 209,* Giuseppe Capogrossi - 1957; *Stenographic Figure Composition*, Jackson Pollock - 1943; *Composition*, Basaldella Afro - 1956; *Vega* Nor, Victor Vasarely - 1969; *SZ1*, Alberto Burri - 1949; *Yellow, red, blue*, Vasilij Kandinskij - 1925; *Composition n.2*, Piet Mondrian - 1920; Suprematist *Composition*, Kazimir Malevich - 1915; *Breton Landscape*, Renato Birolli - 1957). They consisted of high- resolution digital versions of art paintings downloaded from different website collections. The selected artworks belonged to different artistic abstract movements. Abstract paintings were selected over figurative ones in order to facilitate participants' free exploration of each stimulus, without perceptual elements of salience potentially linked to previous experience, e.g., a human figure, an object – which could attract the gaze of the observer. An external geometrical symbol was added in the middle of each image, and the reason was twofold. Participants could have a reference point when orienting in the 360° space, since the perimeter of the painting was lost when the artwork was presented in a 360° format. For the experimenter, this symbol was added as a reference point of visual exploration to compute as Areas of Interests (AOIs) and, to calculate how many participants focused on the central geometrical symbol.

[1] https://www.random.org/lists/.

3.4 Stimuli Used as Emotional Inductors

In order to prime participants with a positive vs. negative affect, specific videoclips were selected. Specifically, only participants in Condition 1 and 2 were preliminary exposed to affective videos, while there was no priming exposure in Condition 3. Videoclips were selected from a public database validated by the Stanford University, which contains 350 videos rated according to their levels of arousal and valence (https://vhil.stanford.edu/360°-video-database/). The two videoclips with, respectively, the highest and lowest level of valence were chosen, for condition 1 and 2. The videoclip for Condition 1, was entitled "Puppy Bowl II) and featured puppies competing in a mock football match. The videoclip for Condition 2, was entitled "The Displaced", and it was a journalistic documentary on three homeless children. The average duration of videos was 8 min.

3.5 Measures

Self-reported Measures

The following self-reported measures were administered to all participants before the experiment started:

- *Questionnaire on art interests* (modified from Chamorro-Premuzic & Furnham, 2004–2005) [21].
- *Desire for Aesthetic Scale* (DPAS) (Lundy et al., 2010) [22].
- *Dispositional Positive Emotions Scale* (DPES); (Shiota et al., 2006; adapted by Chirico et al., 2021) [23, 24].
- *Positive and Negative Affect Scale* (PANAS) (trait version), 10 items [25].
- *Level of knowledge of VR* (previous experiences, known applications)*: ad hoc* questionnaire.
- *Level of knowledge of the artists and the artistic movement* of the chosen paintings: *ad hoc* questionnaires.

Finally, *Positive and Negative Affect Scale* (PANAS) state version was administered twice: before the affective priming and before the contemplation of artworks as a double check measure of the effectiveness of the priming conditions.

Eye-Tracking Measures

Moreover, six different parameters were extracted from the eye-tracking metrics for each painting:

- *Number of fixations:* we expect more fixations for participants in Condition 1 compared to those in Condition 2 and 3; this would indicate the different pattern of visualization of subjects in a positive mood, aimed at a broader exploration of the artistic stimuli.
- *Average duration of fixations*: for this parameter, we expect higher values for Condition 2, indicating a less exploratory visualization's pattern.

- Number *of saccades:* we expect more fixations for participants in Condition 1 compared those in Condition 2 and 3; again, indicating a broader exploration of the stimuli.
- *Average peak velocity of saccades:* also, here, we expect more fixations for participants in Condition 1 compared to those in Condition 2 and 3.
- *Average amplitude of saccades*: this parameter is expected to be higher for participants belonging to Condition 2.
- *Pupil diameter:* pupil dilatation (millimeters) as an indicator of physiological arousal. Participants belonging to Condition 1 and 2 are likely to have higher values regarding pupil dilatation compared to those in Condition 3 because they have been subjected to the induction of a precise emotional state.

In a second phase, the visual pathway of each subject was defined. It was discovered that all participants, at the beginning, focused their attention on the same Area of Interest (AOI). A specific Area of Interest emerged for each painting, thus, resulting into eleven AOIs, based on the absolute fixation counts. Each AOI corresponded to the external symbol added on the original image. The eleven AOIs were automatically visualized by the *Tobii Pro Lab* software in a heatmap, created on the basis of a radius diameter that was set to 90 pixels. The definition of those AOIs was relevant because we run a second specific analysis on AOIs to measure the dispersion of the gazes of participants with respect to each symbol. Four different features of each AOI were computed: (i) *number of fixations in each AOI, (ii) average duration of fixation in each AOI, (iii) the number of visits for each AOI, (iv) the average duration of visit for each AOI.*

3.6 Procedure

Before the experimental session took place, participants have to fill an online survey, created with Qualtrics[2], featuring all the self-reported measures described in paragraph 3.5. All participants in Condition 1 and 2 were primed with a validated affective video before the contemplation of the artworks. Before and after the initial emotion induction, each participant filled the PANAS short state version (10 item) to report their contingent affect. This was used as a double check measure of the effectiveness of the experimental priming manipulation. Then, participants saw all the 11 abstract paintings through the *HTC Vive Pro* viewer. Before the VR session started, an eye tracking calibration procedure had started. During the calibration, participants were asked to look at specific points on the screen, also known as calibration dots, then, the virtual reality session began. Each painting was visualized by participants as a 360° scenario. Participants were completely immersed and surrounded by each virtual environment and were able to explore it freely, walking around the room with the headset on, adapting head's orientation and gaze's direction at will. At the end of this session, a debriefing was conducted (Fig. 1).

[2] https://www.qualtrics.com/it/.

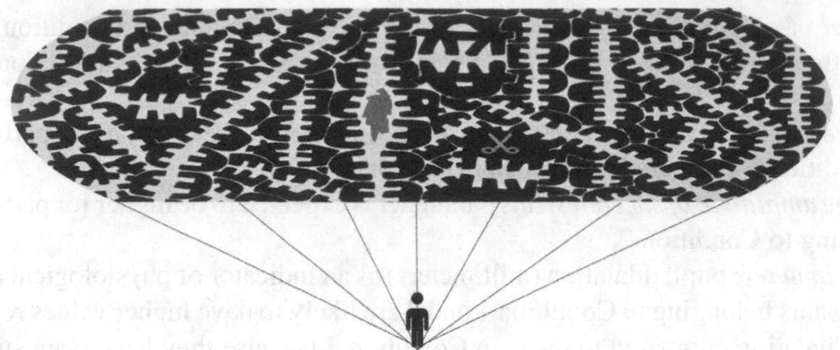

Fig. 1. The figure represents, in a stylized manner, an example of a virtual 360 scenario depicting a painting in which each subject is immersed. The participant is completely surrounded by the virtual environment and can explore it freely.

3.7 Virtual Reality Setup

In the current study, also the priming emotion-induction videos were presented in a 360° VR scenario. The presentation of the works of art in a 360° environment was intended to isolate the participant from potential distractors and to help them focus on the stimulus, by preserving the ecological validity of the study. Moreover, participants could move around the room and freely explore each painting from each point of view. The reason was threefold.

First, recent developments of digital technologies in the field of Virtual Reality (VR), indeed, especially VR galleries and museums, gave the opportunity to study art experience in strongly controlled but still very naturalistic context. There are some studies, attempting to demonstrate that aesthetic experience of paintings is similar in different presentation modes, even if different contexts, real or virtual, hold different features that are able to influence different aspects of an aesthetic experience. However, generally, *aesthetic experience of paintings seems to be more intense in VR than in the computer screen setting* [25].

Then, a recent study [26] also demonstrated the similarity of the distribution of the gazes of the participants involved in a visual exploration of Mondrian's paintings compared to the visual exploration of the same paintings, presented in a virtual reality scenario, in a 360° format. Similarity of viewing patterns between the two conditions suggested that virtual galleries and virtual paintings, as presented in the current study, can be treated as ecologically valid environments, parallel to physical art galleries, demonstrating, from a psycho-physiological point of view, no significant perceptive difference between the enjoyment of a live artwork and the fruition of the same artwork, presented in a virtual environment. Additionally, what VR can guarantee is a greater realism and therefore an emotional involvement closer to what can be experienced in the enjoyment of a live work, compared to a classic computer presentation.

Furthermore, there are many methods that can be used to evoke a user's emotion such as music, video clips, movie, still images (Affective Picture System - IAPS). However, the outcomes from emotion induction studies could sometimes not be entirely accurate since, by using images and video clips that are presented by sitting in front of the computer display, such a setup cannot guarantee that the test subject is actually and exactly focusing on the images or the stimulus.

Finally, grasping the complexity of a positive emotion such as that evoked during an aesthetic experience – awe or the sublime - trying to ensure the emotional intensity of an experience conveyed by this emotion, should require a medium able to resemble its multifaceted nature. From this understanding, recently, VR can represent the ideal medium to induce and enhance those aesthetic feelings thanks to the above-mentioned features it has, that allows the user to feel completely inserted and immersed in the proposed virtual environment [27].

For these reasons, the use of VR, particularly for the purpose of this study, was essential, firstly for the induction of the chosen emotional state and, secondly, for the presentation of the paintings in a 360° format. This setup could guarantee that subjects were actually and exactly able to focus their attention on the stimuli, being fully "immersed" within the 360° virtual environment as soon as they start wearing the VR headset.

3.8 Eye-Tracking Data Acquisition

Data acquisition was performed using the software *Tobii Pro Lab* (trial version).

In a first phase, eleven-time intervals were defined based on the onset and offset of each stimulus and parameters were analyzed considering only these intervals. Among the numerous measures that can be extracted from *Tobii*, those useful for the research objectives were those related to the fixations and saccades.

These metrics were also chosen based on some previous findings.

4 Results

4.1 Self-report Measures

The questionnaires administered before the presentation of the stimuli to the participants revealed that, at the baseline, the motivation to use the works of art and, in general, to practice artistic disciplines was not significantly different between participants belonging to the three conditions. Results from DFAS suggested that the disposition to perceive art and appreciate aesthetic experience did not significantly differ between the three conditions, as showed by the One-Way ANOVA [$F(2,27) = .366$, $p = .697$] conducted with "condition" as independent variable. Additionally, the analysis from DPES scores revealed no significant differences between participants in the general disposition to experience seven distinct positive emotions [$F(2,27) = 1.367$, $p = .272$]. Moreover, two One-way ANOVAs with "condition" as an independent variable and positive affect and negative affect, measured through PANAS SF, did not show any significant differences across conditions at the baseline. Conversely, the two similar One-Way ANOVAs with positive and negative affect as post-induction measure, showed a main effect of "condition" [F (2,27) = 4.314, p = .030], in terms of Negative Affect. Specifically, Tukey's post-hoc comparisons revealed that the negative affect elicited in Condition 2 (M = 10.2, SD = 3.12) was significantly higher compared to Condition 3 (M = 7.50, SD = 2.42) and 1 (M = 6.50, SD = 2.43). Regarding the positive dimension of PANAS SF, even if participants assigned to Condition 1, as revealed by descriptive statistics, reported higher scores in this dimension, a main significant effect of "condition" [F (2,27) = .972, p = .397] was not found. So, if the induction of the negative affect was completely confirmed by the scores obtained by subjects in Condition 2 in the negative dimension of the PANAS, the induction of the positive affect was not significantly detected by the positive subscale of the same tool. This could be due to the small sample size considered in the study.

4.2 Eye Tracking Data

General Overview: Between-Group Effect

Six different parameters were taken into consideration for each painting and participant: *i) average duration of whole fixations, ii) number of whole fixations, iii) number of saccades, iv) average amplitude of saccades, v) average peak velocity of saccades.* We run several One-Way-ANOVAs, with all the values related to the eye-tracking parameters listed above as dependent variable, and "condition" as the independent variable (or fixed-factor). Particularly, we expected to find a significant difference between Condition 1, and Condition 2 in terms of values related to average duration of whole fixations, number of whole fixations, number of saccades, average amplitude of saccades, average peak velocity of saccades. We found out a significant main effect among values related to number of saccades [F (2,27) = 21.50, p < .001], average amplitude of saccades [F (2,27) = 26.46, p < .001], average peak velocity of saccades [F (2,27) = 127.79, p < .001] between the three Conditions. We used Tukey's post-hoc comparison to detect in which Conditions these differences were significant, finding a significant difference, for those parameters, between Condition 1 [Number of saccades (M = 626.90, SD = 98.64); Average amplitude of saccades (M = 13.50, SD = 3.42), Average peak velocity of saccades (M = 1400.83, SD = 278.77)] and Condition 2 [Number of saccades (M = 341.60, SD = 170.35) Average amplitude of saccades (M = 6.49, SD = 2.13), Average peak velocity of saccades (M = 269.39, SD = 131.49)] but also between subjects belonging to Condition 1 and Condition 3 [Number of saccades (M = 254.30, SD = 119.34) Average amplitude of saccades (M = 6.46, SD = 1.56), Average peak velocity of saccades (M = 220, SD = 98.68)]. For values related to average duration of whole fixations [F (2,27) = 6.03, p = .007], significant differences were recorded between Condition 1 (M = 155.90, SD = 18.42) and Condition 2 (M = 193.70, SD = 44.84) but there was also a significant difference, even if lower than the previous one, between subjects belonging to Condition 2 and Condition 3 (M = 151.70, SD = 17.65). We run a One-Way ANOVA to assess a possible difference regarding the pupil's dilation of the subjects, belonging to the three conditions, during the observation of the stimuli. We do not expect homogeneity between the three conditions, assuming a higher pupil dilatation for participants belonging to Condition 1 and 2 compared to those belonging to Condition 3 for a higher level of general arousal given by the induction of two different emotional states, so we expect to reject the null hypothesis, stating that there is no difference regarding the scores, between the three conditions. The p-value, obtained for both pupils' diameter, left and right, is greater than the critical value .05, thus we cannot reject the null-hypothesis and we can assume that there is no difference among participants, belonging to three different conditions, regarding the pupil's dilation of the subjects, during the observation of the stimuli [$F(2,27) = 0.681$, $p = 0.519$; $F(2,27) = 0.308$, $p = 0.739$] (Fig. 2).

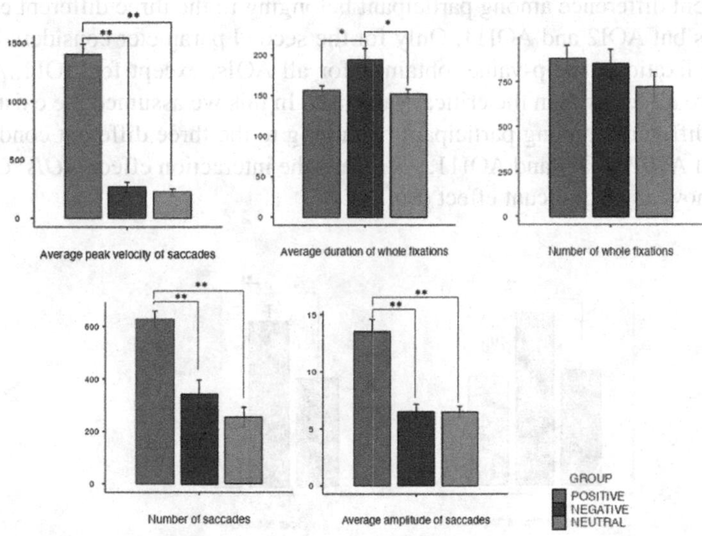

Fig. 2. Plots representing post-hoc comparisons of values related to the five parameters of general analysis (average duration of fixations, number of fixations, average amplitude of saccades, number of saccades, average peak of velocity of saccades for each group (Condition 1, Condition 2, Condition 3). *p. < .05, **p. < .01

AOIs' Analysis

Four different parameters, related to the selected AOIs, were taken into consideration for each painting and participant: number of fixations, average duration of fixations, number of visits and average duration of visits. Four repeated mixed ANOVAs, considering as a between factor the condition each participant belongs to and as a within factor the number of AOIs, were run to look for significant differences among the three conditions, concerning the different pattern of exploration assumed to exist in terms of number of fixations, average duration of fixations, number of visits and average duration of visits. We do not expect homogeneity for those values since it is hypothesized that the pattern of exploration between the participants belonging to each group is different. Additionally, we did not expect a significant interaction effect since we expected homogeneity between participants belonging to the same condition; namely, that each AOI is explored in the same way by participants belonging to the same group. Each mixed

ANOVA revealed a significant main effect for all the parameters considered [F (2,27) = 8.67, p = .001; F (2,27) = 25.2, p < .001; F (2,27) = 11.4, p < .001; F (2,27) = 18.7 p < .001]; however, post-hoc comparisons showed that this significance exists for all AOIs' parameters between Condition 2 and both Condition 1 and Condition 3. We used Tukey's post-hoc comparison to look for the specific AOIs, in which those differences, related to the mentioned parameters, were most significant. For the first, third and fourth parameter, the number of fixations, number of visits and the average duration of visits, the p-value, obtained for all AOIs, except for AOI2 and AOI11, were all lower than the critical value .05, thus we had to reject the null-hypothesis, assuming that there is a consistent difference among participant belonging to the three different conditions for all AOIs but AOI2 and AOI11. Only for the second parameter considered, average duration of fixations, the p-value, obtained for all AOIs, except for AOI2, AOI7 and AOI11, were all lower than the critical value .05. In this we assumed the existence of a consistent difference among participant belonging to the three different conditions for all AOIs but AOI2, AOI7 and AOI11. As regard the interaction effect, *AOIs*Condition*, it did not show any significant effect (Fig. 3).

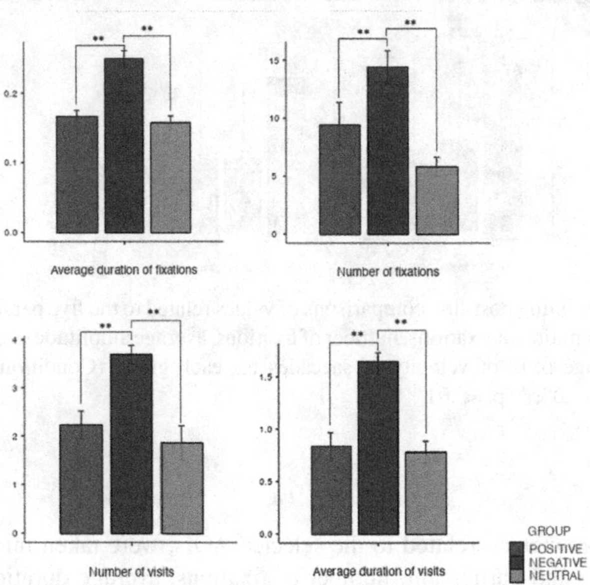

Fig. 3. Plots representing post-hoc comparisons of values related to the four parameters of AOIs' analysis (average duration of fixations, number of fixations, number of visits, average duration of visits) for each group (Condition 1, Condition 2, Condition 3). *p < .05, **p < .01

5 Discussion

The aim of this study was to investigate how the emotional state of the observer, induced in a pre-classification stage of the aesthetic experience, so before observing some works of art, can play a fundamental role in the following visual exploration of the stimuli. As stated by Pelowski et al. [1] through the introduction of the VIMAP model, aesthetic experience could emerge from the reciprocal influence between top-down components, such as the emotional state of the observer, and bottom-up ones, concerning the visual perception of the artwork. Specifically, in the current study, the hypothesis was that, according to the "Broaden and Build Theory" by Barbara Fredrickson [2], individuals induced a different affect are thought to adopt a different pattern of visual exploration of some abstract paintings: subjects in a positive emotional state, are hypothesized to adopt a broader visual pattern of exploration while individuals in a negative emotional state are thought to explore less the paintings and to linger more on some points of it, especially on the center of them. For this purpose, thirty participants, divided into three conditions, were subjected to the induction of a specific emotional state through the vision of some video-clips; ten subjects were assigned to Condition 1, in which they were subjected to the induction of a positive emotional state; ten subjects to Condition 2 in which a negative emotional state was induced; ten to the third Condition, a control one, in which participants were not subjected to the induction of any emotional state. After this first phase, all participants were subjected to the vision of 11 abstract paintings presented in an immersive format.

The movie clips and the presentation of the experimental stimuli were administered through a virtual reality viewer and the gaze of the observer monitored, during the observation of the paintings, through an eye-tracking, integrated to the viewer.

5.1 Eye-Tracking Data: Between-Group Effect and AOI'S Analysis

Two different analyses were run, a general heat-map analysis and a specific AOIs' analysis: the former was performed in order to test if, generally, participants induced a positive affect, visually explore more the abstract paintings compared to those induce a negative emotional state. Eye-tracking data showed that participants belonging to Condition 1 and subjected to the induction of a positive emotional state have significantly lower values regarding the average duration of whole fixations and higher values regarding the number of saccades, average amplitude of saccades, average peak velocity of saccades, especially if compared to the values of subjects belonging to Condition 2, subjected to the opposite emotional state's induction. Values related to the whole number of fixations were found to be not significantly different between the three conditions. Also, data related to the pupil dilatation, recorded in order to check and confirm the induction of the chosen emotional state, do not differ between participants: this could be explained by some previous studies in literature [28], in which the goal was to identify a set of features from pupil size variation and eye tracking to distinguish between neutral and arousal states. In particular, the response to emotional elicitation induced by IAPS images showed significant information from eye gaze patterns, but not significant pupil size differences. What emerges from these preliminary results is that, as expected, people in a positive mood, from a first general analysis, broaden their visual attention, as expected, through decreased time fixation to some parts of the stimuli and generating more frequent saccades to artworks, with higher amplitude and higher speed. On the contrary, we cannot say much of participants in a negative emotional state, because their pattern of exploration was not significantly different from that of the control group condition. So, to identify the parts of each painting to which each group lingers more, we run a second specific analysis in which we identify for each painting an AOI, representing the most fixated point of the painting, at least at the beginning of the exploration, and corresponding to the external symbol added on each painting that is thought to be the first element that attracts the attention of the observer. As claimed above, the definition of those AOIs were relevant because we hypothesized that if, at the beginning, all participants were attracted by them in the same manner, in a second time, participants in a negative mood fixate them more and in a more consistent way because they explored less each painting. This second AOI's analysis indicates that, as expected, participants in a negative emotional state explore more the center of the paintings, corresponding to those AOIs, through increased number and time fixations and by making a higher number and duration of visits directed to them while positive mood group fixate and visit less the center of the paintings, corresponding to the AOIs. Taken together, these two analyses underlined two peculiar different patterns of visual exploration between participants induced a positive emotional state and participants induced a negative emotional state. Indeed, while the former group lingers less on some points of the images, exploring equally the entire surface of the paintings and generally more each stimulus, including the peripheral parts of it, the latter excludes the exploration of the periphery, lingering more on the center of them and generally exploring less each painting. According to the hypothesis proposed by Fredrickson, namely "Broaden-and-Build" theory [2], positive emotions have a broadening effect on the momentary thought-action repertoire, in this case, pushing subjects to visually explore more the stimuli presented in a virtual environment. Foundational evidence for the proposition that positive emotions broaden people's momentary thought-action repertoires comes from two decades of experiments conducted by Isen and colleagues [29] that documented that people experiencing positive affect show patterns of thought that are notably unusual, flexible, creative, integrative, open to information and efficient. The broaden-and-build hypothesis of positive emotions suggests these broadening patterns may have evolutionary origins and adaptive benefits, as also suggested by the Hedonic Contingency Model (HCM) proposed by Wegener and Petty [30]. This model posits that individuals experiencing a positive mood have been conditioned through experience to purposely pursue activities that will perpetuate or elevate their benevolent affective states. Handley [31], for example, found out that individuals who have watched a positively valenced video for fifteen minutes evaluated their preference for future activities based upon a nonconscious and automatic tendency to seek experiences that would sustain their positive mood. Indeed, in a first attempt to test Fredrickson's broaden-and-build hypothesis of positive emotions using eye-tracking as a measure of visual exploration, a group of participants was subjected to the vision of some images presented in a central-peripheral arrays and emotional connotated [32]. Attentional breadth was determined by measuring the percentage viewing time to peripheral images as well as by the number of visual saccades participants made per slide. Consistent with Fredrickson's theory [2], the first study showed that individuals induced into a positive mood, fixated more peripheral stimuli than did control participants; however, this only held true for highly-valenced positive stimuli. So, the HCM theory could explain this effect suggesting that individuals would only broaden to images of similar valence, regardless of their location, in order to maintain their current affective mood. Our study, subjecting all the participants to the viewing of the same stimuli without a central-peripheral subdivision, aims at overcoming the possible confounds postulated by the HCM theory. Since the broader pattern of visual exploration for subjects belonging to Condition 1 – positive mood induction group - was found for all paintings but, from this first analysis, we were not able to say that much about individuals in a negative mood, AOIs' analyses were fundamental for two reasons i) to determine if subjects in a negative mood explore more the center of the paintings– evaluating parameters such as the fixation percentage and the number of visits directed to those AOIs and ii) to define in which paintings this effect was more visible. As revealed by this AOIs' analysis, participants belonging to Condition 2 and subjected to the induction of a negative emotional state, explored more those AOIs, placed in the center of each painting, also increasing the time of their fixations directed to them. They linger more on the center of each painting, leaving out the exploration of the peripheral parts of the stimuli, showing an opposite pattern of exploration revealed from a first general analysis for Condition 1 whose fixations were more focused on the perimeters of the stimuli. We reported below (Fig. 4) two of the three paintings in which the differential visual exploration of the stimuli between participants belonging to Condition 1 and subjected to a positive affect and participants belonging to Condition 2, subjected to a negative affect, was most evident. It is interesting that this effect was found most on these two paintings, one by Victor Vasarely and the second by Piet Mondrian: the composition of these paintings is most characterized by a geometrical configuration, made by straight lines, angles and no rotundities. As proposed by Reber [33] aesthetic pleasure is a function of the perceiver's processing dynamics: the more fluently perceivers can process an object, the more positive their aesthetic response. So, for this reason, the differential exploration between the two conditions is thought to be emphasized.

The interpretative framework arising from our results, thus far, gives a specific role to the emotional state of the observer, as a top-down component, in the way it affects the aesthetic perception of paintings. Thus, the general analysis reporting gaze fixation data, not only supports the Broaden-and- Build model [2] but also highlights the role of a pre-emotional state in which an individual is, as a top-down component, in influencing the following visual exploration of the artwork and in contributing to the emergence of the aesthetic experience.

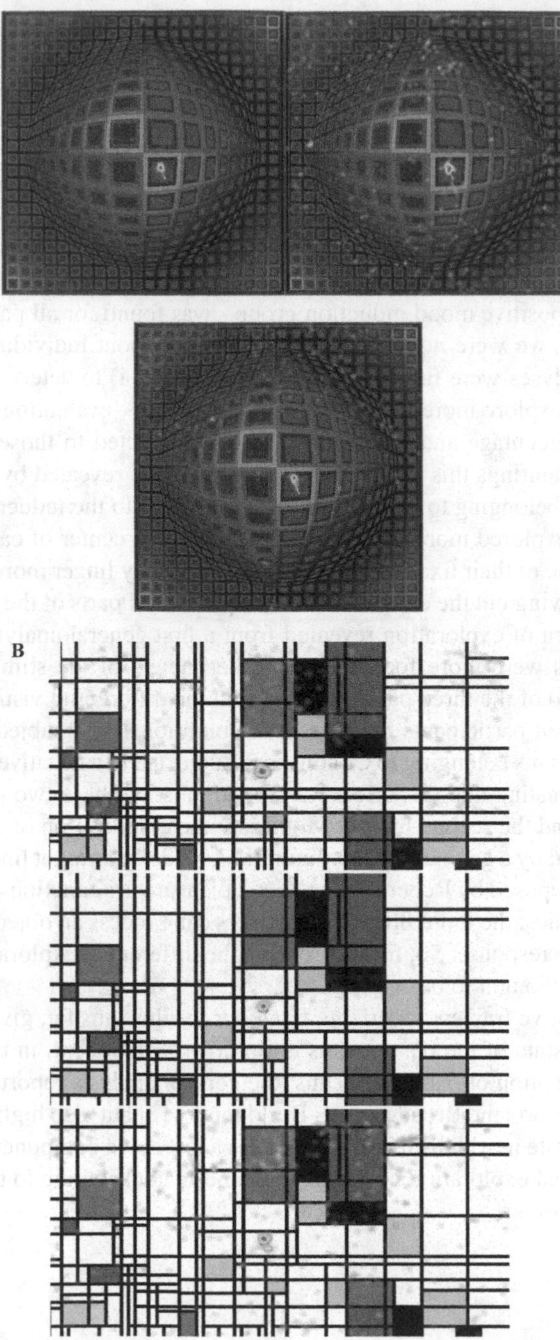

Fig. 4. (A) Right: total number of fixations made by participants belonging to Condition 1, Left: total number of fixations made by participants belonging to Condition 1. In the middle: total number of fixations made by participants belonging to Condition 3. (B) First image: total number of fixations made by participants belonging to Condition 2. Second image: total number of fixations made by participants belonging to Condition 1. Third image: total number of fixations made by participants belonging to Condition 3.

6 Limitations and Future Perspectives

While these findings offer preliminary support that Broaden and Built theory for positive emotions [2] suits also for aesthetic stimuli, demonstrating the broader visual exploration in relation to a positive affect; also supporting the confirmation of the VIMAP model - claiming that aesthetic experience emerges from the contribution of both top-down and bottom-up components - there are several evident limitations to the current study. An important possible confound involves the differential arousal level and emotional content of the stimuli used in the experiment. Berlyne [5] suggests that arousal is a function of collative stimulus properties like novelty, complexity, incongruity, and uncertainty. He posits that moderate levels of arousal are correlated with positive affect whereas high levels of arousal are correlated with negative affect. So, further studies, following this strand, have to consider this arousal and emotional nature of the paintings considered, without taking for granted that the emotional induction, before the presentation of the stimuli lasts for the entire duration of the experimental session and that some paintings, for their representative content, could elicit slight emotional changes into subjects taking part in the experiment. It is therefore suggested that participants judged the types of emotions each stimulus evokes through an additional ad-hoc questionnaire, before and after taking part into the experimental session. Another factor to be taken into consideration is the presentation of those paintings through a virtual- reality viewer. The exploration of some stimuli on a classic screen presentation is different from that in a virtual reality environment. If this modality, on one hand, could stimulate the sense of being inside a work of art, enhancing the power of an aesthetic experience, on the other hand, confounding factors have to be taken into account such as the order of presentation of the images in the sense that stimuli presented at the beginning are more explored due to the novelty factor of a virtual reality experience and stimuli presented at the end of the session could be subjected to a kind of "habituation" effect. This study offers strong support that individuals experiencing an induced positive mood expand their attentional breadth as compared to those experiencing an induced negative mood and to normal control participants. The broader explorative behavior has been demonstrated through some parameters related to the visual exploration, but further studies could take into consideration also parameters related to the movement of the head. Induction of the defined emotional state could be assessed through other different modalities such as music: in this case the induction could last for the entire duration of the experimental session as paintings are progressively presented to the participants [34]. Finally, a more thorough future analysis could be conducted with subjects who are both expert and non-expert in visual arts, to look for potential differences between these two groups and might provide data from a more varied ethnic sample, including data from middle-aged or elderly people.

Acknowledgment. The work has been supported by Fondazione Cariplo, grant: "Promoting Education of Scientific and Technological Societal Issues Through Sublime (PROMETHEUS)" n°: 2019-3536.

References

1. Pelowski, M., Markey, P., Forster. M., Gerger. G., Leder, H.: Move me, astonish me... delight my eyes and brain: the Vienna Integrated Model of top-down and bottom-up processes in Art Perception (VIMAP) and corresponding affective, evaluative, and neurophysiological correlates. Phys. Life Rev. **21**, 80–125 (2017). 359(1449), 1367–1378
2. Fredrickson, B.L.: The role of positive emotions in positive psychology. The broaden-and-build theory of positive emotions. Am. Psychol. **56**(3), 218–226 (2001)
3. Zeki, S., Watson, J.D., Lueck, C.J., Rfiston, K.J., Kennard, C., Frackowaik, R.S.J.: A direct demonstration of functional specialization in human visual cortex. J. Neurosci. **11**, 641–649 (1991)
4. Lasher, M., Carroll, J., Bever, T.: The cognitive basis of aesthetic experience. Leonardo **16**(3), 196–199 (1983)
5. Berlyne, D.E.: Conflict, Arousal, and Curiosity. McGraw-Hill, New York (1960)
6. Martindale, C., Dailey, A.: Creativity, primary process cognition and personality. Pers. Individ. Differ. **20**, 409–414 (1996)
7. Kreitler, H., Kreitler, S.: The model of cognitive orientation: towards a theory of human behaviour. Br. J. Psychol. **63**, 9–30 (1972)
8. Marković, S.: Components of aesthetic experience: aesthetic fascination, aesthetic appraisal, and aesthetic emotion. i-Perception **3**, 1–17 (2012)
9. Darwin, C.: The expression of the emotions in man and animals. University of Chicago Press, Chicago (1965) (Original work published 1872)
10. James, W.H.: What is Emotion? 1884 (1948)
11. Cannon, W.B.: The James-Lange theory of emotions: a critical examination and an alternative theory. Am. J. Psychol. **100**(3–4), 567–586 (1987)
12. Schachter, S., Singer, J.E.: Cognitive, social, and physiological determinants of emotional state. Psychol. Rev. **69**, 379–399 (1962)
13. Scherer, K.R.: Emotion as a multicomponent process: a model and some cross-cultural data (1984)
14. Easterbrook, J.A.: The effect of emotion on cue utilization and the organization of behaviour. Psychol. Rev. **66**, 183–201 (1959)
15. Johnson, K.J., Waugh, C.E., Fredrickson, B.L.: Smile to see the forest: facially expressed positive emotions broaden cognition. Cogn. Emot. **24**, 299–321 (2010)
16. Derryberry, D., Tucker, D.M.: Motivating the focus of attention. In: Neidenthal, P.M., Kitayama, S. (eds.) The Heart's Eye: Emotional Influences in Perception and Attention, pp. 167–196. Academic Press, San Diego, CA (1994)
17. Bylinskii, Z., Borkin, M.A., Kim, N.W., Pfister, H., Oliva, A.: Eye fixation metrics for large scale evaluation and comparison of information visualizations. In: Burch, M., Chuang, L., Fisher, B., Schmidt, A., Weiskopf, D. (eds.) Eye Tracking and Visualization (2015)
18. Brieber, D., Nadal, M., Leder, H., Rosenberg, R.: Art in time and space: context modulates the relation between art experience and viewing time. PLoS ONE **9**(6), e99019 (2014)
19. Leder, H., Goller, J., Rigotti, T., Forster, M.: Private and shared taste in art and face appreciation. Front. Hum. Neurosci. **10**, 155 (2016)
20. Koide, N., Kubo, T., Nishida, S, Shibata, T., Ikeda, K.: Art expertise reduces influence of visual salience on fixation in viewing abstract-paintings. PLoS ONE **10**(2), e0117696 (2015)
21. Chamorro-Premuzic, T., Furnham, A.: Art judgement: a measure related to both personality and intelligence? Imagination Cogn. Pers. **24**(1), 3–24 (2004–2005)
22. Lundy, D.E., Schenkel, M.B., Akrie, T.N., Walker, A.M.: How important is beauty to you? The development of the desire for aesthetics scale. Empirical Stud. Arts **28**(1), 73–92 (2010)

23. Shiota, M.N., Keltner, D., John, O.P.: Positive emotion dispositions differentially associated with Big Five personality and attachment style. J. Positive Psychol. **1**(2), 61–71 (2006)
24. Chirico, A., Shiota, M.N., Gaggioli, A.: Positive emotion dispositions and emotion regulation in the Italian population. PLoS ONE **16**, e0245545 (2021)
25. Jankovic, D.: Art and VR museums: about the aesthetic experience in different contexts (2021)
26. Gulhan, D., Durant, S., Zanker, J.M.: Similarity of gaze patterns across physical and virtual versions of an installation artwork. Sci. Rep. **11**, 18913 (2021)
27. Chirico, A., Yaden, D.B., Riva, G., Gaggioli, A.: The potential of virtual reality for the investigation of awe. Front. Psychol. **7**, 1766 (2016)
28. Lanatà, A., Valenza, G., Scilingo, E.P.: Eye gaze patterns in emotional pictures. J. Ambient Intell. Humanized Comput. **4**, 705–715 (2013)
29. Isen, A.M.: Positive affect and decision making. In: Lewis, M., Haviland-Jones, J.M. (eds.) (1960)
30. Wegener, D.T., Petty, R.E.: Mood management across affective states: the hedonic contingency hypothesis. J. Pers. Soc. Psychol. **66**(6), 1034–1048 (1994)
31. Handley, I.M., Lassiter, G.D., Nickell, E.F., Herchenroeder, L.M.: Affect and automatic mood maintenance. J. Exp. Soc. Psychol. **40**, 106–112 (2004)
32. Wadlinger, H.A., Isaacowitz, D.M.: Positive mood broadens visual attention to positive stimuli. Motiv. Emot. **30**, 87–99 (2006)
33. Reber, R., Schwarz, N., Winkielman, P.: Processing fluency and aesthetic pleasure: is beauty in the perceiver's processing experience? Pers. Soc. Psychol. Rev. Official J. Soc. Pers. Soc. Psychol. Inc.**8**(4), 364–382 (2004)
34. Albertazzi, L., Canal, L., Micciolo, R.: Cross-modal associations between materic painting and classical Spanish music. Front. Psychol. **6**, 424 (2015)

Augmented Reality and 3D Printing for Archaeological Heritage: Evaluation of Visitor Experience

Valeria Garro(✉) and Veronica Sundstedt(✉)

Blekinge Institute of Technology, Karlskrona, Sweden
{valeria.garro,veronica.sundstedt}@bth.se

Abstract. Augmented Reality (AR) and 3D printing have increasingly been used in archaeological and cultural heritage to make artifacts and environments accessible to the general public. This paper presents the case study of the Ljungaviken dog, an archaeological find of dog skeleton remains dated around 8000 years ago. The dog remains have been digitized using 3D scanning and displayed in an AR application. A physical replica has also been created with 3D printing. Both the AR application and the 3D printed copy have been shown in a temporary museum exhibition. In this paper, we present the visitors' experience evaluation based on a study with 42 participants. Aspects being evaluated are related to the realism, enjoyment, and easiness of use of the AR application. Moreover, the two media are compared in terms of understanding, visual quality, and experience satisfaction. The results show an overall positive experience for both the display solutions, with slightly higher scores for the AR application in the comparison. When asked about overall preference, the participants reported similar results between both media. Due to issues of displaying fragile objects in a museum setting, as well as recent restrictions following pandemic closures and availability, the results presented in this paper show a positive alternative towards using digital artifacts to showcase our cultural heritage.

Keywords: Augmented Reality · 3D Printing · Cultural heritage

1 Introduction

In the last decades, several museums have been adopting digital technologies such as Virtual Reality (VR) and Augmented Reality (AR) as an alternative or complementary media to traditional cultural heritage (CH) exhibitions for enhancing the visitors' experience [6]. AR technology allows us to enhance the real world with overlaid digital information, such as interfaces or three-dimensional objects. On the other hand, VR technology presents the user with an immersive virtual world inside a head-mounted display (HMD), for example. In order to display 3D objects or scenes in either AR och VR, they need to be converted into a digital 3D format from information in the real world. There are different methods for

L. T. De Paolis et al. (Eds.): XR Salento 2022, LNCS 13446, pp. 360–372, 2022.
https://doi.org/10.1007/978-3-031-15553-6_25

acquiring 3D models, and one common technique that speeds up the process is digitizing CH artifacts and archaeological finds using 3D scanning devices.

The obtained virtual 3D models are not only featured in digital media but also used for the creation of 3D printed replicas. These replicas can be temporarily displayed in the museums as accurate copies of the original artifacts that have to be removed, e.g., due to being temporarily lent to another exhibition, or because they are too fragile or too valuable to be shown to the general public [22,24]. 3D printing has also been used to support the restoration of damaged objects [4,22] and the accessibility of objects also from a tactile perspective which are either too large or too small to be properly analyzed and understood [16]. The use of 3D copies, both digital and 3D printed replicas, is a valid solution for enlarging the access to museums' storage, as it facilitates the exhibition of CH objects in multiple venues and locations while preserving the original delicate artifacts.

Moreover, VR and AR media can offer an engaging and enhanced experience to the visitor by interaction [6] and providing additional information in a more immersive way compared to more traditional displays of complementary texts and videos. In some cases, the use of VR opens the possibility for the visitor to be immersed in an ancient scenario created by the analysis work of the archaeologists and based on the archaeological remains [18].

Restrictions due to the Covid-19 pandemic have resulted in many museums being closed. As a consequence, CH environments and artifacts usually on display have not been able to be shown to the general public in the same way or not at all during this time. A recent work by Itani and Hollebeek [11] analyzes the impact of the pandemic and highlights how the visitors' requirements are shifting towards viable VR alternatives of the most traditional exhibitions.

In this paper, we present a study in which we compare the visitor assessment of a mobile AR application showing a 3D model of an archaeological find and a 3D printed replica of the object. The overall aim is to explore if there would be a gap in the experience assessment between using digital AR technology and a 3D reconstructed printed object.

Our case study features the Ljungaviken dog, a recent archaeological find in southern Sweden of a dog's skeleton remains dated around 8000 years ago. The original remains of the Ljungaviken dog are currently stored away and not accessible to the general public. During a temporary museum exhibition of this discovery, we carried out an evaluation of the two media experiences. The AR application and the 3D printed replica were compared in terms of ability to understand the archaeological find, their visual quality, and experience satisfaction. The AR application was also evaluated based on realism, enjoyment, and easiness of use.

The remainder of the paper is organized as follows. Section 1.1 presents related work in the area of AR applied to a CH setting. This part also highlights previous work using 3D printing as a means of portraying archaeological artifacts. Section 2 presents the Ljungaviken dog, the archaeological discovery featured in the case study. The pipeline for creating the digital model and the

3D printed replica, as well as the experience evaluation, are presented in Sect. 3. The overall results gathered in the user evaluation are presented and discussed in Sect. 4. Finally, Sect. 5 summarizes the conclusions and highlights ideas for relevant future work.

1.1 Related Work

Several works and case studies have been presented implementing and evaluating the use of AR applications in CH, either as mobile applications or with the use of head-mounted devices. An extensive overview of recent works can be found in the survey by Bekele et al. [6]. This work describes both indoor and outdoor AR solutions, and it identifies three main application areas of AR in CH: the enrichment of traditional exhibitions, the reconstruction of artifacts, and the support for exploration of CH sites.

More recent works have also shown the implementation of AR-based serious games supporting interactive learning activities [14]. This work proposes an interactive AR mobile experience exhibiting historical and architectural content in multiple points of interest distributed in the Hwaseong Fortress in South Korea. Hammady et al. [9] presents an immersive AR application designed to be used with a HMD (Microsoft HoloLens). The authors focus on the storytelling and historical narrative aspects of the application. In this case study, in one of the museum's rooms, the visitors visualize a 3D scene set in ancient Egypt representing a battle narrated by an avatar. The results of the user acceptance evaluation conducted during this study exhibit a high level of engagement and easiness of use. Several other works investigate the level of engagement and satisfaction of the AR applications in the CH context showing an overall positive impact of AR technology [7,10,23].

The use of 3D scanning and 3D printing (digital fabrication) in CH is a well-studied solution that allows the creation of affordable tangible replicas of artifacts of different scales [5,22,27]. 3D printing has also been used in support of restoration of artifacts, for example, by recombining fragments [4] and reconstructing damaged parts [12,25], also based on symmetrical properties [26]. The possibility to interact with 3D printed replicas of fragile artifacts has opened new opportunities for engaging the visitors. An example is shown in [8], in which the authors present a workflow for the development and fabrication of a 3D printed puzzle of an ancient urn.

Moreover, 3D printing has been applied in the construction of trackable objects to be used as markers for AR applications which superimpose on the 3D printed replicas virtual elements such as specific textures [15] or virtual 3D models [13,21].

Some recent works compare the impact of virtual and tangible media on the users. In [17], the authors investigated users' interaction with virtual and 3D printed versions of CH artifacts and how they influence learning aspects. The digital versions of the 3D models have been shown via an immersive AR application (HoloLens) and with a more traditional on-screen application (Sketchfab). The results reveal that all three representations are valid media for achieving learning outcomes. However, differences in the interaction have an impact on the learning process showing higher levels of enjoyment for the HoloLens compared to the other two representations while still achieving learning outcomes comparable to the more traditional screen content of SketchFab. The absence of textural information in the 3D printed representation can be a disadvantage for the critical interpretation of the artifacts. However, tangible media, compared to virtual media, have the unique characteristics of supporting visually impaired people [20]. A study by Ramkumar et al. [19] extends [17] by replicating a similar experimental setting and also investigating users' visual attention using eye tracking. The results confirm the findings in [17] and also indicate similar visual attention comparing virtual and tangible representations.

With this paper, we continue the investigation of comparing the influence of different media. In particular, we are interested in studying the visitors' perception in terms of understanding, visual quality, and experience satisfaction of a CH object displayed as a virtual 3D model on an AR application and replicated with 3D printing technology.

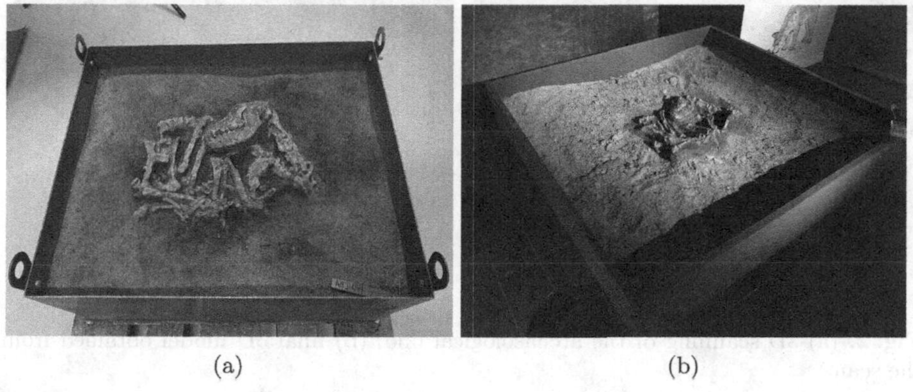

(a) (b)

Fig. 1. Ljungaviken Dog. (a) Original remains currently preserved in grave soil. (b) 3D printed replica installation during the exhibition.

2 The Ljungaviken Dog

The Ljungaviken dog was discovered in 2020 during an archaeological excavation in Ljungaviken, an urban area located east of Sölvesborg, in southern Sweden. The excavation brought to light a village settlement from the Stone Age consisting of several houses and fireplaces. In the vicinity of one of these houses, the archaeologists found skeletal remains of a dog dated around 8000 years old. This find may suggest that the dog was a valued friend of the inhabitants of the village since it was buried near one of the houses together with flints. The archaeologists estimated the dog died at a relatively young age, between one and three years old. The dog's remains are placed on a surface of about 30 × 40 cm, and the height of the withers has been estimated to be around 53 cm. This archaeological find, shown in Fig. 1a, is currently preserved at the Blekinge Museum under special environmental conditions and it is not permanently displayed to the general public due to its fragile nature.

3 Methodology

This section describes the development and evaluation of the 3D replica and AR application. It has four main parts: (1) 3D scanning of the dog's remains, (2) developing the AR application, (3) printing the 3D model, and (4) a description of the questionnaire evaluation conducted with the general public during the exhibition.

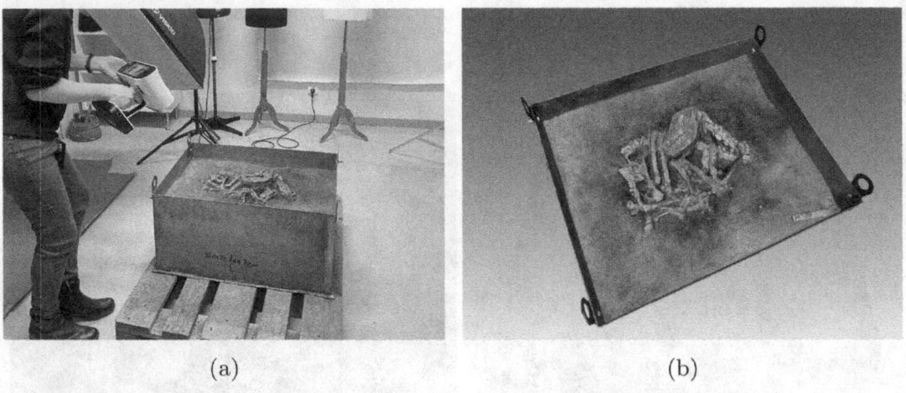

(a) (b)

Fig. 2. (a) 3D scanning of the archaeological find, (b) final 3D model obtained from the scan.

3.1 3D Scanning

The dog remains were digitized using an Artec Leo (Fig. 2a), a structured light 3D scanner that captures both geometry and texture information and has a 3D resolution of up to 0.5 mm. After the scanning acquisition, the data have been processed using the Artec Studio Projects software. We followed the typical processing pipeline to obtain a 3D mesh of the archaeological find. First, we performed a cleaning stage of the scans by removing the base surface and other unwanted elements of the scene. The Leo scanner automatically performs a first alignment of the different scans directly during the scanning, but it is also possible to perform this stage manually via the software. The scans were converted to a single coordinate system via global registration and the final fusion step created the 3D mesh model. After the mesh simplification step, we obtained a model with about 500 thousand triangles on which we applied the high-resolution texture information (8192 × 8192). Finally, the model has been exported in different formats: *glb*, binary GL Transmission Format (glTF), to be loaded in the AR application, and *stl* format for the 3D printing stage. As shown in Fig. 2b, the 3D model includes the whole box in which the bones are preserved, the whole surface measures around 60 × 70 cm.

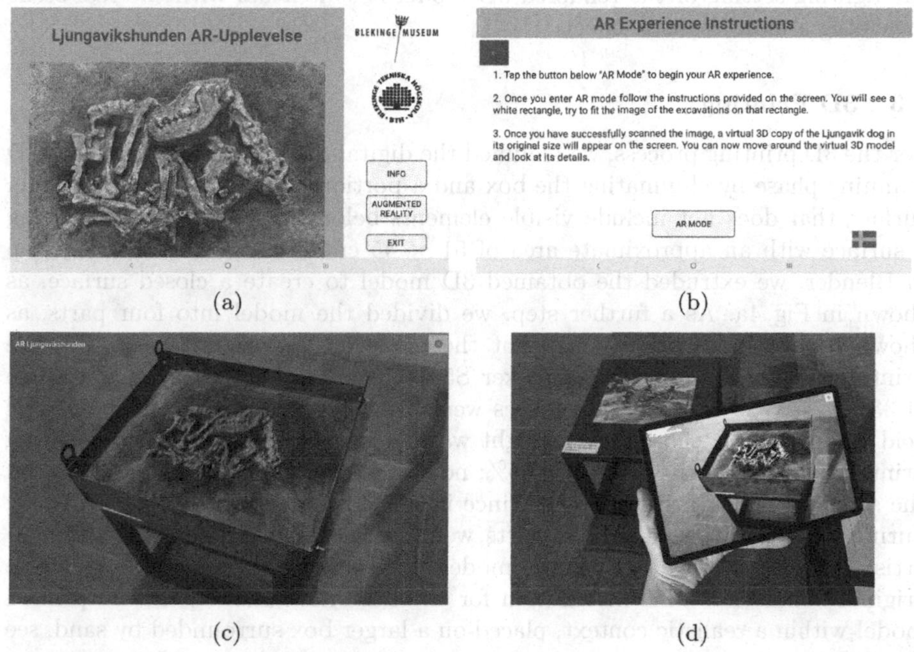

Fig. 3. AR application: (a) initial view, (b) AR experience instructions, (c) example of AR mode view, (d) AR app at the exhibition.

3.2 AR Application

The developed AR application runs on Android mobile devices supporting Google AR platform ARCore [1] and is based on the Sceneform 3D framework [2,3]. During the development phase, we tested the application on different Android tablets, i.e., Samsung Galaxy Tab S4, Tab S7, and Tab S7+. During the exhibition, the visitors could experience the AR application on a Samsung Galaxy Tab S7 with a display size of 11 in.. The initial view of the application displays a photo of the dog and a menu where the visitor can choose to open the AR experience directly or to read a text shortly describing the history of the archaeological find (Fig. 3a). When selecting the AR experience, a first text view displays simple instructions on how to visualize the 3D model (Fig. 3b).

The user can then open the AR mode view and proceed with the AR experience, the application detects a predefined image placed on a plane surface and it automatically displays on top of it the 3D model at its original scale, as shown in Fig. 3c. For the exhibition, we used an A3-size picture of the archaeological excavation as a marker image positioned over a low side table (Fig. 3d). The chosen table setup offers an experience similar to looking at the real artifact. The ARCore Sceneform library provides an automatic lighting estimation, so the lighting setting of the rendered 3D model is contextual with the real scene providing a more realistic effect.

3.3 3D Printing

For the 3D printing process, we modified the digital model obtained from the 3D scanning phase by eliminating the box and a portion of the surrounding terrain surface that does not include visible elements belonging to the dog, obtaining a surface with an approximate area of 51 × 45 cm. As a post-processing step in Blender, we extruded the obtained 3D model to create a closed surface, as shown in Fig. 4a. As a further step, we divided the model into four parts, as shown in Fig. 4b to be able to print the model at its original scale. For the printing phase, we used an Ultimaker S5 3D printer that has a build volume of 33 × 24 × 30 cm. The four pieces were printed with white PLA (polylactic acid) filament; the chosen layer height was 0.1 mm to ensure a high-resolution print. The infill density was set to 5%; no special requirements were needed on the strength of the printed replica since its purpose was exclusively for display during the exhibition. The four parts were assembled and glued together. An artist painted the final 3D printed model to resemble as much as possible the original bones. The final installation for the exhibition showed the 3D printed model within a realistic context, placed on a larger box surrounded by sand, see Fig. 4d.

3.4 Exhibition Evaluation

During the exhibition, the visitors could look at the 3D printed replica of the dog's remains and they could test the AR application. A questionnaire was provided to visitors (over the age of 18) who volunteered to take part in the evaluation stage.

The questionnaire briefly described what AR technology is in order for the participants to have a basic concept understanding in case they were not familiar with AR technology. Moreover, the questionnaire collected information about the participants' prior experience with AR technology. The first set of three questions asked the participants' feedback related to the AR application. In detail, we asked about the level of realism of the 3D model shown by the AR application (Q1), i.e., to what degree they felt the 3D model as being part of the reality, the level of fun of the AR experience (Q2), and the easiness of use (Q3). The second set of questions targeted both the AR application and the 3D printed replica of the dog remains. We asked the participants to rate the degree

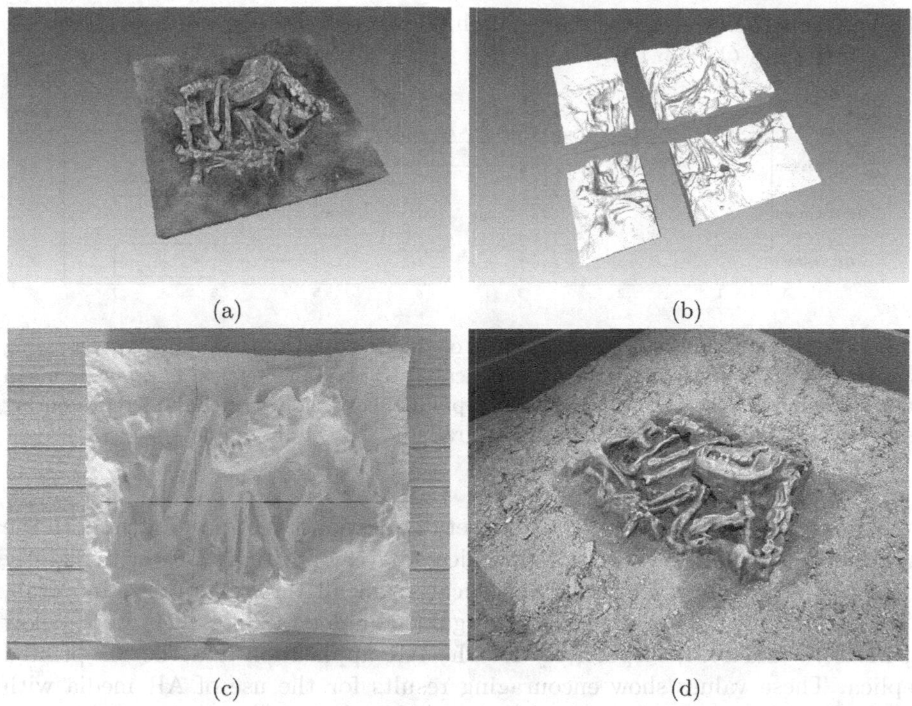

Fig. 4. (a) 3D model used for the 3D printing, (b) 3D model divided in 4 pieces, (c) 3D printed replica before the painting the process, (d) final version of the painted 3D printed replica at the exhibition.

of received understanding of the Ljungaviken dog through the two experiences (the AR application and the 3D printed replica) (Q4), the visual quality of the two models (Q5), and the degree of satisfaction of the two experiences (Q6). All questions were formulated to be answered through a 7-point Likert scale with 1 as the lowest score and 7 as the highest score. As a final question, we asked the participant to indicate which of the two experiences they preferred, the AR application or the 3D printed replica.

4 Results and Discussion

We collected questionnaires from $N = 42$ participants, with an almost equal gender distribution (22 female, 19 male, 1 n/a). The age of the participants spans a range from 18 to 75 with an average age of 46 (7 people did not report their age). Only 21% of the participants had already used AR technology previous to the exhibition, while 50% answered they had never used AR and the remaining 29% did not indicate any preference. Figure 5 shows the results of the first set of questions related exclusively to the AR application. All three assessed factors, i.e., the realism of the 3D model (Q1), the easiness of use (Q2) and enjoyment

(Q3) of the AR experience, obtained high scores with average values of $Q1 = 6.0$, $Q2 = 6.19$, and $Q3 = 6.18$.

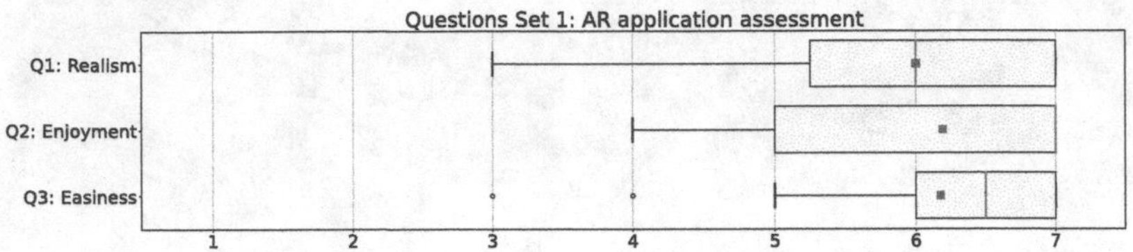

Fig. 5. Boxplot visualization of the results of the first part of the user study assessing the AR application. Median values are indicated by the blue vertical bars, while mean values are represented by the red squares. 7-point Likert scale, with 1 and 7 representing respectively the lowest grade and highest grade. (Color figure online)

Analyzing the results of the second set of questions, shown in Fig. 6, both the AR application and the 3D printed replica got very positive scores with slightly higher average values for the AR application in all three questions. In detail, only the average values regarding the gained understanding (Q4) were below 6, i.e. 5.79 and 5.74, respectively for the AR application and the 3D printed replica. These values show encouraging results for the use of AR media with respect to the more traditional exhibition of physical objects and artifacts since they show similar positive results. This result, together with the high average value obtained for the easiness of use (Q3), can be interpreted as an overall acceptance of the digital media whose use is becoming more and more common in our everyday lives and the absence of relevant hindrance related to the use of the AR technology. We obtained interesting results in particular for Q5 regarding the visual quality of the digital and printed models. The 3D model of the AR application got higher average results (6.20) with respect to the 3D printed replica (6.0). We expected a different trend here with a larger difference in favor of the 3D printed replica that has been painted very accurately and was placed in a realistic scenario surrounded by real sand and soil. Regarding the overall experience satisfaction (Q6), the AR application scored an average result of 6.41 with respect to a lower value (6.05) for the 3D printed model. This result was expected since the AR experience offers a higher interaction. The visitors could look at the 3D model of the AR application from different angles. They could also get close to the virtual 3D object observing details that they could not see by just looking at the 3D printed replica positioned in a large box. Finally, the last question asking which of the two experiences was the preferred experience showed tight results, i.e. 51% for the AR experience and 49% for the 3D replica.

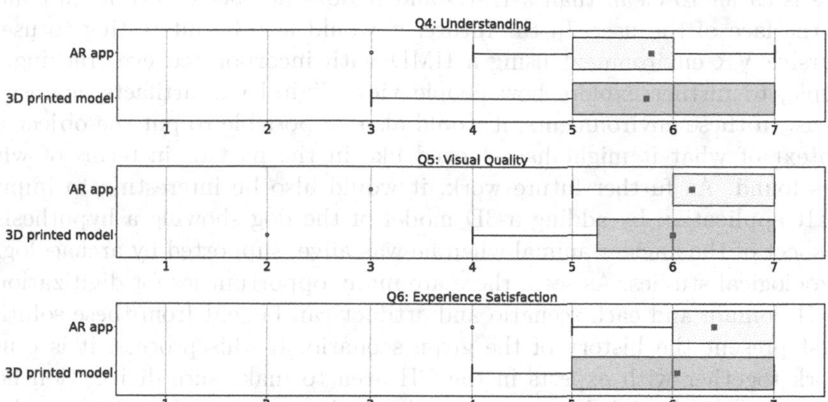

Fig. 6. Comparison between the AR application and the 3D printed model, boxplot visualization. Median values are indicated by the blue vertical bars, while mean values are represented by the red squares. 7-point Likert scale, with 1 and 7 representing respectively the lowest grade and highest grade. (Color figure online)

5 Conclusions and Future Work

This paper has presented a case study exploring user experiences of an AR application and a 3D printed model of an archaeological ecofact in an exhibition setting. Technologies such as AR and 3D printing allow visitors to have experiences that might otherwise not be feasible. Digitization of CH environments and objects is an increasing trend as part of longer-lasting documentation of our historic past. Digitization can also help speed up moments of the documentation process for staff working with a recording of historical sites.

The work presented in this paper includes a pipeline for making a non-accessible archaeological object available to the general public without affecting the original model, which is stored away in the Blekinge Museum archives under special environmental conditions. Digitization of artifacts has also been shown to make museum objects more accessible during the pandemic restrictions. The exhibition's evaluation presented in this paper assessed user experiences of the AR application and the 3D printed model in the Ljungaviken dog case study. The results show that the AR experience received high scores in terms of realism, enjoyment, and ease of use. In terms of comparing the two experiences, they both scored high on understanding, visual quality, and experience satisfaction, with a slightly higher score for the AR media, indicating that both techniques are valuable additions to a museum exhibition setting.

As part of future work, it would be interesting to compare the perceived realism of the real artifact, the AR prototype, and 3D printed replica in further detail. However, then it would be important to carry this out in a way that would not harm the delicate original dog remains. Due to the pandemic, a hand-held AR solution was chosen for displaying the digital representation since a tablet device is easier to clean than a HMD and it does not need to come in contact with the face of the user. In the future, it would also be interesting to use an immersive VR environment using a HMD with incorporated eye tracking, for example, to further explore how people view digital CH artifacts against 3D replicas. In these environments, it would also be possible to put the object into a context of what it might have looked like in the past or in terms of where it was found. As further future work, it would also be interesting to improve the AR application by adding a 3D model of the dog showing a hypothesis of the aspect of the ancient animal when he was alive, supported by archaeological and zoological studies. As seen, there are many opportunities for digitization in the CH domain and each scenario and artifact can benefit from these solutions to best present the history of the given scenario. In this process, it is crucial to work together with experts in the CH area to make sure digitization helps portray accurate knowledge regarding what is known and what the hypotheses are. Either way, the exhibition evaluation presented in this paper has shown that the opportunities for AR and 3D printing provide a very positive experience for the visitors.

Acknowledgement. This work was supported in part by KK-stiftelsen Sweden, through the ViaTecH Synergy Project (contract 20170056). The authors thank Peter Blaschke (BTH Innovation Labs) for the support during the 3D printing phase and Advaith Putta for the help prototyping a first version of the AR application. Moreover, they thank Blekinge Museum and Sölvesborg's Kommun for collaboration and exhibition access.

References

1. Google ARCore. http://developers.google.com/ar. Accessed June 2021
2. Sceneform Maintained SDK for Android. http://thomasgorisse.github.io/sceneform-android-sdk. Accessed June 2021
3. Sceneform SDK for Android. http://developers.google.com/sceneform. Accessed June 2021
4. Arbace, L., Sonnino, E., Callieri, M., Dellepiane, M., Fabbri, M., Iaccarino Idelson, A., Scopigno, R.: Innovative uses of 3d digital technologies to assist the restoration of a fragmented terracotta statue. J. Cult. Heritage **14**(4), 332–345 (2013). https://doi.org/10.1016/j.culher.2012.06.008
5. Balletti, C., Guerra, F., Lorenzon, A.: The venetian galea: from the wooden model to the digital model. In: International Archives of the Photogrammetry, Remote Sensing and Spatial Information Sciences - ISPRS Archives, vol. 43, pp. 1371–1379 (2020)
6. Bekele, M.K., Pierdicca, R., Frontoni, E., Malinverni, E.S., Gain, J.: A survey of augmented, virtual, and mixed reality for cultural heritage. J. Comput. Cult. Herit. **11**(2) (2018). https://doi.org/10.1145/3145534
7. Chung, N., Lee, H., Kim, J.Y., Koo, C.: The role of augmented reality for experience-influenced environments: the case of cultural heritage tourism in Korea. J. Travel Res. **57**(5), 627–643 (2018). https://doi.org/10.1177/0047287517708255

8. Echavarria, K.R., Samaroudi, M., Weyrich, T.: Fracturing artefacts into 3d printable puzzles to enhance audience engagement with heritage collections. J. Comput. Cultural Heritage **13**(1) (2020)
9. Hammady, R., Ma, M., Strathearn, C.: Ambient information visualisation and visitors' technology acceptance of mixed reality in museums. J. Comput. Cult. Herit. **13**(2) (2020). https://doi.org/10.1145/3359590
10. Huang, Y., Rodriguez Echavarria, K., Julier, S.: Engaging audiences with cultural heritage through augmented reality (AR) enhanced pop-up books. In: Spagnuolo, M., Melero, F.J. (eds.) Eurographics Workshop on Graphics and Cultural Heritage. The Eurographics Association (2020). https://doi.org/10.2312/gch.20201292
11. Itani, O.S., Hollebeek, L.D.: Light at the end of the tunnel: visitors' virtual reality (versus in-person) attraction site tour-related behavioral intentions during and post-covid-19. Tourism Manag. **84** (2021)
12. Jo, Y.H., Hong, S., Jo, S.Y., Kwon, Y.M.: Noncontact restoration of missing parts of stone buddha statue based on three-dimensional virtual modeling and assembly simulation. Heritage Sci. **8**(1) (2020)
13. Kobeisse, S., Holmquist, L.E.: Archeobox: engaging with historical artefacts through augmented reality and tangible interactions. In: Adjunct Publication of the 33rd Annual ACM Symposium on User Interface Software and Technology, pp. 22–24. UIST '20 Adjunct, Association for Computing Machinery, New York (2020). https://doi.org/10.1145/3379350.3416173
14. Koo, S., Kim, J., Kim, C., Kim, J., Cha, H.S.: Development of an augmented reality tour guide for a cultural heritage site. J. Comput. Cult. Herit. **12**(4) (2019). https://doi.org/10.1145/3317552
15. Mann, L., Fryazinov, O.: 3D printing for mixed reality hands-on museum exhibit interaction. In: ACM SIGGRAPH 2019 Posters, SIGGRAPH '19. Association for Computing Machinery, New York (2019). https://doi.org/10.1145/3306214.3338609
16. Neumüller, M., Reichinger, A., Rist, F., Kern, C.: 3D Printing for Cultural Heritage: Preservation, Accessibility, Research and Education, pp. 119–134. Springer, Heidelberg (2014). https://doi.org/10.1007/978-3-662-44630-0_9
17. Pollalis, C., et al.: Evaluating learning with tangible and virtual representations of archaeological artifacts. In: Proceedings of the Twelfth International Conference on Tangible, Embedded, and Embodied Interaction, TEI '18, pp. 626–637. Association for Computing Machinery, New York (2018). https://doi.org/10.1145/3173225.3173260
18. Pujol-Tost, L.: Did we just travel to the past? Building and evaluating with cultural presence different modes of VR-mediated experiences in virtual archaeology. J. Comput. Cult. Herit. **12**(1) (2019). https://doi.org/10.1145/3230678
19. Ramkumar, N., Fereydooni, N., Shaer, O., Kun, A.L.: Visual behavior during engagement with tangible and virtual representations of archaeological artifacts. In: Proceedings of the 8th ACM International Symposium on Pervasive Displays, PerDis '19, Association for Computing Machinery, New York (2019). https://doi.org/10.1145/3321335.3324930
20. Reichinger, A., Neumüller, M., Rist, F., Maierhofer, S., Purgathofer, W.: Computer-aided design of tactile models: taxonomy and case studies. In: Proceedings of the 13th International Conference on Computers Helping People with Special Needs, ICCHP'12, vol. Part II, pp. 497–504. Springer, Heidelberg (2012). https://doi.org/10.1007/978-3-642-31534-3_73

21. Scianna, A., Gaglio, G.F., Guardia, M.L.: Augmented reality for cultural heritage: the rebirth of a historical square. In: ISPRS - International Archives of the Photogrammetry, Remote Sensing and Spatial Information Sciences, vol. 4217, pp. 303–308 (2019)
22. Scopigno, R., Cignoni, P., Pietroni, N., Callieri, M., Dellepiane, M.: Digital fabrication techniques for cultural heritage: a survey. Comput. Graph. Forum **36**(1), 6–21 (2017). https://doi.org/10.1111/cgf.12781
23. Wakefield, C., Simons, A., John, D.: Can augmented reality enhance to a greater visitor satisfaction of historical landmarks? In: Rizvic, S., Rodriguez Echavarria, K. (eds.) Eurographics Workshop on Graphics and Cultural Heritage. The Eurographics Association (2019). https://doi.org/10.2312/gch.20191350
24. Wilson, P.F., Stott, J., Warnett, J.M., Attridge, A., Smith, M.P., Williams, M.A.: Museum visitor preference for the physical properties of 3d printed replicas. J. Cult. Heritage **32**, 176–185 (2018). https://doi.org/10.1016/j.culher.2018.02.002
25. Xu, J., Ding, L., Love, P.E.D.: Digital reproduction of historical building ornamental components: from 3D scanning to 3D printing. Autom. Construct. **76**, 85–96 (2017)
26. Zhou, P., Shui, W., Qu, L., Gao, F., Wu, Z.: Case study: missing data computation and 3D printing application in symmetrical artifact restoration. In: Proceedings - VRCAI 2016: 15th ACM SIGGRAPH Conference on Virtual-Reality Continuum and Its Applications in Industry, vol. 2, pp. 63–66 (2016)
27. Ziegler, M.J., et al.: Applications of 3D paleontological data at the Florida museum of natural history. Front. Earth Sci. **8** (2020)

Building Blocks for Multi-dimensional WebXR Inspection Tools Targeting Cultural Heritage

Bruno Fanini(✉), Emanuel Demetrescu, Alberto Bucciero, Alessandra Chirivi, Francesco Giuri, Ivan Ferrari, and Nicola Delbarba

Digital Heritage Innovation Lab (DHILab), National Research Council—Institute of Heritage Science (CNR-ISPC), Napoli, Italy
bruno.fanini@cnr.it,
https://www.ispc.cnr.it/en/2021/06/16/dhilab-digital-heritage-innovation-lab/

Abstract. Data exploration and inspection within semantically enriched multi-dimensional contexts, may benefit of immersive VR presentation when proper 3D user interfaces are adopted. WebXR represents a great opportunity to investigate, experiment, develop and assess advanced multi-dimensional interactive tools for Cultural Heritage, making them accessible through a common web browser. We present and describe the potential of WebXR and a set of building blocks for crafting such immersive data inspection tools, exploiting recent web standards and spatial user interfaces. We describe the current state of the EMviq tool - developed within SSHOC European project - and how it is taking advantage of these components for online immersive sessions. The EMviq tool allows to visually inspect and query an Extended Matrix dataset, allowing to query and explore all the information within the knowledge graph relating to the interpretative datasets - in this paper applied to the case studies of the Roman theatre of Catania and Montebelluna smithy. The main functionalities discussed are spatio-temporal exploration, search and selection of stratigraphic units, and the presentation of metadata and paradata related to the data provenance (both objective and interpretative).

Keywords: WebXR · Web3D · Graph-DB · Immersive VR · Semantic inspection

1 Introduction

The presentation of 3D content and dissemination of interactive applications on desktop and mobile web browsers has undergone major advancements, thanks to the improvement of browsers' capabilities and the introduction of standards and specifications. Web browsers are available on virtually all devices, offering users a way to access interactive applications (web-apps) or tools anywhere, as long as internet (or local network) connection is available. This translates

L. T. De Paolis et al. (Eds.): XR Salento 2022, LNCS 13446, pp. 373–390, 2022.
https://doi.org/10.1007/978-3-031-15553-6_26

into a great opportunity to design, prototype, develop and deploy accessible, universal and interactive web-applications targeting different fields, including Cultural Heritage. Thanks to WebXR specification it is also possible to offer unified presentation on XR devices, including 3 or 6 DoF (degrees of freedom) immersive VR headsets, AR/MR devices and much more. Thanks to its inherent openness and accessibility, the web thus represents a big opportunity for CH to enable universal access to immersive VR tools or experiences, with no additional software required.

Data exploration, specifically dealing with semantically enriched 3D environments, may benefit of immersive VR presentation [35] when providing proper interfaces to final users. WebXR can thus offer a great opportunity to investigate, experiment, develop and assess advanced multi-dimensional inspection tools for Cultural Heritage, accessible through a standard web browser. Emerging research fields like Immersive Analytics (IA) furthermore, are investigating how novel interactions in immersive VR and display technologies can be used to support analytical reasoning and decision making. Such themes - combined with an increased adoption of graph databases in Cultural Heritage - provide a fertile ground (that will be discussed in Sect. 2) to research and investigate WebXR tools for the inspection of semantically enriched multi-dimensional contexts. There are indeed several challenges to face to craft such web-based immersive tools (Sect. 3) and a minimal set of building blocks that can be adopted to facilitate the creation of such class of WebXR tools (Sect. 4).

The paper aims to present the current state of WebXR interaction model for a product of such building blocks and guidelines - called *EMviq*. EMviq is a web-based multidimensional inspection tool, that leverages on the open source framework ATON [16] and the Extended Matrix formalism [6]. More specifically the article will illustrate and discuss how this tool can be used to immersively explore and inspect a digital replica of an archaeological site and its virtual reconstruction, as well as the knowledge graph of all the related information.

2 Related Work

Since the introduction of the first WebVR specification [37], large advancements have been made through the introduction of WebXR [20,25]. The specification aims to unify VR and AR (Augmented Reality) worlds, supporting a wide range of user inputs (e.g., voice, gestures) offering users new models to interact with virtual spaces over the web. WebXR is enabling developers and designers to create seamless immersive applications accessible through common web browsers using consumer-level 3-DoF and 6-Dof HMDs. This is leading to new, innovative experiences built for the web [10,26,30], also fueling content creators who need to assess immersive VR content or applications on the web.

From a user perspective, immersive VR is well known to introduce additional challenges related to navigation techniques, like disorientation and/or motion sickness during the exploration of a virtual environment [23]. This is why there is still a lot of ongoing research and experimentation on locomotion techniques and user interfaces for VR, although we can rely on already established guidelines and techniques [2,3,39]. Furthermore, user interfaces for immersive VR are radically different compared to standard ones: existing literature on 3D UIs [27,40] must be taken into account to craft WebXR applications and tools, especially those aimed at data exploration [21].

Regarding 3D formats' standardization, *glTF*[1] (GL Transmission Format) by Khronos is a royalty-free, open standard designed for efficient streaming and rendering of 3D models and scenes [41]. glTF is an extensible format that facilitates authoring workflows by enabling the interoperable use of 3D content across professionals and applications. Currently, a multitude of 3D modeling software tools (Blender, 3DS Max, Maya, etc.) as well as game engines like *Unreal Engine 4* offer direct export options for glTF, thus boosting the web publishing workflow. Regarding publication of large 3D datasets, open specifications like *3D Tiles* built on glTF developed by Cesium [42] allow to share, visualize and interact with massive heterogeneous 3D geospatial content, high-resolution photogrammetry datasets or BIM [46] on desktop, web, and mobile applications [33]. These standards and open specifications also represent robust foundations to build interoperable Web3D tools, services and applications for Cultural Heritage.

Immersive Analytics is an emerging research field investigating how novel interaction models and display technologies can be exploited to support analytical reasoning and decision making [9,28]. At the intersection of visual analytics and VR, Immersive Analytics (or IA) has gained some traction in the last few years. The main goal is to study advanced and usable UIs (user interfaces) to support collaboration and offer VR users (analysts) ways to query and immerse themselves in complex, or multi-dimensional datasets. A few recent works also focus on immersive analytics on the web, although facing the common challenges related to online deployment. Butcher et al. [4,5] investigated some of the challenges faced by developers in crafting effective and informative immersive web-based 3D visualizations. Other works did investigate proper encoding models for compact, interactive and efficient WebXR analysis of large multi-dimensional datasets related to users' sessions [13,14]. Regarding data exploration using immersive VR, previous work from McIntire [35] did show that using stereoscopic visualization improves people's performance in spatial tasks in more than 60% of the time.

Finally, there is an increased adoption of *graph databases* in the Cultural Heritage field, especially in scenarios where the connections between the information is a valuable aspect. Tools like ResearchSpace [38] (https://researchspace.org) allow to "draw" metadata in a canvas with the metaphor of nodes (semantic building blocks) connected by arches (semantic relations) enabling the production of rich knowledge graphs, suitable for data mining, searching, and interoperation.

[1] https://www.khronos.org/gltf/.

3 Challenges

Designing and creating web-based 4D inspection tools for CH providing support for immersive XR presentation is not an easy task, since it raises multiple challenges. One of the first challenges has to deal with incompleteness, imprecision and heterogeneity of data. Visualization of uncertainty in general, is a complex and persistent challenge [28,43]. Digital representations of archaeological datasets, inherently introduce some uncertainty that needs to be efficiently represented for immersive VR consumption.

Work in [11] highlights grand challenges related to data visualization, semantic knowledge, immersive analytics and more, depicted and divided in multiple topics. Within the scope of interest of this paper we can identify different challenges that seem to affect more the class of tools depicted.

3.1 Spatially Situated Data Visualisation

Exploring 4D scenarios depicting Cultural Heritage contexts enables the interaction between scientific model data driven and the final user with the immediate consequence to bridge heterogeneous data within a VR experience. In the case of virtual reconstruction of "lost" contexts this complexity raises at its maximum level, compelling different contents (objective data, interpretation, reasoning, data workflows, etc.) embedded in different media (text, image, video, 3d models, etc.). The general approach in the scientific community is to formalize this complexity through graph databases that are suitable to define rich connections at ontological level both with conceptual models (CIDOC-CRM) and with customized tools (e.g. ResearchSpace). The ambition of our approach is to use a standardized visual template for graph DB, the Extended Matrix formal language [6], to connect relevant information (contents and containers i.e. 3D models, images, etc.) to simplify the overall record connected to the 3D scenario without reducing the richness of the information. Furthermore, another crucial challenge to face when creating immersive inspection tools for CH, is related to the presentation of information: how to extract and represent complex semantic relationships at runtime in a suitable manner for immersive VR? What kind of approaches should we use?

3.2 Interacting with Immersive Analytics Systems

We primarily use our sight to analyse and interpret data, but what if we could also use our hearing? Through data-audio relationships, we could understand the significance, subject, and location of a particular data point through the loudness, type and direction of the sound, for example. By using multiple senses, we can enhance our ability to process data with more dimensions but what is the right meaning to give to sound within a data analysis session?

3.3 Transitions Around Immersive VR Environments

As highlighted in Sect. 2, within immersive VR contexts, there is a paradigm shift related to the interaction model. The transition between a mostly seated work environment and one requiring more physical involvement (like the one offered by 6-DoF HMDs) represents another crucial challenge. Final users transition from desktop-based tools (where they have expertise) to immersive tools (which may present novel and unfamiliar approaches) also involving different devices (e.g. VR controllers) to query or inspect the immmersive VR environment. Such challenge can affect interaction fluidity, thus possibilities involve the combination of established 3D interfaces and metaphors [27,40].

3.4 Supporting Behaviour with Collaborators

Effective presentation on immersive displays is only one way to gain an understanding of complex data. The increasing demands of large and multidimensional datasets are also making it unfeasible for a single expert to be able to tackle the analysis of large quantities of data. It has become necessary to create multidisciplinary teams with varying areas of expertise and even using different methodologies to solve problems when using these large datasets. Research stretching back over decades has found that collaborative decision making is often more effective than working on problems alone. Hill [22] provides a good review of early research comparing group versus individual performance on different tasks, finding that group performance is generally superior to that of an average individual. Similarly, in comparing collaborative to single user performance on an information visualization task, Mark et al. [34] found that groups worked slower, but produced more accurate results. Recently, Woolley et al. [45] have argued for a group collective intelligence factor that predicts performance on collaborative tasks, and could be improved by using collaborative tools. All these considerations led to new challenges in data visualization, such as determining how to present the data to different users, how to allow simultaneous data manipulation by multiple users, or how to let users socialize, among other challenges [24].

3.5 Software and Hardware Challenges

To the already mentioned challenges, as reported by the taxonomy defined in [11] a more technological topic must be considered, related to issues and constraints raised by software and hardware platforms. One of the main challenges is represented indeed by performance required for a consistent and comfortable experience, when dealing with Web3D limitations in terms of interactive rendering and resources available - especially on mobile devices These are even worsened within immersive XR sessions, introducing additional demands and performance requirements for low-latency communication to deliver a consistent, smooth and acceptable experience for HMDs.

Considering all the previously described challenges, the next section will address a minimal set of building blocks for crafting WebXR inspection tools targeting multi-dimensional CH datasets.

4 Building Blocks for WebXR CH Tools

The goal of this section is to highlight a minimal set of components for crafting WebXR inspection tools for Cultural Heritage. Most of WebXR high-level functionalities are today available through well-known open-source libraries supported by large communities, such as THREE.js (https://threejs.org/), Babylon.js (https://www.babylonjs.com/) and many others. Within the Cultural Heritage field, the open-source framework ATON [16] by CNR ISPC offers developers all the building blocks to support the creation and prototyping of WebXR applications targeting CH, including advanced multi-dimensional inspection tools. These building blocks can be combined and reused to craft immersive 4D tools - or more in general - cross-browser WebXR applications accessible directly online, without any installation required for final users.

Fig. 1. A few examples of basic WebXR components to interact with immersive 3D scenes on the web. Top: wrist spatial UI (left VR hand) with basic buttons and sample measurement in VR. Bottom (left to right): scene 3D query for basic navigation tasks (teleport); query of semantic shapes; customization of wrist spatial UI toolbar (left hand).

Scene-Graphs: these are crucial to design and organize the hierarchy of a 3D scene according to a given set of nodes and relationships. Furthermore, it offers a straightforward way for multi-temporal representations, with each one belonging to a sub-graph, easily manageable at runtime level. This also provides the possibility to reuse shared scene portions for *temporal instancing* [12], with beneficial effects on memory footprint and web browser caching

Semantic-Graph: a graph that allows to organize semantic shapes (or proxies) in a separate manner [7,44]: they typically consist of basic geometries that can be queried at runtime through spatial interaction (ray casting, etc.), assigned to a specific semantic ID. The graph structure allows to organize advanced hierarchies of semantic shapes, including instancing (e.g. series of columns) and more.

Interactive XR Queries: This is crucial to query representation models or semantic shapes in a 3D space. The framework offers BVH (Bounding Volume Hierarchy) trees to spatially index geometric meshes [29], providing efficient WebXR queries for both 3D scene and semantics that can be performed at runtime. This can be employed in different scenarios, including pointing/selection tools attached to the VR camera (view-aligned query), VR controllers (3-DoF or 6-DoF) or tracked hands. Typical usage scenarios range from basic navigation tasks (e.g. teleport), immersive XR measurements, object selection, up to semantic queries (see Fig. 1). Specifically for the ATON framework - and more in general for THREE.js projects - the open-source BVH library[2] offers an efficient implementation applicable to WebXR sessions, or even to perform 4D queries [15].

Navigation: this is indeed a central component for such class of tools, allowing professionals to explore the 3D space using a HMD. Within the ATON framework, different interaction models are automatically enabled, depending on HMD degrees-of-freedom (3-DoF or 6-DoF). A locomotion technique based on teleport [3] is provided with specific transitions to minimize motion sickness [2]. The component automatically adapts to 3-DoF and 6-Dof head-mounted displays, switching pointing/selection methods accordingly, also depending on the presence of VR controllers (see Fig. 1, bottom left).

Spatial UI: this built-in module is specifically designed for immersive XR sessions. It provides components developed on top of established guidelines [1] and design patterns related to 3D user interfaces, including immersive UIs targeting advanced XR tools (professionals) but also virtual museums and applied VR games (wider audiences, see for instance [30]). More specifically, a set of reusable UI elements include 3D panels providing optimized font rendering, toolbars, buttons and labels that can be arranged into the 3D space (see Fig. 1) and highly customized to suit requirements of diverse immersive WebXR applications. Furthermore, given the underneath graph structure, these components can be also attached to other static or dynamic scene nodes (like a virtual hand), providing the basics for the creation of *wrist-UIs* (see [1]) or 3D panels attached to user local VR space.

[2] https://github.com/gkjohnson/three-mesh-bvh.

5 Application Study: EMviq Tool

EMviq (Extended Matrix Visual Inspector and Querier) is a complete, interactive 4D visualization and runtime inspection and interrogation tool[3] for Extended Matrices (EM) developed on top of ATON framework [16] and building blocks described in previous section. The tool focuses on parsing and automatic extraction of runtime data from graph DBs (Extended Matrices) [7], in order to provide an interactive, semantically enriched 4D environment for professionals. The first tool was developed as desktop-based application, already offering immersive VR inspection and advanced query solutions like *spherical peeling* [12] to spatially "carve" proxy-graph (semantic graph) and/or representation models (scene-graph). Within SSHOC european project[4], a completely redesigned tool based on ATON framework was developed, including support for WebXR inspection. The online tool targets real-time Web4D, offering professionals interactive inspection of multi-temporal, semantically enriched virtual environments through a common web browser. The project was designed with ease-of-use in mind and cloud-based integration [12] in order to establish a fast and robust pipeline within multi-disciplinary teams. This section describes and illustrates how WebXR components offered by the framework (see Sect. 4) were applied to a couple of case studies, and how they can be exploited for immersive VR tools on the web.

5.1 The Roman Theatre of Catania

Within the SSHOC project, a virtual reconstruction of the Roman theatre of Catania has been created as an example of an actual transition of archaeological data to the cloud. EM has been applied to the wide and heterogeneous data of the site and the redesigned 4D visualization tool has been used to inspection and interrogation extended matrices connected to the *DAI's norm data systems*[5]. Based on the experience gained on other monuments of ancient Katane [32] the theatre was selected as case study for several reasons. This monument is undoubtedly one of the most interesting Roman theaters, both for its noteworthy size and the exceptional state of conservation. The study of the monument for the elaboration of a 3D reconstruction proposal required a laser scanner survey (see Fig.2). It has been useful to rectify the weaknesses of the graphic documentation available today and has been the starting point for the development of a three-dimensional model which incorporates all the historical archaeological and architectural information available for the structure.

The laser scan revealed the presence of a semicircular cavea with a maximum width of 97 m, and a depth of 51 m and the overall height from the orchestra must presumably have reached 26 m. A third and just as important element was the graphic reproduction of some representative decorative architectural elements

[3] https://github.com/phoenixbf/emviq.
[4] https://sshopencloud.eu/.
[5] https://idai.world/.

Fig. 2. Laser survey of the theatre

such as capitals, columns, cornices, pedestals, friezes, and statues, present within the structure, using an Image Based 3D survey with algorithms from Structure from Motion [18,19].

Once the metric characteristics were acquired, and the data cross-checked with the published material, it was thought opportune to link the hypothetical reconstruction to one of the monument's most interesting phases (see Fig. 3). This construction phase has been dated to within a relatively long period, which began in the Antonine period and probably continued until the Severan period [31]. The hypothesis proposed is the result of a study that uses direct analysis of the remains, integrated with the important contribution offered by the availability of an enhanced observation in a virtual environment. The many information gaps on the archaeological and historical level have been supplemented by a comparative study with other contemporary structures [17].

5.2 Montebelluna Smithy

The Roman forge of Montebelluna is an archaeological site located in the locality Posmon, investigated by the University of Padua Department of Cultural Heritage under the authorization of the Superintendence. The findings have been set up in the Museum of Natural History and Archaeology of Montebelluna.

The site, dating back to Roman times between the first before Christ and the third after Christ, hosts a craft building articulated in a series of rooms and a central open court. This context has provided exceptional data for understanding and reconstructing the articulation of a metallurgical workshop thanks to the

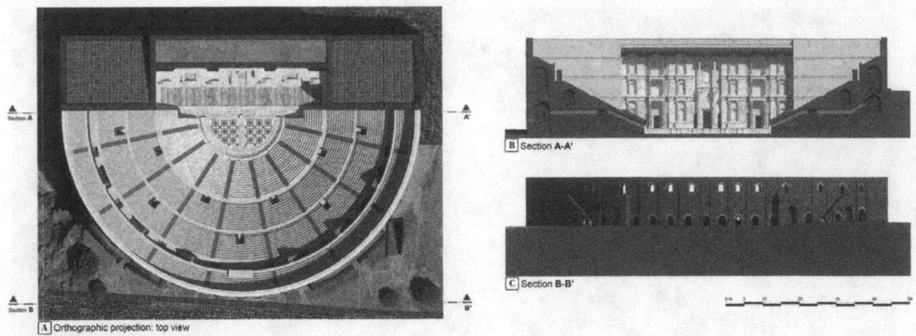

Fig. 3. 3D model of the hypothetical reconstruction of the Roman theatre of Catania: Orthographic views (A) and sections (B, C).

remains of workmanship, iron finds produced in the workshop and traces of furniture, which confirm what is already known from iconographic sources (the stele of blacksmith Ferrario of Aquileia or the stele of Cornelius Atimetus or the marble table from the catacombs of Domitilla).

The Institute of Heritage Sciences of the CNR (National Research Council) developed a reconstructive hypothesis together with the University of Padua and the Museum and Superintendence Office which led to the creation of a web-app to improve the on-site and off-site visit experience of the Roman forge. The reconstruction followed the Extended Matrix methodology including the creation of a digital replica, the drawing of the stratigraphy in 3D and the development of a volumetric reconstructive hypothesis and then a naturalistic representation. The entire project has been developed with software, formats and processes open and validated in previous case studies within the laboratory practice of the Digital Heritage Innovation Lab (DHIlab formerly VHLab).

5.3 Immersive VR Inspection in EMviq

This section illustrates the current development state of EMviq immersive inspection (through WebXR) and its interaction models, based on the building blocks presented in Sect. 4. In order to test and assess inspection tasks, we adopted EMviq tool on the two case studies using Oculus/Meta Quest (1 and 2) and cardboard (android).

Tool Deployment. The Web4D tool is designed to consume a scene ID (mapping an ATON scene descriptor, as JSON file - see [16]) and a matching Extended Matrix (a GraphML file). The scene descriptor defines all representation models for each period, matching the ones defined in the EM file. This approach allows the online tool to load different projects through an identifier (in this case, the scene ID) through an inline parameter, thus providing a way to address not only the tool (EMviq), but also the specific project, resulting in the following URL form:

$$\langle AFinstance \rangle /a/ \langle AppID \rangle /?s = \langle sid \rangle \quad (1)$$

where *AFinstance* is the up and running instance of the ATON framework, the *AppID* identifies the web-application (in this case "emviq") and *sid* represents the scene ID (or project) to load. As a result, the final user can use the built-in web browser and a cardboard, or advanced HMD (e.g. Meta Quest) to inspect the semantically enriched 4D space without any third-party installation (see Fig. 4, A).

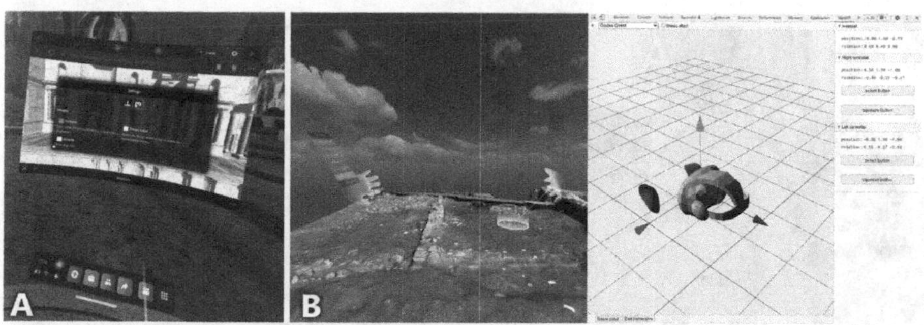

Fig. 4. A) WebXR option in EMviq on official Meta Quest 2 web-browser B) Simulation and testing on desktop Chrome browser through WebXR extension

In order to offer a valid WebXR session, a certified (SSL) domain is required by the API specification: we deployed the EMviq tool on the main instance of the ATON framework[6]. However, even offline extensions - such as Chrome WebXR - allow to launch WebXR presentation on several simulated devices, in order to test and assess the XR session without possessing a real device (see Fig. 4, B). Once the tool has been properly setup and deployed, the immersive VR mode will be simply accessible through a single button.

Querying the Semantic Graph - As already discussed in previous works [7,12] the *proxy-graph* (semantic queryable skeleton) is generated from a given EM using the semantic shapes offered by the ATON framework (see Sect. 4): this allow us to realize the runtime structure comprised by the basic semantic elements of the EM formalism (proxies) that can be queried during the immersive exploration of the 4D environment.

Each proxy referenced in the EM has a unique ID (see [7]) and its geometrical representation (basic 3D shape) is realized through a specific folder, where glTF models with matching IDs are located. Such 3D shapes translate into direct, spatial interface elements for immersive XR queries, to retrieve associated content via proxy ID (e.g. "USV100") at runtime.

[6] https://aton.ispc.cnr.it/.

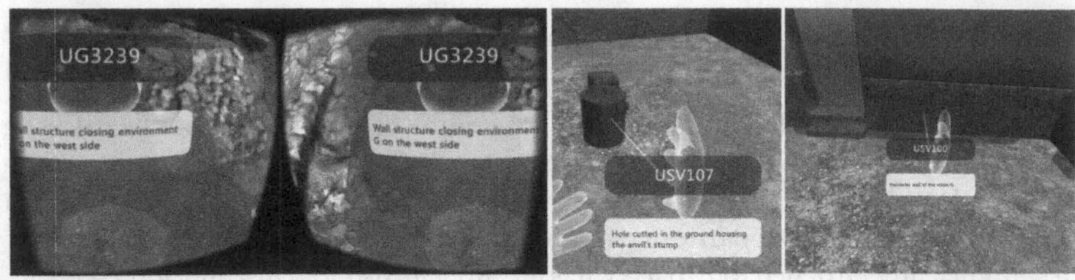

Fig. 5. Left: querying proxies of Montebelluna case study on a cardboard (android smartphone) and through a 6-DoF device (Meta Quest 2 with VR controllers, right)

Fig. 6. A) EMviq teleport interface to navigate the virtual space in VR, using primary controller/hand; B) 2D timeline interface (HTML)

As described in Sect. 4, depending on VR device used, the tool automatically detects if WebXR controllers are available or not. In the first case (e.g. Meta/Oculus Quest) the primary controller is used as pointing tool (see Fig. 5, right) to query the proxy-graph (the hierarchy of semantic 3D shapes extracted from the Extended Matrix). If no controllers are found (e.g. cardboards) head-aligned query mode is automatically enabled (see Fig. 5, left) thus using view-direction to cast 3D ray and query the proxy-graph.

In the current form, the tool presents the proxy ID and its description, exploiting 3D labels during an immersive WebXR session. The spatial UI (see Sect. 4) is exploited on the primary hand/controller to present the ID of the proxy and the extracted description: as spatial element, the user can control and manipulate such information in the 3D space (in this case, information extracted from "USV107" and "USV100" of the Montebelluna smithy). If no controllers are found (e.g. cardboard) such information is displayed alongside view-direction segment (see Fig. 5, left) with customizable distance and size of the Spatial UI element.

Moving Through Space - In order to query and inspect the 4D context in its entirety during an immersive VR session, users should be able to explore both *space* and *time*. Regarding space, EMviq exploits the underneath navigation system provided by ATON (see Sect. 4). More specifically, the primary hand/controller (in this case, right) is used to pick a location and *teleport* in said location using the main select button (white ring, see Fig. 6, A). As provided by the underneath ATON navigation system, the teleport is available on specific surfaces depending on their normal, or alternatively, on predefined locations if navigation constraints are introduced (more details are described in [16]). This model allows the user to move around the semantically enriched space, using a well-known and consolidated teleport technique, widely studied in literature and often adopted for minimizing motion sickness (see [2,3]). For 6-DoF immersive VR devices (e.g. Meta/Oculus Quest) user can also exploit head motions for close inspection within the physical tracked area (e.g. $2m \times 2m$).

Moving Through Time - Data extraction from the graph-DB (EM) also generates a *timeline* that can be used at runtime to move through time. While for the standard (HTML5) interface of EMviq this is quite straightforward - a 2D timeline with selectable periods (see Fig. 6, B) - immersive VR mode requires a totally different approach.

Following existing guidelines (e.g. [1,27]) and previous WebXR interfaces developed on top of ATON framework [16,30], a *wrist UI* timeline panel was introduced (see Fig. 7). Such spatial UI element allows the user to easily select a time period (automatically extracted from the EM) whenever he/she desires during the immersive VR session, using his/her left hand or VR controller. The 3D list is generated dynamically, thus allowing for live reloads of the timeline from the EM (e.g. during cloud-based workflows) during an immersive VR session.

As shown in Fig. 7, the spatial UI element (attached to secondary controller/hand) dynamically builds the interactive timeline layout, easily accessible on the wrist and always within user reach to move through the temporal dimension, while maintaining the same spatial location. Each time period is in fact selectable by the user through the primary controller/hand (see Fig. 7 - top row, middle). This spatial UI element is extremely useful to have a direct and immersive comparison between different time periods of the same context. Furthermore it can be attached or detached at runtime from the wrist, thus allowing to place the 3D timeline anywhere inside the virtual space, depending on custom immersive VR scenarios.

6 Conclusions and Future Developments

We described and discussed WebXR building blocks (Sect. 4) to craft immersive inspection CH tools for semantically enriched environments on the Web.

Fig. 7. The spatial UI (left wrist) to move through time in Montebelluna (top) and Catania theater (bottom) case studies.

There are several challenges to face, ranging from limitations of Web3D visualization, up to how information is presented and which user interfaces adopt to query multi-dimensional environments in immersive VR sessions. Recent literature already offers us guidance and established interaction models to draw from (especially desktop VR applications), in order to build functional tools supporting knowledge extraction in such complex and rich contexts. We illustrated and discussed the current state of EMviq tool for immersive inspection (Sect. 5), employed on two case studies (Catania theater and Montebelluna smithy) and how the building blocks are exploited for WebXR sessions. The possibility to consume such class of tools directly online, through a common web browser and without any third-party installation - represents an incredible opportunity for CH segment to deploy and investigate a cloud-based, web-based XR inspection.

One most important specific question that Immersive Archaeology will have to address is whether and how to visualize data uncertainty [43]. Digital representations of archaeological sites and artifacts, while constantly improving, inherently introduce some measurement uncertainty. Concern over the presentation of such data is not new, and was formally addressed in the London Charter for the Computer-based Visualization of Cultural Heritage [8]. It very important to quickly determine the provenance of any given digital object, and for this goal Extended Matrix approach is very efficient. The question is: how can we distinguish the degree of reliability of the various elements of a virtual reconstruction while navigating the 3D model at run-time? This will be one of the directions in which we will focus our future work: from one side trying to give a measure of the degree of certainty of a virtual reconstruction and from the other finding the most intuitive and effective way to visually represent it.

We plan also to re-design and re-adapt for the WebXR tool a few techniques and lessons learnt in previous desktop VR prototypes of EMviq, already discussed in [12]. More specifically, design and develop novel spatial UIs and visual models suited for WebXR to represent and query *source-graphs* of EMs targeting immersive VR modes (see Fig. 8). The challenges indeed will be not only at presentation level (e.g. avoiding visual clutter, what to present and how) but also overcoming the already discussed technical limitations of the Web, in terms of performance and resources available in a browser.

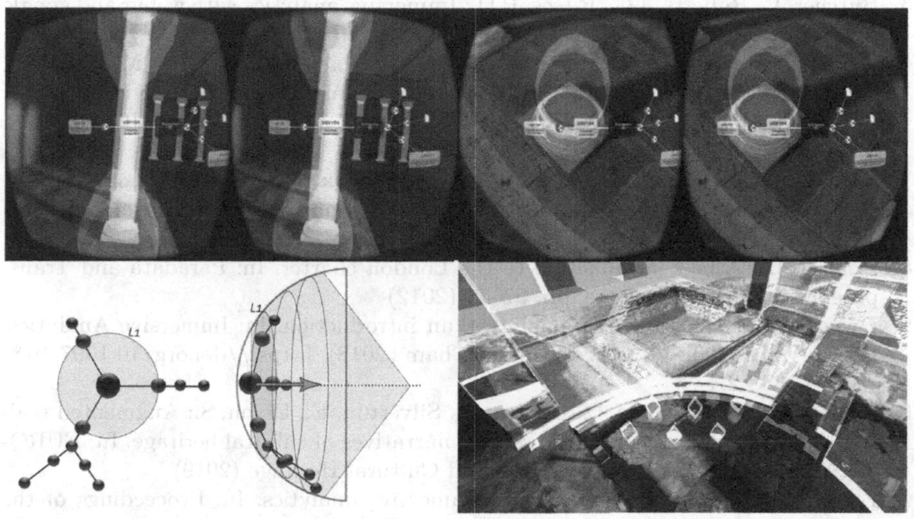

Fig. 8. The first prototype of spatial UI for source-graph presentation in VR, introduced in 2018 and the "spherical peeling" (bottom right).

We plan also an extensive User eXperience (UX) study of EMviq tool and its XR interface elements, mostly targeting professionals working with EM formalism, also including data scientists. Finally, as already anticipated in Sect. 3.4, one of the future direction of development will be focused towards Collaborative Immersive Analytics, since research has proven that groups of people collaborating perform better in a variety of tasks than when alone, producing more accurate results [22]. Immersion also has a positive impact in user performance when used for collaboration [36]. Because of the clear benefit in using collaboration to aid immersive data visualization, it seems useful to extend these tools to support multi-user collaboration (also already provided by the underneath framework [16]) in order to make easier for everyone to have access and foster collaborative discussion processes within this class of data-inspection tools for CH.

References

1. Alger, M.: Visual design methods for virtual reality. Ravensbourne (2015). http://aperturesciencellc.com/vr/VisualDesignMethodsforVR_MikeAlger.pdf
2. Boletsis, C.: The new era of virtual reality locomotion: a systematic literature review of techniques and a proposed typology. Multimodal Technol. Interact. **1**(4), 24 (2017)
3. Bozgeyikli, E., Raij, A., Katkoori, S., Dubey, R.: Point & teleport locomotion technique for virtual reality. In: Proceedings of the 2016 Annual Symposium on Computer-Human Interaction in Play, pp. 205–216 (2016)
4. Butcher, P., John, N.W., Ritsos, P.D.: Towards a framework for immersive analytics on the web. In: Posters of the IEEE Conference on Visualization (IEEE VIS 2018), Berlin (2018)
5. Butcher, P., Roberts, J.C., Ritsos, P.D.: Immersive analytics with webvr and google cardboard. In: Posters of IEEE VIS, pp. 30–32 (2016)
6. Demetrescu, E.: Virtual reconstruction as a scientific tool: In: Münster, S., Friedrichs, K., Niebling, F., Seidel-Grzesinska, A. (eds.) UHDL/DECH -2017. CCIS, vol. 817, pp. 102–116. Springer, Cham (2018). https://doi.org/10.1007/978-3-319-76992-9_7
7. Demetrescu, E., Fanini, B.: A white-box framework to oversee archaeological virtual reconstructions in space and time: methods and tools. J. Archaeol. Sci. Rep. **14**, 500–514 (2017)
8. Denard, H.: A new introduction to the London charter. In: Paradata and Transparency in Virtual Heritage, pp. 57–71 (2012)
9. Dwyer, T., et al.: Immersive analytics: an introduction. In: Immersive Analytics. LNCS, vol. 11190, pp. 1–23. Springer, Cham (2018). https://doi.org/10.1007/978-3-030-01388-2_1
10. Echavarria, K.R., Dibble, L., Bracco, A., Silverton, E., Dixon, S.: Augmented reality (AR) maps for experiencing creative narratives of cultural heritage. In: EUROGRAPHICS Workshop on Graphics and Cultural Heritage (2019)
11. Ens, B., et al.: Grand challenges in immersive analytics. In: Proceedings of the 2021 CHI Conference on Human Factors in Computing Systems, pp. 1–17 (2021)
12. Fanini, B., Demetrescu, E.: Carving time and space: a mutual stimulation of IT and archaeology to craft multidimensional VR data-inspection. In: Luigini, A. (ed.) EARTH 2018. AISC, vol. 919, pp. 553–565. Springer, Cham (2019). https://doi.org/10.1007/978-3-030-12240-9_58
13. Fanini, B., Cinque, L.: Encoding, exchange and manipulation of captured immersive VR sessions for learning environments: the prismin framework. Appl. Sci. **10**(6), 2026 (2020)
14. Fanini, B., Cinque, L.: Encoding immersive sessions for online, interactive VR analytics. Virtual Reality **24**(3), 423–438 (2020)
15. Fanini, B., Ferdani, D., Demetrescu, E.: Temporal lensing: an interactive and scalable technique for web3d/webxr applications in cultural heritage. Heritage **4**(2), 710–724 (2021)
16. Fanini, B., Ferdani, D., Demetrescu, E., Berto, S., d'Annibale, E.: Aton: an open-source framework for creating immersive, collaborative and liquid web-apps for cultural heritage. Appl. Sci. **11**(22), 11062 (2021)
17. Gabellone, F., Ferrari, I., Giuri, F.: The greek-roman theater of taormina: towards a reconstruction proposal. In: Proceedings of the 22nd International Congress Cultural Heritage and New Technologies, CHNT, vol. 22, pp. 8–10 (2022)

18. Gabellone, F., Ferrari, I., Giuri, F.: Digital restoration using image-based 3D models. In: Proceedings of the 1st International Conference on Metrology for Archaeology, pp. 478–482 (2015)
19. Gabellone, F., Ferrari, I., Giuri, F., Chiffi, M.: Image-based techniques for the virtualization of Egyptian contexts. In: Proceedings of IMEKO International Conference on Metrology for Archaeology and Cultural Heritage, Lecce, Italy, 23–25 October 2017, pp. 601–606 (2017). ISBN 978-92-990084-0-9
20. González-Zúñiga, L.D., O'Shaughnessy, P.: Virtual reality... in the browser. In: VR Developer Gems, p. 101. CRC Press, Boca Raton (2019)
21. Hayatpur, D., Xia, H., Wigdor, D.: Datahop: spatial data exploration in virtual reality. In: Proceedings of the 33rd Annual ACM Symposium on User Interface Software and Technology, pp. 818–828 (2020)
22. Hill, G.W.: Group versus individual performance: are n+ 1 heads better than one? Psychol. Bullet. **91**(3), 517 (1982)
23. Ibánez, M.L., Peinado, F., Palmieri, O.: Walking in VR: measuring presence and simulator sickness in first-person virtual reality games. In: Proceedings of the Third Congress of the Spanish Society for Video Games Sciences (2016)
24. Isenberg, P., Elmqvist, N., Scholtz, J., Cernea, D., Ma, K.L., Hagen, H.: Collaborative visualization: definition, challenges, and research agenda. Inf. Visualiz. **10**(4), 310–326 (2011)
25. Jones, B., Waliczek, N.: Webxr device API. W3C Working Draft 10 (2019)
26. Jung, K., Nguyen, V.T., Lee, J.: Blocklyxr: an interactive extended reality toolkit for digital storytelling. Appl. Sci. **11**(3), 1073 (2021)
27. Kharoub, H., Lataifeh, M., Ahmed, N.: 3D user interface design and usability for immersive VR. Appl. Sci. **9**(22), 4861 (2019)
28. Koebel, K., Agotai, D., Çöltekin, A.: Exploring cultural heritage collections in immersive analytics: challenges, benefits, and a case study using virtual reality. Int. Archiv. Photogram. Remote Sens. Spatial Inf. Sci. **43**, 599–606 (2020)
29. Kontakis, K., Malamos, A.G., Steiakaki, M., Panagiotakis, S.: Spatial indexing of complex virtual reality scenes in the web. Int. J. Image Graph. **17**(02), 1750009 (2017)
30. Luigini, A., Fanini, B., Basso, A., Basso, D.: Heritage education through serious games. A web-based proposal for primary schools to cope with distance learning. VITRUVIO-Int. J. Architect. Technol. Sustain. **5**(2), 73–85 (2020)
31. Malfitana, D., Gabellone, F., Cacciaguerra, G., Ferrari, I., Giuri, F., Pantellaro, C.: Critical reading of surviving structures starting from old studies for new reconstructive proposal of the roman theatre of Catania. In: 8th International Congress on Archaeology, Computer Graphics, Cultural Heritage and Innovation, pp. 155–161. Editorial Universitat Politècnica de València (2016)
32. Malfitana, D., et al.: Integrated methodologies for a new reconstructive proposal of the Amphitheatre of Catania. In: 8th International Congress on Archaeology, Computer Graphics, Cultural Heritage and Innovation, pp. 146–154. Editorial Universitat Politècnica de València (2016)
33. Mao, B., Ban, Y., Laumert, B.: Dynamic online 3D visualization framework for real-time energy simulation based on 3d tiles. ISPRS Int. J. Geo-Inf. **9**(3), 166 (2020)
34. Mark, G., Carpenter, K., Kobsa, A.: Are there benefits in seeing double? A study of collaborative information visualization. In: CHI'03 Extended Abstracts on Human Factors in Computing Systems, pp. 840–841 (2003)
35. McIntire, J.P., Havig, P.R., Geiselman, E.E.: Stereoscopic 3d displays and human performance: a comprehensive review. Displays **35**(1), 18–26 (2014)

36. Narayan, M., Waugh, L., Zhang, X., Bafna, P., Bowman, D.: Quantifying the benefits of immersion for collaboration in virtual environments. In: Proceedings of the ACM Symposium on Virtual Reality Software and Technology, pp. 78–81 (2005)
37. Neelakantam, S., Pant, T.: Bringing VR to the Web and WebVR Frameworks. In: Learning Web-based Virtual Reality, pp. 5–9. Apress, Berkeley (2017). https://doi.org/10.1007/978-1-4842-2710-7_2
38. Oldman, D., Tanase, D.: Reshaping the knowledge graph by connecting researchers, data and practices in ResearchSpace. In: Vrandečić, D., et al. (eds.) ISWC 2018. LNCS, vol. 11137, pp. 325–340. Springer, Cham (2018). https://doi.org/10.1007/978-3-030-00668-6_20
39. Prinz, L.M., Mathew, T., Klüber, S., Weyers, B.: An overview and analysis of publications on locomotion taxonomies. In: 2021 IEEE Conference on Virtual Reality and 3D User Interfaces Abstracts and Workshops (VRW), pp. 385–388. IEEE (2021)
40. Riecke, B.E., LaViola Jr, J.J., Kruijff, E.: 3D user interfaces for virtual reality and games: 3D selection, manipulation, and spatial navigation. In: ACM SIGGRAPH 2018 Courses, pp. 1–94 (2018)
41. Robinet, F., Arnaud, R., Parisi, T., Cozzi, P.: GLTF: designing an open-standard runtime asset format. GPU Pro **5**, 375–392 (2014)
42. Schilling, A., Bolling, J., Nagel, C.: Using GLTF for streaming citygml 3D city models. In: Proceedings of the 21st International Conference on Web3D Technology, pp. 109–116 (2016)
43. Skarbez, R., Polys, N.F., Ogle, J.T., North, C., Bowman, D.A.: Immersive analytics: theory and research agenda. Front. Robot. AI 82 (2019)
44. Tobler, R.F.: Separating semantics from rendering: a scene graph based architecture for graphics applications. Visual Comput. **27**(6), 687–695 (2011)
45. Woolley, A.W., Chabris, C.F., Pentland, A., Hashmi, N., Malone, T.W.: Evidence for a collective intelligence factor in the performance of human groups. Science **330**(6004), 686–688 (2010)
46. Xu, Z., Zhang, L., Li, H., Lin, Y.H., Yin, S.: Combining IFC and 3D tiles to create 3D visualization for building information modeling. Autom. Construct. **109**, 102995 (2020)

Comparing the Impact of Low-Cost 360° Cultural Heritage Videos Displayed in 2D Screens Versus Virtual Reality Headsets

Bruno Rodriguez-Garcia[1(✉)], Mario Alaguero[2], Henar Guillen-Sanz[1], and Ines Miguel-Alonso[1]

[1] Department of Computer Engineering, Universidad de Burgos, Burgos, Spain
{brunorg,hguillen,imalonso}@ubu.es
[2] Department of History and Geography, Universidad de Burgos, Burgos, Spain
malaguero@ubu.es

Abstract. The continuous price reduction of head mounted displays (HMDs) raises the following question in the field of cultural heritage: Is it possible to adapt desktop passive virtual reality (VR) 360° experiences for HMDs? This work presents a comparison of low-cost 360° videos of cultural heritage displayed across two devices: a desktop display and an HMD. The study case is the virtual reconstruction of Burgos (Spain) in 1921. The key factors of these videos are short duration, virtual reconstruction based on 3D modelling and photo editing and the inclusion of real actors performing out looping micro stories. The comparison of both displays devices has been carried out by a group of 32 students from the University of Burgos. The validation includes user satisfaction, knowledge acquisition and visual identification. The results are the following: 1) better knowledge acquisition and immersion in the HMD group, 2) better user satisfaction for the desktop group and 3) more fault identification related to the characters for the HMD group. Looking at these results, the most important elements to improve are the integration of characters and increase the length of the videos.

Keywords: Virtual reality · Cultural heritage · Virtual reconstruction · 360° · Low cost

1 Introduction

Much of the cultural heritage has been lost over time. For this reason, the virtual reconstruction of heritage is a necessary tool for transmitting this knowledge, because it allows the transmission of historical knowledge in a very direct and visual way [1]. Virtual reconstruction also brings other advantages to the dissemination of cultural heritage, such as being able to access virtually to places with accessibility problems or restricted access [2]. Consequently, as technology advances, it is more common to carry out virtual reconstructions of heritage. Within this discipline, the creation of virtual reconstructions of heritage through virtual reality (VR) applications, whether interactive or passive, have

L. T. De Paolis et al. (Eds.): XR Salento 2022, LNCS 13446, pp. 391–404, 2022.
https://doi.org/10.1007/978-3-031-15553-6_27

a special importance. This is due to VR allows more immersion for users and the sense of "being there" [3].

Within VR applications we can differentiate between passive and interactive. Passive VR is the one that does not have very limited movement and interaction, otherwise in interactive experiences users can freely interact with the environment. In the VR experiences it is also possible to differentiate between those that are visualized on desktop displays and those that are visualized on head mounted displays (HMDs) [4]. Interactive virtual reconstructions of heritage are usually low-cost due to the low budget that is normally handled in this discipline [5]. Therefore, passive VR experiences find their place in cultural heritage [4].

The rise of low-cost HMDs like Oculus Quest is making these VR experiences widely used in education and cultural heritage [6], causing the transition from desktop passive VR applications to HMDs. This phenomenon raises the following question: Can a passive desktop VR experience be successfully displayed with HMDs with the same knowledge acquisition or user satisfaction?

Other researchers have already worked on porting and comparing desktop passive VR experiences to HMDs. Pietroni [7] in his virtual reconstruction of Villa Livia already adapted a passive VR desktop experience to HMDs. Work has also been done comparing different HMDs, such as Fabola [8] in the virtual reconstruction of the St. Andrews Cathedral or Petreli [9] in the reconstruction of the temple of Mars Ultor and the Dr Jenner's house. Also evaluating the impact of VR to other non-immersive digital methods, for example, the work of Checa [10], comparing a virtual reconstruction in video versus a passive VR HMD experience. But there is already a gap in VR research. Since it has not been investigated whether it is possible to effectively adapt a desktop passive VR experience for HMD.

This work presents the design and validation of the virtual reconstruction of 3 squares from the virtual reconstruction of Burgos in 1921 in 360° video, addressing this issue. This research compares: 1) usability and user satisfaction, 2) acquisition of knowledge, and 3) the visual relevance of the elements included in 360° videos displayed through two devices: a desktop screen and an HMD.

This paper is structured as follows. Section 2 explains the design of the experience, the virtual reconstruction of Burgos in the year 1921, from the choice of the reconstructions to their creation. In Sect. 3, the evaluation method is explained. Section 4 explains the results. Finally, the conclusions of this paper are in Sect. 5.

2 Study Case: Burgos 1921

Burgos is a 1,200-year-old city in Spain. One of its most important monuments is the cathedral, a World Heritage Site. In 2021, Burgos Cathedral turned 800 years old. For these reasons, as part of the centennial celebrations of the cathedral in 2021, 3 virtual 360° reconstructions of the city were created. In these reconstructions 3 squares of the city can be seen as they looked like in 1921.

2.1 Design of the Experience

The 360° video reconstructions want to represent the change in the urban space and the cultural change. In this century, the city has undergone great changes, such as remodelling of buildings, the pavement, the cathedral and even the total remodelling of the interior of its main square. In addition, the city has suffered technological and social changes such as the popularization of the automobile. For this reason, the experience was designed by reconstructing 3 important points of the city, by showing how different squares with different uses have changed. These squares are Santa María Square marked 1 in Fig. 1, Main Square marked 2 and Llana de Afuera marked 3. All the squares. The 3 squares are located around the cathedral of the city.

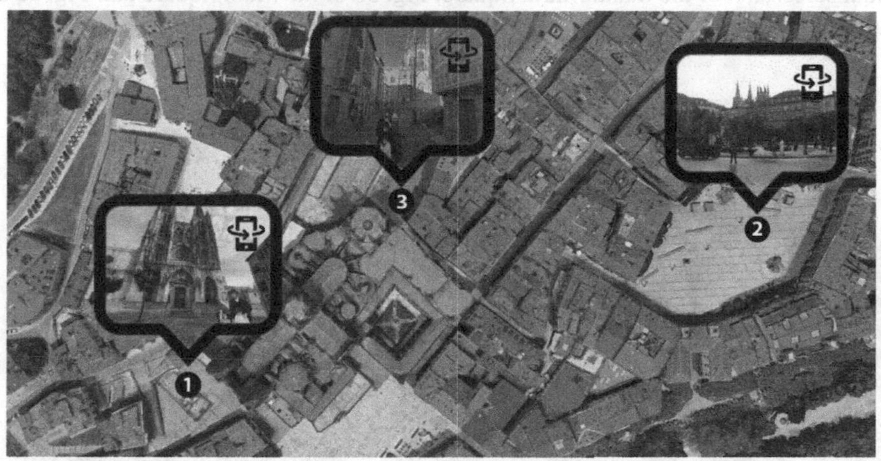

Fig. 1. The 3 squares and their location in Burgos

2.2 Design of the Videos

To represent the changes in the urban space, the buildings have been digitally rebuilt and the squares have been reformed. The cultural change was represented with the inclusion of characters. Through the performance of looping micro-stories distributed throughout the virtual environment, the characters recounted situations of Burgos in 1921, such as waiting to take a photograph in front of the cathedral, as shown in Fig. 2.

Fig. 2. People waiting to take a photo in the reconstruction of Santa Maria square

These 3 virtual reconstructions were designed to be visualized in situ and to compare reality with the reconstruction, by seeing them through a smartphone, or a cardboard. The procedure was proposed thinking of these visualization devices. For this same reason, the duration of each 360° video is short, around one and a half minutes. Figure 3a shows a final screenshot of the Santa María Square, Fig. 3b of the Main Square and Fig. 3c of Llana de Afuera.

Fig. 3a. Screenshot of the virtual reconstruction of Santa María Square

Fig. 3b. Screenshot of the virtual reconstruction of Main Square

Fig. 3c. Screenshot of the virtual reconstruction of Llana de Afuera

2.3 Reconstruction Procedure

The main objective of this procedure was to recreate realistically the city of Burgos in 1921, by optimizing economic resources and with historical accuracy. For this, a procedure that combines several audiovisual techniques seeking a great level in realism with few economic resources was created.

The development process was as follows: 1) documentation, 2) assets creation and characters recording, and 3) digital composition of all the assets. The workflow and relationships between the different techniques are explained in Fig. 4.

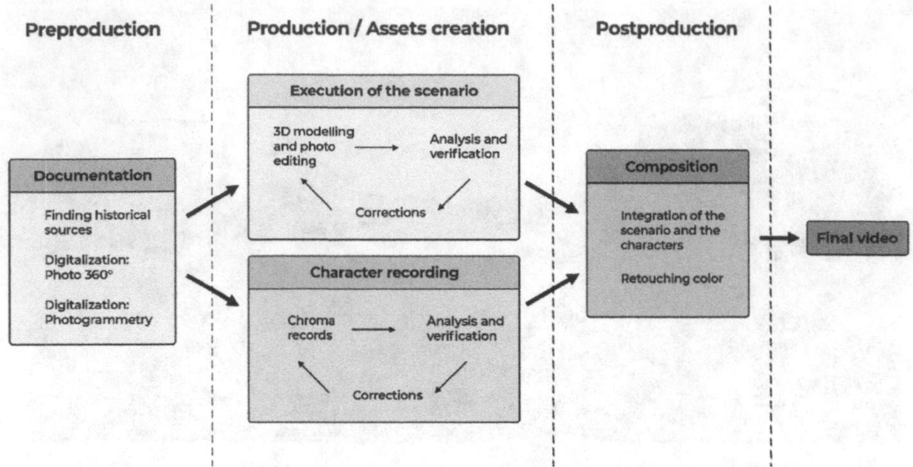

Fig. 4. Workflow used in virtual reconstruction

It is not the first time that this procedure has been used, by separating the creation of the scenario from the inclusion of the characters. Kwiatek [11] has already done something similar in his reconstruction of the Charles Chapel, including real characters on a 360° reconstruction. Also Rizvic [12] did something similar in her reconstruction of Villa Livia.

In the first step of the procedure, documentation, experts in historical analysis located all the necessary documentation, like blueprints and photos, to provide historical accuracy to the reconstruction. At the same time the 3 locations were digitized with 360° photos and photogrammetry. The 360° photos were later used as support for the virtual reconstruction. The parts of the city that had not undergone changes were kept from the 360° photo or slightly edited. Photogrammetry was used to have volume references in the 3D modelling step.

The production step was divided into two branches: the creation of environments and the recording of characters. Two different techniques were used to create the environments. Firstly, 3D modeling for those buildings or objects that had been lost over time. The modeling process used is explained in [13, 14]. This technique was used only in essential cases because it is the most expensive, but it is necessary when there were no remains to date. For the parts of the city that had not changed or changed little, the 360° photo of the squares was digitally edited. Over these images the 3D models were placed replacing remodeled buildings, the pavement or adding vehicles. The characters were recorded with chroma to include them after in the reconstruction. Attention to detail was paid during recording and the actors wore clothing of the 20s in Spain, as seen in Fig. 5.

This decision allowed lower costs and achieved a better historical accuracy with the characters. They were recorded with a common DLSR camera, and their perspective was later corrected in the next step. Also the light was previously calculated depending on where they will be placed. In both processes there was continous historical review.

In the last step of the procedure, the elements produced in the creation of assets were combined, rendering the 3D models on the 360° photos and combining the result with

Fig. 5. Recording of the actors with chroma

the images of the edited squares. Subsequently, the actors were introduced, correcting their perspective digitally to fit them in the reconstruction. The color of all the elements was retouched and matched to achieve the final composition, thus creating the 3 videos of Burgos in 1921.

The software used in the work were Blender for 3D modelling, Adobe Photoshop for photo editing and Adobe After Effects for video editing. The reasons to choose these programs were the low price and the experience of the team with the software.

The localized advantages and disadvantages in this procedure are the follows. It is a low-cost procedure but it achieves a high level of realism. Also, this method can get a high level of historical accuracy in the characters because they can be dressed and checked by experts while recording. This procedure is based on relying on photogrammetry and photo 360° to save modelling resources. For this reason, it can only be applied with heritage that has not been completely lost. 3 videos can be viewed at [15–17].

3 Evaluation

The evaluation was carried out with students of the degree in Media Communication and the Master in Communication and Multimedia Development of the University of Burgos. The group was formed by 32 students with a balanced gender distribution. They had an average age of 23 years, a minimum age of 20 and a maximum of 31. The students were divided equally into two groups, the one that visualized the 360° reconstructions through a high-end HMD (HCT Vive Pro Eye), hereinafter called the HMD group, and the one that did it through a desktop display, hereinafter called desktop group.

Both groups viewed the 360° videos in the following order: 1) Santa Maria Square, 2) Main Square, 3) Llana de Afuera. But the HMD group previously viewed another 1-min 360° video to compensate for the increased acclimatization required by this device

[4]. In this way, the duration of the experience for the desktop group was 4 and a half minutes and the duration of the HMD group was 5 and a half minutes. In Fig. 6 some of the participants of the HMD group can be seen visualizing the experience.

Fig. 6. HMD group students visualizing the experience

After viewing the experience, both groups answered a questionnaire. The survey consisted in a set of questions divided into 4 blocks: usability, knowledge acquisition, visual elements and a suggestion section. To answer the questions, there were 3 possible response options. These responses options are the following: 1) Likert scale from 1 to 5, 2) open questions and 3) question with 2 or 3 options.

The usability block was meant to measure user satisfaction regarding duration and realism. It is also designed to know their estimation of movement and time, to check if there were differences between the two devices. The knowledge acquisition block was set to check which format transmits better historical information. For this, questions ask about the change in the use of the city, but also about the change in some specific elements, such as the cathedral. The visual element block was meant to check which elements have the greatest visual importance for users. Since the characters and the scene have been created separately in the reconstruction procedure, this block has also been divided into two groups. The first set of questions asks about the scenario, and the second about the characters. Finally, a fault identification question has been added to find out possible bugs in the reconstruction procedure. The last block asks users to indicate what things they would like to freely change. This block is intended to detect patterns not evaluated in the previous questions.

Likert scale questions have been used to find out the opinion of users in a standardized way. The scale if the Likert questions was 1 to 5. That is why they have been used in the usability block. The open questions had the objective of not biasing the users' response or not giving them clues about the correct answer. Choice questions were used when questions had very clear possible answers, such as yes or no. All questions can be seen in Table 1.

Table 1. List of questions

Code	*Type*	*Question*	*Posible Answers*
Q1	Usability	Lenght opinion	Likert scale
Q2	Usability	Realism opinion	Likert scale
Q3	Usability	Movement estimation	Likert scale
Q4	Usability	Lenght estimation	Open question
Q5	Knowledge acquisition	What was the use of the Llana de Afuera?	Open question
Q6	Knowledge acquisition	What changes has suffered the Main Square?	Open question
Q7	Knowledge acquisition	What changes has suffered the cathedral?	Open question
Q8	Knowledge acquisition	Have you seen changes in the pavement?	Open question
Q9	Knowledge acquisition	What was the most common vehicle?	Open question
Q10	Visual identification of 3D models	Have you seen the car moving?	Two options
Q11	Visual identification of 3D models	Which square do you think had more trees?	Three options
Q12	Visual identification of 3D models	Can you describe the most common curtains?	Open question
Q13	Visual identification of characters	Have you seen the common characters? Describe them	Open question
Q14	Visual identification of characters	Have you seen childs? Describe them	Open question
Q15	Visual identification of characters	Did you see what the photographer had underfoot? Describe them	Open question
Q16	Visual identification of characters	Have you seen the characters they were reading? Describe them	Open question
Q17	Visual identification of characters	Has any character caught your attention? Describe them	Open question
Q18	Visual elements	Have you seen any error in the reconstruction? Describe them	Open question
Q19	Suggestions	Do you have any suggestions to improve this experience?	Open question

4 Results

Regarding user satisfaction, there are similar results for both groups. In Q1, on the duration opinion, the HMD group achieved an average score of 2.8 against 3.0 for the desktop group. In this question the maximum score, 5 is considered too long and 1 too short. In Q2, on the opinion of realism, the HMD group achieved an average score of 4.12 against 4.18 of the desktop group. The scores of both groups are high and very similar. However, slightly better results can be observed for the desktop group. Doing a deeper analysis in user satisfaction, it can be seen how the HMD have 8 suggestions demanding more interaction compared to 3 of the desktop group. The desire for greater and better interaction which could explain this slightly lower result in the user satisfaction for the HMD group.

In the questions about space-time perception, greater differences can be seen. In Q3, about movement estimation, HMD group has estimated its movement as lower. This group has an average score of 3.7 compared to 4.3 for the desktop group. Regarding the estimation of the duration, Q4, the HMD group has obtained worse results. They have estimated the time at an average of 6.7 min, deviating more than a minute from real time (5.5 m). In contrast, the desktop group has estimated the time at 4.5 min on average, being the correct answer in this case (4.5 m). These two questions have in common a great difference in the dispersion of the answers. In both questions, the HMD group shows a greater dispersion of responses, especially in the movement estimation. This can be seen in Fig. 7, in which the user score is represented on the y-axis and the two groups on the x-axis. This difference in results is probably because viewing through HMDs causes a greater sense of immersion.

The results in the knowledge acquisition questions block are as follows. To compare the results, scores have been normalized, given to the different answer points from 1 to 5. In this block a 1 means a completely wrong and 5 means the correct answer. The HMD group has achieved a better average score, 3.58 compared to 3.28 for the desktop group. But it has had worse scores in Q7, 1.68 vs. 2.06 for the desktop group, and in Q9 with 2.93 vs. 3.37 for the desktop group. These results are plotted in Fig. 8. In this figure the average score of both groups is represented on the y-axis and each question and the total average score on the x-axis. This difference in results could be explained by a greater gaze dispersion for the HMD group. The questions in which this group has had the worst score, Q7 and Q9, are those that ask about specific elements, the cathedral and a car respectively. While those with the highest score asked about urban spaces as a whole, but not for a specific element. This result can be related to the previous section. As there is a greater immersion and dispersion for the HMD group, it is possible that certain elements have gone unnoticed for them.

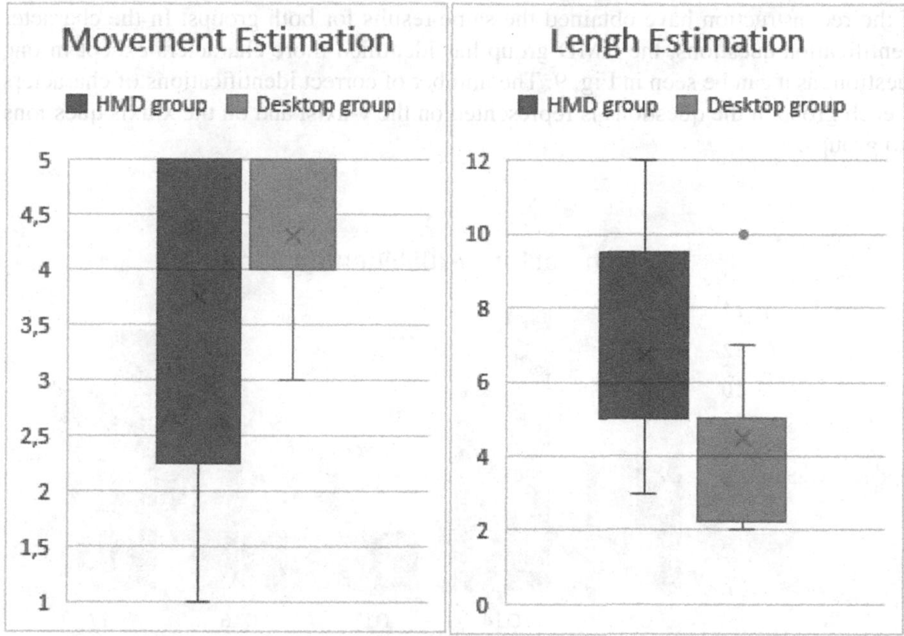

Fig. 7. Comparison of the dispersion of answers between the groups

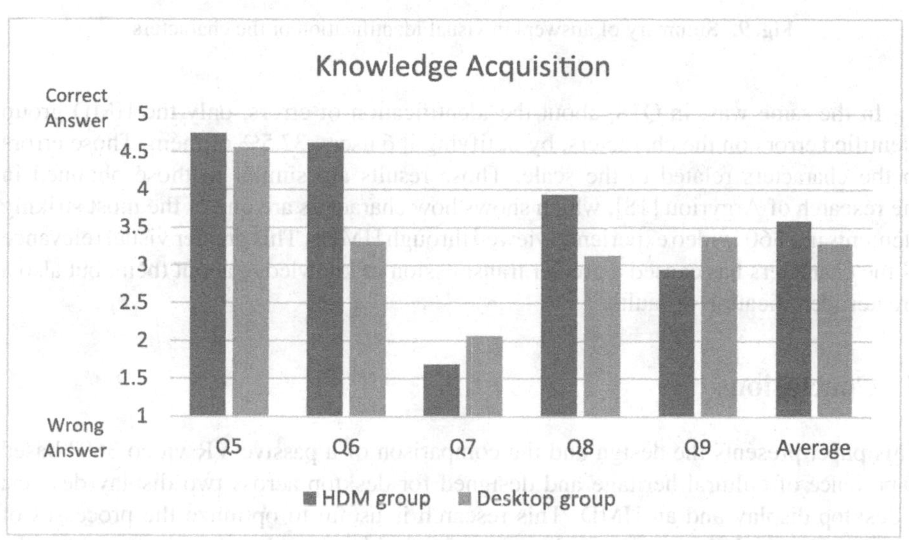

Fig. 8. Summary of answers in the block of knowledge acquisition

Regarding the visual element questions there are also significant differences. The score of this block has been counted giving one point for each correct identification of the users. Half of the block, questions Q10, Q11 and Q12, about the 3D elements of the reconstruction have obtained the same results for both groups. In the character identification questions, the HMD group has identified more characters except in one question, as it can be seen in Fig. 9. The number of correct identifications of characters of each group in the questions is represented on the y-axis, and on the x-axis questions and groups.

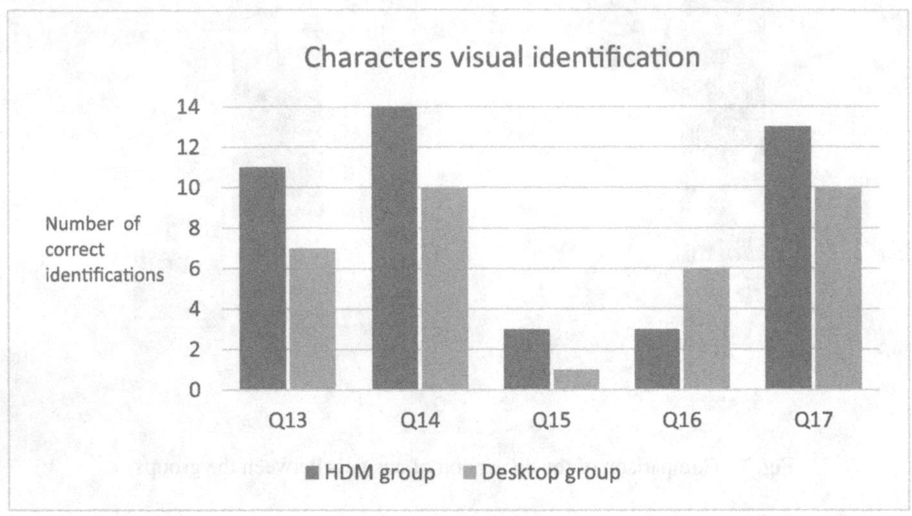

Fig. 9. Summary of answers in visual identification of the characters

In the same way, in Q18, about the identification of errors, only the HMD group identified errors on the characters, by notifying it 6 users, 37.5% of them. Those errors in the characters related to the scale. Those results are similar to those obtained in the research of Argyriou [18], which shows how characters are one of the most striking elements in a 360° video experience viewed through HMDs. This greater visual relevance of the characters has caused a greater transmission of knowledge about them, but also a greater identification of faults.

5 Conclusions

This paper presents the design and the comparison of a passive VR video 360° based experience of cultural heritage and designed for desktop across two display devices: a desktop display and an HMD. This research is useful to optimize the processes of creating passive VR experiences based on 360° video in cultural heritage, where the budget is usually low. The evaluation has been carried out by a group of 32 students from the University of Burgos. These students were divided into two groups of 16. One group visualized the experience through a desktop display, and the other with an HMD. Subsequently, they filled out a questionnaire from which the following results were extracted.

The HMD group presented a much greater dispersion of responses about space-time perception. They had better results in knowledge acquisition too. Finally, the characters had a greater visual relevance for this group. However, the desktop group showed better satisfaction, by having better results in their opinion about the realism and duration of the experience. Also, this group has identified fewer bugs than the HMD group.

Through the interpretation of these results, the following conclusions can be reached. Even though the HMD group has achieved better results in knowledge acquisition, the greater immersion provided by this device has caused worse results in some of these questions. Specifically, those who asked about specific elements of the videos. The greater visual relevance of the characters for the HMD group allows more knowledge to be transmitted through them. But it also makes them identify more flaws and ask for a better integration of the characters. This result may be related to the slightly lower realism score of the HMD group.

The comparison of these 3 videos has been satisfactory, but these results show elements that need to be improved in the procedure: 1) better integration of characters, to avoid reporting bugs related to them and 2) longer video duration to give users more time to focus on details when using an HMD.

Future works will focus on modifying this reconstruction procedure by considering these results to repeat the experiment. In this way, it is wanted to achieve a low-cost reconstruction process of 360° videos suitable for viewing through HMDs. The development of simple interactions will be also considered to increase users' satisfaction in VR experience as previous research has outlined [19, 20].

Acknowledgments. This work was partially supported by the ACIS project (Reference Number INVESTUN/21/BU/0002) of the Consejeria de Empleo e Industria of the Junta de Castilla y León (Spain) and the Erasmus+ RISKREAL Project (Reference Number 2020–1-ES01-KA204–081847) of the European Commission.

7. References

1. Gabellone, F.: Virtual environments and technological solutions for an enriched viewing of historic and archeological contexts. In: First Olympia Seminar, pp. 223–232 (2015)
2. Njerekai, C.: An application of the virtual reality 360° concept to the Great Zimbabwe monument. J. Herit. Tour. **15**, 567–579 (2019). https://doi.org/10.1080/1743873X.2019.1696808
3. Škola, F., et al.: Virtual reality with 360-video storytelling in cultural heritage: study of presence, engagement, and immersion. Sensors (Switzerland) **20**, 1–17 (2020). https://doi.org/10.3390/s20205851
4. Checa, D., Bustillo, A.: A review of immersive virtual reality serious games to enhance learning and training. Multimedia Tools Appl. **79**, 5501–5527 (2019). https://doi.org/10.1007/s11042-019-08348-9
5. Anderson, E.F., McLoughlin, L., Liarokapis, F., Peters, C., Petridis, P., de Freitas, S.: Developing serious games for cultural heritage: a state-of-the-art review. Virtual Reality **14**, 255–275 (2010). https://doi.org/10.1007/s10055-010-0177-3

6. Checa, D., Gatto, C., Cisternino, D., De Paolis, L.T., Bustillo, A.: A framework for educational and training immersive virtual reality experiences. In: De Paolis, L.T., Bourdot, P. (eds.) Augmented Reality, Virtual Reality, and Computer Graphics. LNCS, vol. 12243, pp. 220–228. Springer, Cham (2020). https://doi.org/10.1007/978-3-030-58468-9_17
7. Pietroni, E., Forlani, M., Rufa, C.: Livia's Villa Reloaded: An example of re-use and update of a pre-existing Virtual Museum, following a novel approach in storytelling inside virtual reality environments. In: 2015 Digital Heritage International Congress, Digital Heritage, pp. 511–518 (2015). https://doi.org/10.1109/DigitalHeritage.2015.7419567
8. Fabola, A., Miller, A.: Virtual reality for early education: a Study. In: Allison, C., Morgado, L., Pirker, J., Beck, D., Richter, J., Gütl, C. (eds.) Immersive Learning Research Network. CCIS, vol. 621, pp. 59–72. Springer, Cham (2016). https://doi.org/10.1007/978-3-319-41769-1_5
9. Petrelli, D.: Making virtual reconstructions part of the visit: an exploratory study. Digital Applications in Archaeology and Cultural Heritage. **15**, e00123 (2019). https://doi.org/10.1016/j.daach.2019.e00123
10. Checa, D., Bustillo, A.: Advantages and limits of virtual reality in learning processes: Briviesca in the fifteenth century. Virtual Reality **24**(1), 151–161 (2019). https://doi.org/10.1007/s10055-019-00389-7
11. Kwiatek, K., Woolner, M.: Transporting the viewer into a 360° heritage story: Panoramic interactive narrative presented on a wrap-around screen. In: 2010 16th International Conference on Virtual Systems and Multimedia, VSMM, pp. 234–241 (2010). https://doi.org/10.1109/VSMM.2010.5665980
12. Rizvic, S., Boskovic, D., Bruno, F., Petriaggi, B.D., Sljivo, S., Cozza, M.: Actors in VR storytelling. In: 2019 11th International Conference on Virtual Worlds and Games for Serious Applications, VS-Games 2019 - Proceedings. pp. 1–8 (2019). https://doi.org/10.1109/VS-Games.2019.8864520
13. Bustillo, A., Alaguero, M., Miguel, I., Saiz, J.M., Iglesias, L.S.: A flexible platform for the creation of 3D semi-immersive environments to teach cultural heritage. Digit. Appl. Archaeol. Cult. Heritage. **2**, 248–259 (2015). https://doi.org/10.1016/j.daach.2015.11.002
14. Alaguero, M., Checa, D.: Optimización en proyectos de realidad virtual de bajo presupuesto en la didáctica del patrimonio. Comunicación y Pedagogía: nuevas tecnologías y recursos didácticos. **317–318**, 6–9 (2019)
15. Alaguero, M., Rodriguez-Garcia, B.: Virtual reconstruction of Santa María Square. https://youtu.be/FPCV_JEmBrw. Accessed 17 Mar 2022
16. Alaguero, M., Rodriguez-Garcia, B.: Virtual reconstruction of Main Square. https://youtu.be/btyju8gHNMk. Accessed 17 Mar 2022
17. Alaguero, M., Rodriguez-Garcia, B.: Virtual reconstruction of Llana de Afuera. https://youtu.be/KzqdYP0YPk4. Accessed 17 Mar 2022
18. Argyriou, L., Economou, D., Bouki, V.: Design methodology for 360° immersive video applications: the case study of a cultural heritage virtual tour. Pers. Ubiquit. Comput. **24**(6), 843–859 (2020). https://doi.org/10.1007/s00779-020-01373-8
19. Checa, D., Saucedo-Dorantes, J.J., Osornio-Rios, R.A., Antonino-Daviu, J.A., Bustillo, A.: Virtual reality training application for the condition-based maintenance of induction motors. Appl. Sci. **12**, 414 (2022). https://doi.org/10.3390/app12010414
20. Checa, D., Miguel-Alonso, I., Bustillo, A.: Immersive virtual-reality computer-assembly serious game to enhance autonomous learning. Virtual Reality, 1–18 (2021). https://doi.org/10.1007/s10055-021-00607-1

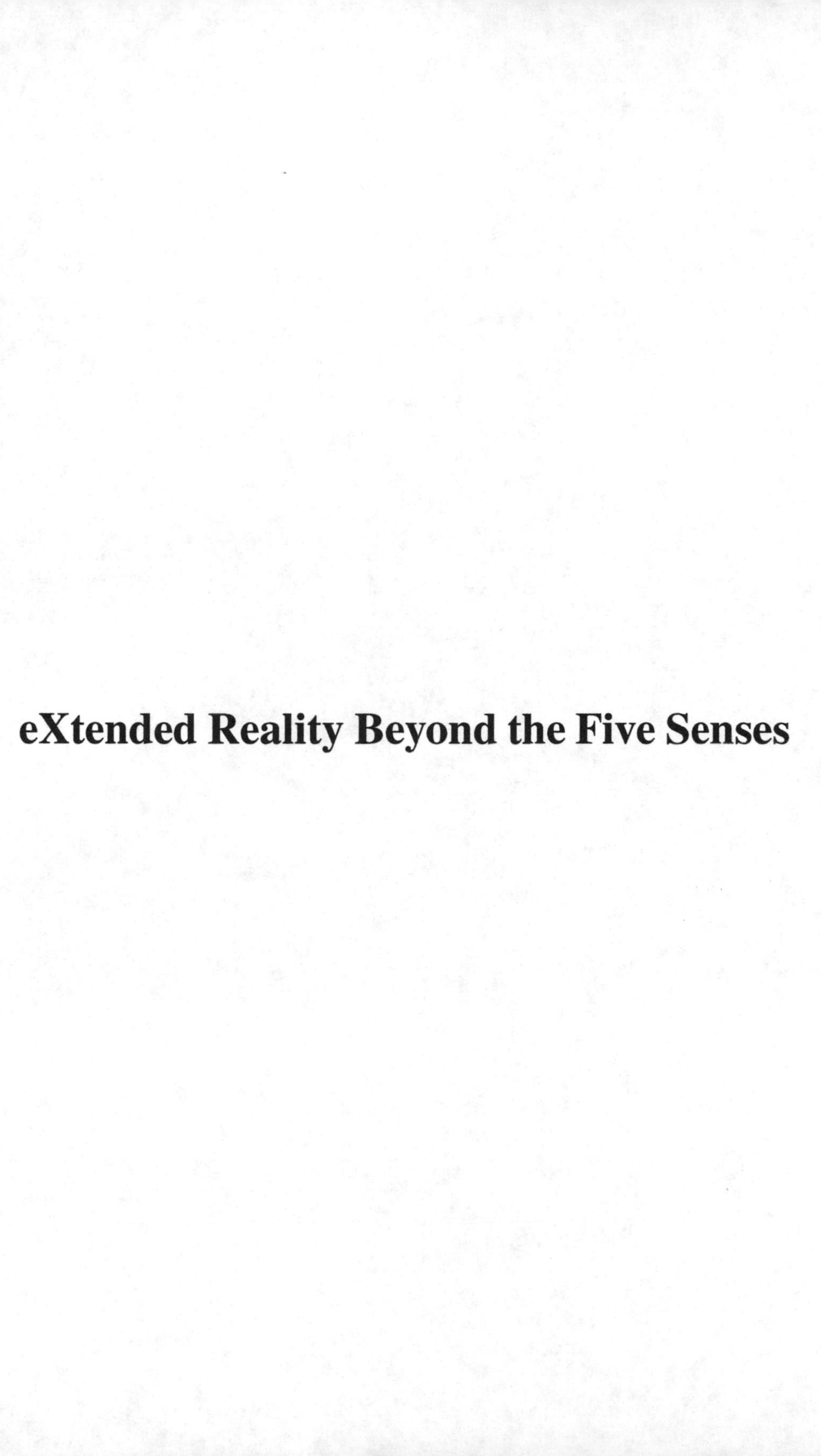

eXtended Reality Beyond the Five Senses

Non-immersive Versus Immersive Extended Reality for Motor Imagery Neurofeedback Within a Brain-Computer Interfaces

Pasquale Arpaia[1,2](✉), Damien Coyle[3], Francesco Donnarumma[4], Antonio Esposito[1,5], Angela Natalizio[6], and Marco Parvis[6]

[1] Department of Electrical Engineering and Information Technology (DIETI), Universitá degli Studi di Napoli Federico II, Via Claudio 21, 80138 Naples, Italy
pasquale.arpaia@unina.it

[2] Interdepartmental Center for Research on Management and Innovation in Healthcare (CIRMIS), University of Naples Federico II, Naples, Italy

[3] Intelligent Systems Research Centre, University of Ulster, Derry, Northern Ireland

[4] Institute of Cognitive Sciences and Technologies, National Research Council (ISTC-CNR), Rome, Italy

[5] Centro Servizi Metrologici e Tecnologici Avanzati (CeSMA), University of Naples Federico II, Naples, Italy

[6] Department of Electronics and Telecommunications (DET), Politecnico di Torino, Corso Castelfidardo 39, 10129 Turin, Italy

Abstract. A sensory feedback was employed for the present work to remap brain signals into sensory information. In particular, sensorimotor rhythms associated with motor imagery were measured as a mean to interact with an extended reality (XR) environment. The aim for such a neurofeedback was to let the user become aware of his/her ability to imagine a movement. A brain-computer interface based on motor imagery was thus implemented by using a consumer-grade electroencephalograph and by taking into account wearable and portable feedback actuators. Visual and vibrotactile sensory feedback modalities were used simultaneously to provide an engaging multimodal feedback in XR. Both a non-immersive and an immersive version of the system were considered and compared. Preliminary validation was carried out with four healthy subjects participating in a total of four sessions on different days. Experiments were conducted according to a wide-spread synchronous paradigm in which an application provides the timing for the motor imagery tasks. Performance was compared in terms of classification accuracy. Overall, subjects preferred the immersive neurofeedback because it allowed higher concentration during experiments, but there was not enough evidence to prove its actual effectiveness and mean classification accuracy resulted about 65%. Meanwhile, classification accuracy resulted higher with the non-immersive neurofeedback, notably it reached about 75%. Future experiments could extend this comparison to more subjects and more sessions, due to the relevance of possible applications in rehabilitation. Moreover, the immersive XR implementation could be improved to provide a greater sense of embodiment.

L. T. De Paolis et al. (Eds.): XR Salento 2022, LNCS 13446, pp. 407–419, 2022.
https://doi.org/10.1007/978-3-031-15553-6_28

Keywords: Brain-computer interface · Extended reality · Motor imagery · Electroencephalography · Haptics · Neurofeedback

1 Introduction

In extended reality, or XR, experiences rely on creating an interactive environment and providing the perceptive consequences of these interactions. In accordance with the predictive coding theory [1], the human brain continuously generates and updates a mental model of the surrounding environment. This happens while receiving sensory stimuli, and, in turn, these models can predict imminent stimuli. In the real world, the movement of the body in space produces a continuous stream of both sensory stimuli and inner stimuli, but the XR community has currently focused on the only sensorimotor contingency as the prominent factor for presence. However, neuroscience has demonstrated that multi-perceptual integration of bodily signals, action, and embodiment are also critical to generate XR experiences [2]. Therefore, to develop novel XR-based applications, enhanced embodied XR experiences are relevant. For instance, this may apply to clinical scenarios, such as post-traumatic stress disorders, eating disorders, phantom limb pain, and autism, since these are related to a dysfunctional bodily self-consciousness. In such a scenario, mental training protocols are widely used.

With specific regards to neuromotor rehabilitation, conventional training protocols are used with the aim of recovering the functional damage or making an optimal use of residual motor assets. Some examples are the "Kabat" method [3], the "Bobath" method [4], and the "mirror therapy" [5]. In the "Kabat" method, the aim is to recover motor functionality through external proprioceptive stimuli by improving the altered movement. In the "Bobath" method, instead, functional recovery is attempted through proprioceptive learning and a tactile, visual and auditory sensory experience. Finally, mirror therapy represents a rehabilitation method that involves moving both injured limbs evenly and symmetrically in front of a mirror. The patient will have to observe the healthy limb, so that it will appear that the paretic limb is moving. This is a way to trick the brain into thinking that the movement is taking place normally and thus exploit the residual capacity of the injured limb by stimulating it with the optical effect of the mirror. Physical effort is also required from the patient in classical rehabilitation. On the contrary, these rehabilitation techniques have been recently combined with Brain-Computer Interfaces (BCI) based on motor imagery, i.e. a cognitive process during which the subject imagines a movement without performing it [6].

Nowadays, innovative systems try to exploit XR in such motor training. In particular, motor imagery is widely exploited in BCIs as a way for control and communication between the brain and an external device [7], and motor imagery-based BCIs are proposed in several fields because the brain activity generated by motor imagery affects the same brain areas involved during the execution of a movement [8]. However, although people have the ability to imagine, they do not get a sense of how they imagine. Therefore, a neurofeedback provided in XR can bridge this gap. Neurofeedback is a process by which the users are provided with feedback as a result of real-time processing of their brain signal. Moreover, neurofeedback reduces the training time required to be able to use the interface and increases the motivation and attention level of the users [9]. In neurorehabilitation, neurofeedback aids the patients in the self-regulation of their brain rhythms. It induces neural plasticity and promotes recovery of the injured motor nerve pathway [8]. The patients can receive multidimensional neurofeedback, i.e., visual feedback and haptic feedback simultaneously, in response to the executed motor imagery task. In this framework, XR technology can be exploited to create an immersive and realistic environment to provide users with sensory feedbacks [10].

Patient comfort is another priority. For this reason, BCIs are often based on electroencephalography (EEG) due to non-invasiveness, wearability, portability, and good temporal resolution [11]. To further enhance wearability and ease of use, the number of EEG channels should be minimized. Three channels is usually considered as a minimum number for motor imagery [12]. A wearable motor imagery-based BCI integrated with the XR aims to be a novel and emerging methodology for motor rehabilitation [13]. Indeed, letting the user become aware of his/her ability to imagine a movement can improve a rehabilitation protocol by engaging the patient during long and exhausting sessions.

In this contribution, both non-immersive and immersive neurofeedback in XR were explored as a means to remap motor imagery into sensory feedback. Notably, visual and vibrotactile sensory stimulation were proposed as a way to "feel" how they imagine movements. The final aim was to improve mental tasks, which are often unperceived and go beyond the five senses. The proposed systems aim to be wearable and portable and they could be suitable for neuromotor rehabilitation even outside a clinical setting. However, as a preliminary study, the systems were tested with healthy subjects. The paper is organized as follows: Sect. 2 presents the BCI system with XR neurofeedback and details both the non-immersive and the immersive version, Sect. 3 reports the results of preliminary tests carried out with these system versions, and Sect. 4 draws some conclusions as well as future steps for further research.

2 Materials and Methods

The present study focuses on wearable and portable BCI integrated with XR as a means to provide multimodal feedback related to motor imagery. This aims to allow the user to become aware of his/her ability to imagine a movement. As a consequence, it promotes the voluntary modulation of sensorimotor rhythms. The system prototypes were implemented with consumer-grade hardware and they are addressed to neuromotor rehabilitation, e.g. post-stroke. In particular, a limited number of differential channels were exploited during signal acquisition. A dedicated virtual environment was developed to provide either visual and haptic feedback to the user. These were modulated according to the ongoing brain activity related to motor imagery. Hence, brain signals were acquired and processed online in order to modulate the feedback in terms of direction and intensity. Two versions of the same system were proposed. In them, the differences were only related to the feedback actuators. In the first version, visual feedback was non-immersive because it was provided through a PC's monitor. Instead, haptic feedback was provided by a vibrotactile suit. In the second version, instead, visual feedback was ported to a virtual reality visor, while the haptic feedback was provided via the visor's controllers. Experiments were carried out according to a standard synchronous paradigm, as detailed hereafter.

2.1 System Implementation

Virtual Environment. The virtual environment for both versions was developed with the Unity Development Platform[1]. Regarding the visual feedback, the scene is represented in Fig. 1. In there, the visual feedback consisted of a virtual ball, which could horizontally roll to the left or to the right side of the scene. Its actual movement was modulated in terms of direction and speed in accordance with the measured brain activity. The edges for the ball movement were marked in the environment with two white lines on the two sides of the scene. Regarding the haptic feedback, the vibration was modulated in terms of direction and intensity according to the measured brain activity. For this modality, the feedback actuators are described below in distinguishing the non-immersive version from the immersive ones. Details about the feedback actuation are thus given along with such a discussion.

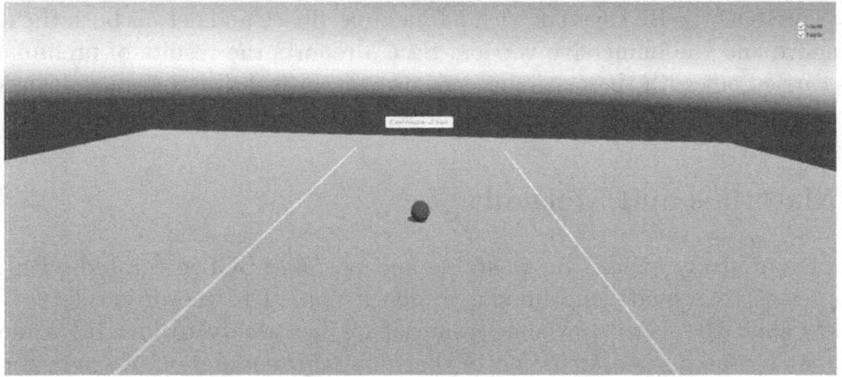

Fig. 1. Scene for the visual feedback within the virtual environment.

[1] https://unity.com/.

Non-immersive Version. Feedback actuators for the non-immersive version were first considered. The visual feedback consisted of a virtual rolling ball on a PC's monitor. This had an LCD 15.6" display (resolution 1920×1080 pixels) with a 60Hz refresh rate. Meanwhile the haptic feedback was provided by the vibrotactile suit from bHaptics Inc[2] (Fig. 2). This consists of a double 5×4 matrix with vibration motors on the front and back of the torso capable of actuating a chest vibrotactile stimulation. The vibration can be modulated in terms of duration, frequency and intensity. The suit communicates via Bluetooth and it was particularly controlled through the Unity application.

The SDK provided by bHaptics was exploited to modulate the suit haptic feedback. Vibration patterns were provided on the front of the torso starting from the center. They moved toward the left or toward the right according to the brain activity. The goal for the user was to maximally activate the haptic feedback on the back of the respective side.

Fig. 2. Wearable haptic suit with a double matrix of vibrating motors for vibrotactile feedback.

Immersive Version. The immersive feedback was provided through the HTC VIVE PRO EYE by HTC Corporation Inc[3]. This consists of a virtual reality headset with dual-OLED 3.5" diagonal displays (resolution 2880×1600 pixels), a 90Hz refresh rate, and a 110° field of view. The wireless controllers with SteamVR Tracking 2.0 sensors provide high definition haptic feedback and they should be held by hands (Fig. 3). In this version, the controllers were employed to provide vibrotactile feedback during the experiments, while participants did not actively interact with the environment through them. Like the suit, the vibration could be modulated in terms of duration, frequency and intensity.

[2] https://www.bhaptics.com/tactsuit/tactsuit-x40.

[3] https://www.vive.com/us/product/vive-pro-eye/overview/.

The SteamVR Unity Plugin[4] was exploited to provide an immersive interaction with the environment in the HTC system. The visual feedback was simply ported on the visor in this immersive version. Meanwhile, for the haptic feedback provided through the controllers, the vibration at the hand corresponding to the motor imagery task was modulated in terms of intensity. Notably, this intensity changed according to the measured brain signals.

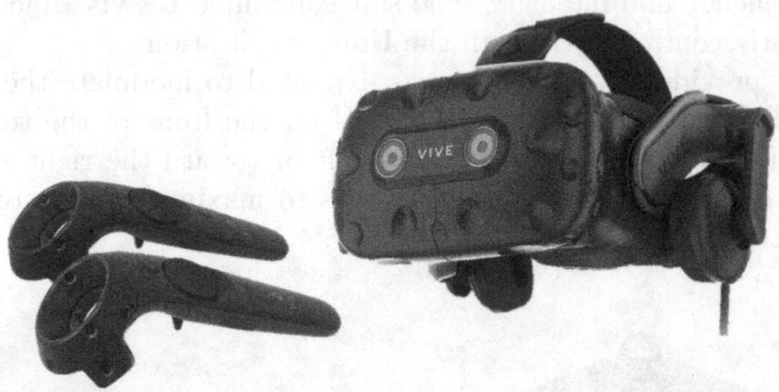

Fig. 3. HTC VIVE PRO EYE virtual reality headset with hands-held controllers.

EEG Acquisition. EEG data were acquired by means of a FlexEEG headset by Neuro-CONCISE Ltd[5] with 3 differential channels over the motor cortex (Fig. 4). In this acquisition system, electrodes are located at FC3-CP3, FCZ-CPZ, and FC4-CP4 by following the standard 10–20 system for EEG recordings [14]. The ground electrode is placed at AFz. Despite the possibility to use dry electrodes, wet ones are generally preferred to ensure good signal-to-noise ratio and high signal reliability. Therefore, conductive gel was used in these experiments. Thanks to its wearable design, FlexEEG was properly embedded with the XR visor. EEG signals were sent to a custom Simulink model by using Bluetooth 2.0 wireless signal transmission and available Simulink APIs. Such a model involved online signal processing and responded to the application's timing.

2.2 Experimental Paradigm

The XR neurofeedback was implemented within a synchronous motor imagery-based BCI. The experiments consisted of two sessions per system version carried out on different days (four sessions in total). Each session involved three runs for calibrating the system and three runs for providing online neurofeedback. About 10min-break was given to the participant between these two phases. A single session lasted about 30min. Each experimental task consisted of imagining left or right hand movement depending on the indication and in accordance with an external timing. The motor imagery task to be imaged was randomized in

[4] http://steamvr.com.

[5] https://www.neuroconcise.co.uk/.

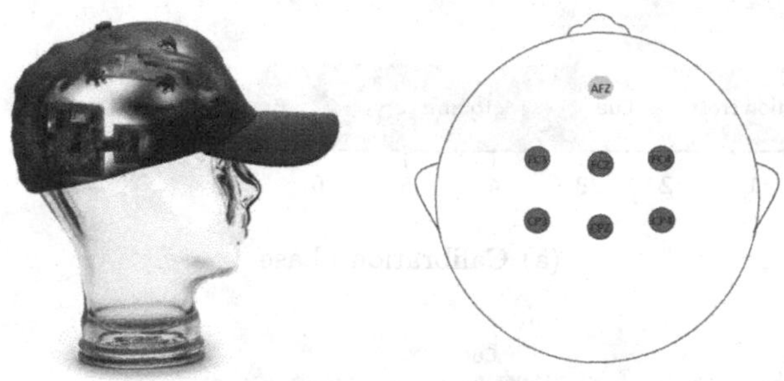

Fig. 4. Wearable and portable electroencephalograph with electrodes over the motor cortex.

order to avoid any bias. A total of 30 trials per run were performed, so that 270 trials were carried out as a whole in both the non-immersive and immersive case. With reference to the standard paradigms of BCI competitions [15], Fig. 5 shows the timing diagrams of a single trial during the calibration phase and online feedback phase, respectively.

During the calibration phase (Fig. 5(a)), the participants performed the pure motor imagery. Each trial started with a relax period during which the participant had to stare at a fixation cross. Then, a cue indicated the trial to be carried out during the following "motor imagery period", lasting 3.00 s. Finally, a break with random duration concluded the trial. These indications always appeared on the PC's monitor. Hence, the calibration phase was non-immersive in both system versions. At the end of all the trials associated with this phase, the recorded EEG signals were exploited in order to train the algorithm for the online phase. In particular, the cross-validation technique was employed to find the 2.00 s time window within the 3.00 s of motor imagery in which the maximum overall classification accuracy and the minimum per-class accuracy difference were achieved. Thus, the algorithm was trained by considering this optimal window.

During the online feedback phase (Fig. 5(b)), EEG signals were classified during motor imagery execution in order to provide simultaneous feedback. After the fixation cross period and the cue, the signals were processed during each motor imagery window using a 2.00 s sliding window with a shift of 0.25 s until the end of the task. It is worth noting that, despite the previous case, the cue indication is here persistent during the whole motor imagery/feedback period. In terms of feedback, the goal for the user was to push the ball over the white line on the respective side of the virtual floor. At the same time, maximum vibration intensity was provided. In order to avoid user frustration and disengagement, the user received the feedback only when the class associated with the measured brain signal corresponds to the indicated task (biased feedback). If instead the assigned class did not match with the task, the ball did not move and the controllers did not vibrate. In any case, the intensity of the feedback was modulated according to the classification score.

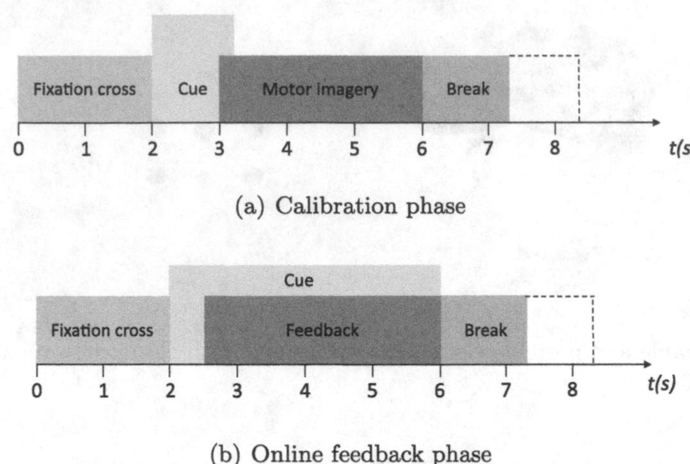

(a) Calibration phase

(b) Online feedback phase

Fig. 5. Timing diagrams for a single experimental trial.

2.3 Signal Processing

The EEG signals were processed to modulate the neurofeedback during experiments, but also to assess the motor imagery capability of a subject after the experiments (offline analysis). In both cases, features were extracted from raw EEG data by means of the filter-bank common spatial pattern (FBCSP) algorithm [16] and then classified with a Naive Bayesian Parzen Window (NBPW) classifier. During online neurofeedback, the assigned class with its associated score were used in order to modulate the feedback direction and speed/intensity, respectively. The online operation of the system, including signal acquisition and processing, was implemented by means of a Simulink model communicating with the Unity application. Meanwhile, Matlab scripts were implemented to train the algorithm for online processing by relying on acquired EEG signals and to analyse these signals after the experiments.

In offline analyses, baseline removal was first applied by considering the 100 ms before the cue. Then, the FBCSP was used. In particular, (i) EEG data were digitally filtered using an array of bandpass filters from 4 Hz to 40 Hz, (ii) the common spatial patterns (CSP) algorithm was exploited for feature extraction, (iii) the mutual information-based best individual features (MIBIF) algorithm was used to select the most important features, and (iv) finally the NBPW was exploited to classify the features related to a specific task and to assign them the most probable class. Note that the CSP uses spatial filters to maximize the discriminability of two classes. Hence, binary classification was considered, but multi-class extensions would be possible as well. As a result of the NBPW, the most probable class and its probability were used to modulate the feedback in the online phase, as already mentioned above. The block diagram of the algorithm is recalled in Fig. 6.

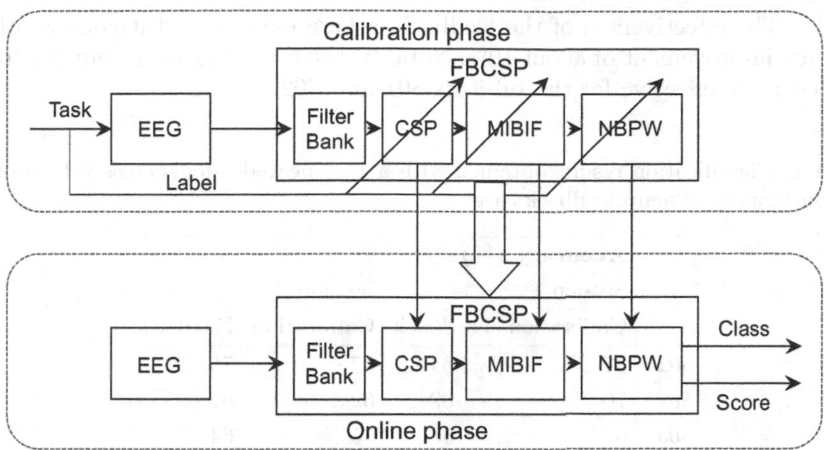

Fig. 6. FBCSP algorithm. EEG: electroencephalography, CSP: common spatial pattern, MIBIF: mutual information-based best individual features, NBPW: naive bayesian parzen window.

3 Results

3.1 Subjects

With the aim of evaluating the effectiveness of the proposed system, four right-handed healthy volunteers participated in the two experimental sessions per each system version (non-immersive and immersive). One subject was male and three were females (mean age 27). The subjects signed an informed consent before participating in the experiments. These were conducted at the Augmented Reality for Health Monitoring Laboratory (ARHeMLab, University of Naples Federico II) in Italy.

3.2 Classification Results

Data from each experimental phase were analysed as described before by applying a 5-folds cross validation with 10 repetitions. For both the calibration and the online phase, an optimal 2.00s-wide time window was selected per each subject. With particular reference to the results of the calibration phase, the criterion for an optimal choice of the time window was to maximize the classification accuracy while trying to also minimize the difference between accuracies per class. Therefore, the same criterion was adopted in also reporting the accuracy associated with the online feedback. These classification accuracies are reported in Table 1 and Table 2 for the non-immersive version and the immersive version, respectively. Each session and phase are considered separately.

It can be thus interesting to compare the two system versions. Referring to mean accuracies associated with the non-immersive case, it can be noted that the one associated with the calibration phases of both sessions resulted from 62%

to 64%. The effectiveness of the feedback is here evident and it consists of an accuracy improvement of about 10%. Notably, the non-immersive neurofeedback resulted more effective for the subjects S01 and S02.

Table 1. Classification results obtained with a 10-repeated 5-folds cross validation in the non-immersive neurofeedback case.

	Accuracy (%)			
	Session 1		Session 2	
	Calibration	Feedback	Calibration	Feedback
S01	57	84	67	75
S02	70	82	62	82
S03	63	68	65	64
S04	57	65	61	76
Mean	62	75	64	74

Instead, for the immersive case, it can be noted that mean accuracies remain between 61% and 66% for both the calibration and online feedback phases. Only in the Session 2, the improvement in mean accuracy is associated with neurofeedback, but due to a lowered accuracy in the calibration phase. Despite the previous case, subjects S01 and S02 are not improving with the immersive neurofeedback. Meanwhile, the improvements associated with S03 and S04 are compatible with the previous case.

3.3 Discussion

As a whole, the results reported above were not capable of proving the effectiveness of the immersive feedback while a substantial improvement was highlighted for the non-immersive case. Despite that, all subjects agreed that the immersive system was helping them to keep higher concentration throughout the experiment. A possible issue related to the immersive version of the system could be that participants were not familiar with using visor before the experiments. In addition, since the calibration phase was always delivered in a non-immersive modality, participants could have been confused when the modality changed during the session. Therefore, an immersive calibration phase could be explored in the future.

A more immersive visual feedback could be also explored. Indeed, the current one simply consisted of a simple porting to the visor of the non-immersive visual feedback, while an updated version could be realised. For instance, in motor imagery-assisted neurological rehabilitation, an embodied feedback could be implemented to perform mirror therapy. Finally, regarding data analysis, more insights could be done by going beyond classification accuracy. For instance, band

Table 2. Classification results obtained with a 10-repeated 5-folds cross validation in the immersive neurofeedback case.

	Accuracy (%)			
	Session 1		Session 2	
	Calibration	Feedback	Calibration	Feedback
S01	69	67	62	63
S02	74	60	63	63
S03	53	63	65	68
S04	63	68	56	69
Mean	65	65	61	66

power could be evaluated to understand if the neurofeedback enhances neurological phenomena associated with movement while keeping the mental workload low.

4 Conclusion

Extended reality has been recently considered in motor training and rehabilitation. Notably, motor imagery can be exploited in brain-computer interface systems integrated with extended reality as a novel way for communication and control of an external device. In doing that, people do not get a sense of their motor imagery capability and a neurofeedback could be exploited to that aim. Thanks to a real-time processing of brain signal, this aims to improve user engagement and hence performance, while reducing the training time.

The current study focused on the design, implementation, and preliminary testing of a wearable and portable brain-computer interface exploiting extended reality for neurofeedback associated with motor imagery. The system was implemented with consumer-grade hardware involving only three differential channels for EEG acquisition. The virtual environment was developed in Unity to provide visual and haptic feedbacks modulated according to the online processing of EEG signals. Both a non-immersive and an immersive system implementation were explored. The feedback was modulated in terms of direction and intensity by means of class and score, respectively. This processing relied on the filter bank common spatial pattern and a Bayesian classifier, which are widely employed in the field of brain-computer interfaces.

Preliminary experiments were carried out according to a standard paradigm for synchronous brain-computer interfaces by involving four subjects in two sessions per each system version. The classification results were thus compared to highlight the better neurofeedback modality. Overall, these preliminary results indicated a greater effectiveness of the non-immersive feedback in comparison with the immersive one, though the immersive environment favored concentration. The reason could be due to a lack of confidence with the visor usage.

Therefore, further experiments could explore an even more immersive virtual scene and a greater number of experimental sessions should be performed with a larger number of subjects as well.

Acknowledgement. This work was carried out as part of the "ICT for Health" project, which was financially supported by the Italian Ministry of Education, University and Research (MIUR), under the initiative 'Departments of Excellence' (Italian Budget Law no. 232/2016), through an excellence grant awarded to the Department of Information Technology and Electrical Engineering of the University of Naples Federico II, Naples, Italy. The authors thank also thank Giovanni D'Errico and Stefania Di Rienzo for supporting system design and data analyses.

References

1. Kok, P., de Lange, F.P.: Predictive coding in sensory cortex. In: Forstmann, B.U., Wagenmakers, E.-J. (eds.) An Introduction to Model-Based Cognitive Neuroscience, pp. 221–244. Springer, New York (2015). https://doi.org/10.1007/978-1-4939-2236-9_11
2. Škola, F., Tinková, S., Liarokapis, F.: Progressive training for motor imagery brain-computer interfaces using gamification and virtual reality embodiment. Front. Human Neurosci. 329 (2019)
3. Kabat, H.: Studies of neuromuscular dysfunction; treatment of chronic multiple sclerosis with neostigmine and intensive muscle re-education. Permanent. Found. Med. Bullet. **5**(1), 1–14 (1947)
4. Kollen, B.J., et al.: The effectiveness of the bobath concept in stroke rehabilitation: what is the evidence? Stroke **40**(4), e89–e97 (2009)
5. Thieme, H., et al.: Mirror therapy for improving motor function after stroke. Cochrane Datab. Syst. Rev. **7** (2018)
6. Pfurtscheller, G., Neuper, C.: Motor imagery and direct brain-computer communication. Proc. IEEE **89**(7), 1123–1134 (2001)
7. Wolpaw, J.R., et al.: Brain-computer interface technology: a review of the first international meeting. IEEE Trans. Rehabilit. Eng. **8**(2), 164–173 (2000)
8. Wen, D., et al.: Combining brain-computer interface and virtual reality for rehabilitation in neurological diseases: a narrative review. Ann. Phys. Rehabilit. Med. **64**(1), 101404 (2021)
9. McCreadie, K.A., Coyle, D.H., Prasad, G.: Learning to modulate sensorimotor rhythms with stereo auditory feedback for a brain-computer interface. In: 2012 Annual International Conference of the IEEE Engineering in Medicine and Biology Society, pp. 6711–6714. IEEE (2012)
10. Elbamby, M.S., Perfecto, C., Bennis, M., Doppler, K.: Toward low-latency and ultra-reliable virtual reality. IEEE Network **32**(2), 78–84 (2018)
11. Teplan, M., et al.: Fundamentals of EEG measurement. Measur. Sci. Rev. **2**(2), 1–11 (2002)
12. Leeb, R., Lee, F., Keinrath, C., Scherer, R., Bischof, H., Pfurtscheller, G.: Brain-computer communication: motivation, aim, and impact of exploring a virtual apartment. IEEE Trans. Neural Syst. Rehabilit. Eng. **15**(4), 473–482 (2007)
13. Cuomo, G., et al.: Motor imagery and gait control in Parkinson's disease: techniques and new perspectives in neurorehabilitation. Expert Rev. Neurotherap. (2022)

14. Klem, G.H., Lüders, H.O., Jasper, H., Elger, C., et al.: The ten-twenty electrode system of the international federation. Electroencephalogr. Clin. Neurophysiol. **52**(3), 3–6 (1999)
15. Brunner, C., Leeb, R., Müller-Putz, G., Schlögl, A., Pfurtscheller, G.: BCI competition 2008–Graz data set A. In: Institute for Knowledge Discovery (Laboratory of Brain-Computer Interfaces), vol. 16, pp. 1–6. Graz University of Technology (2008)
16. Ang, K.K., Chin, Z.Y., Wang, C., Guan, C., Zhang, H.: Filter bank common spatial pattern algorithm on BCI competition IV datasets 2a and 2b. Front. Neurosci. **6**, 39 (2012)

Virtual Reality Enhances EEG-Based Neurofeedback for Emotional Self-regulation

Pasquale Arpaia[1,2(✉)], Damien Coyle[3], Giovanni D'Errico[4], Egidio De Benedetto[1], Lucio Tommaso De Paolis[5], Naomi du Bois[3], Sabrina Grassini[4], Giovanna Mastrati[1], Nicola Moccaldi[1], and Ersilia Vallefuoco[1]

[1] Department of Electrical Engineering and Information Technology (DIETI), University of Naples Federico II, Naples, Italy
pasquale.arpaia@unina.it
[2] Interdepartmental Center for Research on Management and Innovation in Healthcare (CIRMIS), University of Naples Federico II, Naples, Italy
[3] Intelligent Systems Research Centre, Ulster University (UU), NI, UK
[4] Department of Applied Science and Technology, Polytechnic University of Turin, Turin, Italy
[5] Department of Engineering for Innovation, University of Salento, Lecce, Italy

Abstract. A pilot study to investigate possible differences between a virtual reality-based neurofeedback and a traditional neurofeedback is presented. Neurofeedback training aimed to strengthen the emotional regulation capacity. The neurofeedback task is to down-regulate negative emotions by decreasing the beta band power measured in the midline areas of the scalp (i.e., Fcz-Cpz). Negative International Affective Picture System images were chosen as eliciting stimuli. Three healthy subjects participated in the experimental activities. Each of them underwent three VR-based neurofeedback sessions and three neurofeedback sessions delivered on a traditional 2D screen. The neurofeedback training session was preceded by a calibration phase allowing to record the rest and the baseline values to adapt the neurofeedback system to the user. For the majority of sessions, the average value of the high beta band power during the neurofeedback training remained below the baseline, as expected. In compliance with previous studies, future works should investigate the virtual reality-based neurofeedback efficacy in physiological responses and behavioral performance.

Keywords: Brain-computer interface · EEG · Extended reality · Virtual reality · Health 4.0 · Emotion regulation · Neurofeedback

1 Introduction

Neurofeedback is a form of biofeedback based on signals collected from the brain. Typically, electrical activity from the brain is acquired by using electroencephalography (EEG). Brainwave information is provided in real time to the user so they can learn how to self regulate brain electrical activity [1]. This technique proves effective in the treatment of attention-deficit/hyperactivity disorder [2], sleep disorders [3], and in the self-regulation of emotional behavior [4].

L. T. De Paolis et al. (Eds.): XR Salento 2022, LNCS 13446, pp. 420–431, 2022.
https://doi.org/10.1007/978-3-031-15553-6_29

Emotion regulation (ER) is the ability to recognize one's emotions and manage the intensity and duration of emotional experience [5]. Impairment of the ability to regulate affect leads to emotional vulnerability: a high sensitivity to experienc- ing emotions with high degrees of intensity and for a long time. Various cognitive and behavioral strategies can be employed for ER. Typical cognitive strategies are based on shift of attention, distancing, or cognitive reappraisal. The latter proved to be particularly successful and consists in changing the way the person thinks and evaluates the emotionally critical situation in order to modify his/her emotional impact [6]. A specific kind of reappraisal is the reality checking that is the reappraisal of the meaning of the current situation. Physical exercises such as running can be an effective behavioral strategy for achieving emotional modulation [7].

Thanks to the association between emotions and the diverse brain activation patterns [8] and the relations between cerebral damages and emotion perception and expression [9], neurofeedback can be used for the treatment of emotion regulation disorders. Neurofeedback for ER has been successfully applied to treat schizophrenia [10], stress [11], depression [12], and anxiety [14–16]. In [10], functional Near-Infrared Spectroscopy and EEG were employed for the neurofeedback training of eighteen subjects suffering from schizophrenia. The regulation of frontal delta asymmetry allowed to restore the unbalance between the hemispheres. In [11], frontal alpha power and frontal alpha asymmetry based neurofeedback were successfully exploited for stress mitigation. EEG data from 20 participants were recorded in two neurofeedback sessions. In [13], simultaneous real-time Functional Magnetic Resonance Imaging and EEG-based neurofeedback for ER in 16 subjects with major depressive disorder was carried out. Frontal EEG asymmetries in the alpha band and high-beta band were the exploited EEG-related quantities. Significant upregulation was achieved. In [14], the effectiveness of neurofeedback on brain training of ER was proven. By means of a control group, the study separated the effects of neurofeedback and cognitive strategy. In a neurofeedback training to increase frontal alpha asymmetry was exploited for the reduction of negative affect and anxiety. 32 subjects underwent the experimental activities. As a result an increment in alpha asymmetry produced a reduction in both negative affect and anxiety. In [15], alpha, beta and alpha-theta bands measured in Pz and Fz locations were regulated by neurofeedback training in two patients diagnosed with anxiety disorder. Anxiety-related symptoms reduced within a three month period. The case study of a subject with anxiety was presented in [16]. A neurofeedback-based protocol was successfully employed to suppress excessive central high beta activity. Neurofeedback training was successfully employed also in healthy subjects. In [16], long-term effects of neurofeedback training based on frontal beta EEG were evaluated on 25 healthy subjects. Resting-state EEG was recorded prior to neurofeedback training and in a 3-year followup. Neurofeedback training increased Fz beta activity both in short and long-term. In the impact on mood of frontal alpha-activity based neurofeedback was evaluated. 40 healthy females were involved in the experiments and results demonstrated the feasibility of varying frontal alpha asymmetry just in a single neurofeedback session..

Emotion induction mechanisms are often grouped into two classes: passive and active [17]. Traditionally, passive elicitation methods place the user as a mere observer, ignoring the importance of personal meaning in the emotional experience. Active mechanisms are characterised by high ecological validity (meaning the ability of experimental results to be generalisable to the real world outside the laboratory [18]), immersiveness and interactivity.

Among active approaches, Virtual Reality (VR) (and, more in general, eXtended Reality) shows great potential for emotional elicitation, offering motivational and empathy mechanisms that make it an ecologically valid paradigm for studying emotions. The sense of presence offered by VR is the result of a technological simulation consistent with the predictive mechanisms of the brain (body matrix) [19, 20]. VR stimulates a wide range of sensory modalities, integrating proprioception, interoception and sensory information [19].

Although the so-called novelty bias may play a controversial role, various researches show that the use of VR leads to even stronger valence and arousal elicitation with respect to passive methods [21]. Nevertheless, there is a lack of reference datasets and databases in the literature that standardise VR content, which is mandatory for performing comparison studies [22]. This represents the greatest limitation in this line of research to date.

Important but less explored (especially with EEG-BCI) in this context is the use of neurofeedback for ER in VR. In this study, and similarly to what has already been covered in the literature [23], International affective picture system (IAPS) images are exploited as visual stimuli also in the VR environment. The aspect of immersivity and engagement is exploited for the environmental neurofeedback rather than the stimulus delivery mechanism.

The goal of the present study is to explore potential differences between a VR-based and a traditional 2D neurofeedback system, aimed to strengthen the ER capacity. Specifically, three subjects carried out three sessions with the 2D neurofeedback system and three sessions with the VR neurofeedback system. In both systems, feedback training exploits standardised stimuli to elicit specific emotions and EEG signals to provide the feedback. Differences between the two proposed systems were assessed through different self-assessment scales that evaluated both emotional states and systems' usability. In Sect. 2, the overall neurofeedback systems, the experimental campaign for the EEG signal acquisitions, and the statistical and EEG data analysis procedures are presented. The statistical analysis and the EEG data analysis are reported in Sect. 3. Discussions and conclusions are illustrated in Sect. 4 and Sect. 5, respectively.

2 Material and Methods

2.1 VR Neurofeedback System

Two different neurofeedback-based systems were developed: a 2D-neurofeedback system and a VR-neurofeedback system. To induce a certain emotional state to the user, IAPS images [24] negatively polarised on the valence axis (and with. neutral arousal) were used as eliciting stimuli. Since IAPS images are rated according to the circumplex model of affect, the dimensional model is considered as reference theory. Pictures represented scenes of danger, death, violence, disease etc. Pictures were different and randomly presented to participants in order to prevent habituation and familiarity. In the first system, the application dis- plays sequentially on the screen appropriate visual stimuli.

During regulation, the feedback was provided by the colour bar (on the right hand side) and by the frame (placed around the images). Figure 1-a shows the 2D-neurofeedback application.

(a) 2D feedback (b) VR feedback

Fig. 1. 2D (a) and VR (b) feedbacks (Color figure online)

Fig. 2. Colour scale (Color figure online)

In the VR-neurofeedback system, a visual stimulation mechanism using IAPS images was adopted, so that a one-to-one comparison with the on-screen neurofeedback case was straightforward. Specifically, the application immerses the subject in a virtual room (a minimalist office room in which care was taken not to include distracting elements) in which stimuli are displayed on a room wall. In this case, in addition to the traditional thermometer on the side of the image, feedback is provided by changing the colour of the lights in the room. The colour-changing image frame here becomes the entire virtual environment, which modulates its colours in accordance with the subject's feedback. In Fig. 1-b, the VR environment is shown. In both systems, the colour bar can move from down (blue) to up (yellow) according to the registered cortical activation following the colour scale proposed by [25] (Fig. 2)..

The heights of the bars were updated every 1-s according to the level of the EEG feature to regulate. The two proposed applications were developed using Unity [26] (version 2019.4.4f1, Personal 64 bit for Microsoft Windows) as game engine. For the VR system, the HTC Vive Pro 2 [27] was used as VR headset. FlexEEG™ from Neuroconcise [28] was employed for signal recordings. EEG data were acquired from three bipolar channels, namely FC3-Cp3, FCz-Cpz, and Fc4-Cp4 placed according to the International 10–20 Positioning System. Afz is the bias electrode. Electrodes were filled in with conductive gel. The system allows wireless signal transmission via Bluetooth 2.0 and adjustable sampling rate (125 Hz-250 Hz) and ADC resolution (16–24 bits).

EEG signal was acquired, transmitted and real time processed in Matlab environment R2021b version. The EEG system is provided with a Matlab script which allows the parameters setting and a default Simulink model which contains the compiled code to run the FlexEEG. Simulink was employed also for the online processing of the acquired EEG signal. Data were first filtered by using a bandpass filter with cut-off frequencies 20 Hz and 34 Hz, and then 2-s epochs overlapping of 1-s were extracted. Fast Fourier transform (FFT) was then applied to each epoch in order to extract the power values in the considered EEG band. Neurofeedback training focused on the decrease of the high-beta power in midline locations (FCz-Cpz) [29]. For each session, an initial calibration phase was carried out to adapt the neurofeedback session to each participant. 2-min eyes-opened resting state and a task-related baseline were initially recorded [10]. For both phases, the mean high-beta powers of the neurofeedback electrodes were computed and used as the upper and lower limits of the colour scale, respectively. After the calibration phase, the neurofeedback training started. Also in this second phase, EEG data were online processed and the high-beta power computed over the FCz-CPz electrode was used to drive the visual feedback provided to the user. Simulink and Unity communicated via UDP protocol: Unity sent Simulink start and end messages for each task. Simulink returned the values of the reference feature computed in the rest and baseline phases and during the neurofeedback training in order to update the feedback to be provided to the user in real time. In Fig. 3, the overall experimental setup is shown.

2.2 Participants

The present pilot study enrolled three healthy participants (mean age 48.5; two males and one female). All subjects were not familiar with emotion-related BCI experiments and VR systems. All participants gave written informed consent to participate. Ethical approval in accordance with the declaration of Helsinki was obtained from the Ethics Committee of Psychological Research of University of Naples Federico II.

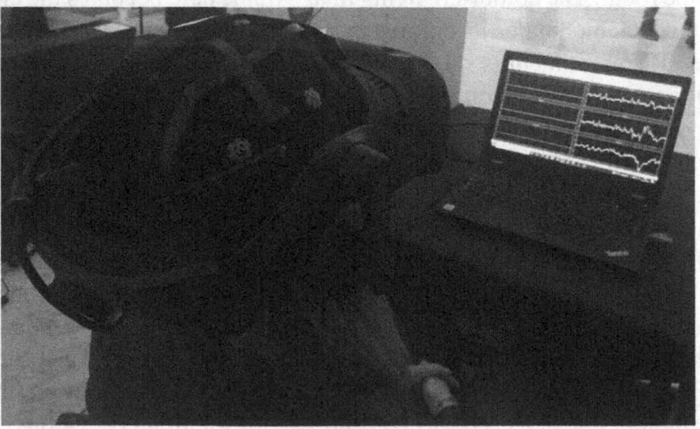

Fig. 3. Experimental setup

2.3 Procedure

The study consisted of six neurofeedback sessions: three sessions via the 2D- neurofeedback system, and three sessions via the VR-neurofeedback system (three days of neurofeedback sessions per week, one session per day). All neurofeedback sessions were carried out at the Arhemlab laboratory of the University of Naples Federico II, in a dark and soundproofed environment to avoid distractions.

Before starting neurofeedback sessions, participants were instructed on the purpose of the experiment and they were given the necessary instructions to conduct the experiment. Subsequently, the participants were asked to sit on a comfortable chair, positioned approximately 70 cm away from a monitor (16″ size), and to wear the EEG cap. The researchers filled the electrodes with conductive gel and visually checked the quality of the EEG signal. After EEG configuration, participants were asked to look at the screen and follow the instructions on it, without moving.

Following [30, 31], a specific neurofeedback experimental protocol was elaborated for this study. The task of the experimental activity was to decrease the beta power value registered along the midline sites of the scalp (compared to the baseline) during the exposure to negative stimuli in a chromatic context that informs the subject about the distance from the target.

Each neurofeedback session was divided in two phases: an initial calibration phase and a NF-training phase. The calibration phase was made of 120-s of opened-eyes resting state and of a negative baseline consisting of the projection of 21 images, each lasting 5-s and preceded by 10-s fixation cross. During the calibration phase, the subjects had to relax themselves and after, to passively watch the projected images.

The training phase was made of 22 trials, fourteen of ER in which the par- ticipants received a feedback about their performance, seven of passive vision during which the participants had only to see the projected images, and a final transfer run in which the subjects had to regulate their emotion but without the feedback.

Regulation trials and only vision trials were randomly shown to participants. Each neurofeedback trial was made of 3-s instruction about the following task, 14-s fixation cross and 20-s image projection. In Fig. 4, the overall experimental procedure is reported.

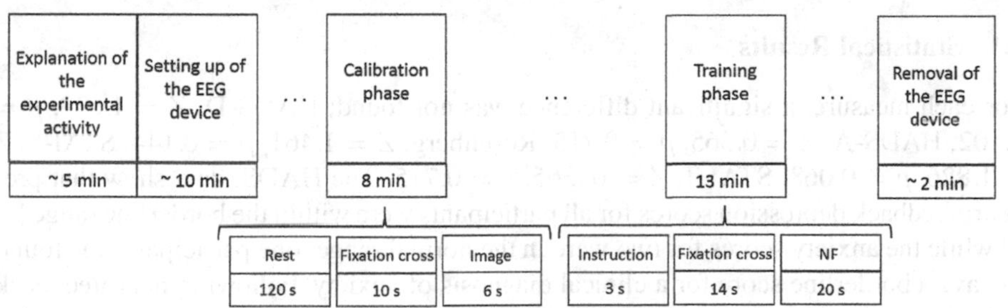

Fig. 4. Experimental protocol

During the training phase, participants had to regulate the felt emotion guided by the provided feedback. In particular, they were instructed to down regulate their target region activity by turning the colour of the frame/room and progress bar to yellow and to hold that level as long as possible. Additional information was not provided to the user. Mental strategy they had to adopt to control the felt emotion was cognitive reappraisal, namely an active cognitive process that allows to change the emotional impact of a situation [32]. Specifically, reality checking was employed. The user was asked to re-evaluate the meaning of the actual situation by thinking: "this is not real", "it is only an image", or "it is not really happening". The subject is required to consider the facts objectively without referring to his opinions, ideas, or beliefs.

The Hospital Anxiety and Depression (HADS) scale [33], the Rosenberg self- esteem (RSE) [34] scale, and the State-Trait Anxiety Inventory (STAI) [35] were employed to assess the levels of anxiety, depression, and self-esteem of the par- ticipants before and after the neurofeedback sessions. The Emotion Regulation Questionnaire (ERQ-10) [36] were administered to participants in order to assess their tendency to regulate their emotions. In particular, ERQ-10 was ad- ministered at neurofeedback starting, at the end of the three 2D sessions and at the end of the three VR sessions. The usability of two proposed neurofeedback systems was evaluated using the System Usability Scale (SUS) [37], Italian version.

2.4 Statistical Analysis

To evaluate whether there was a change in reported levels of anxiety, depression, and self-esteem following the neurofeedback training, the Wilcoxon signed-rank. test was used to analyze the pre- and post- scores of HADS-D, HADS-A, Rosenberg, STAI-S, and STAI-T. Similarly, data of SUS scores (2D versus VR) were analyzed via the Wilcoxon signed-rank test. A Friedman's ANOVA test was computed to compare ERQ-10 scores. Statistical analysis was performed using R Software (version 4.1.1) and a p-value < 0.05 indicated statistically significant differences.

3 Results

3.1 Statistical Results

For each measure, a significant difference was not found; HADS-D, $Z = 1.633$, $p = 0.102$, HADS-A, $Z = 0.365$, $p = 0.715$, Rosenberg, $Z = 1.461$, $p = 0.144$, STAI-S, $Z = 1.826$, $p = 0.068$, STAI-T, $Z = 0 .365$, $p = 0.715$. The HADS. data show that pre-neurofeedback depression scores for all participants were within the borderline range [7, 9] while the anxiety scores for two were in the normal range, one participant was found to have a borderline score for a clinical diagnosis of anxiety. Following neurofeedback training, the depression score reduced for the three participants. A reduction of anxiety was not found. Pre-training scores on the Rosenberg measure of self-esteem were not found to fall below the cut-off for low self-esteem. Althoughugh a significant difference in self-esteem was not found between pre- and post-training scores, two participants had an improved score (with one participant reporting a drop of one point). The pre-training scores on trait anxiety, using the STAI measure, show that all participants had scores suggesting borderline ($n = 2$) to abnormal ($n = 2$) levels of trait anxiety. A reduced score was found for all participants post-training. Notably, the greatest improvement in post-training scores on each questionnaire was found for state anxiety, as measured by the STAI-S.

As regards the usability of the systems, SUS mean score is 56.7 (SD = 26.7) and 59.2 (SD = 29.2) for 2D-neurofeedback and for VR-neurofeedback, respectively. Since SUS scores are above 68, these results indicate a marginally acceptable level of system usability [37]. Moreover, no statistically significant differences between 2D-neurofeedback and VR-neurofeedback in SUS scores were detected by the Wilcoxon signed-rank test ($Z = 0$, $p = 0.1736$).

While a significant reduction in anxiety and depression was not found post- neurofeedback training according to the HADS measures, prior to training the participants' scores were in the borderline range for a diagnosis of depression, and only one was found to have a borderline score indicative of a diagnosis of anxiety. Furthermore, depression scores were lower post-training for all three. Moreover, all three participants were found to have reduced scores on the STAI measure of state anxiety following training. It is tentatively suggested that neurofeedback training to regulate emotion has the potential to reduce state anxiety, and to ameliorate symptoms for individuals who are predisposed to high levels of trait anxiety. However, to test that hypothesis, further research would be required, involving a larger sample. Concerning the ER capacity, the Friedman's ANOVA test did not detect significant differences in the ERQ-10 scale, both the Cognitive. Reappraisal subscale ($p = 0.0821$) and the Emotional Suppression subscale ($p. = 1$), between the means of three evaluations (baseline, at three sessions of 2D-neurofeedback, and at three sessions of VR-Neurofeeback).

3.2 EEG Data Results

For each participant the high-beta power in midline locations (FCz-Cpz) was elaborated. In particular, the median values of the baseline and resting-state were computed for each session. These two values were adopted to evaluate the trend of high beta power during the training session. In particular, the decrement of beta power appeared linked with the increment of valence level within the subject. For the subjects, in the majority of the session, the median of the training values is below the baseline and often even below the resting-state, as shown in Fig. 5a, 5b, and 5c. However, no statistically significant differences in baseline/resting-state power-gap between traditional and VR-based neurofeedback were detected via Wilcoxon signed-rank test ($Z = 12$, $p < = 0.125$). Finally, relevant differences between traditional and VR-based neurofeedback effects were not observed.

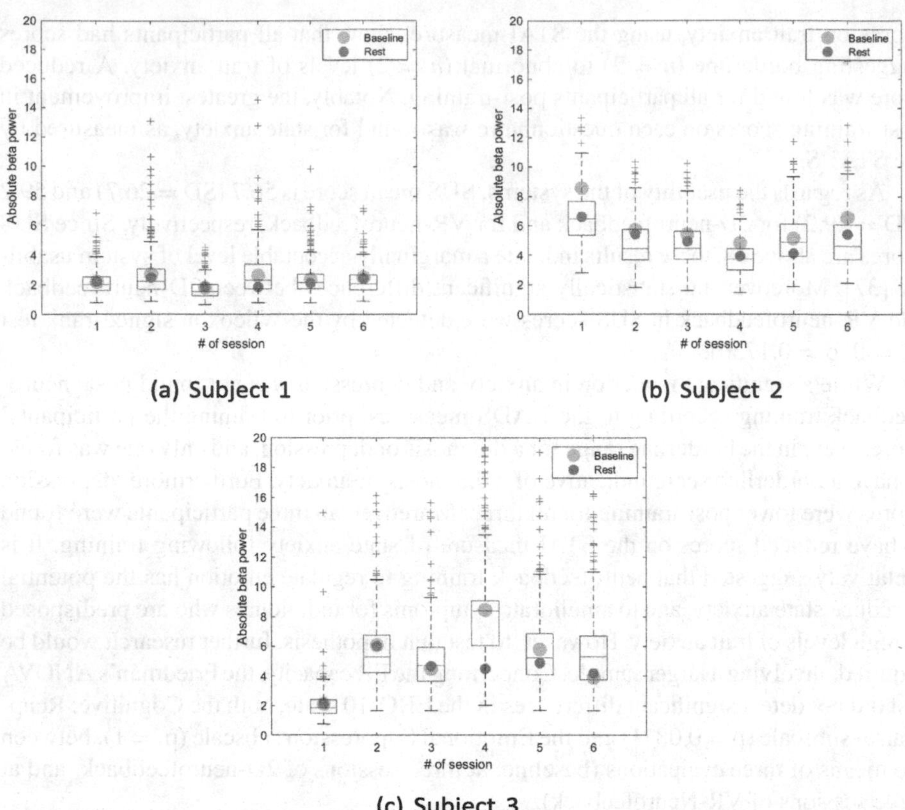

Fig. 5. Boxplot of high-beta power from midline locations (FCz-Cpz) computed during the neurofeedback training for the six sessions (1–3: traditional neurofeedback; 4–6: VR NF). The resting-state and the baseline values are also reported (a) Subject 1, (b) subject 2, and (3) subject 3 community.

4 Discussion

Findings from the scientific literature suggest that a decrease in the high beta power value registered along the midline sites of the scalp are related to improved ER capacity [16]. In accordance with previous studies the average high beta band power value computed during the neurofeedback training remained below the task-related baseline for most of the sessions. From a qualitative analysis the immersive environment provided by the VR system increased the power gap between baseline and resting-state. Despite this difference was not confirmed by statistical analysis this is a promising result by considering also the small sample size.

Concerning the ER capacity, significant differences in the results of the ERQ- 10 scale at the three end point were not found. The reasons can be manifold: the low number of subjects involved in the experimental activities, the reduced number of sessions (both 2D and VR), and the short time interval between the neurofeedback sessions.

Overall, the participants showed interest in the experimental activity and described it as attractive and innovative. All, except one, stated the possibility to use systems frequently in the future. However, they highlighted the need for more time to use the system autonomously, understand fully neurofeedback dynamics and establish a preference for two proposed neurofeedback-systems. These considerations were supported by the results of the SUS scores. In fact, SUS detected a marginally acceptable level of system usability [37] and it did not detect statistically significant differences between the two neurofeedback systems.

The results suggest that VR might improve emotion elicitation methods in laboratory environments in the next decade, and impact on affective computing research, transversely in many areas, opening new opportunities for the scientific However, more research is needed to increase the understanding of emotion dynamics in immersive VR and, in particular, its validity in performing direct comparisons between simulated and real environments.

5 Conclusions

Possible differences between a VR-based and a 2D-based neurofeedback aimed to strengthen the ER capacity were explored. The task of the neurofeedback was to down-regulate negative emotions by decreasing the midline beta power measured in FCz-Cpz. Negative emotions were induced by using IAPS images as eliciting stimuli. Three healthy subjects underwent the experimental activities completing three VR-based and three 2D-based neurofeedback sessions. Each training session started with a calibration phase for recording the rest and the baseline values of the current subject in order to adapt the neurofeedback system to the user. The average high beta band power value computed during the neurofeedback training remained below the baseline for most of the sessions, as expected. The participants showed interest in the experimental activity and described it as attractive and innovative. No statistically relevant differences were found between VR and 2D neurofeedback. Future developments include: (i) expanding the experimental sample, (ii) increasing the number of neurofeedback sessions, and (iii) increasing the interval between sessions. As stated by previous studies, future works should investigate the effectiveness of the VR-based neurofeedback in physiological responses and behavioural performance.

References

1. Enriquez-Geppert, S., Huster, R.J., Herrmann, C.S.: EEG-neurofeedback as a tool to modulate cognition and behavior: a review tutorial. Front. Hum. Neurosci. **11**, 51 (2017)
2. Arns, M., Heinrich, H., Strehl, U.: Evaluation of neurofeedback in ADHD: the long and winding road. Biol. Psychol. **95**, 108–115 (2014)
3. Gomes, J.S., Ducos, D.V., Akiba, H., Dias, A.M.: A neurofeedback protocol to improve mild anxiety and sleep quality. Brazilian J. Psychiatry **38**, 264–265 (2016)
4. Cavazza, M., et al.: Towards emotional regulation through neurofeedback. In: Proceedings of the 5th Augmented Human International Conference, pp. 1–8 (2014)
5. Gross, J.J.: Emotion regulation: current status and future prospects. Psych. inquiry **26**(1), 1–26 (2015)

6. Gross, J.J.: The emerging field of emotion regulation: An integrative review. Rev. General Psychol. **2**(3), 271–299 (1998)
7. Herwig, U.: Modulation of anticipatory emotion and perception processing by cognitive control. Neuroimage **37**(2), 652–662 (2007)
8. Gross, J.J., Feldman Barrett, L.: Emotion generation and emotion regulation: one or two depends on your point of view. Emotion Rev. **3**(1), 8–16 (2011)
9. Hamann, S.: Mapping discrete and dimensional emotions onto the brain: contro- versies and consensus. Trends Cogn. Sci. **16**(9), 458–466 (2012)
10. Fox, N.A.: Dynamic cerebral processes underlying emotion regulation. Monogr. Soc. Res. Child Dev. **59**(2-3), 152–166, 1994
11. Balconi, M., Frezza, A., Vanutelli, M.E.: Emotion regulation in schizophrenia: a pilot clinical intervention as assessed by EEG and optical imaging (functional near-infrared spectroscopy). Front. Hum. Neurosci. **12**, 395 (2018)
12. Hafeez, Y.: Development of enhanced stimulus content to improve the treatment efficacy of EEG–based frontal alpha asymmetry neurofeedback for stress mitigation. IEEE Access **9**, 130 638–130 648 (2021)
13. Davidson, R.J.: Affective style and affective disorders: Perspectives from affective neuroscience. Cogn. Emot. **12**(3), 307–330 (1998)
14. Al-Ezzi, A., Kamel, N, Faye, I., Ebenezer, E.G.M.: EEG frontal theta-beta ratio and frontal midline theta for the assessment of social anxiety disorder. In: 2020 10th IEEE International Conference on Control System, Computing and Engineering (ICCSCE), pp. 107–112. IEEE (2020)
15. Mennella, R., Patron, E., Palomba, D.: Frontal alpha asymmetry neurofeedback for the reduction of negative affect and anxiety. Behav. Res. Ther. **92**, 32–40 (2017)
16. Trystula, M., Zielińska, J., Półrola, P., Góral - Półrola, J., Kropotov, J.D., Pachalska, M.: Neuromarkers of anxiety in a patient with suspected schizophrenia and TIA: the effect of individually-tailored neurofeedback. Acta Neuropsychol. **13**(4), 395–403 (2015)
17. Zotev, V., Mayeli, A., Misaki, M., Bodurka, J.: Emotion self-regulation training in major depressive disorder using simultaneous real-time fMRI and EEG neurofeedback. NeuroImage Clin. **27**, 102331 (2020)
18. Dehghani, A., Soltanian-Zadeh, H., Hossein-Zadeh, G.-A.: Probing fMRI brain connectivity and activity changes during emotion regulation by EEG neurofeedback. arXiv preprint arXiv: 2006.06829 (2020)
19. Moradi, A., Pouladi, F., Pishva, N., Rezaei, B., Torshabi, M., Mehrjerdi, Z.A.: Treatment of anxiety disorder with neurofeedback: case study. Procedia Soc. Behav. Sci. **30**, 103–107 (2011)
20. Engelbregt, H.J., et al.: Short and long-term effects of sham-controlled prefrontal EEG-neurofeedback training in healthy subjects Clin. Neurophysiolo. **127**(4), 1931–1937 (2016)
21. Peeters, F., Ronner, J., Bodar, L., van Os, J., Lousberg, R.: Validation of a neurofeedback paradigm: manipulating frontal EEG alpha-activity and its impact on mood. Int. J. Psychophysiol. **93**(1), 116–120 (2014)
22. Meuleman, B., Rudrauf, D.: Induction and profiling of strong multi-componential emotions in virtual reality. IEEE Trans. Affect. Comput. **12**(1), 189–202 (2018)
23. Kihlstrom, J.F.: Ecological validity and ecological validity. Perspect. Psychol. Sci. **16**(2), 466–471 (2021)
24. Riva, G., Wiederhold, B.K., Mantovani, F.: Neuroscience of virtual reality: from virtual exposure to embodied medicine. Cyberpsychol. Behav. Social Netw. **22**(1), 82–96 (2019)
25. Arpaia, P., D'Errico, G., De Paolis, L.T., Moccaldi, N., Nuccetelli, F.: A narrative review of mindfulness-based interventions using virtual reality. Mindfulness **13**, 1–16 (2021)

26. Rivu, R., Jiang, R., Mäkelä, V., Hassib, M., Alt, F.: Emotion elicitation techniques in virtual reality. In: Ardito, C., etal., (eds.) INTERACT 2021. LNCS, vol. 12932, pp. 93–114. Springer, Cham (2021). https://doi.org/10.1007/978-3-030-85623-6_8
27. Somarathna, R., Bednarz, T., Mohammadi, G.: Virtual reality for emotion elicitation–a review. arXiv preprint arXiv:2111.04461 (2021)
28. Bekele, E., Bian, D., Peterman, J., Park, S., Sarkar, N.: Design of a virtual reality system for affect analysis in facial expressions (VR-SAAFE); application to schizophrenia. IEEE Trans. Neural Syst. Rehabilit. Eng. **25**(6), 739–749 (2016)
29. Lang, P.J., Bradley, M.M., Cuthbert, B.N., et al.: International affective picture system (IAPS): Technical manual and affective ratings. NIMH Center Study Emot. Attent. **1**(39–58), 3 (1997)
30. Bru¨hl, A.B., Scherpiet, S., Sulzer, J., St¨ampfli, P., Seifritz, E., Herwig, U.: Real- time neurofeedback using functional MRI could improve down-regulation of amygdala activity during emotional stimulation: a proof-of-concept study. Brain Topograp. **27**(1), 138–148 (2014)
31. Unity. https://unity.com/ (Access 28 Apr 2022)
32. HTC VIVE PRO 2. https://www.vive.com/eu/product/vive-pro/ (Access 28 Apr 2022)
33. Neuroconcise technology https://www.neuroconcise.co.uk/ (Access 28 Apr 2022)
34. Hammond, D.C.: What is neurofeedback? J. Neurother. **10**(4), 25–36 (2007)
35. Herwig, U., et al.: Training emotion regulation through real- time fMRI neurofeedback of amygdala activity. Neuroimage **184**, 687–696 (2019)
36. Lawrence, E.J., et al.: Self-regulation of the anterior insula: Reinforcement learning using real-time fMRI neurofeedback. Neuroimage **88**, 113–124 (2014)
37. Lazarus, R.S., Alfert, E.: Short-circuiting of threat by experimentally altering cognitive appraisal. Psychol. Sci. Public Interest **69**(2), 195 (1964)
38. Bjelland, I., Dahl, A.A., Haug, T.T., Neckelmann, D.: The validity of the hospital anxiety and depression scale: an updated literature review. J. Psychosom. Res. **52**(2), 69–77 (2002)
39. Rosenberg, M.: Rosenberg self-esteem scale (RSE) acceptance commitment therapy. Meas. Package **61**(52), 18 (1965)
40. Spielberger, C.D., Gonzalez-Reigosa, F., Martinez-Urrutia, A., Natalicio, L.F., Natalicio, D.S.: The state-trait anxiety inventory. Revista Interamericana de Psicologia/Interamerican J. Psychol. **5**(3), 4 (1971)
41. Preece, D.A., Becerra, R., Robinson, K., Gross, J.J.: The emotion regulation questionnaire: psychometric properties in general community samples. J. Personal. Assess (2019)
42. Balzarotti, S., John, O.P., Gross, J.J.: An italian adaptation of the emotion regulation questionnaire. European J. Psychol. Assess. (2010)
43. Brooke, J.: Sus: a quick and dirty'usability. Usability Evaluation Industry **189**(3) (1996)

Psychological and Educational Interventions Among Cancer Patients: A Systematic Review to Analyze the Role of Immersive Virtual Reality for Improving Patients' Well-Being

Maria Sansoni[1(✉)], Clelia Malighetti[1], and Giuseppe Riva[1,2]

[1] Humane Technology Laboratory, Università Cattolica del Sacro Cuore, 20123 Milan, Italy
maria.sansoni@unicatt.it

[2] Applied Technology for Neuro-Psychology Laboratory, Istituto Auxologico Italiano, 20021 Milan, Italy

Abstract. Previous studies show that the lack of information about cancer-related topics (e.g., diagnosis, treatments) and the impact of treatment toxicity on patients' life, may undermine cancer patients' psychological well-being. Psycho-educational interventions are therefore implemented to support the oncological population. This systematic review aims to explore the state of art and effectiveness of psychological and educational interventions implemented using Virtual Reality and designed for pediatric and adult cancer patients. The review was conducted in accordance with the Preferred Reporting Items for Systematic Reviews and Meta-Analyses guidelines (PRISMA), and it was registered with the PROSPERO international prospective register of systematic reviews (registration number CRD42022308402). Twenty studies were included in the review. Our findings show that psychological interventions predominantly use emotion-focused strategies (i.e., distraction) to reduce patients' emotional distress; educational studies prefer, on the contrary, cognitive-behavioral strategies (i.e., exposure) to restructure patients' beliefs, increasing their understanding of the procedure, and reducing situational anxiety. VR could be a promising and effective tool for supporting cancer patients' needs. However, since most of these VR interventions assign the patient a passive role in coping with his or her diagnosis, future research should develop psychological and educational VR interventions that have the primary goal of rendering people with a cancer diagnosis active characters in their psychological well-being, supporting in this way patients' empowerment.

Keywords: Virtual Reality · Cancer · Psychological intervention · Educational intervention · Systematic review · Emotion regulation · Well-being

1 Introduction

Cancer is a life-threatening disease that leads patients to experience emotional distress [1, 2]. The impact of cancer treatments on patients' functionality and appearance adds an extra source of stress in patients' lives [3], contributing to a further decline in their

L. T. De Paolis et al. (Eds.): XR Salento 2022, LNCS 13446, pp. 432–454, 2022.
https://doi.org/10.1007/978-3-031-15553-6_30

mental health [4]. These combined factors undermine patients' well-being (e.g., [5–7]), threaten their compliance [8, 9], endanger treatment outcomes [10], and increase their risk of mortality [11–13]. Additionally, the lack of information about cancer experience and treatment side effects may jeopardize to a greater extent patients' mental health [14], representing one of the unmet needs of this clinical population [15, 16]. Therefore, to support patients' mental health [17], educational (e.g., [18, 19]) and psychological interventions (e.g., [20–22]) are implemented. Psychological interventions buffer patients' emotional distress and reduce negative mood states using emotional, cognitive, or behavioral strategies [23]. Educational interventions are, on the other hand, based on the premise that exposure to care-related information provides coping assistance to patients, by offering answers to their search for information. This process restructures how the cognitive assessment of events is perceived (e.g., being stressful) and, consequently, reduces the associated situational anxiety [24].

Over the last decades, thanks to technological advancement and to the possibility to have affordable devices, health care has witnessed a switch, passing from in-person interventions to therapies that use technological devices. Thus, it is not surprising that the usage of virtual reality (VR) in the medical field has gradually increased [25, 26]. Recent studies have shown that VR is not only broadly used in treating mental health problems [27], but that it is also effective in health care [28]. VR allows the user to navigate and interact in real-time with a 3D environment [29], making it possible for patients to experience situations that would otherwise be impractical or difficult to access [30]. These characteristics are particularly pertinent in the oncological setting, where treatment toxicity (e.g., pain, fatigue, nausea) impairs physical functioning [31, 32] and leads to hospitalizations [33], rendering it complicated for cancer patients to attend in-person therapies or educational training. VR appears as a possible solution to overcome the barriers that oncological treatments create: thanks to VR patients can face situations, as well as receive interventions, without leaving their room, with the quality of an in vivo experience [30], and feeling present in the situation [34]. VR is a particularly suitable tool also for its capability to visually show realistic scenarios to users, through an experiential form of imagery [35]. This quality, combined with a well-structured narrative [36], is very helpful when patients have difficulties picturing the situations they are told to imagine [35], for example when staff explains how the surgical procedure will be performed or how radiotherapy works. Therefore, VR may assist nurses and surgeons in visually showing to patients the steps of the oncological procedure, avoiding misinterpretations, and reducing procedural anxiety [18]. Misunderstandings about treatment benefits and harms can, in fact, lead patients to regret the decision taken and the treatment accepted [37]: when patients do not fully understand the implications of the procedure or have incomplete information about outcomes are more susceptible to regret [38], risking to make poorly informed decisions about their oncological journey. The uncertainty in a negative situation makes the situation more unpleasant [39], potentially causing distress and poor health outcomes [40]. For this reason, being able to overcome this problem would be extremely valuable for patients' well-being. VR is already used in oncological settings. However, its major application is planning or simulating surgeries (e.g., resection of the tumor mass), as well as training residents or medical specialists to implement oncological procedures (e.g., surgery, radiotherapy, etc.) (e.g., [41–46]).

Since VR has the potential to support cancer patients' well-being, this systematic review aims to explore the state of the art of psychological and educational interventions among adult and pediatric cancer patients. It seems, in fact, essential to create an accessible understanding of how VR is used in the psycho-oncological setting, and which are its possible future uses. Hence, our research questions are:

RQ1: Which are the current educational and psychological interventions for cancer patients that use VR for their implementation?
RQ2: Which is the effectiveness of such VR interventions?

Interventions will be considered effective when there is a statistically significant improvement in the measures of interest for the intervention group compared to the control group.

2 Methods

A systematic review of scientific literature has been performed to identify studies that report the employment of psychological and educational VR intervention on cancer patients. This systematic review was conducted in accordance with the Preferred Reporting Items for Systematic Reviews and Meta-Analysis (PRISMA) guidelines [47], and the study was registered in the International Prospective Register of Systematic Reviews (PROSPERO) in 2022 (CRD42022308402). The detailed protocol is available upon request.

2.1 Data Sources and Search Strategy

Data sources were collected on the 14th of January 2022 through a selective computer search in the following databases: PubMed, PsycINFO, and Web of Science (Web of Knowledge). The current systematic review wants to offer a broad panoramic of the current literature: for this reason, we did not define a beginning year of publication for the articles to be included. Each database was searched independently, according to a specific iteration research string:

(Virtual Reality) AND ("Cancer" OR "Oncology" OR "Chemotherapy" OR "Cancer treatment" OR "Cancer care" OR "Cancer support").

To make this study repeatable in the future, detailed results are available in Table 1. The selection of these strings was made in the attempt to capture an extensive range of features regarding VR interventions and cancer patients. This systematic review focused on immersive VR, which comprehends technologies in which users wear head-mounted displays and are surrounded by enclosed virtual environments [48]. In other words, virtual environments are immersive when the user experiences a sense "of being there": the person feels in the virtual environment even if they are physically situated in another place [34]. Citations were retrieved independently for each iterative search crossing all databases. A complete list of citations and abstracts for each database was exported and imported into Rayyan [49] for the title and abstract screening.

Table 1. Detailed search strategy

Detailed search strategy			
Virtual reality AND	PubMed	PsycINFO	Web of Science
Cancer	754	123	1078
Oncology	611	45	227
Chemotherapy	233	20	84
Cancer treatment	503	70	262
Cancer care	186	43	207
Cancer support	273	30	226
Sub Total	2560	331	2084
Total			4975
Duplicates removal			3073
Identified studies for Abstract and Title screen			1902

2.2 Study Selection and Inclusion Criteria

Two reviewers (M.S. and C.M.) independently screened all non-duplicate titles and abstracts, searching for eligible articles. The same reviewers retrieved, and analyzed the full text for all relevant articles, resolving discrepancies by consensus. G.R. was designated as the third reviewer to arbitrate potential differences in agreement.

Participants
We included patients (both pediatric and adult) diagnosed by a practitioner with cancer (all cancer diagnoses and stages were included). Both female and male participants were included. Patients with metastases or undergoing palliative care were included, too. We did not include studies focused on caregivers of cancer patients, oncological professionals (e.g., nurses, surgeons, etc.), or with a mixed sample of participants (i.e., studies that also included cancer patients, but that were not limited to them). In addition to this, we did not include interventions implemented on patients with benign neoplasms, or who have not received a cancer diagnosis yet (e.g., waiting for the biopsy result).

Interventions

We focused on interventions tailored both for cancer treatments (e.g., chemotherapy) and procedures (e.g., subcutaneous port access). We included studies that considered behavioral, emotional, educational, and cognitive interventions (e.g., cognitive restructuring), including those that targeted cancer fatigue and cancer pain. Studies that focused only on the assessment of psychological (e.g., anxiety) or educational (e.g., health literacy) dimensions were not included in the systematic review, but we did include interventions that aimed to improve those features. We did not include studies that focused on neuropsychological functions (e.g., sleep, attention, memory, etc.), and treatments' side effects (e.g., lymphedema, memory impairment, etc.). We excluded studies that were developed to improve surgeons' skills or training, focused on detecting or removing the tumor mass (e.g., computer-assisted surgery, VR to plan post-surgery reconstruction, VR to plan tumor resection, etc.), cancer screening interventions or medical procedures to diagnose cancers (e.g., biopsy).

Methodological Characteristics of the Studies

We included both cross-sectional studies and studies with repeated measures. We included randomized controlled trials, but randomization was not a requirement since it can be difficult to implement within social science intervention research (e.g., ethical reasons) [50]. We did not include qualitative studies. We excluded non-English published studies, studies that used animals, and articles in which the full text was not available. We also excluded the following types of manuscripts: reviews, meeting abstracts, conference proceedings, notes, case reports, letters to the editor, research protocols, patents, editorials, books or chapters, and other editorial materials. We excluded studies that did not use validated measures, and studies that used only some of the items of the validated measure (i.e., when the items used do not allow to calculate the total score or a subscale of the validated measure). In the case of studies with a pediatric population, we only included papers that also provided a self-report measure of the minor. We only included studies that presented a control group of healthy subjects or cancer patients, or studies with repeated measures of the same group of participants (e.g., within-subject design). The included studies needed to compare the experimental condition with a group of participants undergoing the same type of intervention, a different type of intervention, non-intervention, or standard care to point out the effectiveness of the VR condition (Fig. 1).

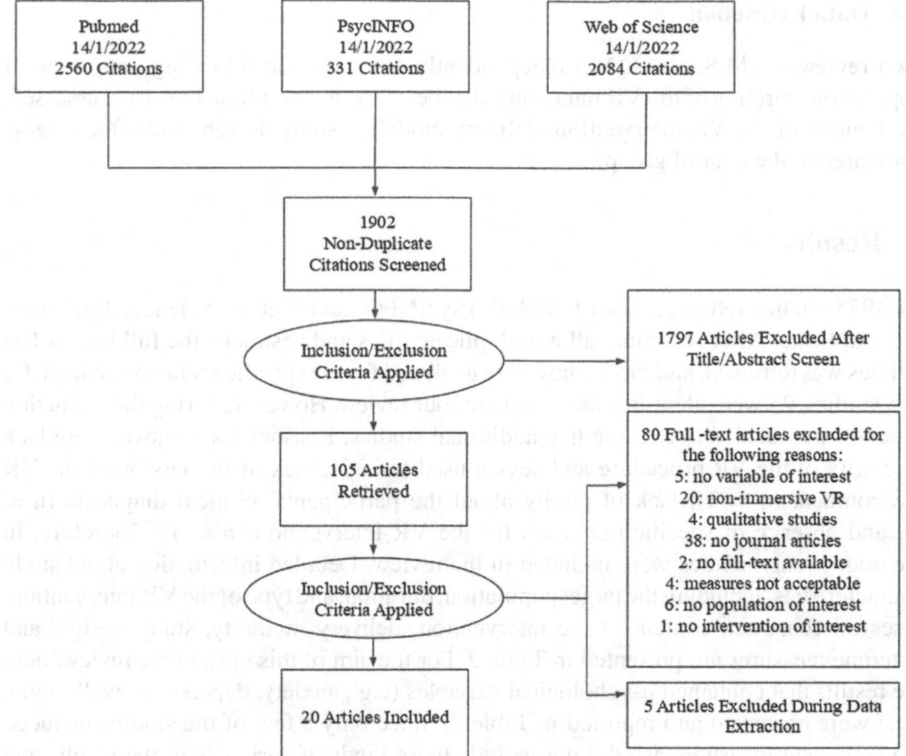

Fig. 1. Flow chart of the systematic review. The figure illustrates the search strategy of the systematic review conducted under PRISMA guidelines

2.3 Risk of Bias Assessment

To assess the risk of bias, the reviewers used the Downs and Black checklist [51]. This checklist provided an overall quality index and four subscales of quality assessment: reporting, external quality, internal validity bias, and internal validity confounding. After assigning the scores to each of the 27 items (answers are scored 0 or 1, except for one item that scored 0–2), a total score was provided. Scores could be "excellent" (24–28 points), "good" (19–23 points), "fair" (14–18 points), or "poor" (14 points or less) [51]. Two reviewers (M.S. and C.M.) independently evaluated the studies for risk of bias, and disagreements were resolved through consensus or the help of the third reviewer (G.R.).

2.4 Data Extraction

Two reviewers (M.S. and C.M.) independently extracted the following data: type of population, duration of the VR intervention, type of VR intervention, construct assessed, the content of the VR intervention, delivery modality, study design, and effectiveness compared to the control group.

3 Results

Of 4975 studies retrieved from PubMed, PsycINFO, and Web of Science, 1902 were non-duplicate. After screening all non-duplicate titles and abstracts, the full text of 105 articles was retrieved, and the studies were analyzed for the specific inclusion criteria. Of 105 studies, 25 were identified as suitable for our review. However, during the extraction process, we decided to exclude five additional studies. Reasons for removal were lack of clarity of the VR procedure and device used (n = 2), lack of immersion of the VR environment (n = 1), lack of clarity about the participants' clinical diagnosis (n = 1), and absence of specific outcomes for the VR intervention (n = 1). Therefore, in the end, twenty studies were included in the review. Detailed information about study characteristics, including the target population, duration, and type of the VR intervention, assessed construct, content of the intervention, delivery modality, study design, and outcome measures are presented in Table 2. For the aim of this systematic review, only the results that contained psychological variables (e.g., anxiety, depression, well-being, etc.) were presented and reported in Table 2. Since only a few of the studies included physiological measures, we did not include these kinds of variables in the results and the table either.

3.1 Study Characteristics

The studies took place in eleven countries: one study took place in Japan [52], one in Spain [53], one in France [54], one in Jordan [55], one in Iran [56], and another in Canada [57]. Two studies took place in China [58, 59], Italy [60, 61], Turkey [62, 63] and Australia [64, 65]. Lastly, six studies took place in the United States [66–71]. There was a variation in sample size between the studies, ranging from 11 [67] to 126 participants [53]. Papers were published within the past 23 years (1999–2022), with over fifteen studies published in the past 3 years [52–66]. About the study design, ten studies were randomized controlled trials (RCT) [53, 55–59, 62–64, 71], two were characterized by a within-subjects design (i.e., repeated measures) [61, 65], four were crossover studies [66, 68–70], one was an observational study [54], one a prospective single-arm study

[52], one an externally controlled trial [60], and one an interrupted time series study [67].

Sample Characteristics
The mean ages of participants ranged from 10 [59] to 72 years [52]. Participants of the studies were both adults [52–55, 58, 60, 61, 66, 68–70] and children/adolescents [56, 57, 59, 62–65, 67, 71]. Only one study [68] specifically focused on older cancer patients of at least 50 years. Most studies were conducted with female and male samples: only five studies were conducted only with female participants [54, 55, 60, 68, 69]. Of all studies, two [52, 61] recruited patients undergoing palliative care, and three focused on patients who were about to start their treatment (e.g., surgery) [53, 58, 65]. Most studies focused on patients on active treatments (e.g., chemotherapy) [54–56, 60, 64, 66–70], and patients undergoing oncological procedures (e.g., access to the venous port) [57, 59, 62, 63, 71]. In terms of diagnosis, nearly all studies enrolled patients with different cancers. Six studies enrolled only a specific oncological population, focusing on people with cervical [54], breast [55, 60, 68, 69], and colon cancer [53].

Characteristics of VR Interventions
The duration of the VR interventions was variable, going from 4–7 min in Tennant et al. [65], to eight sessions of 30-min each, once a week for 2 months in the study by Sharifpour, Manshaee, and Sajjadian [56]. Nearly all studies were psychological interventions (n = 17). These interventions shared the same underlying psychological strategy known as distraction. Distraction was implemented through different scenarios (e.g., naturalistic, games, etc.): some of them were interactive (e.g., [57]), and others were not (e.g., [59]). In general, interventions were tailored to participants' age. Some VR interventions simulated pleasant activities or exposed the person to a relaxing virtual environment. This is the case of Niki and colleagues [52], in whose study the adult patients simulated a trip, visiting a memorable place (e.g., a shrine in Japan where one of the participants had his wedding) or a destination (e.g., a city) that they wanted to explore, but that had never the occasion to. A similar approach was used by Tennant and colleagues [64], who proposed to their young participants a trip to Australian national parks, zoos, or global city tourist spots. The study of Wolitzky and colleagues [71] also offered as a distraction a visit to a zoo. In particular, in this scenario children went to the Zoo Atlanta, and virtually explored the gorilla habitat. Varnier and colleagues [54] used as a distraction a virtual dive with a whale swimming in a peaceful environment. The authors invited the patient to slow down their breathing following the moves of the whale's tale. This type of distraction was tailored for adult participants. Sharifpour and colleagues [56] opted for a VR video showing the young participants a stroll along the beach and a journey to the depth of the oceans. In the study by Semerci, Akgün Kostak, Eren, and Avci [63], always tailored for children, the authors opted for a roller coaster that speeded up and then slowed down in the forest accompanied by slow music. In other scenarios, the type of distraction

was chosen by the participants among different options, according to their interests: Schneider, Prince-Paul, Allen, Silverman, and Talaba [69] allowed their participants to choose between a scuba diving experience, a walk into an art museum or a resolution of a mystery. Two studies by Schneider [68, 70], in addition to the scenarios mentioned above, also added the possibility to explore ancient worlds. These three studies were tailored for adult participants. Schneider [67] proposed different options when implementing the study on the pediatric population: the young patients could, in fact, choose between the experience of riding a magic carpet, solving a mystery, or staying in a haunted mansion. Moscato and colleagues [61] proposed two scenarios that adult participants could watch: the first one was a non-interactive virtual environment characterized by natural and relaxing scenarios (i.e., seascape, park, waterfall, London Bridge, mountain landscape). The second environment was an interactive scenario that consisted of a skill game where the user, surrounded by a calm underwater landscape, had to reproduce an ideogram that represented concepts like friendship, courage, or strength. Mohammed and Ahmad [55] offered as a distraction two scenarios from which adult participants could choose: deep sea diving or sitting on the beach while listening to the "Happy Place" track. Chirico and colleagues [60] opted for interaction with relaxing virtual environments: the participant explored an island, walked through a forest, observed different animals, climbed a mountain, and swam in the sea. Also this type of scenario was tailored to adult participants. Ashley Verzwyvelt, McNamara, Xu, and Stubbins [66] proposed to their adult participants nine different scenarios. They could explore tropical beaches, underwater oceans, take to the stars, discover over sixty different animals, command the weather, take control of the night, or create and shape their own world. Gerçeker and colleagues [62] offered to the children that took part in their study three different environments: swimming with marine animals underwater, riding a roller coaster, and exploring the forest through the eyes of woodland species. Some scenarios implemented the distraction through a game to play with or by watching a video without interacting with it. Hundert [57] and colleagues, for example, proposed as a distraction a game that consisted of aiming rainbow balls at sea creatures as they explored an underwater scenario in search of a treasure. In the study by Wong and colleagues [59], on the contrary, two animated videos of Minions were shown to the patients during the medical procedure to distract them. Both these types of distraction were tailored to children.

Three educational interventions were included in the systematic review. These studies focused on preparing pediatric or adult patients for therapy. In particular, Gao and colleagues [58] focused on radiation therapy, showing to the adult participants the entire radiotherapy process, from the accelerator functioning to the equipment used, while patients lay down on a couch. Tennant and colleagues [65] proposed a similar scenario by showing their young participants a 360° video displaying the radiotherapy procedure. Turrado and colleagues [53] focused on surgery instead. These authors proposed to their adult participants a scenario that revealed the various steps of admission to surgery, from the first interview with the surgeon to the operating room and postoperative recovery.

Regardless of whether they were psychological or educational, the focus of the included studies was mostly pain [52, 54–57, 59, 61–64, 66, 71] and anxiety [52–56, 58–62, 64, 65, 67–71]. Some studies also assessed depression [52, 53, 60, 61], anger [60, 64], fear [57, 58, 62], distress [57, 66, 71], as well as fatigue and tiredness [52, 60, 61, 68–70]. A few studies considered well-being [52, 61], positive mood [64], and other mood states such as tension, vigor, and confusion [60]. For more information about how the studies targeted each of the psychological dimensions, please see Table 2.

Effectiveness of VR Interventions
Four studies reported no significant differences between the VR and the control condition or between the pre-post VR intervention [57, 66, 67, 70]. Other four studies reported mixed results [58, 61, 68, 69], displaying significant improvements for some clinical dimensions but not for others. In particular, Gao and colleagues [58] reported significantly lower anxiety in the VR condition compared to the control group, but they did not find a significant reduction in the fear scores of the VR condition: the fear was lower but not significant. Schneider and colleagues [69] observed a similar trend in their study: a significant decrease in the fatigue scores was observed in the VR condition, but not in the anxiety, which was lower but not significant. Moscato and colleagues [61] reported a significant improvement in pain, depression, anxiety, and well-being scores assessed through the Edmonton Symptom Assessment System. However, no statistical difference was found in depression, anxiety, and pain scores when they used different assessment measures (i.e., Hospital Anxiety and Depression Scale and Brief Pain Inventory). Another study reported mixed results [54]: however, since the authors did not use inferential statistical analysis, it was not possible to describe the results in terms of statistical difference. What we can say is that these authors observed a greater decrease in anxiety in the control condition compared to the VR and a larger improvement in pain in the VR group. According to these findings, VR worked better in the management of pain than anxiety. Eleven studies showed a significant improvement in the VR condition compared to the controls or to the pre-VR assessment [52, 53, 55, 56, 59, 60, 62–65, 71]. Tennant and colleagues [65] showed a significant reduction of anxiety in their pediatric patients. However, this improvement did not last for long and increased again just before the beginning of the cancer treatment.

3.2 Methodological Quality of Studies

As shown in Table 3, the Downs and Black checklist [51] revealed that the methodological quality of studies was mixed. Most studies were classified as “fair” [52, 54, 56, 58, 60–62, 65, 66, 67, 69, 71] implying a medium risk of bias. One study [68] was classified as “poor” implying a high risk of bias, and seven other studies [53, 55, 57, 59, 63, 64, 70] were classified as “good”, implying a mild risk of bias. None of the studies was classified as “excellent” with a poor risk of bias.

Table 2. Studies characteristics according to extraction parameters

Table 2. Studies characteristics according to extraction parameters

Authors(s) and Year	Population	Duration	Type of intervention	Construct of interest assessed*	Content of the intervention	Delivery modality	Study design	Outcome
Niki et al., 2019	Adults (M=72.3 years)	One session of 30 minutes. The session time was extended or shortened according to participants' wishes.	Psychological	Pain intensity, anxiety, tiredness, depression, well-being	VR travel session using Google Earth VR. Participants could freely decide where they wanted to go (memorable places or places that wanted to visit but had never).	Headset HTC VIVE (includes headphones).	Prospective single-arm study	There was an improvement in the variables of interest post-intervention. The participants who went to a memorable place tended to experience more benefits from VR than did those who went to a place they had wanted to go to but never visited.
Hundert et al., 2022	Pediatric (8-18 years)	Same duration of the subcutaneous port access procedure.	Psychological	Pain intensity, fear, distress, pain catastrophizing	EG: Standard care (adhesive topical local anesthetic patches placed before the needle insertion) + VR intervention. The VR scenario consisted of a game that aimed rainbow balls at sea creatures, while participants explored an underwater environment in search of treasure. CG: Standard care + same video of the VR condition implemented through an iPad.	Samsung GearVR™ with Sony MDR 10R Headphones and MOGA PRO™ POWER controller.	RCT	Although not statistically significant, less pain and distress were seen in the VR group compared to the iPad group, while fear scores remained similar between study groups.
Wolitzky, Fivush, Zimand, Hodges, & Rothbaum, 2005	Pediatric (7-14 years)	Same duration of the subcutaneous port access procedure.	Psychological	Pain intensity, anxiety, distress	EG: an exploration of the gorilla habitat at Zoo Atlanta. CG: NO VR intervention. Children in the CG were allowed to play with the VR for a few minutes after the end of the procedure and assessment.	Computer connected to a joystick and a head-mounted display. Participants also wore headphones.	RCT	During the procedure, there was a significant difference between groups on pain and a trend for the retrospective distress rating of the procedure. The children in the EG did not experience as much pain and anxiety and tended to be less distressed than the CG.
Tennant et al., 2021	Pediatric (6–18 years)	4–7 minutes, depending on treatment location	Educational	Anxiety	360 videos recording of actual treatment procedures. Participants viewed two virtual simulation experiences that corresponded to their upcoming procedure: VR CT Simulation [VR CT] and VR Radiation Therapy [VR RAD].	Samsung Gear VR® and Oculus Go® Facebook Technologies	Within-subjects, repeated measures	Significant reductions in child pre-radiation therapy (RT) anxiety levels were observed following the VR CT intervention compared to the baseline measures. On the day of RT commencement, following multiple exposures to VR RAD, children's anxiety showed an increase at follow-up from levels at post-VR CT.
Semerci, Akgün Kostak, Eren, & Avci, 2021	Pediatric (7-18 years)	8 minutes	Psychological	Pain intensity	EG: the VR scenario consisted of a roller coaster that speeds up and slows down in the forest, accompanied by slow music. CG: Standard care (parent's presence during the procedure without local anesthetic patches) + no VR treatment.	Piranha™ VR system. Headphones included.	RCT	There was a significant difference between the EG and the CG: the mean pain score of the children in the CG was significantly higher than that in the EG. The difference observed was quite large and clinically meaningful, with a large effect size reported.

(continued)

Table 2. *(continued)*

Table 2. Studies characteristics according to extraction parameters

Authors(s) and Year	Population	Duration	Type of intervention	Construct of interest assessed*	Content of the intervention	Delivery modality	Study design	Outcome
Schneider, & Workman, 1999	Pediatric (10-17 years)	Same duration of the chemotherapy treatment	Psychological	Anxiety	The VR environment consisted of commercially available scenarios: Magic Carpet®, Sherlock Holmes Mystery®, and Seventh Guest® (a haunted mansion). The VR intervention was implemented only throughout the second chemotherapy (3 chemotherapies in total).	Virtual i-O brand headset connected to a personal computer.	Interrupted time series	Participants showed high levels of anxiety during the initial chemotherapy treatment that decreased during subsequent treatments. However, anxiety levels were not influenced by the VR intervention.
Sharifpour, Manshaee, & Sajjadian, 2021	Pediatric (14–18 years)	8 sessions of VRT (virtual reality therapy), each 30-min long, once a week for 2 months	Psychological	Pain intensity, pain-related anxiety or fear responses in individuals with chronic pain, pain catastrophizing, pain self-efficacy	EG: A VR film was watched offline by the patients using AAA VR Cinema. It showed a stroll along the beach and a journey to the depths of the ocean. CG: No VRT. Participants were put on a waiting list.	Samsung Gear VR headset. Auditory stimuli were included but not played using headphones.	RCT	There was a significant difference in pain scores between the EG and the CG. Moreover, the effect of the treatment remained constant during the first and second follow-up periods.
Ashley Verzwyvelt, McNamara, Xu, & Stubbins, 2021	Adult (26-84 years)	5-15-minutes intervals throughout their infusion (as tolerated). Mean usage: 53.3 minutes	Psychological	Distress, pain intensity	VR room: Nature Treks software. Patients were able to choose between 9 different interactive natural environments: they could explore tropical beaches, underwater oceans, take to the stars, discover over 60 different animals, command the weather, take control of the night or create and shape their own world. Control room: standard treatment room with no windows, equipped with a standard infusion chair, vital signs monitor, and television. Participants in this condition received standard care. Green therapy room: the intervention placed the patient in a window-lined room. Participants could sit facing the large wall of windows overlooking a rooftop garden and picturesque mural. Each of the participants received chemotherapy once in each room.	Oculus Quest Head Mounted Display (HMD), headphones were included.	Crossover design	No significant differences were shown in the changes of pain or distress before and after infusion between the control, Green Therapy, and Virtual Reality rooms.
Tennant et al., 2020	Pediatric (7–19 years)	10 minutes	Psychological	Positive mood, anxiety, anger, pain	EG: Participants viewed one of three immersive 360° virtual simulation experiences, including simulated trips to Australian national parks (i.e. 'Nature experience), Australian zoos (i.e. 'Animal experience), or global city tourist spots (i.e. 'Travel experience). EG: identical content of the VR group presented using the iPad (360° video).	Samsung Gear VR® first-generation mobile HMD. Headphones were included.	RCT	Patients benefited from both Immersive VR and novel iPad intervention with no statistically significant differences found between conditions on child outcomes. However, patients accessing Immersive VR consistently reported greater positive shifts in mood state and reductions in anxiety, anger, and pain when compared with iPad.

(continued)

Table 2. *(continued)*

Table 2. Studies characteristics according to extraction parameters

Authors(s) and Year	Population	Duration	Type of intervention	Construct of interest assessed*	Content of the intervention	Delivery modality	Study design	Outcome
Gao et al., 2020	Adult (18-75 years)	30 minutes	Educational	Anxiety, fear	EG: Advance face-to-face educational meeting to explain the purpose and content of the education before the simulation appointment. The VR program included RT-related content (i.e., RT process, RT equipment, linear accelerator functioning, demonstrations with the radiation beam during the treatment process, and RT positioning). The patient, while wearing VR glasses, was lying on a treatment couch to simulate the RT position. Explanation material was also provided in this condition. CG: Standard care (regular face-to-face education).	Based on the HTC VIVE system the authors developed a VRRT system (Virtual Reality Radiotherapy Simulator) implemented through the use of VR glasses.	RCT	Anxiety was significantly lower in the EG than in the CG. Fear was also reduced, even if the statistical difference was not significant. Comparing the two groups pre- and post-intervention, the EG had a significant decrease in anxiety and fear.
Gerçeker et al., 2021	Pediatric (6-17 years)	Same duration of the access to the venous port	Psychological	Pain intensity, fear, anxiety	EG: Standard care (children and parents were informed 1h before the procedure, and no pharmacological methods were used) + three VR applications: swimming with marine animals underwater (Ocean Rift), riding a roller coaster (Rilix VR), and exploring the forest through the eyes of woodland species. Children could choose the scenario to explore. CG: Standard care.	Samsung Gear Oculus headset	RCT	The study found a statistically significant difference between the EG and the CG in post-procedural pain, fear, and anxiety scores.
Schneider & Hood, 2007	Adult (32-78 years)	Same duration of the chemotherapy treatment (45–90 minutes)	Psychological	Anxiety, fatigue	VR intervention during one chemotherapy treatment and no intervention (standard care) during an alternate matched chemotherapy treatment (e.g., watching television, conversing with others, or reading). When in the VR intervention, participants could choose from four possible CD-ROM–based VR scenarios: deep sea diving (Oceans Below®), walking through an art museum (A World of Art®), exploring ancient worlds (Timelapse®), and solving a mystery (Titanic: Adventure Out of Time®): participants were free to change scenarios at any time.	i-Glasses® SVGA Head-Mounted Display, i-O Display Systems	Crossover design	Patients had an altered perception of time when using the VR, which validates the distracting capacity of the intervention. However, the analysis demonstrated no significant differences in symptom distress immediately or two days following chemotherapy treatments.

(continued)

Table 2. *(continued)*

Table 2. Studies characteristics according to extraction parameters

Authors(s) and Year	Population	Duration	Type of intervention	Construct of interest assessed*	Content of the intervention	Delivery modality	Study design	Outcome
Chirico et al., 2020	Adult (18-70 years)	20 minutes	Psychological	Mood states (i.e., tension, depression, anger, vigor, fatigue, and confusion) and anxiety.	VR condition: participants used the VR for 20 minutes to experience the relaxing landscapes created on the Second Life® platform. In particular, they could explore an island, walk through a forest, observe different animals, climb a mountain, and swim in the sea. MT condition: an mp3 reader and headphones were provided to the patients, after 5 min from the start of the chemotherapy infusion. Patients listened to 20 min relaxing music, pre-taped by an expert music therapist. Control condition: standard care (patients were free to choose different activities during treatment, including conversation and reading).	Head-mounted glasses (VuzixWrap 1200 VR) with a head motion tracking system. A controller to interact with the virtual environment was also included.	Externally controlled trial	Both VR and MT were useful interventions for alleviating anxiety and for improving mood states in cancer patients during chemotherapy. Moreover, VR seems more effective than MT in relieving anxiety, depression, and fatigue.
Schneider, Prince-Paul, Allen, Silverman, & Talaba, 2004	Adult (18–55 years)	Same duration of the chemotherapy treatment (45–90 minutes)	Psychological	Anxiety, fatigue	Participants received the VR intervention during either their first or second chemotherapy treatment, and they were free to change scenarios if they wanted (deep sea diving, walking through an art museum, or solving a mystery). During the control condition, subjects received standard care (pre-treatment teaching, obtaining venous access, administering chemotherapy, providing homecare instructions, and administering antiemetic medications). Each of the participants experienced both conditions.	Sony PC Glasstron PLM-S700 headset. Headphones were included.	Crossover design	Significant decreases in fatigue occurred immediately following chemotherapy treatments when participants used the VR intervention. Anxiety scores were lower following the use of VR, but no significant differences were found.
Mohammad & Ahmad, 2019	Adult (18-70 years)	15 minutes	Psychological	Pain intensity, anxiety	EC: Morphine + VR intervention. Participants chose from two scenarios on a CD-ROM: deep sea diving "Ocean Rift," or sitting on the beach with the "Happy Place" track. CG: Morphine alone + no VR intervention.	Head-mounted display with headphones (model not specified).	RCT	The study findings showed that one session of the immersive VR plus morphine made a significant reduction in pain and anxiety self-reported scores, compared with morphine alone.
Wamier et al., 2021	Adult (43-67 years)	10 minutes. However, the VR intervention could be renewed if the procedure lasted longer.	Psychological	Pain intensity, anxiety	EG: VR intervention (Aqua 10 French Version) consisting of a virtual dive with a whale swimming in a peaceful environment. The patient was invited to slow down his breathing following the moves of the whale's tale. EG: Nitrous oxide (N2O) conscious sedation.	Goggles harboring a smartphone and earphones (no model specified).	Observational Study	The mean anxiety score was 2.9 before and 2.7 at the peak in the EG versus 4.1 and 1.6, respectively in the CG. The mean pain score was 1.0 before, 3.1 at the peak, and 0.4 after the procedure in the EG, vs 1.8, 2.0, and 0.6 respectively in the CG.

(continued)

Table 2. *(continued)*

Table 2. Studies characteristics according to extraction parameters

Authors(s) and Year	Population	Duration	Type of intervention	Construct of interest assessed*	Content of the intervention	Delivery modality	Study design	Outcome
Moscato et al., 2021	Adult (18-70 years)	The authors did not set a minimum or a maximum time of VR usage/ number of sessions: patients used the headset at home for 4 days in moments of psychophysical discomfort (e.g., pain and growing anxiety), whenever they wanted.	Psychological	Pain intensity, anxiety, tiredness, depression, well-being	The VR included both an IS and a NIS. The NIS consisted of immersive 360° videos with different natural and relaxing scenarios, such as a seascape, a park, a waterfall, the London Bridge, and a mountain landscape. The IS consisted of a basic skill game called "Yuma's World": the user, surrounded by a calm underwater environment, had to reproduce with the controller a displayed "Kanji" (i.e., an ideogram that represents concepts like friendship, courage, and strength). On day 1 the participants could only watch the NIS, to familiarize themselves with the VR. From day 2 on, participants were free to choose the type of scenario.	Mirage Solo VR Headset. A remote controller was included.	Within-subjects, repeated measures	Depression, anxiety (assessed with the HADS), and pain (assessed with the BPI) did not change significantly between days one and four. However, pain, depression, anxiety, and well-being (assessed with the ESAS) collected immediately after the VR sessions showed a significant improvement.
Schneider, Ellis, Coombs, Shonkwiler, & Folsom, 2003	Adult (50-77 years)	Same duration of the chemotherapy treatment	Psychological	Anxiety, fatigue	Participants were randomly assigned to receive the VR treatment during either their first or next chemotherapy treatment. VR condition: Participants chose from 3 CD-ROM-based scenarios (Oceans Below®, A World of Art®, or Titanic: Adventure Out of Time®); they were free to change the VR scenarios. Control condition: standard care (e.g., pre-treatment teaching, obtaining venous access, administration of antiemetic medication).	Sony PC Glasstron PLM- S700. The sense of touch is involved through the use of a computer mouse that allows for the manipulation of the image.	Crossover design	The results demonstrated a significant decrease in anxiety scores immediately following chemotherapy treatments when participants used VR. No significant changes were found in the fatigue values. There was a consistent trend toward improved symptoms on all measures 48 h following completion of chemotherapy.
Wong et al., 2021	Pediatric (6-17 years)	5 minutes before the PIC + total duration of the procedure	Psychological	Anxiety, pain intensity	EG: 2 animated videos from "Minions" were selected and shown to the participants (from 5 minutes before the PIC procedure started to its end) CG: Standard care (phlebotomists explained and performed PIC. The patients were comforted verbally but no VR intervention was implemented).	Google cardboard goggles were used.	RCT	Participants in the EG demonstrated a significantly greater reduction in pain and anxiety levels compared with the CG.
Turrado et al., 2021	Adult (26-94 years)	16-34 minutes	Educational	Anxiety, depression	EG: The participants were exposed to a realistic environment in which they could experience the various steps of their admission to surgery, from the first interview with the surgeon to admission into the surgical ward, the operating room, and the postoperative recovery room.	Bluebee™ Genuine VR 3D Glasses	RCT	After exposure to VR, anxiety and depression rating scales decreased significantly.

EG= Experimental Group, CG= Control Group, IC= Informed Consent, MT=Music Therapy, IS= Interactive Scenario, NIS=Non-Interactive Scenario

* We only reported some of the variables the studies assessed (i.e., self-reported psychological variables). For more details about the rest of the variables, please see the original papers.

Table 3. Risk of bias assessment using the Downs and Black checklist (1998)

Table 3. Risk of bias assessment using the Downs and Black checklist (1998)

	Niki et al., 2019	Hundert et al., 2021	Wolitzky, Fivush, Zimand, Hodges & Rothbaum, 2005	Tennant et al., 2021	Semerci, Akgün Kostak, Eren, & Avci, 2021	Schneider & Workman, 1999	Sharifpour, Manshaee, & Sajjadian, 2021	Ashley Verzwyvelt, McNamara, Xu, & Stubbins, 2021	Tennat et al., 2020	Gao et al., 2020	Gerçeker et al., 2021	Schneider & Hood, 2007	Chirico et al., 2020	Schneider, Prince-Paul, Allen, Silverman, & Talaba, 2004	Mohammad & Ahmad, 2019	Varnier et al., 2021	Moscato et al., 2021	Schneider, Ellis, Coombs, Shonkwiler, & Folsom, 2003	Wong et al., 2021	Turrado et al., 2021
Question 1	1	1	1	1	1	1	1	0	1	1	1	1	0	1	1	1	1	1	1	1
Question 2	1	1	1	1	1	1	1	1	1	1	1	1	1	1	1	1	1	1	1	1
Question 3	1	1	0	1	1	1	1	1	1	1	1	1	1	1	1	1	1	1	1	1
Question 4	1	1	0	1	1	0	0	1	0	1	0	0	0	0	0	0	1	0	0	1
Question 5	0	0	0	0	0	0	0	0	0	0	0	1	1	0	1	1	1	0	1	0
Question 6	1	1	1	1	1	1	1	1	1	1	1	1	1	1	1	0	1	1	1	1
Question 7	1	1	1	1	1	1	1	1	1	1	1	1	1	1	1	0	1	0	1	1
Question 8	1	1	0	1	0	0	0	0	0	0	0	0	1	1	1	1	0	1	1	1
Question 9	0	1	1	1	1	1	0	1	1	0	1	1	1	1	1	1	1	0	1	1
Question 10	1	1	0	0	1	0	1	0	1	1	1	0	1	1	0	1	0	0	1	1
Question 11	1	1	0	1	1	1	1	0	1	0	1	1	0	0	0	1	1	0	1	1
Question 12	1	1	1	1	1	1	1	1	1	1	1	1	1	1	1	1	0	1	1	0
Question 13	1	1	1	1	0	1	0	1	1	1	1	1	1	1	1	1	1	1	1	1
Question 14	0	0	0	0	0	0	0	0	1	0	0	0	0	0	0	0	0	0	0	0
Question 15	0	1	0	0	0	0	0	0	0	0	1	0	0	0	0	0	0	0	0	0
Question 16	1	1	1	1	1	1	1	1	1	1	1	1	1	1	1	1	1	1	1	1
Question 17	0	0	0	0	0	0	0	0	1	1	0	0	0	0	1	1	0	0	0	0
Question 18	0	0	0	1	1	0	1	1	1	1	0	1	1	0	1	1	0	0	1	1
Question 19	1	1	1	1	1	1	1	1	1	1	1	1	1	1	1	1	1	1	1	1
Question 20	1	1	1	1	1	1	1	0	1	1	1	1	1	1	1	1	1	1	1	1
Question 21	1	1	1	1	1	1	1	1	1	1	1	1	1	1	1	1	1	1	1	1
Question 22	1	1	1	1	1	1	1	1	1	1	0	1	1	1	0	1	1	1	1	1
Question 23	0	1	1	0	1	0	1	1	1	1	1	1	0	1	1	0	0	1	1	1
Question 24	0	0	0	0	0	0	0	0	0	0	0	0	0	0	1	0	0	0	1	0
Question 25	0	0	1	0	0	0	0	0	1	0	0	1	1	0	0	0	1	0	1	0
Question 26	0	1	1	1	1	1	0	1	1	0	1	1	1	1	1	1	1	0	1	1
Question 27	1	0	0	0	1	0	0	0	0	0	1	0	0	0	1	0	0	0	0	1
TOTAL SCORE	17	20	15	18	19	15	15	15	21	17	18	19	18	17	20	18	17	13	22	20

NOTE: 0 = No/Unable to determine, 1 = Yes. Only question 5 could be answered 0 = No, 1 = Partially, 2 = Yes, Cut-off total score: 24–28 points (excellent), 19–23 points (good), 14–18 points (fair), 14 points or less (poor)

4 Discussions

To the best of our knowledge, this is the first systematic review to offer a comprehensive panoramic of VR interventions implemented both with adult and pediatric cancer patients. Twenty studies were eligible for the review, and they included both educational and psychological VR interventions. The majority of these interventions showed complete or partial effectiveness of VR, demonstrating that this technology is an optimal delivering modality for psycho-educational interventions. Most studies we included in the systematic review carried out psychological interventions. The common thread between these interventions is the use of distraction as a strategy to reduce patients' distress during medical procedures and treatments. VR distraction has been identified as a promising emotion-focused method aiming at improving tolerance during medical procedures, mostly by reducing the distress and pain that patients experience [72]. According to Lazarus and Folkman's stress and coping model, when people acknowledge that there is nothing they can do to change a stressful situation, they tend to adopt emotion-focused coping strategies (e.g., distraction) to regulate their emotional response [73]: distraction diverts attention away from unpleasant stimuli toward intriguing ones, reducing tension and anxiety [70]. The mechanism behind the functioning of distraction is that human beings have the cognitive resources to process a limited pool of information: using the capacity for one activity limits their availability for another task, preventing other information from being processed and accessing consciousness [74]. VR is a tool of choice in achieving this goal thanks to the possibility of visually showing to the participant the distractor, and offering a sense of presence in the situation. When in the virtual environment, participants have the opportunity to interact with the distractor (e.g., playing the role of a character in the distracting virtual environment), or to just be receptive to the virtual world without interacting with it (e.g., watching a relaxing scuba dive in the ocean). In both cases the individual makes changes in their mental health in a passive way: VR distraction works due to the inability of our mind to manage so much information at the same time, not because the individual is actively involved in improving their own mental health (e.g., by learning how to cope with anxiety or self-regulate emotional distress). The perception of control over a patient's own change improves disease management, health status, and medication adherence [75], variables that are particularly important in cancer care. For this reason, further research should compare VR distraction with other coping strategies that engage patients in a more active way, in order to investigate which is the most effective and has long-term effects on patients' well-being. Problem-focused coping, for example, includes adaptive strategies that focus on reducing or eliminating stressors through the implementation of active behaviors [76]. In this context, problem-focused coping renders the individual actively engaged in the promotion of their mental health, and could be an important factor to develop interventions that make patients feel empowered. Another important element that emerges from this review is that educational tasks represented only a small part of the interventions implemented using VR. Even if the lack of information has been identified as an unmet need of the cancer population [15, 16], educational interventions are still limited. Results from this review show that VR educational interventions are effective both for children and adults and that they can reduce patients' emotional distress by improving patients' knowledge and understanding. Johnson and colleagues [77] underline that patients themselves identify VR as an appropriate and important educational tool to include in cancer care for improving patients' understanding. Specifically, patients consider VR particularly effective in reducing anxiety thanks to the ability to recreate the spatial and acoustic aspects of cancer therapy. Educational studies generally exploit the cognitive-behavioral strategy known as exposure. Exposure-based techniques are broadly used in treating anxiety disorders: by confronting the feared stimuli and incorporating corrective information in the memory, exposure-based techniques decrease the distress experienced, disconfirming the dysfunctional associations [78]. In the educational studies we included, the authors used what we could define as an "informative exposure". Patients are exposed through VR to a simulation of the real experience they will face once the treatment will start: by doing that, they not only reduce the uncertainty associated with the procedure but also acquire the knowledge to predict the steps they will go through. This exposure process allows the patients to restructure their expectancies, reducing the anxiety experienced before the beginning of the treatment. In medical settings where the in vivo exposure (e.g., doing with the patients a tour of the surgical room) may be time-consuming and not always possible, the benefits of adopting VR are numerous. This technology creates an immersive experience, giving the patient the feeling of being in the treatment: the patient can wander around the virtual room and view the therapy from various perspectives. Using VR also decreases the risks (e.g., contamination) associated with physically going to a sterile operating room, radiotherapy vault, or chemotherapy chair, it decreases the amount of time needed in doing the same process in person, and the human and economic resources necessary to do that. VR exposure has recognized effectiveness, greater than in vivo exposure [79], and similar to the classical evidence-based interventions with no VR exposure [80]. By virtue of exposure effectiveness, and the importance that educational interventions have in rendering patients empowered and involved in their treatment, it is extremely important to include psycho-education in cancer care and the optimal tool to reach this goal is VR.

The studies included in this review are not without their limitations. First, only half of the studies included an assessment of the adverse events that may have taken place during the VR intervention. This appears as an extremely important element to incorporate in VR interventions due to the cybersickness (i.e., nausea, headache, and dizziness) that users may experience during or after VR immersion [81]. Secondly, the studies often did not include visual material (e.g., photos, screenshots, videos) to offer more insights into the VR environments used for the intervention. The absence of a clear understanding of how the scenario looks and its specific characteristics may affect the replicability of the results, and increase the risk of bias. A third limitation is the small sample size that characterized some of the studies. Although the difficulties that clinical researchers have in recruiting patients are well recognized, when the samples are very small it is hard to draw firm findings. Thus, to assess effectiveness in a variety of therapeutic contexts, and to make concrete and stable conclusions to refer to the population of interest, future large-scale research comparing VR to other technologies is needed. Lastly, an additional limitation to these studies is that confounders are often not made explicit nor taken into account during the analysis, increasing the risk of bias of the studies. This is especially true when VR interventions are implemented for the length of the medical procedure because VR exposure is performed "as long as the procedure execution". Being implemented from a human being on another human being, a medical procedure rarely lasts the same amount of time for different people, leading participants to different exposures both to the VR and to the control condition. Therefore, it would be essential to keep this element into account both in the analysis and in the confounders' assessment in order to increase the methodological quality of these interventions.

In conclusion, VR seems to be a promising tool for supporting cancer patients' well-being. Two main focuses emerged from this systematic review: psychological interventions predominantly used emotion-focused strategies (i.e., distraction) to reduce patients' emotional distress, while educational studies employed cognitive-behavioral strategies (i.e., exposure) to restructure patients' beliefs towards oncological treatments and reduce their anxiety. However, if on the one hand educational VR interventions support cancer patients in actively acquiring skills for coping with their diagnosis, on the other hand, psychological VR interventions surprisingly do not, assigning a passive role to the patient. For a greater adherence to medical treatments and a meaningful enhancement of patients' psychological and physical well-being, psychological VR interventions need to switch their locus of control from an external to an internal focus, empowering patients. Psychological VR interventions have the potential to become the means to achieve patients' empowerment, assisting them in discovering and using their own intrinsic potential to master their cancer diagnosis. When patients receive a cancer diagnosis, they feel powerless and hopeless: psycho-oncological VR interventions need to fit into this point, accompanying the patient in regaining a perception of control over their life. This will allow the clinical research to have a real impact on the clinical practice and on patients' well-being. Therefore, future research should focus not only on improving the methodological quality of the studies but also on developing new interventions that can fulfill this essential and profound switch. It is the will of our team to develop VR experiences that embrace this change of mindset: starting from the results of this systematic review, we will harmonize psychological and educational tasks within the same VR intervention, with the aim of making the patient an active character of their own well-being [82].

References

1. Linden, W., et al.: Anxiety and depression after cancer diagnosis: prevalence rates by cancer type, gender, and age. J. Affect. Disord. **141**(2–3), 343–351 (2012)
2. Akechi, T., et al.: Major depression, adjustment disorders, and post-traumatic stress disorder in terminally Ill cancer patients: associated and predictive factors. J. Clin. Oncol. **22**(10), 1957–1965 (2004)
3. Rhoten, B.A., Murphy, B., Ridner, S.H.: Body image in patients with head and neck cancer: a review of the literature. Oral Oncol. **49**(8), 753–760 (2013)
4. Bacon, C.G., et al.: The impact of cancer treatment on quality of life outcomes for patients with localized prostate cancer. J. Urol. **166**(5), 1804–1810 (2001)
5. Taghian, N.R., et al.: Lymphedema following breast cancer treatment and impact on quality of life: a review. Crit. Rev. Oncol. Hematol. **92**(3), 227–234 (2014)
6. Vakalopoulos, I., Dimou, P., Anagnostou, I., Zeginiadou, T.: Impact of cancer and cancer treatment on male fertility. Hormones **14**(4), 579–589 (2015). https://doi.org/10.14310/horm.2002.1620

7. Vonk-Klaassen, S.M., de Vocht, H.M., den Ouden, M.E.M., Eddes, E.H., Schuurmans, M.J.: Ostomy-related problems and their impact on quality of life of colorectal cancer ostomates: a systematic review. Qual. Life Res. **25**(1), 125–133 (2015). https://doi.org/10.1007/s11136-015-1050-3
8. Greer, J.A., et al.: Behavioral and psychological predictors of chemotherapy adherence in patients with advanced non-small cell lung cancer. J. Psychosom. Res. **65**(6), 549–552 (2008)
9. Markovitz, L.C., Drysdale, N.J., Bettencourt, B.A.: The relationship between risk factors and medication adherence among breast cancer survivors: what explanatory role might depression play? Psychooncology **26**(12), 2294–2299 (2017)
10. Pham, H., Torres, H., Sharma, P.: Mental health implications in bladder cancer patients: a review. Urol. Oncol. Semin. Orig. Investig. **37**(2), 97–107 (2019)
11. Karvonen-Gutierrez, C.A., et al.: Quality of life scores predict survival among patients with head and neck cancer. J. Clin. Oncol. **26**(16), 2754–2760 (2008)
12. Satin, J.R., Linden, W., Phillips, M.J.: Depression as a predictor of disease progression and mortality in cancer patients a meta-analysis reply. Cancer **116**(13), 3304–3305 (2010)
13. Pinquart, M., Duberstein, P.R.: Depression and cancer mortality: a meta-analysis. Psychol. Med. **40**(11), 1797–1810 (2010)
14. Mesters, N., et al.: Measuring information needs among cancer patients. Patient Educ. Couns. **43**(3), 253–262 (2001)
15. Harrison, J.D., et al.: What are the unmet supportive care needs of people with cancer? A systematic review. Support. Care Cancer **17**(8), 1117–1128 (2009)
16. Stead, M.L., et al.: Lack of communication between healthcare professionals and women with ovarian cancer about sexual issues. Br. J. Cancer **88**(5), 666–671 (2003)
17. Singer, S., Das-Munshi, J., Brahler, E.: Prevalence of mental health conditions in cancer patients in acute care-a meta-analysis. Ann. Oncol. **21**(5), 925–930 (2010)
18. Wang, L.J., Casto, B., Luh, J.Y., Wang, S.J.: Virtual reality-based education for patients undergoing radiation therapy. J. Cancer Educ. (2020). https://doi.org/10.1007/s13187-020-01870-7
19. Lovell, M.R., et al.: A randomized controlled trial of a standardized educational intervention for patients with cancer pain. J. Pain Symptom Manage. **40**(1), 49–59 (2010)
20. Barrera, I., Spiegel, D.: Review of psychotherapeutic interventions on depression in cancer patients and their impact on disease progression. Int. Rev. Psychiatry **26**(1), 31–43 (2014)
21. Guo, Z., et al.: The benefits of psychosocial interventions for cancer patients undergoing radiotherapy. Health Quality Life Outcomes **11** (2013)
22. Zhang, M.F., et al.: Effectiveness of mindfulness-based therapy for reducing anxiety and depression in patients with cancer a meta-analysis. Medicine **94**(45) (2015)
23. Jassim, G.A., et al.: Psychological interventions for women with non-metastatic breast cancer. Cochrane Datab. Syst. Rev. **5** (2015)
24. Belleau, F.P., Hagan, L., Masse, B.: Effects of an educational intervention on the anxiety of women awaiting mastectomies. Can Oncol Nurs J **11**(4), 172–180 (2001)
25. Pensieri, C., Pennacchini, M.: Virtual reality in medicine. In: Handbook on 3d3c Platforms: Applications and Tools for Three Dimensional Systems for Community, Creation and Commerce, pp. 353–401 (2016)
26. Riva, G.: Applications of virtual environments in medicine. Methods Inf. Med. **42**(5), 524–534 (2003)
27. Kim, S., Kim, E.: The use of virtual reality in psychiatry: a review. J. Korean Acad. Child Adolesc. Psychiatry **31**(1), 26–32 (2020)
28. Chirico, A., et al.: Virtual reality in health system: beyond entertainment. A mini-review on the efficacy of VR during cancer treatment. J. Cell. Physiol. **231**(2), 275–287 (2016)
29. Riva, G.: Virtual reality in psychotherapy: review. Cyberpsychol. Behav. **8**(3), 220–230 (2005)

30. Riva, G.: Virtual reality: an experiential tool for clinical psychology. Br. J. Guid. Couns. **37**(3), 337–345 (2009)
31. Abrahams, H.J.G., et al.: Risk factors, prevalence, and course of severe fatigue after breast cancer treatment: a meta-analysis involving 12 327 breast cancer survivors. Ann. Oncol. **27**(6), 965–974 (2016)
32. Murphy, B.A., Gilbert, J., Ridner, S.H.: Systemic and global toxicities of head and neck treatment. Expert Rev. Anticancer Ther. **7**(7), 1043–1053 (2007)
33. Feliu, J., et al.: Prediction of unplanned hospitalizations in older patients treated with chemotherapy. Cancers **13**(6) (2021)
34. Riva, G., Davide, F., Ijsslsteijn, W.: Being there: Concepts, effects and measurements of user presence in synthetic environments. In: Studies on New Technologies & Practices in Communication, 2003 edn. (2003)
35. Botella, C., et al.: Virtual reality and psychotherapy. Stud. Health Technol. Inform. **99**, 37–54 (2004)
36. Gorini, A., et al.: The role of immersion and narrative in mediated presence: the virtual hospital experience. Cyberpsychol. Behav. Soc. Netw. **14**(3), 99–105 (2011)
37. Diefenbach, M.A., Mohamed, N.E.: Regret of treatment decision and its association with disease-specific quality of life following prostate cancer treatment. Cancer Invest. **25**(6), 449–457 (2007)
38. Stryker, J.E., et al.: Understanding the decisions of cancer clinical trial participants to enter research studies: factors associated with informed consent, patient satisfaction, and decisional regret. Patient Educ. Couns. **63**(1–2), 104–109 (2006)
39. Wallis, J.D.: Orbitofrontal cortex and its contribution to decision-making. Annu. Rev. Neurosci. **30**, 31–56 (2007)
40. Gustafson, A.: Reducing patient uncertainty implementation of a shared decision-making process enhances treatment quality and provider communication. Clin. J. Oncol. Nurs. **21**(1), 113–115 (2017)
41. Beyer-Berjot, L., et al.: A virtual reality training curriculum for laparoscopic colorectal surgery. J. Surg. Educ. **73**(6), 932–941 (2016)
42. Lee, C., Wong, G.K.C.: Virtual reality and augmented reality in the management of intracranial tumors: a review. J. Clin. Neurosci. **62**, 14–20 (2019)
43. Mazur, T., et al.: Virtual reality-based simulators for cranial tumor surgery: a systematic review. World Neurosurg. **110**, 414–422 (2018)
44. Quero, G., et al.: Virtual and augmented reality in oncologic liver surgery. Surg. Oncol. Clin. North Am. **28**(1), 31 (2019)
45. Schreuder, H.W.R., et al.: An "intermediate curriculum" for advanced laparoscopic skills training with virtual reality simulation. J. Minim. Invasive Gynecol. **18**(5), 597–606 (2011)
46. van Ginkel, M.P.H., et al.: Bimanual fundamentals: validation of a new curriculum for virtual reality training of laparoscopic skills. Surg. Innov. **27**(5), 523–533 (2020)
47. Moher, D., et al.: Preferred reporting items for systematic reviews and meta-analyses: the PRISMA Statement. PloS Medicine **6**(7) (2009)
48. Mills, S., Noyes, J.: Virtual reality: an overview of user-related design issues revised paper for special issue on "Virtual reality: User issues" in interacting with computers, May 1998. Interact. Comput. **11**(4), 375–386 (1999)
49. Ouzzani, M., et al.: Rayyan-a web and mobile app for systematic reviews. Syst. Rev. **5** (2016)
50. Deeks, J.J., et al.: Evaluating non-randomised intervention studies. Health Technol. Assess. **7**(27), iii–x, 1–173 (2003)
51. Downs, S.H., Black, N.: The feasibility of creating a checklist for the assessment of the methodological quality both of randomised and non-randomised studies of health care interventions. J. Epidemiol. Commun. Health **52**(6), 377–384 (1998)

52. Niki, K., et al.: A novel palliative care approach using virtual reality for improving various symptoms of terminal cancer patients: a preliminary prospective, multicenter study. J. Palliat. Med. **22**(6), 702–707 (2019)
53. Turrado, V., et al.: Exposure to virtual reality as a tool to reduce peri-operative anxiety in patients undergoing colorectal cancer surgery: a single-center prospective randomized clinical trial. Surg. Endosc. **35**(7), 4042–4047 (2021)
54. Varnier, R., et al.: Virtual reality distraction during uterovaginal brachytherapy applicators' removal: a pilot comparative study. Brachytherapy **20**(4), 781–787 (2021)
55. Mohammad, E.B., Ahmad, M.: Virtual reality as a distraction technique for pain and anxiety among patients with breast cancer: a randomized control trial. Palliat. Support. Care **17**(1), 29–34 (2019)
56. Sharifpour, S., Manshaee, G., Sajjadian, I.: Effects of virtual reality therapy on perceived pain intensity, anxiety, catastrophising and self-efficacy among adolescents with cancer. Couns. Psychother. Res. **21**(1), 218–226 (2021)
57. Hundert, A.S., et al.: A pilot randomized controlled trial of virtual reality distraction to reduce procedural pain during subcutaneous port access in children and adolescents with cancer. Clin. J. Pain **38**(3), 189–196 (2022)
58. Gao, J., et al.: Pilot study of a virtual reality educational intervention for radiotherapy patients prior to initiating treatment. J. Cancer Educ. (2020). https://doi.org/10.1007/s13187-020-01848-5
59. Wong, C.L., et al.: Virtual reality intervention targeting pain and anxiety among pediatric cancer patients undergoing peripheral intravenous cannulation a randomized controlled trial. Cancer Nurs. **44**(6), 435–442 (2021)
60. Chirico, A., et al.: Virtual reality and music therapy as distraction interventions to alleviate anxiety and improve mood states in breast cancer patients during chemotherapy. J. Cell. Physiol. **235**(6), 5353–5362 (2020)
61. Moscato, S., et al.: Virtual reality in home palliative care: brief report on the effect on cancer-related symptomatology. Front. Psychol. **12** (2021)
62. Gerçeker, G.O., et al.: The effect of virtual reality on pain, fear, and anxiety during access of a port with huber needle in pediatric hematology-oncology patients: randomized controlled trial. Eur. J. Oncol. Nurs. **50** (2021)
63. Semerci, R., et al.: Effects of virtual reality on pain during venous port access in pediatric oncology patients: a randomized controlled study. J. Pediatr. Oncol. Nurs. **38**(2), 142–151 (2021)
64. Tennant, M., et al.: Exploring the use of immersive virtual reality to enhance psychological well-being in pediatric oncology: a pilot randomized controlled trial. Eur. J. Oncol. Nurs. **48** (2020)
65. Tennant, M., et al.: Effects of immersive virtual reality exposure in preparing pediatric oncology patients for radiation therapy. Tech. Innov. Patient Supp. Radiat. Oncol. **19**, 18–25 (2021)
66. Ashley Verzwyvelt, L., et al.: Effects of virtual reality v. biophilic environments on pain and distress in oncology patients: a case-crossover pilot study. Sci. Rep. **11**(1), 20196 (2021)
67. Schneider, S.M., Workman, M.L.: Effects of virtual reality on symptom distress in children receiving chemotherapy. Cyberpsychol. Behav. **2**(2), 125–134 (1999)
68. Schneider, S.M., et al.: Virtual reality intervention for older women with breast cancer. Cyberpsychol. Behav. **6**(3), 301–307 (2003)
69. Schneider, S.M., et al.: Virtual reality as a distraction intervention for women receiving chemotherapy. Oncol. Nurs. Forum **31**(1), 81–88 (2004)
70. Schneider, S.M., Hood, L.E.: Virtual reality: a distraction intervention for chemotherapy. Oncol. Nurs. Forum **34**(1), 39–46 (2007)

71. Wolitzky, K., et al.: Effectiveness of virtual reality distraction during a painful medical procedure in pediatric oncology patients. Psychol. Health **20**(6), 817–824 (2005)
72. Indovina, P., et al.: Virtual reality as a distraction intervention to relieve pain and distress during medical procedures: a comprehensive literature review. Clin. J. Pain **34**(9), 858–877 (2018)
73. Lazarus, R.S., Folkman, S.: Stress, Appraisal, and Coping (1984)
74. Kahneman, D.: Attention and Effort, vol. 1063 (1973)
75. Nafradi, L., Nakamoto, K., Schulz, P.J.: Is patient empowerment the key to promote adherence? A systematic review of the relationship between self-efficacy, health locus of control and medication adherence. PLoS ONE **12**(10), e0186458 (2017)
76. Morris, N., et al.: The relationship between coping style and psychological distress in people with head and neck cancer: a systematic review. Psychooncology **27**(3), 734–747 (2018)
77. Johnson, K., et al.: Learning in 360 degrees: a pilot study on the use of virtual reality for radiation therapy patient education. J. Med. Imaging Radiat. Sci. **51**(2), 221–226 (2020)
78. Kaczkurkin, A.N., Foa, E.B.: Cognitive-behavioral therapy for anxiety disorders: an update on the empirical evidence. Dialog. Clin. Neurosci. **17**(3), 337–346 (2015)
79. Bouchard, S., et al.: Virtual reality compared with in vivo exposure in the treatment of social anxiety disorder: a three-arm randomised controlled trial. Br. J. Psychiatry **210**(4), 276–283 (2017)
80. Opris, D., et al.: Virtual reality exposure therapy in anxiety disorders: a quantitative meta-analysis. Depress. Anxiety **29**(2), 85–93 (2012)
81. Caserman, P., Garcia-Agundez, A., Gámez Zerban, A., Göbel, S.: Cybersickness in current-generation virtual reality head-mounted displays: systematic review and outlook. Virtual Reality **25**(4), 1153–1170 (2021)
82. Sansoni, M., et al.: Mitigating negative emotions through virtual reality and embodiment. Front. Hum. Neurosci. **16**, 916227 (2022). https://doi.org/10.3389/fnhum.2022.916227

Author Index

Aitmagambetov, A. Z. I-104
Alaguero, Mario II-391
Alce, Günter I-18
Aliprandi, Federico II-178
Alsaleh, Saleh I-296
Ambrosini, Emilia I-3
Amditis, Angelos I-239
Ameglio, Enrico I-200
Angeloni, Renato II-329
Arifin, Samsul I-229
Arlati, Sara I-3
Arpaia, Pasquale II-407, II-420
Augello, Agnese I-219

Baldassa, Andrea II-128
Baldi, Vincenzo I-63
Barba, Maria Cristina I-162
Bassano, Chiara I-130
Battegazzorre, Edoardo I-200
Bekhter, Danylo II-3
Biffi, Emilia I-3
Blehm, Dascha II-3
Bordegoni, M. II-271
Bottino, Andrea I-200
Bracco, Fabrizio I-130
Breitkreuz, David II-287
Bucciero, Alberto II-373
Buonocore, Sara II-306
Bustillo, Andres I-121

Caggianese, Giuseppe I-219
Cannavò, Alberto I-77
Capasso, Irene I-130
Capece, Nicola I-63
Capolupo, Alessandra II-254
Carpentieri, Bruno I-174
Carulli, M. II-271
Catapoti, Despina II-211
Chardonnet, Jean-Rémy II-17
Checa, David I-121, II-63
Chen, Yang II-89
Chessa, Manuela I-130
Chiarello, Sofia I-335
Chirico, Alice II-341
Chirivi, Alessandra II-373
Cirulis, Arnis I-37
Clini, Paolo II-329
Colombo, Daniele I-3
Colombo, Vera I-3
Combe, Théo II-17
Corchia, Laura I-335
Coyle, Damien II-407, II-420

D'Angelo, Andrea II-79
D'Errico, Giovanni I-162, II-420
Daineko, Ye. A. I-104
Danglade, Florence II-198
De Benedetto, Egidio II-420
De Cet, Giulia I-324, II-128
De Paolis, Lucio Tommaso I-92, I-162, I-335, II-63, II-420
Del Vecchio, Vito I-312
Delbarba, Nicola II-373
Demetrescu, Emanuel II-373
Di Domenico, Simone Gerardo I-63
Di Giovanni, Daniele II-79
Di Gironimo, Giuseppe II-306
Donnarumma, Francesco II-407
du Bois, Naomi II-420

Erics, Zintis I-37
Erra, Ugo I-63
Esposito, Antonio II-407

Faggiano, Federica I-335
Fajar, Muhamad I-229
Fanini, Bruno II-373
Farinella, G. M. I-139
Farrugia, Jean-Philippe II-198
Ferrari, Ivan II-373
Frontoni, Emanuele II-329
Fumagalli, Alessia I-3

Gadia, Davide II-178
Gainley, P. I-139, I-147
Gallo, Luigi I-219
Garro, Valeria II-360
Gastaldi, Massimiliano II-128

Gatteschi, Valentina I-77
Gatto, Carola I-92, I-162, I-335
Gavalas, Damianos I-249, II-211
Genz, Fabio II-44
Gilio, Gabriele I-63
Giuri, Francesco II-373
Grassini, Sabrina II-420
Grazioso, Stanislao II-306
Guarneri, Massimiliano II-79
Guillen-Sanz, Henar I-121, II-34, II-391

Hackman, Lucina I-154
Hanserup, Felicia I-18
Hensen, Benedikt II-3
Hufeld, Clemens II-44

Ipalakova, M. T. I-104
Iqbal, Y. I-139, I-147

Jenek, Tomasz I-48

Karampidis, Konstantinos I-185
Karaseitanidis, Ioannis I-239
Kasapakis, Vlasios II-211
Katika, Tina I-239
Kavakli, Evangelia II-211
Klamma, Ralf II-3
Kołecki, Jedrzej I-113
Köse, Ahmet I-296
Koutsabasis, Panayiotis I-249, II-211
Kranzlmüller, Dieter II-44
Krauss, Oliver II-236
Kulakayeva, A. E. I-104

Lamberti, Fabrizio I-77
Lazoi, Mariangela I-312
Lebert, Déborah II-198
Lezzi, Marianna I-312
Liaci, Silvia I-335
Livatino, S. I-139, I-147
Logothetis, Ilias I-185
Lucesoli, Matteo II-224

Macis, Luca I-77
Maggiorini, Dario II-178
Maik, Mikołaj I-48
Malighetti, Clelia II-432
Malinverni, Eva Savina II-224, II-329
Mameli, Marco II-161
Mancini, Adriano II-329
Manfredi, Gilda I-63
Manzanares, María Consuelo Saiz II-34
Martinez, Kim I-92, II-34
Mastrati, Giovanna II-420
Mayer, Anjela II-17
Meinberger, Sebastian II-3
Merienne, Frédéric II-198
Migliorini, Massimo II-79
Miguel-Alonso, Ines I-121, II-63, II-391
Mishra, Rakesh II-287
Moccaldi, Nicola II-420
Mohamed, M. I-147
Molteni, Franco I-3
Mondellini, Marta I-3
Monterisi, Cristina II-254
Morana, G. I-139, I-147
Müller, Maike II-287
Mulliri, Maurizio II-224
Murtinger, Markus II-79

Nannipieri, Olivier I-273
Natalizio, Angela II-407
Nguyen, T. H. I-147
NicDaeid, Niamh I-154
Nobre, Renato Avellar II-178
Nossa, Roberta I-3
Nuccetelli, Fabiana I-162
Nuzzo, Benito Luigi I-162

Orsini, Federico I-324
Ovtcharova, Jivka II-17

Paladini, Giovanna Ilenia I-162
Palm, Kornelia I-18
Palma Stade, Tobías II-109
Palmieri, Francesco I-174
Palumbo, Giovanna I-3
Pandiani, Delfina S. M. II-101
Papadourakis, Giorgos I-185
Parvis, Marco II-407
Pauls, Aleksandra II-329
Pedrocchi, Alessandra I-3
Pescarin, Sofia II-101
Petlenkov, Eduard I-296
Piccinini, Fabio II-224
Pierdicca, Roberto II-161, II-224, II-329
Pizzolante, Marta II-341
Plouzeau, Jérémy II-198
Praschl, Christoph II-236

Quattrini, Ramona II-329

Regal, Georg II-79
Reni, Gianluigi I-3
Rinaldi, Vincenzo I-154
Ripamonti, Laura Anna II-178
Riva, Giuseppe II-432
Rodríguez-Garcia, Bruno II-34, II-63, II-391
Rosati, Riccardo II-161
Rosenberg, Louis B. I-263
Rossi, Riccardo I-324, II-128
Rossini, Mauro I-3

Sacco, Marco I-3
Sansoni, Maria II-432
Saputra, Karen Etania I-229
Schrom-Feiertag, Helmut II-79
Sobociński, Paweł I-48
Solari, Fabio I-130
Spadoni, E. II-271
Stegelmeyer, Dirk II-287
Strada, Francesco I-200
Sumerano, Giada I-335
Sundstedt, Veronica II-360
Szrajber, Rafał I-113

Tagliabue, Mariaelena II-128
Tang, LiTing II-150
Tarantino, Eufemia II-254
Tauro, Giovanni I-3
Tepljakov, Aleksei I-296
Thiele, Erik II-236
Tonetto, Flavio II-161
Tsepapadakis, Michalis I-249
Tsoy, D. D. I-104
Turello, Simone I-200

Udjaja, Yogi I-229

Vallefuoco, Ersilia II-420
Vasic, Bata II-329
Vasic, Iva II-329
Vianello, Chiara II-128
Vidakis, Nikolas I-185
Viola, Eros I-130
Vosinakis, Spyros II-211

Walczak, Krzysztof I-48
Wang, JiaYu II-141
Williams, K. I-147
Wiśniewska, Aneta I-113
Wojciechowski, Adam I-113

Zhang, YanXiang II-89, II-141, II-150
Zingaretti, Primo II-161
Zocco, A. I-139, I-147

Printed in the United States
by Baker & Taylor Publisher Services

Printed in the United States
by Baker & Taylor Publisher Services